Purity, Sacrifice, and the Temple

Purity, Sacrifice, and the Temple

Symbolism and Supersessionism in the Study of Ancient Judaism

JONATHAN KLAWANS

OXFORD
UNIVERSITY PRESS

2006

OXFORD
UNIVERSITY PRESS

Oxford University Press, Inc., publishes works that further
Oxford University's objective of excellence
in research, scholarship, and education.

Oxford   New York
Auckland   Cape Town   Dar es Salaam   Hong Kong   Karachi
Kuala Lumpur   Madrid   Melbourne   Mexico City   Nairobi
New Delhi   Shanghai   Taipei   Toronto

With offices in
Argentina   Austria   Brazil   Chile   Czech Republic   France   Greece
Guatemala   Hungary   Italy   Japan   Poland   Portugal   Singapore
South Korea   Switzerland   Thailand   Turkey   Ukraine   Vietnam

Published by Oxford University Press, Inc.
198 Madison Avenue, New York, New York 10016

www.oup.com

Oxford is a registered trademark of Oxford University Press

Library of Congress Cataloging-in-Publication Data

Klawans, Jonathan.
Purity, sacrifice, and the temple: symbolism and supersessionism in the study of ancient
Judaism / Jonathan Klawans.
    p.   cm.
Includes bibliographical references and index.
ISBN-13 978-0-19-539584-6

1. Sacrifice—Biblical teaching.   2. Purity, ritual—Biblical teaching.
3. Temple of God.   4. Temple of Jerusalem (Jerusalem).
5. Sacrifice—Judaism—History of doctrines.
6. Purity, ritual—Judaism—History of doctrines.   I. Title.

BS680.S2K53 2005
296.4'92—dc22   2004066297

Preface

My interest in sacrifice began in all the wrong ways. Already as a graduate student, I found that reading about sacrifice provided an intellectual escape from research into impurity and sin in ancient Judaism. At the time, I reveled in the fact that books on sacrifice were concerned with violence at the origins of religion, while books on purity spoke about hierarchy and symbolism in more advanced religious systems. It was only a few years later when I began to wonder whether there was any good reason that books on sacrifice looked so different from books on purity. With that question in mind, I was on my way toward conceiving this project. As a matter of course, this book covers some of the same ground as *Impurity and Sin*. But this work is more directly interested in symbolism and more thoroughly tracks the ways in which various biases (Jewish, Christian, and other) continue to impact on the discussion of ritual structures in the Hebrew Bible and ancient Judaism. I am gratified with the reception accorded to *Impurity and Sin*. If this project seems like an unlikely successor to my first book, I hope that it will be considered a worthy one.

During the years of research and writing that led to the completion of this book, I was helped by many institutions and individuals. Most important, I was granted two semesters of leave from Boston University; the first was funded by the university's Humanities Foundation, and the second was a standard sabbatical from the College of Arts and Sciences. At Harvard University's Divinity School, I was given the opportunity to teach a seminar on purity and sacrifice in ancient Judaism. At the Hebrew College in Newton, Massachusetts, I was given the opportunity to teach a six-week adult education course on prayer and sacrifice in Jewish thought. In addition to my regular teaching responsibilities at Boston University, I also had the opportunity to coteach a course with my colleague Kathe Darr, entitled "Priests and Prophets in Ancient Israel." I thank the students in all these courses, and I thank the institutions for giving me these opportunities. I also thank Boston University's College of Arts and Sciences, and the Elie Wiesel Center for Judaic Studies, for sponsoring a short trip to Israel in June 2003. Though the main focus of that trip was a speaking engagement regarding *Impurity and Sin,* I was able while I was there to track down a number of resources helpful for this project as well. Finally, close to the completion of this book, Boston University's Humanities Foundation funded one year's worth of access to Harvard's libraries, for which I am grateful.

Preliminary versions of some sections of this book were presented during annual meetings of the American Academy of Religion, the Association for Jewish Studies, and the Society of Biblical Literature. Aspects of these presentations subsequently appeared as articles in the *AJS Review, Harvard Theological Review, New Testament Studies,* and *Religious Studies Review,* all cited in the bibliography. I thank the editors of these journals for granting permission to rework material from these articles into chapters 1, 2, and 7 of this work.

A large number of colleagues have helped me in various ways as this manuscript took shape. For reading drafts of articles or book chapters and offering many helpful suggestions, I thank Gary A. Anderson, David Bernat, Marc Bregman, Katheryn Pfisterer Darr, Paula Fredriksen, Maxine Grossman, Naomi Koltun-From, Frank Korom, Jon D. Levenson, Joel Marcus, John McKenna, Scot McKnight, Simon B. Parker, Kimberley Patton, Eyal Regev, and Jeffrey L. Rubenstein. Christine E. Hayes and David P. Wright both read drafts of the complete work and offered much helpful advice. I also thank anonymous reviewers for Oxford University Press and the aforementioned journals for their helpful suggestions. A number of others helped in sundry ways, by facilitating or participating in conversations on purity, sacrifice, or some other matter such as metaphor, that proved fruitful to me and benefited my completion of this book: Kim Haines-Eitzen, Martha Himmelfarb, Steven T. Katz, Andrea Lieber, Stephen Prothero, Gary Rendsburg, Alan F. Segal, and David Weiss-Halivni. Some teachers of mine from many years back ended up helping me in ways they may not even be able to recall, by offering reading suggestions and other advice that eventually proved helpful to this project: Edward Greenstein, John Stratton Hawley, and Wayne Proudfoot. Thanks are also due to Cynthia A. Read for her unfailing support, back when I could hardly articulate clearly what it was I intended to do. Linda Donnelly deftly guided the book through production; Ingrid Anderson worked diligently on the indexes. Credit for whatever is done right in this book is to be shared among all those who have helped me in this project; the blame for all that is wrong is mine alone.

Credit for much of the early progress on this book is due to the late John Clayton. The Englishman in him kindly predicted that all would work out very well. The Texan in him pushed me to get this project underway. I wish he were here to see it. Credit for all the later progress is due to my wife, Helaine, and our son, Ari. My wife's kindness and patience gave me time to write. Our son's happiness—for which we are ever thankful—inspired me to complete it, so that I could spend more of my time with him. Alas, life brings the good and bad much faster than I have been able to write. This book is dedicated to my late father, Harold L. Klawans, M.D. The last time he and I ate lunch together, we spoke about some of my ideas about the relationship between purity and sacrifice. Although we never had the chance to discuss these matters again, I know that a number of lessons I learned from him over the years are reflected here. He should have lived to see this book, to say nothing of the many other even more important things he has missed since 1998.

Contents

Note on Translations, Transliterations, and Citations

Translations of the Hebrew Bible and the New Testament follow—with some modifications—the New Revised Standard Version Bible (NRSV).

Other translations of ancient texts are cited in the notes when used. Unless otherwise noted, translations of rabbinic texts are my own, though the standard translations by Danby and Epstein (cited in the bibliography) have been consulted.

Abbreviations of biblical and other ancient texts generally follow, with some slight modifications, the *The SBL Handbook of Style: For Ancient Near Eastern, Biblical and Early Christian Studies*, edited by Patrick H. Alexander, John F. Kutsko, James D. Ernest, Shirley A. Decker-Lucke, and David L. Peterson (Peabody, Mass.: Hendrickson, 1999). Transliterations follow this handbook's general-purpose style. Citations also generally follow this handbook, with some slight and generally self-explanatory simplifications. Series titles (often abbreviated) have been provided in the bibliography only for those works, such as text editions and commentaries, that are typically shelved together in research libraries. Series titles for scholarly monographs have not been provided unless the information is necessary for identifying or locating the volume.

Purity, Sacrifice,
and the Temple

Introduction

Purity, Sacrifice, and Evolutionist Analysis

This book sets out to reexamine modern scholarly approaches to ancient Judaism's temple cult. In part I, we will evaluate current scholarship on purity and sacrifice in the Hebrew Bible. In part II, we will evaluate scholarship concerning ancient Jewish views of the temple cult in Jerusalem. The common denominator of parts I and II—and the thesis of this book—is the claim that scholarly understandings of Jewish cultic matters have been unduly influenced by various contemporary biases, religious and cultural. For some interpreters, ancient Jewish sacrifice was but one small step away from the chaotic violence that typified human origins. For others, the temple cult was destined to be replaced—superseded—by other less bloody rituals that would prove to be of greater value, both spiritually and symbolically. The problem with interpretations like these is not just that they are biased. They are also methodologically unsound. But most important, they are also simply inadequate and inaccurate understandings of the evidence before us.

One problem with such readings is that they are conspicuously selective. Scholars will find symbolism in many rituals, but not in sacrifice. They will grant that many ancient Jews did offer symbolic or "spiritualized" understandings of the temple cult. But scholars generally attribute these attitudes only to those philosophers, mystics, sectarians, or later Christians or rabbis who stand outside of the cult in place or time. Practically anyone could understand the cult symbolically, with the exception of the priests and pilgrims who willingly and happily performed cultic rituals.

Another problem with current scholarly approaches is that they often assume what they should be trying to prove. Instead of tracing the history of ideas on the basis of datable evidence, all too often evidence is dated by virtue of the perspectives it is perceived to express. Texts are plugged into preconceived conceptions of religious history, where trajectories are assumed to run from primitive, pre-Israelite cult practices to ancient Jewish symbolic or "spiritualized" understandings of sacrifice, culminating in the nonsacrificial practices of contemporary Christianity and Judaism. When texts concerning ancient Judaism's sacrificial cult are placed within such broad, evolutionary schemes, it should come as no surprise that selective and biased readings of the earlier evidence can result. As we will see throughout this book, various forms of religious and cultural supersessionism have prevented scholars from seeing the temple as a powerful source of meaning and symbolism for those who believed in it. This project seeks to expose and counter such approaches, by taking a fresh look at a broad array of evidence concerning ancient Judaism's temple and cultic practices.

Because we are covering a large body of literature, composed over a long span of time, the argument will have to unfold gradually. But we can introduce and illustrate the approach taken here by starting at the beginning, looking at the selectivity and biases that characterize scholarly analyses of two cultic ritual structures of the Hebrew Bible: sacrifice and purity.

That sacrifice and ritual purity are structurally interrelated can hardly be denied: the two are juxtaposed in the biblical book of Leviticus, with sacrifice treated (primarily, but not exclusively) in chapters 1–10, and purity treated (again, not exclusively) in chapters 11–15. In Leviticus, it becomes clear that ritual purity is the prerequisite for those who would come to the sanctuary to offer sacrifices, for those priests who regularly officiate at sacrifices, and for any animals that are to be offered as sacrifices. Ritual impurity, by definition, is associated with those phenomena that are barred from the sanctuary. Sacrifice, also by definition, involves many activities that—especially according to the priestly traditions—can take place *only* in the sanctuary.

The idea that ritual purity is a fundamental prerequisite for sacrifice is reflected in ancient Jewish literature as well. Indeed, virtually every ancient Jewish literary treatment of cultic themes in ancient Jewish literature, from the Hebrew Bible through rabbinic literature, treats both purity and sacrifice, if it treats one of them at all. This is true of the biblical book of Ezekiel, and of ancient Jewish works such as *Jubilees*, the *Temple Scroll* (11QT), and *Miqsat Ma'aseh ha-Torah* (4QMMT). It is also true of rabbinic works, including the Mishnah, the Tosefta, and the Sifra. The two ritual structures of purity and sacrifice are virtually inseparable. The reason for this, as Philo put it so clearly, is that purity is required of those who offer sacrifices (*Special Laws* 1:256–261).

As the anthropologist Victor Turner (1920–83) advised some time ago, sacrifice should be understood as a process with several stages.[1] Turner was following his predecessors Henri Hubert (1872–1927) and Marcel Mauss (1872–1950)—about whom we will have much more to say later. Hubert and Mauss devoted part of their classic 1898 essay *Sacrifice: Its Nature and Functions* to describing the processes of "sacralization" and purification that precede sacrifice.[2] With regard to the Hebrew Bible and ancient Judaism, that process of sacrifice can be said to begin with the processes of ritual purifi-cation. Clearly, an integrated analysis of purity and sacrifice is a desideratum.

Yet, surprisingly, one would be hard pressed to find current scholarly works on the Hebrew Bible or ancient Judaism that approach ritual purity with the understanding that it is the prerequisite to sacrifice or that approach sacrifice with the understanding that ritual purity is what leads up to it. The ritual structures may have been integrated in ancient times, but they are hardly integrated in the current scholarly discussion. Typically, monographs and thematic treatments are devoted to only one or the other of these ritual structures.

Some scholarly works, to be sure, treat both purity and sacrifice—even with regard to the Hebrew Bible. But these tend not to be monographs but rather one or another of two genres with an entirely broader focus altogether. General treatments of biblical religion will as a matter of course include introductory surveys of both purity and sacrifice in general.[3] But textbooks, understandably, have their limits. To find single works in which these two topics are subjected to detailed scholarly analysis, one must turn to the nu-merous commentaries on the biblical books of Leviticus and Numbers. Be-cause Leviticus in particular treats both purity and sacrifice, one would expect to find in the commentaries discussions that approach the two ritual struc-tures with similar methods and attitudes. But a review of the commentaries on Leviticus provides further confirmation of the divide separating purity from sacrifice in the current scene: biblical scholars, if they treat both at all, still tend to treat purity and sacrifice rather differently.

Since Mary Douglas wrote *Purity and Danger* in the 1960s, most scholars studying the dietary laws and the purity system(s) of ancient Israel have rec-ognized the need to treat these as symbolic structures.[4] The laws serve func-tions, to be sure, but they also may express some fundamental ideas about the body, cosmology, and perhaps even justice.[5] Jacob Milgrom's recently com-pleted magisterial commentary on Leviticus in the Anchor Bible series is a case in point. As we will see in chapter 1, Milgrom's treatment of the purity laws is complex and sympathetic—precisely what one would expect from a scholar who has digested the thrust of *Purity and Danger*. He argues for an elaborate thesis on the symbolic nature of the ritual purity system in general. Moreover, he pays the dietary rules in particular a high compliment by arguing that their ultimate basis is an ethical one.

Yet when biblical scholars turn back to the first ten chapters of Leviticus, Mary Douglas's general insights are no longer considered terribly informative. Comparatively speaking, scholarship on the Hebrew Bible exhibits very little interest in analyzing sacrificial rituals in the way Douglas analyzed the purity rituals—recognizing the possibility that the ancient Israelite sacrificial rules could profitably be analyzed as a symbolic system.[6] There are, of course, symbolic explorations of a "piecemeal" sort: for instance, one can find ex-aminations of the symbolic value of the color red in the red heifer ritual.[7] There are also, to be sure, symbolic explorations of the most general sort: for example, one can find studies that look through and beyond the details of varied sacrificial rites and narratives and find a fundamental sameness in them all, which can then be analyzed symbolically, as in the works of René Girard.

While biblical scholars frequently approach purity rites as a symbolic system, what we generally find in analyses of sacrifice in ancient Israel is, rather, a concern with origins. And this concern takes two forms. One is the standard discussion—found in numerous commentaries—of the basic theories (about which we will have more to say below) that sacrifice originated as offerings of food for the gods, as gifts to the gods, or as communion with the gods. The other is René Girard's search for the original murder that accounts for all subsequent sacrificial rituals. Again, Milgrom's commentary is a case in point. Although he endorses no single theory on the origins of sacrifice, his treatment of the ritual concedes that the interesting issue is not what sacrifice actually means for the ancient Israelites, but rather how sacrifice came about in the first place.

The question of the origins of sacrifice is certainly one of the more important—and justifiably fascinating—questions in the field of religious studies. Yet this fascination with the origins of sacrifice is, in actuality, notoriously selective. Theorists arbitrarily assume that the origin of religion is to be found in sacrifice. Biblical commentators, following suit, exhibit a greater interest in the origins of sacrifice than in the beginnings of other ritual structures. When dealing with the food laws or the purity systems, biblical scholars have long avoided getting sidetracked by explorations into the origins of dietary restriction or the menstrual taboo. When dealing with circumcision in the Hebrew Bible, very few have felt the need to explore the early history of human body marking. But when it comes to sacrifice, the interest shifts to questions of origins. Biblical scholars seem to get along just fine without "theories" concerning most of the rites in the Hebrew Bible, but when it comes to sacrifice, everyone wants a "theory."

Our concern here is not to evaluate this search per se but to evaluate its impact on biblical studies. It is my contention that the search for the origins of sacrifice should remain largely irrelevant to the work of biblical commentators, who ought rather to be interested in understanding the developed sacrificial system of ancient Israel in its context. The quest for origins is not merely irrelevant; its impact on biblical studies has been largely detrimental. When the search for origins predominates, the search for any contextual understanding of ancient Israelite sacrifice is eclipsed. Moreover, all too frequently interest in the origins of sacrifice results in an evolutionist analysis.

Evolutionism is a difficult phenomenon to define precisely, and there is some dispute among scholars as to the pertinence of the referent to certain theorists. Nonetheless, the term is commonly used to describe a broad array of theories of history—often pertaining to the origin of religion—that trace a more or less linear evolution of human civilization along intellectual, ethical, and religious lines.[8] Inspired by G.W.F. von Hegel's philosophy of history and Charles Darwin's theory of biological evolution, evolutionist theories came into prominence in the late nineteenth and early twentieth century with the works of E. B. Tylor (1832–1917) and James G. Frazer (1854–1941).[9] Perhaps the most notorious example of evolutionist theory is Frazer's book *The Golden Bough* (published in various forms between the 1890s and 1920s), which traces human development along three successive stages, from an original primitive magic through a later religious stage, culminating in modern science. Surely one of the most pernicious of these evolutionist approaches was expressed in Friedrich Delitzch's "Babel und Bibel" lectures (delivered 1902–4), which understood the gradual and eventually complete de-Judaization of religion as a positive development.[10] Evolutionist theories, however, need not be as purely linear as Frazer's or as patently offensive as Delitzch's. Like Hegel, evolutionist theories often trace temporary regressions and wrong turns (these are analogous to Hegel's stage of "antithesis"). Like Darwin, evolutionist theories often trace the "survival" of aspects of early thought in later societies. The evolutionism of William Robertson Smith (1846–94), as we will see below, exhibits both of these traits. Yet on the whole, evolutionist theories posit broad, definitive, and positive development of human civilization. The theories, moreover, exhibit the presumption of intellectual and ethical superiority of the author's position. Typically, the highest rung on the evolutionist ladder is occupied by whatever perspective the author advocates, be it monotheism, Christianity, or science.

With regard to sacrifice in particular, evolutionist analyses look something like this. Scholars first speculate on what sacrifice meant, at its origins: for instance, sacrifice was originally understood as divine food. Then scholars find only the faintest echoes of such primitive ideas in the Hebrew Bible: for instance, at least the Israelites—unlike their neighbors—didn't really conceive of sacrifices as divine food anymore.[11] The achievement of the Israelites, according to this evolutionist approach, lies precisely in the fact that sacrifice no longer means to them what it meant to those who preceded them. For those who take the evolutionist approach, sacrifice remains in ancient Israel as a meaningless, vestigial ritual, a relic from a more primitive era.[12] Many theorists find further support for such a claim by asserting that the ancient Israelite prophets were already attuned to the futility of sacrificial worship.[13] This kind of evolutionism is in evidence in much of the current work on ancient Israelite sacrifice.

There is, with regard to sacrifice, yet another sort of evolutionist argument. This second sort of evolutionism—which can also be termed "supersessionism"—appears primarily in works of scholarship dealing with later periods of Jewish history. Where one sort of evolutionism begins with the supposition that ancient Israel demonstrated a marked development over the paganism that preceded it (by moving, ever so slightly, away from a literal, mechanical understanding of sacrifice), this second sort of evolutionism is predicated on the assumption that ancient Jewish sacrifice was itself superseded by something better that came later.

Within the Christian tradition, of course, it is often understood that the Jewish sacrificial cult was superseded by Jesus' sacrificial death. Within the New Testament, this perspective is laid out most clearly in the epistle to the

Hebrews. Ancient Israel's sacrificial service is described in the letter as offering ineffective atonement (Heb. 7:18); its numerous priests limited by their mortality (7:23), and their sanctuary a mere copy of the true temple in heaven (8: 1–5). Jesus' priesthood, however, offers an ever-effective atonement (9:12), a perfect sacrifice (9:14) offered in the true holy place (9:11) by the single eternal and true high priest (7:16–17, 21).[14] This ideology often emerges in scholarship on two New Testament narratives in particular (neither of which are even alluded to in Hebrews): the Last Supper and Jesus' overturning the tables in the temple. According to this approach, the temple incident symbolizes or enacts Jesus' rejection of Jewish sacrificial worship.[15] The eucharistic traditions of the Last Supper then constitute an efficacious symbolic act that "inverts" and "replaces" Jewish sacrifice.[16] The reason for all this is that Jewish sacrificial worship was indeed flawed: for some, sacrifice is deemed spiritually inadequate;[17] for others, the temple is deemed too hierarchical or exclusive.[18] Perhaps the fullest attack on the Jewish temple in current scholarship is to be found the works of Robert G. Hamerton-Kelly, who, following René Girard, indicts the temple as a place of violence, vengeance, and victimage.[19] Hamerton-Kelly's judgment is atypically extreme. But as we will see throughout this book, criticisms of sacrifice and the temple are the rule, and sympathetic treatments are the exception. Scholarship on the New Testament tends to adhere to the rule, often in line with traditional Christian criticisms of sacrifice. This perspective has affected scholarship on the Hebrew Bible as well, as can be seen, for example, in treatments of biblical sacrifice that conclude with reference to the New Testament book of Hebrews.[20]

We cannot suppose, however, that this kind of argument is made by Christian scholars alone. A number of Jewish scholarly approaches to either ancient Israelite or ancient Jewish sacrifice are marked by a similar assumption that sacrifice was destined to be replaced by something better that came later. Already in the Middle Ages, the forward-thinking philosopher Moses Maimonides (1135–1204) famously developed an historicist—or evolutionist—approach to ancient Israel's sacrificial laws. In his *Guide of the Perplexed* (III:32, 69b) Maimonides compares the sacrificial laws to mother's milk (cf. Hebrews 5:11–14!) and claims that God suffered sacrificial worship to remain as a "divine ruse" whose purpose was to eliminate idolatry.[21] The ideal form of worship is prayer, for, as the prophets have shown, sacrifices are inadequate, and God "can dispense with them" (III:32; 72b). Maimonides' approach is fascinating in its own right and was highly controversial in its day. Less than thirty years after his death, Maimonides' *Guide* was banned by French rabbis—and copies were burned in Montpellier.[22]

Yet Maimonides' approach was never rooted out. It came to life again in the nineteenth century with the birth of the reform movement in Germany, which advocated that the traditional liturgy be stripped of references to sacrificial worship. Indeed, practically from the very beginning of modern synagogue reform, rather contentious disputes arose over what to do with sacrificial language in the traditional Jewish liturgy.[23] Some reformers who were more moderate advocated subtle changes, such as rephrasing hopes for the restoration of sacrifices into nostalgic memories of sacrifices offered long ago (and this is still done in contemporary American Conservative prayer books). Other more radical reformers advocated a fuller elimination of sacrificial terms and references (as is still done in contemporary American Reform and Reconstructionist prayer books). These disputes can in no way be separated from Jewish scholarly approaches to sacrifice, because the history of modern Jewish historical scholarship is wrapped up in the history of synagogue reform, in figures such as Abraham Geiger.[24] We should therefore not be surprised that a good deal of Jewish scholarship on the Hebrew Bible or ancient Judaism operates on the assumption that sacrifice is hopelessly outmoded and meaningless. In 1869, with reference to his own edition of the prayer book, Geiger wrote: "even if it be assumed that, in ancient times, sacrifice was an adequate expression of the adoration of God, sacrifice has long since made way for a more spiritual worship service, and its reintroduction is unthinkable."[25] More recently, a similar perspective on sacrifice led Elias J. Bickerman to conclude an essay entitled "The Temple" with the judgment that the Roman emperor Titus (who as a Roman commander supervised the destruction of the Jerusalem temple in 70 C.E.) was "certainly the greatest religious reformer in history."[26] Obviously, Maimonides' approach remains compelling for modern Jewish exegetes and theologians who deny the traditional Jewish view that sacrificial worship is destined again to become the norm for Jewish worship.[27] We will see the continued impact of this understanding of matters throughout this book, but especially in chapter 1, with regard to the Hebrew Bible, and in chapter 6, with regard to the history of early rabbinic Judaism.

The view that ancient Jewish sacrifice was destined to be replaced by a morally superior mode of worship like prayer is, in fact, structurally akin to the argument that the temple was destined to be spiritualized by the eucharist. In both cases, what becomes important in subsequent religious developments is also seen as inherently superior, of greater spiritual and even symbolic value. Both of these arguments are frequently bolstered by the claim that ancient Israelite sacrifice was itself an activity that was morally superior to that which preceded it. Perhaps inspired by the world wars and genocides of the last century, a number of scholars have been impelled of late to search for the origins of human violence. Curiously, it is not uncommon for scholars to tie the origins of human violence to the early history of sacrificial practice. Needless to say, there is little evidence for the claim that sacrifice originated in efforts to respond to or curb early human violence: how could there be evidence for such a theory? There is even less evidence that today's postsacrificial humanity is any less violent than it was before sacrifice began or while sacrifice was widely practiced. But the frequency with which such assertions are made (as we will see below) reflects a third, distinctively modern bias against sacrifice—one that differs from, but nonetheless now supports, the Christian and Jewish biases we have just discussed. This is the claim that sacrifice is inherently violent and immoral.

None of these perspectives, true or not, are of use when trying to determine what ancient Israelite sacrifice meant to those Israelites who believed in its efficacy. But all of these perspectives play a significant role in the current discussion of the themes we will consider. As we will see in chapter 1, they lurk behind the fact that while purity rites are generally treated fairly and sympathetically today, sacrifice still tends to be dismissed with derision.

To put these religious and scholarly approaches in their place, it might be helpful to consider some arguments long ago raised in *defense* of sacrifice. It is well known, but not always sufficiently appreciated, that the history of animal sacrifice in the West did not end with the destruction of the Jerusalem temple. Sacrificial rituals continued to be practiced throughout the Roman Empire until the fourth and fifth centuries of the Common Era. Then, as Christian leaders and emperors became more and more powerful, they began closing pagan shrines. Greco-Roman religious life began to face its end, but it didn't go without a fight. Among the philosophers who defended the old religions was one Platonius Sallustius—a friend and ally of the emperor Julian, who briefly reinstated the old Roman cults from 361 to 363 C.E. This Sallustius authored a tract, *On the Gods and the World*, which is little read or known today.[28] But it contains some rather sharp arguments in defense of sacrifice. First, Sallustius notes that it is fitting to give to the gods *in kind*, as they have provided. They have given life, and life should be given to them. Sallustius goes on to challenge the presumed superiority of prayer: "Prayer without sacrifice," said Sallustius, "is only words" (*On the Gods* 16). Or, in the words of the modern cliché, talk is cheap. Sacrifice, however, costs.

The goal here is not to defend the practice of sacrifice, or to denigrate the practice of prayer. But Sallustius's defense of sacrifice—with its biting critique of prayer—ought to help us appreciate that polemics can be written the other way around. Had the history of religion turned out differently from the way it did, perhaps someone would have to write a book about the fact that scholars denigrate prayer more than they should. But that's not how things worked out.

The Scope and Structure of the Book

This project seeks to reach beyond the current antisacrificial bias. In particular, we seek to trace and counter the various evolutionist approaches that seem to predominate over current scholarly understandings of ancient Israelite and Jewish cultic matters. This book consists of two parts, with a rough chronological divide between them. In part I, we focus on biblical Israel, while in part II we will focus on the literature of ancient Judaism (Second Temple and rabbinic periods). In part I, we will see how the selective (and often evolutionist) fascination with the origins of sacrifice has had a detrimental effect on scholarly understandings of biblical Israel. In part II, we will see how various Christian and Jewish ideas about the replacement of sacrifice (or its "spiritualization") have impacted negatively on the understandings of a whole array of ancient Jewish texts dealing with cultic matters. Parts I and II address two different epochs, in chronological order: biblical Israel and ancient Judaism.

But within each of the two parts, we address our topics not chronologically but thematically. The order in which matters are presented allows for the smoothest presentation of the particular arguments: as we will see, the understanding of the prophets (chapter 3) depends on the analysis of the Pentateuch (chapter 2), and the interpretation of the New Testament (chapter 7) builds on the surveys of the rabbis (chapter 6) and Qumran (chapter 5). Certainly thematic clarity ought to have at least as strong a claim over a book's structure as chronology has. Moreover, siding with thematic clarity over chronology has the added advantage of aiding in the effort to eschew evolutionist analyses. A chronological presentation can lead to the *impression* that one has traced a linear development. It is hoped that the book's thematic analysis will lead to the conviction that evolutionist constructions have had too great a hold over scholars of biblical Israel and ancient Judaism.

In chapter 1, we will survey a number of theoretical approaches to purity and sacrifice, with an eye toward those theorists whose work has had a significant impact—for better or for worse—on the understanding of the cultic rituals of the Hebrew Bible. As we will see—and as I have already intimated—scholarly approaches to ancient Israel's cult rituals tend to be unintegrated (separating purity from sacrifice) and differentiated (understanding purity symbolically and sacrifice historically). Over the course of this chapter, we will review the theoretical works on purity and sacrifice that currently loom over the discussion. We will also look back to a time when things were very different, in order to reflect better on why things might be the way they are today.

In chapter 2, we will turn to the biblical rituals themselves, and offer a preliminary effort toward understanding purity and sacrifice in ways quite different from those that are more common. We will seek to reach beyond the current antisacrificial bias, by studying sacrifice and purity in tandem, using similar methods, with a willingness to grant that sacrificial rules could be just as symbolic as purity rules are generally understood to be. The integrated symbolic approach to both purity and sacrifice offered here will work toward understanding what ancient Israelites might have believed about the purpose and meaning of their sacrificial cult. In particular, we will see that much of the symbolism can be understood in light of two central theological ideas— *imitatio Dei*, and the concern to attract and maintain God's presence dwelling in the sanctuary.

In chapter 3, we will turn to the prophetic literature, with an eye toward reexamining the kinds of challenges raised there to the sacrificial system. Certain prophetic passages are seemingly critical of the cult—and indeed, such passages in part motivate the dominant antisacrificial bias. As we will see, however, the prophets do not in fact reject the practice of sacrifice or its meaning, although there are indeed a number of reasons why the prophets took a particular interest in the sacrificial practices of their contemporaries.

In part II, we will bring the analysis of part 1 to bear on an understanding of Judaism in the Second Temple and early rabbinic periods. After briefly reviewing a number of recent works that treat understandings of the cult in ancient Judaism (introduction to part II), we will examine our themes as they are developed in ancient Jewish literature in general (chapter 4), in the Dead Sea Scrolls in particular (chapter 5), in rabbinic literature (chapter 6), and in the New Testament (chapter 7).

In chapter 4, we will discuss two overarching ancient Jewish understandings of the temple: (1) that the temple represented the cosmos and (2) that the Jerusalem temple was understood as the earthly analogue of the heavenly temple. All too often, these ideas are understood as "desacralizations" of the temple or as "spiritualizations" of the cult. I will argue, however, that these two notions help us understand what the cultic rituals meant in that time for those Jews who remained loyal to the temple and its practices. As we will see, these two ideas continue and develop the understandings of purity and sacrifice to be traced in chapter 2: the concerns with *imitatio Dei* and attracting the divine presence. We will also see that the two symbolic approaches to the temple—that it represents the cosmos or corresponds to a heavenly analogue—do not constitute criticisms of the temple.

In chapter 5, we will evaluate the criticisms leveled against the temple in ancient Jewish literature, particularly among the texts discovered at Qumran. As we will see, the Dead Sea sectarians built on and developed the prophetic tradition (discussed in chapter 3) in order to articulate a sharper criticism of the Jerusalem temple, its practice, and its personnel. After carefully schematizing the various antitemple polemics, we will consider the degree to which the Qumran sectarians rejected the temple. We will then consider the question of whether the Qumran sectarians replaced the temple—even provisionally—in some fashion. As we will see, the Qumran sectarians emulated the temple in a number of ways, but they did not consider their communal rituals or institutions to be effective replacements for the temple. Nor did they "spiritualize" sacrifice. The scholarship that magnifies and even praises the sectarian rejection of the temple has fallen into the trap of endorsing the ancient and modern rejections of the temple. Instead of endorsing such criticism, I will suggest that the criticism needs to be more carefully scrutinized.

In chapter 6, we consider the approach to the temple taken in rabbinic literature. Our first task will be to consider the degree to which the rabbis adopted the criticisms of the temple articulated at Qumran. We will then consider the ways in which the rabbis responded to the destruction of the temple in 70 C.E. As we will see, like the Qumran sectarians before them, the rabbis ascribed cultic significance to a number of extratemple rituals, without maintaining that the temple has been effectively replaced or superseded by something else. Again, scholars who themselves appear reluctant to recognize the temple's meanings have mistakenly attributed to the rabbis a number of antitemple ideas that are in truth not to be found in rabbinic literature.

In chapter 7, we will consider the approach to the temple taken in the New Testament. We will focus in particular on two events said in the Synoptic Gospels to have occurred in Jesus' last days: the New Testament narratives concerning Jesus' overturning the tables in the temple and his institution of the eucharist at the Last Supper. Many scholars view both of these events as articulating criticisms of or even rejections of the Jerusalem temple. Here too,

I will argue, biases against the temple and its cult have exerted too much influence on the discussion. We will consider alternative interpretations of both narratives, building on the conclusions of the previous three chapters. We will conclude this chapter with a brief survey of some New Testament texts that do criticize the temple, such as the book of Hebrews. Thus we will conclude with the beginnings of the antisacrificial biases that we have briefly discussed here.

It is hoped that each of the following chapters will shed light on its stated topic and that therefore the book as a whole will contribute to the understanding of our themes in selected literature stretching from the Hebrew Bible through the Talmud. But I also hope to drive home a number of more general methodological points. First, the project will argue for the importance of analyzing sacrifice in particular in a balanced and fair manner, using methods consistent with those applied to other related ritual structures (such as ritual purity). Second, I will continuously point out—and refute—a number of evolutionist theories or assumptions that continue to predominate, or at least crop up in, the scholarly discussions of our themes in the various literatures we will survey. Third, the work will highlight some of the ways in which the study of Judaism and Christianity in antiquity continues to be too heavily influenced by contemporary religious and cultural perspectives toward—and critiques of—sacrifice.

The field of religious studies is probably destined to be populated by scholars who adhere to a large or small degree to the religions they study. It would be hypocritical of me to decry this phenomenon, for I cannot rightfully wish things were otherwise without wishing myself out of work. Moreover, it has also long been known that atheistic and secularist biases can produce their own distortions of religious phenomena—the figures of James Frazer and Sigmund Freud may come to mind.[29] But I think that those of us who study the history of Judaism and Christianity while maintaining a commitment to one tradition or the other can do better than we have done. In this book, I will try to do my part, by identifying in particular a number of scholarly understandings of various ancient Jewish and early Christian texts that, in my view, too closely reflect certain religious attitudes—both Jewish and Christian—toward ancient Judaism's sacrificial cult.

PART I

Purity and Sacrifice in Biblical Israel

I

Sacrifice and Purity

The Twisted Fortunes of Related Ritual Structures

Approaches to Purity, Theories of Sacrifice

In order to understand better the difference between the ways in which purity and sacrifice are studied by contemporary biblical scholars, we would do well to review the theoretical works that currently have the broadest impact on the study of these topics. With regard to purity, the theoretical work that still dominates the discussion is Mary Douglas's *Purity and Danger*, first published in 1966. With regard to sacrifice, the theoretical works most frequently cited in the commentaries are René Girard's *Violence and the Sacred* and Walter Burkert's *Homo Necans*, both of which appeared in 1972. There are of course other significant works in the field (some of which will be discussed below), but it is fair to say—especially with regard to Douglas and Girard—that their impact on biblical studies has been unmatched. Girardian readings of the Hebrew Bible and the New Testament can easily be found, and no one would dare to write on ritual purity in Leviticus without citing *Purity and Danger*. The strange thing is that it is difficult to imagine two books more fundamentally different than *Purity and Danger* and *Violence and the Sacred*.

Mary Douglas and the Rehabilitation of Purity

Mary Douglas's *Purity and Danger* is a complex work that defies brief treatment. However, as fuller treatments of her work can easily be found, a few brief remarks should suffice for our purposes of tracing the varied approaches taken to purity and sacrifice in recent years.[1] Before Douglas, there was a time when conceptions of defilement were treated with outright disdain. Scholars and thinkers of such stature as Frazer and Robertson Smith lacked all patience for the avoidance behaviors of the Hebrew Bible, and they could barely conceal their disdain. Other scholars were perhaps less disrespectful but no less dismissive. In his *Elementary Forms of Religious Life*, Emile Durkheim (1858–1917) drove a wedge between the "Negative Cult" and the "Positive Cult," with the former serving primarily a functional purpose, while only the latter could be deeply expressive or symbolic.[2] At about the same time—and making matters even worse— Sigmund Freud (1856–1939) famously compared religious avoidances with the obsessive behavior of psychotics in his *Totem and Taboo*.[3] Whether they were seen as the products of primitive fears or primeval obsessions, ritualized avoidances were dismissed by many as irrational, pointless, and just plain foolish.

For the sake of illustration, we paraphrase here Robertson Smith's approach to the "taboos" of Leviticus, as spelled out in an appendix to his *Lectures on the Religion of the Semites*.[4] Robertson Smith begins by observing correctly that taboos often revolve around matters that are natural, innocent, and even necessary: sex, birth, death, and disease. Robertson Smith then asserts that such beliefs arose among "savages" who believed that birth, death, and sex involved "the action of superhuman agencies of a dangerous kind."[5] The person whom the Israelites deemed to be ritually defiled, their predecessors deemed to be truly in danger. According to Robertson Smith, the approach taken by Israel's predecessors "is not scientific, but it is perfectly intelligible, and forms the basis of a consistent system of practice."[6] But the Israelites, according to Robertson Smith, should have known better:

> Rules like this have nothing in common with the spirit of Hebrew religion; they can only be remains of a primitive superstition, like that of the savage who shuns the blood of uncleanness, and such things, as a supernatural and deadly virus....
>
> The irrationality of laws of uncleanness, from the standpoint of spiritual religion or even of the higher heathenism, is so manifest, that they must necessarily be looked on as having survived from an earlier form of faith and society. And this being so, I do not see how any historical student can refuse to class them with savage taboos. The attempts to explain them otherwise, which are still occasionally met with, seem to be confined to speculative writers, who have no knowledge of the general features of thought and belief in rude societies.[7]

This is the situation to which Douglas addressed her work, and it is fair to say that she did so with a certain degree of success.

For our purposes, four aspects of Mary Douglas's *Purity and Danger* remain of lasting importance—in part because of the influence her work has had on Milgrom and other interpreters of Leviticus's purity laws. First, against especially Robertson Smith and Frazer, Douglas argued that avoidance behaviors could no longer be dismissed as something inherently or distinctly primitive. Douglas shows that our own notions of hygiene are not necessarily any more rational or objective than the religious conceptions frequently dismissed as irrational.[8] Second—again against Frazer and Robertson Smith—Douglas argued that avoidance behaviors could no longer be treated in a "piecemeal" fashion, on a one-by-one basis. If Frazer could try to collect and analyze taboos in an encyclopedic fashion—comparing, for instance, various cultures' attitudes toward blood or hair—Douglas's work argued persuasively that the avoidances of any religious tradition or culture had to be treated *systemically* or *structurally*.[9] Third—and here her criticism applies more widely—the ritual system once described must then be understood as a symbolic expression.[10] Thus, for instance, Douglas's famous chapter on the abominations of Leviticus treats the biblical dietary laws as a self-contained ritual system that expresses fundamental ideas about ancient Israelite cosmology. In contrast to Robertson Smith, Douglas looked for an explanation of biblical dietary laws not by looking back at pre-Israelite dietary restrictions but rather by appealing to Israel's own account of God's creation of the cosmos.[11] Fourth—and for our concerns, finally—Douglas argued that purity symbol systems serve identifiable social functions. Far from being meaningless vestiges, these rules serve not only to express an idea but also to impose or reinforce it. In some cases, these behaviors serve to draw external boundaries, such as prohibiting exogamy. In others, pollution ideas serve to highlight internal distinctions in status, or to control certain undesirable behaviors.[12]

Purity and Danger, in short, is a passionate defense of ritual in general, and purity rites in particular. Douglas argues that purity rites should not be understood as empty vestiges or irrational obsessions. The rituals work together to form expressive symbolic systems, which not only articulate ideas but also serve to enforce them. *Purity and Danger* demonstrates persuasively that previous treatments of purity rites were plagued by two demons: antiritualism and evolutionism. Antiritualism was in evidence in Frazer's and Robertson Smith's problematic assumption that anyone who adhered to rituals of avoidance must have been erroneously persuaded of their automatically effective result. Why else would people persist in avoiding an obviously harmless substance, such as pork, unless they were duped into believing that the avoidance achieved some magical aim? Not only has Douglas answered that question but also she has correctly identified the misguided, biased motivation behind it.[13] Antiritualism was also in evidence in the commonplace critique of ritual as empty formalism, an insufficient expression of the interior and true thoughts of the person.[14]

Evolutionism was in evidence, for example, in Robertson Smith's tracing of a more or less linear development from earlier primitive beliefs in the automatic, magical, effectiveness of ritual (by primitives and early ritualists), first to the recognition (ostensibly by the Hebrew prophets) that what really matters is not external ritual but interior disposition. The final step for Robertson Smith would be, apparently, the elimination of the silly original ritual altogether. Evolutionism was also in evidence in the assumption that the move away from ritual defilement was paralleled with a move toward ethics. Thus the primitive magician lacked ethics, the Hebrew prophets taught them, while we moderns finally learned them. Douglas argues passionately that such schemes are both inaccurate and biased.

While *Purity and Danger* remains focused on its stated subject, Douglas ventures to speak of ritual in general: "ritual focuses attention by framing; it enlivens the memory and links the present with the relevant past. In all this it aids perception."[15] With the understanding that ritual purity is the prerequisite for sacrifice, it is rather obvious that what Douglas has to say about ritual purity in particular—to say nothing of what she says of ritual in general—would apply to sacrifice as well. In fact, outside the field of biblical studies, one can find a number of analyses that apply Douglas's methods, with some success, to the study of sacrifice. Such works include Luc de Heusch, *Sacrifice in Africa*, as well as what Marcel Detienne, Jean-Pierre Vernant, and their colleagues at the Paris Center for Comparative Studies of Ancient Societies have produced in *The Cuisine of Sacrifice among the Greeks*. In biblical studies, however, such treatments are much more rare, though not entirely unknown.[16] Yet to my knowledge, none of these applications of Douglas's methods to biblical sacrifice attempt to account for both purity and sacrifice at one and the same time. Had Douglas followed up her work on purity with a subsequent volume—entitled *Sacrifice and Safety*—then perhaps the history of the study of sacrifice would have been different. But as it happened, Douglas did not directly treat sacrifice in Leviticus until quite recently (and we will briefly consider her new work toward the end of this chapter).

Claude Lévi-Strauss, Totemism, and Metaphor

Lurking in the background of Douglas's *Purity and Danger* are the works of another figure who straddled anthropology and religion, Claude Lévi-Strauss. In a number of ways, his *Totemism* and *The Savage Mind*—both of which first appeared in 1962—are important preludes to *Purity and Danger*. Like Douglas, Lévi-Strauss argued that evolutionist approaches to primitive society were highly flawed. Throughout his work, Lévi-Strauss insisted that

> these people whom we usually consider as completely subservient
> to the need of not starving, of continuing able just to subsist in very
> harsh material conditions, are perfectly capable of disinterested
> thinking; that is, they are moved by a need or a desire to understand
> the world around them, its nature and their society. On the other
> hand, to achieve that end, they proceed by intellectual means, exactly
> as a philosopher, or even to some extent a scientist, can and
> would do.[17]

In *Totemism* and in *The Savage Mind*, Lévi-Strauss also argued passionately and persuasively that ritual structures once derided as irrational and primitive—such as totemism—were in fact complex and meaningful structures. Like

Douglas, Lévi-Strauss insisted that the individual rules cannot be understood when one is isolated from the other, but only when the rules are studied together as a system.[18] Only then can the symbolism be understood. Once their structural and symbolic nature is properly appreciated, then, finally, "primitive" rules of avoidance can be understood in their original complexity.

Yet, unlike *Purity and Danger*, Lévi-Strauss's work contributes very little in any direct way to an understanding of ancient Israel. In fact, the overall impact of his work on the study of sacrifice in particular was largely negative. Lévi-Strauss was not interested in situating ritual structures (or myths, for that matter) in specific contexts; he was, rather, in search of revealing the ways in which rituals (and especially myths) articulate a universal, dialectic mode of thinking.[19] Thus in order to apply it to any specific case, Lévi-Strauss's wild and radical structuralism needs to be domesticated.[20] But that is not the only problem. We also must be aware that Lévi-Strauss's application of his method was quite selective. He obviously preferred myth to ritual, as is demonstrated by the subjects of most of his studies throughout his career. In his later works, hostility toward ritual is painfully expressed, notably in the "Finale" to his four volumes of *Mythologiques*. When compared to myth, ritual comes off as "a bastardization of thought."[21] But even in Lévi-Strauss's earlier work—which displays some sympathy to ritual—his approach to ritual was also selective, matching the overall biases I have been tracing here.

As noted already, *Totemism* and *The Savage Mind* analyze "primitive" systems of avoidance behaviors, demonstrating that the rules, when taken as a whole, exemplify a rational and symbolic mode of thinking. In Lévi-Strauss's mind, it is imperative to recognize the metaphoric nature of totemic rules:

> Totemism is based on a postulation of homology between two parallel series—that of natural species and that of social groups—whose respective terms, it must be remembered, do not resemble each other in pairs. It is only the relation between the series as a whole which is homomorphic: a formal correlation between two systems of difference, each constituting a pole of opposition.[22]

In other words, we cannot hope to understand totemism if we remain focused on any supposed relationship between a specific clan and its totem. The trick to understanding the symbolism of totemism is to acknowledge its systemic nature, whereby the relationship between a set of clans is expressed through the analogy (i.e., the metaphor) in the relationship between their respective totems. In its simplest form, as group X is to group Y, so too is the totem of X to the totem of Y. This is what Lévi-Strauss means when he refers to totemism as metaphorical. And because he views metaphor as foundational and cognitive, when he describes totemism as metaphor, he is paying it a high compliment.[23] All this is well and good, and we can see how these works lead toward some of the key insights of *Purity and Danger*.[24]

When, however, Lévi-Strauss turned his attention to sacrifice—which he did only briefly—an entirely different instinct seems to have taken over.[25]

Lévi-Strauss does not compare sacrifice to totemism; he contrasts them. And sacrifice comes off looking worse by far. Unlike totemism, sacrifice cannot be a complex symbolic system because it is based not on symbolism but substitution. Lévi-Strauss takes as his starting point—and his guiding example—a description of the sacrifice of a cucumber in Evans-Pritchard's *Nuer Religion*.[26] Just as a cucumber in this instance stands for an ox, so too in all sacrifice does the victim stand for something else. But in this case, the symbolism is not metaphorical but *metonymic*: "the two systems [sacrifice and totemism] are therefore opposed by their orientation, metonymical in one case and metaphorical in the other."[27] There is no metaphorical system of relations, as in totemism, just the plain and simple relation—one that is nonmetaphorical and not so rational—between the sacrifice and whatever it substitutes for. Just as "metaphorical" for Lévi-Strauss is a compliment, its antonym—"metonymical"—is derogatory. In the end, while totemic systems "belong to the levels of language" and "aim to make sense," sacrifice is a discourse "wanting in good sense for all that it may frequently be pronounced."[28]

It is disappointing that the same Lévi-Strauss who argued in his *Totemism* that animals are "good to think"[29] would treat sacrifice so callously in *The Savage Mind*. His explicit disdain for sacrifice finds an unfortunate tacit support in Douglas's benign neglect of the same rite—although she cannot be blamed for Lévi-Strauss's hostility. But when the two viewpoints are taken together, one could too easily think that structural anthropology cannot contribute to an understanding of sacrifice.[30] One could also too easily think that while evolutionist analyses of purity were wrong, perhaps evolutionist analyses of sacrifice were not. Whatever the explanation, the tone of *Purity and Danger*, which looms large over current treatments of biblical pollution, is largely absent from the current discussion of biblical sacrifice.

René Girard and the Assault on Sacrifice

Reading the works of René Girard is an experience altogether different from that of reading a work by Douglas. While Douglas is an anthropologist, speaking about what various peoples do (or did), Girard is a literary critic, analyzing first and foremost the myths that various peoples have composed. Where Douglas speaks of Africa and Polynesia in addition to the Hebrew Bible, Girard limits his observations primarily to the classics of the Western literary tradition, in particular the Bible and the Greek myths. Where Douglas seeks to understand the symbolism and function of purity systems by placing them in their social contexts, Girard takes his cue from Freud and Lévi-Strauss, and seeks to uncover the fundamental idea that lies behind all sacrificial rituals: he seeks to reveal, as he puts it, "the unity of all rites."[31] But the greatest difference is this: where *Purity and Danger* seeks to rehabilitate purity rituals from the slanders heaped upon them, *Violence and the Sacred* is nothing short of an indictment of sacrificial rituals. It is therefore disappointing that many biblicists have chosen to develop Girard's ideas or depend on his interpretations.[32]

In a nutshell, Girard's argument runs as follows.[33] Like Freud, Girard finds that a crime lies at the heart of religion. But for Girard, the crime that explains sacrifice is not a sexually motivated act of patricide but a collective murder by a frenzied mob of an arbitrarily chosen hapless victim. How does this crime come about? The first step is to understand that rivalry is part of human nature. This rivalry manifests itself in what Girard calls "mimetic desire," the innate tendency for one person to want what another already has.[34] It is a short step—in a primitive world—from desire to violence, and soon enough, one of our two primeval competitors has killed the other. Because the victim has family and friends who naturally seek vengeance, this first murder does not end things but rather leads to a cycle of "reciprocal violence."[35] The violent cycle of vengeance repeatedly spirals out, widening and intensifying, until it reaches a crisis. What finally puts an end to the cycle of vengeance is an act of "unanimous violence."[36] Acting now as one, the community spontaneously channels all blame and all violence onto a single person, who is chosen arbitrarily to become the mob's victim. This is what Girard calls "generative scapegoating," and it is this murder that gives rise to sacrificial rites.

In Girard's scheme, the act of sacrifice is productive—or "generative"—in a number of ways.[37] First and foremost, this final act of brutality puts an end to the seemingly endless cycle that preceded it. Second, the act's very success spawns imitation, albeit on a smaller scale. Because the destructive cycle of violence has now ended, the relieved community will naturally reenact this event. But from now on, the community will make a secondary substitution, utilizing an animal victim that can be more readily disposed of—because no one will seek vengeance for it. Hence the origin of sacrifice. On the one hand, ritual sacrifice reenacts the scapegoating that preceded it. But, more important, ritualized sacrifice serves to prevent the cycle of violence from breaking out again. And there is still another way in which the original act of scapegoating is generative. Because human culture can flourish only once the cycle of violence is broken, the act of generative scapegoating bequeaths to humanity not only sacrifice but all forms of ritual, myth, and social structure. Girard's scheme, in the end, accounts for the origin "of all those cultural forms that give man his unique humanity."[38]

Girard's tale is a hybrid Western myth. It begins like the story of Cain and Abel and it reaches a climax that comes out of *The Bacchae*. It ends, however, with something of a happily ever after. This is, of course, just a thumbnail sketch, and not an altogether sympathetic one. But if one can muster an ounce of sympathy for sacrificial rituals, it is difficult to conjure much more than that for Girard's analysis of sacrifice. Girard, in fact, does not hide his disgust for sacrificial rites, which he refers to as "abhorrent."[39]

To be sure, Girard does believe that sacrifice has a positive function: it seeks to end violence.[40] But sacrifice is in reality ill suited to that task; systems of justice—which develop later—are much more effective.[41] Moreover, Girard insists that the victims of "generative scapegoating" are chosen arbitrarily: the origin of sacrifice is then not only violent but actually unjust. Thus, despite its positive goal, sacrifice is ineffective and immoral. Sacrificial rites also have a negative function: to whatever degree they achieve their goal, they do so only by concealing their true nature.[42] The performance of sacrifice led to the development of sacrificial myths, which appear to relate the origins of sacrifice but in fact conceal its true origin. If the genesis of sacrifice—in violent, unanimous scapegoating—were revealed, the cycle of mimetic violence would begin anew. Thus the myths and rituals divert attention from what really happened. To this task of deception, sacrifice and religion in general are all too well suited, to wit the fact that we never knew what had been concealed until Girard revealed it. Thus sacrifice fails in its true goal and succeeds only insofar as it deceives.

Girard's scheme has numerous methodological faults, many of which have been pointed out before.[43] His scheme is thoroughly reductionist: the essence of all myth and ritual is sacrifice, and sacrificial ritual boils down to criminal violence. Girard's real interests are, moreover, suspiciously selective. After paying lip service to some anthropological work, he focuses on biblical narratives and Greek myths. The traditions of Arabia and India play no role, and presumably contribute nothing to our understanding of how sacrifice began. Moreover, Girard's reading of myth and ritual is in truth an elegant argument *ex silentio*. By claiming to reveal what pre-Christian myth and ritual seek to conceal, Girard can develop his own account that finds confirmation precisely in the fact that what he reveals is not actually articulated straightforwardly in these rituals and myths. Those scholars who think that sacrifice can be explained by interpreting the evidence are simply being fooled by the sources, the purpose of which is to mislead. In this respect, Girard's reading is not only distinctively Christian but also notably Gnostic.[44] But Girard's reading offends not only by being methodologically flawed; not unlike Robertson Smith's approach to ritual impurity, Girard's take on sacrifice exhibits tendencies that are antiritualist and evolutionist.

Evolutionism abounds in Girard's work, and it takes a number of forms. One is to view sacrifice as a primitive but failed attempt to achieve what our systems of justice are devoted to:

> There may be a certain connection between all the various methods
> employed by man since the beginning of time to avoid being caught up
> in an interminable round of revenge. They can be grouped into three
> general categories: (1) preventive measures in which sacrificial rites
> divert the spirit of revenge into other channels; (2) the harnessing
> or hobbling of vengeance by means of compensatory measures, trials
> by combat, etc., whose curative effects remain precarious; (3) the
> establishment of a judicial system—the most efficient of all curative
> procedures.
>
> We have listed the methods in ascending order of effectiveness.
> The evolution from preventive to curative procedures is reflected
> in the course of history or, at any rate, in the course of the history of
> the Western world. . . .

The curative procedures employed by primitive societies appear rudimentary to us. We tend to regard them as fumbling efforts to improvise a judicial system.[45]

This argument has all the hallmarks of evolutionism. Like Frazer's work, this construct is largely the result of the theorist's creativity, not real history.

A second form of evolutionism is even more problematic. Girard's reading is distinctively Christian, and notably supersessionist. The supersessionistic nature of Girard's project becomes most clear when he turns to Christian narratives and finds *only* in them the revelation of what all earlier myths and rituals conceal. Thus, the Gospels outdo all previous mythology.[46] But Girard not only lifts the Gospels above the mythology of religions that are no longer among us; by seeing the Gospels as the only texts that are truly revelatory, Girard is led to view Christianity as the necessary completion of Judaism.[47] Even more troubling is the fact that in his analysis of Jesus' death, Girard squarely places much of the blame on Jewish authorities and on the (Jewish) crowd, without entertaining the possibility that postcrucifixion conflicts between Jesus' followers and other Jews may have had an impact on how the passion narratives were constructed.[48] What is latent in Girard's work becomes more explicit elsewhere: there are some who push the Girardian approach further, articulating interpretations of sacrifice that explicitly (as opposed to implicitly) impute to ancient Jews a fair degree of guilt for the killing of various innocent victims in the first century C.E. and earlier, through the killing of Jesus, and more simply through the performance of ancient Israelite ritual.[49]

Girard's antiritualism is evident first in his disdain for sacrifice as immoral: all sacrifice involves the killing of *innocent* victims.[50] Girard's starting point is, in truth, that sacrifice is *injustice*. Clearly concerned with the violence of the twentieth century, Girard assumes that there is a fundamental connection between the human proclivity for (unjust) violence and animal sacrifice.[51] But this assertion is by no means obvious, correct, or even helpful. As Bruce Chilton recently put it, "Girard makes sacrifice in the ancient world the scapegoat for violence in modern experience."[52] In fact, the assertion is itself antipriestly, to say the least: whenever one puts the "innocent victims" of sacrificial ritual in the foreground, there must be, lurking in the background, a cadre of "guilty priests." Can this really help us understand sacrifice? But Girard's antiritualism extends further. Girard in fact dislikes impurity as much as he dislikes sacrifice: throughout his work, impurity is equated with violence.[53] Thus, to his credit, we can say that Girard's approach does take both purity and sacrifice into account. But in Girard's case, his wider vision detracts from his argument. Indeed, when we telescope his disdain for sacrifice with his reductionist claims regarding the "unity of all rites," we find a charge against all rites.

Eventually, it becomes clear that Girard's antiritualism drives his evolutionism. Defending his historicist approach, Girard avers that

the relative failure of Frazer, Freud, or Robertson Smith is no
reason to regard their insistence on getting to the bottom of things as
foolish or outdated. To assert that there is nothing to be gained by
seeking out the function and origin of ritual is to say that the language
of religion is destined to remain forever a dead letter, a kind of
gibberish—cleverly codified, perhaps, but devoid of any real
meaning.[54]

Here we have it. Unless we can understand its history, ritual is and remains a
meaningless gibberish. While his intentions sound laudable, in fact his un-
derlying assumptions here prove to be *both* evolutionist and antiritualist.
Ritual obviously means nothing today, Girard says, so the only hope is to
resort to history. Only then can we understand how things evolved from what
was originally misguided but explainable to what is now a dead letter. In the
final analysis, Girard's take on sacrifice—far from breaking new ground—
really just brings us back to Robertson Smith on taboo. But Girard's work
does reveal what had been concealed. The fascination with origins is motivated by an evolutionist bias. The *only* way to understand it is to get to the
bottom of it. This motivating bias characterized Robertson Smith's take on
Israelite taboos a century ago. And it characterizes much current work on
Israelite sacrifice today.

Walter Burkert and the Primitive Hunter

It is certainly a remarkable coincidence that Walter Burkert published his
theory on the origins of sacrifice—entitled, *Homo Necans: The Anthropology of
Ancient Greek Sacrificial Ritual and Myth*—in the same year René Girard
published *Violence and the Sacred*. In this work, Burkert sets out, like Girard, on a
quest to reveal the concealed origins of sacrificial practices. Burkert similarly assumes the centrality of ritual killing: the first subheading of the first
chapter of *Homo Necans* is "Sacrifice as an Act of Killing." Like Girard, Burkert's
concern with violence in the contemporary world translates into a distaste
for sacrifice: Burkert's own summary of his theory is entitled "The *Problem*
of Ritual Killing."[55] Considering the similarities—both coincidental and sub-
stantive—it is not all that surprising that the two theories are commonly
paired.[56] It is also not surprising that the two authors themselves felt a sense of
kinship with each other.[57]

Yet there are differences between the two, and for the most part where they
differ it is to Burkert's benefit. Primarily, of course, they differ in the thrust of
the theory. Where Girard gives priority to an original act of scapegoating,
Burkert argues that sacrifice constitutes a ritualization of the hunt. While
Burkert's works are infused with a concern for elucidating the nature of human evolution, he manages to theorize about sacrificial origins without falling
into an evolutionist approach. In fact, Burkert repeatedly and pessimistically
denies that humans have made as much progress as we may tend to hope,
especially when it comes to violence.[58] Burkert's work is also less reductionist

than Girard's: Burkert recognizes the difference between scapegoat rites and whole burnt offerings, and he denies that a single explanation works for all sacrificial rites.[59] And he doesn't begin to go as far as Girard's "unity of all rites." To the contrary, Burkert endorses contextual, functionalist approaches, taking a decided step back from Lévi-Strauss in the direction of Douglas—though he remains focused on his quest for origins.[60] Burkert is also less critical of sacrifice in general: while he focuses on sacrifice as killing, he legitimates sacrifice by tying it to hunting, which of course was necessary at one time for human survival.[61]

While Burkert expands the scope from Girard's exclusive focus on killing, he is still too focused on the supposed shock and horror of killing.[62] Whether this focus will help us understand the origins of sacrifice we may never know. But surely such a focus cannot help us explain an entire sacrificial process (to say nothing of preliminaries such as ritual purification). Indeed, precisely because he is more methodologically sound in his quest for origins, Burkert's works are equally less relevant for an understanding of the sacrificial process as described in Leviticus. Like Lévi-Strauss, Burkert's work on sacrifice—as interesting as it is—is a dead end for those interested in ancient Israel. Whether or not sacrifice originated in hunting practices, it is difficult to imagine how the sacrifice-as-hunting thesis can shed light on the killing of domesticated animals by a pastoralist society such as ancient Israel.[63]

Having established the disparity between the theoretical treatments of purity and sacrifice, we are positioned to observe how this disparity is reflected in current exegetical work on Leviticus. Significantly, a number of modern commentaries exhibit some sort of disparity between their treatments of purity and sacrifice.[64] But to illustrate the case, we turn to what is surely the greatest academic treatment of Leviticus, Jacob Milgrom's three-volume, 2,700-plus-page Anchor Bible commentary.

Ritual Purity and Sacrifice in Jacob Milgrom's Leviticus

Milgrom's volumes engage much of the current theoretical work on purity and sacrifice, with both positive and negative results. On the positive side, we finally have a comprehensive, learned, scholarly commentary on Leviticus that is informed by the advances made by anthropologists and other experts in religious studies. But on the negative side, we also have a commentary that reflects the methodological disparities characterizing the current study of purity and sacrifice.[65] Briefly put, while Milgrom treats ritual purity thoroughly and sympathetically, his treatment of sacrifice leaves something to be desired. Of course, as noted already, Milgrom's work is hardly unique in this respect. But precisely because his work is so detailed—and because it is destined to be a major tool for the study of Leviticus for generations to come—it is fitting to devote attention here to ways in which the common methodological disparities manifest themselves in Milgrom's work.

Ritual Purity

Jacob Milgrom's treatment of the ritual purity laws is sophisticated and sympathetic. For our purposes, there are two important characteristics of Milgrom's approach to ritual purity, both of which result from lessons drawn in part from Douglas's *Purity and Danger*. First, Milgrom insists on the structural—"systemic"—nature of the ritual purity rules.[66] Tellingly, he speaks of ritual purity regulations as a "system" throughout his commentary, and he draws certain implications from that assumption. In particular, Milgrom is willing to infer the existence of all sorts of purity rules, even though they are not explicitly stated in the Hebrew Bible. For instance, Leviticus 15 does not explicitly require that women immerse themselves upon the completion of their menstrual periods, a fact that frequently surprises those who know that this is one of the few ritual purity rules that many traditionally minded Jews still follow to this day. What are we to make of the absence of this requirement? Interestingly, Leviticus 15:16 requires a man to bathe upon purification from semen defilement, even though that particular form of defilement lasts for only a single day. Moreover, Leviticus 15:21 requires a man to immerse if he had come into contact with his wife while she was ritually impure. If the men in these cases are required to immerse themselves, does it not stand to reason that those who were purifying themselves from even more severe forms of impurity—like that which results from menstruation—must also immerse? Milgrom applies precisely this kind of logic to this case and some others as well.[67] The validity of this approach is not the present concern. What is important for our purposes is to underscore that his approach operates on the assumption that the ritual purity rules form a coherent system that is governed by its own internal logic. Therefore, the scholar-reader of Leviticus who is equipped with the proper understanding of the system's principles can fill in many of the regulations left unarticulated. The reader of Milgrom's commentary can best appreciate this aspect of his approach by examining the various charts and diagrams occupying some twenty pages of *Leviticus 1–16*. These charts map out the various ways in which distinct substances defile, and then indicate the ways in which one might purify oneself from such defilements.[68] Virtually every chart has items marked in brackets. These brackets enclose data that are not mentioned as such in Leviticus but result from logical deductions like the one just paraphrased.

A second ramification of Milgrom's systemic approach to ritual purity is found in his argument that the system *as a whole* can be understood symbolically. According to the laws of the Pentateuch, a number of natural processes and substances bring about ritual defilement, including childbirth (Lev. 12:1–8), certain skin diseases and other fungi (Lev. 13:1–14:32), genital discharges (Lev. 15:1–33), the carcasses of certain impure animals (Lev. 11:1–47), and human corpses (Num. 19:10–22).[69] In his discussions of the various substances that bring about ritual defilement in the Hebrew Bible, Milgrom sets out to find a single common denominator that underlies all of the rules. In the end he does find one; and then, not unlike Douglas, he argues that the entire system has a single symbolic focus: the "common denominator" of the purity system is, in Milgrom's view, death.[70] Each substance that defiles is just one or two steps removed from representing the process of death or the forces of death.

Not all are convinced by this explanation. We will review the details in the next chapter when we analyze biblical purificatory and sacrificial rituals more closely. It is not important for our purposes here to evaluate whether Milgrom's single symbolic common denominator is correct. Rather, what is important to note is how indebted Milgrom's approach is to Douglas. Milgrom speaks consistently of a system that is symbolic in nature and can be explained by appeal to a single idea. This is not unlike how Douglas treats the dietary prohibitions in the famous third chapter of *Purity and Danger*. Significantly, while Milgrom criticizes Douglas on many points of detail, he also recognizes the debt his interpretation of ritual purity rules owes to hers.[71]

Sacrifice

Milgrom's approach to sacrifice is altogether different, virtually the inverse of the way in which he approaches ritual impurity. While Milgrom recognizes that sacrificial rules constitute a system,[72] he denies to that system any real meaning. Moreover, his treatment of sacrifice is highly evolutionist. When it comes to understanding sacrifice as a phenomenon, he seems more interested in what happened before Leviticus and after and less interested in what is going on within the text itself. In this respect, Milgrom's work is in line with—and very likely influenced by—the current search for origins that seems to predominate in much of the current discussion on sacrificial rituals.[73] With regard to sacrifice, the influence of Douglas on Milgrom is not in evidence.

Milgrom begins his discussion of theories of sacrifice by quoting a rabbinic text that he believes—erroneously, as it turns out—"clearly implies that the sacrifices were not ends in themselves but were divinely ordained in order to wean Israel from idolatry."[74] The passage in question is a rabbinic comment on Leviticus 17:3–7, the passage requiring that all slaughter take place at the tent of meeting (*Lev. Rabbah* 22:8; ed. Margulies 2:516–517).[75] Milgrom continues, quoting the following extract: the matter "may be compared to a king's son who was addicted to carcasses and forbidden meats. Said the king: Let him always eat at my table and he will get out of the habit." The text continues, explaining that the son in the parable represents the Israelites, who were accustomed to performing idolatrous worship when they were enslaved in Egypt. God requires, therefore, that they slaughter animals for food only at the tent of meeting (that is, in God's presence) so that they will break their idolatrous habits and perform their sacrificial worship properly. This text, however, does not "clearly imply" that sacrifice itself is only a means to an end, as Milgrom asserts. The means to the end of weaning Israel from idolatry is the requirement that all slaughter take place at the tent of meeting, just as the means to the end in the parable is the requirement that the son eat only at the king's table. The parable does not imply that sacrifice in general is destined to end, any more than it implies that the king's son is supposed to learn eventually to live without eating. The text operates on the assumption that sacrifice—like eating—is a given, something that neither the son nor the king can live without. That this particular rabbinic comment was concerned with the restriction of slaughter to the sanctuary (and not the eventual abolition of sacrifice) can also be seen in the fact that the text explicitly cites Leviticus 17:7. Moreover, the editors of Leviticus Rabbah placed this passage in the midst of other passages commenting on Leviticus 17:3–7, and not among passages speaking of sacrifice in general.

Milgrom then cites the medieval Jewish philosopher Maimonides, who certainly exhibits, in Milgrom's phrase, "an uneasiness with sacrifice." As we discussed already, Maimonides' historicist (or evolutionist) approach to sacrifice was highly controversial in its own day. Indeed, the controversy continued down through the Middle Ages, coming to a head again with the rise of movements advocating synagogue reform. Significantly, the passage Milgrom quoted from Leviticus Rabbah has itself played a role in these medieval and modern Jewish debates about the future of sacrifice. The philosopher and exegete Isaac Abarbanel (1437–1508) quotes a version of the Leviticus Rabbah passage in the introduction to his commentary on Leviticus, where he defends Maimonides' approach. Interestingly enough, Maimonides himself did not quote the Leviticus Rabbah passage in his own historicist interpretation of sacrifice. Scholars have continued to debate whether the passage really means what Abarbanel (and now Milgrom) says it means. And this debate typically is but an aspect of the larger debate on the role sacrifice should play in Jewish liturgy and eschatology.[76] The upshot is this: Leviticus Rabbah 22:8 doesn't "clearly" imply anything. Milgrom's reading of this passage is clearly shaped by those exegetes who took Maimonides' side in the debate about the future of sacrifice. Yet one can certainly wonder whether the fourth- or fifth-century rabbis responsible for Leviticus Rabbah 22:8 really meant what the Maimonidean medievals and reforming moderns make them say.[77]

But Milgrom's approach is not problematic only on these grounds. In truth, Maimonides' evolutionist argument is no more relevant to the scholar of Leviticus than René Girard's approach to sacrifice, or Robertson Smith's approach to ritual purity. The priestly traditions, after all, understand sacrifice as if it were "an eternal law" meant to last "throughout the generations forever" (e.g., Exod. 12:17).[78] Citing Maimonides' evolutionist scheme—or even its ostensible rabbinic precursors—is no different from concluding a treatment of sacrifice in the Hebrew Bible with a discussion of the New Testament book of Hebrews.[79] The Christian belief that sacrifice was destined to be replaced by Jesus' death is surely irrelevant. The modern Jewish belief that sacrifice was destined to be replaced by prayer is no more relevant.

From this problematic first paragraph, Milgrom's treatment of sacrifice continues along evolutionist lines. He briefly summarizes some of the theories of sacrifice, including the understandings of sacrifice as feeding the gods, as effecting unity with the gods, and as giving gifts to the gods. Milgrom explicitly denies that any theory except the last illumines sacrifice in ancient Israel.

He grants, as he must, that the Hebrew Bible is full of sacrificial idioms based on the idea that sacrifices are divine food, including "my table" (Ezek. 44:16), "the food of his God" (Lev. 21:22), and "my food" (Num. 28:2). Moreover, the tabernacle was furnished with a *table* (Exod. 25:23–30) on which *bread* was regularly offered (Lev. 24:5–9). But he dismisses the notion that Israelites thought they were sustaining their God: "these words, objects and mores are only *fossilized vestiges* from a dim past, which show no life in the Bible."[80]

Milgrom's discussion continues, treating various theories of sacrifice, including René Girard's and Walter Burkert's. He regards the former as "remote from explaining biblical sacrifice" while suggesting that the latter "may prove to have penetrated deepest into the mystery of sacrificial origins." Milgrom concludes that "no single theory can encompass the sacrificial system of any society, even the most primitive." He wraps up his discussion by quoting an anthropologist's assertion that "sacrifice is a flexible symbol which can convey a rich variety of possible meanings."[81]

While this last sentiment may be on the right track, Milgrom's approach to sacrifice generally proceeds along other lines. Truth be told, his approach to sacrifice is suspiciously like Robertson Smith's treatment of purity rules. For Robertson Smith, taboos made sense only when people really thought that the sources of defilement were demonic and dangerous; for Milgrom, sacrifice really only made sense when people literally believed they were feeding the gods. For both Robertson Smith and Milgrom, ancient Israel represents a stage beyond that, when the literal meanings no longer applied but ancient rituals survived nonetheless as fossilized vestiges. The final stage of intellectual and ritual development comes when the primitive ritual—taboo, for Robertson Smith; sacrifice, for Milgrom—is dispensed with altogether.[82]

Milgrom's evolutionism is not limited to his approach to sacrifice. He also approaches purity rules from an evolutionist perspective—tracing developments from idolatrous conceptions of the demonic toward Israel's symbolic and ethical understandings of the rites.[83] The difference is that Milgrom argues at the same time that the purity rules take on new meanings in ancient Israel, expressing fundamental ideas about life and death, and Israel's relationship to God. But while ritual purity rules become a true symbolic system for ancient Israel, the sacrificial rules largely remain as a "fossilized vestige." The development in this case is a negative one: sacrifice no longer has the foolish, literal meanings it once had for pre-Israelite idolaters.

Milgrom's argument suffers because his approach to sacrificial language is itself rather problematic. Running through his commentary is the presumption that linguistic usage develops in one direction, from the literal to the metaphorical. Many of his arguments for the claim that the Priestly source (P) predates the Holiness Code (H) are predicated on the assumption that terms (such as "purity") which are to be taken literally in P are to be understood metaphorically in H.[84] Other developments can also be traced by following the process of metaphorization: from Deuteronomy to the Holiness Code, as well as developments within the Holiness Code tradition itself.[85] Indeed, Milgrom's general approach to the relationship of the various strands of the Pentateuch has justly been called evolutionist,[86] and the assumption that language develops from literal to metaphorical is a consistent aspect of his approach.

Milgrom's denigration of sacrifice goes hand in hand with his assumption that metaphor is a relatively late development in human thought. As I have argued and will continue to argue, a full contextual understanding of sacrifice in ancient Israel requires that we remove both sacrifice and metaphor from evolutionist schemes like Milgrom's that place literal understandings of sacrifice in a primitive stage of human development and metaphor in a relatively late stage. The problem with such schemes is that by nature they preclude the possibility that sacrifice was understood symbolically by those Israelites who practiced it. The origin of the ritual is set back in a pre-metaphorical era, and symbolic thought—the essence of metaphor—enters only later. It should be clear that such constructions of the remote past are ideologically biased and methodologically flawed. We have also seen how they can be arbitrarily selective: why is it that ritual purity becomes a symbolic system while sacrifice does not? The answer to this question lies, in part, in the degree to which contemporary approaches to ritual structures like purity and sacrifice are culturally conditioned. But in order to understand that, we would do well to look back to a time when things were very different.

Looking Back: A Different Time, a Different Attitude

William Robertson Smith, Taboo, and Communion

As we have seen, the recent theoretical works on sacrifice and purity treat their topics separately and differently. It is therefore significant to note that there was a time—just over a century ago—when the prominent approach to purity and sacrifice was practically the reverse of what it is today. We have already quoted from and discussed William Robertson Smith's dismissal of the ritual purity legislation of the Hebrew Bible. The passage from *Lectures on the Religion of the Semites* quoted above represents an evolutionist approach to ritual at its worst. It is all the more striking, therefore, to realize that Robertson Smith's approach to sacrifice was notably more sympathetic, even while it was only slightly less evolutionistic.[87]

Robertson Smith described sacrifice first and foremost as an act of communion:

> The leading idea in the animal sacrifices of the Semites, as we shall see by and by, was not that of a gift made over to the god, but of an act of communion, in which the god and his worshippers unite by partaking together of the flesh and blood of a sacred victim.[88]

According to Robertson Smith, other notions of sacrifice developed around this original idea. The understanding of sacrifice as giving something to the deity presupposes a number of technological, social, and theological developments that must have come later, including the invention of agriculture, the idea of private property, and the notion that the deity owns and rules the land.[89] The expiatory role of sacrifice is also a by-product of the original notion of communion: by renewing the kinship between the sinner and the deity, sacrificial acts can function in a piacular role, without any connotation of gift or payment.[90] Robertson Smith, however, does not view these moves from the original idea in a positive light. He is particularly critical of the notion of private property, which "materializes everything that it touches" and renders traditional sacrificial practices useless to the task of reaching "spiritual conceptions of the deity."[91] Nonetheless, the original idea of sacrifice as communion was never entirely eliminated. Above all, it remains in evidence in ancient Israel in the joyful and social performance of, and sharing of, what Robertson Smith referred to as the *zevah* sacrifice (also known as the peace-offering; Lev. 3:1–17).[92]

In reaching his understanding of sacrifice, Robertson Smith takes several steps, not all of which are on solid ground. Robertson Smith must first posit, following Julius Wellhausen (1844–1918), that the idea of sacrifice as an act of expiation was a relatively late development.[93] Robertson Smith must also posit the widespread existence of a certain form of totemism whereby an animal representing the deity was consumed, along with its blood.[94] Neither of these positions is fully justifiable, and the second in particular is highly problematic, being based on the weakest of evidence.[95]

Robertson Smith's approach to sacrifice is, of course, highly evolutionist. Throughout his work, he traces developments from the simple to the sophisticated, from lower to higher, from the material to the spiritual.[96] His overall estimation of the early human capacity for thought is quite low.[97] Moreover, his evolutionism is distinctly supersessionist as well: historical analysis here serves as a Christian apology (despite the fact that Robertson Smith himself was tried as a heretic).[98] But his approach to sacrifice exhibits an evolutionism of a different sort from that seen above in his treatment of purity rules. While purity rites remain in ancient Israel as a meaningless vestige, soon to be dispensed with altogether, sacrifice serves in ancient Israel as a meaningful ritual, one that exemplifies all that is good in ancient religion:

> The sacrificial meal was an *appropriate* expression of the antique *ideal* of religious life, not merely because it was a *social* act and an act in which the god and his worshippers were conceived as partaking together, but because, as has already been said, the very act of eating and drinking with a man was a *symbol* and a confirmation of fellowship and mutual social obligations.[99]

Sacrifice, being social and symbolic, is not just appropriate but even possesses a "sacramental efficacy."[100] As he traces evolutionary developments that culminate in Christianity, Robertson Smith at the same time emphasizes a certain degree of continuity, by isolating communion as the key motivation of sacrifice from the beginning: "the more ancient idea of living communion between the god and his worshippers, which fell more and more into the background under the theory of sacrificial gifts, contained an element of *permanent truth* wrapped up in a very crude embodiment."[101] While purity rituals were an illogical dead end, sacrificial rituals were from the beginning on the right track—along a winding road, perhaps—leading to their fulfillment in Christianity. Thus, again unlike purity rules, sacrificial practices and ideas were worthy of sustained analysis: over half of Robertson Smith's *Lectures* treats sacrifice,[102] while the treatment of purity is relegated to an appendix. And it is certainly no small coincidence that the central role assigned to sacrifice in antiquity—communion—was "congenial to the Christian faith as he understood it."[103]

It is difficult to overestimate the historical significance of Robertson Smith's work for the field we now call religious studies. Robertson Smith had direct impact on, among others, Emile Durkheim, James Frazer, Sigmund Freud, Henri Hubert, and Marcel Mauss.[104] In many cases, it is precisely in our fields of interest—purity and sacrifice—that Robertson Smith influenced these scholars the most. His emphasis on the social origins of sacrifice—and, by extension, all religion—had a profound impact on Durkheim and his associates.[105] Robertson Smith's interest in totemic origins had profound influence, for better or for worse, on Frazer and Freud.[106] By emphasizing the inadequacy of Tylor's sacrifice-as-gift theory to a social context—where sharing is paramount—Robertson Smith can be seen as a precursor to Marcel Mauss's work *The Gift*, which does away with simple understandings of giving altogether. Yet influence can breed disagreement. Just as Douglas has successfully controverted Robertson Smith's approach to purity, so too have many others—as we will see soon—demonstrated the inadequacy of Robertson Smith's approach to sacrifice. But it is not only his theory that has been rejected. The entire idea of giving pride of place to sacrificial practice *as understood by ancient Israel* seems entirely out of fashion with the origins-obsessed works of recent years. Instead, we find that the fashion in biblical studies today is a complete inversion of Robertson Smith's approach one century ago, with scholars like Milgrom approaching sacrifice the way Robertson Smith approached purity.

Hubert, Mauss, and the Gifts of Their Collaboration

Less than a decade after the original publication of Robertson Smith's *Lectures*, Henri Hubert and Marcel Mauss published in 1898 what remains one of the most remarkable essays on sacrifice ever written.[107] More than a century later, the brief essay continues to receive praise from anthropologists, classicists, and even some biblicists.[108] It has safely been called "the most frequently cited theoretical work on sacrifice ever written."[109] For our purposes, there are three fundamental contributions of the work, each of which provides an important and lasting corrective to Robertson Smith. First, Hubert and Mauss criticize the evolutionist scheme at the heart of Robertson Smith's project (by the time they wrote, James Frazer had already developed these ideas further).[110] Not only is there not enough evidence to posit that the origin of sacrifice is to be found in totemism but also there is not enough evidence to support any scheme that prioritizes a single idea of sacrifice (such as communion) and then views all other motivations (such as expiation) as developments or by-products.[111] In a particularly prescient passage, Hubert and Mauss forswear drawing any implications for the history of sacrifice from the chronologies of the biblical texts inferred by the biblical critics:

> even if we believe that Biblical criticism can provide the history of the texts, we refuse to confuse this history with that of the facts. In particular, whatever may be the date of Leviticus and of the Priestly Code in general, the age of the text is not, in our view, necessarily the age of the rite. . . . [The rites] existed before they were recorded.[112]

This brings us to their second contribution: that ancient sacrifice cannot be reduced to any single motive. Hubert and Mauss doubt on phenomenological grounds that the idea of communion can ever be fully separated from expiation, or vice versa: elements of sharing and separation seem to be present in all sacrificial rites to a greater or lesser degree.[113] Against the textual history of Wellhausen and the evolutionary construct of Robertson Smith, Hubert and Mauss maintain, in short, that sacrifice must be studied "in its original complexity."[114]

The third remarkable aspect of their contribution for our purposes is their widening of the scope of sacrifice, beyond the killing and beyond the consumption. Hubert and Mauss conceive of sacrifice as a broad process consisting of several stages. In addition to killing and consumption, this scheme of sacrifice consists of processes of sacralization and desacralization, or more simply, entry and exit.[115] Figuring prominently in the rituals of entry are, of course, the biblical rites and concepts of ritual purification.[116] Unlike Robertson Smith, Hubert and Mauss do not dismiss these rituals as meaningless survivals. They are seen, rather, as part and parcel of the sacrificial process: "all these purifications, lustrations, and consecrations prepared the profane participant for the sacred act, by eliminating from his body the imperfections of his secular nature, cutting him off from the common life, and introducing him step by step into the sacred world of the gods."[117] In its fullest form, this process of becoming sacred is, in fact, something akin to becoming divine: the priest "is obliged to become a god himself in order to be capable of acting upon them."[118] We will return to this important idea in the next chapter.

There are other contributions of this essay: some see in it, in fact, the seed of structuralism.[119] But there are also important shortcomings. Surely their attempt to speak of a universal structure, while focusing primarily on Semitic and Hindu models, brings the charge of ethnocentrism.[120] It should be no surprise that their model applies neither to Africa nor to Greece.[121] The chapter "Sacrifice of the God" seems overly focused on Christian models of the sacrificial ideal.[122] Indeed, as Ivan Strenski has shown, Hubert and Mauss's work on sacrifice can be situated in specific moral and political concerns of late nineteenth-century France.[123] Surely their valorization of sacrifice reflects ideologies of the time when—leading up to World War I—sacrifice (especially self-sacrifice) was considered a civic virtue.[124] Yet these concerns are not as typically European or as distinctively Christian as some have assumed. In fact, their particular interpretation of sacrifice—which mediates between expiation and communion, and which identifies a self-serving aspect to sacrificial acts— actually challenges contemporary Roman Catholic and Protestant approaches to these matters.[125] More than anything else, Hubert and Mauss's work emulates and aligns itself academically, morally, and politically with the work of the French Jewish expert of Indian religion Sylvain Lévi (1863–1935).[126] Lévi was a teacher of both Mauss and Hubert, and he published his *La Doctrine du Sacrifice dans les Brahmanas* in 1898, the same year as Hubert and Mauss's essay. Lévi was also an active member of various Jewish social, religious, and academic organizations. True to the life and work of their teacher Lévi, Hubert and Mauss articulate a theory of sacrifice that is sympathetic to ritual and equally sympathetic to biblical and postbiblical Jewish sources. More important, Hubert and Mauss's joint studies of Hindu and Semitic ritual—simply by pairing the Hebrew Bible with the Vedas—formulate a critique of racist, anti-Semitic conceptions of Aryan superiority, which were already gaining ground in their day.[127]

In a way, then, we can accurately say that Hubert and Mauss's classic work is just as engaged in the issues of concern to late nineteenth-century France as Girard's work is engaged in the moral concerns of his time and place.[128] But there are two significant differences. First, it is easier—hopefully—to sympathize with the universalist moralizing of Hubert and Mauss than with the blunt antiritualist biases of Girard. Second, and more important, Hubert and Mauss's methods withstand the test of time *in their application to the biblical evidence*. Their aim of analyzing the *entire process* of sacrifice in its "original complexity"—whatever its motivation—provides a firm foundation for the analysis of sacrifice in ancient Israel. We will see in the next chapter just how productive an approach that starts like theirs can be.

Emile Durkheim and the Elementary Form of the Current Scene

If Hubert and Mauss's approach was so productive and sound, why then has it not been emulated in studies of sacrifice in ancient Israel, especially as it is so frequently cited and praised? To answer this question, we need to trace briefly what happened to their theory in the field of religious studies on the one hand and in biblical studies on the other. To start with the latter: it was generally ignored. The most influential twentieth-century works on sacrifice in ancient Israel—including the works of George Buchanan Gray, Roland de Vaux, and Jacob Milgrom—say little if anything about Hubert and Mauss, even as they take up and critique Robertson Smith's theories. The reason for this is actually not so difficult to isolate. The biblicists tend to be concerned with theories of *origins*, and Hubert and Mauss explicitly eschew any such concerns. To those who persist in explaining sacrifice in ancient Israel by constructing broader evolutionist histories of the rite, Hubert and Mauss's essay must seem beside the point.

In the broader field of religious studies, the impact of Hubert and Mauss has been limited by two factors. For those like Burkert and Girard who are interested in origins, Hubert and Mauss's essay is either ignored (as in Burkert's *Homo Necans*) or criticized for not seeking to understand origins (as in Girard's *Violence and the Sacred*).[129] But another reason for the limited impact of Hubert and Mauss's work is, ironically, the way in which their work was mediated to the general public by their own teacher in the most famous work to emerge from the Durkheimian group, Durkheim's own *Elementary Forms of the Religious Life.*

It is becoming increasingly clear that Durkheim owed a great debt to Mauss and Hubert, and not just vice versa.[130] But while we appreciate Hubert and Mauss's impact on Durkheim, we must at the same time contemplate the disservice that *Elementary Forms* does to *Sacrifice: Its Nature and Function.* Briefly put, Durkheim's *Elementary Forms* forges something of a forced communion between the theories of Hubert and Mauss on the one hand and Robertson Smith on the other. In my view, the effects of this union were largely negative.

Following Hubert and Mauss, Durkheim rejects the centrality of communion, and he likewise exhibits an interest in the purificatory rites that precede sacrifice.[131] But where Hubert and Mauss find a place for expiation alongside communion, Durkheim emphasizes the connection between the notions of communion and oblation, recognizing that in a social context, it is difficult to separate the giving from the sharing.[132] Durkheim here paves the way for Mauss's later essay, *The Gift*, which argues, with attention to sacrifice, that all forms of giving are based on assumptions that gifts will be reciprocated. In these and other respects, Durkheim criticizes the work of Robertson Smith. But in agreement with Robertson Smith—and in disagreement with Hubert and Mauss—Durkheim takes up the matter of totemism and the question of origins, presenting an analysis decidedly more evolutionist than that of Hubert and Mauss.[133] What is more—and what is particularly significant for our concerns—Durkheim once again drives a wedge between the various aspects of the sacrificial process that Hubert and Mauss wished to integrate.

The rites that Hubert and Mauss classify as "the entry"—the first step of the sacrificial process—Durkheim classifies as the "negative cult." Durkheim thus takes a decided step back toward Robertson Smith and his radical separation of irrational and vestigial conceptions of defilement from what he saw as the symbolic ritual par excellence, sacrifice. Granted, Durkheim's analysis is not a full throwback to Robertson Smith's understanding of taboo. Durkheim does defend the negative cult against the charge of irrationality, and he also cites Hubert and Mauss and notes approvingly that these rites serve important functions leading toward the positive cult.[134] Moreover, we cannot forget that prohibitions regarding sacred things do serve a central role in Durkheim's overall definition of religion. Yet it is equally clear that for Durkheim, the referent "negative cult" is an evaluative one. Compared to the "positive cult"—of which sacrifice is a supreme example—the "negative cult" is merely a preliminary.[135] It is the positive cult that proves worthy of detailed analysis, with Durkheim devoting to the positive cult roughly four times the space allotted to its negative preliminary. Moreover, it is the positive cult that serves the ultimate function of creating the sacred principle, which in Durkheim's view is the personification of society itself. Thus the positive cult is not only functional but also symbolic.[136]

Durkheim's logic is rather shaky here, and his overall approach is subject to due criticism.[137] But the circularity of Durkheim's reasoning is not of interest to us. What remains significant is the fact that by introducing the terms "negative" and "positive," and by evaluating the two categories accordingly, Durkheim effectively undid what should have been one of Hubert and Mauss's more lasting contributions. It is to Durkheim's (dis)credit that after him the field of religious studies has maintained, for the most part, this distinction between the positive and negative cult. The significant difference is that the heirs of Durkheim—including Douglas and Lévi-Strauss—evaluated avoidance behaviors positively and sacrifice either negatively or not at all. But the contrast drawn crudely by Robertson Smith—which was broken down for a brief moment by Hubert and Mauss—was reestablished by Durkheim. And so it remains.

Accounting for the Current Scene

So the question arises: Why is it that some of the very same scholars who look at the food laws and the purity regulations, and see the need to find a key to unlock a complex symbolic system, look at sacrifice as a fossilized vestige, one that is finally bereft of whatever foolish meanings it once had? If the ritual purity system—the prerequisite for sacrifice—can be understood as symbolic, does it not stand to reason that the sacrificial system(s) also might be?

Significantly, this current state of affairs seems to be relatively distinct to biblical studies. Outside the narrow (and often nonsecular) confines of biblical studies, sympathetic analyses of sacrificial rituals are actually *de rigueur*. In classical studies, Marcel Detienne, Jean-Pierre Vernant, and their colleagues at the Paris Center for Comparative Studies of Ancient Societies have produced an impressive collection of essays, *The Cuisine of Sacrifice among the Greeks*. These essays are interested not in origins but rather in elucidating what sacrifice meant to those ancient Greeks who practiced it. The same can be said of Luc de Heusch's *Sacrifice in Africa*, which takes lessons from *Purity and Danger*. But within biblical studies, Mary Douglas's latest treatment of Leviticus—to which we will turn toward the end of this chapter—is one of the few analyses of the Hebrew Bible that fits the bill. For a variety of reasons, scholars of the Hebrew Bible are willing to study purity with some sympathy, leaving little patience for sacrifice.

One reason for this phenomenon is the simple fact that in the field of religious studies today, purification and sacrifice are generally considered to be two distinct topics. This is perhaps best exemplified by the fact that a number of the most frequently cited theoretical works in the field (e.g., the classic works by Douglas and Girard) are devoted primarily, if not entirely, to one or the other of these subjects. But the hard-and-fast bifurcation of purity and sacrifice—though it is certainly a factor—is insufficient to explain the difference in the ways they are treated in biblical studies. The same bifurcation is in evidence in classical studies, for instance, where we have Robert Parker's *Miasma* (treating purity) and Detienne and Vernant's collection of essays *The Cuisine of Sacrifice among the Greeks*. Yet in classical studies, we don't find the same significant dissimilarity between the ways these rites tend to be treated.

In addition to the general separation of purity from sacrifice in the field of religious studies, another explanation for their being treated differently also recommends itself. Purity rituals in the form of baptism remain a part of Christianity, and purity concerns relating to both the body and diet remain a part of Judaism. But truly sacrificial rituals do not play a role in contemporary Jewish or Christian practice. Of course, certain Christian traditions foster sacrificial understandings of the eucharist. And the traditional hope for the restoration of sacrificial service is maintained by Orthodox Jews. Even so, Christianity in general and modernist forms of Judaism are predicated upon the replacement of blood sacrifice by something better that came later: Jesus' death and/or the eucharist, in the case of Christianity; prayer, in the case of (modernist) Judaism. Thus we should not be at all surprised when ancient Israelite sacrifice is dismissed as a vestige from the remote past by either Christian or (modernist) Jewish scholars. But this factor too is not a fully sufficient explanation, for if it were, we would certainly have expected to see the same bias at work a hundred years ago in biblical studies. But in the case of Robertson Smith, for example, we saw that quite the reverse was the case: he viewed sacrifice with some sympathy, and purity with no sympathy at all.

There is a third factor, one that has something to do with the changing fashions of popular and, by extension, scholarly society. We began this chapter by quoting Robertson Smith's derision of biblical taboos. We also mentioned that he was one of a number of scholars of the Victorian age who exhibited an interest in and a disdain for such "primitive" taboos. But while we have already noted how Robertson Smith's interpretation of sacrifice was congenial to his Christianity, we have not yet fully contextualized his derision of taboo.

Such things, of course, are often best seen in hindsight, and perhaps with some cultural distance as well. Thus it took the perspective of a later, marginal figure like Franz Steiner (1909–52) to put his finger on what lay behind Robertson Smith's take on taboo. Steiner was a Jewish refugee from Nazi-occupied Czechoslovakia who spent the war years in Oxford, where he eventually served as lecturer in anthropology from 1949 to 1952.[138] Toward the end of his short and tragic life, he delivered a series of lectures on taboo. Mary Douglas, not so coincidentally, was one of his students—and she has recently acknowledged her debt to Steiner once again.[139] His posthumously published book *Taboo* was long out of print, but it may now get the attention it truly deserves.

Steiner's *Taboo* traces the scholarly interest in its stated topic, from the British "discovery" of Polynesia through Robertson Smith and Freud. Steiner emphasizes the degree to which the late nineteenth-century discussion of taboo was influenced by the distinctively rationalist approach to religion that dominated intellectual circles of that time. But then Steiner emphasizes another factor:

> there is yet another side to the Victorian interest in this problem, and one which cannot be overlooked. Victorian society itself was one of the most taboo-minded and taboo-ridden societies on record. It must not be forgotten that scholars like Frazer grew up among people who preferred, in certain circumstances, to say "unmentionables" rather than "trousers."[140]

The disdainful fascination with taboo was a Victorian problem indeed.

It is tempting to take the hint from Steiner and try to reflect on precisely why it is that in our own day sacrifice is treated with such disdain in the popular and scholarly mind. This is, however, dangerous territory: the quest is not unlike the Girardian one, which seeks to reveal what is concealed, and finds proof in the lack of evidence. But it is difficult to avoid the realization that our own society is marked by an ambivalence toward the killing of animals that is not unlike the Victorian ambivalence toward taboo. Our society— and much of our scholarship—recoils from "primitive" sacrificial practices, but at the same time, our own food supply is remarkably susceptible to significant ethical charges. We can begin, of course, by noting that the slaughterhouse is surely no more of a welcome place for an animal than an ancient temple.[141] But the ethics of contemporary food can be impeached in a variety of ways. Besides the treatment of animals, one can raise questions concerning the labor practices of agricultural and meat-packing industries, to say nothing of fast-food chains. Moreover, these industries can be accused of deceiving children through advertising in much the same way the smoking industry has.[142] On the other hand, one can identify another realm of sacrificial practice—one even more hidden from view. On a daily basis, in public and private institutions, animals are subjected to pain and death by respected and trained professionals, all under the justification of an ideology that is essentially sacrificial: better them than us. I refer, here, to animal testing (a practice that, just to make it clear, I do not categorically oppose).[143] With some frequency, animal research is conceived of as a sacrificial practice and even described in such terms.[144] Moreover, anyone familiar with the ways animal deaths are routinized in laboratories, hospitals, and biology classrooms can recognize that even if ritual sacrifice were entirely eliminated, one could certainly still question whether modernity has brought any improvements at all to the lives of animals.

I have no interest here in reviewing or taking a side in any of the complicated moral and philosophical questions concerning the ethics of our food supply or our treatment of animals. Rather, I simply wish to suggest that, fifty years from now, if a perspicacious figure like a Franz Steiner were to look back on our society and its scholarly products, he or she might find it rather strange that so much ink was spilled on the violent and primitive nature of sacrifice, even while other ancient rituals were understood to be symbolic in nature. Fifty years from now, this selective interest in the (im)morality of sacrifice might look quite a bit the way the Victorian obsession with taboo looks to us today.

Recent Steps in the Right Direction

We have devoted the bulk of this chapter to documenting and tracing the history of a disparity in the ways sacrifice and purity have been treated by anthropologists, biblicists, and other theorists. It would be unfair not to recognize, however, that a number of works produced over the last generation or so have in one way or another bucked the trend we are tracing. Some of these works—like that of Edmund Leach—have consciously attempted to apply the insights of structural analysis to the study of biblical sacrifice. Others—like Howard Eilberg-Schwartz's work *The Savage in Judaism*—have not really contributed to the discussion of sacrifice per se but rather provide helpful treatments of other matters, such as metaphor. None of these works presents an analysis that studies both purity and sacrifice as part of a single ritual process, using the same methodological assumptions. But each in its own way constitutes a step in the right direction, toward a sympathetic, symbolic understanding of at least one of these ritual structures.

Edmund Leach, "The Logic of Sacrifice"

The British anthropologist Edmund Leach (1910–89) was, like Mary Douglas, a theorist with a strong interest in biblical studies; he too felt that anthropological method could be quite productive when applied to biblical texts. Generally speaking, Leach advocated a method that fused Durkheim's functionalism with Lévi-Strauss's structuralism.[145] In this respect, too, his overall approach was not all that different from Douglas's, even though the two did not always see eye to eye.[146] In one of his general works on rituals and symbolism, Leach devoted a chapter to biblical sacrifice that looks something like the kind of treatment Douglas could have written, had she chosen to do so.[147] Like *Purity and Danger*, Leach's essay operates under the assumption that the sacrificial rules constitute a symbolic system. What is more, the title of the chapter—"The Logic of Sacrifice"—must be taken as a deliberate refutation of Lévi-Strauss's dismissive approach to sacrifice noted earlier. One further contribution of the essay pertains to its rehabilitation of metaphor with regard to sacrifice. Believing that rituals are by nature symbolic and expressive, Leach asserts—again *contra* Lévi-Strauss—that sacrificial rituals are metaphorical.[148]

Leach observes in this essay that the "theory" that understands sacrifice as a gift is itself a metaphor. This understanding of sacrifice is based on the fact that various societies have chosen to describe their offerings as gifts to the deity. But how can gods—who dwell beyond the realm of pure human experience—accept such gifts from people in any literal sense? As Leach points out, the understanding of sacrifice as giving requires a number of "metaphorical associations," not so much on our part as interpreters but on the part of those who originally described sacrifice as giving in the first place.[149] We can easily push this observation one step further: *all* of the well-established "theories" of sacrifice—as a gift to the gods, as communion with the gods, as food for the gods—are based on those "metaphorical associations" that people who offered sacrifices made themselves.

Theorists and commentators from Tylor to Milgrom have fallen into a trap. Presuming primitives to be incapable of metaphorical thought, scholars have taken sacrificial metaphors—like "gift" and "feeding the gods"—and have literalized them into theories of dubious value. Of course we cannot preclude the possibility that at various points in human history these notions were understood in some literal fashion. But even so, Leach's essay helps put the lie to evolutionist constructions of the history of sacrifice that are predicated on the assumption that sacrifice first had a simple, exclusively literal meaning that was metaphorized only later. Rather, we must seek to understand sacrifice with the assumption that it was, from the beginning, a symbolic action—and it is by sympathetically understanding sacrificial metaphors that we can begin to appreciate the symbolism of sacrifice.

The brief essay is well worth reading, but its overall contribution—aside from the methodological points just summarized—remains limited. In formulating his understanding of sacrifice as communication, Leach focused primarily on rites of initiation and atonement, but, as we will see in the next chapter, these are not necessarily the central motivations for sacrifice in ancient Israel. Although Leach adopted Hubert and Mauss's contention that sacrifice is about communication, Leach did not follow their example in making the effort to interpret the entire sacrificial process. The purity rules play practically no role in Leach's analysis. To be fair, Leach's analysis is not meant to be a complete interpretation. The essay is presented as a model of the kind of analysis that can be done when one realizes that "attention to small details really matters."[150] And the essay remains a model—perhaps most of all it demonstrates that the methodological fusion of functionalism with structuralism holds great promise for the study of ancient Israel's sacrificial rituals. But the application of that method to the *entire process* of sacrifice has not yet taken place.[151]

Howard Eilberg-Schwartz, The Savage in Judaism

In one sense, Howard Eilberg-Schwartz's book *The Savage in Judaism* provides yet another example of the phenomenon we have been tracing. Here too is a work that seeks to study ancient Jewish ritual practice in light of anthropology—one that treats purity rites as a complex symbolic system and gives sacrifice relatively scant attention or sympathy. While sacrifice is treated as a side issue in chapters 5 and 7 of *The Savage in Judaism*, purity and impurity are the central theme of the entire second half of this book. But more significant is the disparity in the ways purity and sacrifice are treated. According to Eilberg-Schwartz, the ritual purity rules constitute a complex system that has varied layers of symbolic meaning. His discussion of these meanings will prove useful in the discussion of the ritual purity system in the next chapter. By contrast, Eilberg-Schwartz believes that sacrifice is a much simpler system based on the idea of substitution. Considering the overall influence of structuralism on Eilberg-Schwartz, it should not come as such a surprise that Lévi-Strauss's disdain for sacrifice has rubbed off on the author of *The Savage in Judaism*.

Yet what is something of a pleasant surprise is the fact that Eilberg-Schwartz does spend a good deal of time discussing animal metaphors in ancient Israel. Eilberg-Schwartz isolates a number of metaphors that appear in ancient Israelite prophecy and poetry—such as the image of God as Israel's shepherd in Psalm 23—and he argues that many of these metaphors can be used to enhance our understanding of ancient Israelite ritual. For example, Eilberg-Schwartz draws a parallel between the prominence of the metaphorical description of Israel as God's herd on the one hand and the fact that domestic livestock constitutes ideal food, according to Leviticus 11.[152] Similarly, in his chapter entitled "The Fruitful Cut," he examines the parallel between the circumcision of Israelite boys at the eighth day (Gen. 17) and the prohibition of the consumption of the fruit of young trees, the initial produce of which is referred to as "foreskin" (Lev. 19:23–25). Both are to be understood by the idea—made explicit only with regard to the trees—that circumcision is meant to ensure fertility.[153] Instead of dismissing metaphors as some ornamental description of prior laws, Eilberg-Schwartz argues that ritual can be understood as the "actualization of metaphor."[154] In other words, it is not the ritual that explains the metaphor but the opposite: the metaphor allows us to understand the ritual's symbolic value in ancient Israelite society.

Not all of Eilberg-Schwartz's examples are equally persuasive, yet he has demonstrated a way of trying to come to grips with sacrifice in ancient Israel. As we will see, there are a number of sacrificial metaphors in ancient Israelite prophecy and poetry that are not fully utilized in the attempt to understand sacrifice. Yet, under the influence of Lévi-Strauss, Eilberg-Schwartz seems to believe that sacrifice is something of an exception—a ritual that cannot be explained in quite this manner.[155] As I will argue in the next chapter, however, it is best not to see sacrifice as an exception or as resistant to this kind of analysis. Rather, sacrifice too can be understood as an actualization of metaphor. In the final analysis, Eilberg-Schwartz's work, even while it exhibits some of the biases we have been tracing, is also on a methodological level an important step in the right direction.

Bruce Chilton, The Temple of Jesus

One of the few recent works devoted to sacrifice in ancient Judaism that manages to move the discussion forward in an informed way is Bruce Chilton's book *The Temple of Jesus*. This book is notable for its even-handed and theoretically informed evaluation of biblical sacrificial rituals. Chilton helpfully reviews various theories of sacrifice, and presents a pointed critique of the Girardian approach.[156] Another strength of this book is its breadth—Chilton moves from an informed discussion of theories of sacrifice, through the Hebrew Bible, to sources pertaining to the first century, including Josephus, the New Testament, and even rabbinic literature. Importantly, Chilton recognizes that there are two ritual structures related to the temple—purity and sacrifice—and both topics figure in his analysis. In the course of it all, Chilton presents a rather complicated and novel approach to Jesus' overturning the tables in the temple, which we will consider in some detail toward the end of this book.

Chilton also understands sacrifice symbolically, endorsing the works on sacrifice produced by the French classicists in *The Cuisine of Sacrifice among the Greeks*. In fact, Chilton suggests that we would do well to replace the Girardian focus on violence and death with the classicists' focus on food:

> in sacrifice, consumption is probably a better metaphor to describe
> what is happening than death; the passing of the victim rarely
> arouses interest, while its preparation and its disposal, to the advan-
> tage of people or the gods, are specified. What happens most
> nearly approximates a meal, and sacrificial practice—in the type and
> preparation of food and its consumers—is often associated with
> culinary practice.[157]

There is some degree of truth to these claims: sacrifice in the Hebrew Bible is about much more than killing, and eating too plays a role (as emphasized long ago by Robertson Smith). Chilton is surely correct to critique Girard, and he is correct to praise Detienne, Vernant, and their colleagues. Their morally neutral theory of sacrifice as food is a welcome respite to Girardian readings of ancient Judaism. One advantage of the "sacrifice as a meal" metaphor over the "sacrifice as killing innocent victims" metaphor is that the question of the innocence or guilt of the animal becomes irrelevant. The animal is not innocent or guilty: the animal is food. This assumption promises to lead to a more balanced assessment of the Hebrew Bible and ancient Judaism than the Girardian approach allows.

Chilton missteps, however, when he assumes that what ought to transfer to ancient Israel is the classicists' conclusion—that sacrifice is primarily about food—as opposed to their method. The classicists reach their conclusion about the centrality of "cuisine" to Greek sacrifice only upon detailed analysis of sacrificial rites as preserved in ancient Greek literature and art, as well as folk customs persisting in modern Greece. Their method is well defined,[158] and worthy of emulation. But it is a mistake to think that their conclusion can be applied blindly to ancient Israel. Consumption *may* be a prominent metaphor for sacrifice in ancient Israel, but it is hardly *the* prominent metaphor, especially considering the significant role played by the burnt offering, none of which is eaten (at least not by people). Moreover, even if consumption is *the* prominent sacrificial metaphor in the Hebrew Bible, that doesn't mean it remains the central understanding centuries later in ancient Judaism. A full understanding of the meanings of sacrifice in the Second Temple period—which is also part of Chilton's project—must be based not on an anthropologically informed reading of the Hebrew Bible but on careful analysis of symbolic meanings ascribed to sacrifice in ancient Jewish literature such as Josephus and Philo.[159] While Chilton effectively critiques the works of the Girardians, his own analysis falls short in its effort to study ancient Israelite sacrifice with the analytic depth it deserves. Chilton's analysis is even more problematic when it comes to his specific understandings of sacrificial practice in ancient Judaism and early Christianity; but discussion of these matters will find its place in the second part of this work.

Mary Douglas, Leviticus as Literature

Perhaps the most promising recent treatment of sacrifice is that found in Mary Douglas's latest work on Leviticus, *Leviticus as Literature*.[160] Douglas's goal in this work is to comment on Leviticus as a whole, and to "reintegrate the book with the rest of the Bible."[161] But if in her previous works on purity systems Douglas set out to comment on complete ritual structures, here the structure that most captivates her is that of the book of Leviticus itself. The central idea of this book is that "Leviticus exploits to the full an ancient tradition which makes a parallel between Mount Sinai and the Tabernacle."[162] So Leviticus's structure maps out the Israelite tabernacle as described in Exodus. Leviticus 1–17 conforms to the outer court; Leviticus 18–24 then maps out the inner court; and Leviticus 25–27 conforms to the holy of holies.[163] Each set of rules laid out in Leviticus—sacrifice, food laws, purity laws, the Holiness Code—can be understood in light of this overarching analogy.

In chapter 4 of *Leviticus as Literature*, we have, for the first time, Douglas's own treatment of biblical sacrifice, and it is characterized by all that is good in the anthropologist's approach to rituals. She operates under the assumption that ritual structures convey meaning: even sacrifice is "philosophy by enactment."[164] She eschews itemized solutions, and searches for "integrated" (i.e., systemic) ones.[165] She breaks down boundaries, and draws on the full resources of the Hebrew Bible in order to figure out what that philosophy being enacted by sacrifice might have been. The central insight here—and it's a good one—is that the same tripartite scheme involved in the analogy between Sinai and the tabernacle can be mapped onto the carcass of an animal offered for sacrifice.[166] The beauty of the theory is that everything finds its place: the prohibited fats serve to mark out the boundaries between three sections of the carcass, each of which corresponds to one of the three realms of the tabernacle. Typically, her theory is quite comprehensive. Her interest in animal parts extends as far as the lobe over the liver (e.g., Lev. 3:15), to which she assigns a meaning by drawing an analogy between sacrificial remains and the prophetic doctrines of the remnant of Israel.[167] She eventually works into her theory the prohibitions of leaven and honey (Lev. 2:11–12).[168] One idea sure to raise some eyebrows is her suggestion that a Hebrew term usually translated as "legs" (כרעים) really means "genitals," allowing for an understanding of sacrifice that highlights ideas pertaining to fertility.[169] Douglas's work is not for the squeamish—but how else will Leviticus ever be understood? Commentators will no doubt question many of her specific claims. But taken as a whole, this single chapter is probably as important as any that's been written on Leviticus, perhaps since the third chapter of *Purity and Danger*. Just as that chapter has had a substantial and lasting impact on the ways people look at Leviticus 11–15, chapter 4 of *Leviticus as Literature* deserves to have the same impact on the ways people look at Leviticus 1–10. Perhaps more scholars will now entertain the possibility that ancient Israelite sacrificial rules were as symbolic and expressive as the food laws are commonly believed to be.

Some two decades ago, G. S. Kirk published an important evaluation of Douglas's methodology as it pertains to sacrificial rituals in general (and Greek rituals in particular). Though the article is in some respects dated now, one key issue raised by Kirk deserves to be noted here. While endorsing Douglas's structural insights, Kirk calls for some middle ground between the "piecemeal" solutions that Douglas rejects and the single-principle theories that she often espouses instead. What Kirk would like to see is "the careful restatement of functionalism in relation to those accidents, confusions, syncretisms, and historical changes that make religion in particular, including its rituals and the practice of animal sacrifice not least of all, such a multifarious and often contradictory affair."[170] From *Purity and Danger* through *Leviticus as Literature*, Douglas has frequently championed new and fascinating ideas that she then—at least so it seems to many of us—pushes too far. Can the dietary laws of Leviticus 11 be explained any more on a one-by-one basis? Probably not. Can they all be explained by the single elegant idea that the abominations of Leviticus cohere perfectly with the categories of creation laid out in Genesis 1? Again, probably not. Or, now, can the rules of sacrifice be explained by the single idea that we are to superimpose a map of the tabernacle onto the sacrificial animal? Yet again, probably not. I suspect that Douglas is aware of this point, but she leaves it to the rest of us to work out the details.

Moving Forward: Toward a Consistent Approach to Related Ritual Structures

How are we then to proceed in the study of purity and sacrifice? The method that recommends itself is a hybrid of the best methods discussed earlier. Put simply, one needs to begin like Hubert and Mauss's *Sacrifice* and then proceed like Douglas's *Purity and Danger*, taking into consideration, though, the modifications suggested by Kirk. Moreover, the final product would not look like the broad comparative theorizing that characterizes *Purity and Danger*, because we will remain focused on the Hebrew Bible and ancient Judaism. Once we apply Douglas's assumptions and interpretive methods to a single society, the final product would, rather, look something like what Detienne, Vernant, and their colleagues produced in *The Cuisine of Sacrifice Among the Greeks*.

To understand biblical sacrifice in such a way, one must recognize the utter irrelevance to biblical studies of theories pertaining to the origins of sacrifice. This does not involve advocating the abandonment of the search for origins altogether. We must simply recognize that the only way to draw any connection between biblical studies on the one hand and theories of origins on the other is to formulate an evolutionist analysis, moving backward from Leviticus or forward from some preconceived notion of what primitive sacrifice must have been like. Either kind of approach is both biased and flawed.

At the same time—and for the same reason—questions pertaining to the aftermath of Israel's sacrificial cult must also be put aside. For an understanding of sacrifice in ancient Israel, it does not matter that according to Maimonides, sacrifice was destined to be replaced by prayer. It does not matter that according to Hebrews, sacrifice was destined to be replaced by Jesus' death. And it does not matter that according to Girard, Jesus' death finally put the lie to deceptive rituals of sacrifice. Looking back at ancient Israel from the presumption of intellectual, ethical, and religious superiority is not the way ancient Israel will truly be understood or properly evaluated.

We would also do well to put aside altogether the search for a theory of sacrifice. The term "theory" is problematic first and foremost because of its singularity. As commonly recognized, no single theory seems to explain all of the sacrifices in ancient Israel, let alone other societies.[171] This, however, is easily rectified—we could just as well speak of "theories." But the term and the quest associated with it remain problematic because the common method of sacrificial theorizing is flawed. The search for a theory of sacrifice almost always involves the selective literalization of a single sacrificial metaphor. First, one places emphasis on a single metaphor by which sacrifice is understood— for instance, sacrifice as a gift. Then one assigns priority to a literal understanding of that metaphor—for instance: originally people mistakenly thought they were *really* giving to their gods. This process is doubly flawed. The selection of one metaphor over others is often arbitrary, and the literalization of the metaphor is often not warranted. Moreover, this sort of theorizing, as we have seen, all too easily becomes evolutionist, assuming a historical move from the literal to the metaphor. This manner of theorizing also, by nature, precludes the possibility that sacrifice was ever understood as truly symbolic. In one stage we have a simple literal understanding, and in another we have *merely* a metaphorical one. To understand sacrifice in its context, we must rehabilitate sacrificial metaphors. We can no longer assume that such metaphors are vestiges from a bygone era, giving us hints of what earlier generations may have assumed. We must recognize, rather, that sacrificial metaphors are windows into the ways the rite was symbolically understood by those who used such metaphors in relation to their performance of sacrifice.

In addition to abandoning evolutionist constructs in various guises, in order to understand sacrifice in ancient Israel, we need to expand the scope to encompass the related ritual structures of the priestly code, especially the purity rules. Expanding the scope in this matter brings two advantages. As we have argued all along, ritual purification is a key step of the broader sacrificial process. Thus we cannot hope to explain sacrifice when disregarding ritual purity. Second, by integrating the two structures that have so typically been separated in scholarly analyses, we stand to benefit by applying to sacrifice the sympathy and the methodology that have productively been applied to ritual purity in recent decades.

Thus we need to begin to look for ways in which the entire symbolic process of ancient Israelite sacrifice—beginning with rites of purification—can be accounted for. We need to account for its *original complexity* by trying to isolate some ways of highlighting the connections between its various aspects. Yet, following Kirk, we have to avoid the temptation of finding satisfaction with any single answer. We need to recognize that both purity and sacrifice are multivalent entities, even though they are deeply connected ones. Thus the search for theories will be replaced here with a search for what can accurately be called "organizing principles."[172] These organizing principles will need to be concerns central to the priestly traditions of the Pentateuch, which will help us understand better the dynamic between the systems of sacrifice and defilement. One organizing principle is the concern with imitating God. Another organizing principle is the concern with attracting and maintaining the presence of God within the community. By focusing on these two concerns, we will be able to analyze the two sets of ritual structures—sacrifice and defilement—in tandem. We will, moreover, be able to do so using the same methodological assumption, which allows for the possibility that sacrificial rules could well be just as symbolic as purity regulations are commonly believed to be. That is precisely the agenda for the next chapter.

2

The Sacrificial Process of Ancient Israel

Studying Biblical Rituals and Texts

The purpose of this chapter is to present an analysis of purity and sacrifice in the Hebrew Bible, one that avoids the methodological problems addressed in chapter 1: the separation of ritual purity from sacrifice, and the relatively hostile treatment that sacrifice then typically receives, at least when compared with the treatment accorded ritual purity. In order to achieve a more balanced approach to sacrifice, we will seek here to isolate symbolic meanings in sacrificial rituals, after attempting to analyze the sacrificial process as a whole.

Although we have already surveyed many methodological issues with regard to the study of purity and sacrifice in general, a few critical questions remain that pertain specifically to the study of rituals in the Hebrew Bible. Before we can embark on a detailed analysis of purity and sacrifice in the Hebrew Bible, we must briefly address some of these questions. These include: (1) the relative dates of the components of the priestly material in the Pentateuch; (2) the application of ritual studies to the gap-ridden accounts of rituals in the Hebrew Bible; and (3) the relationship between priestly materials and prophetic materials. We will briefly take up the first two questions here; we will consider the relationship between prophetic and priestly texts in the next chapter.

Dating Components of the Priestly Tradition

To the degree that one can speak of a standard approach to *anything* in biblical studies, it has become accepted to identify two distinct strands in the priestly materials of the Pentateuch: the Priestly strand (P: roughly Lev. 1–16) and the Holiness Code (H: roughly Lev. 17–26).[1] The Holiness Code was first recognized as a distinct source in 1877 by August Klostermann (who gave the section the name *Heiligkeitsgesetz*).[2] Building on Klostermann's work, Wellhausen's famed historical reconstruction of events placed H before P: the Holiness Code was one source among many that were incorporated into the postexilic Priestly strand.[3] For the most part, scholars who accept the distinction between P and H have followed Wellhausen in viewing H as prior to P. This dating of the sources has been questioned, however, first by Israel Knohl and then by Milgrom.[4]

The central problem with most efforts of assigning dates to the priestly traditions is that they are evolutionist. Going back to the early days of biblical criticism, Wellhausen believed that P (which incorporated an earlier H) represented the ritualistic turn away from prophetic ethics—the devolution that is characteristic of Second Temple Judaism. This kind of argument was turned on its head by Yehezkel Kaufmann and those who followed him (including, among others, Menahem Haran, Israel Knohl, Jacob Milgrom, and Moshe Weinfeld). In short, the Kaufmann school maintains that the ritualistic, nonethically oriented priestly traditions were early, and preprophetic. Thus, in this reconstruction of things, the Israelite tradition and subsequent Judaism develops in a relatively linear fashion, with an ever-improving trajectory running from the priests through the prophets and culminating in later Judaism.[5] Either way, the argument remains evolutionist: When P is seen as preprophetic, it is because the author traces an evolution toward the ethical and from the ritual; when P is seen as postprophetic (and postexilic), the evolution is away from ethics and toward ritual.

Wellhausen's anti-Semitism (or anti-Judaism) and his evolutionism (whether Hegelain or not) are well known and need not be rehearsed here.[6] Kaufmann's work, of course, exhibits no trace of hostility toward the later Jewish tradition. But his work is by no means free of all of the shortcomings of Wellhausen. Evolutionism abounds in Kaufmann's work, and it remains a central facet of practically all scholarship associated with the "Kaufmann school."[7]

Evolutionist arguments are particularly conspicuous in the recent efforts of current heirs of the Kaufmann school (especially Knohl and Milgrom) to assert that H is actually later than P, not earlier. According to Knohl, the regulations of the Priestly strand "are not at all designed to establish social order, righteousness, or justice; they all relate exclusively to the ritual-cultic sphere."[8] Over and against P's lack of interest in ethics, Knohl argues that the Holiness School (H) heralds a great "innovation" with its "infusing of holiness with moral content."[9] Somewhat ironically, Knohl's evaluation of the priestly tradition (when separated from the Holiness Code) is almost every bit as hostile as Wellhausen's. Compared to Knohl's assessment, Milgrom's view is not as black and white: Milgrom argues that P was indeed interested in ethics. But Milgrom too posits that H is characterized by a number of marked ethical advances over P.[10]

These reconstructions falter in two ways. First, the evolutionist model is inherently flawed. As we have seen throughout chapter 1, evolutionist models are posited on unsubstantiated assumptions about how things change over time. Just as Wellhausen had his reasons for supposing that Second Temple Judaism was in a state of moral decline, so too Milgrom and Knohl have their reasons for arguing that First Temple Israelite tradition exhibited a linear, positive, ethical development over time. Of course, their arguments aren't purely evolutionist: on the whole, Knohl's careful identification of H-sounding redactional material in various P texts is compelling, and Milgrom too gathers much evidence to the effect that H is a later textual layer than P. But these textual arguments are put to evolutionist ends: their historical reconstructions are based on the assumption that what is more ethical must be later, and what is earlier is deemed subject to due criticism. While Milgrom's and Knohl's constructions are less hostile to the Israelite/Jewish tradition, generally speaking, Mary Douglas, for one, is right to emphasize that these approaches are quite hostile to P in particular: she correctly accuses these approaches of "P-baiting."[11]

A second problem with the theory of ethical evolution from P to H is raised by Knohl's own hypothesis—which has been endorsed to some degree by Milgrom—that H is to be credited with the redaction of P.[12] If in fact H (or some later reviser of H) was also responsible for the redaction of P, then we need to recognize that we are in something of a bind when it comes to evaluating P over against H. If we know P only through they eyes of H, how can we be so sure that we have enough of P to judge it on its own terms? Is it not possible, as Milgrom suggests, that H omitted P's ethical code and replaced it with its own version?[13] We can't know, and that is precisely why the evolutionist arguments made by Milgrom and Knohl regarding P and H fall short on evidential grounds as well: we lack the material from P that we would need in order to make such a comparison.

So how then are we to proceed? In my view, the fact that so much of the discussion of the priority of P versus H (or vice versa) is evolutionist in nature should give sufficient cause to be wary. Instead, we should follow the model proposed by Rolf Rendtorff and Joseph Blenkinsopp—and recently put to service by Douglas—that the priestly traditions (both within and without Leviticus) ought to be interpreted as we have them, and as an integral part of the Pentateuch as a whole.[14] Blenkinsopp's advice is apt:

> After working through the writings of what may be called the
> Kaufmann school, one is tempted to suggest that it would be more
> profitable to put one's time and energy into a positive and unpre-
> judicial assessment of P as a religious text, an assessment based on
> a synchronic reading without reference to the circumstances of
> its composition and reception, rather than attempting to refute
> Wellhausen's arguments by means of chronological displacement.[15]

I will not, therefore, account here for the distinction between P and H, for I am convinced by the arguments of Blenkinsopp and Rendtorff that the priestly traditions of the Pentateuch need to be studied as a whole, regardless of the history of their component parts.

Ritual Studies and Gap-Ridden Biblical Rituals

Even when we take the priestly traditions as a whole, the biblical descriptions of sacrificial rituals remain gap-ridden. As a result, a number of scholars—like Jonathan Z. Smith—claim that the biblical material is too incomplete to be considered a good subject for ritual studies:

> we don't have ritual texts in the Bible. We have very poor ethnographic descriptions. You cannot perform a single biblical ritual on the basis of what is given to you in the text. If you can't perform it, then by definition it is not a ritual. The biblical texts are scattered, theoretical reconstructions of what may have happened.[16]

This particular kind of caution is also endorsed by Rolf Knierim, in his microcommentary on Leviticus 1:1–9, where he disparages the possibility of structural interpretations of biblical texts.[17] On the other hand, we have those—like Mary Douglas—who carry on with the task of applying anthropological insight to the ritual fragments preserved in biblical texts, with results that are pleasing to many (though not, of course, to those who advocate the position of J. Z. Smith). It is difficult to imagine that this debate will ever be resolved fully. Douglas's and Leach's achievements do not convince Smith that we have enough data; Smith's methodological claims have not encouraged Douglas or others to give up their task. There are those, like Frank Gorman, who try to steer a middle course—by obeying the rules of both anthropology and philology.[18] But it's a difficult synthesis to forge, and I am not so sure we can fully understand any biblical ritual if we consider our subject bounded by the particular books, chapters or even verses that may constitute the focus of one biblical commentary or another.[19]

But how can we answer J. Z. Smith's challenge? First, Milgrom in his commentaries has modeled one method of filling in the gaps. By employing Milgrom's "systemic analysis," one can draw analogies among parallel texts, and suppose that if a certain action is required in ritual A, then perhaps it is also required in ritual B. A second helpful tool is imagination: some of what is left unstated in any given biblical ritual text can be filled in simply by trying to picture the process being described. And a third argument against Smith pertains to ethnography in general: gap-filling, by whatever method, is to some degree inevitable. No one can possibly ever witness a complete ritual, from all angles. From the simple, inevitable, blink of the eyes to the inherent limits of any one person's placement and vision—all descriptions of ritual are incomplete.[20] It's a question of degree, not a question of absolutes. The methodological questions raised by those concerned with the purity of ritual studies as a field cannot be dismissed out of hand. Nonetheless, the application of methods of ritual studies onto the texts of the Hebrew Bible cannot be ruled out in advance.

The Sacrificial Process, Part 1

We are now set to proceed with a synchronic reading of the priestly traditions, one that seeks to describe and understand the meaning of the *entire process* of sacrifice, beginning with the process of ritual purification. Yet while we attempt to describe and account for the broad process of sacrifice, we cannot at the same time review and account for all types of Israelite sacrifice.[21] As we have noted, sacrifice is a "multivalent entity."[22] Sacrificial rituals in ancient Israel involved select animals, as well as wine, incense, grains, and bread; details will be provided as necessary, while the focus remains, for the purposes of this work, on animal sacrifices.[23] More specifically, this analysis will pertain most directly to the daily burnt offering (Exod. 29:38–42; Num. 28:3–8; cf. Lev. 1:1–17). As indicated at the end of the previous chapter, instead of putting forth a theory, we will identify and illustrate two "organizing principles," two concerns central to the priestly traditions of the Pentateuch, each of which will help to understand better the dynamic between the systems of sacrifice and defilement. One organizing principle is the concern with imitating God. Another organizing principle is the concern with attracting and maintaining the presence of God within the community. By focusing on these two concerns, we will be able to analyze our two sets of ritual structures—sacrifice and purity— in tandem. We will, moreover, be able to do so using the same methodological assumption, which allows for the possibility that sacrificial rules could well be just as symbolic as purity regulations are commonly believed to be. Since ritual purification is one of the first steps of this sacrificial process, we begin the analysis with some reflections on the nature and meaning of ritual defilement.

Ritual and Moral Impurity

Fundamental to the argument being made here is the distinction between two types of defilement, which will be referred to as "ritual impurity" and "moral impurity." More detailed descriptions of this distinction can be found elsewhere.[24] But because the distinction pertains to this argument, we rehearse here (with minimal annotation) the basic contours of the two types of defilement.

As commonly understood, "ritual impurity" refers to the sort of defilement described in Leviticus 11–15 and Numbers 19. This defilement results from direct or indirect contact with any one of a number of natural processes and substances, including childbirth (Lev. 12:1–8), certain skin diseases (13: 1–46; 14:1–32), funguses in clothes (13:47–59) and houses (14:33–53), genital discharges (15:1–33), the carcasses of certain animals (11:1–47), and human corpses (Num. 19:10–22). Paradoxically, ritual impurity also comes about as a by-product of some sacrificial procedures (Lev. 16:28; Num. 19:7–8). The durations of these impurities differ, as do the requisite cleansing processes— but the intricacies of these laws are not our concern here.[25] In general, however, there are three distinct characteristics of ritual impurity: (1) the sources of ritual impurity are natural and more or less unavoidable; (2) it is not sinful to contract these impurities; and (3) these impurities can convey an impermanent contagion to people (priests and Israelites) and to many items within close proximity.

(1) That the sources of ritual impurity are natural is really quite clear. Birth, death, sex, disease, and discharge are part of normal life. Ritual impurity is also generally unavoidable. While certain defiling substances are relatively avoidable (e.g., touching carcasses), discharge, disease, and death are inescapable. Some ritual impurities are not just inevitable but obligatory. All Israelites (priests included) are obligated to reproduce (Gen. 1:28, 9:7). All Israelites (except the high priest) are required to bury their deceased relatives (Lev. 21:10–15; cf. 21:1–4). Priests are also obligated to perform cultic procedures that leave them defiled as a result (Lev. 16:28; Num. 19:8).

(2) It is not a sin to contract these ritual impurities. This idea proceeds logically from the observations drawn above. While priests must limit their contact with corpse impurity (Lev. 21:1–4), it is not prohibited for them to contract other impurities (22:3–7). To be sure, priests are sternly warned against eating sacred food or entering sacred precincts when in a state of ritual impurity (Lev. 7:19–21, 22:3–7). Yet the primary concern incumbent upon the priests is not to avoid ritual impurity at all times but to safeguard the separation between ritual impurity and purity (Lev. 10:10; cf. Ezek. 44:23). By extension, Israelites are obliged to remain aware of their ritual status, lest they accidentally come into contact with the sacred while in a state of ritual impurity (Lev. 15:31). Of course, refusal to purify oneself would constitute a transgression (Num. 19:20). But this does not make being ritually impure sinful in and of itself. As long as Israelites remain aware of their status—and do what is necessary to ameliorate the situation—there is little chance of danger or transgression.

(3) The third characteristic of ritual impurity is that it conveys to persons (priests and Israelites, men and women) an impermanent contagion. This is obviously true of the ritual impurity that Israelites contract from direct or indirect contact with a ritually impure carcass or another ritually impure Israelite. In such a case, the period of defilement can be as brief as the time lasting until sunset (Lev. 11:24; 15:7; Num. 19:22). The same holds for persons who engage in permitted sexual relations (Lev. 15:16–18). A man who has sexual contact with a menstruant or a person who comes into contact with a corpse will be ritually impure for a week (Lev. 15:24; Num. 19:11). Other defiling conditions can result in even longer periods of defilement. Menstruation lasts roughly a week, but the defiling state left after giving birth lasts, in its less severe form, either thirty-three or sixty-six days (Lev. 12:1–8). Finally, irregular genital flows (for both men and women), scale disease, and house funguses last an unspecified amount of time. But even these forms of impurity are conceived of as impermanent—that is why the biblical tradition records purificatory procedures for all of them. There is no form of ritual impurity that does not have purificatory procedures, from waiting until sundown

to bathing bodies, washing clothes, and performing sacrificial rites. Even when long lasting, the status of ritual defilement is an impermanent one.[26]

The Hebrew Bible is concerned with another form of purity and impurity, often referred to as "moral." (Some scholars draw this distinction in different terms, speaking of "permitted" [ritual] and "prohibited" [moral] impurities.[27]) Moral impurity results from committing certain acts so heinous that they are considered defiling. Such behaviors include sexual sins (e.g., Lev. 18:24–30), idolatry (e.g., 19:31; 20:1–3), and bloodshed (e.g., Num. 35:33–34). These "abominations" (תועבות) bring about an impurity that *morally*—but not *ritually*—defiles the sinner (Lev. 18:24), the land of Israel (Lev. 18:25, Ezek. 36:17), and the sanctuary of God (Lev. 20:3; Ezek. 5:11). This defilement, in turn, leads to the expulsion of the people from the land of Israel (Lev. 18:28; Ezek. 36:19). The bulk of the references to these ideas can be found in priestly traditions (especially the Holiness Code) and in the most priestly of prophetic books, Ezekiel. Additional articulations of the notion or echoes of it can be found in various strands of biblical tradition.[28]

There are a number of important differences between moral and ritual impurity. (1) While ritual impurity is generally not sinful, moral impurity is a direct consequence of grave sin. (2) A characteristic feature of moral impurity is its deleterious effect on the land of Israel. Ritual impurity, in contrast, poses no threat to the land. (3) While ritual impurity often results in a contagious defilement, there is no personal-contact contagion associated with moral impurity. Moral impurity does defile the sinners themselves (Lev. 18:24, 19:31; cf. Gen. 34:5; Deut. 24:1–4). But one need not bathe subsequent to direct or indirect contact with an idolater, a murderer, or an individual who committed a sexual sin. (4) While ritual impurity results in an impermanent defilement, moral impurity leads to a long-lasting, if not permanent, degradation of the sinner and, eventually, of the land of Israel. (5) While ritual impurity can be ameliorated by rites of purification, that is not the case for moral impurity. Moral purity is achieved by punishment, atonement, or, best of all, by refraining from committing morally impure acts in the first place.

(6) Since moral impurity does not produce ritual defilement, sinners—in contrast to those who are ritually impure—are not excluded from the sanctuary. In the case of the suspected adulteress (Num. 5:11–31), the woman is brought into the sanctuary itself in order to determine her moral status. It also appears that Israelite murderers sought sanctuary *in the sanctuary* (Exod. 21:14; cf. 1 Kgs. 1:50–53 and 2:28–30). Moral impurity does indeed defile the sacred precincts (e.g., Lev. 20:3). But the effect of moral impurity does not penetrate the holy realm by the entrance of sinners into it. Moral impurity is a potent force unleashed by sinful behavior that affects the sanctuary even from afar, in its own way.

(7) In addition to these phenomenological differences between ritual and moral defilements, there are also terminological distinctions drawn in the texts themselves. Although the term "impure" (טמא) is used in both contexts, the terms "abomination" (תועבה) and "pollute" (חנף) are used with regard to the sources of moral impurity, but not with regard to the sources of ritual

TABLE 2.1. Ritual and Moral Impurity

Impurity Type	Source	Effect	Resolution
Ritual	Natural processes and substances such as birth, death, bodily flows, certain animal carcasses, human corpses	Temporary, contagious defilement of persons and objects	Ritual purification, which can include bathing, waiting, and sacrifices
Moral	Sins: idolatry, sexual transgression, bloodshed	Long-lasting defilement of sinners, land, and sanctuary	Atonement or punishment, and ultimately, exile

impurity. For all of these reasons, it is imperative to distinguish between moral and ritual impurity. And to help clarify the distinction between ritual and moral impurity, the basic differences are summarized in Table 2.1.

In the priestly traditions of the Pentateuch, it is *ritual* purity that is the prerequisite for the performance of sacrificial ritual. Curiously, *moral* purity is not explicitly required of those who would offer sacrifices. Still, the moral purity system does intersect with the sacrificial process, in ways that will become clearer at the end of this chapter. For now, we note what this chart already intimates: ritual impurity poses a threat to the sanctuary by virtue of the fact that those who are ritually impure must be kept away from the sacred precincts. Moral defilement poses a threat to the sanctuary as well, though this threat is operative whether or not the sinners in question come to the temple. The purity systems intersect with sacrifice also when it comes to their resolution: the procedures of ritual purification as well as the process of atonement from sin involve, in part, sacrificial acts.[29]

Ritual Purity, Sacrifice, and Imitatio Dei

For ancient Israel, the sacrificial process can be said to begin with *ritual* purification. Ritual purity is the prerequisite of those who come to the sanctuary to offer sacrifices, of those who regularly officiate at sacrifices (priests), and of any animals that are to be offered as sacrifices. We briefly noted in the previous chapter that a number of theories have been advanced in the attempt to account for the varied nature of the substances viewed as ritually defiling in Leviticus 11–15 and Numbers 19. One popular theory focuses on death as the common denominator of the ritual purity system. The most articulate champion of this view currently is Jacob Milgrom, who, after reviewing the sources of ritual defilement, states:

> the common denominator here is death. Vaginal blood and semen represent the forces of life; their loss—death. . . . In the case of scale disease [i.e., "leprosy"], this symbolism is made explicitly: Aaron prays for his stricken sister, "Let her not be like a corpse" (Num. 12:12). Furthermore, scale disease is powerful enough to contaminate

by overhang, and it is no accident that it shares this feature with
the corpse (Num. 19:14). The wasting of the body, the common
characteristic of all biblically impure skin diseases, symbolizes the
death process as much as the loss of blood and semen.[30]

The importance of death as a common denominator of the avoidance regulations in priestly traditions can also be seen, perhaps, in the blood prohibition
(Lev. 17:10–14), in the elimination of carnivores from the diet of ancient Israel,
and in the abhorrence of pigs, which played a role in Canaanite chthonic
worship.[31] The purpose of the system, as Milgrom says elsewhere, is to drive a
wedge between the forces of death, which are impure, and the forces of life,
which, like God, are holy.[32]

Milgrom's impurity-as-death "theory"[33] is by no means entirely new.
Milgrom notes that other scholars have focused on death in order to understand ritual impurity in ancient Israel.[34] Indeed, regarding the ancient Israelite system, this view can be traced back at least as far as Alfred Edersheim
(1825–1889).[35] But Milgrom has advanced the theory in a number of new
ways. In his commentary, the theory comes across as remarkably comprehensive. Moreover, he draws on anthropological and ethnographic works that
identify a similar problematization of death in other purity systems.[36] Yet the
view of death as impure and corpses as defiling is by no means universal:
some societies concerned with defilement problematize death, while others do
not.[37] Just as there are no universal taboos, so too there is no universal theory
of impurity.

While few scholars deny the importance of death-avoidance to the biblical
purity system, some questions remain. One question concerns the relationship between death-avoidance and sex-avoidance. A second question concerns
sacrifice. Indeed, the centrality of death to the ritual purity system brings
us to a riddle at the heart of our concerns. Why, if the ritual purity system is
concerned with keeping death out of the sanctuary, does the sacrificial system
involve precisely the opposite: the killing of animals, *in the sanctuary?*[38]

Regarding the relationship between death and sex, the death-avoidance
theory may well explain why individuals become ritually defiled when genital
fluids are lost through nonsexual discharge from the body—surely the potential for life is lost in such situations. But it remains unclear whether or
not the fear of death really explains why sex and birth *always* defile, even when
no mishap occurs. Moreover, why is it that the only substances that flow from
the body and defile are sexual or genital in nature? Even blood flowing
from the veins of a dying person is not ritually defiling. A number of scholars
have convincingly argued, against Milgrom, that the overarching concern with
death-avoidance does not fully explain the particular concern with genital
discharges. Tikva Frymer-Kensky and David P. Wright, among others, emphasize the important role that attitudes toward sexuality (but not necessarily
gender) play in ancient Israel's perceptions of defilement.[39] Both of these
scholars argue, with different emphases, that both death *and* sex figure in the
ritual purity system of ancient Israel, and that the system serves to highlight

the differences between persons and God. Because God is eternal, God does not die. As Wright puts it, "the mortal condition is incompatible with God's holiness."[40] Because God has no consort, God cannot have sex. Therefore, as Frymer-Kensky puts it, "in order to approach God, one has to leave the sexual realm."[41]

By separating from sex and death—by following the ritual purity regulations—ancient Israelites (and especially ancient Israelite priests and Levites) separated themselves from what made them least God-like. In other words, the point of following these regulations is nothing other than the theological underpinning of the entire Holiness Code: *imitatio Dei* (Lev. 11:44–45, 19:2, 20:7, 26). Only a heightened, god-like state—the state of ritual purity—made one eligible to enter the sanctuary, God's holy residence on earth. Here we come back to Hubert and Mauss and their classic essay on sacrifice where, with regard to the process of "sacralization," they said: "all that touches upon the gods must be divine; the sacrifier is obliged to become a god himself in order to be capable of acting upon them."[42] The applicability of this observation to the priestly materials of the Pentateuch ought now be manifest.

Yet we are still left with a problem: if death is defiling (and banned from the sacred) why does killing animals find a central place within the sacred? The answer to the riddle lies, in part, in the fact that the kind of death that occurs in the sanctuary is not a natural kind of death but a highly controlled one. Sacrifice is frequently described (or derided) as "violent"; and it certainly is, at the very least, deadly and bloody. But the violence of sacrifice is not random or indiscriminate: animal sacrifice in ancient Israel proceeds only in a very orderly and controlled way.[43] The domesticated animals fit to be offered as sacrifices have no power whatsoever to resist: "like a gentle lamb led to the slaughter" (Jer. 11:19). That is why, at least in ancient Israel, sacrifice is very little like the hunt: the sacrificial animals chosen cannot put up much of a fight.[44]

As we will soon see, in ancient Israel, sacrifice involves—in part—the controlled exercise of complete power over an animal's life and death. This is precisely one of the powers that Israel's God exercises over human beings: "the Lord kills and brings to life" (1 Sam. 2:6; cf. Deut. 32:39). But exercising control over the death of a subordinate being is not the only aspect of sacrificial ritual that can be understood in light of *imitatio Dei*. Indeed, we will soon see that a great many facets of sacrificial ritual—from the selection of animals to be sacrificed to the dissection and consumption of the animals on or near the altar—can also be understood in this light.

Domestication, Sacrifice, and Imitatio Dei

Ritual purity is not the only prerequisite for sacrifice, nor is it the only prerequisite that may help us understand better the nature and meaning of ancient Israel's sacrificial process. Before an Israelite could offer anything as a sacrifice, the Israelite would have to acquire whatever items, animal or vegetable, are to be offered. In a society such as ancient Israel, in which many (if not most) were agrarians and pastoralists, it behooves us to reflect on whether we can learn something about sacrifice by understanding better the relationship between Israelites and their animals.

In his essay "The Domestication of Sacrifice," Jonathan Z. Smith offered the tantalizing suggestion that sacrifice might be understood as a "meditation on domestication."[45] Smith here is at once criticizing the theories of René Girard and Walter Burkert and offering something of an alternative. Smith points out that "animal sacrifice appears to be, universally, the ritual killing of a domesticated animal by agrarian or pastoralist societies."[46] Smith even entertains the possibility that animals were originally domesticated so that they could be sacrificed.[47] Leaving the question of origins aside, I wish to ask what we can learn about ancient Israelite sacrifice if we were to meditate on the process of domestication as a prerequisite for sacrifice.

We must, however, exercise some caution when trying to make use of Smith's insights for an understanding of the Hebrew Bible. Smith offered his account of sacrificial origins as a kind of "jeu d'esprit."[48] When pressed in the conversation that followed the paper, he asserted that he doesn't even believe his own theory.[49] In contrast to Burkert and Girard, Smith emphatically—and very seriously—rejected altogether the enterprise of theorizing about the origins of sacrifice.[50] It is ironic, therefore—but true nonetheless—that Smith's reflections on the process of domestication and its relation to sacrifice make an important contribution to an understanding of sacrifice in the Hebrew Bible. The reason for this is obvious: not only do domesticated animals play a key role in ancient Israelite sacrifice but also metaphors comparing ancient Israelites to their domesticated animals play a key role in ancient Israelite theologizing: "The Lord is my shepherd," the psalmist famously noted (23:1). Smith's essay—mind-game or not—may help us indeed.

Before we go further, some clarification is in order. What precisely is domestication? Smith provides the helpful definition: "domestication may be defined as the process of human interference in or alteration of the genetics of plants and animals (i.e., selective breeding)."[51] A useful recent work by the biologist Bruce D. Smith provides further details of this process, which, as he puts it, results in the "human creation of a new form of plant or animal."[52] As B. D. Smith ably demonstrates—in a manner clear even to the nonscientist—a domesticated plant or animal is "identifiably different from its wild ancestors and extant wild relatives."[53] The origins of this process are not our concern, any more than the origins of sacrifice. What is important here is the fact that domestication by its nature involves human control over a plant's being or an animal's life and death. While this is true of plants (which were sown, grafted, and reaped by human farmers), it is even more dramatically true with regard to animals. By keeping animals penned up, separating herds, rationing their feeding, selectively killing some and selectively allowing others to breed, herders exercise a rather striking amount of control over the animals in their possession.[54] In light of what we have already observed regarding ritual purity, sacrifice, controllability, and death, it is certainly worth thinking about the relationship between sacrifice and domestication in ancient Israel.

Ancient Israelites were no exception to the general rule noted by J. Z. Smith: their animal sacrifices consisted of domesticated species. But only certain domesticated animals were allowed on the altar. Pigs, of course, were out of the question, as were the other carnivores and omnivores whose consumption were proscribed in Leviticus 11 and Deuteronomy 14. Israel's dietary rules also banned the consumption of horses, camels, and donkeys (which were nonetheless kept by them and used for transportation).[55] But Israel's altar was subject to greater restriction that Israel's table.[56] Israel's animal sacrifices came primarily from the herd and flock—cattle, sheep, and goats—along with certain species of domesticated birds. Thus Israel's sacrificial offerings involved animals that are by nature docile, defenseless, and communal (living and reproducing in flocks and herds).

We should not be surprised that ancient Israelite literature makes generous use of metaphors involving its favorite domesticated animals.[57] As any reader of the Bible knows, these metaphors are rather prominent, and a good number of them depict God as Israel's shepherd: "for He is our God, and we are the people He tends, the flock in his care" (Ps. 95:7).[58] In the capacity of shepherd, God is depicted as protecting, guiding, feeding, even slaying his flock.[59]

> The Lord is my Shepherd, I shall not want.
> He makes me lie down in green pastures;
>   He leads me beside still waters...
>
> (Psalms 23:1–2)
>
> He will feed his flock like a shepherd;
> He will gather the lambs in his arms,
>   and carry them in his bosom
>   and gently lead the mother sheep.
>
> (Isaiah 40:11)

> I myself will be the shepherd of my sheep, and I will make them lie
> down, says the Lord God. I will seek the lost, and I will bring back
> the strayed, and I will bind up the injured, and I will strengthen
> the weak, but the fat and the strong I will destroy. I will feed them
> with justice.
>
> (Ezek. 34:15–16)

The activities ascribed to God in these and other passages constitute the necessary preliminaries to the sacrificial act. Before any animal can be sacrificed, it must first be protected when born, fed, and then finally guided to its place of slaughter. What is more, because maimed animals are unfit for the altar (Lev. 22:18–25), the careful shepherd will keep an eye toward protecting the animals that are fit for sacrifice. Because Israelites are prohibited from offering an animal and its offspring on the same day (Lev. 22:28), shepherds cannot lose track of the familial relationships within their herds and flocks. Because the art of herding is selective breeding—choosing which males will be allowed to reproduce with which females—shepherds will, therefore, as a matter of course, make the "life-and-death" decisions for their herds and flocks.

Israel's sacrificial system presumes that Israelites themselves will be doing some good tending of their herds or flocks: if they did not, there would be nothing left to offer. Israel's theologizing frequently depicts God performing precisely that role vis-à-vis Israel, tending the flock. Thus it stands to reason that, on some level, ancient Israelites understood tending their own flocks in light of this analogy: as Israel is to Israel's herds and flocks, so too is God to Israel, the flock of the Lord. The prophetic and hymnic metaphors based on this analogy—as well as other metaphors we will examine below—provide a clue as to the ways ancient Israelites may have understood their rituals. More specifically, taken as a whole, these metaphors provide further confirmation of the case I am making: the process of sacrifice can be understood as an act of *imitatio Dei*.

Before reviewing other aspects of the sacrificial process, we need to counter two tropes in biblical scholarship—reflections on sacrifice that are based, in part, on judgments concerning Israel's attitude toward animals. The first misconception is the idea that because humans in the beginning were vegetarians, sacrifice therefore is something that was not originally intended, or at least less than ideal.[60] It is true that Genesis 1:29–31 (cf. Gen. 9:1–11) mandates that humans and animals are to eat only plants (even while humans are told to lord over both animals and plants in Gen. 1:28). While this diet is, strictly speaking, "vegetarian," even "nonviolent," one should wonder whether these terms accurately and objectively describe the diet imagined in Genesis 1 and 2, which seems to consist exclusively of *raw* plants.[61] This diet also excludes, it would appear, dairy products, bread, and anything else that requires human effort or cooking. From a canonical perspective, agriculture begins with the expulsion from the Garden (Gen. 3:17–19), and cuisine begins even later. What is more, also from a canonical perspective, animals were sacrificed by Abel (4:1–5) and Noah (8:20) before permission was granted to eat animals (9:1–3). There is, therefore, no direct correspondence between the permission to eat animals and the understanding that one must sacrifice them.

A second misconception concerning biblical attitudes toward animals and animal sacrifices also concerns the Genesis narratives. It is sometimes suggested that the Hebrew Bible has a stated preference for animal over vegetable offerings, reflecting the preference of herding over agriculture.[62] This is ostensibly borne out by the Cain and Abel story—where the agrarian Cain kills the pastoralist Abel after the former's sacrifice has been rejected by God (Gen. 4:1–8). This is also borne out, ostensibly, by the fact that the first two chapters of Leviticus detail sacrificial rules beginning with larger animals and working down to grain. But interpretations of sacrifice that pit herders against farmers overlook two indisputable facts. First, the sacrificial rituals of the priestly traditions routinely involve offerings consisting of animals *and* grains, along with wine, oil, and other sundry products (e.g., Exod. 29:38–42; Lev. 24:5–9; Num. 28:1–8). Second, the literary and archaeological evidence for ancient Israel suggests that herders and farmers worked together: the ancient Israelite economy was neither entirely nomadic nor exclusively agricultural.[63] These two facts are two sides of the same coin: the social life of ancient Israel involved both plants and animals, and its cultic ritual reflects that symbiosis.

Imitating God in the Sanctuary of God

It has now been established that two preliminaries for the sacrificial process can be understood in light of *imitatio Dei*. Ancient Israelites understood the chores related to the raising of and caring for domesticated animals—even though these are not rituals per se—by analogy to their relationship with God. The ritual purifications that were the prerequisites for encountering the sacred can also be understood in light of the notion of *imitatio Dei*.

Another preliminary for sacrifice can similarly be understood, and must be noted briefly here. The priestly texts that tell us of Israelite sacrifice imagine these rites taking place in the desert tabernacle. Of course, Israelite sacrifice will also find its place in the Solomonic temple (and, to be sure, elsewhere as well).[64] It is therefore significant to note that a good deal of archaeological and literary evidence *suggests* that ancient Israelites—following ancient Near Eastern myths and models—conceived of their cult places as representing the cosmos.[65] As we will see in chapter 4, this idea is more clearly articulated in later ancient Jewish texts. But there are hints of this notion in the biblical record too. Indeed, as Jon D. Levenson has pointed out, the language and structure of the tabernacle (and temple) construction narratives carefully recall the language and structure of Genesis 1.[66] Thus by building their cult site, the Israelites themselves construct a miniature cosmos. Of course, this in turn means that the priestly traditions understand tabernacle and temple construction as acts of *imitatio Dei*. The question we will now consider is whether other aspects of sacrificial ritual can be understood in the same light.

Breaking down ancient Israel's sacrificial process into discrete steps is not as simple a task as it may seem. Henri Hubert and Marcel Mauss spoke of three major stages of the sacrificial process: entry, victim, and exit.[67] More recently, Gary Anderson breaks the process into six steps: (1) bringing the animal into the sanctuary; (2) laying hands on the animal; (3) slaughtering and cutting the animal; (4) tossing the blood; (5) burning the animal, in part or in whole; and (6) the disposal of the remains.[68] Erhard Gerstenberger, in his Leviticus commentary, lists nine steps: (1) selection of the sacrificial animal; (2) transfer of sin through laying of hands; (3) immolation; (4) blood aspersion; (5) flaying and dividing the animal; (6) altar preparation; (7) burning parts of the animal; (8) cleansing entrails; and (9) burning the rest of the animal.[69] The two larger lists are similar but not identical. Following closely the syntax of Leviticus 1:3–9, Gerstenberger separates the killing and the flaying into two steps (see Lev. 1:5–6). He adds a reference to preparing the altar (Lev. 1:7) and distinguishes between two stages of burning (Lev. 1:8 and

1:9b). Importantly, Gerstenberger correctly extrapolates that certain actions are presupposed by the text: in order to bring a fit animal for sacrifice, one must select a proper animal from the herd or flock.[70] Gerstenberger's list also *interprets* laying hands on the sacrificial animal (Lev. 1:4) as an act of transfer, a view that others have questioned. Of course, neither of these two lists is entirely complete. The process of ritual purification is not included, nor is the equally important process of acquisition. In order to sacrifice an animal, one must of course have one; in order to *select* an animal, one must have more than one.

We will discuss here many, but not all, of the steps just noted. Our concern is not so much to account for every detail of the sacrificial process as to demonstrate the kind of interpretation that can be offered when one attempts to account for the broad sweep of the sacrificial process. If the analysis falls short of explaining every aspect of the ritual as described in Leviticus 1:3–9, at least I can claim that it accounts for much that is usually left out of other analyses. In this section, we will discuss those aspects of the sacrificial process that can be understood in light of the notion of *imitatio Dei*. Other aspects of the process will be discussed later in this chapter. Still other aspects of the process—notably the rite of laying a hand on the sacrifice—will be discussed in chapter 3, for reasons that will become clear.

Coinciding with the process of ritual purification comes a process of selection: the offerer or the officiating priest for each sacrificial ritual must *select* the animal that is to be sacrificed. Any animal offered must be without blemish (Lev. 1:3). While this regulation is repeated many times in the Priestly strand,[71] one finds the definition of what constitutes a blemish in a text usually attributed to the Holiness Code (Lev. 22:17–28).[72] Here we find that animals brought to the altar must be free of at least the following defects.

> (22) Anything blind, or injured, or maimed, or having a discharge, or an itch, or scabs—these you shall not offer to the Lord. . . . (23) An ox or a lamb that has a limb too long or too short[73] you may present for a freewill offering; but it will not be accepted for a vow. (24) Any animal that has its testicles bruised or crushed or torn or cut you shall not offer to the Lord; such you shall not do within your land.

It is commonly pointed out that it is fitting for animals offered on the holy altar to be perfect and whole.[74] It is equally important to recognize, however, that this stipulation does not only concern the animal: it requires the offerer to carefully examine the animal destined for sacrifice. These regulations, moreover, don't only apply at the moment of sacrifice. Prudent shepherds will properly care for their flocks, watching for blemishes that have appeared, trying to prevent others from coming about, and perhaps even controlling the breeding of those animals born with defects. As we have also already mentioned, Leviticus prohibits offering an animal and its offspring on the same day (Lev. 22:26–28). This regulation requires of all offerers of sacrifice, priestly and otherwise, to remain keenly aware of the familial relationships among the animals to be offered as sacrifices.

Even after the offerer has eliminated unfit animals in accordance with these regulations, presumably more than one fit animal is left in the herd or flock—and that's when the selection of the animal truly takes place.[75] The closest we come to a description of this aspect of the sacrificial process is in Exodus 12, where the Israelites' selection and watching over the animal to be consumed as a Passover offering (12:6) is juxtaposed with God's guarding and watching over Israel in preparation for the tenth plague (12:42). Indeed, the sacrificial narrative in Exodus 12 is infused with intimations of Israel acting in imitation of God.[76] The idea that Israelites could imitate God by selecting things is, of course, evident elsewhere. The book of Leviticus itself more than once draws a connection between the human capacity to make distinctions and the divine power to do the same (Lev. 10:10; 11:46–47). Clearly, the process of selection too can be understood in light of the concern to imitate God.

We have already mentioned that exercising control over the life and death of the animal can be understood in light of *imitatio Dei*. Once the animal is killed, a number of steps immediately follow: the blood of the animal is manipulated in various ways (Lev. 1:5) and then the priests flay and cut up the offering (Lev. 1:6). We skip for a moment the complex questions concerning blood and focus on the priest's separating of the carcass into its constituent parts. Although the basic regulations for this process—specifying which parts belong where—are laid out in Leviticus and elsewhere, there are very few descriptions of the image of an offerer or priest looking into the innards of an animal. The only relevant passages I know of can be found in Jeremiah, the Psalms, and a few other places, which speak of God, who "examines the kidneys and heart."[77] In most English editions of the Hebrew Bible, the phrase is translated figuratively, which obscures the sacrificial nature of the metaphor being employed in these passages.[78] The idea that ancient Israelites believed the heart to be the center of thought (e.g., Deut. 8:5 and 1 Kgs. 2:44) is beside the point. The figurative translations conceal the fact that the organs being examined are, regardless of their function, ones that figure prominently in sacrificial rituals (e.g., Lev. 3:4, 10, 15). Can we infer from these images that the priest—by looking into the animal—is doing divine work?

We now turn back to the matter of blood,[79] which is daubed on the altar by a priest (Lev. 1:5). A number of prophetic passages also imagine God manipulating blood. Such images appear particularly in passages depicting God as the divine warrior.[80] This phenomenon, incidentally, constitutes one of many interrelationships in the Hebrew Bible between sacrificial ideologies and the notion of holy war.[81] Isaiah 63:1–6, for instance, depicts God wearing a bloodstained garment—would not the priestly garments be stained with blood?[82] What is more, other sacrificial terms appear in this passage: God "spatters" the blood (63:3), and the prophet here uses the same verb used commonly in sacrificial contexts (e.g., Lev. 4:6, 6:20). When the prophet complains that there is no "helper" (סומך; Isa. 63:5), he uses another term commonly used in sacrificial contexts (e.g., Lev. 1:4).[83]

A similar depiction of God manipulating blood in the performance of sacrifice can be found in Isaiah 34:6–7:

(6) The Lord has a sword; it is sated with blood,
      it is gorged with fat, with the blood of lambs and goats,
      with the fat of the kidneys and rams.
For the Lord has a sacrifice in Bozrah,
      a great slaughter in the land of Edom.
(7) Wild oxen shall fall with them,
      and young steers with the mighty bulls.
Their land shall be soaked with blood,
      and their soil made rich with fat.

This passages and still others like them[84] are striking in their depiction of God performing sacrificial behaviors with blood.

Once the animal is dissected, various parts of it are consumed in one way or another. While parts of the altar or sanctuary are doused with the blood of the animal, the fat, meat, and organs of the animal are either consumed in the flames of the altar or eaten by the priests. These aspects of sacrifice, too, can be well understood in light of *imitatio Dei*. A number of biblical scholars have struggled with the idea of a God who eats, and it may now come as little surprise that many argue that Israelites could not have believed in such an idea. For instance, according to Menahem Haran, references to sacrifices as "God's food" (e.g., Lev. 3:11) and to the altar as God's "table" (e.g., Ezek. 41:22; Mal. 1:7) are "fossilized" usages that are "clearly based on a very ancient and elementary conception of the world and could not possibly be the products of Israel's own cultural *milieu*."[85]

Perhaps the biblical God doesn't rely on food the same way people do (Ps. 50:12–13), but God certainly does "consume"—and the difference between "eating" and "consuming" exists only in our translations, not in the original Hebrew. Throughout biblical narrative, God appears to the Israelites as a "consuming fire." In the context of holy war, God will travel with and before the Israelites as a "consuming fire" to devour Israel's enemies.[86] Strikingly, God also appears as a "consuming fire" in a number of sacrificial narratives concerning the offerings of (among others) Moses, Aaron, David, Solomon, and Elijah.[87] By "consuming" and burning elements of sacrificial offerings, the offerers of sacrifice in ancient Israel are imitating activities often ascribed to God in narratives in which God's presence during a sacrifice is explicitly described.

We have seen that the typical ancient Israelite sacrifice involves the performance by Israelites and priests of a number of activities that can be understood well in the light of the concern to imitate God. The process of ritual purification may well involve the separation of people from those aspects of humanity (death and sex) that are least God-like. The performance of pastoral responsibilities—caring, feeding, protecting, and guiding—can easily be understood in light of *imitatio Dei*, as can the more dramatic acts of selective breeding. Closer to the altar, the selection, killing, dissection, and consumption of sacrificial animals are also activities that have analogues in the divine realm. God too selects, kills, looks inside things, and appears on earth as a consuming fire. Indeed, the concern with imitating God serves as a symbolic underpinning of much of the sacrificial process.

Sacrifice and Metaphor

It is likely that some will resist the suggestion that sacrificial rituals can be better understood in light of the notion of *imitatio Dei*. It is also likely that some will resist this analysis because of its unabashed use of images culled from the Psalms and prophetic literature in order to understand the rituals dryly laid out in Leviticus. Some might suppose that passages like Jeremiah 11:20 (in which God examines the kidneys and heart) or Isaiah 40:11 (in which God the shepherd gathers, guides, and feeds his flock) do not really concern sacrifice at all because they are just metaphors. We cannot, however, be so quick in labeling these images as metaphors and then dismissing them from a discussion of the meaning of sacrificial rituals. First of all, it is worth keeping in mind that as long as the date of Priestly strand(s) of the Pentateuch remains a debated issue, it can by no means be assumed that the (presumably metaphorical) passages in Jeremiah (or even the Psalms) are later than the (presumably literal) descriptions of sacrificial rituals in Leviticus. Of course, this observation is really only relevant if we operate under the standard assumption that metaphors involve secondary and nonliteral usages that in some way extend beyond the original, literal usage of the terminology in question. The more time one spends reflecting on metaphor, however, the more one is impelled to rethink simplistic approaches.[88]

This book began with the observation that antisacrificial biases in contemporary scholarship have hindered the understanding of sacrifice in ancient Israel. It can equally be said that the understanding of sacrifice has suffered because of antimetaphorical biases in scholarship. There is a longstanding tradition in Western philosophy—going back all the way to Aristotle—that disparages metaphor as something that is merely ornamental.[89] For some decades, however, a number of philosophers, linguists, and anthropologists have worked to rehabilitate metaphor, arguing that metaphor is cognitive, meaningful, often primary and foundational, and so pervasive as to become inescapable.[90] Nonetheless, very few works that set out to study ancient Israelite ritual in general (to say nothing of sacrifice in particular) seek to make use of biblical metaphors in their analysis.[91] In general, the study of Israelite sacrifice has suffered because antimetaphorical biases in biblical scholarship have eliminated sacrificial metaphors from the discussion.[92]

It is no longer sound to assume that metaphor is historically secondary. Quite often the reverse can be demonstrated, even within the Hebrew Bible.[93] One stunning example is the "dry bones" vision in Ezekiel 37. Here we find a metaphorical reference to the resurrection of the dead that by virtually all accounts precedes by hundreds of years the time when ancient Israelites literally believed in any notion of resurrection of the dead.[94]

It is also no longer methodologically sound to dismiss metaphor as merely ornamental. At the very least, metaphor—when it can be demonstrated to be in existence—must be taken seriously. It must also be recognized that metaphor, even when it can be demonstrated to be historically secondary, frequently *expands* the meanings and usages of words and concepts, thereby influencing both behavior and beliefs.[95] Consider, for instance, one of the few biblical metaphors that is generally treated properly: the prophetic comparison of God's covenant with Israel to a marriage between a man and a woman (e.g., Hos. 1:2–3:5). This is clearly metaphorical, yet most scholars are willing to grant that this metaphor in particular *expands* our understanding of ancient Israelite perceptions of what a covenant meant. Scholars don't dismiss Hosea's marriage as mere metaphor, and Jeremiah 11:20 ought not be dismissed either. It is one thing to label Jeremiah 11:20 and similar passages as metaphor—this could well be justified. It is quite another thing to go further and assume that these passages contribute nothing to our understanding of ancient Israelite sacrifice. If rituals (sacrifice included) mean anything at all, they involve metaphors, practically by definition.[96] Why dismiss one set of metaphors from the discussion of another? Considering that a fair amount of evidence can be marshaled in defense of the argument that the notion of *imitatio Dei* informed ancient Israelite approaches to sacrifice, the prophetic images that depict God in sacrificial terms or in pastoral roles ought to be looked at very seriously. These may well be root metaphors that contribute to our understanding of what sacrifice meant to ancient Israelites.

Sacrifice, then, ought to be understood *metaphorically*—and I use the term advisedly.[97] There is an analogy at the heart of sacrifice.[98] The offerer and priest play the part of God, and the domesticated animals—from the herd and the flock—play the part of the people (and particularly Israel). The analogy, of course, is not perfect: people don't *really* become divine in the process of imitating God. They can merely aspire briefly to play on the human level roles otherwise played by God on the divine level.[99] But this problem is inherent in and characteristic of metaphor: analogy is not identity.[100] If Jonathan Z. Smith is right, the problem is also inherent in ritual: "ritual is a means of performing the way things ought to be in conscious tension to the way things are."[101]

There will continue to be those who insist that ritual in general—to say nothing of biblical sacrifice in particular—lacks any inherent symbolic meaning.[102] Perhaps the pivotal theoretical work in this respect is Frits Staal's essay, "The Meaninglessness of Ritual." The debate on whether ritual is symbolic or not is sure to continue, and those seeking the final word will not find it here. My sympathy for those who seek to find symbol in ritual—including Mary Douglas, Clifford Geertz, Edmund Leach, Victor Turner, the early Claude Lévi-Strauss, and others—should already be clear enough. Still, assuming for a moment that we accept Staal's interpretation of Hindu rites, does that mean that biblical rites are necessarily similar in their essential nonsymbolic nature? The case for the symbolic or nonsymbolic nature of rituals needs to be made on a case-by-case basis. Moreover, the claim that rituals are nonsymbolic in essence is a claim pertaining to origins—it cannot be denied that, at the very least, some rituals are infused with symbolic meanings in certain religious traditions (the Israelite tradition no doubt included). Even if some cultures' rituals remain free of symbolic explanation, that fact does not eliminate the possibility that symbolism looms large in others. Even if it could be established that rituals were *originally* arbitrary, that does not preclude the possibility that developed religious systems infuse rituals with symbolism. Since we are interested here in a developed ritual system, it matters little that symbolism may be secondary, and it matters even less that symbolism may be absent elsewhere.

Those who focus on ritual as activity remind us, at the very least, that ritual is not only symbolic but functional as well. Following Victor Turner, I believe scholars must recognize both, and distinguish between, symbolic and functional meanings, without denying the possibility of either one.[103] Rituals— sacrifice included—are multivalent entities, whose levels of meaning cannot be reduced to any single idea or purpose.[104] With this thought in mind, we return to our analysis of the sacrificial process, and introduce our second "organizing principle"—one that highlights connections between purity and sacrifice but also one that focuses more on what sacrifices were perceived to have achieved for ancient Israelites.

The Sacrificial Process, Part 2: Attracting and Maintaining the Divine Presence

Our first organizing principle—*imitatio Dei*—allows us to understand better the relationship between the Israelites' pastoral activities and their depictions of God as a shepherd. Moreover, the principle provides a fuller understanding of many aspects of the sacrificial process, from ritual purification to the consumption of the offering. Yet *imitatio Dei* does not exhaustively explain sacrifice in ancient Israel. The principle also does not, for instance, fully explain other important matters, such as the determination of which parts of the animal are placed on the altar and which are given to the priests.[105] It also cannot fully answer important questions concerning the agricultural offerings on the one hand and blood symbolism on the other. It also does not serve to explain fully the purposes or functions of the sacrificial act: what is achieved by this act of imitation? I doubt that any single theory, principle, or metaphor will ever explain all this. The *function* of the sacrificial act can, I believe, be better understood when we bring to the discussion our second organizing principle: the priestly traditions' overriding concern with the divine presence dwelling among Israel, in the sanctuary.[106]

That the priestly traditions of the Pentateuch are concerned with the presence of God in the community of Israel need hardly be stated. Practically from the first ritual legislation incorporated into the Priestly strand (Exod. 20:24) through the end of Leviticus (26:11–12), the concern with the presence of God runs throughout. This concern is articulated in the command to build the sanctuary: "make them build me a sanctuary and I will dwell among them" (Exod. 25:8). Upon the construction of the tabernacle, we are told that "the glory of the Lord fills the tabernacle" (Exod. 40:35; cf. 1 Kgs. 8:10–11). According to many interpreters, various elements of the tabernacle serve to symbolize the notion of God's presence there.[107] Of course, the term "tabernacle" (מִשְׁכָּן), with its connotation of indwelling—itself testifies to the importance of this concern.[108] Moreover, the priestly traditions' favorite term for the sacrificial act—"offering" (קָרְבָּן), with its connotation of closeness and nearness—is likely expressive of the same concern.[109] We also ought to recall that our most detailed sacrificial rules—along with the rest of the book of Leviticus—are said to have been spoken to Moses, by God, *from the Tent of Meeting* (Lev. 1:1).

How does the concern with the divine presence help us understand the sacrifice? A number of years ago, Baruch Levine suggested understanding sacrifices, particularly the burnt offerings, as an effort to attract the deity.[110] This dynamic is borne out by a host of biblical narratives that describe God's presence appearing—usually as a consuming fire—immediately upon the proper performance of some sacrificial rite. This description applies, at least roughly, to the covenant ratification ceremony at Sinai (Exod. 24:17); the ceremony of Aaron's investiture (Lev. 9:22–24); the sacrifice offered by Samson's parents (Judg. 13:19–21); the sacrifices David offered at Araunah's threshing floor (1 Chr. 21:26; but cf. 2 Sam. 24:25); and, perhaps most dramatically, the narrative of Elijah's confrontation with the priests of Baal (1 Kgs. 18:38).[111] According to Gary Anderson, this same dynamic is operative in the prophetic literature of the postexilic period, whose message is: rebuild the temple, seek to restore the presence of God, and then things will begin to improve.[112]

The notion that sacrifice functions as an invitation or as a means of attracting the divine presence is also reflected in other sources from the ancient Near East, perhaps most notably in the often-quoted passage from the eleventh tablet of the standard Babylonian (Ninevite) version of the Epic of Gilgamesh:

> (155) I let out to the four winds and I offered a sacrifice. (156) I made an offering at the mountain top. (157) I set up cult vessels by sevens. (158) Under them I poured reed, cedar and myrtle. (159) The gods smelled (its) sweet savor. (161) The gods, like flies, around the offerer gathered.[113]

Perhaps the clearest articulation of the same dynamic in a biblical ritual text can be seen in Exodus 29, where the sacrifice to be offered twice daily is referred to as a "pleasing odor to God" (29:41). What is more, the performance of this regular daily sacrifice is explicitly connected to the notion of the perpetual maintenance of the presence of God within the sanctuary (29:42–46):

> (42) It shall be a regular burnt offering throughout your generations at the entrance of the tent of meeting before the Lord, where I will

meet with you, to speak to you there. (43) I will meet with the
Israelites there, and it shall be sanctified by my glory.... (45) I will
dwell among the Israelites and I will be their God. (46) And they
shall know that I am the Lord their God, who brought them out of
the land of Egypt that I might dwell among them; I am the Lord
their God.

Not only does the daily offering attract the divine presence but also its proper
performance serves to maintain that presence among the community.[114]

This overriding concern with the attraction and maintenance of the divine
presence can also be understood, in a way, as a common denominator of many
of the older, well-known "theories" (or metaphors) of sacrifice. For instance,
the bestowal of gifts and the provision of food can easily be understood as
aspects of more general concerns with attraction and maintenance. Similarly,
those aspects of sacrifice that are sometimes explained in light of "communion" (e.g., the sharing of sacrificial meat) or "blood-ties" (e.g., the daubing of
blood upon both persons and the altar) can possibly be understood as expressions of the concern to establish a sense of connection between the people and
the deity, whose presence the people hope to attract and maintain among them
for perpetuity.

There is a further value in elevating the concern with the attraction and
maintenance of the divine presence to the level of an "organizing principle."
Like the notion of *imitatio Dei*, the concern with the attraction and maintenance of the divine presence allows us to draw additional connections between the interrelated structures of purity and sacrifice. The notion of *imitatio
Dei*, as we have seen, allowed us to see that the ritual structure of sacrifice is
intimately connected to the structure known as *ritual* purity. Our second
organizing principle, however, allows us to see the deep connection between
the structure of sacrifice on the one hand and the structure of *moral* defilement on the other.

As noted above, the notion of moral defilement concerns the idea that
certain grave sins are so heinous that they are considered defiling. The
problem with these three sins—idolatry, sexual transgression, and murder—
and the reason why they bring about exile is that God finds them so abhorrent
that He will not and cannot abide on a land that becomes saturated with the
residue left by their performance. This concern is very clearly articulated
toward the end of the book of Numbers (35:30–34):

(30) If anyone kills another, the murderer shall be put to death....
(31) Moreover you shall accept no ransom for the life of a murderer
who is subject to the death penalty; a murderer must be put to death.
(33) You shall not pollute the land in which you live; for blood
pollutes the land, and no expiation can be made for the land, for
the blood that is shed in it, except by the blood of the one who shed
it. (34) You shall not defile the land in which you live, in which I
also dwell; for I the Lord dwell among the Israelites.

The thrust of the passage is this: murder morally defiles the land, and this phenomenon poses a threat to the maintenance among Israel of the presence of God. In a sense, we could say that murderers themselves become abominations (תועבות). These grave sinners threaten to saturate the land with their sin, which poses a threat to the sanctuary. Indeed, it is precisely this ramification of Israel's performance of grave sin that is depicted quite dramatically in Ezekiel 8–11. Upon Israel's continued performance of grave sins—again, primarily idolatry, sexual transgression, and murder—the divine presence (called in Ezekiel the "glory" [כבד]) departs from the sanctuary.

We can now, perhaps, see even more clearly the differences between ritual and moral defilements. Ritual defilement concerns those things that threaten the status vis-à-vis the sacred of the individuals directly affected. Those who are ritually defiled, those whom they ritually defile, and those animals that, when dead, are considered ritually defiling—all of these are banned from the sanctuary. If that ban is violated, the presumption is that the danger that ensues falls upon those who transgressed the boundary: "thus you shall keep the people of Israel separate from their impurities, so that they do not die in their impurity by defiling my tabernacle that is in their midst" (Lev. 15:31).[115] The moral defilements, however, work very differently. The moral defilements threaten not only the status of the individuals in question but also the land and in turn the sanctuary itself. Unlike the ritual impurities, the moral impurities bring with them not just the danger that sacred precincts might be violated but also the threat that God will depart from the sacred precincts altogether. As already emphasized, the moral impurities, unlike the ritual impurities, are referred to as abominations. These things are repugnant to God; they are repulsive, repellent. So we can also now see better how the moral defilements are related to sacrifice. Abominable acts undo what properly performed sacrifice does. Sacrifice attracts and maintains the divine presence; moral defilement resulting from grave sin repels the divine presence.

The idea that sacrifice and sin are related in some way has long been recognized and emphasized. Indeed, many discussions of sacrifice are dominated by concerns with guilt, scapegoating, and expiation. It certainly cannot be denied that a number of sacrificial rituals described in Leviticus in particular serve an expiatory role on some level (Lev. 1:4; Lev. 4; Lev. 16). But the typical understanding of the way daily sacrifice and grave sin are related is, I believe, backward. It is not that the daily sacrifice undoes the damage done by grave transgression. Quite the contrary: grave transgression undoes what the daily sacrifice produces. And the difference between the two formulations *is* important. What it boils down to is whether sacrifice is considered, in and of itself, a productive act. Those who argue that expiation is at the core of all or most sacrificial rituals ultimately view sacrifice not as something productive in its own right but as a correction or a reversal of something else that was wrong. One well-known and useful commentary uses the following sequence of verbs in discussing sacrifice: "restore," "correct," "undo," "reverse," and "cleanse."[116] This is typical of a host of scholars in biblical studies who view sacrifice as primarily a response to transgression.[117] Other scholars, however, such as George Buchanan Gray, Yehezkel Kaufmann, Baruch Levine, and more recently Gary Anderson and Alfred Marx, each in their own way emphasize the joyful and productive nature of much of Israelite sacrifice.[118] These scholars, I believe, put us in a better position to understand the biblical descriptions of the daily burnt offering (Exod. 29:38–45; Num. 28:3–8), which are completely devoid of any concern with expiation. The purpose of the daily burnt offering—and perhaps some other sacrifices as well—is to provide regular and constant pleasing odors to the Lord, so that the divine presence will continually remain in the sanctuary.[119]

Conclusion

The goal of this chapter has been to present an analysis of purity and sacrifice in the Hebrew Bible, one that avoids the methodological problems addressed in chapter 1: the separation of ritual purity from sacrifice, and the relatively hostile, evolutionist treatment that sacrifice then typically receives, at least when compared to the way ritual purity is handled. I have suggested that the ancient Israelite sacrificial process, broadly conceived, can be more fully understood if we keep in mind two overriding concerns of the priestly traditions: the desire to imitate God and the concern to attract and maintain the presence of God. Accordingly, ritual purification involves a process of separating from those aspects of humanity that make one least God-like, as a preparation for the performance of a number of sacrificial behaviors (selecting, killing, looking into, and consuming) that are much more God-like. The pastoral responsibilities that Israelites would enact with regard to their domesticated animals—some of which, inevitably, would be offered for sacrifice—also can be understood in light of the notion of *imitatio Dei*.

Along the way, I have offered some thoughts on the role of metaphor and symbol in ancient Israelite ritual and thought—arguing against those who dismiss the symbolic understandings of ritual. Throughout this chapter, the analysis has drawn on prophetic and hymnic descriptions of God, many of which utilize sacrificial terms in their descriptions of divine activity. Other passages utilize pastoral images in their descriptions of God's relation to Israel. On the whole, these passages bolster the claim that Israelites understood much of the activity related to sacrifice in a symbolic or metaphorical way. There is an analogy at the heart of sacrificial activity, and it is expressed in these prophetic and hymnic passages: as God is to Israel, so is Israel to their domesticated animals.

The analogy at the heart of sacrifice can be fully appreciated only when both halves receive equal consideration: as God is to people, so too—during the process of sacrifice—is the people of Israel to the domesticated animals offered for sacrifice. Indeed, one value of understanding sacrifice metaphorically is that we are encouraged to think of the roles played by both the people and the animals. Theories of sacrifice that identify the (usually innocent) animal with the (usually guilty) offerer without identifying the offerer with something or someone else—as analogy would require—can only hope to explain half of sacrifice, if even that much. Another value of the approach suggested here is that we can understand the aspects of sacrificial rituals discussed above without making recourse to scapegoating or even expiation. Indeed, the daily burnt offering in particular can well be understood as morally neutral: there are not necessarily any innocent victims here, any more than there are any guilty priests. What we have, rather, are animals symbolically representing Israelites at the same time that the Israelites and priests stand in for God.

We also reviewed some theories regarding the function of Israelite sacrifice. One function of the sacrificial imitation of God is to send up pleasing odors that will attract and maintain the continued presence of God in the sanctuary, in the midst of Israel. Animal sacrifice, however, has its nemesis: the grave sins that are viewed as morally defiling (idolatry, sexual transgression, and murder) have the capacity to undo the good that sacrifice does. While properly performed sacrifice attracts and maintains the divine presence, the grave sins that produce moral defilement have the capacity to repel the divine presence.

We have seen throughout that sacrifice and defilement are intricately interrelated. When we examine these structures in light of the concerns of *imitatio Dei* and attracting and maintaining the divine presence, we are able to identify a number of important connections between ritual and moral impurity on the one hand and sacrifice on the other. When we examine sacrificial and defilement systems at the same time, we cannot help but conclude that ancient Israelite sacrificial rituals may well be just as much of a symbolic system as ancient Israelite purity rules are commonly believed to be. Moreover, keeping all of these concerns in mind may well help move us in the direction of understanding sacrifice not only as a meaningful and symbolic act but as a productive act as well. Ancient Israelites conceived of sacrifice not primarily as a solution to the problem of transgression but rather as a pro- ductive expression of their religious ideals and hopes: the imitation of the divinity, in order to maintain the divine presence among them.

This analysis puts the lie to the unsound disparity (discussed in chapter 1) that remains too entrenched in the scholarly and popular minds alike: while ancient Israelite purity rules are widely recognized to be symbolic, ancient Israelite sacrificial rules are widely dismissed as vestigial and therefore meaningless. The selective killing of animals for the sake of worshiping God may never sit well with those of us raised in modern nonsacrificing religious traditions. But the selective denigration of sacrifice by moderns who use ani- mals without living with them should not sit well with us either. Those who approach sacrifice in ancient Israel with the presumption that sacrifice is primitive and unethical cannot help us understand what sacrificing meant to ancient Israel. Ancient Israel was a culture that not only lived with animals but thought and theologized with them too.

We have, however, left one significant issue unaddressed: if we are indeed to understand the sacrificial process in light of images culled, in part, from prophetic literature, why is it that the biblical prophets seem to object to sacrifice? We take up this question in the next chapter.

3

Rethinking the
Prophetic Critique

We turn in this chapter to a consideration of the biblical prophets'
approaches toward cult in general and sacrifice in particular. We do
so for a number of reasons. As is well known, a number of the
prophets appear to criticize cultic practice: "for I desire steadfast
love, and not sacrifice" (Hos. 6:6). These prophetic statements are
certainly significant, and no analysis of sacrifice in the Hebrew Bible
can be considered complete without addressing this issue. What is
more, there can be little doubt that a good deal of the hostility toward
sacrifice, on the part of scholars and others—which we traced in
chapter 1—is motivated at least in part by these passages.[1] If, after all,
the prophets did want to abolish sacrifices, then surely there must
have been something truly wrong with them! We begin this discussion by looking briefly at the classic scholarly works that have greatly
influenced the current discussion.

   We have already mentioned the work of Wellhausen in connection with the classic, evolutionist approaches to the composition of
the Priestly strand in the Pentateuch. There can be no doubt that
Wellhausen's contempt for priests, their rigidity, and the cult goes
hand in hand with his reverence for the prophets, their spirit, their
authentic religion, and their ethics.[2] The priest-versus-prophet
dichotomy finds its truly classic and most influential expression,
however, a few years later in the work of Wellhausen's younger contemporary, Max Weber (1864–1920). Weber devoted a portion of
his *magnum opus*—a massive and unfinished work entitled *Economy
and Society*—to an examination of the sociology of religion.[3] Within
that work-within-a-work (now widely available as its own book) we
find sections devoted to the exposition of the roles of the priest on
the one hand and the prophet on the other. Weber famously—and

rather dryly—described the priesthood as "the specialization of a particular group of persons in the continuous operation of a cultic enterprise, permanently associated with particular norms, places and times, and related to specific social groups."[4] The prophet, in contrast, was presented as "a purely individual bearer of charisma, who by virtue of his mission proclaims a religious doctrine or divine commandment."[5] Needless to say, an antipriestly bias predominates in such definitions, which were frequently evolutionistic, and not limited to Wellhausen or Weber.[6] Peter Berger's diagnosis—offered in 1963—remains apt:

> Developed by nineteenth-century Protestant scholarship, an image of the Old Testament prophets has so successfully filtered down to the religiously interested laity that it is quite difficult for anyone ever subjected to a Protestant Sunday school to think in other terms. One of the stereotypes connected with this image is the notion of the prophets as opponents of the priests, brave individualists defying the religious authorities of their time. It does not require great sophistication in the sociology of knowledge to guess why this image was developed by Protestant scholars (though perhaps psychological gifts too may be needed to interpret the rather strange affinity of German university professors, mostly teaching in theological faculties of established churches, for prophets as against priests!). In any case, during the period that the Wellhausen school dominated Old Testament scholarship, the notion that priests and prophets were fundamentally opposed attained almost axiomatic status.[7]

It also should be noted for the record that these approaches are not exclusively Protestant. As we have observed already, an analogous bias (but not, of course, a Protestant one) runs through the works of the Kaufmann school that trace evolutions from early, priestly (ritual) texts through later prophetic (moral) texts to the final synthesis of the two in the Holiness Code. In this case, the negative evaluation of P serves both to bolster its antiquity and to provide the stepping-stone for a positive evolution toward prophecy and beyond.[8] For the most part, however, the works of Kaufmann and the school associated with him step back from the absolute opposition of priests and prophets.[9] Indeed, most scholars today reject both Wellhausen's judgments and Weber's dichotomy, though it is not at all uncommon to find surveys of priests and prophets that dialogue with—even if only for the purposes of illustration—Weber's dramatic contrasts.[10]

But not all who discuss Weber's dichotomy consider it a fossilized vestige from bygone days. In a provocative survey of the issues we are considering in this chapter, Ronald S. Hendel has recently called for a return to Weber's dichotomy: "Where the priests see a correspondence and mutuality between ritual and ethics, the classical prophets *contrast* the ethical with the ritual."[11] Hendel also states, with regard to the ostensible prophetic condemnations of sacrifice: "although many scholars in recent years have attempted to read these passages as something less than a rejection of ritual, I would agree with William McKane that these scholarly attempts do not do justice to the texts."[12] McKane, in turn, advocates a return not so much to Weber as to Wellhausen:

> The prophet is a man of sorrows. . . . In so far as the prophet suffers rejection and knows the anguish of an isolation which is not self-imposed, but arises out of a concern for a community which cannot be reached, he walks along a *via dolorosa* and is enrolled in the fellowship of the sufferings of Jesus. Buber is to be listened to when he urges that the prophets are the great renewers of the religion of the Old Testament, and they should be allowed to do this work in every age.[13]

Those who disparage the achievements of the prophets—by downplaying their dispute with the priests—serve, in McKane's view, to deny them "the heroic dimensions which Wellhausen coveted for them."[14] McKane's appeal to Martin Buber's work *The Prophetic Faith*[15] hardly mitigates the fact that what we have here is a typically Protestant reading of the "Old Testament," couched in distinctly theological terms, expressing particularistic Christian concerns.

Despite the excesses of the passage just quoted, the possibility that some contemporary apologia for priests or sacrifice are themselves biased is not a charge that we can safely ignore. We will therefore consider Hendel's and McKane's criticism of current work in due course. But before we can determine whether Weber was right or not, we must survey the biblical evidence, and consider the arguments that have been offered against the idea that prophets opposed the priests and rejected sacrificial ritual. I will then try to offer my own contribution to the understanding of this important question.

The material we need to consider here can be conveniently broken up into four units. In the first, we review the array of passages attributed to various prophets that appear to reject priestly cultic rituals. We also will evaluate in this section some of the ways scholars typically approach these passages. In the second section we consider the impact that one generally overlooked issue could have on understanding the prophetic critique of sacrifice: what is the effect of theft on a sacrificial system predicated on proper ownership of cultic offerings? In the third and fourth sections, we consider closely two significant prophetic texts that offer rejections of and/or alternatives to the temple in Jerusalem: Jeremiah's so-called temple sermon (Jer. 7:1–15 and 26:1–24) and Ezekiel's vision of the future temple (Ezek. 40–48). We focus on these passages not only for their significance within the Hebrew Bible, which can hardly be denied. The additional justification for analyzing these passages closely extends from the fact that each of them has a distinct afterlife in the literature we will consider in part II of this book. Jeremiah's temple sermon has no doubt impacted the Gospels' traditions concerning Jesus' action and statement in the temple precincts (see discussion in chapter 7). Ezekiel's temple vision no doubt influenced much of the literature from Qumran—in particular, the *Temple Scroll*, which presents a similar (but by no means identical) alternative, ideal vision of the temple's structure (see discussion in chapter 5).

The Prophets and the Cult: Some General Considerations

We turn now to consider the prophets' relationship to ancient Israel's sacrificial practice. Of course, this topic is too large to be addressed thoroughly in a brief survey. A full assessment of these matters would require one to analyze each passage in the context of a broader treatment of the prophet who ostensibly uttered the words in question—and we can hardly do that here. Indeed, each prophetic book presents its own challenges. Virtually all of the prophetic books—as is now recognized—are composites of one sort or another.[16] But text-critical problems are only the beginning. A host of issues prevents one from generalizing the experience or message of ancient Israel's prophets. Indeed, were it not for the coincidence of canonization and the influence of tradition, we might more easily recognize that these figures have much less in common than is often supposed.

We know of some prophets—like Samuel and Elijah—primarily from stories told about them in the Deuteronomistic history.[17] We know of others—like Amos, Hosea, and Micah—primarily from collections of oracles which they or their later disciples bequeathed to us. We know of still others—like Jeremiah and Ezekiel—from lengthier books incorporating both oracle and narrative, whose transmission histories are all too unknown to modern scholars. Within this array of material, we find figures early and late—stretching from the early days of the monarchy (e.g., Samuel) down past the destruction of the first temple, and into the early Second Temple period (e.g., Haggai). We hear of figures from the northern kingdom of Israel (e.g., Elijah, Hosea) and from the southern kingdom of Judah (Isaiah). We hear of figures who were urban, wealthy, and well connected, like Isaiah, and figures who were presumably rural, poor, and of negligible social status, like Micah. Some of these differentiations might well match those advanced by social scientists in the distinction between "peripheral" and "central" prophets.[18] And as we will see momentarily, these figures had various relations with other Israelite institutions, like the priesthood and the monarchy. A complete analysis of prophecy and the cult in ancient Israel would need to account for these and other social variables. Various studies on prophecy—both brief and long—work toward this end.[19]

But a comprehensive focus on one phenomenon or theme also brings its dangers. Recent thorough treatments of sacrifice have not dealt adequately with purity; recent specialized analyses of ritual purity have ignored moral purity. A fundamental claim of this project is that there is a distinct advantage to trying to grasp an image of a broader scene, even if in widening the scope one must be satisfied with a slightly less focused picture. On its own, this goal justifies the attempt to make some generalizations concerning prophecy and the cult. And there is a further reason for treating the prophetic critique of the cult as a general topic, one that is validated by the nature of the evidence we are about to survey. The ostensible prophetic condemnation of contemporary sacrificial practice has a remarkable resilience: passages condemning the cult and giving priority to righteousness over sacrifice appear throughout the prophetic corpus, in narrative and oracular texts, attributed to figures who could be described as either central or peripheral, from various periods of Israelite history, from the north and south.

One such denunciation of sacrificial practice is attributed to the early prophet Samuel, in the later Deuteronomistic narrative of his condemnation of Saul's failure to eradicate the Amalekites: "has the Lord as great delight in burnt offerings and sacrifices as in obeying the voice of the Lord? Surely to obey is better than sacrifice, and to heed than the fat of rams" (1 Sam. 15:22–23). An eighth-century B.C.E. prophet with a somewhat less tortured relationship to the monarchy ostensibly uttered similar words: "what to me is the multitude of your sacrifices? Says the Lord; I have had enough of burnt offerings of rams and the fat of fed beasts; I do not delight in the blood of bulls, or of lambs, or of goats" (Isa. 1:11). A seventh-century Judean successor declared: "your burnt offerings are not acceptable, nor are your sacrifices pleasing to me" (Jer. 6:20). The eighth-century northern prophet Hosea is said to have declared: "I desire steadfast love and not sacrifice, the knowledge of God rather than burnt offerings" (Hos. 6:6). Hosea's southern contemporary Amos is similarly reputed to have said: "I hate, I despise your festivals, and I take no delight in your solemn assemblies. Even though you offer me your burnt offerings and grain offerings, I will not accept them. . . . But let justice roll down like waters, and righteousness like an unfailing stream" (Amos 5:21–24).

These and other passages like them—including Micah 6:6–8, Jeremiah 7:21–23, and Psalms 40:6—do indeed have their distinct concerns. It is no coincidence that Samuel calls for obedience (שמע), while Amos calls for justice (צדק) and Hosea calls for steadfast love (חסד).[20] Each of these emphases relates to the prophet's concerns in the situation at hand: Saul's disobedience as perceived by the Deuteronomist; Israel's social injustice as perceived by Amos; and the people's religious infidelity as perceived by Hosea. But clearly the passages share a concern as well: the belief that, in the words of some later sage, "the sacrifices of the wicked are an abomination to the Lord" (Prov. 15:8; 21:27). Taken as a whole, the passages have common features and themes.[21] Clearly, what we have here is a prophetic trope, one that deserves to be analyzed as such.

How can we make sense of this repeated condemnation of sacrifice in particular? Did the prophets oppose the cult and reject sacrificial practice? One way to approach this question is to note the limitations of Weber's ideal types. The most direct challenge to the Weberian dichotomy emerges from the fact that many prophets were themselves priests, or at least actively engaged in priestly and sacrificial acts.[22] Jeremiah was descended from priests (Jer. 1:1), as was Ezekiel (Ezek. 1:1–3). Prophetic heroes like Moses, Samuel, and Elijah are remembered as actively performing sacrificial offerings (e.g., Exod. 24:4–8; 1 Sam. 3:1, 7:10, 9:14; 1 Kgs. 18:30–39). It is sometimes surmised that

Isaiah—whose call vision is situated in God's sanctuary (Isa. 6:1)—may have been of priestly descent himself, though the evidence in this regard is certainly inconclusive.[23] Without any doubt later prophets such as Haggai, Zechariah, and Malachi were actively involved in the restoration of sacrificial worship in the early Second Temple period.[24] Under the influence of Sigmund Mowinckel (1884–1966), the designation "cultic prophet" has also been applied to additional biblical figures, including Nahum, Habbakuk, and Joel, among others.[25] If prophetic activity could be cultic, and prophets themselves priestly, could their rejection of sacrifice really have been complete?

But this argument does not solve the matter. There can be little doubt that ancient Israelite reality was more complex than Weber's ideal types might suggest. Nonetheless, it cannot be denied that prophets repeatedly voiced opposition to sacrificial practices, often at cult sites. The facts that some prophets performed sacrifices and others were descended from priests do not eliminate altogether the need to acknowledge that Amos (7:10–17), Micah (3:12; cf. Jer. 26:18–19), Jeremiah (7:1–15), and probably other prophets as well certainly raised the ire of priests whom they encountered.

Another direct challenge to Weber's dichotomy comes from the other direction: if one looks in the right place (e.g., Lev. 19), one can easily find within the priestly traditions ideas and ethics that cohere with the prophetic message. We already have noted and discussed Mary Douglas's work in rehabilitating the scholarly attitude toward the priests: "one serious look at Leviticus shows that there is no lineup of priest and prophet, and no conflict between internal versus external religion, or justice versus ritual."[26] But we still need to be careful: granted that priests too were just and good, was there really then no dispute between them at all?

A different approach to our question is to identify aspects of the prophetic books that seem to mitigate the claim that the prophets categorically rejected sacrifice. There is truth to the often-repeated observation that the prophets do not *only* raise objections to sacrifice: Amos objects to the Israelites' festivals (Amos 5:21), and Isaiah objects to their prayers (Isa. 1:14–15). Is it conceivable that the prophets have categorically opposed all forms of worship? If they didn't oppose all prayer, could they really have opposed all sacrifice?[27] Against this argument one could note that it does not account for two related factors: (1) sacrifice was the central official form of worship for ancient Israel; and (2) the prophetic statements exhibit a particular focus on sacrifice, an interest that is not fully explained by observing that the longer passages also include references to festivals and prayer. Shorter condemnations focus exclusively on sacrifice, and we find no one-line passages that oppose prayer to justice, or the festivals to loving-kindness.

There is also some truth to another argument: a number of the prophets envision temples and sacrifices in their eschatological visions.[28] Isaiah and Micah famously depict a future in which peoples of many nations would turn their swords into plowshares and come to worship the Lord at the temple in Jerusalem (Isa. 2:1–4; Mic. 4:1–5). Is it really conceivable that an exclusively nonsacrificial form of worship is imagined here? Jeremiah speak more specifically of sacrifices in the future (Jer. 17:26, 33:17–18). If there is any doubt about these figures, surely Ezekiel—to say nothing of the early Second Temple cult prophets—approved of sacrifice both in theory and in practice.

But even this argument does not solve the problem. If anything, the fact that some prophets speak of sacrifice in the future illustrates the broad, complex nature of prophecy in general: prophecy, as Anderson reminds us, "is not systematic theology."[29] We surely cannot assume that all prophets agreed on this point. After all, prophets didn't argue *only* with priests: they often disputed with other prophets (e.g., Jer. 18:18, and 28:1–17).[30] With regard to sacrifices, the prophets who speak explicitly in favor of contemporary and future sacrificial practice are not those prophets whose works condemn sacrificial practice most severely.

There is one factor that still cannot be overlooked: prophets were prone to hyperbole.[31] What seems like a categorical rejection can probably be better understood as a prioritization. The "not . . . but . . ." form appears, for instance, in Proverbs 8:10, which presents the following advice: "take my instruction, not silver." As Alexander Rofé helpfully points out, the sage here is not likely to be advocating a categorical rejection of money.[32] Rather, the verse states that following divine teaching is better than pursuing wealth. While there is truth to this point, it still doesn't solve the problem entirely: are we to understand that the priests and prophets had different priorities? If so, why, and what were they?

Jacob Milgrom has suggested another argument in the attempt to mitigate the claim that the prophets categorically rejected all sacrifice. Milgrom's argument is focused in particular on Jeremiah 7:21–22 and Amos 5:22–25, passages that deny that Israelites offered sacrifices in the wilderness. The prophets in these passages speak of divine disinterest in the burnt offerings and the well-being sacrifices in particular. As it happens, these two offerings are juxtaposed in priestly traditions that concern voluntary offerings brought by individuals (Lev. 17:8; 22:17–30). Milgrom therefore concludes that Amos and Jeremiah "have nothing whatever to say concerning the fixed Temple sacrifices such as the *tamid* [daily offering]. Rather they turn to the people and urge them to renounce their individual offerings because this ritual piety is vitiated by their immoral behavior."[33]

This argument is unconvincing. That Jeremiah's emotional prose or Amos's parallelistic poetry should be interpreted in light of a limited and technical priestly usage is highly unlikely. These passages do not come off sounding nuanced or narrow in focus. On the whole, the prophets use a host of sacrificial terms (compare Hos. 4:8); and some speak generally of the animals being offered (e.g., Isa. 1:11, Mic. 6:7). Jeremiah himself elsewhere includes a reference to frankincense in one of his cultic condemnations (Jer. 6:20). Given that the incense altar was located in the inner parts of the sanctuary (Exod. 30:1–10, Lev. 4:7), the prophet cannot, by Milgrom's own interpretation, be speaking of individual offerings.[34] In most cases, the prophets probably utilize any one or another combination of terms in order to connote the complex system of sacrifice in general.[35] Moreover, it is important to keep in mind that

both Amos (7:10–17) and Jeremiah (7:1–15, 26:1–24) uttered their condemnations at public cult places, enraging local priests. This too suggests that the
prophets' denunciation of cultic practice had an institutional focus.

So, then, how to explain the prophetic interest in condemning contemporary sacrificial practice? Perhaps the most common approach is to suggest in
some way that the prophets are not objecting to sacrifice per se but to cultic
abuse: sacrifice as performed in an inappropriate manner by unrighteous people. This argument can actually take a few distinct forms, though often treatments of the issue will incorporate both sides of the coin. One form of the
argument is put succinctly by de Vaux: "the prophets are opposed to the formalism of exterior worship when it has no corresponding interior dispositions
(Isa. 29:13)."[36] The other is stated with equal economy by Heschel: "when
immorality prevails, worship is detestable."[37] The common denominator here
is that proper worship presupposes moral righteousness. The difference between the two formulations is whether the problem is individual or communal:
the distinction between exterior practice and interior motive is a personal problem; but if prevalent immorality renders sacrifice inefficacious, then even the
offering of a well-intentioned individual could be rejected in a sinful age. Despite this potential difference between the two arguments, many formulations
hover between the two, or incorporate both aspects in one way or another.[38]

There is undoubtedly some substance to these approaches. Importantly,
these arguments go a long way toward breaking down Weber's ideal types and
allow for the recognition that priests too may have had similar ethical concerns.
Nonetheless, one must recognize that Hendel and McKane have a point when
they suggest that contemporary ideas of religious piety have impacted the
discussion.[39] If Weber and Wellhausen articulated an approach to prophecy
that was too close for comfort to their conservative Protestant backgrounds and
biases, then we must be equally on guard against the possibility that scholars
have articulated positions that are in line with contemporary Jewish, Catholic,
or Protestant perspectives. Certainly we should be suspicious when scholars—
anachronistically—insert into the discussion distinctions between ritual and
ethics, interiority and exteriority, or letter and spirit. That the ritual-versus-
ethics distinction cannot apply in full is readily apparent when one considers
that many prophets opposed idolatry and theological infidelity with great ve-
hemence. To sacrifice an animal to Baal is a ritual crime, not a moral one.[40] It
is equally evident that distinctions of interiority versus exteriority, or of letter
versus spirit, are foreign to the concerns of ancient Israelite prophets. The
prophets speak primarily against external behaviors performed by groups of
people: they despised the external unrighteousness of the many, and therefore rejected the external sacrifices of all. Part of what we find here—when
the question is phrased in terms of individual, internal dispositions—is that the
scholarly dispute on Israelite ritual has become the arena for contemporary
theological disputes on the place of ritual and morality. In all too many cases,
one finds that scholars understand the prophets to express precisely what one
can easily recognize as a contemporary religious attitude to the question of
ethics and ritual.[41]

There is another problem with these approaches, one that brings us closer to our concerns. To suggest that the prophets rejected the cult because they presupposed proper intention or a certain moral disposition is to suggest either that the priests did not make any such presuppositions or that there was no substantial dispute between the priests and the prophets on this matter. If we incline toward minimizing the dichotomy, then what Hendel and McKane have argued comes back to haunt us: why all this prophetic fuss if there was no substance to the dispute? If we incline toward resurrecting the dichotomy, then we are only a few steps away from the old, biased, evolutionist, antipriestly perspectives that I have been arguing against all along. Would the priests have thought it was acceptable to offer sacrifices while committing transgressions?

How then can we make progress in accounting for the prophetic critique of Israel's cultic practice? Is the situation hopeless—is it simply impossible to answer the question without "overstepping the proper limits of criticism?"[42] While we can hardly avoid bias altogether, we can make some progress if we avoid using anachronistic theological distinctions. A more significant step can be taken if we recognize the problematic and biased nature of some of the scholarly terminology frequently used with reference to priests and prophets. If indeed sacrifice in particular, and ritual in general, can be understood as symbolic action—as I argued in the previous chapter—then it becomes all the more interesting to note that many thematic discussions of prophecy in biblical Israel point out that the prophets were wont to perform "symbolic acts" in order to dramatize and illustrate their message to the Israelite people.[43] It suffices for our concerns to note only a few of the more famous actions: Hosea marrying a prostitute to symbolize Israel's infidelity (Hos. 1:2); Isaiah walking barefoot and naked to symbolize Egypt's impending doom (Isa. 20:1–6); Jeremiah wearing a yoke to symbolize God's desire for the nations to submit to Babylon (Jer. 27:1–15). What is seldom appreciated in the context of this theme is that the very existence of this phenomenon proves that the prophets were aware of and sympathetic to symbolic behavior. By referring to the prophets' behavior as "symbolic action" while dryly describing cultic behavior as "ritual," scholars force a divide between, and prevent a comparison of, two phenomena that are not altogether different. But surely, Weber might object, there is a difference between a passionate, spontaneous, individual symbolic act and a communal cultic one. To counter that argument, one must remember that Hosea married a prostitute (Hos. 1:2)—possibly two (Hos. 3:1–3)—and remained so married for some time. Isaiah, it is said, walked naked and barefoot *for three years* (Isa. 20:3). Jeremiah must have worn that yoke for some time as well (Jer. 28:10). The historicity of such claims is not my concern; I simply call attention to the fact that one can safely wonder whether all symbolic actions were truly spontaneous or free of regulation.[44] A repeated symbolic action is hardly all that different from a ritual. This suggests to me that it is indeed unlikely that prophets categorically opposed ritual in general or even sacrifice in particular. The suggestion that the prophets opposed sacrifice because they denied the efficacy of ritual really makes them out to be the hypocrites that the priests are commonly assumed to have been: how could the prophets believe in the efficacy of their own symbols but deny efficacy to ritual? The prophets did not, it must be clear, oppose ritual as such. The question is why they were dissatisfied with the practice of sacrifice as they knew it.

This is the challenge: to try to understand the prophetic critique, in terms that are neither entirely anachronistic nor unduly aligned with contemporary theological positions. What is more, an equal part of the challenge is coming to terms with these passages in such a way that one can at the same time make good sense of both the prophets and the priests. We must reject out of hand explanations that make the priests into immoral mechanists, and we must equally reject explanations that leave one thinking that the priests and the prophets were never in any real conflict at all—just some simple misunderstanding or slight shift in emphasis. We also do well to keep in mind the advice of H. H. Rowley: "to think of prophets only in terms of the best and priests only in terms of the worst is unwise. There were good prophets and good priests, and while there was undoubtedly a difference of emphasis between them, they were all exponents of the same religion."[45]

Priests, Prophets, Sacrifice, and Theft

Some further reflection on the nature of sacrificial ritual may help to understand better the nature of the prophetic critique. Whether we focus on sacrifice as gift, as communion, as expiation—or in the ways I suggested in the previous chapter—sacrifice nonetheless involves at least in part the transfer of property from layperson to priest, and from priest to God. Fundamental to the proper workings of such a system, then, is due ownership of what is offered. For how can a gift be a true expression of anything if what is given was stolen in the first place? The significance of this question is, unfortunately, rarely recognized. Among the theorists, Marcel Mauss's contribution stands out as one of the few to treat sacrifice as it relates to issues of property and ownership.[46] But Mauss's treatment of theft is all too brief, and no one, to my knowledge, has followed through with the agenda he lays out with regard to the issues of our concern. In the current climate, theorists under the influence of René Girard and Walter Burkert seem to be too concerned with the origins of sacrifice to give the practical concerns of developed sacrificial systems enough attention. Among the biblical exegetes, the issue of ownership has been noted by, among others, James Barr, Roland de Vaux, and Jacob Milgrom.[47] All three have emphasized that biblical regulations presuppose that one owns what one sacrifices—but a sustained treatment is wanting.[48] Even recent attempts at examining the nexus between sacrifice and economics in ancient Judaism[49] do not address this issue: what happens when what is given to the deity was itself stolen from someone else? As important as this idea may be to an understanding of sacrifice, we address the issue in this section because it is fundamental to understanding the prophetic critique.

The biblical evidence regarding the potential impact of theft on the sacrificial system is complex and varied. We should not necessarily expect that priests and prophets, wise men and royal historians would agree fully on such matters. Nonetheless, we find a rather surprising consistency of concern with the problem of sacrificing stolen goods.

Within the priestly material, a number of regulations *imply* that proper sacrificial worship presupposes proper ownership of what is being offered. First, sacrifices in ancient Israel are to come from domesticated animals and grains (Lev. 1:2, 10, 14; 2:1, 4, 5). Of course, domesticated animals and grains—which are reared by people—can be properly owned while they are still living, as opposed to fish and game, which can only be duly owned once they are dead. As Milgrom and Barr have suggested, the exclusion of fish and game from the sacrifices of ancient Israel may well go hand in hand with ancient Israel's emphasis on sacrifice as a gift, of something properly owned, to God.[50]

A second way in which the priestly traditions may imply that proper sacrifice presupposes proper ownership is through the rite of laying a hand on the sacrificial offering. According to Leviticus 1:4 (cf. 3:2, 8, 13; 4:4, 24, 29), individuals bringing sacrifices must lay a single hand on the sacrifices they bring. Interpreters commonly assimilate this practice to those rites that require the placement of *two* hands on the offering, as specified in Leviticus 16:21 (cf. 24:10, Num. 27:18, 23, Deut. 34:9). For some interpreters, all of the hand-laying rites are then taken as connoting some notion of transfer, as when the sins are transferred onto the scapegoat in Leviticus 16:21.[51] Other interpreters view all of these rites as representing substitutions: just as the goat is substituted for Israel in Leviticus 16, so too the animal is substituted for the offerer in Leviticus 1.[52] Rolf P. Knierim suggests that the rite is "a distinct act by which the animal is officially surrendered to its subsequent sacrificial death."[53] David P. Wright, however, has argued that the rite of laying a single hand on the sacrifice in Leviticus 1 needs to be distinguished from the rite of laying two hands on the sacrifice in Leviticus 16.[54] Drawing on biblical and ancient Near Eastern sources, Wright argues that the two-handed rite conveys a notion of designation, as in the case when the high priest selects the scapegoat (Lev. 16:21) or as when Moses appoints Joshua as his successor (Num. 27:18, 23, Deut. 34:9; cf. Lev. 24:14). Since Aaron does not himself embody evil, the placement of his hands on the scapegoat in Leviticus 16 cannot be understood as an act of transfer.[55] According to Wright, while the laying of two hands connotes designation, the laying of a single hand conveys the notion of ownership. The rite is not intended to express some abstract identification between the offerer and the offering—it is not intended to say "This offering represents me." Rather, the statement is more concrete and practical. The offerer puts his single hand on the offering to state: "This offering is mine."[56]

A third way in which the priestly traditions presuppose proper ownership is the fact that property crimes of various types constitute one of the few realms of moral transgression for which sacrificial remedies are explicitly provided in Leviticus (5:20–26). The priestly traditions' selective interest in property crimes suggests the issue was of particular significance to the sacrificial system.[57]

The effect of this evidence from the priestly traditions is cumulative: there seems to be a sustained concern with proper ownership of sacrificial offerings. In order to find clear and explicit treatments of this theme, however, we must look beyond the priestly traditions. We find the clearest evidence for the concern with properly owned sacrifices in two vital narratives of the Deuteronomistic history. Each of these narratives, interestingly enough, addresses the shortcomings of a monarch: Saul in the first instance, David in the second.

When Saul is sent out to destroy the Amalekites and all that was theirs (1 Sam. 15:2–3), he spares King Agag and the best of the sheep and cattle (1 Sam. 15:8–9). The prophet Samuel confronts Saul, who then claims that the animals were spared by the Israelites in order to sacrifice them (15:15). This excuse brings on the aforementioned well-known harangue "Has the Lord as great delight in burnt offerings and sacrifices as in obeying the voice of the Lord?" (15:22–23). Many interpreters of this passage highlight "the long tradition of prophetic attack on hollow cultic practice."[58] But this interpretation overlooks an essential point. Samuel's outburst appears in a context in which Saul has proposed to "sacrifice" to God goods that were supposed to be banned and certainly do not belong to the king. According to the narrative, God wanted these animals destroyed; how can such refuse ever constitute a proper gift?

If this were an isolated incident in the Deuteronomistic history, this reading of it could easily be called into question. It happens, however, that what we find implied in the narrative of Saul's rejection is explicitly stated in another tradition concerning Israel's next monarch. Following David's ill-advised census of the Israelites, David is told to set up an altar on the threshing floor of Araunah the Jebusite (2 Sam. 24:18; cf. 1 Chron. 21:18). When the kindly Araunah (called Ornan in 1 Chron. 21) offers David both the site and oxen to sacrifice, David protests: "no, I will buy them from you at a price. I cannot sacrifice to the Lord my God burnt offerings that have cost me nothing" (2 Sam. 24:24; 1 Chron. 21:24). If what's given to you constitutes an inappropriate offering to God, how much more so what is stolen!

In the prophetic literature we find the most explicit and powerful condemnation of the practice of sacrificing to God *matériel* that has been acquired through immoral means. It is precisely this element of the prophetic critique that is too often missed. The bulk of Amos's famous condemnation of the Israelites focuses on economic transgressions: "they sell the righteous for silver, and the poor for a pair of sandals" (2:6). The prophet then highlights the fact that economic sin spoils sacrificial worship (2:8):

> They lay themselves down beside every altar
>   on garments taken in pledge
> and in the house of their God they drink
>   wine bought with fines they imposed.

The power of the image conjured by Amos is the irony of the wealthy Israelites worshiping God with goods stolen from the poor. In a more straightforward

way, the same concern is articulated in Isaiah 61:8: "for I the Lord love justice;
I hate robbery with a burnt offering (נזל בעולה)."[59]

An extended passage from the late prophet known as Malachi may also
address some of these concerns. The prophet describes various scenarios in
which priests present unfit offerings to the Lord. The priests—who are accused of despising God's name (1:6)—make a practice of offering as sacrifices
animals that are lame, sick, blind (1:8), or even stolen (1:13). These are offerings that even the Persian governor would reject, let alone God (1:8). In
response to this, the prophet presents God's retort: "if only you would lock the
doors, so that you would not kindle fire on my altar *at no cost* (חנם)!" The
common translation—"in vain" or "useless"[60]—misses what I understand to
be the proper connotation (and an equally attested meaning) of the Hebrew
word in question: the fact that the sacrifices described have no value or cost to
the person offering them. The term—"without cost"—is the same word used
in 2 Samuel 24:24, quoted above. This meaning also explains better the
various aspects of what the prophet is complaining against: the sacrifices
brought are offerings that have little inherent value (1:8, 13), little real value to
the offerer (because they were stolen; 1:13), or less value than that which the
offerer originally promised to bring (1:14). They are all offerings brought
without due cost, and they are all offerings that God finds detestable.

All too often, scholars approach these passages—and prophetic literature
in general—with the assumption that sacrifice and ethics are distinct matters,
with one evaluated negatively and the other positively. Others may assume
that ritual sacrifice is rejected because it is an improper or ineffective way to
atone for ethical sins such as theft. Yet it is important to note that a number
of the classic statements erroneously taken as "rejections of sacrifice" are in
context juxtaposed with expressions of concern over the economic exploitation
of the poor (Amos 5:23 is preceded by Amos 5:10–11; Isa. 1:11–15 is followed by
1:17; Jer. 6:20 is preceded by 6:13). This raises the strong possibility that these
passages too can be understood similarly: the prophets' "rejection" of sacrifice was deeply connected to their belief that Israel was economically rotten to
the core.

What the foregoing survey demonstrates—albeit briefly—is that when it
comes to sacrifice, ethics and rituals are intricately and inherently connected.
Indeed, when we take the issue of ownership into consideration, the dichotomy
between ethics and ritual collapses. The sources surveyed above point to the
conclusion that for Israelite priests, prophets, and court historians, improper
ethics render ritual sacrifice ineffectual, not because God doesn't like the idea of
sinners atoning through ritual, and not because God would simply prefer to
dispense with the ritual in the hopes that the people would simply seek righteousness apart from the cult. The objection to sacrifice rests the assumption
that God detests the facts of the situation at hand. One who has taken unjustly
from the poor cannot properly *give* anything, and therefore the "sacrifice" offered by such a person is anathema.

Precisely this perspective is articulated in the often-quoted passages from
Proverbs that condemn as "abominations" the offerings of the wicked (15:8;

21:27). These are the closest we come in the Hebrew Bible to any statement concerning the ritual status of such sacrifices: as "abominations," these sacrifices are morally offensive, and ritually deficient as well. These statements are, however, imprecise in and of themselves. What precisely happens if such an abomination were brought into the temple? Would the offering be considered as if it were physically blemished (Lev. 1:3; cf. Ben Sira 34:21)? Would the temple be defiled in any way? While the biblical passages remain ambiguous, we will see in part II that Jews of later periods struggled to answer the questions left hanging here. Of course, all will continue to agree that it is improper to sacrifice stolen goods; but only some will reach the conclusion that tainted offerings were not only improper but defiling. We have no reason to suppose there was a dispute over this particular matter in the days of the prophets, but it is possible—even likely—that priests and prophets didn't see eye to eye on all matters pertaining to the ownership of sacrifices. Even if, as I have argued, priests and prophets agreed in principle that one should not sacrifice stolen goods, there remains room for disagreement on: (1) the definition of theft, and (2) the way one deals with the concern.

We noted above that the priestly texts do *imply* that sacrifice presupposes proper ownership. But there is a striking difference between what is implied in priestly texts and what is stated all too clearly in prophetic ones. Exaggeration, as we have already observed, is a key characteristic of prophetic outbursts. Who wasn't a thief in Amos's conception of things? The prophets presume all to be guilty of—or at least culpable for—the crimes they find in their society.[61] Is it not possible that the priestly cult as envisioned in Leviticus operated, if not on a presumption of innocence, at least on a different (and lesser) presumption of guilt? Perhaps priests believed—in *principle*—that the referent "thief" should be used more sparingly than the prophets were wont to do.

We also can assume that prophets and priests would have dealt with the problem of theft differently. The prophets find guilt everywhere and therefore preach wrath to, and call for atonement from, everyone. Of course the priests did not envision all as innocent; that is why the cultic traditions implement rituals of atonement. The rituals of Leviticus, however, approach this question differently: a balance is struck between communal atonement (esp. Lev. 16) and personal atonement (Lev. 4–5). Some time ago, the idea of atonement by rituals of sacrifice was rather unpopular—indeed, this was an essential aspect of Wellhausen's assault on priesthood and cult.[62] A number of subsequent writers have stepped away from Wellhausen's stark assessment, presenting more sympathetic and nuanced understanding of the ways sacrifice effects atonement in ancient Israel.[63] Here, too, we have an inescapable religious debate: some (Protestants, liberal-modernist Jews) may be uncomfortable with fixed rituals of atonement; others (Catholics, more traditional Jews) may insist that such things are right and necessary. Surely, the priests *believed* in the efficacy of the atonement rituals their texts preached. Just as likely, they *believed* that it was right and proper to bring sinners to the sanctuary—not to defile it, or to offer stolen goods—but to effect atonement and, hopefully, bring about a change in behavior. But the only way this can be done is to allow also for the possibility that one offering or another now and then might just be tainted by the sins previously committed by the person now wishing to atone.

We cannot here enter a full discussion of these matters—but we can observe that once the question concerning ownership of sacrifices is raised, more than one principled answer can be offered, especially if the question is pushed to the extreme. Some may want to advocate that any theft or economic wrongdoing could threaten to bring down the entire system (e.g., Amos). This could lead either to a rejection of current sacrificial practice or to a prediction of doom for the places where that practice occurs (as we will see momentarily). A more limited view, one that allows for sacrificial restitution and individual atonement, can also be imagined. The priestly desire to keep the central religious institutions open and operative may not have been motivated exclusively by desire for personal gain. The cultic allowance for personal acts of atonement at the sanctuary, *by sinners*, can also be understood as an ethical position.

Jeremiah's Temple Sermon: Institution as Symbol

The book of Jeremiah is a complex compilation of poetry and prose, prophecy and narrative.[64] Those who are at all familiar with the book will not be surprised that what scholars refer to as the temple sermon is recorded not once but twice. The reader first encounters the temple sermon in Jeremiah 7:1–15, with minimal narrative context: the prophet is simply told to go to the house of the Lord and to proclaim divine judgment there (7:2). The reader finds the expanded narrative—along with a summarized version of the sermon—in Jeremiah 26:1–24 (in the Greek versions, the narrative appears in chapter 33).[65] The sermon is perhaps best known for the fact that the prophet's condemnation of the temple as a "den of robbers" (Jer. 7:11) was, according to the New Testament, quoted by Jesus in his condemnation of the temple (e.g., Mark 11:17). But our analysis here is motivated primarily by fact that the traditions concerning Jeremiah's sermon provide opportunity for further reflection on the nature of the prophetic critique of sacrifice.

According to Jeremiah 26:1, the prophet was summoned to deliver his sermon at the beginning of the reign of King Jehoiakim (Josiah's son); following scholarly convention for dating the Israelite kings, the sermon would therefore have occurred sometime around 609 B.C.E. To be sure, there are very good reasons to question whether Jeremiah 7:1–15 accurately records the words of the prophet and whether Jeremiah 26:1–24 accurately provides their setting. Of course, the stylistic differences between the prose sermon and the poetic oracles contained elsewhere in Jeremiah 1–25 provide one cause for concern.[66] The powerful Deuteronomistic influences on both chapters provide another.[67] The curious, and possibly crucial, role played by Jeremiah's scribe Baruch (Jer. 36:4, 43:3; 45:1–5) in shaping the book we have—or at least parts of it—provides yet a third source of concern.[68] Obviously, the more the story is shaped to fit a later perspective, the less likely it is that some historical event has been accurately recorded. Yet a number of scholars are less skeptical of the historicity and authenticity of the temple sermon.[69] In truth, it matters very little for our purposes whether or not Jeremiah 7:1–15 accurately preserves the prophet's speech or whether Jeremiah 26:1–24 records its true historical context. I am satisfied to analyze and comment on the sources as we have them, and to assume that we learn, at the very least, something about the ways the prophetic tradition remembers Jeremiah's condemnation of, and conflict with, some of his cultic contemporaries. Even so, as we examine closely the sermon and its narrative, we will note a few aspects of these traditions that challenge the view that these passages are fully Deuteronomistic. The purpose, however, is not to argue for the historicity of the sermon but simply to understand it better.

The longer version of Jeremiah's sermon begins with a call to repentance (7:3), followed by a warning not to believe the deceptive words: "the temple of the Lord, the temple of the Lord, the temple of the Lord" (7:4). Apparently, we have here a reference to the people's belief in the inviolability of Zion, as expressed, for example, in Psalms 46 and 48: because God dwells in the sanctuary, it cannot be conquered or destroyed (cf. Jer. 14:13).[70] The paragraphs that follow amplify this theme: the people are called again to repent (7:5), and they are assured that if they do what is right and good, then the Lord will indeed dwell among them (7:6–7).[71] Following another reference to the people's belief in deception (7:8), the prophet declares:

> (9) will you steal, murder, commit adultery, swear falsely, make offerings to Baal, and go after other gods that you have not known, (10) and then come and stand before me in this house, which is called by my name, and say, "We are safe!"—only to go on doing all these abominations? (11) Has this house, which is called by my name, become a den of robbers in your sight? You know, I too am watching, says the Lord. (12) Go now to my place that was in Shiloh, where I made my name dwell at first, and see what I did to it for the wickedness of my people Israel. (13) And now, because you have done all these things, says the Lord, and when I spoke to you persistently, you did not listen, and when I called you, you did not answer, (14) therefore I will do to the house that is called by my name, in which you trust...just what I did to Shiloh.

The prophet's comparing the present temple to the destroyed cult place of Shiloh (1 Sam. 4–6; Ps. 78:56–72) is certainly jarring. Far from being inviolable, Zion will be destroyed for the people's sins just as Shiloh was.

It is precisely the prophet's similar declaration in 26:6—"I will make this house like Shiloh, and I will make this city a curse"—that brings about the events told in that chapter. According to the narrative, Jeremiah's preaching against the temple and capital city meets with objections from the priests, prophets, and all others who are there listening (26:7–9). Since the people believe it a capital offense to speak such treasonous words, a trial ensues (26:10–19). The hearing is finally resolved in Jeremiah's favor when the officials and people remember the precedent of the prophet Micah, who a century before similarly spoke dire words against Jerusalem (26:18, quoting Mic. 3:12).[72] Jeremiah is let go. But we are then told of another, less fortunate prophet named Uriah, who similarly spoke against Jerusalem and its temple. Unlike Jeremiah—who enjoyed the protection of Ahikam, son of Shaphan (26:24, see also 2 Kgs. 22:12–13)—this prophet was killed (Jer. 26:20–23). Apparently, precedent meant more when one had powerful patrons.

It is surely significant that the temple sermon, in its longer version (7:1–15), is situated in a context in which we find passages that are not unlike Hosea 6:6 in their apparent condemnation of the people's sacrifices (Jer. 6:20, 7:21–22). This strongly suggests that, at least on a redactional level, Jeremiah's ostensible rejections of sacrifice are to be understood in ways spelled out here: God does not reject sacrifice per se; God rejects the people's presumption that the temple and its service can be taken for granted. If scholars are correct in assuming that Jeremiah argues here with those who believe in the inviolability of Zion, we should keep in mind that this doctrine—correct or not—is rooted in a number of ancient theological traditions that manifest themselves in the symbolism of the temple and its ritual. The temple is God's abode, the sacrifices are divine service; the sanctuary complex represents the cosmos, and what takes place there involves *imitatio Dei*.[73] Jeremiah accepts all of this—except that he insists on the conditional, covenantal aspect of God's relationship with Israel.[74] If Israel violates that relationship—by committing theft, idolatry, sexual sin, and murder (7:9)—then the temple and the sacrifice that is performed there will be of no avail. For Jeremiah, the rejection of sacrifice (6:20) must be closely related to his warning that the temple would be destroyed (7:1–15).[75]

A second important aspect of these traditions is that Jeremiah gives prominence to the problem of theft. He famously refers to the sanctuary as a "den of robbers" (7:11), but even more striking is the juxtaposition of theft with more severe crimes in 7:9–10: "will you steal, murder, commit adultery, swear falsely, make offerings to Baal, and go after other gods that you have not known, and then come and stand before me in this house?" Of course, other traditions juxtapose theft and murder (e.g., Exod. 20; Deut. 5). But this case includes a distinct emphasis on stealing. Theft—and no other lighter crimes— is immediately juxtaposed with the severest of sins (idolatry, sexual transgression, and murder). Moreover, theft is referred to twice in three sentences. This may add further confirmation to the case made above: theft poses a particular problem for all those concerned with sacrifice in general (cf. Jer. 6:13, 20). The prophets' rejections of sacrifice are connected to their belief that economic transgressions render sacrificial offerings not just invalid but offensive.

A third realm of significance for our purposes emerges from a brief consideration of the traditions' relationship to Deuteronomistic concerns.[76] We have already noted that Deuteronomistic language and ideas appear throughout these passages. The prophet's call to care for the widow, orphan, and stranger (7:6) recalls Deuteronomic advice (Deut. 10:18, 27:19). The prophet's concern with the *place* where God's *name* dwells (Jer. 7:11, 12, 14) likewise recalls a frequent Deuteronomic concern (Deut. 12:14). Moreover, the conditional, covenantal theology expressed in the sermon coheres with what we find frequently in the fifth book of the Torah (Deut. 4:1–14; 6:1–15, etc.).[77] But several aspects of these traditions do not cohere so well with Deuteronomy. The aforementioned explicit references to the dwelling of God's *name* are balanced by passages that seem to speak more plainly of God's presence in the sanctuary (7:3, 7). These references to God dwelling in the sanctuary (if that is, indeed, how we are to understand 7:3 and 7) recall priestly discussions of the matter (e.g., Exod. 25:8).

It is also curious that the prophet's memory of Shiloh's destruction does not match perfectly with the Deuteronomistic telling of that event. In 1 Samuel, the Philistine defeat of the Israelites and the capture of the ark are explicitly blamed on the sinfulness of Eli's sons, priestly scoundrels who took for themselves the best of what the people had given to God (1 Sam. 2:12–17, 27–36). Jeremiah, however, is not remembered as having directed any blame for this event on any particular line of priests. Of course, it is surely significant that Jeremiah—as a priest from Anathot (Jer. 1:1; 32:1–4)—was apparently descended from the remnants of Eli's priestly line (1 Sam. 2:36; 1 Sam. 22: 18–23; 1 Kgs. 2:26–27). In placing blame for Shiloh's fall on the people of Israel (as opposed to the sons of Eli) Jeremiah's temple sermon echoes not the Deuteronomistic tradition, but an alternative narrative, preserved in Psalms 78:56–72:

> (56) Yet they [the people of Israel] tested the Most High God,
>   and rebelled against him.
>   They did not observe his decrees. . . .
> (59) When God heard, he was full of wrath,
>   and he utterly rejected Israel.
> (60) He abandoned his dwelling at Shiloh,
>   the tent where he dwelt among mortals,
> (61) and delivered his power to captivity,
>   his glory to the hand of the foe.

As in Psalm 78, the prophet blames Shiloh's fall not on the guilt of Eli's sons but on the sins of the nation as a whole. It is reasonable to believe that priests— especially those related to Eli's descendants—might have found this interpretation of the events more congenial than the Deuteronomistic tradition.

The concerns of the temple sermon diverge from distinctly Deuteronomistic ideas in a third way, moving again toward concerns that can safely be attributed to priestly circles. The prophet's attitude toward sin and its effect on the sanctuary reflects the notion of moral defilement, whereby grave sin— idolatry, sexual transgression, and bloodshed—defiles both the sanctuary and land, leading to God's withdrawal from the sanctuary and Israel's exile from the land. Although we do not find explicit reference to the *defilement* of the sanctuary here, the three cardinal sources of moral defilement are mentioned

(7:9, along with theft) and referred to as abominations (7:10). What is more, the sermon rehearses some essential outcomes of moral impurity: the sanctuary is rendered useless (7:11), destined for destruction (7:14), and the people are to be exiled (7:15). Significantly, what is missing here—explicit reference to the defiling nature of the crimes at hand—appears elsewhere in Jeremiah. The land is defiled by adultery (3:1–2, 9; cf. Deut. 24:1–4; Num. 35:33) and idolatry (Jer. 2:7); the latter defiles the sanctuary as well (7:30; cf. 19:13, 32:34). The people have defiled themselves in much the same way (2:23).

One aspect of what we observed in the previous chapter bears repeating here. According to the Priestly strand and the Holiness Code, moral defilement threatens what is supposed to result from the proper performance of sacrificial ritual. In the absence of grave sin, the regular and proper performance of sacrificial service attracts and maintains the dwelling of the divine presence in the sanctuary. Moral defilement—brought about by actions God finds utterly repugnant—threatens to undo this state of affairs. It stands to reason that in the presence of grave sin, sacrifice is no longer adequate to the task of attracting and maintaining the divine presence among the people of Israel. The notion that moral defilement affects the sanctuary is predicated on the idea that the temple is the locale for the divine-human encounter, and therefore the symbol of the divine-human relationship. Sin, by leaving its stain on the sanctuary, becomes the moral barometer of the people of Israel.[78] Needless to say, this barometer operates by evaluating the moral status of the community as a whole, not the status of individual worshipers.[79] An important aspect of understanding the prophetic critique in general—and Jeremiah's temple sermon in particular—is to appreciate that when prophets speak of the futility of the temple or its cult, they are not necessarily criticizing ritual as much as they are evaluating the current state of Israel's relationship to God.[80]

This survey is not meant to argue that we can situate Jeremiah among the priests of his day—surely Jeremiah was in conflict with priests, as he was in conflict with prophets and many others.[81] But it is equally important to recognize that much of what we find here—including, significantly, the conditionality of the dwelling of the divine presence and the problem posed to the sanctuary by grave sin—are issues that are not distinctively Deuteronomistic. Nor are they perspectives that can be seen as inherently anticultic or antipriestly.[82] Indeed, the traditions we have examined here are roughly commensurate with the traditions we examined in the previous chapter, even if we cannot fully identify Jeremiah's sermon with the (presumably) priestly understanding of moral defilement. The Holiness Code—in that it allows for and is worried about the potential defilement of the land and sanctuary by sin—contains within it the seeds of the temple sermon's rejection of a sin-infested cult and morally defiled temple. Moreover, the articulation of the notion of moral defilement in priestly traditions demonstrates that priests (at some point) also rejected the doctrine of Zion's inviolability, just like the prophet who is remembered for delivering a sermon in the temple precincts in the early days of the reign of King Jehoiakim.

Ezekiel: The Prophetic Critique in Transformation

In this final section, we consider the attitude toward the temple cult expressed in the prophetic writings attributed to the prophet Ezekiel. In this section, too, the analysis is motivated by a desire not only to survey the prophets' stance toward the cult, but also to lay the groundwork for later chapters. We will soon see (in chapter 5) that the book of Ezekiel had a tremendous impact upon many ancient Jews, particularly some groups that articulated rejections of the Second Temple (including the sectarians at Qumran). In this section, however, we focus on the book of Ezekiel, and the attitude it expressed toward the sacrificial cult of its day.

Little doubt exists that the book of Ezekiel has developed since the time the historical prophet walked on Babylonian soil.[83] Different versions of the book are extant, and there are some good reasons to suspect the work of later editors, especially in the last nine chapters.[84] Of course—as is the case with Jeremiah—there are scholars who defend not only the literary unity of the book but its essential historicity as well.[85] Some even continue to maintain a connection between the historical prophet and the later chapters of the prophetic book.[86] Again, these issues are not of the utmost importance for our concern here, which is to comment on the book of Ezekiel's contribution to the prophetic stance toward the cult.

We should not expect to find in the present book of Ezekiel any passages quite along the lines of those we have examined already. After all, Ezekiel *obviously* did not reject the cult: this priest in exile (Ezek. 1:1–3) ostensibly had an elaborate vision of how the temple would eventually be rebuilt, and how its priests would perform animal sacrifice (Ezek. 40–48). But we will see that Ezekiel has critical things to say about the temple as he knew it, and not only because the Israelites were sinful. Thus we will observe in Ezekiel a critique of the cult of his day, subtly expressed, that is qualitatively different from what we have seen before. It is also significant that some of this criticism is expressed in passages that could easily be mistaken for priestly literature. Indeed, if any figure calls into question Weber's dichotomy, it is Ezekiel. The case for whether a figure like Habakkuk was a cult prophet is surely debatable. But the case for Ezekiel is all but closed, unless one seeks to deny the authenticity of all of Ezekiel's cultic aspects.[87] Yet as Marvin Sweeney correctly observes, the effort to take the priest out of the prophet Ezekiel is motivated by an all-too-religious adherence to Weber's dichotomy.[88]

The connections between Ezekiel and the priesthood—or, better, between the prophetic book and priestly traditions—are extensive, well documented, and undeniable.[89] According to the superscription (Ezek. 1:3), Ezekiel himself was a priest—and there is little in the book to question that fact. Ezekiel's interest in cultic matters runs deep—from his detailed description of sin in the temple (8:1–11:25) to his comprehensive depiction of the temple to come in the last nine chapters. Just as the priestly traditions exhibit a distinct interest in the divine presence, so too Ezekiel concerns himself with the comings and goings of God's "glory" (e.g., 8:6). There is also, importantly, an undeniable link between Ezekiel and the Holiness Code.[90] This is most apparent in the fact that we find in Ezekiel a sustained interest in the notion of moral defilement. Like the Holiness Code, Ezekiel exhibits a particular interest in Israel's "abominable" sins of idolatry (8:9–18), bloodshed (11:6–7), and sexual transgression (22:10). These transgressions have a defiling impact on the sanctuary (5:11) and the land (36:17), leading to the departure of God's "glory" (8:6, 11:22–23) and the exile of the people from their land (11:9–10).

But perhaps the most priestly of passages in Ezekiel is the prophet's vision of the future temple. No doubt the thoroughgoing interest in the temple, its service, and priestly prerogatives appears distinctly P-like in style, form, and content.[91] Indeed, those who endeavor to isolate the date of the priestly traditions usually base their argument in part on the date of these chapters. Wellhausen, for instance, predicated his late dating for the priestly traditions in part on his assumption that Ezekiel must precede them.[92] Kaufmann, on the other hand, turned this argument on its head, dating P based in part on the assumption that P must precede Ezekiel.[93] I have already expressed my avowed disinterest in solving such questions—and my equally avowed suspicion that such questions can be duly answered without articulating an evolutionist view of Israelite religion. There is, however, an important aspect of these approaches that impacts on our concerns: if one can postulate a development from the Priestly strand to Ezekiel (or vice versa), one has also identified a divergence, be it slight or significant, between Ezekiel and the Priestly strand. How, then, are we to understand the divergence between Ezekiel 40–48 and the priestly traditions?

There was a time when chapters 40–48 of Ezekiel were not among the well-studied portions of this prophetic book.[94] Fortunately, however, that is no longer the case. Studies by Moshe Greenberg, Jon D. Levenson, Kalinda Rose Stevenson, and Jonathan Z. Smith (to name a few) are now readily accessible and facilitate a sustained comparison between the prophet's vision of the temple's future and the priestly remembrance of the tabernacle's past.[95] As has been frequently noted, Ezekiel's vision and the priestly tradition differ in no small respect. In general, Ezekiel articulates rules that are stricter than their priestly counterparts. For instance, compared with priestly traditions, Ezekiel seems to require an extra week of purification from corpse impurity before a priest can participate in the cult (Ezek. 44:25–27; cf. Num. 19:10–13). But a number of the rules are not just stricter: they articulate a social agenda vastly different from what we find in the priestly traditions of the Pentateuch. Precisely for this reason, Stevenson speaks of Ezekiel's vision as one not of "restoration" but of "transformation," the implication being that Ezekiel seeks not a return to some ideal past but the establishment of something entirely new.[96]

On the level of structure, Ezekiel's new social program is in evidence in the massive gates he imagines surrounding the temple (40:20–23). These gates—one of which is to remain shut (44:2)—symbolize controlled access, and the legislation that the prophet provides is similarly meant to restrict access to the sacred precincts.[97] A number of details are worthy of note. Strikingly, Eze-kiel simply bans foreigners from entering or otherwise bringing offerings to the sanctuary (Ezek. 44:6–9). The contrary view—permitting and even requir-ing the participation of "strangers"—is expressed more than once in priestly materials (Lev. 17:8; Num. 15:14–16, 27–29).[98] Ezekiel also places a number of restrictions on Israelites. Since the sacred precincts are vastly expanded (to five hundred square cubits; 42:16)—and since various land allotments around the sancta are given to the priests, Levites, and the prince (45:1–5, 7)—Israelites are left with a limited area in the vicinity of the temple in which they are per-mitted to live (45:6). More significantly, the prophet imagines the sacrificial altar being placed within sacred precincts (40:47, 43:13–27), an area which only priests may enter (44:15–16). Thus Israelites are denied direct access to the altar (in contrast to Exod. 40:29) and no longer permitted to slaughter their own offerings (Ezek. 44:11; in contrast to Lev. 1:5).[99] A second ramification of Ezekiel's placement of the altar is the fact that individual offerings—those that the Israelites would themselves bring (e.g., Lev. 1:2)—seem to be dispensed with.[100] The prophet's legislation concerns only the public offerings brought by the priests (45:18–25) and other sacrifices brought by the prince (46:11–15).[101] Ezekiel also—in comparison with priestly materials—restricts the roles of Levites (44:10–14) and confines the priesthood to the descendants of Zadok (44:15–16; cf. 1 Kgs. 1:7–8, 2:26–27).[102] Finally, as is well known, be-cause he imagines a "chief" (NRSV: "prince"), there does not seem to be any place in Ezekiel's program for a powerful Davidic monarch.[103]

Significantly, a few aspects of Ezekiel's vision seem to predict or accu-rately reflect the social reality of the early Second Temple period: the priestly leadership was restricted to the Zadokite line, and the community eventually established itself as a theocracy. Whether by priestly or Persian design, the Davidic monarchy disappeared. Thus certain political aspects of Ezekiel's vi-sion have an aura of reality about them.[104] A few other aspects of Ezekiel's vision—ones that did not become reality—are notably idealistic, even egali-tarian: land is allotted to all tribes in a relatively equitable fashion, ensuring shared access to the sea (48:1–7, 23–29), and a portion is even set aside for the resident aliens (47:21–23).[105]

Yet, despite these observations, the fact remains that much of Ezekiel's vision is neither egalitarian nor reflective of what we know to be First or Second Temple practice. Indeed, Ezekiel's vision of "transformation"—as Stevenson helpfully calls it—can be understood as a critique of the cult of the past. The temple that has been destroyed (as well as, perhaps, the temple that has just been rebuilt) is in Ezekiel's estimation vastly inadequate—structurally and otherwise—to the task of maintaining the requisite holiness of God's residence.[106] Ezekiel's is not just a vision of what will be but equally a vision of what should have been. This vision of the future contains within it a critique of the past. It's a different kind of critique from the others we have seen, but it's a prophetic critique of a temple nonetheless.

A second important conclusion can be reached if we look back at the priestly traditions. Over and against the exclusive ideal of Ezekiel's vision, the priestly traditions maintain a sacrificial system that is open to the participation of Israelites and aliens. In addition, according to priestly traditions, the Israelites remain unrestricted in choosing their residence. By all accounts, the Second Temple period priests followed not Ezekiel in these matters but the priestly traditions of the Pentateuch. And while the high-priestly line was indeed Zadokite for much of the Second Temple period, it is not at all clear that non-Zadokite priests were banished from sacred service; there is certainly no reflection of that in other late biblical traditions (e.g., 1 Chron. 24:1–31).[107] Regardless of what one believes about the historical relationship between Ezekiel and the priestly strands in the Torah, one must recognize that once both traditions existed, the powers that were decided to side with Leviticus and Numbers against Ezekiel 40–48. We can safely assume that early Second Temple priests played some role in the canonization—and centralization of—Leviticus and Numbers, and the relative ostracizing of Ezekiel 40–48. We can therefore safely conclude that when it comes to the disputes we have covered in this section, we find a radical reversal of what is commonly presumed to be the norm. Here we find anonymous priests defending what would strike us as just and good—openness and inclusion—against the vision of an exclusivist prophet.[108] Indeed, the thrust of the last two sections could lead one to suggest, with some irony, that it is Jeremiah and not Ezekiel who was truly the most priestly of prophets—if not in literary style, then perhaps in ideological perspective.

Conclusion

We have examined in this chapter a number of issues revolving around the prophets' critique of the cult and the various approaches taken to this question by contemporary scholars. We began by observing—in agreement with most contemporary scholars—that neither Julius Wellhausen's evolutionist history nor Max Weber's ideal typology provides an adequate foundation for understanding the complex dynamic between priests and prophets in ancient Israel. Yet we then observed—in partial agreement with Ronald Hendel and others who would bring us back to the approaches of Wellhausen or Weber—that many contemporary responses to the older approaches are also inadequate. Some approaches seek to maintain a qualitative difference between the prophets and the priests, and do so by predicating that early priests composed dry ritual texts, and that later prophets infused these rituals with a sense of morality. This approach—articulated by Kaufmann and those who follow him—has the advantage of being less black and white than Wellhausen's and Weber's. It also has the advantage of being free of the hostility toward later Judaism that motivated earlier approaches. Yet this approach still operates on an inadequate, evolutionist theory. Many other approaches to the question of the prophetic evaluation of the cult also smack of apology. By defending the prophets' interest in ritual or the priests' interest in ethics, scholars breaking down Weber's typology can sometimes be heard to express interpretations of the matter that seem all too familiar to those conversant with contemporary religious approaches to ethics and ritual. That the prophets opposed ritual only when performed in a state of moral turpitude, or that they drew a contrast between exterior ritual expression and interior spiritual disposition—these answers, even if they are an advance over Wellhausen and Weber, are suspicious in their own right as well.

I have endeavored in this chapter to steer a middle course between the classic contrasts and more contemporary efforts to smooth things over. As we have seen, the problem of biased terminology applies not only to the use of theologically charged terms (like "interior" and "exterior" or "letter" and "spirit") but even to seemingly dry scholarly discourse: the common distinction made between priestly "ritual" and prophetic "symbolic action" illustrates the degree to which our academic terminology may predispose one to see differences where the situation is really rather similar.

We have also seen that some things become clearer when one ignores categorical distinctions and focuses instead on the details of the situation at hand. I suggested that many of the prophetic oppositions to sacrifice can be understood as a reflection of their social and economic message. But the prophets did not object, in the abstract, to the idea of sinful people worshiping God. And the (external) ritual is not rejected because of an (interior) ethical wrong. Rather, the prophets—or, at least, some of them—found sacrifice offensive because they believed that those who were offering gifts had themselves stolen them. The concern with property renders it impossible altogether to distinguish between a ritual violation and an ethical wrong. Sacrificing a stolen animal is, at one and the same time, both ethically and ritually wrong.

As argued above, an important aspect of the prophetic critique becomes clearer when one recognizes that both priests *and* prophets accepted various symbolic understandings of both the temple and its service. Thus a prophet's condemnation of the temple—and prediction of its destruction—could mean very simply that the prophet believes that doom is immanent, and that neither sacrifice nor anything else will avert the decree. Moreover, prophets like Jeremiah and Ezekiel, in particular, fully accepted a number of doctrines usually associated with priestly tradition. Both apparently believed that God dwelled in the sanctuary, and both recognized the dangers associated with the notion of moral defilement: when sin defiles the land and temple, the divine presence will depart.

Finally, we considered the attitude toward the cult expressed in the works attributed to the most priestly of prophets, Ezekiel. Here, too, we found a sharp critique of the cult, though it concerns issues distinct from those of other prophets, and is expressed in a vastly different—even priestly—style. Nonetheless, here too we can identify a decided dispute between priestly and prophetic circles, even if the boundaries seem blurred.

In short, I believe that the disputes between priests and prophets were indeed real, though they defy simple generalization. These debates also defy simple linear historical constructions. Attempts by either Wellhausen or Kaufmann to trace ethical developments or ritual declines fail on grounds of bias and method. We simply cannot date texts on the basis of any preconceived notion of how religious traditions do or should develop. Moreover, we cannot assume that all the differences between our sources can be explained by positing that they emerged in distinct historical periods. While scholars will continue to argue about the dates of our texts and the various strands that can be discerned within them, it must be recognized that too much of this business is circular. The relationship between Ezekiel 40–48 and the Priestly strand is a case in point: how can we really know which text was written first? How can we know for certain which text was edited later? We cannot know.

There are, however, some things we can discern about ancient Israel; and these should affect how we approach the questions considered in this chapter. First, it is undeniable that all of the sources we have—priestly ones and prophetic ones—experienced protracted periods of textual development. Second, it is equally undeniable that there were various distinct social groupings in ancient Israel, clans of priests and circles of prophets among them. Thus we do well to recognize that any reconstruction of the situation ought not be linear but rather grid-like. The biblical tradition comprises various preexilic priestly and prophetic traditions that have been transmitted, redacted, and glossed by various priestly and prophetic scribal circles in exilic and postexilic milieus. What these sources provide, therefore, are assorted windows into disputes among ancient Israelites; and these windows are half-open and partially curtained ones at that.

When we survey the sources accordingly, we can reconstruct a sketchy picture of priests and prophets in disagreement. To get a fuller picture, we cannot selectively take certain prophetic texts at face value. We must avoid simple categorizations, be they religious or scholarly. And we must try to read priestly texts with the sympathy that some prophetic texts may and certain scholarly approaches do mean to deny them. When we do all this, we can imagine a situation where prophets and priests—and others too, to be sure—argued about the various issues we have covered in this chapter.

While we do well to assume that both priests and prophets would have rejected offerings of stolen goods, we can safely suppose that priests and prophets might have defined theft differently. A prophet like Amos saw theft in economic inequality. Priests, by contrast, would likely have defined theft in a more restricted fashion. We similarly do well to assume that priests and prophets—especially Jeremiah and Ezekiel, among the latter—agreed on a number of symbolic and theological understandings of sacrifice. Yet we can again safely suppose that priests and prophets might have drawn some lines differently. Jeremiah and Ezekiel, fed up with the sin they saw everywhere around them, leaned more toward giving up on the situation. Their contemporary priests, however, may still have had reserves of patience for atoning Israelites. Ironically, some of the sharpest ideological disputes are between the priestly traditions and Ezekiel. Here, too, there is broad agreement on the need to maintain the sanctity of God's earthly residence. But where Ezekiel preached a safer system characterized by the exclusion of Israelites and foreigners, the priestly traditions articulated a more open system, characterized perhaps by a greater chance that the temple's offerings could be corrupted in some way.

In a number of studies, Moshe Greenberg has helpfully recognized the tension between reality and idealism in the biblical tradition.[109] Greenberg speaks in these studies of "the ideal of power in the law" as contrasted with the "reality of power in the prophets."[110] Greenberg refers here to the fact that while priestly tradition assumes that priests, kings, and judges will do what is right and good—and legislates accordingly—it is the prophets who recognize that power corrupts. Without arguing these points, I believe that what we have seen in this chapter points to the inversion of these perspectives when we focus not on the leaders but on the people. The prophets hold the people to an ideal moral standard, while the priests seek to operate and maintain social institutions that serve these people's needs. Greenberg helpfully concludes his study by noting that the legacy of these disputes carries on into the Second Temple period.[111] As we will see in part II, he is right about that, too.

The Second Temple, Symbolism, and Supersessionism

Introduction to Part II

In the second part of this book, we focus on ancient Jewish attitudes toward the Second Temple. The following chapters will be fully informed by the lessons learned in part I. Here too we will see the benefit of studying purity and sacrifice as related ritual structures, utilizing the same assumptions and methods. Symbolic understandings of the temple cult will remain of interest, and it will not be assumed that those who speak symbolically are also speaking critically about the cult. We will also recognize the need to eschew evolutionist approaches, which continually crop up in the scholarship, especially toward sacrifice.

The project is bounded by a number of limits, chronological, practical, and thematic. We are interested in the later Second Temple period (c. 300 B.C.E. to 70 C.E.), but we cannot cover all material relating to sacrifice and purity in ancient Jewish sources. Thankfully, there is little need to review here some topics that are well covered elsewhere. For instance, excellent scholarship exists on the architecture and structure of the Second Temple. These works analyze the literary evidence (especially Josephus, *Jewish War* 5:184–287, and Mishnah Tractate *Middot*) along with the results of recent archaeological surveys to give us a picture of the Second Temple in its physical glory.[1] In addition, a number of other writers have described the day-to-day practice of the Second Temple, based on the descriptions in, among other sources, Mishnah Tractate *Tamid* and book 1 of Philo's *Special Laws*.[2] Curiously, a number of scholarly works of one sort or another contain descriptions of fictionalized visits to the temple.[3] Thankfully, with the existence of these vivid accounts—as well as other helpful general treatments[4]—we have no reason to survey here either the physical structure of the temple or the nature of its daily ritual. We can focus, therefore, on the issues of our concern: what the temple meant to ancient Jews who worshiped there, and the reasons many scholars have been reluctant to recognize the varied religious meanings of ancient Jewish sacrificial service.

As is widely recognized, the temple was the fulcrum of ancient Jewish religion. The centrality of the temple as a social institution can hardly be denied, and certainly any responsible survey of ancient Judaism devotes at least a chapter to discussing the social and religious importance of the Second Temple to ancient Judaism.[5] Jewish people living throughout the ancient world maintained ties with the Jerusalem temple, whether by making an occasional pilgrimage to the temple or by paying the half-shekel temple tax.[6] Many Jews living within the land of Israel maintained their ties to the temple by even more frequent visits, and by sending or bringing their biblically mandated agricultural donations and other votive offerings.[7] But the temple's centrality was not only manifest in the economic sphere. The temple was the location of political, judicial, and religious decision-making, serving as an assembly, court, school, and, perhaps, library.[8] Even after the temple's destruction, the continued importance of the institution can be seen in the physical decoration and structural orientation of ancient synagogues: long after 70 C.E., these buildings commonly faced Jerusalem and were adorned with temple motifs. The importance of the temple is enshrined in scholarly discourse through the near-consensus periodization of ancient Jewish history into the "First" and "Second Temple" periods.

But it is not primarily these aspects of the temple that give rise to much of the scholarship on the Second Temple, although most of the items just mentioned are widely acknowledged and discussed in the scholarly literature. Much of the scholarship on the Second Temple—like, indeed, much of the scholarship on ancient Judaism in general—serves not primarily to analyze the stated topic but rather as a backdrop for something else, whether it is the study of the New Testament, rabbinic Judaism, or, ever more commonly, the Dead Sea Scrolls. Scholars of the New Testament, of course, are obligated to try to make sense of the tantalizingly brief narratives of the Last Supper and Jesus' overturning the tables in the temple. Scholars of rabbinic Judaism must make sense of the rabbinic response to the destruction of the temple—indeed, for many scholars, the response to 70 C.E. is what makes rabbinic Judaism what it was. Scholars of the Dead Sea Scrolls have no choice but to understand why it is (or at least seems to be) that the sectarians withdrew from the Jerusalem temple. The problem is that there is a difficulty inherent in all three of these endeavors, one that has hindered scholarly understanding of the Second Temple and its ritual practices: it is all too easy for the temple to play the role of antagonist in the drama of the development of whatever phenomenon primarily interests the scholar, be it rabbinic Judaism, the New Testament, or the Dead Sea Scrolls.

As we will see later, scholars of the New Testament all too commonly find something truly flawed in the Second Temple, be it the moral corruption of the priests, the ostensibly offensive nature of the purity system, or the inherent inefficacy of sacrificial ritual. Christianity, in these analyses, makes a decided advance by "spiritualizing" the temple or by providing an ever more effective and meaningful service in the eucharist. Of course, in order to speak of a spiritualization of sacrifice (or of any ritual for that matter) one must assume that that particular ritual lacks all spirit (or meaning) to begin with.[9] In a similar vein, scholars of the Dead Sea Scrolls commonly assume that the temple that the sectarians rejected was indeed worth rejecting, for any one of the reasons just noted, or perhaps others too (we will schematize their antitemple polemics in chapter 5). So the sectarians, too, may have "spiritualized" the temple, or in some other way provided a better alternative. Finally, for reasons already mentioned in part I, scholars of rabbinic and postrabbinic Judaism have also all too frequently operated on similar biases, positing that rabbinic Judaism makes a moral advance over ancient Judaism, replacing the sacrificial service with the rabbinic "service of the heart."[10]

The evolutionism that is all too common in these interrelated fields has led to the manifestation in scholarly discourse of a number of specific interpretive oversights and errors. First, while there is much literature devoted to the Second Temple and its symbolic significance, surprisingly little of that scholarship even attempts to connect the adduced meanings of the temple to an understanding of the rituals that took place there. Thus while one can find many analyses of the "cosmic symbolism" of the Second Temple, one can hardly find an analysis that attempts to connect directly the temple's purificatory or sacrificial rituals to such cosmic symbolism.[11] The reluctance to recognize that sacrifice itself could have meaning for those who practiced it remains regnant. Of course, this phenomenon goes hand in hand with evolutionist arguments: as a meaningless vestige, sacrifice was destined to disappear.

A second problem pertaining to many of these analyses is the fact that when symbolic meanings of the temple (and in rare cases, of sacrifice itself) are identified, they are ascribed not to those Jews who believe in the temple and its sacrifices but to those who ostensibly spiritualize it or reject it.[12] According to this approach, symbolic understandings of the temple—as representing the cosmos, for instance—are attributed to diaspora Jews removed from the temple's reality, mystics removed from all reality, or Christians and schismatics who no longer believe in the temple's legitimacy or efficacy. As we will see, especially in chapter 4, there is little justification for this. The rush to ascribe symbolic understandings of the temple to those who ostensibly reject the temple is a reflection of the degree to which scholarship on these matters remains influenced by the various antisacrificial biases we have been tracking in this book.

A third problem is closely related to the second. Just as scholars too often ascribe any temple-related symbolic discourse to those who ostensibly reject the temple, so too scholars too frequently ascribe moral sensibilities to those who reject the temple but not to those who adhere to it. The problems discussed in chapter 3 appear also in scholarly discourse on the ancient period: the morality of those neoprophetic voices that criticize the temple is generally left unquestioned, and the immorality of those priests and others who maintain the temple in all its hierarchical exclusivity is often assumed.[13] Those who reject the temple or managed to survive it are able to develop meaningful, moral, and more inclusive modes of worship. Compared to these sensitive visionaries, temple-centered Judaism is understood to be decidedly lacking in morality and meaning.

And there is a fourth problem: just as scholars tend to attribute all symbolic understandings of the temple to those Jews who reject it in some fashion, scholars then tend to group disparate symbolic approaches together, without recognizing the practical and theoretical differences between them. Some Jews imagined that the earthly temple represented the entire cosmos. Other Jews imagined that the earthly temple corresponded to a heavenly temple *within* the cosmos. But scholarly discourse tends to lump these—and other—distinct ideas together as "cosmic symbolism." We will see, however, that a fuller understanding of ancient Jewish meanings ascribed to the temple is predicated on a more precise analysis of these distinct ideas.

A fifth problem is similar to the fourth. Just as scholars have not distinguished adequately between various "cosmic" symbolisms, so too scholars could distinguish better the various charges that are raised against the temple by certain groups of ancient Jews. In the effort to bolster the antitemple camp—and perhaps unduly influenced themselves by the various antisacrificial biases we have traced here—some scholars seem too quick to group together various polemics that are best seen separately. For some, the criticisms are grouped together in order to make the case that the temple or its personnel were in fact corrupt. For others, the criticisms of the temple once grouped together are all seen as examples of "spiritualizations" of sacrifice. To be sure, there are certain common threads to these antitemple polemics (at least those that *are* antitemple), and we can hardly suggest that the temple was a pristine place where nothing went wrong. Nonetheless, it is my belief that scholarly analysis could benefit from a clearer differentiation and schematization of these various views.

Finally, more attention must be paid to the various ways ancient Jews (and, indeed, early Christians) attempted to channel the sanctity of the temple into other realms of daily life, such as eating and praying. These efforts—also too commonly described as "spiritualizations"—are not criticisms of the temple, nor are they attempts to replace it. As we will see, these efforts are merely further attestations of the temple's meaning and significance.

I will bolster these claims throughout the rest of this book. But before developing these arguments, it will be worthwhile to review two recent works, each of which presents a synthesis of the understandings of the temple in ancient Judaism. Because we will be able to rely on these works for what they do well, these works deserve attention here. But neither of these works is entirely free of the problems spelled out above, and so I hope these brief reviews will further underscore the need for the analysis that follows.

C. T. R. Hayward, *The Jewish Temple*

One helpful survey of the meanings attributed to the temple (and secondarily to sacrifice) in ancient Judaism can be found in *The Jewish Temple: A*

Non-Biblical Sourcebook, by C. T. R. Hayward. This work—aimed at the student and scholar alike[14]—surveys a number of the important Second Temple period texts, with an eye toward helping others understand and appreciate the meanings attributed by ancient Jews to the temple during its last centuries of existence. The work focuses primarily on the symbolic meanings ascribed to the structural elements of the temple and its personnel. Hayward devotes time and attention to two central ideas: (1) that the temple was understood as a symbolic representation of the cosmos, and (2) that it was understood as an earthly counterpart to a temple in heaven.[15] Of course, sacrifice plays a role in his analysis, as it must, but it is fair to say that illuminating the symbolic understandings of sacrifice per se is not Hayward's primary focus. The work provides helpful analyses and bibliography—and I acknowledge my debt here.

As its title suggests, Hayward's book seeks to present and comment on nonbiblical texts, understood here in the sense of the Protestant canon. No chapters focus on either the New Testament or the Hebrew Bible, while two chapters focus on the "apocryphal" Wisdom of Ben Sira (which, of course, is biblical for Catholics and others). But the Protestant Bible is not the only boundary drawn in this nonbiblical sourcebook. Three other realms of literature are not treated systematically: rabbinic sources, the Dead Sea Scrolls, and the various documents speaking of ascent to a heavenly temple. Presumably, rabbinic literature is not treated systematically because these sources are beyond the chronological bounds Hayward sets for his study.[16] It is less clear why Hayward doesn't devote more time to descriptions of the heavenly temple. Perhaps it was determined that these sources have been handled adequately elsewhere.[17]

Hayward does tell us why Qumranic literature gets scant attention: the Dead Sea sectarians rejected the Jerusalem temple, believing instead that their community functioned as a temporary stand-in for the current defiled temple.[18] Hayward is certainly correct that much of the Qumranic literature criticizes the structure, practices, and priesthood of the Second Temple. But the exclusion of *all* Qumranic literature from a survey of ancient Jewish understandings of the temple is a methodologically flawed move, in at least two ways. First, even if Hayward's view of the sectarian community-as-temple idea is correct (we will turn to this question in chapter 5), the idea that *all* of Qumranic literature agrees with this principle remains to be demonstrated.[19] As we will see, many Qumranic texts provide insight into ways in which the temple and its sacrificial service were understood by many ancient Jews, including the *Songs of the Sabbath Sacrifice* and, of course, the *Temple Scroll.*

The second problem here is Hayward's well-intentioned assumption that an exploration of the Jerusalem temple should "focus upon people and writings which were favorably disposed towards it."[20] Hayward's survey provides an important antidote to the often anticultic approaches taken to this material. Hayward is correct when he implies that a lack of contemporary scholarly sympathy for the subject is often manifest in a scholarly focus on those texts that were critical of the institution in question. But in my view, the problem is not that scholars have studied these critical texts too much, it's that

they have allowed themselves to be persuaded by these texts that the temple
was a flawed institution. As we will see in the following chapters, there is
much to be learned from a sympathetic reading of the critical literature.[21]
Still, Hayward's sourcebook is commendable and extremely helpful with regard to what it does cover, and this analysis builds productively on his work.

Francis Schmidt, *How the Temple Thinks*

Another important recent work that seeks to present a synthesis of ancient
Jewish understandings of the temple and temple service is Francis Schmidt's
How the Temple Thinks. Considering all that has been noted in earlier chapters
regarding Durkheim, Hubert, and Mauss, it is certainly fitting to point out
that Schmidt holds a chair in the history of Judaism at the École Pratique des
Hautes Études. Indeed, in more ways than one, Schmidt is the heir to their
tradition.[22] In *How the Temple Thinks* we find a generally sympathetic, non-
evolutionist look at ancient Judaism, one that is informed by the insights of
functionalist anthropology.

    Schmidt helpfully and correctly rejects the idea—believed by many, but in
fact supported by little evidence—that the Second Temple was an institution
in decline.[23] Schmidt also correctly criticizes those who describe the alleged
Qumranic or Christian rejections of the temple as "spiritualizations" of the
cult.[24] He correctly identifies the two biases that motivate such approaches.
Christian theology, predicated on the replacement of Jewish sacrifice by the
death of Jesus, is one important motive.[25] The modernizing tendencies of
Reform-minded Jewish scholars, who viewed with favor the destruction of the
temple and its replacement by the synagogue, is another.[26] Thus Schmidt's
work provides an important corrective to much of the biased work that pro-
poses to describe the Second Temple but in fact criticizes it.

    Schmidt's work is particularly important in its demonstration that the
temple has meaning—in his words, it has its own "thinking." Thus Schmidt
correctly argues that when those living outside the temple seek to imitate
its sanctity, they are not criticizing or replacing the temple, they are emulating
it; we will return to this issue now and again. But Schmidt's understanding
of the temple's thought is rather narrow. Schmidt believes the fundamental purpose of the institution is "to prevent the mixing of orders," which is
achieved by "establishing over the natural and social world a control according
to the categories of the sacred and the profane, of the pure and the impure."[27]
In other words, the temple seeks to symbolize and enforce social hierarchies.
It is here, of course, that his indebtedness to the functionalist tradition becomes most clear.[28] Yet in my view, Schmidt has mistaken the means for the
ends: classification is not a goal in and of itself. Indeed, although it is sympathetically written, *How the Temple Thinks* can still be taken as an indictment
of the Second Temple. It comes off, in Schmidt's telling, as an institution
interested primarily in control and hierarchy. The temple and its priests were
particularly obsessed with the exclusion of foreigners (mistakenly deemed in

Schmidt's analysis to be inherently impure).[29] Moreover, in his overly sim-plified analysis of the conflicts of the Second Temple period, all seems to hinge on whether or not sacrifices may be offered at the temple by or for Gentiles.[30]

While the priestly traditions do of course speak with frequency of dis-tinctions between the holy and profane, the pure and the impure (Lev. 10:10), it is a mistake to assume that the distinction is the purpose of, or the symbolic thinking behind, the temple or the sacrificial process. As I argued in chapter 2, the sacrificial process is about much more than making distinctions and enforcing hierarchies. Indeed, it is now widely recognized that the function-alist thrusts of Mary Douglas's early work may not apply at all to the Hebrew Bible or ancient Judaism. The ritual purity system is simply not as well suited to the task of establishing distinctions and maintaining hierarchies as the reader of Douglas's *Purity and Danger* may assume. For instance, according to rabbinic literature (e.g., *m. Pesahim* 7:3–6; *m. Hagigah* 3:6–8), the ritual purity rules were *relaxed* at the times of the festivals in order to accommodate the throngs of pilgrims whose observance of the rules could not be easily ensured or regulated.[31] This kind of leniency—and there is no reason to doubt the reasonable and practical rabbinic record on this matter—is difficult to as-similate if Schmidt's application of Douglas's early work to the practice of the late Second Temple is to be accepted.

Other similar leniencies are to be found as well. Compared to the "thinking" of other ancient temples, the Jerusalem temple could be seen as rather tolerant of jumbled categories and mixed multitudes. Exclusions of foreigners or the uninitiated from temples were commonplace in the ancient world,[32] and at least the Jerusalem temple allowed for foreign offerings and donations to be received and recognized. Indeed, we know for certain that there were ancient Jews who considered the temple's practice too lenient with regard to who was admitted and how far.[33] There may have been similar disputes—with some taking a more lenient view—concerning the entry of women into the sanctuary as well.[34] Certainly the Jerusalem temple's practice and "thinking" were relatively lenient when compared with other temples imagined by ancient Jews, such as that imagined in the *Temple Scroll* (on which see chapter 5) and that imagined in the concluding chapters of Ezekiel (discussed in chapter 3). Schmidt overlooks too much of this in his earnest focus on what the Jerusalem temple purportedly excludes, because of his belief that exclusion is the *raison d'être* of the institution altogether.

Ironically, Schmidt's work depends on and develops those aspects of *Purity and Danger* that even Douglas herself would no longer apply to the Jewish purity and sacrificial systems. Schmidt's book appeared (in its first, French edition) in 1994, just a few years too soon to make use of Douglas's more recent and provocative works on purity. Importantly, these publications undercut her original (and more typically functionalist) contributions to the field.[35] At the same time, Schmidt virtually ignores those aspects of Douglas's early work that have proven most helpful to us: the effort to find symbolic meanings in ritual structures. Thus in a work devoted to uncovering the thinking of the temple, we find little attention paid, if any, to notions such as *imitatio Dei*, the divine presence, or to the cosmic symbolisms we will analyze in especially the following chapter. In the final analysis, Schmidt's work is too entrenched in the less helpful aspects of the functionalist tradition to be of much help in reaching the goals of the following chapters: uncovering the symbolic meanings of purity, sacrifice, and the temple in ancient Judaism.

Part II: Scope and Structure

In the chapters that follow, we will survey various approaches to the temple taken by ancient Jews, with the hope of understanding these matters a little differently from previous analyses. This can be achieved, first and foremost, if we consistently question whether certain sources are in fact critical of the temple. The only way to avoid *assuming* that sources are critical of the temple is to reevaluate them. Second, we will do well to eschew evolutionist approaches, whether these endorse the Christian replacement of the temple by Jesus' death or the (modernist) Jewish replacement of the temple by statutory prayer.

We will first consider two major symbolic approaches to the temple taken by various groups of ancient Jews (chapter 4). We will then consider the criticisms of the temple articulated in the literature discovered at Qumran (chapter 5). In the final two chapters we will consider, respectively, the evidence of rabbinic literature (chapter 6) and the Gospels (chapter 7). In the first instance, we will consider the rabbis' approach to the destruction of the temple. In the second, we will consider Jesus' approach to the temple in the last generation of its existence.

We will find that the various religious and cultural ideologies asserting that the temple has been outmoded or replaced—that is, *superseded*—have prevented scholars from seeing the temple as a powerful source of meaning and symbolism for those ancient Jews who believed in it. As a result, a number of facets of ancient Judaism have been misconstrued, misunderstood, or simply ignored. We will see that when symbolic understandings of the temple are found and discussed, such approaches are all too often attributed by scholars not to those who believed in the rituals of the temple but to those prophets, mystics, philosophers, or religious revolutionaries who allegedly rejected, opposed, or wished in some way to transcend the sacrificial cult. In the scholarly discussion, temple symbolism seems to reign everywhere but in the temple. In short, religious and cultural ideologies of supersessionism have prevented scholars from coming to grips with various symbolic understandings of the cult and its ritual as expressed in biblical and ancient Jewish literature.

4

Temple as Cosmos or Temple in the Cosmos

Priests, Purity, Sacrifice, and Angels

In this chapter, we consider two important symbolic approaches to purity, sacrifice, and the temple. While related, the two approaches to be studied here are in fact distinct. The first idea understands the temple as a symbol of the cosmos;[1] the second concern understands the earthly temple as an analogue to a sanctuary located in heaven.[2] The goals here will be to carefully schematize, analyze, and trace the relationship between these two notions.[3]

There is, in fact, much confusion regarding these ideas in the scholarly literature. For one thing, it remains rather common for these notions to be confused or jumbled together under a single discussion concerning "cosmic symbolism,"[4] heaven-earth "correspondence,"[5] or simply "temple symbolism."[6] Even some scholars who do differentiate between the two concepts do not generally explain well enough the distinct implications of the two approaches.[7] Yet as we will see, it is imperative to distinguish carefully between those sources that describe the temple as representing cosmos and those that describe a temple *in* heaven to which the Jerusalem temple constitutes an earthly analogue. While the two ideas are not contradictory, there are many tensions between them, and, as we will see, it is a general rule that ancient Jewish sources will articulate only one or another of these approaches, and not both.

Of course, the difference between the two notions can be seen most easily on the level of symbolism. When the earthly sanctuary is seen as an analogue to the heavenly one, then we do not generally find emphasis on the notion that the temple represents the cosmos. After all, if there is a temple *in* heaven, then the earthly sanctuary represents not the entire cosmos but just the most sacred part of it.

Conversely, when (as in Philo) the earthly temple represents the cosmos, then there is not necessarily any heavenly temple per se.

But this difference is by no means the most significant. The notion of the temple as cosmos is perfectly in line with the idea that the divine presence dwells within the sanctuary.[8] Indeed, while the cosmic symbolism of the temple structure is not in all ways explicitly spelled out in biblical priestly texts, scholars frequently argue—as pointed out in chapter 2—that various elements of the sanctuary's structure, decoration, and mythology operate with the understanding that God's presence dwells within the sanctuary that symbolizes the cosmos. On the face of it, it would appear that the notion of a temple in heaven raises a challenge to the idea of God's presence residing in the earthly temple. Many scholars assume that the notion of a temple in heaven serves to undercut the importance or sanctity of the earthly temple, by asserting that God's true location is in the heavens above, and not the temple below.[9] Yet there is very little evidence to support this contention. In many instances, the heavenly sanctuary above is believed to correspond to the temple below. Therefore, just as God dwells in the heavenly sanctuary, so too some divine being—some aspect of God—is understood to dwell in the heavenly temple's earthly analogue. It would appear then that an important prerequisite to the idea of the earthly temple *corresponding* to a heavenly one is a developed theology of divine emanation: while God dwells in the heavenly temple, the earthly temple is the residence of a divine emanation, be it God's "presence," "name," or Logos.

A theology of divine emanation is not the only prerequisite for the belief of a temple in heaven. A heavenly temple must have heavenly priests—angels—who serve the God worshiped there as priests serve in an earthly temple. In all cases, where we find a belief of a temple in heaven, we will also find a developed angelology. On the other hand, in the absence of a developed angelology, we are more likely to find evidence for the notion of the temple *as* cosmos, as opposed to a temple *in* the cosmos. For instance, the priestly theology of the Pentateuch remains perfectly intelligible without any developed notion of heavenly hosts or angels. A well-developed angelology, however, is an absolute prerequisite for the notion of a heavenly temple.

A further difference can be seen in the understandings of ritual purification and sacrifice. In chapter 2, I suggested that two themes—*imitatio Dei* and the desire to attract the divine presence—help us to appreciate the symbolic significance and the interconnection between ritual purity and sacrifice. When the temple is conceived as a symbol of the cosmos, we find a good deal of continuity with the biblical tradition as we have understood it: if the temple symbolizes the cosmos, then maintaining the temple can easily symbolize maintaining the world, and the sacrificial activity that takes place there can be seen on some level as part of that effort.[10] The purity required for entering the temple can still be understood similarly as well. By separating from substances associated with death and sex, priests and pure laypeople attempt to emulate divine attributes, in order to encounter God's presence in the temple.

The notion of *imitatio Dei* and the concerns with presence theology can also be related to the idea that the earthly temple corresponds to a heavenly one. In this symbolic scheme, the priests are frequently understood as behaving in ways that are analogous to the angels. Just as angels attend to God's throne in heaven, so too do the priests manage the sacrificial worship on earth. Similarly, the priestly concerns with ritual purity are often explicitly understood as efforts to imitate the nature of the angels. Strictly speaking, purity and sacrifice in this perspective are to be understood in light of not so much the notion of *imitatio Dei* as a notion of *imitatio angeli*.

This distinction leads to a question concerning the *meaning* of sacrifice. If the temple represents the cosmos, then sacrifice too can be understood as some form of divine work. But when the earthly temple is seen as an analogue of a heavenly one, earthly sacrifice is seen to correspond to some sort of heavenly worship. This leads, on the one hand, to some curious speculation concerning what in fact is offered in heaven. On the other hand, this correspondence leads away from symbolic understandings of sacrifice, strictly speaking: the ritual does not, in this view, stand for something else but constitutes an earthly analogue to a rather similar activity as carried out in heaven, by the angels.

Despite the differences between these two notions, it is important to emphasize that the notions are not completely incompatible. Nor does the mere presence of the aforementioned prerequisites necessarily lead directly to the notion of a temple in heaven. Philo, as we will see, presents both an emanational theology and a developed angelology, but he does not present us with any visions of a temple in the heavens. Indeed, there are many overlapping aspects of these notions as developed by ancient Jews. In both cases, ritual purity can be understood as a process that allows for a symbolic transformation of a pure person into an angelic or divine-like being. In one instance, the transformation may allow one to participate in and exercise control over the cosmic activity that takes place in the temple. In the other instance, the transformation may permit the person to be admitted, by analogy, to the heavenly sanctuary. Similarly, we will find in both approaches the potential for understanding much of the sacrificial process as imitating God or divine beings. Still, the similarities of these notions do not justify the confusion of them we find all too often in the current literature on the subject.

The Temple as the Cosmos

We embark on our analysis by looking at those writers who emphasize the idea that the temple represents the cosmos. We will first consider the approach taken by Josephus, for his is perhaps the clearest and simplest articulation of these ideas, all the while remaining closest to what we have already seen in the priestly traditions. We then turn to Philo, whose approach when compared to Josephus echoes an even greater number of ideas that we have seen already in the Hebrew bible, but at the same time Philo breaks even more new ground. We will then consider the scanty but tantalizing evidence attesting to the persistence of this notion among Jews living in the rabbinic period and beyond. At that point we will turn back to consider the various sources that articulate the idea that the earthly temple corresponds to the heavenly one.

The Temple as the Cosmos according to Josephus

Perhaps the clearest ancient Jewish articulation of the idea that the temple represents the cosmos is to be found in the writings of Josephus.[11] He alludes to the idea now and again in his *Jewish War,* and he returns to the idea in his *Antiquities.* In his earlier work, Josephus describes the temple in its glory, as a prelude to his telling of its destruction (*JW* 5:184–237; see also 4:324). In his later work, Josephus paraphrases the priestly traditions' accounts of the tabernacle, its sacrificial service, and the purity laws in the context of his paraphrase of the Pentateuch (*Ant.* 3:102–279).[12] In both of these works, the thrust of Josephus' accounts is descriptive: for the most part he tells his readers what the structures looked like, and what the practices were, as he understands them.[13] At certain points, however, Josephus breaks off his dry description with an interpretive discourse. For instance, in his depiction of the temple in *Jewish War,* Josephus attributes cosmic significance to various aspects of the structure. The veil hanging above the temple gate itself symbolizes the universe (5:212–213). The twelve loaves placed on the table symbolize the zodiac and the months, while the *menorah* (i.e., candelabrum) symbolizes the seven planets (5:218).

Josephus presents a more comprehensive treatment of these themes in his *Antiquities,* where he is apparently responding to unspecified calumnies uttered against the temple by those hostile to the Jewish people (3:179; cf. *Against Apion* 2:109–111). He says that the tabernacle and its contents are all designed "to recall and represent the universe" (εἰς ἀπομίμησιν καὶ διατύπωσιν τῶν ὅλων; *Ant.* 3:180). The division of the tabernacle into three realms, two of which are generally approachable, corresponds to the fact that while the land and water are accessible to people, the heavens are not (3:181; cf. 3:123). Turning to the priestly vessels and offerings, Josephus suggests again that the twelve loaves represent the months, while the seven lights of the menorah represent the planets (3:146, 182). Josephus similarly interprets the tabernacle's coverings (3:132) and its decorative tapestries (3:183), as well as the priestly garments (3:183–187).[14]

Josephus is by no means alone in offering these kinds of interpretations, and parallels to many of his symbolic analyses can be identified in the earlier writings of Philo and in the later writings of the rabbis.[15] There seems to have been a particular fascination among ancient Jews with the priestly garb.[16] The Wisdom of Ben Sira (from the early second century B.C.E.) describes Aaron's "perfect splendor" (45:8) and even more carefully describes the high priest Simon's appearance as "like the morning star among the clouds" (50:7).[17] Yet Ben Sira stops short of explicitly ascribing cosmic symbolism to the priestly vestments—the implication, though, is that the garb casts a cosmic appearance.

Similarly, the *Letter of Aristeas*—a work of uncertain date, but probably from the second century B.C.E.—describes the appearance of a high priest Eleazar and claims that one who saw him in his glorious clothing would think he encountered a "man from outside the world" (ὥστε νομίζειν εἰς ἕτερον ἐληλυθέναι ἐκτὸς τοῦ κόσμου; 99).[18] Again, the clothing here does not explicitly represent the universe but serves to cast an otherworldly impression.

We can find a more explicit reference to the cosmic symbolism of the priestly garb in the Wisdom of Solomon (18:24), a work of uncertain date that most certainly is earlier than Josephus.[19] But, as we will see, it is in the works of Philo that we find many similar—and some practically identical—cosmic interpretations of various aspects of the temple, and not just the priestly garb. Yet, as we will also see, Philo's approach is different enough that we have reason to assume that Josephus did not draw his interpretations directly from Philo.[20] We will also see that similar (and again in some cases identical) interpretations were offered in rabbinic literature—and there is little cause to believe that rabbinic authorities were directly familiar with either Philo or Josephus. Thus what Josephus tells us about temple symbolism may reflect some common understandings in his day.

It is also important to emphasize here that Josephus' approach accords with what many scholars believe to be the general symbolic understandings of temples in the ancient Near Eastern world, ancient Israel included.[21] We have already noted the general ancient Near Eastern idea of the temple representing the cosmos—a notion that many biblicists find to be reflected in the accounts of the wilderness tabernacle, the Solomonic temple, and even the Garden of Eden narratives.[22] Josephus' explicit testimony in this regard can then be seen on some level as tentative support for these approaches. Working from the other direction, these scholarly approaches to the biblical sources lend credence to the idea that Josephus' work in this regard is not creative but conservative. It is hardly likely that Josephus created anew among Jews an analogy that is well attested in ancient Near Eastern literature.

We also noted, in chapter 2, that the idea of the temple as cosmos is itself related to the all-important notion of *imitatio Dei*. Just as God creates the world, so too people create the earthly symbol of that world, the temple—an analogy implied by parallels between the language and structure of the creation and tabernacle-construction narratives.[23] While Josephus does not to my knowledge directly connect all these themes together, it is interesting and important to note that Josephus emphasizes *imitatio Dei* as *the* overall motivation and justification for Jewish religious practices (*Ant.* 1:23–24):

> Our legislator, on the contrary, having shown that God possesses the
> very perfection of virtue, thought that men should strive to participate
> in it, and inexorably punished those who did not hold with or
> believe in these doctrines. I therefore entreat my readers to examine
> my work from this point of view. For studying it in this spirit,
> nothing will appear to them unreasonable, nothing incongruous with
> the majesty of God and His love for humanity; everything, indeed,

is here set forth in keeping with the nature of the universe (τῇ τῶν ὅλων φύσει σύμφωνον).[24]

The juxtaposition of cosmic significance with *imitatio Dei* could possibly also represent an aspect of Josephus' work that is more conservative than creative.

Josephus in at least one other way implies that sacrificial practice—or at least part of the process—is to be understood as *imitatio Dei*. As noted above, the historian suggests that just as heaven is closed off to people, so too is a portion of the earthly temple closed off to all but priests (*Ant.* 3:181). Indeed, Josephus emphasizes the relative sanctity of the priests, and notes on more than one occasion the role of the ritual purity laws in establishing that higher level of sanctity (*Ant.* 3:258, 276). What is left unclear in Josephus' works is whether this sanctity can itself be understood in light of the notion of *imitatio Dei*—as I argued with regard to the biblical traditions—or whether Josephus would have seen priests as angels, as we will see in other Jewish works of Josephus' day.[25]

We can identify yet another aspect of Josephus' treatment of these matters that accords with the general approach running through scripture and ancient Jewish literature. First, Josephus says quite clearly in his biblical paraphrase that when the Israelites construct their model of the universe, God demonstrates approval by taking residence there (*Ant.* 3:202–203; cf. Exod. 40: 33–34).[26] But—again, as in the priestly traditions—Josephus does not view God's presence in the sanctuary as Israel's irrevocable prerogative. Throughout *Jewish War*, Josephus takes a particular interest in describing gory events taking place in or near the temple (e.g., 4:151, 313), and he says explicitly that the city and temple were desecrated by this Jewish-instigated bloodshed (2:455; 4:150).[27] The historian—here speaking more like a prophet[28]—also says quite clearly that God departed from the sanctuary (5:412; 6:300; cf. *Ant.* 20:166), a reality that reflects the deity's disgust with the people's behavior (*JW* 2:539; 5:19; 7:328).[29] Here too we see further aspects of Josephus' theologizing that are deeply rooted in biblical traditions as we have already understood them.

The Cosmic Temple and the Logos-Priest according to Philo

The well-known philosopher Philo of Alexandria, of the early first century C.E., treats both purity and sacrifice now and again throughout his works.[30] There are, however, a number of his treatises that present sustained explanations of these matters, including especially the second book of his *Life of Moses* (esp. 71–160) and the first book of his *Special Laws*.[31] Philo's approach to our themes is remarkable for a number of reasons. First and foremost, we will find in Philo knowledge of and interest in both of the themes explored in chapter 2: in his own way, Philo understands the sacrificial process as imitating the divine, and as playing a role in maintaining a holy presence on earth. Second, Philo exhibits a broad interest in the details of the sacrificial process, beginning with ritual (and moral) purification. Indeed, Philo consistently views both ritual and moral purity (and he clearly distinguishes between these ideas) as prerequisites to sacrifice, and his overall interpretive scheme applies, at least in part, to purification and sacrifice. Thus, preceding Hubert and Mauss by nineteen hundred years, Philo may well present the first truly integrated interpretation of the entire sacrificial process, beginning with ritual and moral purification.

Philo's works are also significant for our purposes because his approach to ritual is extremely sympathetic: he is open to and fascinated by symbolic understandings of priestly rites. As is well known, Philo is wont to entertain rather fantastic, allegorical, interpretations of many biblical themes.[32] Yet Philo's interpretations of ritual are not exclusively allegorical, nor are they entirely symbolic in any narrow sense. He does not let his allegorical interpretations lead to any rejection of sacrifices on the literal, performative level.[33] Indeed, Philo made pilgrimage to the temple on at least one occasion (*On Providence* frag. 2, 64). Thus his approach to purity and sacrifice can be rather practical too. When explaining, for instance, the reasons why there are no trees within the temple complex (*Spec. Laws* 1:74–75; cf. Deut. 16:21),[34] Philo presents a number of justifications that are not really symbolic but rather "functionalist," or even simply practical. Philo suggests that the pleasure trees provide is incompatible with the "sacred austerity" of the temple. Second, Philo points out that vegetation requires fertilization—which comes from excrement—and bringing such substance into the sanctuary would be most unseemly. Third, plants are either of no use (producing no fruit) or a potential source for distraction for those who would seek their fruit. Fourth, the presence of much growth would give opportunities to thieves and others to hide from unsuspecting victims. Finally, Philo points out that the absence of trees allows all who visit an unobstructed view. These explanations, while typically Philonic, are hardly allegorical. Yet, as we will see, Philo approaches many other aspects of the sacrificial process in a more symbolic manner. On the whole, therefore, Philo's approach to our concerns involves an interplay of practical and symbolic explanations.

For all these reasons, those interested in the meanings ascribed by ancient Jews to sacrificial rituals would do well to pay due attention to Philo's works. Yet the question then arises: is what we find in Philo characteristic of ancient Judaism in general or uniquely his own? Or, as Erwin Goodenough famously argued, is Philo representative of a thoroughly Hellenized Judaism that is generally unknown from other literature but in evidence particularly in the archaeological record?[35] In response partially to Goodenough's provocative theses, a number of (especially Jewish) scholars endeavored to demonstrate that Philo's theology and practice were largely commensurate with what we find in rabbinic literature.[36] Going one step further in a slightly different direction, Isaac Baer tried to identify within Philo's works evidence for the antiquity of the theurgic approach to sacrifice taken by medieval Jewish mystics.[37] It has even been argued that what we find in Philo represents the reemergence of ancient royal cultic ideologies.[38] The true state of affairs is probably more complicated than any single one of these approaches. In some respects Philo's works appear idiosyncratic, but in others he may well present ideas that were known to—and in some cases even expressed by—other ancient Jews.[39] We should therefore proceed with the willingness to identify within Philo's works both reflections of notions one can find elsewhere, and the expression of ideas that are possibly unparalleled.

Prominent among Philo's multifarious interpretations of cultic rites is the notion that many aspects of the temple's ritual and structure are to be understood as representing elements of the cosmos.[40] Philo, tellingly, emphasizes this point when he introduces his most detailed and sustained discussion of sacrificial matters in the first book of *Special Laws* (1:66–67):

> The highest, and in the truest sense the holy, temple of God is, as we must believe, the whole universe, having for its sanctuary the most sacred part of all existence, (namely) heaven; for its offerings, the stars; for its priests, the angels who administer His powers as unbodied souls, not compounds of rational and irrational nature, as ours are, but with the irrational eliminated, all mind through and through, pure intelligences, in the likeness of the One. There is also the temple made by hands; for it was right that no check should be given to the forwardness of those who pay their tribute to piety and desire by means of sacrifices either to give thanks for the blessings that befall them or ask pardon and forgiveness for sins.[41]

This passage is characteristically dualistic, even allegorical. Yet it is not without its practical concerns: Philo recognizes general human motivations for sacrifice (thanksgiving and forgiveness), and the latter obviously has no exact analogue in the cosmic realm.

Philo supports his general thesis by arguing that various aspects of the temple's structure, decoration, and furniture are to be explained as representing parts of the cosmos. In *Special Laws*, Philo turns first to the priestly garb, which itself symbolizes the universe (1:82–97).[42] Philo also ascribes cosmic significance to the twelve loaves (1:172) and elsewhere claims that the incense burned in the inner altar represents the four elements (*Who Is the Heir* 196–197). In one place, he even interprets the qualities of the animals offered for sacrifice in light of the cosmic elements they represent (*QA Gen.* 3:3; but see *Spec. Laws* 1:162–165). In his treatment of the tabernacle in *Life of Moses*, Philo similarly points out the cosmic significance of a number of sacred items. While Philo entertains the idea that the two cherubim symbolize the two hemispheres surrounding the earth (*Moses* 2:98), he prefers to explain these as representing the creative and kingly aspects of the divine (2:99). The altar and menorah are, however, explained cosmically, with the former representing the earth and water in their central location, and the latter representing the seven luminaries (2:101–103). Again, the priestly garb is analyzed in detail, with cosmic symbolism as the main feature (2:109–135). Philo presents a similar set of interpretations of cultic matters in *Questions and Answers on Exodus*, particularly from 2:51 through 2:124, which treats Exodus 25:7–28:38.[43] Again, the cosmic symbolism of priestly garb figures prominently in the extant portions of the work (2:107–124), though the symbolisms of the menorah (2:73–81), veil (2:91–93), and other items are also noted.[44]

While for Philo the entire temple symbolizes the cosmos, it is also appropriate for the high priest himself to wear a garment symbolizing the cosmos.[45] It reminds the priest to remain worthy of the world for which he offers sacrifice, and to have the world with him as he does so (*Spec. Laws* 1:96). Philo also suggests that the cosmic symbolism has a universalistic significance: the priest is to offer prayer and sacrifice on behalf of the entire world (1:97; cf. 2:163–167; *Moses* 2:134–135).[46] Philo adds that by wearing the world, the priest also transforms himself from human nature into cosmic nature— indeed, the priest himself becomes a small world (*Moses* 2:135). In Philo's cosmic allegory quoted above (*Spec. Laws* 1:66–67), the role played by the angels in heaven is played by the priests on earth. This approach is found not only in Philo but also in other ancient Jewish literature, as we will see. This idea cannot be found—at least not explicitly—in the priestly traditions of the Pentateuch, where angelology and other beliefs in intermediary figures are downplayed (except, of course, for the idea of the divine presence). There are hints even in the Pentateuch that ancient Israelites believed in such figures (e.g., *Gen.* 6:1–4), but the priestly traditions focus on the need to establish a sanctuary in which the worship of God by people imitating God's nature will attract the divine presence to dwell among them. The cosmic symbolism is implied but not generally spelled out. In the later literature, such as Philo and Josephus—as well as in earlier ancient Near Eastern texts—we find that the cosmic symbolism becomes overt. It is with explicit cosmic symbolism (as opposed to what remains implicit in the Hebrew Bible) that we find room for what Philo believes: the idea that the role of the priests on earth is analogous to the role of angels in heaven.

While the conceptual transformation involved in this development should not be underestimated, it is also important to appreciate that the desire and willingness to see priests as earthly counterparts to the angels involves by necessity the willingness to recognize divine behavior within priestly rituals and roles. As Philo himself says:

> [the high priest is] endowed with a nature higher than the merely human and to approximate the Divine, on the borderline, we may truly say, between the two, that people may have a mediator through whom they may propitiate God and God a subordinate to employ in extending the abundance of his boons to men. (*Spec. Laws* 1:116; cf. *On Dreams* 2:185–189)

In other words, the understanding of priests as analogous to angels also exhibits certain significant continuities with the biblical understanding of sacrifice as *imitatio Dei*.

For Philo, a number of priestly restrictions are understood in this light. We can begin by noting the regulations limiting the priests and prohibiting the high priests from mourning (Lev. 21:1–3, 10–11): Philo's statement quoted above relates to these rules in particular. Priestly perfection is also manifest in the marriage restrictions (Lev. 21:7–8, 13–15; *Spec. Laws* 1:102; *On Dreams* 2:185) and in the laws concerning priests with physical deformities (*Spec. Laws* 1:80–81, 117–118). For Philo, priestly holiness exemplifies the general endeavor to emulate the divine, a desire that comes naturally to people (*The Sacrifices of Abel and Cain* 68). Thus while the laws he describes apply especially to priests—and particularly to the high priest—all people in their own way are to emulate this priestly purity when they approach the sanctuary to worship (*Spec. Laws* 2:163–164). By doing so, the entire nation becomes more priestly, and by extension, more divine-like.

Various aspects of the sacrificial process are understood by Philo in this light. He says a number of times that anyone who offers sacrifice must be pure in both body and mind (*Spec. Laws* 1:256): "the law would have such a person pure in body and soul, the soul purged of its passions and distempers and infirmities and every viciousness of word and deed, the body of the defilements which commonly beset it." With regard to bodily purity, Philo recognizes that the sources of ritual defilement are natural and unavoidable (*Spec. Laws* 1:119, 257). Philo takes a particular interest in the defilement resulting from contact with the dead, noting that when the soul departs the body, the corpse that remains is now deprived of the divine image (3:207). Philo also suggests that the purificatory procedures—which, in the case of corpse impurity, involve water and ash—serve to remind the person who would worship to remember what substances the body is composed of (1:261–266; but cf. *On Dreams* 1:81–84). Thus, to avoid ritual defilement is to shun what is natural but ungodly; the maintenance of ritual purity involves recognizing and confronting the difference between persons and God.

The worshiper, however, must be pure with respect to not just the body but also the soul. Philo consistently and explicitly views both ritual and moral purity as prerequisites for the sacrificial process.[47] Of course, compared to the body, it is the soul that represents the most divine aspect of the person (*Spec. Laws* 1:269). The various (bodily) ritual purity laws are therefore to be explained by virtue of the fact that the purity of the body is analogous to and represents what is more important, the innocence of the soul (1:258).[48] Conversely, ritual impurity represents transgression (1:209; cf. *Unchangeableness of God* 131–137). It stands to reason, therefore, that the sacrifices offered by sinful people are unacceptable to God (*Spec. Laws* 1:270–272, 281; *Moses* 2:107–108), and individual sinners are to be barred from the sanctuary (*Spec. Laws* 1:159, 270, 324–325; 3:89).[49] Some sacrificial procedures are also understood as symbolizing the importance of worshiping in innocence. Philo compares the priestly examination of the sacrificial animal to the person's examination of his own soul (1:260), and he even interprets the rite of laying a hand upon the sacrificial animal as testifying to the offerer's innocence (*Spec. Laws* 1:202–204).[50]

Philo in this respect forges a synthesis between the prophetic and priestly traditions—but it's a synthesis that, like much else in Philo, contains some idiosyncratic elements.[51] We have already noted that the prophetic literature and priestly traditions agree on the fact that the performance of grave sin can (morally but not ritually) defile the sinner, the land, and the sanctuary. Philo seems familiar with the biblical notion of moral defilement (especially but not exclusively in *Spec. Laws* 1:257–272). But the philosopher's approach is not in all ways typical.[52] Instead of focusing on the impact moral defilement may have on the land and sanctuary (as in the priestly and prophetic traditions), Philo's central concern is on the effect moral defilement may on the individual sinner's soul. Thus an issue of communal concern becomes an issue of individual concern. Moreover, the explicit ban on sinners in the sanctuary— the inevitable result of Philo's approach—is not known from either rabbinic literature or Josephus.[53] Indeed, it is quite difficult to imagine how such a ban could have been enforced, if it ever existed apart from Philo's wishes. At any rate, it remains to state the obvious: for Philo, both bodily and moral perfection are preliminaries for sacrifice, and both make the person—priest or layperson—more divine.

But it is not just the preliminaries to sacrifice that are understood by Philo as aspects of a divinization (albeit a qualified one). A number of sacrificial behaviors themselves are also understood by him as actions that emulate the divine. Philo notes that just as those who offer sacrifices must be pure and whole, so too the animals brought for sacrifice must be free of blemishes (*Spec. Laws* 1:166). The priests, therefore, carefully examine the offering's physical state, just as they inquire of the offerer's moral state; all this to express symbolically that God sees all, and will turn away from any improper offering (166–167). Philo also suggests that the division and dissection of the animal represents God's own ability to divide into powers and potencies (209). Philo elsewhere emphasizes—when discussing Abraham's cutting various animals into two parts (Gen. 15:10)—that God alone has the capacity to divide things perfectly evenly (*Who Is the Heir* 130, 141–142). Sacrificial cutting is an attempt, therefore, to emulate an activity that only God does perfectly. Finally, the requirement to maintain an everlasting flame is understood as emulating God's permanence (1:285). Indeed the sanctuary's fire is no mere human flame but a divine one, of incorruptible nature (*Moses* 2:158).[54]

To be sure, Philo does not attempt to explain all aspects of the sacrificial process in light of the concern to imitate the divine. We have already noted that he understands the laying of hands as a statement of innocence (1:203). He also understands the washings of the animal's belly as a cleansing of lust, and the washing of the feet as representing the soul's ability to leap from earth to heaven (1:206–207; cf. *On the Migration of Abraham* 67). Philo identifies various other layers of symbolism in the choice of animals selected for sacrifice (1:162–165) and in the choice of which limbs and organs are designated for the priest or the altar (1:145–151). But the existence of these other symbolisms does not mitigate the fact that for Philo—just as in the priestly traditions—one important symbolic aspect of sacrificial practice is *imitatio Dei*.

Philo's approach is not just in continuity with the priestly traditions but also on some level in tension with it, for this philosopher makes frequent and explicit reference to the roles of mediator figures. Those offering sacrifice—and especially those who officiate—do become more divine in the process, but in truth they become more like God's angels or subordinates than they become like God. For Philo, this is particularly true of the way he conceives of the high priest. We have already noted how, for Philo, the high priest becomes—through various ritual restrictions, and by being adorned in his own special way—particularly close to the divine. He becomes God's mediating servant (*Spec. Laws* 1:114–116) and even his own microcosmos (*Moses* 2:135). In this respect, Philo builds on and develops an attitude that appears in Ben Sira and *Aristeas*: the idea that the high priest has an extraworldly nature and appearance (Ben Sira 45:8–12, 50:5–11; *Aristeas* 96–99). More characteristically Philonic is the view that the high priest is the Logos (*On Dreams* 1:215; *On the Migration of Abraham* 102).[55] Again, we find that Philo specifically—and the other sources mentioned more generally—exists in constructive tension with the earlier priestly traditions of the Pentateuch. The priestly understanding of sacrificial activity as *imitatio Dei* is continued and developed in these notions of *imitatio angeli*.

These ancient Jewish interests in angels and divine potencies also exist in some tension with the earlier priestly concerns to maintain the divine presence within the sanctuary. Philo says quite clearly that it is not God himself who dwells in the sanctuary but an "image of divine excellence" (*Who is the Heir* 112–113). Of course, to whatever degree the high priest represents—or in fact *is*—the Logos, here too we find an interest in a divine entity dwelling in the sanctuary. This is not the place to consider the general controversies surrounding the nature and origins of Philo's understanding of the Logos.[56] But we must consider the degree to which Philo's statements regarding the Logos in the temple reflect earlier understandings of God's presence within the sanctuary.

While the priestly traditions in the Pentateuch speak of God's presence dwelling in the sanctuary, the Deuteronomic traditions tend to emphasize the dwelling of God's *name* in the sanctuary (e.g., Deut. 12:5, 11). Whether this difference is simply semantic or expressive of some significant theological dispute remains unclear. Some scholars emphasize the difference between priestly and Deuteronomic traditions on this point (usually positing also a linear development).[57] One commentator, for example, says: "by speaking instead of God's *name* as dwelling in the chosen place, Deuteronomy seeks to correct the impression that God Himself literally dwells there: only His name 'dwells' there, whereas God Himself is in Heaven."[58]

Yet there is reason to wonder whether the difference between the priestly and Deuteronomic traditions is really all that great, or even drawn so neatly. Certainly the Deuteronomistic tradition—in evidence most famously in 1 Kings 8:27—maintains that God's real dwelling is in heaven (cf. Deut. 26:15).[59] But Deuteronomy itself still speaks of the altar as "before the Lord" (e.g., 12:7, 27:7).[60] Other texts, too, seem to use the referents interchangeably (e.g., Jer. 7:7, 12).[61] On the other hand, we find in the priestly tradition references to God's "glory" dwelling among the people (Exod. 40:34), with the implication that God may be elsewhere too.[62] Certainly it is highly unlikely that the priestly tradition thought that God dwelled *only* or *exclusively* in the sanctuary. As we have seen, regardless of what the priestly traditions say about God dwelling in the sanctuary, what the priestly strands depict—and depict more than once—is a fiery presence *coming down from heaven* (Exod. 24:17; Lev. 9:24, etc.). At the most we find separating the two strands a shift in emphasis and differing concerns with proper expression—but not a hard-and-fast distinction between a concrete theology (in P) and an abstract one (in D). Indeed, until we know better what it means for God's name—or is it God's *Name*?—to dwell anywhere, we shouldn't draw too sharp of a contrast between these two strains of Israelite tradition.

The significance for all this for our purposes is the possibility that Philo's concept of the Logos dwelling in the sanctuary may not be all that different in essence from earlier understandings of God's name, glory, or presence dwelling there. Of course, Philo's expression is decidedly Hellenistic—and perhaps distinctly Philonic in its particular complexity. But even when he depicts the Logos dwelling in the temple, Philo may be presenting a sacrificial ideology that is representative of broader streams of the Jewish tradition.[63]

Philo's approach to purity, sacrifice, and the temple is truly remarkable. His approach is integrated, sympathetic, and symbolic. Moreover, his approach exhibits a number of continuities with earlier ancient Jewish and even Israelite traditions. And this is particularly fortunate for us, since he also presents us with the most sustained and sophisticated analysis of purity and sacrifice in ancient Jewish literature. Philo sees ritual (and moral) purification as part of a process of divinization that leads to the sacrificial encounter with God's earthly presence. Jean Laporte has suggested that while Philo's approach to purity is typically Jewish, his approach to sacrifice is not.[64] This may be true of the sacrificial themes Laporte focuses on. But when we consider the themes that Philo uses to connect purity and sacrifice together—in particular his modification of *imitatio Dei*—we find that Philo's approach accords well with earlier views. In short, while many of his expressions are deeply Hellenistic, and aspects of his approach are probably idiosyncratic, Philo may well help us understand better one of the dominant symbolic approaches to these matters in ancient Judaism: the idea that the temple represents the cosmos, and the priests serve as its angelic caretakers.

The Cosmic Temple in Rabbinic and Medieval Judaism

Tracing echoes of these notions in subsequent Jewish literature is a complicated process. Indeed, tracing practically *any* nonlegal matter in rabbinic sources can be most difficult, for while the legal sources are (relatively) well organized—reaping the benefits of having been systematically studied in the medieval and early modern ages—the realm of nonlegal *aggadic* sources is both rather chaotic in its nature and less well studied.[65] As a result, the contemporary scholar is left all to often to rely on inadequate printed editions that are either difficult to find or cumbersome to use or both. Scholarship can benefit in general from the two prodigious attempts at synthesizing aggadic materials—Louis Ginzberg's *Legends of the Jews* and H. N. Bialik and Y. H. Ravnitzky's *Sefer Ha-Aggadah*—but, alas, neither treats the themes that interest us in any great detail.[66] Indeed, while there are some thorough thematic surveys tracing the idea of a temple *in* the cosmos in rabbinic literature,[67] there are precious few studies devoted to tracing the idea of the temple as representing the cosmos in rabbinic literature.[68] Nonetheless, we can say a few things about the persistence of these ideas in Jewish literature beyond the time of Josephus and Philo.

A number of rabbinic traditions speak quite generally about the cosmic significance of the temple. In some sources, the city of Jerusalem and its sanctuary are referred to as the "navel of the earth" (טבור הארץ; cf. Ezek. 38:12),[69] a metaphor that emphasizes not only the temple's centrality but also its function as the point of connection between the created world below and the creator above.[70] A number of sources also speak of the "foundation stone" (אבן שתיה)—a rock located within the temple's inner courts that, according to tradition, was the keystone from which the entire world was formed.[71] Indeed, some sources refer to both concepts (e.g., *Tanhuma Qedoshim* 10 [ed. Buber 39b]):

> Just as the navel is in the center of a person, so the land of Israel is
> the navel of the earth, as it is said, "those who live at the navel[72] of the
> earth" (Ezek. 38:12). . . . The land of Israel sits in the center of the
> world, Jerusalem in the center of the land of Israel, the temple in
> the center of Jerusalem, the sanctuary in the center of the temple, the
> ark in the center of the sanctuary, and the foundation stone—from
> which the world was formed—sits in front of the sanctuary.

These traditions—while important for understanding the cosmic significance ascribed to the temple in the rabbinic period—stop short of claiming that the temple *symbolizes* the cosmos, and therefore they are not directly parallel to or dependent upon the traditions preserved by Philo and Josephus surveyed earlier.

We noted in chapter 2 that a homology between the creation of the world and the building of the tabernacle is implied in biblical narrative, though no explicit statement to this effect can be found in scripture. Various rabbinic traditions notice and develop the analogy. For instance, one tradition preserved in both *Midrash Tanhuma Pequday* 2 (in traditional editions only) and *Numbers Rabbah* 12:13 presents an extended comparison of the seven-day creation of the earth with the process of building the tabernacle, because the tabernacle is parallel to the world.[73] Other traditions similarly compare the creation of the world with the building of the tabernacle, or view the creation of the world as completed by the construction of the tabernacle, all to the effect of emphasizing in only a rather general way the cosmic significance of

Israel's holy place of worship.[74] Very few rabbinic sources take this analogy one step further, identifying the specific points of comparison between the cosmos and the sacred precincts. Nonetheless, we find a few rabbinic sources that interpret one or another of the tabernacle's (or temple's) features as symbolic of an aspect of the universe. For instance, the menorah, with its seven branches, is once again compared to the planets (*Num. Rabbah* 15:7; *Targum Pseudo-Jonathan* to Exod. 39:37); the temple's marble appears to look like water (b. *Sukkah* 51b; see also b. *Hagigah* 14b), and the tabernacle's golden hooks (Exod. 26:6) are remembered as resembling the stars (*Exod. Rabbah* 35:6; *Num. Rabbah* 12:8; *Song Rabbah* 3:25 [to *Song* 3:11], and *Pesikta de-Rab Kahana* 1:3 [ed. Mandelbaum 7–8]).[75] For the most part, however, the developed temple-as-cosmos analogy that we find in Josephus and Philo (and in the literature of the ancient Near East) seems unknown in later rabbinic sources.

But there is one striking exception. One curious midrashic work—of unknown date or provenance—contains within it a fully developed symbolic analysis of the tabernacle's structure, remarkably reminiscent of Josephus and Philo. This work is known as *Midrash Tadshe* (i.e., Midrash "Sprout") for its opening exegesis of Genesis 1:11. The work is traditionally attributed to a tannaitic figure named Phineas ben Yair, who is remembered for his stringent piety and ascetic behavior (e.g., m. *Sotah* 9:15; b. *Hullin* 7a–b; *Gen. Rabbah* 60:8). *Midrash Tadshe* says explicitly that the tabernacle represents the universe. Moreover, the thesis is developed fully: the holy of holies is compared to the heavens, the inner court to the earth, the courtyard to the sea, the twelve oxen (1 Kgs. 7:25) to the zodiac, and so forth (*Tadshe* 2).[76] A subsequent passage (*Tadshe* 11) also develops the symbolism of the menorah as compared to the seven planets.

The antiquity of the work as we have it, let alone its attribution to Phineas ben Yair, is extremely doubtful. Certain aspects of the work betray familiarity with medieval Jewish mysticism—for instance, *Tadshe* 2 compares a measurement of ten cubits with the ten *sephirot* (divine emanations) known from *Sefer Yetzirah* and other medieval mystical texts.[77] Indeed, in the late nineteenth century, Abraham Epstein attributed the work as we have it to the eleventh-century mystic and exegete Moshe ha-Darshan.[78] Yet as Epstein also demonstrated, the work draws on various older traditions, and it seems certain that at least some passages are based closely upon traditions also preserved in *Jubilees*. For instance, *Tadshe* 6 notes that the twenty-two generations from Adam to Jacob correspond to the same number of species created by God in the first six days (see *Jub.* 2:23). *Tadshe* 8—which relates the days of the months on which Jacob's sons were born—bears a striking, but inexact, resemblance to traditions also preserved in *Jubilees* 28:11–24.[79] To explain these correspondences without positing the antiquity of *Midrash Tadshe*, Epstein suggested—implausibly, but not impossibly—that various rabbinic authorities continued to have access to the book of *Jubilees*, in its original Hebrew, well into the Middle Ages.[80] Where Epstein recognized parallels between *Midrash Tadshe* and Philo as well, he posited that Phineas ben Yair edited an expanded edition of *Jubilees*, based in part on Philo's works. Moshe ha-Darshan, in turn, based *Midrash Tadshe* on this expanded edition of *Jubilees*.[81]

It was nearly sixty years before *Midrash Tadshe* was thoroughly reexamined by Samuel Belkin.[82] Belkin was willing to accept that Moshe ha-Darshan was responsible for *Midrash Tadshe* as we have it, but he was unwilling to accept Epstein's hypotheses concerning a medieval Hebrew expanded edition of *Jubilees*. Belkin—who authored various monographs on Philo—was not one to shortchange the parallels between Philo and *Midrash Tadshe*. Indeed, as Belkin's thorough review demonstrates, the Midrash exhibits many more parallels with Philo than with *Jubilees*. For instance, the very first lines of the work—which question why the heavenly bodies were not created until the fourth day—bears striking resemblance to Philo's *On the Creation* 45. Of course, as we have noted, the Midrash's symbolic treatment of the tabernacle parallels Philo much more than *Jubilees*. Yet Belkin did not believe that Philo was read by Jews in the Middle Ages. Instead, Belkin proposed that the parallels between Philo and *Midrash Tadshe*—such as those dealing with the symbolism of the tabernacle—are to be explained by the fact that both are based on a common tradition of allegorical midrash that dates back to the Hellenistic period.[83]

More recently, it has been noted that a number of passages from *Midrash Tadshe*—including those positing a correspondence between the tabernacle and the cosmos—appear in a curious Byzantine work, *The Christian Topography of Cosmas*. Was this medieval Christian work known to the author of *Midrash Tadshe*?[84] In a response to this suggestion, it has been noted that the correspondence between the tabernacle and the cosmos is also articulated in early medieval Jewish liturgical poetry, including especially a *piyyut* attributed to Eliezer b. Kallir.[85] And so the transmission history behind *Midrash Tadshe* remains unclear. Perhaps the author of *Tadshe* knew of such *piyyutim*; perhaps he had access to the *Christian Topography*; or perhaps all three of these texts testify to a greater medieval Jewish and Christian interest in the cosmos-tabernacle analogy.

Unfortunately, *Midrash Tadshe* has not been well studied of late, and the questions pertaining to this text's date and provenance remain unanswered. But in a way, we can reach the same general conclusion regardless of how these questions are resolved. If indeed *Midrash Tadshe* (or, what is more likely, just certain parts of it) should prove to be of genuine early rabbinic provenance, then we could demonstrate that *some* rabbis continued to reflect on the temple as cosmos symbolism that we also know of from Josephus and Philo. On the other hand, if *Midrash Tadshe* were proven to be entirely medieval in origin, then we would be faced with the question of explaining medieval Jewish knowledge of specific textual traditions that can be traced back to Philo and *Jubilees*.[86] In this case, we might then be forced to reach practically the same conclusion that we would have to reach if the antiquity of *Midrash Tadshe* were proven: at least *some* ancient Jewish authorities in the rabbinic period continued to reflect on and transmit traditions concerning the tabernacle's cosmic symbolism.

One final realm of evidence may well testify to the significance of the temple-as-cosmos notion in the memory of Jews living in the rabbinic era. Tourists, students, and even scholars are often baffled when confronted with the image of a zodiac on the mosaic floors of ancient Jewish synagogues.[87] Pictorial depictions of the zodiac have been uncovered in least six synagogues from the Byzantine period: Beth Alpha, Hammath-Tiberias, Huseifa, Na'aran, Sepphoris, and Khirbet Susiya.[88] In addition to these, an aniconic listing of the zodiac signs appears on the mosaic floor of the Ein Gedi synagogue. For our purposes, what is striking about these mosaics is that—without exception—they also display an interest in temple imagery. At Beth Alpha, Hammath-Tiberias, and Na'aran, the zodiac panels are placed directly below an image of the ark flanked by two menorahs. At Sepphoris, the zodiac also appears below an ark flanked by two menorahs, but there are other scenes depicting sacrificial practices between the ark panel and the zodiac panel. But even on the other floors, the menorahs are never too far away from the zodiac. What to make of this juxtaposition?

It is certainly possible that that the zodiac images symbolize the calendar or even serve to aid the communities in their determination of seasons and times.[89] Problematic for this theory is the often-noted fact that a number of these mosaic floors are misaligned:[90] the corner panels depicting the four seasons are not placed alongside the corresponding months, except at Hammath-Tiberias and Sepphoris. Moreover, this theory fails to explain adequately the consistent appearance of specific astral symbols, including Helios, in the center of the zodiacs: there's no practical purpose for *this* image. A number of church mosaics—including the nearby and contemporary monastery of Kyria Maria at Beth-Shean—depict the zodiac as a series of seasonal labors, and again there is little reason to discern a practical purpose here.[91] Perhaps, therefore, the calculation of time is not the only impetus behind these mosaics. It has also been suggested that for some of these mosaics, the menorah-flanked ark may represent the holy of holies, while the zodiac may represent the hall of the sanctuary in which the twelve loaves were placed, alongside many other items interpreted cosmically by Philo, Josephus, and others.[92] Without necessarily endorsing the latter proposal in all its intricacy, it certainly remains quite possible that there is some connection between the juxtaposition of the temple and zodiac images on temple floors and the understanding of the temple as representing the cosmos. Indeed, virtually all sources (even *Midrash Tadshe* 2) that understand the temple as representing the cosmos find some correspondence between one of the temple's twelves and the zodiac. Thus, considering all that we have reviewed in this chapter, it is possible that the frequent juxtaposition of zodiac and temple imagery demonstrates the continued familiarity with and belief in the notion expressed centuries earlier by Philo and Josephus: the temple represents the cosmos.

In the final analysis, the evidence from *Midrash Tadshe*, the synagogue floors, and other miscellaneous literary sources certainly suggests that some Jews continued to understand the temple (or tabernacle) as representing the universe, well into and beyond the rabbinic period. At the same time, we must remain cautious, for the bulk of rabbinic traditions concerning the tabernacle or the temple are either unfamiliar with or unconcerned with this cosmic symbolism. The rabbinic sources, as I will soon show, are much more concerned with a different symbolic approach to the temple: that the earthly one corresponds to and represents the temple in heaven.

A Temple in Heaven

The idea that the earthly temple represents the cosmos is not the only way ancient Jews conceived of a temple-centered correspondence between heaven and earth. The other way this connection was understood was by positing that the earthly temple correlates to a heavenly one. According to this perspective, the earthly temple represents not the entire cosmos, but only part of it: God's heavenly dwelling. And the priestly, sacrificial worship on earth is understood to correspond to and in some way emulate the angelic praise of God in the heavens. A number of texts testify to this idea, including various sources from the Pseudepigrapha, the Dead Sea Scrolls, and rabbinic literature. 1 Enoch and the Testament of Levi each describe the vision of a heavenly temple as seen by an earth-born visionary during an ascent to heaven.[93] The idea of a temple in heaven also runs through the Songs of the Sabbath Sacrifice, a work known from fragmentary manuscripts uncovered at Qumran and Masada. While this work does not describe a heavenly journey per se, it does describe in detail the ways the angels worship God in the heavenly temple. Among rabbinic literature, we find scattered references to heavenly sanctuaries in various midrashic and talmudic sources. In addition, the notion permeates the mystical Hekhalot texts. Unfortunately, however, the current understanding of the nature and history of the heavenly temple idea is rather limited. Again, contributing to the problem is the fact that much of the scholarly literature on this notion is imprecise.

In fact, ancient Jewish literature knows of two distinct ways temples of one sort or another are conceived or seen in heaven. The manner that is of significance here is when those on earth imagine the ways in which the angels worship God in a heavenly temple (we will survey the key examples below). But in a number of instances, ancient Jewish literature imagines a seer taken to heaven to be shown there models or images of the temple, in order to illustrate the way the temple is to be constructed on earth (e.g., 2 Baruch 4:5; Philo, Life of Moses 2:74–76; Pseudo-Philo, Biblical Antiquities 11:15; cf. Wisd. Sol. 9:8). These sources and others like them constitute a tradition elaborating on tantalizingly vague biblical passages such as Exodus 25:9, which says that Moses was shown in heaven an image or a model (תבנית) of the sanctuary he was to build on earth (see also Exod. 25:40, 26:30, 27:8). Scriptural tradition also indicates that David was somehow privy to such knowledge, which he passed to his son Solomon, in writing (1 Chron. 28:11–20). Finally, the most important scriptural tradition regarding a heavenly image of an earthly temple is surely Ezekiel's elaborate vision of the future temple (Ezek. 40–48, discussed in chapter 3).

Over time, a corollary version of this kind of tradition developed. By combination of the accounts concerning Moses' vision of the tabernacle's patterns with Ezekiel's vision of the future temple, a set of traditions emerged that imagined that a glorious new temple was in heaven, ready and waiting to descend to earth at the end of days, and able to be seen by those visionaries who ascend to heaven (e.g., *1 Enoch* 90:28–37; 2 Baruch 4:1–6; 2 Esdras 10: 25–28; cf. the *Temple Scroll* XXIX:9–10 and *The New Jerusalem* texts from Qumran).[94] These sources, too, reflect the idea that God may choose to show a prophet a heavenly model of a temple that is meant to exist on earth. This is vastly different, however, from the idea that there is *ongoing angelic worship of God* in a *permanent heavenly temple* that can be visited by those earthly beings privileged to ascend to it.

George Buchanan Gray pointed out quite some time ago that sources like Exodus 25:9 (which speak of the sanctuary's pattern) cannot be taken as the background to, or as evidence for, the notion that a permanent temple exists in heaven, in which God is worshiped by the angels.[95] Unfortunately, Gray's observation has not received the attention it deserves, and jumblings of the various notions appear in scholarly literature,[96] and even in current editions of the Pseudepigrapha.[97] Scholars would do well, however, to follow Gray's admonition: the appearance of one idea in no way suggests the appearance of another.[98] Philo, for instance, will elaborate on the idea that Moses saw heavenly images or patterns of the earthly temple (*Moses* 2:74–76; cf. *QA on Exod.* 2:52, 82, 90), even while at the same time Philo does not appear to believe in the existence of a heavenly temple.[99] Similarly, passages such as 2 Baruch 4:1–6—which describes a temple in heaven ready for descent to earth—cannot be used as evidence for the belief of a temple *in* heaven in which angels worship God on a regular basis. The two motifs are, to be sure, explicitly linked together—possibly for the first time— in Hebrews 8:1–5 (which we will examine in chapter 7); but the linkage is not inherently necessary, and it is improper, based on the appearance of one of these two ideas to presume the presence or influence of the other. It is also improper to assume that one idea develops from the other.[100]

A further problem encountered in the scholarship tracing the history of these notions is the frequent assumption that one or another of these ideas is in some fashion an articulation of an antitemple or antipriestly perspective. This erroneous assumption is particularly common in scholarship regarding the idea of a temple in heaven—indeed practically every text to be surveyed below is assumed without proper cause to be critical of the Jerusalem temple, its ritual, or its personnel.[101] The assumption that this idea is inherently critical of the temple can perhaps be traced to the fact that the early Christian leader Stephen was said to have appealed to the idea of a heavenly temple in the course of his criticism of the earthly temple (Acts 7:48–50). But Stephen's speech—which we will turn to briefly toward the end of this book—ought not be the basis on which the entire idea is evaluated. Indeed, there is nothing inherently anti-temple in the idea of imagining that the earthly sanctuary has an analogue in heaven. But to justify this argument, we must turn now to the texts themselves.

1 Enoch: *A Primeval Visit to a Temple in Heaven*

To study ancient Jewish conceptions of a temple in heaven, the best place to begin is with the depiction of Enoch's ascent in the *Book of Watchers* (*1 Enoch*

1–36).[102] An emerging scholarly consensus dates the work to some time in the third century B.C.E., based in part on the fragmentary evidence from Qumran.[103] Yet there is much that remains unclear concerning this work's origin and social location. The main issue that concerns us, however, is whether or not the work intends to articulate a criticism of the earthly priesthood or temple.

Expanding on Genesis 6:1–4, 1 Enoch relates how various angels consorted with earthly women. These angels morally defiled themselves in their sexual activity (9:8, 10:11, 12:4, 15:3–4, 19:1), with the result that they are expelled from heaven (14:5).[104] Enoch then ascends to heaven in part to intercede on behalf of the sinful angels. In the course of his travels, Enoch travels to and is admitted into God's heavenly temple (14:8–25). There he sees a structure built of marble and crystal (14:10) that exudes, paradoxically, both heat and cold, from fire and ice (14:13). This description builds on Ezekiel in particular (see Ezek. 1:4, 13, 22, 27 for the juxtaposition of fire and ice) as well as, more generally, ancient Near Eastern depictions of storm-like theophanies.[105] Like the earthly temple, the heavenly temple appears to have three zones, with God in the innermost chamber.[106] While the earthly cult is ministered by priests, the heavenly worship is carried out by cherubim and other angels (14:12, 18).[107] And just as on earth, the heavenly temple is an exclusive place: only the purest can be admitted to God's presence (14:21). As Watchers relates, Enoch's ascent constitutes the first stop on a tour whose itinerary also includes visits to the center and ends of the cosmos. Presumably, the center of the cosmos is the place where the earthly temple will eventually be built (26:1–6).[108] Yet whatever he learns from the rest of the tour, surely Enoch's ascent to heaven serves to highlight the fact that the fallen angels—for whom he was asked to intercede—are no longer fit to encounter God's presence or to perform heavenly worship (15:1–7).

Although there are some dissenting voices, a number of interpreters believe that the Book of Watchers takes "a dim view of the Jerusalem temple and its cult."[109] The arguments in favor of such a view include (1) Enoch visits a heavenly temple, and not an earthly one;[110] (2) the sins of the angels are to be understood as analogous to sexual sins of earthly priests, as explicitly noted in other texts such as T. Levi (see below);[111] and (3) the seer's ascent begins not from Jerusalem but from Mount Hermon (well to the north of Zion).[112]

There is no evidence within the Book of Watchers to defend the claim that visions of a heavenly temple constitute a critique of the earthly one. The idea that God resides in heaven does not undercut the possibility of God's presence, glory, or name dwelling in an earthly temple. The Book of Watchers begins with a reminder that God has the capacity to move from heaven to earth (1:3–4; cf. 4Q 201 I:5–6). Of equal importance is the fact that Watchers is set back in the time of Enoch, when—even according to the priestly Pentateuchal traditions—God has not yet caused a divine presence to reside in an earthly sanctuary. Enoch cannot visit an earthly temple, for none exists in his day.[113] It is conceivable that God could have traveled to earth to meet with Enoch—as Nickelsburg suggests[114]—but the idea that Enoch is taken up to heaven is not invented by an author who seeks to criticize the earthly temple: Enoch's being taken to heaven is the one scriptural "fact" (Gen. 5:24) that 1 Enoch has to work with! Even if we are to understand that God resides in the heavenly temple exclusively and not ever in any earthly analogue, it is important to recognize that this is not really a criticism of an earthly temple— it's a criticism of the earth.

While it would appear logical to assume that an earthly temple would be more prone to pollution than a heavenly one, that logical *assumption* is undercut, not supported, by 1 Enoch. According to this text, the heavenly temple, no different from the earthly one, is prone to pollution by a fornicating priesthood. Why this necessarily constitutes a criticism of an earthly temple is unclear to me. It is certainly true that the angels in the heavenly temple are analogous to the priests in the earthly one. But the narrative of some sinful angels is no more antipriestly than it is antiangelic. Finally, we probably should not make too much of Enoch's ascent to heaven from Mount Hermon (as opposed to Zion). Zion is not even the highest mountain in Jerusalem, let alone the region; the obvious significance of Hermon is its height.[115] The *Book of Watchers* itself considers Jerusalem to be the center of the world (1 Enoch 26).[116]

The *Book of Watchers* relates how Enoch, in his day, encountered God in a heavenly temple, at a time when that heavenly temple was nearly polluted by fornicating angels. That God is in heaven in Enoch's day does not preclude or limit his capacity to dwell on earth in some fashion, at a later time. That *some* of God's own angels will fall into transgression certainly does not constitute a prediction that *all* earthly priests will inevitably fall short. But if they should, they will be following in the footsteps of beings greater than they. The *Book of Watchers* can still be read as a critique of the temple, but it would have to be granted that there is no intrinsic need to read the text in such a fashion.

The Testament of Levi: *A Priestly Patriarch in the Angels' Temple*

Whatever its origin and purpose, 1 Enoch is the earliest exemplar of a literary tradition that was to extend down through the ancient period, and well into the Middle Ages. The *Book of Watchers'* account of a visit to the heavenly temple is developed in various ancient apocalyptic texts, and even later documents of Jewish *Merkabah* mysticism. We cannot and need not review all this material, but we must turn our attention here to a document that is clearly of import—the *Testament of Levi*—which tells of an ascent to the heavenly temple, by a paradigmatic priestly figure.

The questions surrounding the origin and purpose of the *Testaments of the Twelve Patriarchs* (of which *T. Levi* constitutes a part) are even more complicated than the questions concerning 1 Enoch.[117] The *Testaments* are known primarily from various medieval Greek manuscripts that clearly exhibit Christian characteristics: *T. Levi* 4:4, for instance, speaks of the impaled son of God. Many scholars believe that the Christian-sounding passages constitute glosses to an essentially Jewish text, and that these were added in late antiquity or the middle ages by the Christian scribes who preserved the work.[118] Others, however, find that the Christian elements predominate, and that therefore in their current form the *Testaments* constitute a largely Christian work, albeit one that develops earlier Jewish traditions.[119] Prominent among the Jewish traditions behind *T. Levi* is the so-called *Aramaic Levi Document*, preserved fragmentarily at Qumran and in various medieval manuscripts.[120] The extant Aramaic material—that which is undoubtedly Jewish in origin— does not preserve an account of Levi's ascent to a heavenly temple. Still, we have reason to turn here to Levi's ascent as described in *T. Levi*, even though the *Testaments* may have been thoroughly Christianized. We do so because when it comes to the passage describing Levi's ascent, there is good reason to think that we are dealing with some authentic ancient Jewish material.[121]

T. *Levi*'s description of the patriarch's vision is not unlike what we find in 1 *Enoch*.[122] *T. Levi* describes the seer's ascent from a high mountain (2:6), through the heavens to the cosmic holy of holies (3:4), where he sees God, as worshiped by the angels. Again, the visionary passes through a meteorologi- cally phenomenal combination of fire and ice (3:3). Once more, the temple in heaven is like the earthly temple; it's a multichambered structure, with limited access even among the angels to its innermost recesses (3:2–8). With- out undermining these similarities, Levi's vision is, in some important ways, more detailed than Enoch's. For one thing, we find in *T. Levi* what may be the earliest explicit reference to *seven* heavens, something that will become stan- dard in Jewish mysticism of the rabbinic period.[123] We also find in *T. Levi* a more developed association between priests and angels: *T. Levi* 8:1–19 tells of a subsequent vision during which the patriarch is anointed with oil and dressed in priestly garb.[124] The overall thrust of these visions is clear: in doing their cultic duties, the priests are emulating angels, in a manner in which their progenitor was instructed by angels. Indeed, as the document says later, earthly purity is in emulation of heavenly purity (14:3).

Perhaps the most important detail provided in *T. Levi* is the first explicit reference to a sacrificial service in the sixth heaven, where (3:5–6): "(5) there are the angels of the presence of the Lord, those who minister and make propitiation to the Lord for all the sins of ignorance of the righteous, (6) and they offer to the Lord a pleasant odour, a reasonable and bloodless offer- ing."[125] There are a number of remarkable facets to this passage. Of course it must first be pointed out that the reference to a "reasonable and bloodless offering"—which recalls Romans 12:1—is surely a Christian gloss.[126] But one should also note that the image of a temple in heaven (let alone one with a sacrificial service of any sort) contradicts the rather clear thrust of Revelation 21:22, in which an early Christian seer relates that there is no temple in the heavenly Jerusalem. Thus there is reason to take seriously the possibility that the essence of the report here is, at origin, a Jewish one, made safe for Christianity by the assertion that the heavenly worship is "reasonable and bloodless."

T. *Levi* reports that the sacrificial service takes place not in the highest heaven but in the one immediately below that. There is no chance that any slight to sacrifice is intended by this—in fact, this placement shows that the author remains familiar with the structure of the earthly temple as laid out in the various accounts, including the priestly traditions. The earthly sacrificial altar is not located in the holy of holies but outside it (Exod. 40:29). This fact may help explain why most visions of the heavenly temple don't mention any sacrifice in heaven at all. Some believe that the paucity of images of heavenly sacrifice is to be explained by the fact that those who imagine a temple in heaven are those who are deprived of participation in the temple on earth.[127] I see no justification for this assumption. We have very few reliably ancient Jewish images of the heavenly temple, and it bears repeating that even *T. Levi* may not be such a reliably ancient Jewish vision. Those visions that we do have do not undoubtedly emerge among groups who have turned away from, or been forced out of, the earthly temple, despite frequent assumptions to this effect. There is in fact a much simpler reason why most visions of heaven do not dwell on heavenly sacrifice: in these visions the emphasis is on the holy of holies itself—in which no sacrifice takes place, either in heaven, or on earth.

When it comes to evaluating the attitude expressed in *T. Levi* toward the priesthood, much of what was said above with regard to *1 Enoch* also applies. There is nothing inherently antitemple about envisioning a temple in heaven. This is particularly the case when the figure depicted as seeing such a temple is one who lived long before any earthly temple was constructed. Just as Enoch lived long before any priestly tabernacle (let alone temple) was constructed, so too did Levi. The possibility of a divine presence dwelling in an earthly temple is by no means precluded in *T. Levi* (see 5:2).

There is nothing inherently antipriestly in *T. Levi* either. It is true that the sins of future priests are foretold (14:1–8). The sins include not just the sexual matters that we might expect (following *1 Enoch*) but also various other transgressions. Perhaps with the sins of Eli's sons in mind (1 Sam. 2:12–17), the priests are warned against theft (14:5). And with various priestly and prophetic precedents in mind, Levi is warned that these transgressions will lead to the moral defilement of the temple (15:1). Of course these concerns are all scriptural, even priestly.[128] To be sure, distinctly Christian elements are to be found here too, especially in the prediction that the priests will kill a savior (14:4) and possibly also in the expressed hope for a new priesthood (8:14, 18:2–14; cf. Hebrews 4:14–7:28).[129] But Robert Kugler and others are able to discern perfectly Jewish motives for imagining a seer envisioning a new priesthood coming in to replace a sinful and dispossessed predecessor: this, after all, is precisely what was understood to have occurred by the majority of Jews who eventually recognized the legitimacy of the non-Zadokite Hasmonean priesthood in the late second century B.C.E.[130] It is interesting that *T. Levi* does not "predict" that some righteous group of priests will be cut off from the earthly temple, as it very well could have were it of interest (and were the document sectarian). To the contrary, *T. Levi* seems remarkably uninterested in Zadokite or any other specific line of priestly descent—perhaps any worthy descendant of Levi is supposed to qualify.[131] Regardless of whether one agrees with Kugler in his belief that the original *Testament of Levi* was composed to support the Hasmonean priesthood, one must admit that there is nothing antitemple or even antipriestly about a document "predicting" priestly transgression and subsequent changes to the priestly lineage. In this too *T. Levi* is much like its predecessor, *1 Enoch*: the antitemple and anti-priestly messages found there are more in the minds of the interpreters than they are in the nature of the text at hand.

The Songs of the Sabbath Sacrifice: *In Praise with the Priestly Angels*

Alongside *1 Enoch* and *T. Levi*, a third roughly contemporary document provides important information about ancient Jewish conceptions of a heavenly temple. But unlike *1 Enoch* and *T. Levi*, the *Songs of the Sabbath Sacrifice* was unknown to later Jews or Christians, in any language or form, until various manuscripts were unearthed at Qumran in the 1950s. Shortly thereafter, a single copy was discovered at Masada, bringing the total number of known copies to ten: eight from Qumran cave 4 (4Q 400–407) and one each from Qumran cave 11 (11Q 17) and Masada (Mas 1k).[132] While we are fortunate to have ten manuscripts of the work, we are rather unfortunate in the state of those manuscripts: even when all the copies are superimposed, we are left with much less than half of the original work. Because the *Songs* are poorly preserved, any analysis remains provisional and tentative. For all we know, we may well lack the material that is truly important for understanding the entire work.

The paleographers have assigned dates to the various manuscripts ranging from 75 B.C.E. to 50 C.E., with the bulk of the Qumran manuscripts being dated to the earlier period.[133] Thus we must suppose that the work was composed by around 100 B.C.E., and possibly earlier than that. It is generally agreed that the work contained thirteen songs, each of which accompanied the burnt offering for one Sabbath over the course of thirteen weeks of the year.[134] These songs depict angelic worship in a heavenly temple, though the extant fragments do not relate how this heavenly knowledge was revealed: there is no frame narrative of a heavenly ascent by a biblical hero, as in *1 Enoch* or *T. Levi*. The heading for each song indicates not only the number of the Sabbath (one to thirteen) but also its precise day of the month—for instance, the first song is to be recited on the first Sabbath, which is on the fourth day of the first month (4Q 400 frag. 1, I:1). This kind of calendrical precision—which ties given Sabbaths to fixed days of the week and month—presupposes the 364-day, 52-week calendar also known from *Jubilees*, *1 Enoch*, *Aramaic Levi*, the *Temple Scroll*.[135]

This is pretty much where scholarly agreement ends. Although the bulk of the manuscripts do come from Qumran, a number of scholars—Carol Newsom prominent among them—currently believe that the *Songs* were, like *Jubilees* and the *Aramaic Levi Document*, composed not by the Qumran sectarians themselves but by an earlier group.[136] Others, however, maintain that the document is in fact sectarian in origin.[137] Among other matters, this dispute revolves around (1) whether or not sectarian terminology appears in the work in significant measure, and (2) the fact that one manuscript was discovered at Masada. If we had even a single complete manuscript of the *Songs of the Sabbath Sacrifice*—from Qumran or even elsewhere—we might be able to say much more about its nature and origin, and whether the work was composed at Qumran, edited by the sectarians, or simply used by them.

Perhaps the most interesting characteristic of this ongoing debate for our purposes is how little it seems to matter for many scholars in their evaluations of the *Songs'* attitude toward the temple cult in Jerusalem. Of course, for those who view the work as sectarian, its antitemple nature is self-evident. It is also not at all uncommon for scholars to point to the *Songs* as evidence for the claim that contemplation of a heavenly temple is itself indicative of an anti-temple perspective.[138] Even scholars who question the sectarian origin of the work do not hesitate to understand it as aligning well with the sectarian rejection of the temple cult in Jerusalem.[139] Yet the question of whether the work is inherently critical of the temple remains important, and open for debate. There are some scholars, such as Esther Chazon, who argue that what we find here may well reflect broader trends in ancient Judaism.[140] If the sectarian origin of the work remains uncertain, then certainly we ought not take its vision of a heavenly temple as evidence that such depictions are inherently schismatic. The questions we can ask are these: what is the nature of the *Songs'* heavenly temple? What can we say about the document's attitude toward an earthly temple?

The extant portions of the *Songs of the Sabbath Sacrifice* seem to do little else but describe the celestial worship of God, as carried out by the angels.[141] This worship is located in a heavenly sanctuary—variously referred to as the "temple" (מקדש; e.g., 4Q403 frag. 1, I:42) and "tabernacle" (משכן; 4Q403 frag. 1, II:10), among other terms.[142] The celestial temple appears to have many, if not all, of the structures and implements of the earthly temple, including gates (שערי מרום; 4Q400 frag. 1, II:4), a curtain (פרוכת; Q405 frag. 15–16, II:3), and an inner room (דביר; 4Q 400 frag. 1, I:4). These are serviced by angelic beings dressed in various priestly vestments including ephods (4Q405 frag. 23, II:5) and breastplates (4Q405 frag. 41, 2).[143] This heavenly priesthood, like the earthly one, is also concerned with purity: there is no defilement among the holy ones above (4Q400 frag. 1, I:15–16),[144] just as there is to be no defilement in the temple below. The final two songs describe various heavenly sacrifices (זבחי קדושים; 11Q17 IX:4), which include grain offerings (מנחותם; IX:4), libations (נסכיהם; IX:5), and even whole burnt offerings (כליל; 4Q405 frag. 23, I:5–6). Like their earthly counterparts, the heavenly sacrifices please God through their pleasant odor (11Q17 IX:5).[145] Taken all together, the *Songs of the Sabbath Sacrifice* are certainly the most sustained and detailed reflection on the correspondence between heavenly and earthly worship we have in all ancient Jewish literature. Like their earthly analogues, the angels offer their sacrifices to God, dressed like priests, in a state of purity, in a heavenly temple.

Curiously, the angelic praise of God is often described but never directly quoted (e.g., 4Q400 frag. 2, II:1–5).[146] It is possible that the angels' silence in the heavenly sanctuary above is to be understood in relationship to the priestly silence in the earthly temple. There is indeed some intriguing evidence (e.g., *Aristeas* 92, 95) suggesting that the temple priests performed the sacrificial service in silence.[147] Therefore, the angels' silent praise may yet provide another way in which heaven and earth correspond in the *Songs of the Sabbath Sacrifice*. On the other hand, it is possible that the *Songs'* reticence to quote the angels may be a reflection on the inherent inequality of human and divine praise: how can lowly humans quote the angelic praise directly?[148]

Indeed, the correspondence between heaven and earth in the *Songs of the Sabbath Sacrifice* is frequently inexact. Reasonably enough, much of the *Songs'* description of the heavenly temple draws not only on the priestly tabernacle traditions, but also on Ezekiel's visions of the divine chariot.[149] The sevenfold structure of the heavenly temple (שבעת קדשי רום; 4Q403 frag. 1, II:11), with its multiple "royal sanctuaries" (היכלי מלך; 4Q400 frag. 1, I:13), does not exactly correspond with any known description of the earthly temple, scriptural or otherwise.[150] Unlike their earthly counterparts, the structures of the heavenly temple are themselves animate, and participate in the celestial worship (4Q405 frag. 19).[151] The heavenly temple also contains a multiplicity of divine chariots, which seem to retain their capacity for movement (11Q17 VII; 4Q405 frags. 20–22).[152] Finally, there seems to be some reflection on the inequality of the celestial and human priesthoods, for in the second song, unidentified would-be celestial worshipers ask: "how shall we be accounted among them? And how shall our priesthood (be accounted) in their dwellings?" (4Q400 frag. 2, 5–6). For some scholars, this passage provides evidence that the human priesthood compares unfavorably to the heavenly one.[153]

Understanding the passage just quoted is in fact more challenging than it may at first seem. First, it is by no means clear who is speaking: for all we know, the angelic beings could be reflecting on *their* inadequacy. Moreover, there is some compelling evidence that the *Songs* describe some sort of transformation, whereby human beings are incorporated into the heavenly realm (4Q400 frag. 1, I:3).[154] Because of the fragmentary nature of our manuscripts, we cannot be certain whether the statement just quoted reflects an early part of that transformation, a challenge that is subsequently overcome. Finally, it is essential in this case to remember that one cannot take liturgical self-deprecation as an objective evaluation of a worshiper's moral state. Some of the greatest biblical heroes—such as Jacob (Gen. 32:10) or Isaiah (Isa. 6:5)—question their worthiness but are granted divine contact just the same. Prayer texts are not objective or doctrinal statements, and cannot be interpreted as such.[155] Even if some real deprecation is intended here, the passage could be a reflection on the inherent inequality of humans and angels—indeed, it seems that the *Songs* decidedly step back from the idea that humans can become just like angels.[156] In this case too the passage ought not be taken as critical of any single group of people (e.g., priests) in particular. Whoever these worshipers are, the fact that they question their worthiness during the process of their transportation or transformation certainly cannot be taken as evidence that there is any harsh criticism of the earthly priesthood in the *Songs*.

In general, we also cannot be quick to assume that the inexactitude of the heaven–earth correspondence reflects poorly on earthly priests or temples.[157] For one thing, not all is serene in the heavens—the *Songs* speak of celestial

warfare (מלחמת שחקים; 4Q402 frag. 4, 10). More important, we look in vain in
the extant fragments for any explicit condemnation of the earthly temple, its
priests, or its offerings. We will take up the sectarian rejection of the temple in
chapter 5, and we will see that the developed sectarian literature articulates a
number of distinct polemics against the current temple, its purity, its practice,
and its personnel. But the *Songs of the Sabbath Sacrifice* exhibit nothing of the
sort. There is no explicit reference to priestly sin, or to the impurity (ritual or
moral) of an earthly temple. Indeed, the only potentially divisive issue here is
the fact that the *Songs* follows the 364-day, 52-week calendar, but there is no
hint here of any polemic on this matter. Of course, for all we know about
ancient Jewish calendars, it is quite possible that priestly authorities followed
a 364-day calendar in the temple for some portion of the Second Temple
period. But more important for our concerns is the fact that one can imagine
a work such as the *Songs of the Sabbath Sacrifice* serving not to critique the
earthly temple but serving to bolster beliefs in the temple's efficacy and
sanctity by arguing that the earthly service emulates a divine one. In other
words, instead of intending to replace the sacrificial service for those who
opposed it, the songs could have been meant to accompany the physical,
earthly rituals as practiced in the temple.[158] Our extant sources do not allow
us to know with certainty what a mystical text composed by an officiating
Second Temple priest might have looked like. But if we wanted to imagine the
characteristics of such a text, we might do very well to think of something
along the lines of the *Songs of the Sabbath Sacrifice*.

As many scholars have observed, an interesting analogue to the *Songs* can
be found in the traditional Jewish prayer known as the *qedushah*.[159] In its
various forms, this prayer typically involves reciting two biblical doxologies,
each believed to be quotations of angelic speech (Isaiah 6:3: "Holy, Holy, Holy
is the Lord of Hosts..." and Ezekiel 3:12: "blessed be the glory of the Lord
from his place").[160] Thus this prayer involves the human imitation of audi-
ble angelic praise. Of course, as with much of Jewish liturgy, the origins of the
qedushah are obscure.[161] Yet there is general agreement that at least some
form of the prayer dates back to the Second Temple period, because parallels
abound in a wide range of ancient sources. Perhaps the closest and most
verifiably ancient of these ostensible parallels can be found among the allegedly Jewish prayers preserved in the *Apostolic Constitutions*.[162] It is also
argued that the *qedushah* lay behind the traditional Christian liturgical *Sanctus*,[163] as well as ancient Jewish mystical hymns known from the *Hekhalot*
literature.[164] Others find evidence for the antiquity of the *qedushah* in various
prayers from Qumran in general and in the *Songs of the Sabbath Sacrifice* in
particular.[165]

The significance of all this for our purposes is the fact that the Jewish
liturgical *qedushah*—like the *Songs*—involves human imitation of angelic
worship. Yet the traditional Jewish liturgy is by no means hostile to the temple
or animal sacrifice. To the contrary, the traditional liturgy contains many
prayers that explicitly hope for the return to Jerusalem, the rebuilding of the
temple, and the resumption of animal sacrifice. Thus it would be foolhardy to

interpret the *qedushah* in its liturgical context as antitemple, despite the fact that the *qedushah* too betrays some knowledge of an imbalance between heavenly and earthly worship: presumably, heavenly angelic worship is a constant—but the human imitation of it takes place at limited times, in certain circumstances.[166] By extension—and by analogy—the evidence of the *qedushah* lends support to the general argument that there is nothing inherently antitemple in the imaginations of angelic worship in the *Songs of the Sabbath Sacrifice* either. Indeed, all these sources may well testify to a general trend among various groups of ancient Jews to imagine that earthly worship can emulate angelic devotion in the heavens.[167]

Any assessment of the nature and purpose of the *Songs of the Sabbath Sacrifice* is, in the end, limited by the unfortunately poor condition of the surviving manuscripts. It remains possible that the work was composed at Qumran, and reflects—in an extremely muted way—the sect's antipathy toward the Jerusalem temple. But it is at least equally possible—if not more possible—that the work originated in circles sympathetic to and perhaps even active in the earthly temple. This position—currently espoused by only a minority of scholars—deserves, at the very least, greater attention and consideration.

Envisioning the Heavenly Temple in Rabbinic Sources

As noted above, a number of challenges confront the scholar who wishes to trace the history of nonlegal (*aggadic*) themes in rabbinic sources. But the situation with regard to the particular theme we are tracing here is somewhat more fortunate. The foundation for scholarly study of the idea of a heavenly temple in rabbinic sources was set in the 1930s, with the appearance of Avigdor Aptowitzer's now classic essay on the topic.[168] The broad interest in Jewish mysticism, generated in large part by the brilliant works of Gershom Scholem,[169] spawned further work on this theme, and eventually inspired the publication of excellent scholarly editions of the early Jewish mystical texts.[170] Events in the Middle East have also come to play a decided role here: in the wake of Israel's conquest of East Jerusalem in the Six-Day War of 1967, Jewish scholarship on all matters relating to Jerusalem flourished, and studies of the heavenly Jerusalem (with its temple) were not left behind.[171]

A significant number of rabbinic traditions speak of some sort of heavenly temple. While detailed descriptions are scarce, statements asserting the existence of a temple in heaven can be found in the Talmud (e.g., *b. Hagigah* 12b; *b. Sanhedrin* 94b; *b. Menahot* 110a; *y. Berakhot* 4:5, 8c/40–41), in the better known midrashic collections (e.g., *Gen. Rabbah* 55:8, 69:7; *Mekilta de-Rabbi Ishmael Shirah* 10), and in a host of other lesser known texts, of the sort collected in Adolph Jellinek's *Beth ha-Midrasch*.[172] These traditions cannot all be reliably dated to the rabbinic period, but certainly a number of them are at least amoraic, if not tannaitic, and parallels for the idea, as we have seen throughout this chapter, go back well into the Second Temple period.[173]

The rabbinic traditions are an odd lot, and we can hardly be certain that there was any unanimity on the idea in general, or with regard to its particulars. For instance, the traditions differ on the location of the heavenly temple: was it in the fourth heaven, as asserted in the Talmud (b. Hagigah 12b), or in the seventh, as assumed in the Hekhalot literature?[174] Moreover, here, too, we must be careful to distinguish between various types of heavenly sanctuaries. While the traditions just noted speak clearly of a functioning temple in heaven, there are other traditions in rabbinic sources too that describe not a heavenly temple per se but heavenly models of the earthly tabernacle shown to Moses for purposes of illustration, prior to the construction of Israel's earthly sanctuary (e.g., b. Menahot 29a).[175] Moreover, in rabbinic literature too we find the idea that the eschatological temple has already been constructed, and waits in heaven ready to descend to earth at the appointed time (בנוי ומשכלל לעתיד לבוא; e.g., Sifre Deut. sec. 352, ed. Finkelstein 410).[176] Indeed, the diversity of the rabbinic traditions concerning heavenly temples cannot be underestimated. We remain focused here—as throughout this section—on those traditions that imagine there being a temple in heaven, in which angels worship God, just as priests would administer service to God in an earthly sanctuary.

The rabbinic traditions differ, curiously, on when the heavenly temple was established. It would seem reasonable to assume that a heavenly temple would be eternal, compared to the earthly temple that was built and destroyed in time. Most rabbinic sources give us no reason to question this assertion. A few rabbinic sources suggest, however, that the heavenly temple was constructed at the same time as the earthly one: "said Rabbi Simon: When the Holy One, blessed be He, told Israel to build the tabernacle, he hinted to the angels that they too should build a tabernacle. So when the tabernacle was constructed below, one was constructed above" (Num. Rabbah 12:12).[177] A talmudic tradition (b. Ta'anit 5a) reflects on the other end of this remarkable heaven-earth correspondence:

> Rabbi Nahman asked Rabbi Isaac: What is the meaning of the verse (Hos. 11:9) "The Holy One is among you and I will not come to the city"?[178] Can it mean that because the Holy One is among you, I will not come to the city!? Rabbi Isaac answered: Thus said Rabbi Yohanan: The Holy One, blessed be He, said: "I will not enter Jerusalem below until I enter Jerusalem above."[179]

Therefore, just as the divine presence is in exile from the earthly sanctuary, so too is it absent from the heavenly one.[180] Certainly these traditions can hardly be taken as criticisms of the earthly temple in comparison with the heavenly one. Indeed, these sources should raise questions among those who generally assume that visions of heavenly temples constitute criticisms of the earthly temple or responses to its destruction. In these remarkable sources, the heaven–earth correspondence is taken so far that the impact of the earthly destruction is felt in the heavenly one.

A number of the rabbinic traditions also take the heaven–earth corre-spondence so far as to reflect on the nature of heavenly sacrifice. A few talmudic sources note the presence of a sacrificial altar in heaven, upon which an angelic being would present offerings. For instance, the tradition noted above in *b. Hagigah* 12b (attributed to the amoraic sage Resh Lakish) locates the heavenly Jerusalem in the fourth heaven, where one also finds that "the temple and altar are built, and Michael, the great prince stands and offers up an offering upon it" (cf. *b. Menahot* 110a). A few midrashic sources take this notion even one step further, spelling out that what is offered on the heavenly altar are the souls of the righteous (*Num. Rabbah* 12:12).[181] One medieval midrashic source—*Midrash be-Khokhmah Yesod ha-Aretz*—says that the sac-rifice of the righteous souls began only after the destruction of the temple: before that, the likenesses of animals were offered above, just as animals were below.[182] As far as the sources we have surveyed so far indicate, I can hardly disagree with Ephraim Urbach in his assessment that the notion of a heavenly Jerusalem—with its temple—is a reflection not of opposition to the Jerusalem below but of love toward what existed on earth.[183]

Of course, any full discussion of the idea of a heavenly temple in rabbinic literature must take into consideration the evidence from the *Hekhalot* texts.[184] These texts present the most thoroughgoing reflection on the divine temple in rabbinic literature (as broadly defined). It also appears that they draw produc-tively on various earlier sources, including possibly the *Songs of the Sabbath Sacrifice*.[185] A particular focus of these texts is on the nature of the divine praise, as performed by the heavenly angels. This broad interest in angelic praise contrasts sharply with a lack of interest in heavenly sacrifice. Indeed, we noted above that some (but by no means all) Second Temple period texts exhibit a reluctance to describe any corporeal sacrifice in heaven. While this is not true of the midrashic tradition in general, it is certainly true of the *Hekhalot* texts.[186]

This reticence has been explained variously: some have entertained the possibility that the groups who composed these texts were opposed to the sacrificial cult, or believed that sacrifice was too unseemly for the heavenly realm.[187] As for the possibility that sacrifice was viewed as inappropriate for heaven—one must simply recall, as pointed out by Andrea Lieber, that the *Hekhalot* traditions in particular are chock-full of unseemly violence: many of these texts describe the gruesome fate that awaits the unfit visitor to the heavenly abode.[188] As for the possibility that the mystics opposed sacrifice, we simply cannot rush to *assume,* as too many scholars do, that the visions of heavenly temples in apocalyptic or mystical traditions emerge from groups that reject the temple. On the one hand, as we noted above, the midrashic traditions in general preserve a host of speculations on the heavenly temple, none of which can be definitively seen as antitemple, antipriestly, or anti-sacrifice. On the other hand, the *Hekhalot* texts are ridden with curious mysteries and lacunae. As is well known, the paradoxical *descent* (as opposed to *ascent*) to the heavenly throne remains unexplained.[189] Too many questions remain about the genre and provenance of the *Hekhalot* texts to reach definitive conclusions regarding what is absent from the texts. Finally, it bears repeating that the absence of sacrifice from the heavenly altar may simply reflect the fact that the heavenly altar described was believed to correspond not to the outer earthly altar (on which sacrifice was performed) but the inner earthly altar (on which only incense was burned). There is no sacrifice in the seventh *hekhal*, just as there is no sacrifice in the holy of holies on earth.

With or without descriptions of heavenly sacrifice, surely the *Hekhalot* literature builds productively on many temple-related traditions.[190] Most obviously, the term *hekhal* is among the names used of the earthly temple in biblical and rabbinic texts (e.g., 1 Kgs. 6:3; *m. Pesahim* 4:9). A number of the figures mentioned in the *Hekhalot* are also described as priests, including Rabbi Ishmael ben Elisha, who is also remembered as having served in the temple (*Hekhalot Rabbati* 9:1; cf. *b. Berakhot* 7a).[191] Another cultic aspect of these texts is the emphasis on ritual purity as a prerequisite for admission to the heavenly temple.[192] There are too many references to list, but among the better known instances is the narrative embedded in *Hekhalot Rabbati* (20:1–4), which involves Rabbi Nehunia ben ha-Kanah being dismissed from heaven at the moment the sages bring his earth-bound body in contact with a piece of cloth that itself has been brought into contact with a woman of questionable status with regard to ritual purity.[193] Again, in general, the purity of those who ascend is compared to the purity of the angels.[194] Related to this is the idea that just as earthly beings below are susceptible to ritual defilement, so too are the angels above.[195] Although ritual purity is required in the temple above (just as it would be in the temple below), it is not in and of itself sufficient: in contradistinction to rabbinic law concerning the earthly temple (but in agreement with the approach of Philo and others), those to be admitted to the heavenly temple must be free not only of ritual defilement but of all sin and moral taint as well (*Hekhalot Rabbati* 15:2–3; *Synopse* secs. 119–200). But even in this aspect of the traditions, it is most difficult to find in this literature any explicit condemnation of earthly priests, earthly temples, or animal sacrifice.

Of course, another question that remains unresolved is the relationship between the mystics, as recorded in the *Hekhalot* literature, and the sages, as recorded in rabbinic literature. Gershom Scholem famously argued that the *Hekhalot* texts preserve the authentic, historical mystical experiences of rabbinic sages.[196] More recent studies have demonstrated decided differences between the mystical practices of the tannaitic sages (as recorded especially in *t. Hagigah* 2:1–7) and those of the mystics (as recorded in the *Hekhalot* literature).[197] Indeed, it is asserted with some frequency that the rabbis suppressed, or at least frowned upon, these mystical traditions, for one reason or another.[198] Yet, with regard to our concerns, this dispute hardly makes a difference. As we have seen, the *Hekhalot* texts do not contain the only echoes of the idea of a heavenly sanctuary in rabbinic literature. Thus even if the *Hekhalot* texts cannot be attributed to rabbinic sages—and even if some of these texts were suppressed by the sages—we would still have to grant the fact that a number of rabbinic authorities reflect on the notion of a heavenly temple. Certainly it is intriguing that the most explicit descriptions of the inner workings of the heavenly temple, with its altar and angel-priests, are to be found not in the *Hekhalot* writings but in other midrashic works, including even the canonical (but medieval) collections such as *Midrash Rabbah*. Even the Babylonian Talmud itself contains two different explicit traditions speaking of the angelic prince Michael offering sacrifices on a heavenly altar (*b. Hagigah* 12b, *b. Menahot* 110a). On this we do better to follow David Flusser and Shmuel Safrai, who both argue that the notion of a heavenly temple was common to many groups of ancient Jews, the rabbis no doubt included.[199]

Conclusion

In this chapter, we surveyed a number of sources pertaining to two symbolic approaches to the temple that were predominant among Jews in the ancient period. These two notions are distinct, even though they tend to get jumbled in the scholarly literature. According to the first notion—in evidence in Josephus, Philo, rabbinic literature, and elsewhere—the temple was understood to represent the entire cosmos. According to the second notion—in evidence in apocalypses, liturgical texts, rabbinic literature, and elsewhere—the earthly temple, ministered by priests, was believed to correlate to a heavenly temple, ministered by angels. When fully developed, both of these notions allow for symbolic understanding of various aspects of the sacrificial process, purity and sacrifice included.

In the works of Josephus, we observed the confluence of two concerns: the historian consistently understood the temple and its furnishings as representative of the cosmos, and at the same time he consistently saw the temple as the earthly location of God's presence. In both of these matters, Josephus' approach can be seen as largely commensurate with biblical theology. Though he does not explicitly attribute symbolic significance to either purity or sacrifice, we could surmise that he would have been perfectly willing to interpret these rituals in the manner implied by his overall symbolic and theological approaches to the temple.

In the works of Philo, we observed a more developed and detailed exposition of the temple-as-cosmos idea. Philo's exhaustive treatments of the matter incorporate practically every structural element of the sanctuary, as well as virtually every aspect of sacrificial ritual. Indeed, Philo's is the most thorough symbolic exposition of sacrificial ritual known from ancient Jewish times. For the philosopher, much of the sacrificial process can be understood in light of the notion of *imitatio Dei*. And his approach includes purity as well: ritual and moral purification render one more divine-like and, as such, more fit to enter the sanctuary, in which the Logos resides. With his complicated understanding of divine emanations, Philo's approach also exhibits an interest in a divine presence dwelling in the earthly sanctuary. Of course, certain aspects of this approach—especially as it pertains to the Logos—are distinctly Philonic. On the other hand, the general understanding of ritual purity—and in some cases, moral purity as well—as emulating angels is in evidence in other texts reviewed earlier, and may well have been a common one among ancient Jews. Philo's interest in a divine emanation dwelling in the temple is perhaps the most conservative of his ideas, going back to both the priestly and Deuteronomic traditions.

While we find relatively few detailed developments of these themes in later Jewish literature, we noted a number of tantalizing hints suggesting that the interest in the understanding of the temple as representing the cosmos did not disappear. In addition to scattered references in relatively datable rabbinic texts (such as the Babylonian Talmud and the midrashim), we noted the remarkable echoes of Philo's symbolic exposition in the mysterious *Midrash Tadshe*. If this work itself is not evidence of rabbinic interest in the temple-as-cosmos idea, it strongly suggests that there was some such tradition upon which this work could build. We also noted the rather common juxtaposition of cosmic and cultic symbolisms on the floors of late-antique synagogues in the land of Israel. Taken together, the evidence strongly suggests that the idea of the temple as cosmos remained of significance to Jews, even long after the destruction of the temple in 70 C.E.

Turning to the texts that speak of a temple in heaven, we find a different way of approaching the earthly temple in a symbolic fashion. According to this approach, the earthly temple corresponds to the heavenly one. While the angels minister to God in the temple above, the priests coordinate his worship in the earthly temple below. Once again, we can trace a broad continuity from the apocalypses through various liturgical and mystical texts of the rabbinic period. Again, we find that the overarching symbolism pertains to the aspects of the sacrificial process as well. In practically all of these documents, preserving purity serves to emulate the angels; and just as the angels (as well as the select few mortals permitted to ascend on high) encounter the divine in the temple above, so too can the pure encounter a divine presence in the temple below. Thus while we have already observed that some understand purity in light of the notion of *imitatio Dei*, here one could say that purity is understood in light of a not-so-different notion of *imitatio angeli*. For reasons that are not entirely clear, a number of texts decline to speculate on the nature of the heavenly service. For those that do, vocal praise is one common motif, but a number of texts do assert that there was an altar in heaven, on which the ministering angels presented some kind of offerings.

While some scholars assert that the ascent visions in *1 Enoch* or *T. Levi* served to undercut the significance of the earthly temple, I have argued that it is just as likely that quite the opposite is the case: envisioning a temple in heaven can give authority and meaning to its earthly analogue, the Jerusalem sanctuary. This appears to be true of the *Songs of the Sabbath Sacrifice* and the *Hekhalot* literature as well: here we find that the speculation of what happens on high reinforces the significance of earthly emulations down below. No hint of criticism here. While certain aspects of priestly practice were criticized in various apocalypses—including *1 Enoch* and *T. Levi*—there is nothing inherently critical in the ascent vision per se.

Of course, not all Jews were supporters of the Second Temple. Indeed, as we will see in the next chapter, a number of texts articulate specific charges against the temple, its practice, and its personnel. The problem that has been encountered in this chapter is that scholars have assumed such criticism to be present, even in the absence of good evidence for the claim. The documents surveyed above are frequently assumed to be critical of the temple or its ritual, apparently because hostility toward the temple and its cult remains among us. In contrast, it is better to understand the themes we have studied as two fundamental, symbolic understandings of the temple, both of which are generally favorable to the sanctuary's personnel and its ritual practices. The first notion posits that the temple, its structures and rituals, symbolize the cosmos; the other posits that the Jerusalem temple, along with its personnel and practices, is the earthly analogue of heavenly phenomena. In both cases the temple has cosmic significance, and its ritual has symbolic value.

5

Sinful People, Impure Priests, and Inadequate Structures

The Temple as Defiled and Rejected

We turn in this chapter to a consideration of the various charges raised against the temple and its priesthood during the Second Temple period. It is well known that various groups of Jews—including, certainly, the Dead Sea sectarians—expressed dissatisfaction with the temple, its practices, or its priests. According to many interpretations, the historical Jesus as well, to say nothing of subsequent Christians, was displeased with the temple or its priests, though in the case of Jesus, at least, the record is less clear. Even in rabbinic literature we find some criticisms of the temple, though these sources were committed to writing only centuries after the temple was destroyed. We will consider the rabbis' and Jesus' approach to the temple in chapters 6 and 7. Here we will focus on the various antitemple polemics articulated in the literature from Qumran.

As with all matters concerning the Dead Sea Scrolls, the bibliography on attitudes toward the temple and sacrifice is extensive.[1] But as I argued in the introduction to part II, a number of problems appear now and again in the scholarship on these matters. As we will see, evolutionist concerns and biases against the temple—with their hallmark catchphrase, "spiritualization"—show up with some frequency. Moreover, even more problematic is the unmeasured evaluation of the sectarians' own attitudes toward these matters. Scholarship on the scrolls often describes the sect as if they were satisfied with their extratemple rituals. Yet as we will see below, there is some significant evidence to the contrary.

Not all of the documents to be reviewed here were necessarily composed at Qumran, but we focus on those documents that either were likely composed by the sect (e.g., the *Rule of the Community*) or exhibit at least some sectarian tendencies and were probably held in great esteem by them (e.g., the *Temple Scroll*). Certainly each document has its own complex history, and thus the evolving shape of the library as a whole over the centuries the sect thrived is a phenomenon that cannot be denied. Yet, in keeping with the tenor of this entire book, the goal here is not to plot points with documents and then draw straight lines of religious history. We will put aside here questions concerning, for example, the date of the composition of the *Temple Scroll* or the place of 4QMMT in the sectarian library. Regardless of when these documents were composed, they would appear to be of importance to the sect, and they will be analyzed accordingly.

We put these questions aside, in part, because the standard approaches to these matters are based on two kinds of arguments, both of which can be considered evolutionist. First, scholars who attempt to reconstruct the development of the sect on the basis of the nature of the literature found there typically operate on the assumption that the less pronounced the sectarian tendencies, the earlier the document.[2] While such a linear development remains possible, other possibilities also present themselves: perhaps the sect moderated after a period of time, or perhaps there were phases—possibly, for example, during the Herodian construction projects—when the group was interested (even just potentially) in participating in cultic ceremonies or cooperating with other Jews.[3]

Another kind of evolutionism can be seen in the nitty-gritty of Qumran studies: paleography. It is a fundamental tenet of Dead Sea Scrolls scholarship that the manuscripts can be dated rather precisely, by means of paleography, to within approximately twenty-five years.[4] The typologies on which these judgments are based allow primarily for chronological variance. No room is left for regional differences, nor is allowance made for the possibility that some groups or scribes might choose self-consciously to archaize.[5] Indeed, the precision assumed by the Dead Sea Scrolls paleographers is much greater than what is assumed in medieval Hebrew codicology or ancient Greek papyrology.[6] I am not qualified to review the data or evaluate the consensus on these matters, other than to note that the presumption of *linear* development is deeply suspicious, and rooted in attitudes toward history that can rightly be questioned.[7]

As we review the arguments raised against the Second Temple at Qumran, we must also consider whether or not there is a qualitative difference between what we will see in this chapter and what we have encountered already in earlier chapters. It will be helpful at this point to introduce some vocabulary employed by social scientists. In a classic work cited with some frequency by scholars of ancient Judaism, Bryan R. Wilson introduced a distinction between "reformist" sects and "introversionist" ones.[8] Reformist ideology articulates criticism in the hopes that things will change. This criticism can be quite pronounced, but it stops short of advocating withdrawal from the general society. A group with an "introversionist" ideology, however, turns into itself, rejecting entirely the hope that society outside the sect can be redeemed or reformed. With regard to the situation we are considering, Wilson's term "reformist" can be taken to refer to ancient Jewish criticisms of the temple, its practice, and its personnel that stop short of either boycotting the temple or establishing institutional alternatives. Wilson's term "introversionist" is of less use, because these groups' self-perception is of less interest here than their attitudes toward the temple specifically. Therefore, in the analysis that follows reformist views will be contrasted with with "rejectionist" ones. A rejectionist approach not only criticizes the current temple as inadequate in some way but also takes the critique to the next level by boycotting the temple and possibly by establishing some sort of alternative.

We have already encountered those who would categorize the prophets' message as rejectionist, and I have argued at length that prophetic literature articulated criticism without advocating a boycott of or alternative to the temple cult. We have also encountered those who would describe the apocalyptic or mystic visionaries who imagine a temple in heaven as rejectionist, and I have argued that envisioning a temple in heaven need not pose any practical challenge to the earthly temple, and certainly need not involve calling for a boycott of the temple.

At Qumran, however, it does appear that we find all we need to label the group as rejectionist. The criticisms leveled against the temple, its practices, and its personnel are numerous and apparently operated on a number of distinct levels simultaneously. Although the evidence for the sectarian boycott of the temple is not unquestionable, we will find that there is strong evidence to suggest that they explicitly saw their own community as an alternate for the temple. Yet we will also see that they did not view this situation as ideal. Once again, antitemple biases among scholars have clouded the picture. Some scholars recognize that the sectarians viewed their communal replacements for the temple as provisional, for they hoped for a return to a temple-based reality. What is rarely recognized, however, is the fact that the sectarians saw their situation not only as provisional but also as comparatively deficient. While some describe the sectarians as if they were confident that their powers of atonement exceeded that of the temple, we will see below that the sectarians were *not* satisfied with their temple-free existence. We will turn to this point toward the end of this chapter, after we have more fully catalogued the various charges raised against the temple in the Qumran literature.

The Temple as Morally Defiled

One of the more prevalent charges raised against the temple during the Second Temple period is the claim that the sanctuary was morally defiled, as a result of grave transgression. Of course, this charge is hardly novel. The idea that the temple has been or could be defiled by sin is one that is articulated in the Pentateuch as well as prophetic traditions. It is also a notion that appears with some frequency in the Dead Sea corpus, including the following passages: (1) *Temple Scroll* (11QT) LI:11–15, which states that bribery and judicial deceit "defiles the house"; (2) *Damascus Document* (CD) IV:20, V:6–9, which asserts that certain sexual sins defile the sanctuary"; (3) *Pesher Habakkuk*

VIII:8–13, to the effect that the "wicked priest" became arrogant, stole the wealth of the poor, and defiled the temple through abominable deeds; and (4) *Pesher Habakkuk* XII:6–10, which similarly speaks of the wicked priest's defilement of the temple by sin, again juxtaposed with reference to his thievery and greed.[9]

There are additional passages from the scrolls that can be understood similarly: (5) A curious parabiblical work known either as *4QApocryphon of Jeremiah C^e* or *4QPseudo-Moses^e* (4Q390) speaks of the people's sins, predicting that they will steal, oppress one another, and defile the sanctuary (frag. 2, I:9). Like the *Pesher Habakkuk*, this document too juxtaposes violent property crimes and the defilement of the sanctuary.[10] (6) As reconstructed, a further passage from other copies of the same work appears to restate the prophetic concerns with the defilement of the sanctuary by sin (4Q385a frag. 3a, C:6–7; 4Q387 frag. 1, 4; 4Q388a frag. 3, 5).[11] (7) In CD VI:11–17, which we will analyze in greater depth below, we find the suggestion that the temple has been morally defiled by virtue of the fact that stolen property—which is impure (V:15)—has been offered there. (8) CD Ms B XX:22–23 refers to the "House of Peleg," which departed from the holy city at the time when Israel sinned and defiled the sanctuary. The juxtaposition of impurity and sin suggests that moral impurity is of concern here.[12] (9) The *Temple Scroll* warns against sacrificing a pregnant animal (LII:5–7), for doing so is an "abomination."[13] The use of the term "abomination" suggests that such a sacrifice is not only sinful but also odious and therefore a threat to the maintenance of God's presence in the sanctuary—that is, such an offering threatens to morally defile the temple.[14] The interpretation (and even the reading) of some of these passages remains in doubt. It is clear nonetheless that the idea that the temple could by defiled by sin remained of interest—and presumably of importance—to the Qumran sectarians.[15]

Curiously, a number of the passages just cited express in one way or another the idea that the people or the priests could defile the temple by their greed. The juxtaposition of greed with the defilement of the sanctuary is a motif that also appears in other ancient Jewish literature, including rabbinic sources and the New Testament. The phenomenon calls for further attention and comment, for, as we will see, a number of distinct attitudes toward tainted wealth were articulated in these various sources.

In *Jubilees* 23:21 we are told of a future sinful generation that will

> lift themselves up for deceit and wealth so that one shall take
> everything of his neighbor; and they will pronounce the great name,
> but not in truth or righteousness. And they will pollute the holy
> of holies with their pollution and with the corruption of their
> contamination.[16]

As is well known, multiple copies of *Jubilees* were uncovered at Qumran, and we should not therefore be surprised by the strong resemblance between this passage and the above-cited selections from the *Pesher Habakkuk*, especially with regard to the juxtaposition of greed with defilement of the sanctuary. But there is one important difference: while the *Pesher Habakkuk* focuses on the sins of the wicked priest, *Jubilees* seems to direct its attention more broadly at the sinful generation. It's not just the priests who can defile the temple though theft.

We find a similar passage in *T. Levi* 14:5–15:1:

(14:5) You will rob the offerings of the Lord and steal from his portions and before sacrificing to the Lord take the choice things, eating contemptuously with harlots; (6) you will teach the commandments of the Lord out of covetousness, pollute married women, defile virgins of Jerusalem, be joined with harlots and adulteresses, take to wives daughters of the Gentiles, purifying them with an unlawful purification, and your union will be like Sodom and Gomorrah in ungodliness; (7) and you will be puffed up because of the priesthood, exalting yourselves against men; and not only thus, but puffed up also against the commandments of God; (8) you will mock the holy things, jesting contemptuously.

(15:1) Because of this, the temple which the Lord will choose, will be desolate in uncleanness, and you will be captives throughout all the Gentiles.[17]

The sequence of events is complicated, and it is not precisely clear whether the sins mentioned in 14:5 have an immediate causal effect on the destruction and desolation of the sanctuary as mentioned in 15:1. Still, this passage, like others noted above speaks of greedy priests and their ill effect on the sanctuary. It therefore needs to be considered as a possible parallel attestation to the idea that the sanctuary could be morally defiled by the greed of the priests. Similarly curious passages—with many of the same interpretive problems—occur in *Assumption of Moses* 5:1–5, 7:1–10.

Finally, sexual sins, unbridled greed, and sanctuary defilement are all juxtaposed yet again in passages from *Psalms of Solomon*.[18] It would appear that the sexual sins are the text's primary concern: the morally defiling effect of sexual sins is emphasized in 2:11–13 and 8:9–13, 21–22. But in 8:11, the people are also condemned for greedily plundering the temple's wealth. Moreover, the first psalm mentions only greed and theft, and it explicitly speaks also of the defilement of the sanctuary by sin (1:4–8; cf. 2:3). It is *possible* that sexual sins are the immediate cause of the sanctuary defilement, for the sins in question were committed in secret (1:7; cf. 8:9). But it is also quite possible that in this case it is the theft and plundering that is hidden from God and causes the defilement of the sanctuary. Either way, we at least have yet another juxtaposition of greed with sanctuary defilement, one that is not limited in scope to the behavior of the priests.

Whence comes this juxtaposition of greed and sanctuary defilement? One possibility is that an exegetical process lay behind this idea, though I know of no early ancient Jewish evidence for it. In Deuteronomy 25:13–16, the prohibitions against having unfair weights and measures leads to the general warning that (v. 16) "all who do these things—who act deceitfully—are an abomination to the Lord your God." The term "abomination" is, of course, used with some frequency with regard to the well-documented sources of moral defilement (idolatry, sexual sin, and murder). For the later rabbis, the use of the term "abomination" in the context of greed appears to have motivated their considering greed too to be a source of moral defilement (*Sifra Qedoshim* perek 4:1, on Lev. 19:15 [ed. Weiss 88d–89a] and *Mekilta de-Rabbi Ishmael, Yitro*, sec. 9 [ed. Horovitz/Rabin 238]).[19] Perhaps for earlier ancient Jews too—as for the later rabbis—the Deuteronomic reference to avarice as abomination led to the idea that this sort of behavior could defile the sanctuary.

Another possibility concerns the themes developed in chapter 3. It is essential to remember that sacrifice is an economic activity: temple offerings consist of goods that are supposed to be duly owned by those who offer them. This concern helps understand the prophets' critique of their contemporaries' sacrifices. The sacrifices of the sinful are detestable because one who has taken unjustly from the poor cannot properly *give* anything, since that person has no right to what has greedily been taken. But what happened if such offerings were in fact given to the temple? These stolen, tainted, animals would be slaughtered in the sacred realm; their blood would be daubed on the altar, and their meat would be burned on it or consumed by the priests. It is therefore not difficult to imagine that some ancient Jews would consider the possibility that the temple could be morally *defiled* by economic sin. Taking the prophetic condemnatory rhetoric one step further, the offerings tainted by greed are not only detestable, they are even defiling, albeit in the moral sense.

If we turn back to the Dead Sea Scrolls, we find a distinct development of this theme. It is well known that the Qumran sectarians held themselves to rather high standards of economic righteousness—well beyond, we can presume, what was common among even other ethically minded ancient Jews.[20] One manifestation of the sect's economic standards is their unease with "evil wealth," a concern that runs through the Qumran corpus, permeating especially the *Damascus Document*.[21] In CD, one stated reason for the concern with wealth is the fact that greed is seen as a key motivator for sinful behavior. Greed can motivate people to steal (CD VI:16), to violate the Sabbath (X:18, XI:15), and even to kill (XII:6–7). Avarice is also commonly juxtaposed with sexual sins (IV:15–18; B XIX:19 // A VIII:5).[22] The strong sectarian interest in the purity and integrity of their communal property is particularly manifest in the gradual incorporation of the property of initiates, as described in the *Rule of the Community* (1QS V–VI). These procedures illustrate well their idealistic attempt to remain free from the ill-gotten gains that pervade (and possibly defile in some way) the economy outside the sect.

The sectarians appear to have developed the concern with defiling wealth in two ways. First, the concern is generalized: the entire populace has been infected by greed. Second, they advocate a strict removal from the greater society, in order to protect themselves from this evil wealth. And what has any of this to do with the sanctuary? If the entire economy outside the sect is tainted, then it stands to reason that the sacrificial cult too has been sullied. Indeed, the frequency with which greed is juxtaposed with sanctuary defilement in the Qumran corpus confirms this supposition, especially when combined with their overall attitude toward the temple as we are tracing it here.

In the *Damascus Document* we find further evidence that the sectarians perceived a causal connection between what they perceived as the greedy behavior of the populace on the one hand and the defilement of the sanctuary on the other. In the legal material, we find a ruling that prohibits donating "to the altar" anything that has been taken by force (CD XVI:13–14).[23] This passage explicitly addresses the issue that connects greed with sanctuary defilement: the possibility that gifts of the greedy—which are, no doubt, stolen— could be given to the temple.[24] Presumably, many ancient Jewish authorities, learning their lessons from the prophets, would have agreed that individuals should not donate to the temple what they stole from others (cf. Ben Sira 34:21–27). What is remarkable about CD XVI:13–14 is that the ruling confirms the supposition that CD is concerned with the direct and deleterious impact that misappropriated wealth can have on the sanctuary.

One further passage from CD treats this theme, and although the passage is rather obscure, it appears to bring together two important ideas: (1) that evil wealth taints the sanctuary, and (2) that as a result, the sectarians are to shun the temple altogether (VI:11–21; cf. 4Q266 frag. 3, II:17–25):[25]

> (11) and all who have been brought into the covenant (12) so as not to
> enter the sanctuary to light his altar *at no cost*,[26] and to be "closers of
> (13) the door" of whom God said, "Who of you will close my door
> and not light my altar (14) at no cost?" (Mal. 1:10)—if they do not take
> care to perform according to the meaning of the Torah during the
> time of evil and to separate (15) from the sons of the pit and to
> refrain from the wicked wealth which is impure due to oaths and
> bans (16) and from the property of the sanctuary, [for] they "[the sons
> of the pit] steal from the poor of his people, preying upon widows
> (17) and murdering orphans" (Isa. 10:2); and to distinguish
> between the impure and the pure and make known [the difference]
> between (18) the holy and the profane, and to observe the Sabbath day
> in its exact detail, and the appointed times (19) and the day of the
> fast as it was found by those who entered into the new covenant in
> the land of Damascus (20) to offer up the holy things in accordance
> with their detailed requirements, to love each man his brother (21) as
> himself and to support the poor, destitute, and stranger.[27]

The passage is in part an exegesis (a "pesher" of sorts) of Malachi 1:10, and it would appear that CD understands the Malachi verse in the way I proposed in chapter 3: the concern is not with offerings made "in vain" but with offerings that have been acquired unethically. Such offerings have become the norm for the evil people who frequent the temple (V:16). Therefore, those who have entered the covenant are told to shun completely the defiled wealth of the wicked (VI:15; cf. 1QS V:20).[28] And the only way for them to do so is to act as "closers of the door," by agreeing not to enter the temple altogether.[29]

It would appear that tainted wealth is considered to be a source of *moral* defilement for CD, though the clear marker for this notion—sanctuary defilement—is not explicitly mentioned. It is also possible that here too we are already dealing with the more fully developed sectarian notion of defilement that is characteristic of the *Rule of the Community*, in which case the defilement spoken of here would have both ritual and moral characteristics. Either way, because the temple's economics are tainted, there is no way to offer a valid offering. Proper sacrificial worship—as envisioned in CD VI:20–21—is dependent upon due care for the poor and the stranger. But those tainted by evil wealth presumably do not dutifully care for those less fortunate than they. While other concerns too are addressed (like Sabbath observance), it seems that the passage at hand dismisses the current temple as inherently impure, in part because its economic basis is ethically tainted. While the *Pesher Habakkuk* focuses on the sins of the wicked priest, the *Damascus Document* casts a broader scope, indicting the entire economic and sacrificial system. But these and the other assorted passages are commensurate. The temple is defiled, in part because it has been defiled by greed and ill-gotten gains: "would that someone would shut the door."

The concern that the temple could be defiled by sin and that this would lead to destruction, exile and the departure of the divine presence is expressed in a good deal of biblical and ancient Jewish literature. *Jubilees* 23:21—quoted earlier—is immediately followed by the assertion that the generation being spoken of will be afflicted, exiled, and destroyed (23:22). Similarly, *T. Levi* 14:5–15:1, in emphasizing the deleterious effect of sin on the sanctuary, underscores that the result of it all is the desolation of the sanctuary. What we don't find in these texts is the call to abandon the morally defiled temple *in advance* of its punitive destruction. Indeed, while the *Psalms of Solomon* warns against the defilement of the sanctuary, this work also asserts that God's presence has not yet departed (7:1). Clearly, there is no call here to abandon the temple just yet. But this is precisely what we do find in the sectarian literature, especially in the *Damascus Document*: the temple is defiled by various transgressions (1QpHab VIII, XII; CD V:6; XX:23). The righteous ones left the temple long ago (CD XX:22), and the members of the sect are to enter a covenant agreeing not to go there now (VI:11–12). When we read this evidence alongside the other antitemple polemics that we will survey in this chapter, the evidence becomes cumulative, supporting the claim that the critiques raised here are "rejectionist" ones, not "reformist" ones.

Perhaps the rejectionist nature of what we find here can be seen even more clearly if we compare the sources just surveyed with a nonsectarian source, one that develops the concern with tainted wealth in a way that is thoroughly different. In the Wisdom of Ben Sira, we find a passage remarkable for its developed synthesis of the prophetic rhetoric concerning justice (e.g., Amos 2:6–8) with the wisdom traditions' abhorrence of the offerings of the wicked (Prov. 15:8; 21:27):[30]

(34:21) If one sacrifices ill-gotten goods (ἐξ ἀδίκου),
      the offering is blemished (μεμωμημένη);
(22) the gifts of the lawless are not acceptable (οὐκ εἰς εὐδοκίαν).
(23) The Most High is not pleased with the offerings of the ungodly,
      nor for a multitude of sacrifices does he forgive sins.
(24) Like one who kills a son before his father's eyes
      is the person who offers a sacrifice from the property of
      the poor.
(25) The bread of the needy is the life of the poor;
      whoever deprives them of it is a murderer.
(26) To take away a neighbor's living is to commit murder;
(27) To deprive an employee of wages is to shed blood.

Ben Sira asserts unquestionably that those who steal from the poor are in no position to offer a worthy sacrifice to God. Thus this passage further confirms my suspicion that ancient Jews in general—and in the second century B.C.E. in particular—were concerned with the possible impact that tainted wealth may have had on the temple and its offerings. What we don't find here is any development of this theme along rejectionist lines. If there is some cumulative, defiling effect that this behavior can have on the sanctuary, Ben Sira leaves it unmentioned. Ben Sira remains focused on sinful individuals, whose offerings are deemed invalid or profane—but notably they are not impure (ritually or morally). There is no stated concern with the possibility that tainted offerings could defile the temple, and no indication here that the righteous should avoid the temple. To the contrary, Ben Sira advises his readers to give to the temple willfully and generously (35:10–12), for the sacrifices of the righteous are pleasing indeed (35:8–9). This kind of balanced assessment is precisely what is lacking in those sources that reject the temple as morally defiled, such as we find in the *Damascus Document*.

The Temple as Ritually Defiled

Another charge raised against the temple in a number of Qumran texts concerns the ritual defilement of the temple. This phenomenon has been well studied, particularly as it relates to the various purity laws preserved in 4QMMT and the *Temple Scroll* XLV:7–LI:10.[31] Curiously, this charge is raised only rarely in so many words. But one such warning is presented at the very beginning of the *Temple Scroll*'s lengthy collection of purity laws: 11QT XLV: 7–10 warns men against defiling the temple by entering it less than three full days after a seminal emission. A similar general warning can be found at the conclusion of this section of the scroll (11QT LI:6–10; see also XLVII:3–6). There can be little doubt that the various and numerous purity issues raised in these and other sectarian documents (e.g., 4QToharot) would have had considerable impact on the sectarian attitude toward the temple. We cannot by any means list here all of the issues at stake, but we can identify some of the major points of contention.

One reason the sanctuary was considered ritually defiled was because people deemed by the sect to be ritually impure were allowed to enter into it. It appears that the sect adhered to rather strict laws of ritual impurity: for instance, in the passage just alluded to, 11QT XLV:7–10 states that a man who has had a seminal emission is barred from the temple for three days, while the legal precedents in the Pentateuch speak of only a day-long impurity (Lev. 15:16; Deut. 23:10–11).[32] The *Temple Scroll* is also stricter in comparison to rabbinic literature in its emphasis that the impurity in question lasts until sunset (11QT XLV:9; cf. L:4, 15, and 4QMMT B15, 72).[33] Rabbinic literature, in contrast, allowed a person who had immersed to enter parts of the temple immediately thereafter, even if that person's state of ritual impurity technically lasted until sundown (the so-called *tevul yom*; see, e.g., *m. Kelim* 1:5).[34] In addition to asserting longer periods of defilement for some already-known ritual impurities, the Qumran documents also introduce new sources of ritual defilement. For instance, they appear to have considered the blind to be ritually impure (11QT XLV:12–14), though it is possible that these persons are banned not because they are ritually impure per se but because their inability to see could lead to their accidental defilement of the temple precincts (cf. 4QMMT B 49–54).[35] If, as I have argued elsewhere,[36] the sectarians considered sinners in general as if they were *ritually* (and not just *morally*) defiling, then we would find yet another reason why the sect considered the temple impure. No doubt the temple was frequented—and thus, defiled—by those considered sinful according to sectarian standards.

The legal documents from Qumran also raise concerns with the ways certain purification procedures were practiced. A number of texts treat the red heifer rite of Numbers 19, and these documents appear to emphasize that those involved with the preparation are considered ritually impure until evening (4QMMT B 13–17; 4Q277 frag. 1).[37] As is well known, this position contrasts sharply with the practice as remembered (or imagined) by the rabbis. According to *m. Parah* 3:7, the persons involved with the rite are to bathe and immediately resume their duties, because ritual purity can be partially achieved by washing alone (without waiting until sunset). The ramifications of this kind of dispute are also rather serious: this rite yields the purification waters used for the amelioration of corpse impurity, which is the most severe and most contagious form of ritual defilement. If the rite were performed incorrectly, then presumably all of the people from the priests on down would then be in a state of ritual defilement. By their entering the temple in such a state, the temple itself has presumably been rendered ritually defiled as well.

A third kind of ritual purity dispute concerns realms of space: the *Temple Scroll* suggests to us that the sect had an "expansive" approach to the sacred realms, believing that the various sources of ritual impurity (however understood) would have to be kept farther from the temple and even from the city of the sanctuary than we would have otherwise thought.[38] For example, in the case we have been considering, 11QT XLV:11–12 bans men defiled by semen not just from the temple but from the city of the sanctuary. In the *Damascus Document*, we find a related prohibition against having sexual relations in the city of the sanctuary (CD XII:1–2; 4Q 271 frag. 5, I:17–18). Assuming the current temple did not follow the laws as stipulated by the *Temple Scroll*, we can presume that the scroll's stringencies lead to the idea that the temple has been ritually defiled by the admission of ritually impure persons to Jerusalem and its environs.

The *Temple Scroll* emphasizes again and again that its concerns with ritual purity are related to the fact that God's name, presence, or glory is to dwell in the sanctuary (XLV:12–14, XLVI:4, 8, 11–12; XLVII:3–4, 10–11, 18; LI:7–10; cf. XXIX: 3–10). In these passages, the scroll uses the terms "name" and "glory" interchangeably, frequently making use of the causative form of "dwell."[39] We have reviewed already the biblical foundations of this view, and the *Temple Scroll*'s approach seems largely consistent with the biblical evidence.[40] The fact that the *Temple Scroll* emphatically refers to the dwelling of God's name, presence, or glory as a future *possibility* strongly suggests that the document does not believe that the current temple merits this divine endorsement. Presumably, that is because, according to the rules of the *Temple Scroll*, the present temple would be considered ritually defiled. Yet while the *Temple Scroll*'s ritual purity rules appear to differ from those of other ancient Jews— leading to a critical evaluation of the current temple—the essential theology of the *Temple Scroll* seems largely consistent with other biblical, ancient Jewish, and rabbinic documents.[41]

Of course, there is nothing inherently anti-temple in the concerns of 11QT and 4QMMT that the temple could be defiled—ritually or morally—by violations: after all, Leviticus is similarly concerned with the potential defilement of a sanctuary. But 4QMMT is clearly a polemical document, rejecting opposing views that are presumably the ones in practice at the temple at the time of its composition (whenever that was). The date of the *Temple Scroll*—to say nothing of the sources on which it is clearly based—remains a completely open question, and for all we know the purity laws of 11QT could have been composed by priests in the third century B.C.E., describing their practice in a Jerusalem temple at that time.[42] Yet the *Temple Scroll* too—at least in its final form—is surely critical of the current temple (as we will see below), and it is therefore reasonable to read the document with the assumption that it is not describing current temple praxis. Yet I must emphasize that we can only *infer* that these documents—in the forms that we have them—would have articulated boycotting the temple of their day. It's a good inference, but it remains an inference just the same.

I have so far suggested that the Qumran texts raise two distinct charges against the temple, related to purity: that the temple was morally defiled by sin, and that it was ritually defiled by other violations. When analyzing elsewhere the purity rules and the use of related terminology in sectarian documents such as the *Rule of the Community* and the *Thanksgiving Hymns*, I found strong evidence that the sectarians did not distinguish between ritual and moral defilements in the same way that most other Jews did, at least with regard to their distinct approach to sin and sinners.[43] Yet as we have just seen, those Qumran documents that speak most clearly and frequently of the temple and its practice—CD, 4QMMT, 11QT—tend to use purity terms in their traditional ways, referring to what we can reasonably identify as "ritual" or "moral" concerns.

The Temple as Ritually Inadequate

Many other temple-related legal disputes between the sect and their contemporaries fall under a different category, by virtue of the fact that they do not concern purity per se. It is important for the sake of accuracy and clarity to emphasize that violation of these rules would not have led—even in the sectarian perspective—to the defilement of the sanctuary. Indeed, unlike the case of the defilement of the sanctuary (whether ritual, moral, or both) there is less with regard to these disputes that would inherently lead to a boycott of the temple.

We find a number of disputes regarding sacrificial practice in 4QMMT and the *Temple Scroll* that do not concern purity per se. Such concerns include, for example, the prohibition of leaving cereal offerings overnight (4QMMT B 9–13; 11QT XX:12–13),[44] the requirements that fourth-year produce and certain tithes be given to the priests (4QMMT B 62–64),[45] and the various sacrificial procedures spelled out in much of the *Temple Scroll* (11QT XI: 9–XXIX:10).[46] It is certainly striking that the eighteen columns of the *Temple Scroll* devoted to laying out these rules do not preserve any warnings that the temple would be defiled by improper practice. Thus there is no indication that violation of these rules may have defiled the temple. It must also be noted that while certain laws in 4QMMT are specifically said to lead to defilement, others are not. It is therefore essential to recognize the different nature of such issues, and the possibility that the inherent force of such disputes is less than those concerning impurity. On the other hand, we cannot preclude the possibility that debates over such matters may have led in part to a break between the sect and the larger Jewish polity: after all, according to 4QMMT, the issues listed are the reasons why the group separated from the rest of the people (4QMMT C:7–8). But even if these issues were decisive for 4QMMT, they may or may not have been as decisive for the authors or transmitters of 11QT.

Another example of a dispute unrelated to purity between the sect and other Jews concerns the Zadokite priesthood. It has long been assumed that the sect formed in response to the removal of the Zadokite high priestly dynasty in the wake of the Maccabean wars.[47] This view found support in various references to Zadokite priests (e.g., 1QS V:2, 9), as well as the supposition that Qumran was founded in the latter part of the second century B.C.E. This long-held view has come under increased scrutiny of late. With the publication of the Cave 4 copies of the *Rule of the Community*, it became clear that the concerns with Zadokite priests were relatively later glosses added to an already existing sectarian work.[48] Reexamination of the archaeological evidence has led to the conclusion that the site was not in fact settled before 100 B.C.E.[49] It has also long been known—though often overlooked—that in CD III:21–IV:4, the term "Zadokite" functions in a nonliteral fashion: the reference to these priests in Ezekiel 44:15 is decoded so that it refers to the "chosen ones of Israel" who will stand at the end of days.[50] The evidence is certainly quite problematic for those who seek to explain Qumran origins with regard to priestly disputes in the mid–second century. On the other hand, the evidence that Zadokites were—*at some point*—given specific powers or pre- rogatives remains strong (1QS V:2, 9). This development could have been a matter of contention between the sect and the contemporary (non-Zadokite) priestly establishment. If there was such a dispute, it was another that had nothing to do with purity, be it ritual or moral.

Perhaps the most significant example of a temple dispute not related to purity is the fact that 4QMMT, 11QT, and other Qumran documents (including the *Songs of the Sabbath Sacrifice*) follow a 364-day, 52-week, "solar" calendar,[51] while the temple authorities appear to have adhered to some sort of lunar-solar calendar.[52] A number of matters regarding this calendar dispute require brief clarification here. First, when discussing the 364-day, 52-week, "solar" calen- dar, it is essential to avoid the term "solar" altogether or at least put the word in quotation marks. Simply put, that's because the 52-week calendar only approximates the solar year. That the solar year is closer to 365.25 days was well known already in antiquity, as attested by the institution of the Julian calendar, with its quadrennial leap year in 46 B.C.E., and the subsequent reform of the 365-day Egyptian civil calendar in 22 B.C.E.[53] Indeed, with these and other calendar reforms and disputes, practically anyone living in the Mediterranean world in the late first century B.C.E. would have been made aware of the fact that the 364-day calendar does not keep up with the sun, the stars, or the seasons. Despite this knowledge, there is no known system of intercalating the 364-day, 52-week calendar. This calendar holds many attractions: the year divides evenly into four seasons of ninety-one days (exactly thirteen weeks); the holidays fall on the same days of the week each year; and the system of twenty-four priestly courses comes full circle every six years.[54] Add a day here, or a week there, and one or more of these attractions is lost. Indeed *Jubilees* 6:31–32 explicitly prohibits making any adjustments whatsoever.[55] As a result, it is not true to assert that the 364-day "solar" calendar coordinates heaven with earth any better (or with less human intervention) than a lunar- solar one.[56]

There is also no evidence to the effect that calendar disputes led directly to any accusation that the temple was defiled, whether ritually or morally.[57] Moreover, there is reason to wonder whether a calendar dispute on its own would even have impelled one group to shun a temple run in accordance with the calendar of another. True, such a disagreement would lead to the cele- bration of major festivals on different days—indeed, the little information we have on specific calendar disputes among ancient Jews tends to focus on specific holidays (e.g., 1QpHab XI:4–8; *m. Rosh ha-Shanah* 2:8–9). But the holidays—though of great significance—represent, when added together, a proportionally small percentage of the days of the year. Since we have no evidence that ancient Jews counted the days of the week differently, the scheduling of Sabbath or weekday rituals was not affected by these calendar disputes. Any disagreement over when the day begins (morning or evening) would be equally irrelevant, as practically all temple rituals take place during the daytime. Thus even when calendar disputes were looming—or even raging—the temple was run most of the time according to the rules of *both* calendars: that is, on most given days, the priests in the temple were doing nothing particularly special, which is just what either calendar would legislate for that day. This point is not of minor significance: while we could assume that Jews adhering to one calendar might avoid the temple on the holidays as being celebrated in accordance with another calendar, there is no reason to assume that a calendar dispute on its own would necessarily lead to a boycott of the temple on all days.[58]

It is certainly not the case that all of the temple-related legal disputes between the Qumran sectarians and other ancient Jewish groups concerned purity, whether ritual or moral. And this point too is by no means insignificant. Scholars have generally assumed—rightly enough, in my view—that the purity-concerned Qumran sectarians would have shunned a temple that they considered to be both ritually and morally defiled. The same presumption however, does not necessarily apply to those temple disputes that do not concern purity, such as those we have reviewed here. But while potentially of less significance in and of themselves, such disputes could certainly serve to supplement a rejectionist ideology. As if adding insult to injury, once the temple were considered morally or ritually defiled, it could easily stand accused of a host of other lesser transgressions such as those mentioned here.

The Temple as Structurally Inadequate

There is nothing new in the belief that the Second Temple was structurally inadequate. In the early days of the Second Temple—or even before the temple was constructed, if the traditional dating is to be accepted—the prophet Ezekiel or subsequent disciples imagined a future temple of ideal design and enormous size. It was argued in chapter 3 that Ezekiel's vision must be taken on two levels: while it expresses hope for a glorious future, it levels criticism at both the First and Second temples, which certainly fail by comparison. The temple that was destroyed was woefully inadequate, and the temple that had been rebuilt could hardly have surpassed it.

As the Second Temple period progresses, we find similar statements regarding future temples, and these can, for the most part, be understood likewise. In some cases (e.g., 1 *Enoch* 90:28–37, 2 Esdras 10:25–27, 42–44) we are told little more than that a future temple will replace the current one. In some other cases, we are told that the temple of the future will be constructed of jewels, or exhibit other extraworldly characteristics (2 Esdras 10:55; Tobit 13:16–17).[59] A glorious new temple is also imagined in the *New Jerusalem* texts from Qumran (1Q32, 2Q24, 4Q554–555, 5Q15, 11Q18), which imagine a city with a golden wall (11Q18, frag. 10), jewel-encrusted structures (4Q554 frag. 2, II:15), streets paved in white stone, alabaster, and onyx (5Q15 frag1, I:6–7), and a temple whose construction is similarly radiant (2Q24 frag. 3; frag. 8).[60]

On the one hand, these sources can be understood like Ezekiel's vision: since neither the past nor present temples exhibit such characteristics, they are surely inadequate by comparison. On the other hand, the fantastic nature of these visions serves to exculpate the people. After all, they were never asked to build jewel-encrusted temples, nor could they have done so had they even wished to. The people cannot be faulted for not being able to produce the wonders that God can. Moreover, the inadequacy of the present and past temples is inherent: the people didn't render them inadequate by breaking the laws or defiling them in some way. Therefore, to the degree these visions imagine a wondrous future temple, they step away from the kind of vision that Ezekiel had, one that shakes a finger at the past as much as it points toward the future.

In some respects, the *Temple Scroll* might appear to present a similarly wondrous vision of an expanded future temple. Yet it is virtually certain that the temple being spoken of throughout the scroll is not the eschatological temple, of the sort imagined in the *New Jerusalem* texts.[61] According to 11QT, the temple being described is to last for quite some time, until the coming day when God will construct his own sanctuary (XXIX:9–10).[62] Meanwhile, the temple being described throughout the document was supposed to have been built long ago, and it should at any rate already be in existence (XXIX:3–8).

The temple imagined in the *Temple Scroll* is entirely unlike any other known from ancient Jewish literature.[63] In size, the temple's outer court is practically the dimensions of the current old city of Jerusalem (XL:9).[64] In structure, the temple is unique in being surrounded by three concentric square courts (other temple plans allow for just two courts).[65] The *Temple Scroll's* sanctuary exhibits a number of other distinct features, such as its curious golden staircase (XXX:3–XXXI:9).[66] Indeed, the temple envisioned in the *Temple Scroll* is beyond comparison to the tabernacle or the Solomonic temple (as known from the Hebrew Bible), to the Second Temple (as known from Josephus or rabbinic literature), or even to the eschatological temple envisioned in Ezekiel 40–48.[67] All these—and certainly any temple that existed when the *Temple Scroll* was composed—fall short by comparison. And yet the temple envisioned is not *entirely* fantastic: it is not encrusted with jewels or built of golden walls—nor will it descend from heaven. The temple of the *Temple Scroll* is an impressive structure, but it is not a divine one.

There is a tendency to describe the laws and practices laid out in Qumranic literature (including especially 4QMMT and 11QT) as stringent.[68] Certainly there are any number of stringencies in the *Temple Scroll*.[69] Yet it is equally important to recognize that sectarian law is not always stringent, whether compared to the Hebrew Bible or rabbinic literature.[70] Indeed, there are a number of "liberal" or "lenient" tendencies in the *Temple Scroll*—and these seem to get mentioned much less frequently. First, it is worth noting that the expanded temple complex—which serves, to be sure, to protect the sacred center—also provides more Israelites with greater access to holy space than any other temple plan known. There's plenty of room in this temple for the women and children who are permitted to enter the outer court (see XXXIX:7–8). The throngs of pilgrims can enter from all directions, through the outer courts' twelve gates, one designated for each tribe (11QT XXXIX:11–13; XL:13–XLI:11).[71] Indeed, 11QT's interest in all twelve tribes (in a noneschatological text) seems remarkably inclusive, especially if this document does stem from the early Second Temple period. The *Temple Scroll* also gives these pilgrims more reason to come: there are more festivals than we know from other calendars, and there are more sacrifices offered—including especially those sacrifices in which all Israelites participate (e.g., 11QT XIX–XXI).[72] The *Temple Scroll* also legislates that certain sacrificial portions be given to the Levites, something that neither biblical nor rabbinic law provides (LX: 6–9).[73] One final inclusive or lenient tendency requires mention here: in contrast to other sectarian literature, we do not find in the *Temple Scroll* any intimation that sinners were ritually impure or otherwise excluded from the sacred precincts. In these ways, the *Temple Scroll* can be understood as being true to its priestly origins: it seeks to balance the protection of sacred space and the priestly hierarchy with a concern for the inclusion of all Israel. The current temple in Jerusalem falls short in the *Temple Scroll*'s estimation for many reasons, not all of which are stringencies on the part of the scroll.

In comparison to the temple described in the *Temple Scroll*, the present temple is defiled (both ritually and morally); its ritual is not being properly performed, and its calendar is wrong. But even if the temple authorities were to change all that and follow the rules as stated in the *Temple Scroll*, it still wouldn't suffice, because the structure itself is not large enough, nor is it built to code. So while the *New Jerusalem* texts and those like it are less critical of the past and present than Ezekiel 40–48, the *Temple Scroll* is every bit as critical, if not more so. There's really no hope for the present temple, other than for it to be rebuilt from the ground up.

Having surveyed the rejectionist polemics articulated at Qumran, we take a moment to note the difficulties inherent in associating these views with other known groups (e.g., Essenes or Sadducees) or placing these perspectives within any specific social context of the late Second Temple period. The reality of Second Temple Judaism was likely more complex than Josephus'—or many modern scholars'—descriptions of the past allow. Surely the various sects—including the Pharisees, the Sadducees, the Essenes, and the Dead Sea Sect—evolved over time. The sectarians of the first century B.C.E. may or may not have had the same opinions on these matters as the sectarians (or the Essenes) of the first century C.E. Moreover, the temple itself was in a state of great change and development. The structure was thoroughly rebuilt during the reign of Herod (37–4 B.C.E.), and during and after Herod's reign, many high priests came and went. As a result, it is virtually impossible to know precisely what the temple practice was at any given time. So the likelihood remains that the Dead Sea sect's relationship with the temple changed over time, depending on the circumstance.[74]

Still, it is with regard to the temple that we find the greatest of contrasts between the Pharisees and Sadducees on the one hand and the rejectionist attitudes of CD, 4QMMT and the *Temple Scroll* on the other: we have no reason to suppose from any of our sources regarding the Pharisees or Sadducees that either group rejected the temple in any way, at any time. As Philip Davies noted some time ago, "despite a range of differences over Temple cultic procedure with the Sadducees, the Pharisees never abandoned the Jewish temple to their opponents, and vice-versa."[75] But we cannot generalize from the Pharisees and Sadducees to the Qumran sectarians: it must equally be remembered that neither the Pharisees nor the Sadducees established communes out in the desert. Nor did either group leave behind traditions claiming that the temple was ritually or morally defiled already, in their day. As we have seen, the Dead Sea sect did indeed abandon the temple at some point during this period: the various complaints we have surveyed here coalesce into a coherent, sectarian, rejectionist ideology.

Replacing the Temple

We will now consider an issue that is in some respects the result of all (or most) of the foregoing: the idea that because the temple was rendered useless, some sort of replacement was therefore found. There are essentially two distinct ways in which various scholars suggest that the Dead Sea sectarians replaced the Jerusalem temple. One view, articulated by a small minority of scholars, holds that the sectarians performed their own sacrificial worship at Qumran. The other view, articulated by many more scholars, holds that the sectarians conceived of their own community as a temple, in which nonsacrificial acts— sometimes called "spiritual" sacrifices—were performed.

Sacrifice at Qumran?

There is a small but vocal group of scholars who maintain that the sectarians performed sacrifice at Qumran.[76] The archaeological evidence comes primarily from bone burials uncovered at the site.[77] The literary evidence for this claim comes primarily from Josephus' *Antiquities* 18:19, which suggests that the Essenes performed sacrifices on their own (ἐφ' αὐτῶν τὰς θυσίας ἐπιτελοῦ-σιν).[78] Josephus' testimony only pertains to the degree to which one accepts the Essene hypothesis, a question we simply cannot enter into here. Still, I cannot agree with those who interpret Josephus' statement to the effect that the Essenes offered only "spiritualized" sacrifices on their own.[79] Josephus speaks explicitly and plainly of *sacrifices*, and thus we need to entertain the possibility that the Essenes—and perhaps the very Essene-like Dead Sea sectarians—did perform actual sacrificial rituals on their own. Scholars ought not to dismiss the question out of hand by asserting that the possibility is not a likely one or that Josephus must have been mistaken.[80] After all, we do know that at various times in the Second Temple period, groups of Jews established temples and practiced sacrifice outside of Jerusalem.[81]

Still it must also be said that the case for sacrifice at Qumran is not very strong. No sacrificial altar has been uncovered at the site, and the incense altar alleged to have been discovered there is too small to have been of any use in communal worship.[82] The bone burials—though curious—do not provide solid evidence of sacrificial practice, for no known Jewish sacrificial custom requires such burials.[83] It is therefore more likely that the burials reflect some ritualized eating practice.[84] The possibility cannot be precluded that the sectarians performed those sacrificial practices that need no altar, like the red heifer ritual of Numbers 19.[85] But this question is an ancillary one: according to both rabbinic and Samaritan evidence, the ashes produced from a single red heifer could last hundreds of years.[86] Thus even *if* the sectarians performed this rite and used red heifer ashes in their purification rituals, they may have only performed the sacrificial rite itself once in a generation, if even that frequently. Therefore, on the basis of the evidence that has come to light thus far, it cannot be demonstrated convincingly that the sectarians performed any regular sacrificial service at Qumran.

The Community as a Temple

But we need not suppose that sacrifice was performed at Qumran in order to determine whether or not the sectarians viewed the temple as if it had been replaced. The other way the temple could have been replaced at Qumran is if the sect viewed their community as a substitute for the temple.[87] According to this approach, the Qumran sectarians replaced the temple and its sacrificial activity with their own kinds of worship—all too often referred to as "spiritual" sacrifices.[88] According to different interpreters, the sect's ostensible replacement(s) for sacrifice consisted of their prayers, righteous deeds, or even exegetical activity.[89]

A number of passages are typically understood to express the idea that the community constituted some kind of a temple, including especially *4QFlorilegium* (4Q174), along with selections from the *Rule of the Community*. Discussions also typically catalogue what are really corollaries to this main idea: sectarian purity practices, or the various ways in which the sect described their rituals in cultic terms.[90] Indeed, there is strong evidence within the Qumran literature to the effect that the community viewed one or another of its activities as taking on cultic significance, and we will review much of this evidence toward the end of this chapter. We focus for now, however, on passages that have been understood to speak explicitly about the community as some sort of a temple.

The fragmentary document known as *4QFlorilegium*, preserved only in one copy, consists of a thematic collection of eschatological pesher-like commentaries on assorted biblical passages, notably verses taken from Nathan's prophecy concerning King David's dynasty and the king's desire to build a house for God (2 Sam. 7:10–14).[91] The document is widely acknowledged to be sectarian in origin, and generally dated to the Herodian period.[92] 4QFlorilegium quotes 2 Samuel 7:10, which speaks of a place to be established in which the people will dwell secure, free from the interventions of evil oppressors (I:1–2). This verse is then juxtaposed with Exodus 15:17 ("The Sanctuary, Oh Lord, which Your hands have established"). It appears that the document seeks to describe an eschatological temple that will be kept free from the intrusion of various foreigners or those of questionable birth (I:2–4).[93] The major interpretive difficulties begin a few lines later (I:6–7), where, according to one classic reading, the document speaks again of the eschatological temple, this time with the phrase *miqdash adam* (מקדש אדם; often understood as referring to a "human temple"). Within this temple—which is often described as a "spiritual" one— the people will offer up acts of Torah (מעשי תורה) in lieu of sacrifices.[94]

Needless to say, this controversial interpretation has not been universally accepted. Some time ago, Yigael Yadin and David Flusser both argued that 4QFlorilegium imagined a concrete eschatological temple built by God (as suggested I:1–2), which would in the end of days be a sanctuary "among the people."[95] Thus these interpreters would place 4QFlorilegium alongside the various apocalyptic and rabbinic sources that speak of a temple in heaven that is ready and waiting to descend to earth for human use at the end of days. Because such a temple is also envisioned in the *Temple Scroll* (XXIX:9–10) and in the *New Jerusalem* texts, we can be certain that this idea was known at Qumran. Despite its divine origins, this temple will be concrete, and the sacrifices offered there will be real.[96] Allied with this view is the understanding of 4QFlorilegium I:7, which speaks of what will be offered at the *miqdash adam* not as acts of Torah (תורה) but as acts of *todah* (sacrificial thanksgiving; תודה).[97]

More recently, a number of interpreters have suggested that the *miqdash adam* is not to be identified with the eschatological temple explicitly mentioned earlier in the document. This opens up a number of distinct possibilities for understanding the sanctuary spoken of in 4QFlorilegium I:6–7 as referring to (1) the man-made temple of Solomon;[98] (2) a man-made temple yet to be built along the lines of the *Temple Scroll*;[99] (3) a human temple established by the Qumran community, not instead of the future temple but in anticipation of it;[100] or, as a purposely polyvalent term, (4) not only the human temple (as in possibility 3) but also the temple of Adam, the holy place that will signify the fulfillment of God's original creation.[101] Other alternatives—combining one or another of the interpretive options surveyed—have also been considered.[102]

Regardless of how the phrase *miqdash adam* is to be understood, it must be emphasized that any suggestion that the document imagines or hopes for a *permanent* nonsacrificial temple is extremely problematic. The evidence, rather, points in a different direction. Most likely, the sectarians saw their temple-free existence as a *provisional* response to an undesired circumstance.[103] This can be seen most clearly in those eschatological passages from the Qumran sectarian literature that conceive of a future physical temple, in which tangible sacrifices consisting of animal and vegetable will be offered. The *War Scroll*, for instance, imagines future priests administering burnt offerings and other sacrifices in the sanctuary, with the intent to send up the pleasing odor to atone for the people (1QM II:4–6; see also 1QM VII:10–11).[104] The *Psalms Pesher* (4Q171) foretells that the congregation of the poor will inherit the high and holy mountain—presumably the locale of the temple (III:10–11). As mentioned above, the *Temple Scroll* also speaks explicitly of a future temple (XXIX:10), and even though this structure is to be built by God, we cannot presume to say, without explicit evidence, that this temple would not involve sacrificial practice.[105] The *New Jerusalem* texts from Qumran also imagine a future rebuilt temple, with an altar (11Q18, frag. 13, 4), on which sacrifices will be offered (frags. 16–17 II/I:1–5). And certainly it is also relevant to note that the sectarians looked forward to the coming of two messianic figures, one of whom was to be a priest (CD XIV:19; 1QS IX:11).[106] We can safely conclude, therefore, that to whatever extent the sectarians saw their community as a stand-in for the temple, it was surely understood as a provisional situation.

Obviously, a number of challenges face interpreters of *4QFlorilegium*. It remains possible (but not likely) that the document imagines an eschatological temple consisting not of bricks and mortar but of people, where offerings consist not of tangible sacrifices but of righteous deeds. Disputes over the meaning of the curious phrase *miqdash adam* are sure to continue, and scholars will still disagree over whether this phrase refers to the eschatological temple mentioned earlier in the document or to some other temple. In light of all this, we ought not consider *4QFlorilegium* to be solid evidence in favor of the theory that the sectarians viewed their community as a temple.

But the community-as temple theory can still find support in the *Rule of the Community*, where we find a cluster of passages speaking of the establishment of a holy house in the desert that will serve to effect atonement (VIII:5–7, 8–10, with supralineal gloss, and IX:3–5; see also V:5–6).[107] In IX:4, the means by which this atonement is achieved is specified further, but the passage is not entirely clear. For most, the passage is taken to mean that the sect will atone "without the flesh of burnt offerings or the fat of sacrifices."[108] Some read the passage as if it says that atonement by other means is "better than burnt offerings."[109] Still others read the passage as if to say that atonement is still achieved "by means of" or "through the flesh of burnt offerings."[110] One would think that the difference between these translations ought to be rather significant, but, surprisingly, even some who opt for the more neutral translations still insist that the "blood sacrifices have been replaced indefinitely by 'spiritual sacrifices'" and therefore the Jerusalem temple has been "superseded."[111]

The passage is indeed rather complicated, as a number of translators note in one way or another.[112] What cannot be denied is that the sect's own behaviors are described in sacrificial terms. What has not been fully proven is whether or not there is even an explicit replacement here, let alone a "spiritualization" or a "supersession." But even if there is a replacement meant here, it is surely a provisional one: for the sectarians, the expectation of a future temple remains paramount.[113]

The provisional nature of what is spoken of in the *Rule of the Community* can be confirmed in a number of ways. First, the location in the desert (1QS

VIII:14) strongly suggests a temporary, provisional situation. Some have glorified the desert as a pure or idyllic place, building on passages such as Jeremiah 2:2 and Hosea 2:12–16.[114] Others have supposed that a retreat to the wilderness is an explicitly antitemple move.[115] The latter interpretation is difficult to defend: why a retreat from general society can be seen as specifically antitemple is not very clear. The desert, moreover, is not generally viewed in an idyllic fashion: Shemaryahu Talmon is correct to emphasize the exceptional nature of those passages that appear to idealize the desert.[116] The thrust of the biblical evidence leads decidedly in a different direction: the desert is a place of refuge and punishment. Indeed, the fact that the sect viewed itself as living in *exile* certainly suggests that they were experiencing punishment (e.g., 1QpHab XI:6; 1QM I:2; cf. CD VI:5).[117] A number of passages from Qumran literature confirm that they too viewed the desert in this manner (e.g., CD III:6–9).[118] In line with this perspective, the *Temple Scroll* eliminates the wilderness narrative altogether. And, contrary to some interpretations, the scroll does not give great emphasis to the priestly traditions concerning the tabernacle's dimension or materials of construction.[119] Thus here, too, we find further confirmation that the Dead Sea sectarians viewed their establishment in the desert not as a new ideal but as a temporary refuge.

Curiously, the *Rule of the Community* speaks of the institution in the desert as a bifurcated house: there is to be, for example, a "holy house for Israel" and a "holy of holies for Aaron" (1QS VIII:5–6, cf. VIII:8–9, IX:6). For those who interpret the community as a temple, these are typically understood as referring to two of the temple's courts.[120] This bifurcation, however, does not match the description of any known sanctuary, whether from the priestly traditions, Ezekiel, Josephus, the *Temple Scroll*, or rabbinic literature. The temples described in all these sources have at least three zones, or even more, depending on how and what one counts. Jacob Licht, noting other problems with the terms in these passages, suggests that the bifurcation is analogous to the rabbinic distinction between lesser and greater sacrifices (e.g., *m. Zevahim* 5:1–8), here applied not to distinctions of space but to the different statuses of priests and Israelites. Thus for Licht, the passage does not articulate a homology between the community and a physical temple at all.[121]

Without going as far as Licht, there are indeed a number of important ways in which the temple-community homology at Qumran is incomplete— and it is not the case that in all ways the community is evaluated better than the temple. Another important way in which the homology is incomplete is terminological: with the exception of the problematic *miqdash adam* phrase in *4QFlorilegium*, the passages typically cited in discussions of the Qumranic community-as-temple concept make use not of the specific word for sanctuary (מקדש) but the more ambiguous and multivalent term, "house" (בית; e.g., 1QS VIII:5–6, IX:6).[122] This is true even in the *Damascus Document*, where the one (possible) reference to the community as a temple speaks of the establishment of a "sure house in Israel" (CD III:19).[123] Yet the term "sanctuary" (מקדש) is used nine distinct times in CD (I:3, IV:1, 18, V:6, VI:12, 16, XII:1, 2, XX:23) with at least one additional usage in the 4Q manuscripts (4Q266 frag. 6,

II:4).[124] If the author(s) of CD wanted to say that the community was truly a temple, why not use the word?

It is appropriate that the sectarians stopped short of referring to their community as a sanctuary, because presumably they knew better than anyone that the analogy was inexact. Licht helpfully referred to this homology as a sectarian "slogan," drawing a comparison with the passages that refer to the community as an "eternal planting" (VIII:5, XI:8; cf. 1QH^a XIV:15).[125] No one, of course, expects the comparison between the community and a plant to be exact.[126] Scholarship, however, has been too taken with the literalization of the "house" slogan to recognize the intended inexactitude of the homology being drawn. In a characteristic assessment, Lawrence Schiffman states that the sect's stringent purity laws—with the gradual admission of initiates and the expulsion of sinners for periods of time—can "only be understood if the sect itself was regarded as a Temple and, therefore, it was obligatory to maintain Temple purity laws within the context of the life of the group."[127] This observation is commonplace, and certainly true to an extent: but it is equally important to note that we know of no sanctuary—whether from the priestly traditions, Ezekiel, Josephus, the *Temple Scroll*, or rabbinic literature—that allowed people to enter only after *years* of purification. The ability of the temple-community analogy to explain the specific purity practices of the sect has been overemphasized.

Another difference between the temple and the Qumran community— even in their own estimation—can be seen when we consider their attitude toward the divine presence. We can be certain that the concept of God's presence dwelling in an earthly temple was known at Qumran. The notion pervades the *Temple Scroll*, as we have seen, to say nothing of the Pentateuch, the various books of which were also in ample supply at Qumran. The notion is also in *Jubilees*—and we find some key phrases even on extant fragments from Qumran (4Q216 IV:5; see also, as restored, I:7, II:9–10 and IV:5–7; cf. *Jub.* 1:1–16).[128] The idea of a divine presence dwelling in the *heavenly* sanctuary is also asserted in the *Songs of the Sabbath Sacrifice*, as discussed in the previous chapter. Yet none of the texts that are generally understood to express the notion that the community is a temple explicitly asserts that the divine presence, glory, or name now dwells among the community. The closest we come to something along these lines are the references to the holy angels residing among—or fighting alongside—the elect at the end of days (1QSa II:8–9; 1QM VII:6, XII:7–8).[129] While these passages apply clearly to the future, other texts speak suggestively of angels residing among the community in the present age (e.g., 1QS XI:7–8, 1QH^a XI:21–22, XIV:13).[130] Indeed, some texts suggest that the community viewed themselves as holy beings, perhaps on a par with these angels (e.g., 1QS VIII:17).[131] But even so, there is a clear difference between dwelling among the angels and dwelling among a divine presence. It is therefore jarring—but perhaps not surprising—that some scholars assert that the Qumran sectarians believed that the divine presence dwelt among them at Qumran at the present age.[132] It is certainly reasonable to assume that the sectarians believed that the divine presence had already departed from the ritually and morally defiled temple in Jerusalem: presumably they would not have shunned a temple in which the divine presence still resided. But even if God's glory is no longer at the temple, this hardly means that the divine presence now dwells with them at Qumran. Here, too, we find that scholars assume an equivalence between the Qumran community and the temple that is well beyond what is claimed in the Qumran texts themselves.

We come across a similar problem when we consider scholarly evaluations of the sectarian approach to atonement. It is commonplace to find in scholarship forceful descriptions of the sectarian confidence in their ability to atone for Israel. Some scholars say that the sectarians could provide effective atonement just as if they had participated in the temple cult.[133] Other scholars go even further, to suggest that the sectarian power of atonement exceeded that of any temple.[134] A detailed comparison of biblical, Qumranic, rabbinic, and other approaches to atonement is out of the question here, but a few observations can be offered: where the priestly traditions posit sacrificial atonement for a host of sins—and "excision" (כרת) for other extreme violations— the penal code of the *Rule of the Community* considers primarily three kinds of punishment: reduction in rations for fixed terms, separation from the pure food of the community for fixed terms, and expulsion from the community altogether (1QS VI:24–VII:25, VIII:16–27).[135]

On the one hand, even expulsion from the sect is surely more lenient than biblical excision (whatever precisely that was),[136] but for our purposes what is important is that the various forms of sectarian punishment are more severe than the requirement of a sin-offering. Indeed, it is commonly acknowledged that sectarian law was more stringent in these matters than biblical or rabbinic law.[137] To take a specific example: a number of property crimes, even when committed willingly, are resolved in the priestly traditions by repayment, a fine, and a reparation offering (Lev. 5:20–26). Rabbinic literature follows suit, similarly legislating repayment, a fine, and a reparation offering for crimes, including willful robbery (*m. Bava Qamma* 9:7, *m. Zevahim* 5:5; *Sifra Dibura de-Hobah* parashah 13). Yet when considering even lighter offenses with regard to property, the *Rule of the Community* legislates a year-long separation from the pure food of the community, along with a reduction in rations (1QS VI:24–25). The *Damascus Document* similarly assigns lengthy periods of probation, even for sins committed unwillingly (4Q266 frags. 10–11; 4Q270 frag. 7, I:15–19; cf. CD XIV:17–24).[138] Of course, more serious crimes would be punished more severely, especially when committed willfully (e.g., 1QS VIII:16–24).[139]

It seems curious to me that so many scholars find reason to emphasize and praise the sectarian power to effect atonement, even while the strict nature of sectarian punishment is all too obvious (and widely recognized). A more balanced assessment, however, would require that the strict nature of sectarian punishment be brought to bear on any evaluation of the sectarian viewpoint on atonement. To whatever degree the sectarian position on punishment is a more stringent one, it is equally predicated on possessing a lesser power to effect atonement. The penal laws of 1QS—whose punishments typically take a long time to work off—clearly suggest that the sect did *not* claim to possess the powers of atonement that the priestly traditions of the Pentateuch claim for the cult. We must conclude, therefore, that the sectarians did *not* believe they had the power to effect atonement, at least not in a very expeditious manner, which is what one would expect from a temple.

In an important recent study of prayer at Qumran, Eileen Schuller has demonstrated how the confident, triumphant sectarian statements on determinism (e.g., 1QS III:15–16; 1QH^a IX:9–10; CD II:6–10) find a counterweight in the various sectarian prayers that beg God for atonement and purification (e.g., 1QH^a XIX: 32–34):[140] if the sectarians had full confidence that they were predetermined to be the sons of light, what need have they of further atonement or purification? Similarly, even though we are led to believe that the outcome of the final war of the sons of light against the sons of darkness is predetermined, the *War Scroll* states that the high priest is to pray for victory (1QM XV:5).[141] Certainly the sect expressed strong deterministic beliefs, but this did not prevent them from experiencing moods of doubt and composing prayers that step back decidedly from what a simplistic description of their determinism would lead us to expect. While we may wish to continue describing Qumran *doctrine* as deterministic, a fuller analysis of Qumran *religion* would have to take account of these disparate tendencies.

We face, I think, a similarly complex situation when evaluating the Qumranic notion that the community is to be compared to a temple. This comparison is not a doctrine—it is a "slogan," as Licht correctly noted quite some time ago. And it is not just a slogan but also a metaphoric one that purposely utilizes the more ambiguous term ("house") over the specific term ("sanctuary"). Like all comparisons—indeed, like all metaphors—the analogy can only be pushed so far. In my view, when it comes to comparing the sectarian community to a temple, scholars have not exercised due restraint. The slogan indicates that sectarians saw their community as a provisional replacement for a temple, even though their provisional replacement fails by comparison to a temple itself. While the community takes on certain characteristics of the temple, the texts themselves do not assert that the community is better than or even as good as a temple would be. Indeed, compared to the temple that they themselves envision in the *Temple Scroll*, the community offers limited access to the divine presence and relatively inadequate means of achieving atonement.

Imitating the Temple and Its Priests

Having demonstrated the fundamental differences between the ways the community imagined a temple and conceived of itself, we will now consider briefly the aforementioned corollaries to this idea: the fact that the community appears to take on itself certain cultic restrictions and also describes various aspects of its ritual and social structure in cultic terms. Certainly the sectarian concern with purity is the most prominent of these ideas, and it is frequently asserted that their concern with purity reflects their self-understanding as a temple.[142] Though less frequently emphasized, it is also true that the various stages of joining the community are described in cultic terms: the (presumably male) initiate who joins the community "*offers* himself" (המתנדב; 1QS V:1; cf. Exod. 25:2).[143] This offering is by no means "spiritual" in nature: the initiate gives his money and possessions to the community.[144] The sectarians' continued attention to the distinctions among priests, Levites, and the rest of Israel also fits into this mold.[145]

But if they didn't view themselves as a true temple, then how to explain these phenomena? As we will see here and in chapters 6 and 7, the Qumran sectarians were by no means alone in describing various ritual behaviors in cultic terms, or in maintaining purity beyond the boundaries of the temple.[146] With regard to the maintenance of ritual purity, we should consider—in addition to the evidence from Qumran—Josephus' and Philo's testimony regarding the Essenes (e.g. *JW* 2:119–161), Philo's description of the Therapaeutae (in *Contemplative Life*), and the rabbinic descriptions of the "fellowship" (*haburah*; see *t. Demai* 2:2–12). Regardless of one's position on the Essene hypothesis, it is virtually impossible to read all of this evidence as speaking of the Qumran sectarians exclusively: certainly a number of groups in the Second Temple period sought actively to maintain rather high levels of ritual purity, especially when eating or praying. Significantly, other literary evidence suggests to us that we cannot restrict such concerns to isolated groups of pietists. A number of sources testify that individual ancient Jews would perform some rite of purification—from immersing to handwashing—especially before either eating or praying (Tob. 2:9, Jdt. 12:7, 2 Macc. 12:38, *Aristeas* 305, *Sib. Or.* 3:591–593, Mark 7:1–23).[147]

Evidence for this effort can be found in nonliterary sources as well: we know from the archaeological record that the concern with ritual purity was felt well beyond the bounds of the temple. Ritual baths have been discovered in a number of Second Temple period Jewish settlements, and not just in proximity to Jerusalem.[148] And it may be significant that ritual baths have been identified near three synagogues in Israel commonly dated to before 70 C.E.[149] Another characteristic archaeological find are stone vessels, which were in use in the late Second Temple period, again well beyond Jerusalem and its environs. Indeed, such vessels turn up particularly in places where we know that Jews lived, and are rare in places of Samaritan or Gentile settlement.[150] We know from rabbinic literature (e.g. *m. Ohalot* 5:5) and the New Testament (John 2:6) that at least some ancient Jews considered stone vessels to be immune from ritual defilement. Thus here, too, the literary evidence for concern with ritual purity goes hand in hand with the archaeological record. When we put all this evidence together, it appears that efforts to maintain levels of ritual purity beyond the bounds of the temple were common among ancient Jews.[151]

Scholars have disputed the nature and purpose of such efforts. Some have dismissed the rabbinic evidence as wildly impractical—and therefore historically baseless.[152] Others have suggested that the Qumran sectarians may not have eaten their daily food in a state of ritual purity either.[153] Yet the literature and the archaeology of Qumran would suggest that purity matters were taken there seriously—and literally.[154] The tannaitic sources are reasonable enough too, especially when we keep in mind that the early rabbinic literature—and possibly other ancient Jews as well—probably accepted the quasi-purity of the *tevul yom* (one who has already immersed), rendering day-to-day life much simpler for those who have contracted minor defilements.[155] Moreover, with regard to handwashing, for instance, we need not suppose that purity rites were performed only when conditions allowed for a constant or complete level of ritual purity to be maintained. Just as traditional Jews today wash their hands before eating, even when otherwise ritually defiled, ancient Jews may have sought states that were, strictly speaking, states of quasi-purity. This is not to suggest, however, that the possibility of maintaining true ritual purity was an unlikely one. Maintaining ritual purity may have been difficult, but it ought not be dismissed as impossible.

In a classic treatment of purity in ancient Judaism, Gedaliahu Alon supposed that there were two general trends regarding ritual purity among ancient Jews in the Second Temple period.[156] The first trend—which Alon termed "minimalist"—operated on the general assumption that purity concerns were limited to the temple, its environs, and those who intended to visit there. The second trend—which Alon termed "maximalist"—sought to expand the realm of purity well beyond the confines of the temple. In Alon's view, the Essenes (as known in Alon's day only from Josephus and Philo) were in the maximalist camp, while the Sadducees were in the minimalist one. The Pharisees were divided on the issue, though the dominant trend led in the direction taken by the Sadducees.[157]

In Alon's day, he argued against his erstwhile disputant, Adolph Büchler, who had earlier questioned the idea that the rabbinic sources regarding the *haburah* could accurately reflect the situation in Israel before 70 c.e.[158] Of course, both scholars authored their studies on these matters well before the discovery of the literature from Qumran, and well before the archaeological record on ritual baths and stone vessels was so clear. The evidence available to us today should suggest that we are best off making precisely the opposite presumption that Büchler did. Indeed, if anything, what the record lacks is any explicit statement to the effect that ritual purity is to be maintained only in the temple or its environs: it is not Alon's "maximalist" view that requires evidence, it's the "minimalist" one. As recent surveys of ancient Jewish approaches to purity and holiness suggest, a good deal of evidence, both literary and archaeological, can be marshaled to bolster the claim that many Jews—and certainly not only Pharisees or Essenes—practiced forms of ritual purification, regardless of whether they lived near Jerusalem and irrespective of whether trips to the temple were in their immediate plans. And they did so *before* the destruction of the Second Temple.[159]

And how are we to explain these efforts? Quite possibly, one purpose is to be found in the dictum of Exodus 19:6: "and you shall be for me a kingdom of priests and a holy nation."[160] But we must be careful here: it has recently been argued that the Exodus verse in question has been of greater interest and importance to modern scholars (especially from the Reform or liberal tradi-tions) than it was to the ancient sources.[161] Even if the verse in question may not have been utilized so frequently in the justification of these efforts, the sentiment that the reformers found in the verse—that nonpriests too can seek purity and holiness—does indeed appear to be a widespread phenomenon, well documented in the sources, requiring analysis and explanation.[162] Again, we need not suppose that those who emulated priestly purity necessarily thought of themselves as real priests or ascribed to themselves all of the obligations of the priests. The point was not to act *just like priests* but to act *priestly*.[163]

In ancient Judaism, ritual purity is not an end in and of itself. The biblical notion that purity is the prerequisite for sacrifice is echoed in a great deal of Second Temple Jewish literature, recent objections notwithstanding.[164] This much is stated explicitly by Philo, on more than one occasion (e.g., *Special Laws* 1:256, with regard to ritual and moral purity), and it is strongly implied in Josephus' juxtaposition of the ritual purity laws with his description of sacrifice (see esp. *Ant.* 3:258, and *Ag. Ap.* 2:198).[165] Moreover, we have seen in chapter 4 that many apocalyptic and rabbinic visions of visits to the heavenly temple are preceded by some form of purification, again underscoring the conceptual link between purity and encountering the sacred.[166] Ritual purity remained for ancient Jews, first and foremost, the prerequisite for encoun-tering the sacred, whether that meant entering the earthly temple, the heav-enly one, or—at Qumran—the earthly, temporary, and inadequate substitute for the currently defiled Jerusalem temple.

It appears that ritual purity in the Second Temple period was increasingly considered to be an appropriate prerequisite for other behaviors—such as prayer and eating—that were at the same time increasingly considered sacred. In the application of ritual purity rules to meal practices and prayer, we see the effort to channel some of the temple's sanctity to these other realms. When we keep in mind that sacrificial practice often involved eating—and very likely involved prayer as well—we can understand that the ascription of temple purity to prayer and eating was not something that came out of nowhere. Precisely because these activities were already associated with the temple, it was natural for people living beyond the temple to ascribe sanctity to them.

One thing about these efforts is perfectly clear: they do not necessarily set up an alternative to the cult or critique it in any way. There is nothing in-herently antitemple in ascribing cultic significance to activities that are not, strictly speaking, sacrificial or cultic in nature. Nor can we understand these efforts as "spiritualizations" of sacrifice. To the contrary, what we find here could perhaps be better described as the "sacrificialization" of modes of worship that do not involve the performance of sacrifice. And what might be the purpose of directing temple sanctity to new contexts or describing extra-cultic activity in sacrificial terms? The point is to make a rather straightfor-ward statement: "this too is divine service."

In his study of the sanctity of ancient synagogues, Steven Fine lays the groundwork for a proper understanding and evaluation of this phenomenon.

As he demonstrates, long before the destruction of the temple in 70 C.E., one can begin to see a process whereby synagogues came to be viewed as holy places, by virtue of the activities—prayer and Torah study—that take place there. The evidence for this phenomenon includes inscriptions referring to synagogues as holy places, as well as—in later periods—various temple-related decorative motifs (such as were mentioned in chapter 4).[167] Fine introduces two terms to describe this phenomenon: first, he speaks of the "templization" of synagogues and other spaces; second, he describes the process as one of *imitatio templi*.[168] Both of these terms mark a significant advance over the common descriptions of such phenomena, whether as "spiritualizations" of sacrifice or as replacements for the temple. The term *imitatio templi* helpfully drives home the point that the effort of channeling the sanctity that pertains to the temple (and its sacrificial cult) to other forms of worship is not a critique of the temple, any more than an act of *imiatio Dei* involves a critique of God.

The term "templization" also marks an advance. The difference between speaking of the templization of synagogues or the "sacrificialization" of prayer on the one hand and the spiritualization of sacrifice on the other is significant, and cuts to the heart of this analysis. The more common referents presuppose that the temple or sacrifice is the inactive, direct object of the process. When we speak of "templization," we understand and emphasize that the sanctuary and its sacrificial ritual are the active forces motivating their imitation. They are imitated precisely because they are meaningful and powerful. Imitation, in and of itself, is not evidence of claims of supersession.

Once again, an insufficient appreciation of the complexity of metaphor has also impinged on the discussion. The Qumranic usages of cultic terms with regard to sectarian rituals and functions have typically been understood as if the metaphors in question operate in only one direction: with the temple being replaced or spiritualized by something else. But as I have already argued, metaphors are often—and here, too, very likely—two-way streets. Thus by describing its activities in cultic terms, the group is at the same time asserting the significance of the cult. This side of the equation has been missed in much of the scholarship, where antisacrificial, antipriestly, or anti-temple biases continue to predominate.

The sect at Qumran considered their food and drink to be holy, and maintained their ritual (and moral) purity in order to preserve the sanctity of their meals. In their emulation of cultic behavior, and in their desire to seek purity and sanctity beyond the confines of Jerusalem, the sect was not unique at all. In these respects, they were part of a broader trend in ancient Jewish piety. The sectarians were distinct for their stringent praxis, and possibly unique in their fusion of ritual and moral purity concerns. And, as argued above, their purity concerns have the added significance of being part of a broader self-understanding. Since the Jerusalem temple was ritually and morally defiled, the sectarians withdrew from it, considering their own pure community to be a temporary alternate to the currently defiled temple. And yet in their own estimation, their pure community was entirely inferior to a real temple.

Conclusion

Over the course of this chapter, we reviewed a number of specific charges raised in the Qumran literature against the temple, its practices, and its personnel. We observed that according to some texts, the temple was considered morally defiled by sin, while other texts suggest that the Jerusalem temple was ritually defiled by lax standards or incorrect practices. We also observed that a number of charges raised against the temple do not concern a notion of purity at all: disputes concerning the calendar and certain sacrificial practices, for example, also lead to anti-temple polemics. But in these cases the precise implications are not so clear. While disputes about purity can be presumed in many cases to lead to avoiding or boycotting the temple, the implication of these nonpurity disputes is less obvious. We also observed, finally, that the *Temple Scroll* in particular also raises a sharp criticism against the temple: that it is structurally inadequate.

Some argue that the sectarians not only boycotted the temple but also established their own alternative at Qumran. Some even suppose that sacrifices of some sort were performed there. While this possibility cannot be dismissed out of hand, the evidence for it is not altogether compelling. A more common approach is to suppose that the Qumran sectarians considered their own community to be a replacement for the temple. The evidence for this view is more compelling, but with two important qualifications: First, the community very clearly viewed their extratemple ritual life as provisional. They certainly expected that in the future the temple would be run according to their will and animal sacrifice would be performed there as a matter of course. Second, it is also important to emphasize that the sectarians did not view their own institutions as in any way better than a proper temple would be. Indeed, they did not even view their own institution as an equivalent for the current temple, defiled as it was. While scholars frequently assert in strong terms the sectarians' power to effect atonement without sacrifice, a careful reading of the literature itself suggests that precisely the opposite was the sectarian perspective.

The sectarians did, of course, understand many of their ritual behaviors in cultic terms, and they did maintain high levels of purity, even though they were not in close or frequent proximity to the Jerusalem temple. These aspects of their religious behavior, I argued, can be understood fully in line with the arguments presented here. While these behaviors are sometimes interpreted as aspects of an antitemple or antipriestly approach, there is really no reason to interpret them that way. To the contrary, extra-temple, nonpriestly purity was a common aspect of religious behavior in ancient Judaism. The evidence from Qumran in this respect is hardly exceptional; it is, rather, quite typical. We will see further evidence of this claim in chapters 6 and 7.

In the course of the analysis here, too, we can see that antisacrificial biases have negatively impacted the discussion of these matters. Surely the Dead Sea sectarians had their disputes with the Jerusalem temple, its practices, and its priests. Too many scholars, however, have made them out to be the prototypes of later Christians, even modernist Jews, who would come to view sacrifice and the temple as something of the past. But the sectarians were not Christians, and they were not modernist Jews either. The sectarians were hardly critical of sacrifice per se, nor did they "spiritualize" the cult, though many scholars seem to wish that they did. The sectarians also did not view their own community as better than a temple: they did not assert that the divine presence dwelled among them, and they did not claim to possess powerful means of atonement. They did not view the temple, sacrifices, and the priesthood as things of the past. The idea that the sect's austere desert existence was a better alternative than a proper temple comes not from the Dead Sea corpus, but from the scholars of that corpus. As we will see in the next two chapters, the Dead Sea corpus is hardly unique in being interpreted in such ways.

6

The Purity of the Second Temple in Rabbinic Literature

In this chapter we consider the approaches taken in rabbinic literature toward the Second Temple.[1] We have already had occasion to discuss some aspects of the rabbinic view. In chapter 4, we observed that the rabbis were indeed familiar with and remained interested in the two symbolic approaches to the temple prevalent during Second Temple times: the idea that the temple represented the cosmos, and the idea that the earthly sanctuary corresponded to a heavenly one. With this established, we will focus in this chapter particularly on those sources that in some fashion constitute parallels to—or perhaps even responses to[2]—the evidence we considered in the previous chapter. We observed in chapter 5 that the Dead Sea sectarians considered the Second Temple to have been both ritually and morally defiled, and both ritually and structurally inadequate. The sectarians, therefore, boycotted the temple, offering their own worship as temporary and unequal substitutes. Our goal in this chapter will be to assess what the rabbis thought when they looked back on the Second Temple, now that it was destroyed. Had the temple been defiled in some fashion? Was the temple that was lost adequate to its task? Are substitutes to be found in the meantime?

In the first section that follows, we will consider whether the rabbis thought the Second Temple had been defiled, and if so, in what fashion. We will also survey the rabbinic sources claiming that the Second Temple was morally corrupt, and we will consider whether or not this memory of the temple's corruption compares with what the Qumran sectarians had to say about the temple in their day. As we will see, even when the rabbis agreed with others that temple authorities could from time to time commit moral wrongs, the implication of this concern in rabbinic sources differs greatly from what we saw, especially, in the Dead Sea literature. In the second section, we will consider the rabbinic approach to a matter that seemed to be of particular concern to the Qumran sectarians: the fear that the temple had been morally defiled by the greedy behavior of the priests and even the populace. In order to evaluate the rabbinic approach to this question, we will survey the rabbinic ideas concerning three related matters: (1) the gifts given to the temple by wealthy aristocrats; (2) the status of sacrifices that consist of stolen goods; and (3) the temple tax. Again, we will find that the rabbinic stance on these related issues is remarkably lenient, quite different from what we find in the Qumran literature. In the third section, we will inquire as to how the rabbis responded to the destruction of the temple and the fact that the temple rituals could no longer be performed in their day. It will be demonstrated briefly that rabbinic literature is infused with the hope—and the confidence—that the temple will ultimately be rebuilt. We will then consider the question as to whether the rabbis sought and found temporary or permanent substitutes for the temple cult, such as statutory prayer or maintaining purity beyond the bounds of the temple.

This chapter will conclude with reflections on some of the scholarly constructions of early rabbinic history and theology. As we will see, it is rather common for scholars to argue that rabbinic attitudes toward the temple articulate a sustained (and rather delayed) response to the destruction of the temple in 70 c.e. Eventually, so it is believed, the rabbis "got over" the temple, accepting prayer or other behaviors as full substitutes for the temple that was lost. When, however, we compare the attitudes toward the temple expressed by the rabbis with the evidence from earlier periods—especially with regard to the imitation or emulation of the temple—we can see that a good deal of the rabbinic approach to purity, prayer, and the temple was very likely already a part of the predestruction approach to these matters as well. In my view, the common antisacrificial biases we have seen already have negatively impacted the discussion here too.

Moral Defilement and the Corruption of the Second Temple

In the previous chapter, it was argued that the polemics against the Second Temple proceed at Qumran on two levels simultaneously: some sources indicate that the temple was considered to be ritually defiled, while others considered it to be morally defiled. In order to assess the rabbinic approach to the Second Temple, we need to review and reconsider briefly the rabbinic approach to ritual and moral defilement.

In *Impurity and Sin and Ancient Judaism*, I demonstrated that the rabbis continued to be interested in the notion of moral defilement.[3] I also demonstrated that for them—unlike the Qumran sectarians—the notion remained a restricted one. The tannaim carefully compartmentalized their treatments of ritual and moral impurity, so as to maintain a strict separation between the two concepts. Moreover, the tannaim were very circumspect in their approach to moral defilement. In their view, moral impurity was caused primarily by the sins explicitly so described in the Hebrew Bible: idolatry, sexual sin, and murder. To this short list the rabbis also added from time to time other sins, typically ones explicitly described as "abominations" in scripture: so, as noted earlier, judicial deceit becomes a source of moral defilement in the *Sifra* (*Qedoshim* perek 4:1, on Lev. 19:15 [ed. Weiss 88d–89a]; cf. 11QT LI:11–16), and arrogance becomes a source of moral defilement in the *Mekilta de-Rabbi Ishmael* (*Yitro*, sec. 9, [ed. Horovitz and Rabin 238]; cf. 1QpHab VIII:8–13).[4] Still, when compared to the Qumran material, the rabbis view relatively few transgressions as possible sources of moral defilement.

For the most part, the effects of moral defilement for the rabbis also remain close to what the scriptural precedents would cause us to expect: the land and sanctuary are morally defiled by sin, and this leads in turn to the departure of the divine presence, destruction, and exile. Again, when we compare the rabbinic and Qumranic approaches to the *effects* of moral defilement, we find an interesting contrast, one hitherto unnoticed: virtually all the discussions of moral defilement that appear in the Qumran literature concern the morally defiling effect of sin upon the *sanctuary*, with very few texts referring to the defilement of the *land* (but see, e.g., 11QT XLVIII:10–11).[5] In the rabbinic sources we find basically the opposite phenomenon. The standard expressions of moral defilement in the tannaitic sources are expressed in one of two ways: in the longer form—which we encounter in the "Akiban" midrashim (especially the *Sifra* and the *Sifre* to Deuteronomy)—we hear that sin "defiles the land, profanes the name (of God), causes the divine presence to depart, brings the sword upon Israel and exiles them from their land" (e.g., *Sifra Qedoshim* perek 4:1). In the shorter form—which we encounter in the *Mekilta de-Rabbi Ishmael*, the Tosefta and the two Talmuds—we hear that sin "defiles the land and causes the divine presence to depart" (e.g., *Mekilta Bahodesh* 9).[6] In neither case is the moral defilement typically said to affect the sanctuary. On only a few occasions is the defilement of the sanctuary explicitly mentioned in its own right (e.g., *Sifra Qedoshim* parashah 4:8, on Lev. 20:3 [ed. Weiss, 91c]), despite the fact that the rabbis do with some frequency relate that the temple was marred from time to time with corruption and sin. As we will see, for the rabbis, the Second Temple may have been morally corrupt, but it was not morally impure.

In what follows, we will review a representative sample of rabbinic sources that are critical of the Second Temple, its practices, and its personnel. Indeed, we can, without too much difficulty, find some rabbinic sources that tell of priestly corruption and immorality.[7] A number of these sources indict the moral standards of those who officiated at the Second Temple. A remarkably small number of these sources implicate the ritual standards of the Second Temple. While some sources suggest that the sanctuary was defiled by these violations, most of the traditions do not focus on this particular point. Though this catalogue can't be exhaustive, I hope that it includes the most significant sources.

We begin with an account preserved in the Mishnah (*m. Keritot* 1:7), which relates that in the later days of the Second Temple, the price of sacrificial birds became prohibitively expensive. Responding to the situation, Rabban Simeon ben Gamaliel purportedly issued a decree dramatically reducing the number of sacrifices certain women would have to bring, thereby immediately reducing the demand for birds, and their price. As we will see in the next chapter, this story is frequently cited by scholars who wish to assert that the Second Temple was in fact a corrupt institution, governed by greedy priests who overcharged the populace. This story, however, is nothing of the sort. Priests are not mentioned per se, nor is it necessary to assume that anything other than typical market factors (i.e., the relationship between supply and demand) have driven the price up. The problem is solved here not by condemning priests or other merchants for overcharging the rest of Israel but by adjusting the law so as to decrease demand for sacrificial birds. As expected, decreased demand brings a lower price. The rabbinic story tells us nothing other than the fact that certain rabbinic figures were remembered as having been sensitive to the pricing of sacrificial animals, and savvy enough to understand that these prices were driven by factors relating to the open market.

As has often been observed,[8] the depiction of the temple in the Mishnah is rather idyllic: we find various descriptions of festivals and offerings, all colored by a rosy nostalgia (see, e.g., *m. Bikkurim* 3:2–8; *m. Sheqalim* 5:1–6; 6:1–6; *m. Yoma* 1:1–7:5; *m. Sotah* 3:1–3; *m. Negaim* 14:1–10, *m. Parah* 3:1–11, in addition to the entire tractate *Tamid*).[9] Precisely for this reason, some have claimed these sources in general (and tractate *Tamid* in particular) to be authentic accounts of the temple's practice, finding their origin in priestly tradition.[10] Regardless of when and where these traditions originated, it is important to note that the priests are hardly presented in an entirely positive light in the Mishnah: they are depicted as if they were subservient to the sages, a status that their alleged lack of education caused them to deserve (e.g., *m. Yoma* 1:3; cf. *b. Yoma* 18a). Moreover, priests are conspicuous by their absence in *m. Avot* 1:1, which traces the chain of tradition from Moses to the early rabbinic sages—a phenomenon often understood as an antipriestly polemic.[11] Still, as far as the Mishnah is concerned, the priests were not criminals. What is more, we do not find in the Mishnah a single reference to the moral defilement of the sanctuary by sin, whether committed by priests or others. Given all this, I think the story in Mishnah *Keritot* has been largely misread: it's not a story of priestly corruption or extortion at all. The price of birds went up due simply to some shortage, caused in part by women who were so scrupulously bringing all the offerings required of them (rosy nostalgia again, no doubt).

When we look beyond the Mishnah, we do begin to find a number of sources that explicitly charge the priests of the Second Temple with committing various crimes. Indeed, a number of early rabbinic sources raise a specific charge against the priesthood: that the high priestly office was essentially for sale. Along with this come more general charges of greed, gluttony, and corruption. For instance, we find the following tradition in *Sifre Numbers*, sec. 131 (ed. Horovitz 173):

Therefore it is said: "Behold I give him [Phineas] my covenant of peace" (Num. 25:12): this teaches us that from him arose eighteen high priests during the time of the First Temple; but during the time of the Second Temple, there arose from him eighty priests. Because they sold it [the priesthood] for money, their years were cut short. It happened that one sent with his son two measures of silver, filled with silver, and with silver measuring instruments. Then it happened that one sent with his son two measures of gold, filled with gold, and with gold measuring instruments. It was then said: "The foal trumped the candelabrum."[12]

The tradition suggests that the Second Temple priesthood was available to the highest bidder, and as a result priestly reigns became shorter. The point of the peculiar folk saying with which this story concludes is that one bribe can be easily followed by another larger one, and only the larger bribe will get the desired result.[13]

Curiously—and typically—the parallel accounts do not contain all of the same details. Among other differences, we should note the following: in *Leviticus Rabbah* 21:9, the entire tradition is attributed to the fourth-generation amora, Rabbi Berachiah, who quotes it in the name of the third-generation amora, Rabbi Levi (thus despite its appearance in the *Sifre*, the tradition may or may not be tannaitic).[14] We are also told in *Leviticus Rabbah* that some say there were eighty-three high priests in the Second Temple period. Moreover, we are reminded that Simon the Just served forty-five years, which serves to emphasize how short the rest of the high priests' reigns were. In the Palestinian Talmud, we are told that some say there were even eighty-five high priests (*y. Yoma* 1:1, 38c/562). In the Babylonian Talmud, we are told that some say there were actually more than three hundred priests, and that when one accounts for the few priests (such as Simon) who served for many years, we are left with most priests serving only a year or less (*b. Yoma* 9a). Only the version of the tradition preserved in the Babylonian Talmud fails to connect explicitly the shortening of priestly tenures to the sale of the office. But in this case, the Babylonian version is immediately preceded by a tannaitic tradition (*b. Yoma* 8b, attributed to Rabbi Judah) that speaks of precisely the same phenomenon: that the priesthood of the Second Temple was for sale, and the office changed hands annually. We also find elsewhere in the Babylonian Talmud two references to the priesthood of a Joshua ben Gamala, who was appointed to the high priesthood when his wife, Martha (the daughter of Boethus), delivered three *kabs* of golden dinars to the king (*b. Yoma* 18a; *b. Yebamot* 61a; cf. *m. Yebamot* 6:4).[15] That the priesthood in the Second Temple was for sale seems to be common knowledge among later rabbinic sources, midrashic and talmudic.

It is not our concern here to evaluate the historicity of these sources. To be sure, there are various legendary features in these traditions—such as, for instance, the claim that the priesthood of Johanan (i.e., John Hyrcanus?) lasted eighty years (*b. Yoma* 9a). There are also polemic levels to these stories, as is commonly pointed out.[16] A complete analysis of the rabbinic traditions concerning wicked priests would reckon with the tales' narrative qualities, and study them in their literary context as well.[17] Moreover, there are some historical confusions or inaccuracies: in the traditions just noted, we are told that Martha delivered the gold to King Yannai (presumably, Alexander Janneaus), but, according to Josephus, a Jesus son of Gamaliel (presumably the rabbis' Joshua ben Gamala) served over a century later, during the reign of Agrippa II (*Ant.* 20:213). Yet the general thrust of these traditions—that the high priesthood was for sale—is known also from other ancient sources.[18] We could point first to 2 Macc. 4:7–8, which relates that Jason occupied the priesthood by bribing Antiochus Epiphanes, only to be outbid himself a short time later—"The foal trumps the candelabrum," to quote the rabbinic folk saying—by his own messenger, Menelaus (2 Macc. 4:23–24). Closer to the tannaitic period, we could point to a number of passages in Josephus that also testify to the fact that high priests engaged in bribery (e.g., *Ant.* 20:205)—though we would not know from Josephus that the priesthood was for sale.[19] For what it's worth, we also find references to the sale of the priesthood in a homily by John Chrysostom.[20] Of course, we should not forget the more generalized traditions in evidence in apocalyptic literature and Qumran, to the effect that the temple was defiled or corrupted by priestly greed. But for our purposes it doesn't really matter if it was true that the high priesthood was for sale; what is interesting is the fact that the tannaim and later sages can talk now and again about priestly corruption, without ever coming to the conclusion that such behavior would *defile* the temple.

Rabbinic memories of priestly greed are not limited to buying the priesthood for money. Two distinct tannaitic traditions—also frequently cited in New Testament scholarship, as we will see—describe certain priestly families or even specific priests as particularly greedy or gluttonous. One tradition, which appears in both *b. Pesahim* 57a and *t. Menahot* 13:21, describes how some priests would steal sacrificial portions from others. These accounts are followed by a song of woes, attributed to Abba Saul ben Buthnit in the name of Abba Joseph ben Hanin (both presumably early tannaim):[21]

> Woe is me because of the House of Boethus, woe is me for their lances!
> Woe is me because of the House of Hanin, woe is me for their slander!
> Woe is me because of the House of Kathros, woe is me for their pen!
> Woe is me because of the House of Ishmael ben Phiabi, woe is me for their fist! For they are high priests, and their sons are treasurers; their sons-in-law are officers and their slaves beat the people with canes.[22]

In *b. Pesahim* 57a, this hymn is followed by yet another tradition speaking of priestly gluttony, one that imagines the temple itself crying out over a series of sinful, gluttonous high priests (cf. *b. Keritot* 28a–b).[23]

Our Rabbis taught: The temple court cried out four cries.

The first: "Depart from here, sons of Eli!"—for they defiled the sanctuary of God. And it cried out again: "Depart from here Issachar of the village of Barkai!"—for he honored himself and profaned sacred things (*for he wrapped his hand in silks to perform the service*).[24]

And the court cried out again: "'Lift up your heads, oh gates,' (Ps. 24:7) and let enter Ishmael ben Phiabi, the disciple of Phineas, so he may serve as high priest."

And the court cried out again: "'Lift up your heads, oh gates,' (Ps. 24:7) and let enter Yohanan ben Narbai, the disciple of Pinkai, and he will fill his stomach with sacred offerings." It was said of Yohanan ben Narbai that he would eat three hundred calves, and drink three hundred barrels of wine, and eat forty *seahs* of birds for dessert. They said that all the days of Yohanan ben Narbai there were never any sacrificial leftovers in the temple.

The first of these traditions is clearly a series of complaints against various crooked and otherwise unsavory high priests. The second of these traditions has posed some problems: while the first two cries are explicitly negative, the second two appear on the surface to be positive, welcoming these priests into the temple, as the traditional Jewish understanding of the passage would have it (so, e.g., Rashi to *b. Pesahim* 57a).[25] Yet the traditional understanding is questionable on a number of grounds: the juxtaposition of the two traditions in *b. Pesahim* 57a—and the general context there—suggests a generally negative attitude.[26] The list of cries is followed by a series of negative statements regarding Yohanan ben Narbai, and it is preceded by the first tradition quoted above, which condemns the house of Ishmael ben Phiabi. I suggest that the reason why the gates must lift their heads is not to welcome the priests but simply to make room for them: the point of the joke is that without the gates' lifting up their heads, there would be no room for these priests to enter—their gluttony being imagined as having led to an extreme corpulence.

Remarkably, each of the dynasties listed in the first source can be identified with a specific priestly family also mentioned in Josephus' *Antiquities*.[27] Moreover, in some of these instances, Josephus too speaks of these priests' greedy behavior. We are even told that Ishmael ben Ph(i)abi sent slaves to appropriate priestly dues (*Ant.* 20:181).[28] Of the priests mentioned in the second source, only Issachar of Barkai is unattested outside rabbinic literature.[29] The sins of the sons of Eli are, of course, recorded in scripture (1 Sam 2:15–17, 22; cf. *b. Yoma* 9a). Josephus also speaks of one Ananus, son of Nebedeus, as having served under Herod (*Ant.* 20:103). On the whole, the correspondences are striking enough that Daniel R. Schwartz suggests that Josephus and the rabbis both independently drew on a third antipriestly source.[30]

Again, our concern here is not with historicity. What interests me is the way in which the rabbis approach their memories of priestly corruption. Once again, we find that the rabbis could speak in detail about priestly greed and corruption, without indicating that such behavior defiled the sanctuary. The only explicit reference to sanctuary defilement concerns the sons of Eli, but we are not told which of their crimes leads to this condition. According to 1 Samuel, Eli's sons are said to have conspired to appropriate for themselves the best of what was offered to the sanctuary and to have slept with women at the entrance to Shiloh's sanctuary (1 Sam. 2:15–17, 22; cf. b. Yoma 9a). Their pollution of the temple is likely connected to their sexual misconduct, for in this they are unique among the priests condemned in these passages, just as they are the only ones condemned for defiling the sanctuary. The pollution of the temple here can therefore be understood in one of two ways: either they defiled the temple ritually by having sexual relations in close proximity to the sacred precincts, or they defiled the temple morally by committing sexual transgression. Possibly we are to understand the sanctuary defilement here on both levels. Regardless, once again we find that neither the tannaim nor the later amoraim—unlike the earlier apocalyptic and sectarian texts—explicitly refer to Second Temple priestly greed or corruption as a possible cause of sanctuary defilement.

Perhaps the closest we come to finding a source that accuses the priests of defiling the sanctuary by their greed is a tradition preserved in Tosefta Menahot 13:18–22. First we are told of various priestly acts of theft and greed (13:18–21); indeed, this much of the source constitutes a parallel of b. Pesahim 57a, down through the song of woes. The Tosefta then concerns itself (13:22) with the reasons for the destruction of various sanctuaries. According to Yohanan ben Torta (early second century C.E.), Shiloh was destroyed because of the mistreatment of the sacrifices; the First Temple was destroyed on account of bloodshed, idolatry, and sexual transgressions. The question is then asked, why was the Second Temple destroyed, even though these grave sins were not generally committed? According to the Tosefta, the people were lovers of money and hated each other without cause.[31] While the tradition does juxtapose memories of priestly greed with the assertion that greed caused the temple to be destroyed, it lacks two significant features. First, the priests are not blamed exclusively for this circumstance, and second, there is still no explicit reference in either case to sanctuary defilement.

We do find a small number of sources that accuse the priests of sanctuary defilement, only in connection with a much graver charge, murder. A story preserved twice in the Tosefta (t. Yoma 1:12, t. Shebuot 1:4), once in Sifre Numbers (sec. 161; ed. Horovitz 222), once each in the Palestinian and Babylonian Talmuds (y. Yoma 2:2, 39d/568–569; b. Yoma 23a–b), tells of two priests who raced toward the altar and began to fight, presumably over who got there first, with the result that one killed the other.[32] The story continues, supposing (rather preposterously) that the priests, led by a Rabbi Zadok, thought they now had to measure the distances between the corpse, the sanctuary, and the court in order to determine for which area of the temple the ritual of the "strangled heifer" (Deut. 21:1–9) would be performed. Then the victim's father, noticing his son still convulsing, announces to the priests that because his son remains (barely) alive, the knife has not been defiled. In case the point is missed, we are then told explicitly that the temple priests were more concerned with the ritual purity of a knife than they were with an act of murder committed by one of their own, in the temple itself.

For our purposes, what is particularly relevant is the final paragraph, as presented in the Tosefta and *Sifre* on Numbers: "and so it is written, 'Moreover, Manasseh shed so much innocent blood that he filled Jerusalem from one end to the other' (2 Kings 21:16): from this they said that for the sin of bloodshed the divine presence departed and the sanctuary was defiled." So here we find an explicit ascription of callous and murderous behavior to priests. Moreover, the accusation is juxtaposed with a concern for sanctuary defilement: presumably, just as the First Temple was morally defiled by Menasseh's murderous behavior, so too was murderous behavior a cause of the Second Temple's defilement by sin and subsequent destruction. Of course, the act of murder leaves in its wake a corpse in the temple court, so *ritual* defilement probably occurred here as well.[33] Nonetheless, the juxtaposition of murder with sanctuary defilement—especially in a narrative that we know shortly precedes the temple's destruction (and, presumably, the departure of God's presence)—surely suggests that *moral* defilement is the prime concern here.

Indeed, we know the tradition concerns moral defilement because, in the rabbinic understanding of these matters, the ritual defilement of the sanctuary would not lead to the departure of the divine presence. As far as the rabbis are concerned, the ritual defilement of the sanctuary—while serious—is a condition that can be ameliorated, and even tolerated. It can be ameliorated, quite simply, by cleaning it up: in *m. Hagigah* we are told how after a pilgrimage festival, the temple courts would be cleaned and purified (3:7–8). This was necessary because, as we are told in the previous passage (3:6), various purity rules were relaxed at the time of the festivals, in order to allow for general participation on the part of Israel.[34] (Again, I am not concerned with the historicity of these practices but with the ideology that emerges from the ways the rabbis remember or imagine that things happened.) The rabbinic tolerance of the ritual defilement of the temple can also be seen in the traditions concerning a Passover that occurs in a state of ritual defilement. According to Numbers 9:10–13, individuals who become ritually impure by contact with a corpse are to delay their performance of the Passover sacrifice by one month. According to *m. Pesahim* 7:4–6, if the majority of the people (or if the priests) became so defiled, Passover would proceed at its proper time, with the rites being performed in a state of ritual defilement (cf. *m. Temurah* 2:1). As far as the rabbis are concerned, *moral* defilement is frequently connected to the nation's calamities. However, *ritual* defilement—even of the *temple*—was a much less serious matter. Indeed, perhaps more than anything else, this is really the point of the whole story in *t. Yoma*: the ritual purity of the knife was—quite mistakenly—more important to these priests and sages than the moral defilement of the sanctuary.

Before leaving this story, we must note the disparities between the story about Rabbi Zadok and the final paragraph quoted above, concerning the sins of Manasseh and the defilement of the sanctuary. The tradition regarding

Manasseh is not integral to the story itself, and indeed it does not appear in either of the talmudic versions of the tale (y. Yoma 2:2, 39d/568–569; b. Yoma 23a–b). Moreover, whereas the story concerns the Second Temple, the tradition about Manasseh concerns the First. This distinction is by no means incidental, since the rabbis frequently contrasted the First and Second temples, not least with regard to the causes of their destruction (e.g., t. Menahot 13:22).[35] While we are led to believe in the tradition quoted above that Manasseh's bloodshed was sufficient to cause the divine presence to depart from the First Temple, we should certainly question whether the murder of a single priest could possibly cause the same consequence for the Second Temple. Presumably, the story is meant to illustrate the kind of bloodshed that occurred in the Second Temple period—and the callousness with which such was treated, by priests and sages alike. Yet, if bloodshed in general was the cause of the destruction of the Second Temple, we cannot necessarily infer from this source that the rabbis believed that all the bloodshed was committed by priests, any more than we should suppose that all the bloodshed was condoned or overlooked by sages like Rabbi Zadok.

One further rabbinic tradition explicitly connects the defilement and destruction of the temple with activities that took place there: a rather late tradition (a discussion between two Palestinian amoraim, Rabbi Yudan and Rabbi Aha), preserved in the Palestinian Talmud (y. Ta'anit 4:6, 69a/735) as well as various midrashic sources.[36] The tradition is concerned with the murder of the righteous priest Zechariah by a mob acting on the order of King Joash, the son of Jehoiada. According to the biblical account, the murder took place in the court of the house of the Lord (בחצר בית ה; 2 Chron. 24:20–22). The rabbinic tradition, however, locates the murder within the priestly court, which suggest that priests were responsible. Moreover, in the fuller rabbinic accounts (e.g., y. Ta'anit 4:6, 69a/735), the killers—here specified only as "Israel"—are charged with seven transgressions: "they killed a priest, a prophet and a judge; they shed innocent blood; they defiled the court; and it happened on both Sabbath and on the day of Atonement."[37] On the one hand, we find here, too, in this late source, the concern that murder committed within the temple morally defiles it, in advance of—and presumably leading to—the temple's destruction. On the other hand, and once again, the tradition regarding bloodshed in the temple concerns not the Second Temple but the First.

We turn, finally, to consider briefly the most thorough talmudic text treating the destruction of the Second Temple, the narratives collected in b. Gittin 55b–56b. Full analyses of these stories can be found elsewhere,[38] so we can focus on what relates to our theme: the issue of transgressions being committed in or near the temple, by temple authorities, prior to its destruction. Indeed, an important scene in this narrative is located in the temple itself. The story concerns an unnamed man whose servant was supposed to invite his friend, Qamza, to a banquet but instead invited the host's enemy, coincidentally (or folkloristically) named Bar Qamza. Scorned by his accidental host, and ignored by sages who were also present, Bar Qamza resolves to betray Jerusalem to its enemies. He therefore brings an offering from the emperor to

Jerusalem, and while in transit he purposely blemishes the animal. The authorities then face the question: should they, for the sake of peace, offer the
(slightly) blemished animal? A sage by the name of Zechariah ben Avkulos[39]
objects: "should they say that blemished animals may be offered on the altar?"
When it is suggested that Bar Qamza be killed, to prevent the emperor from
discovering what had happened, the same sage objects: "should they say that
one who blemishes [a sacrificial animal] is killed?" The amora Rabbi Yohanan
is then quoted as saying—surprisingly—that Rabbi Zechariah's meekness
"destroyed our temple, burned our sanctuary, and exiled us from our land."[40]

On the one hand, the story hardly speaks favorably of the temple: and in
this case, we must surely admit that the temple is implicated in its own destruction. But at the same time, it must be emphasized that the prime cause of
the situation—and indeed, the overall message of the tale—is the senseless
hatred, the hardening of hearts, between Bar Qamza and his host (Qamza
himself is not implicated in the story). This is the reason for the temple's
destruction, as is made clear in statements found at the beginning and end of
the tale.[41] It is also important to note that the condemnation of the temple
offered here is entirely self-critical. In typical fashion, the rabbis imagine that
the temple was controlled by rabbinic sages; and it is these figures who allow
certain legal and extralegal concerns to let the situation to spin out of control.
The blame placed on Rabbi Zechariah by Rabbi Yohanan is meant surely to
emphasize that the crisis could have been prevented, that the enmity between
Bar Qamza and his host need not have caused the temple's destruction. Indeed,
a second reason for the temple's destruction as related here—as also in *t. Yoma*
1:12—would be the authorities' misplaced priorities. They should indeed have
let the concern for peace trump the fear of offering a blemished animal. In this
respect, the story can be read as if it were less about criticizing the temple of old
and more about warning the sages of its own day against undue caution in the
face of a crisis, or perhaps undue punctiliousness toward relatively minor
matters.[42]

It remains important to emphasize what we don't find here: there are no
guilty priests (other than the sages), and there was no defilement of the
sanctuary per se. Moreover, while the temple is implicated in the events
leading to the destruction, the temple is not seen as the prime cause. Indeed,
one would look far and wide—and in vain—for traditions that explicitly, exclusively, or even primarily, blame the *Second* Temple's destruction on what
happened there. Yet the rabbis explicitly blame the destruction of the *First*
Temple on its moral defilement (as we have seen), and the rabbis are willing to
blame the calamitous events of 70 c.e.—at least for homiletic purposes—on
any one of a whole host of possible transgressions, including senseless hatred
and greed (e.g., *t. Menahot* 13:22, *b. Yoma* 9a), and even on the failure to recite
the *shema* or educate children (e.g., *b. Shabbat* 119b).[43] Of course, all of these
traditions are homiletic, not historical, in nature. Taken in isolation from each
other, these homilies—particularly those collected in *b. Shabbat* 119b—can
seem preposterous; taken together, they share the common denominator that
the destruction was the consequence of transgression (see e.g., *b. Berakhot* 3a).

What is important for our concern is the fact that the rabbis seem willing to blame the Second Temple's destruction on almost anything but the defilement of the temple, whether it be moral defilement caused by widespread grave sin such as bloodshed or the ritual defilement of the temple caused by a lackadaisical or lenient approach to ritual purity.

It may prove instructive at this point to compare the rabbinic approach to sanctuary defilement to that of Josephus. As noted earlier, Josephus was deeply concerned with the purity of the sanctuary. A number of times in his works, Josephus explicitly says that God's presence departed from the Jerusalem temple, as a result of its defilement (*JW* 5:412; 6:300; *Ant.* 20:166). What is more, Josephus on a number of occasions spells out the cause of the sanctuary's defilement: bloodshed in or near the holy precincts (e.g., *JW* 4:200–201, 5:402, 6:110; *Ant.* 20:165). Thus, we could say that Josephus and the rabbis share a particular concern that bloodshed in proximity to the temple might defile it. But Josephus' view is not entirely like that of the rabbis. In tannaitic literature, we generally find that the departure of the divine presence is said to follow the defilement *of the land*.[44] Josephus says nothing about the defilement of the land but seems particularly concerned with the desecration *of the temple*. On the one hand, perhaps we can't make too much of the fact that the rabbis rarely speak of the moral defilement of the sanctuary. The notion is not entirely unknown to them, and moreover, because the temple is located on the land, the temple would be defiled by virtue of the fact that the land was defiled by those sins—primarily idolatry, sexual transgression, and bloodshed—that cause moral defilement. While all this remains true, the rabbinic reluctance to speak explicitly and frequently about the defilement of the temple by sin calls for an explanation.

Yet there is a further difference between Josephus and the rabbis regarding these matters. For Josephus, bloodshed in the sanctuary—sanctioned by temple authorities—is viewed as a prime cause for God's departure from the Second Temple and, subsequently, the Jews' devastating defeat (*JW* 5:402–403, 412; *Ant.* 20:165–166). The rabbinic sources quoted above, however, do not allow us to draw the same conclusions: some sources (not all that many) do speak of the defilement of the sanctuary by murder in proximity to it, leading to the temple's destruction. But these sources generally speak explicitly of the First Temple, not the second. Indeed, we could just as well say that the rabbis exhibited restraint also with regard to the ways they spoke about the Second Temple's destruction. They surely could have developed the idea that God's presence had departed from a morally defiled temple, by building on the same biblical models that lay behind Josephus' theology (e.g., Ezekiel 8–11). Like Josephus, the rabbis could have blamed the Second Temple's destruction primarily or even exclusively on bloodshed committed there, and they could have directed their blame toward a single social group, such as the temple authorities or a band of rebels. But the rabbis chose not to do any of these things.

The rabbinic reluctance to speak of the temple's defilement can also be seen by contrast with Qumran. We observed that a good number of Qumranic sources explicitly connect the moral defilement of the sanctuary with economic transgression. The rabbis, however, do not reach this conclusion. Even when they do speak of priestly corruption taking place in or near the temple, the rabbis do not speak of the temple's defilement by priestly bribery or gluttony. Of course, the rabbinic approach to the *ritual* defilement of the temple is also more lenient than what we find at Qumran. The sectarians viewed the temple of their day as not only morally but also ritually defiled. There is nothing in rabbinic sources to suggest that there was any widespread systematic violation of ritual purity laws, leading to the temple's defilement. Indeed, if anything, the stories we surveyed above suggest that the rabbis believed the temple authorities—including the rabbinic sages among them such as Zadok and Avkulos—were too focused on the ritual purity of the temple, and not attentive enough to other more weighty matters.

So how do we account for the fact that the rabbis were comparatively so reluctant to speak of the ritual or moral defilement of the sanctuary? I suggested in *Impurity and Sin* that the tannaitic approach to ritual and moral defilement should be seen as distinctly nonsectarian.[45] We find confirmations of the nonsectarian nature of the rabbinic attitude in the sources we have just reviewed. The sectarians themselves believed the temple was defiled (both ritually and morally), which led to their separation from the temple. Josephus, of course, was no sectarian, but his account serves to direct blame for the temple's destruction toward specific subgroups of the ancient Jewish polity who were ostensibly responsible for the temple's defilement. The rabbis appear to have carefully avoided reaching the conclusion that the Second Temple was destroyed because some particular group defiled it in some way. The rabbis spoke of the morally defiling effect of sin on the sanctuary only rarely, and typically with regard to the *First* Temple. The rabbis certainly don't blame the destruction on any widespread failure to adhere to ritual purity laws either.

As we have seen in the narrative sources just surveyed, if the rabbinic sources direct blame for the Second Temple's destruction on anything in particular, it is toward (what they perceive as) misplaced priorities—priests and sages who were more concerned with the ritual purity of a knife than they were with murder, or more concerned with blemished offerings than with peace among nations. It is certainly worth considering whether these rabbinic *aggadot* also reflect the nonsectarian or even antisectarian attitudes of the rabbinic sages.[46] As we will see in the next section, tannaitic *halakha* is remarkably lenient when it comes to issues concerning the interplay of greed, corrupt wealth, and sacrificial offerings. Here, too, we may find that rabbinic sources articulate a subtle but determined refutation of many of the rejectionist critiques of the temple that were discussed in the previous chapter.

The Purity of the Second Temple

The quest for rabbinic references to the defilement of the sanctuary by sin did not yield much fruit. It would appear then, that in rabbinic memory, the

Second Temple was considered to be a rather pure place, *despite its flaws.* I illustrate this theme in this section by examining three issues that could have been seen as potential sources of sanctuary defilement, had the tannaim chosen to view them that way. The three potentially problematic issues are: (1) the status of aristocratic wealth in general, as it relates to the sacrificial system; (2) the question of whether sacrificing stolen goods posed a threat to the temple's purity, and (3) the universal application (at least in theory) of the temple tax. While the first issue is largely nonlegal (*aggadic*), the second and third issues will take us into the realm of tannaitic *halakha.*

The Gifts of Aristocrats

As we might expect, rabbinic sources assert, on more than one occasion, the obvious truism that contributions to the temple from the poor often involved greater *sacrifice* on their part than the offerings of the wealthy (*b. Menahot* 104b): "Rabbi Isaac said: what makes the meal offering different so that with respect to it, it is said 'soul' (Lev 2:1). The Holy One, Blessed be He, said: Who is likely to bring a meal offering? The poor. Therefore I will praise him as if he offered his soul." As far as the rabbis were concerned, the contributions of the poor were particularly praiseworthy.[47]

But alongside the rabbinic traditions praising offerings from the poor, we find a number of other sources that explicitly praise the generous contributions of wealthy aristocrats. An early tannaitic catalogue of such donations is recorded in *m. Yoma* 3:9–10 (cf. *b. Yoma* 37a–38a, *y. Yoma* 3:10, 41a/576):[48]

> (9) And there was an urn there, in which there were two lots. These were made of boxwood, but ben Gamala made them of gold, and they would remember him with praise. (10) Ben Qatin made twelve spigots for the laver, which only had two, and he also made a device for the laver,[49] so that its water would not be disqualified overnight. King Monobaz made all the handles for the implements of the Day of Atonement of gold; Helena his mother constructed a gold lamp over the entrance of the sanctuary, and she also made a gold tablet on which the portion of the suspected adulteress was written. Nicanor—miracles occurred with regard to his doors, and he was remembered with praise.

The bulk of these figures are known to be royal or aristocratic. King Monobaz and Queen Helena of Adiabene were royal converts to Judaism,[50] and (Joshua) ben Gamala—whom we have already discussed—served as a high priest. We have no other information regarding ben Katin, but presumably he too was a high priest, by virtue of the juxtaposition with ben Gamala. Certainly the Nicanor who adorned the main gate of the temple with doors of Corinthian bronze was no pauper either.[51]

Some of these aristocrats were also remembered for their righteousness: Queen Helena's piety was legendary (*m. Nazir* 3:6, *b. Sukkah* 2b). But the rabbinic recollection of aristocratic wealth was not limited to those donors who had some claim to righteousness. The ben Gamala whose gifts are recalled here in praise is also recalled as having arrived at his high priestly office through bribery (e.g., *b. Yoma* 18a, discussed above). Yet gifts to the temple were remembered as coming from people even more corrupt, as evidenced by the amoraic traditions relating to King Herod's rebuilding of the temple. Herod's temple was praised as the most beautiful building ever: "whoever has not seen Herod's temple has not seen a beautiful building" (*b. Bava Batra* 4a, *b. Sukkah* 51b). Moreover, the king's work proceeded, according to legend, with God's help: traditions preserved in *b. Ta'anit* 23a (and *Lev Rabbah* 35:10) claim it rained only at night during the Herodian reconstruction project. Yet the Babylonian Talmud describes Herod's sinful behavior with no hesitation, which the rabbis remember as including killing the remaining Hasmoneans, preserving the last princess's deceased body in honey, and—though this point is questioned—having intercourse with her body. To top it off, because the rabbis questioned his legitimacy, Herod then is remembered as massacring all of the sages save one (*b. Bava Batra* 3b). Again, this account is hardly historical in the strict sense of the word. But that hardly matters: what is significant for our purposes is that the rabbis of the Babylonian Talmud remember Herod as a terrible human being—and on that much all would agree—and at the same time (and on practically the same page) they approve of Herod's rebuilding of the temple.[52] The discussion of these matters includes a tellingly practical statement: "if it were not for royalty the temple would never have been built" (*b. Bava Batra* 4a).

Yet the rabbinic position is not just practical, it is also ideological: not unlike their relative containment of accusations of moral defilement, the rabbinic approach to Herod's role in rebuilding the temple provides a stark contrast to what we find in Qumran. In the *Pesher Habakkuk*, for instance, we find a condemnation of a wicked priest (or priests) whose moral crimes render the temple itself inadequate for further ritual use. Whatever the wicked priest's (or priests') moral transgressions were, Herod was surely no better in any sense. He was probably a lot worse, though we really have no way of knowing. Still, the difference between these two literatures emerges not from the consideration of different situations but from different attitudes toward the same basic situation: that the temple's sacrificial worship is or could be tainted by sinful aristocrats. At Qumran, this situation was perceived to undermine the entire sacrificial system. For the rabbis, however, a wicked ruler could not by his own actions invalidate the entire temple.

All of the material we just reviewed is rather late, stemming from well into or even beyond the amoraic period. We cannot be certain of whether earlier tannaim would have approached these matters in the same way as the later amoraim, though we have no reason to assume there was any dramatic change. Indeed, if anything, the earliest rabbinic source—the Mishnah—is even more unequivocal in its protemple stance than the later sources are. Presumably these sages too came to terms with the fact that their beloved and lost temple had largely been constructed by a ruthless despot. In the next section, we will try to find confirmation of this by reviewing some legal positions in the Mishnah and other tannaitic sources that treat a different, but related, matter: the question of whether the temple and its service could be tainted or defiled by the offering of ill-gotten goods.

The Sacrifices of Thieves and Robbers

As I argued in chapter 3, a number of biblical sources imply that proper sacrifice presupposes due ownership of what is being offered. On this point, priests and prophets seem to agree. Indeed, when it comes to sacrificial ownership, it is difficult to distinguish at all between a ritual violation and an ethical wrongdoing. Sacrificing a stolen animal is, at one and the same time, both ethically and ritually wrong. We have already seen this theme developed in the Qumranic literature, to the effect that the temple was seen as a morally defiled place of evil wealth, serviced by wicked priests. But we have also seen more sober developments of the theme, notably Ben Sira 34:21–35:13. The rabbinic approach will prove to be much more like the latter.

There can be no doubt that concerns with property and ownership played a role in shaping the rabbinic treatment of sacrificial rules.[53] So it should come as no surprise that the rabbis believe it improper to sacrifice an animal that belongs to someone else. A statement preserved anonymously in the *Sifra* apparently puts it simply enough. In a commentary on Lev 1:10 ("If his offering is from the herd"), we are told that the purpose of the phrase *"his offering"* is "to exclude what has been robbed" (להוציא את הגזול).[54] A small number of other traditions to the same effect can be isolated.[55]

These traditions find their fullest expression in Maimonides' medieval code of Jewish law, *Mishneh Torah*, which explicitly says: "one who steals (הגונב) or robs (הגוזל) and then offers a sacrifice—it is disqualified (פסול)" (*The Book of Sacred Service* [*Sefer ha- Avodah*], Laws of Altar Prohibitions 5:7). As we will see, two aspects of Maimonides' statement are unparalleled in the rabbinic traditions he seeks to paraphrase, and these differences set the agenda for an analysis of the rabbinic approach to these matters. One problematic aspect of Maimonides' ruling is his assertion that the prohibition applies equally to both what has been *stolen* (in secrecy, and without violence) and what has been *robbed* (openly and violently). Of the small number of rabbinic traditions that speak of such matters, only one of them discusses the sacrificial status of an animal that has been stolen nonviolently (*Sifre Zutta Shelach* 15:3, ed. Horovitz 281). Another problematic aspect of Maimonides' ruling is his assertion that both types of stolen animals would be categorically disqualified as improper offerings.

Curiously, we do not find anywhere in the Mishnah a categorical statement to the effect of Maimonides' ruling, excluding either the stolen *or* robbed sacrifice. Yet we do find in the Mishnah a number of passages treating disqualified sacrifices. These discussions typically contain rote lists of excluded offerings, such as that found in *m. Zevahim* 9:3:

These are the offerings whose disqualification did not occur in the sancta: that which has committed bestiality or been subject to bestiality, or set aside [for the purposes of idolatry], or worshiped [idolatrously], or used as a the fee [for a prostitute] or the purchase [of a dog],[56] or that was cross-bred, or torn, or born not through the womb, or has a blemish.

Similar lists of disqualified sacrifices appear frequently in tannaitic literature.[57] Yet, it is intriguing that not a single one of these lists actually includes stolen or robbed animals, even though related themes—such as animals once used to pay prostitutes—are considered (we will consider these exclusions later). We are certainly not to think that the list quoted above is meant to include all animals tainted by sin. Unattributed, tannaitic traditions in the *Sifra* and the Babylonian Talmud explicitly deny that all such animals would be excluded, and assert, for example, that an ox that was used to plow alongside a donkey—in violation of Deuteronomy 22:10—could constitute a perfectly valid offering.[58] We can also be certain that theft and robbery were concerns of the tannaim, for much of tannaitic civil law treats these matters. Moreover, the chapter of Mishnah treating the rules concerning ritual objects for the holiday of Sukkot considers the status of palm braches and citrons that were robbed (*m. Sukkah* 3:1–5). A number of other tannaitic and amoraic sources even treat the matter of the robbed sacrifice, as we will see. Yet we find no ruling that categorically deems all robbed or stolen sacrifices to be disqualified (פסול).

The consistent failure to include stolen or even robbed sacrifices in the tannaitic lists of excluded offerings provides justification to question whether such offerings were in all cases disqualified by the tannaim. Indeed, we find confirmation that some questioned or limited the exclusion in *m. Gittin* 5:5 (cf. *m. Eduyyot* 7:9), which preserves a tradition attributed to the first-century tanna Yohanan ben Gudgeda. Legendary for his observance of purity laws (*m. Hagigah* 2:7), this figure is also remembered as having been a Levite who served in the temple (*b. Arakhin* 11b; *t. Sheqalim* 2:14). The tradition attributed to him considers the status of a sin-offering that is robbed (החטאת הגזולה), albeit unbeknownst to the community. In this case, the sacrifice is not disqualified; and it is even deemed to effect atonement "for the sake of supporting the altar" (תקון המזבח).[59] It is not at all clear how one ought to extrapolate from this ruling: does it apply *only* to the sin-offering or *even* to the sin-offering? Does it apply *only* to what is robbed or *even* to what is robbed, including, therefore, one that is stolen? And can the guiding principle—supporting the altar—apply to other cases? Some of these issues are addressed, but not resolved, in the Babylonian Talmud's discussion of the passage (*b. Gittin* 55a–b). What is important for our concerns is that we find here a Mishnaic tradition attributed to an early tannaitic sage—one believed to have served in the temple—that explicitly rejects the idea that all robbed sacrifices are disqualified, and even goes so far as to suggest that at least some robbed sacrifices can be perfectly effective.

Yet, as we have already observed, other tannaitic sources are more decided on the matter: the stolen sacrifice is to be excluded. Perhaps the most informative discussion of this issue in rabbinic literature can be found in the Babylonian Talmud. In *b. Sukkah* 29b–30a, the sages take up the mishnaic tradition prohibiting the use of a robbed palm branch on the holiday of Sukkoth (*m. Sukkah* 3:1). The amora R. Yohanan argues in the name of the tanna R. Simeon ben Yohai that using a robbed palm branch would constitute a violation of the principle prohibiting "a precept fulfilled through a transgression." In support of that contention, the sage appeals to the first chapter of Malachi, which we have discussed already: "It is said, 'You bring what has been robbed (הגזול) or is lame or sick' (Mal 1:13): What is robbed is similar to the lame; just as the lame animal lacks a remedy, so too the robbed animal lacks a remedy."[60] Just like the robbed palm branch, the robbed sacrifice is rejected because a commandment cannot be fulfilled through a transgression. The passage continues, questioning whether the issue of despair (יאוש) has any impact on this ruling. According to rabbinic law, when an object is lost or stolen, once the original owner despairs of ever receiving the object back, ownership then transfers to the new owner—even if the new owner robbed the object in the first place (*m. Bava Qamma* 10:2). But according to *b. Sukkah* 30a, even if the original owner despairs, sacrificing a robbed animal still violates the principle of fulfilling a precept by committing a transgression.[61] Yet rabbinic opinion was divided on this matter too. In the talmudic discussions of *m. Gittin* 5:5 (*b. Gittin* 55a–b), it becomes clear that those who do not disqualify all robbed sacrifices are guided in part by the principles concerning despair: because the original owner has given up his claim, there's no reason to exclude the robbed offering, for it is now duly owned by the thief.[62]

The talmudic passage comparing the robbed palm branch to the robbed sacrifice continues (*b. Sukkah* 30a), presenting a further tradition condemning the offering of robbed animals. Commenting on Isaiah 61:8 (that God "hates robbery with a burnt offering"), the following parable is presented—and again (at least in the printed editions) the tradition is attributed to Rabbi Yohanan in the name of Rabbi Simeon ben Yohai.

> The matter is likened to an earthly king who passed a toll-booth, and told his servants to pay the collectors. They said to him: "But [what is collected from the] the toll is entirely yours!" He said to them: "Let all who pass by learn from my example, and not evade paying the toll." Similarly, the Holy One, blessed be He, said: "I the Lord hate robbery with a burnt offering" (Isa. 61:8): Let all learn from my example, and keep themselves clear of robbery.[63]

Like the other sources quoted above, this one too condemns offering robbed goods. But despite the fact that the offerings are condemned, we are not told here that such offerings are, from a strictly halakhic perspective, disqualified or ineffective in all cases. Indeed, the aggadic force of the various traditions in *b. Sukkah* is underscored by the fact that they appeal to passages from the prophets, not the Pentateuch. Altogether, *b. Sukkah* 29b–30a can be read alongside passages like *m. Gittin* 5:5: people must know, as we are told in *b. Sukkah* 30a, that offering robbed sacrifices is most improper. But, as we read in *m. Gittin* 5:5, temple authorities should not presume to exclude all such offerings from the temple. Indeed there is a simple, practical concern here: how can the temple authorities presume to know that one offering or another happened to have been stolen or robbed? What is not known to them—as *m. Gittin* 5:5 stipulates—will not harm the integrity of the temple or its sacrificial service.

It bears repeating that virtually without exception, the sources that do exclude the robbed sacrifice refer only to what is robbed (violently), not to what is simply stolen. It is therefore reasonable to suppose that when our texts exclude sacrifices that are robbed, they mean to exclude *only* sacrifices that were robbed, permitting those that were just stolen. Certainly we cannot be sure that they all intend to categorically disqualify both types of theft (as, again, Maimonides would have it). Indeed, a careful reading of the earlier sources demonstrates that Maimonides' position on the matter—the explicit categorical disqualification of robbed and stolen sacrifices—has little support from tannaitic or amoraic sources.

The rabbis' circumspect approach to the matter of ill-gotten sacrifices can also be seen in their treatment of the Deuteronomic prohibition against bringing to the sanctuary the "fee of the prostitute or the purchase of a dog" (Deut. 23:19).[64] The Mishnah consistently limits the possible applicability of these prohibitions in a number of ways (*m. Temurah* 6:1–4; cf. *t. Temurah* 4:1–10, *b. Temurah* 28a–31b). First, both prohibitions apply only in cases of barter: if money is used to pay the prostitute or to purchase a dog, the money itself is not tainted (6:2, 4; cf. *t. Temurah* 4:2). Second, the barter must involve animals or commodities the like of which can be used on the altar: items such as sheep, wine, flour, oils, and birds (*m. Temurah* 6:4). Moreover, the rabbis interpret the terms *"fee* of the prostitute" and *"purchase* of the dog" in an exclusive manner: the prohibition applies only if one barters to pay a prostitute her *fee* or to *purchase* a dog: if one were to barter to purchase a prostitute (as one would buy a slave) or if one were to barter to pay a fee for a dog's service (to pay the owner for some work the dog could perform) then the prohibition would not apply (6:3; cf. *t. Temurah* 4:2). As with many prohibitions that the rabbis seek to limit, the rulings apply only to the bartered animal itself, not to any offspring the animal may have (6:4; cf. *t. Temurah* 4:3).

Many of these prohibitions—even in the Mishnah itself—are justified exegetically. For instance, the limiting of the prohibition to the harlot's *fee* and to the dog's *purchase* (but not vice versa) is based on the fact that Deut. 23:19 says that "both of them" (שׁניהם) are abhorrent. This is taken to mean (*m. Temurah* 6:3) that only two things are prohibited (the *fee* of the prostitute and the *purchase* of the dog), not four, as the count would be if we were to include also the *purchase* of the prostitute and the *fee* of a dog). The exclusion of the animal's offspring is also justified exegetically, being based on the reference to *them* (in, again, Deut. 23:19: "both of them"). The application of the prohibition to fowl is also justified exegetically, though this particular exegesis defies simple paraphrase (*m. Temurah* 6:3).

The degree to which these mishnaic laws are explicitly exegetical is important to note because there is one essential aspect of the biblical verse that is virtually ignored in the Mishnah, and certainly not exploited to any full potential in the more thorough exegetical treatments (such as *Sifre Deuteronomy*, sec. 261). That ignored or overlooked aspect of Deut. 23:19 is the statement that both the harlot's fee and the dog's purchase are *abominations* (תועבות) to the Lord. The Hebrew Bible, of course, consistently refers to many behaviors—particularly idolatry, incest, and murder—as abominable. Indeed, in the Holiness Code and prophetic literature, this term often appears with regard to acts deemed to be morally defiling. Now and again, the tannaim choose to interpret an appearance of this term in one context or another as a cause to determine that other behaviors too are morally defiling. As I have mentioned earlier, arrogance and judicial deceit are both determined to defile the land and cause the departure of the divine presence (in the *Mekilta* and *Sifra*, respectively), and in both cases, the exegetical basis for such statements is the appearance of the term "abomination" in juxtaposition with the behavior in question (Prov. 16:5 and Lev. 19:15, respectively).[65]

The same exegetical potential is present in Deuteronomy 23:19. Had the rabbis wanted to expand the force of the prohibition, they could have drawn analogies between this and other prohibitions concerning abominable behavior. In *Sifre Deuteronomy*, sec. 261 (On Deut. 23:19; ed. Finkelstein 283–284), the phrase "abomination to the Lord" is commented upon—but only to draw a comparison with similar prohibitions pertaining to excluded sacrificial offerings, such as that contained in Deut. 17:1 (see *Sifre Deut.*, sec. 147, on 17:1; ed. Finkelstein 201–202). Despite the fact that the Deuteronomic prohibitions we have been discussing pertain to abominable deeds, the sacrificial offerings that are tainted by their association with such deeds are not themselves deemed to be abominable or even impure (ritually or morally): such sacrifices, as we have seen throughout, are at most disqualified, and a surprising number of such offerings are in fact permitted.

Two further points require emphasis. The fact that the entire issue we have addressed—concerning stolen or robbed sacrifices and the other tainted offerings—has been phrased in terms of "disqualification" is notable, and in and of itself marks a contrast on these matters between rabbinic literature and the literature from Qumran. I have noted earlier and argued elsewhere that the rabbinic sages compartmentalized ritual purity issues on the one hand from issues concerning morality and moral impurity on the other.[66] We find further confirmation of this phenomenon in the sources we have analyzed here, which suggest that the rabbis do not concern themselves with the possibility that tainted or sinful offerings could threaten the ritual purity of the temple worship.

Even more important, all of the exclusions we have discussed so far apply only to the animal, and not to the person who would offer the tainted offering. This much is stated explicitly in *Sifre Deuteronomy* (secs. 147, 261; on Deut.

17:1 and 23:19; ed. Finkelstein 201–202, 283–284). In fact, the tannaitic discussions of sacrificial disqualifications in general distinguish quite carefully between those that apply to the offerer and those that apply to the offering (*m. Bekhorot* 7:7). It seems reasonable to infer that if a priest who committed manslaughter or sexual sins is not excluded from participating in sacrificial service (*m. Bekhorot* 7:7), then neither is the thief or robber. Indeed, as I have demonstrated elsewhere, sinners were not considered ritually impure in tannaitic *halakha*, and there is no evidence to the effect that sinners were systematically or generally excluded from participation in the temple cult.[67]

In the Mishnah (*Bikkurim* 1:1–2), robbers are explicitly excluded from bringing first fruits to the temple. The exclusion is explained here exegetically: because scripture says, "the first fruits of *your* land" (Exod. 23:19), one who doesn't duly own land from which first fruits emerge is not to bring offerings from such land to the temple. But later in the same tractate (2:3), it is noted that the rules concerning first fruits are exceptional in this matter: the robber would be still be obligated to pay the tithe and heave-offering. Here too we find that there is no consistent concern with the possibility that robbed or stolen goods donated to the temple threaten the integrity or purity of the temple worship. There is also no concern that robbers or thieves themselves posed such a threat.

A tannaitic source preserved only in the Babylonian Talmud confirms that thieves were not barred from participating in the cult. Moreover, this source suggests to us the reasoning behind this leniency (*b. Eruvin* 69b):

> [Commenting on Leviticus 1:2: "When a person from among you brings a sacrifice of cattle"] *"From* among you," and not from all of you, thus the apostate is excluded [and is therefore forbidden to bring a sacrifice]. "From *among you*": among *you* I made this distinction, but not among the nations [and therefore all Gentiles may send offerings to the temple]. . . . "*Of* cattle": to include people who make themselves like animals. From here we learn: they accept sacrifices from the sinners of Israel, so that they may repent, with the exception of an apostate, one who pours wine libations, and one who violates the Sabbath in public.[68]

According to this tannaitic tradition—and I cannot find any dissenting voice in this regard—sacrifices were accepted from practically all sinful Israelites, thieves and robbers no doubt included. And we are not talking about merely allowing repentant sinners to enter the sanctuary in order to offer their sin-offerings. Of course those people are welcome—that's the whole point of having sin-offerings. This passage is not concerned with the obvious, and sin-offerings are not mentioned anywhere in the text. It speaks, rather, of accepting *any* sacrifices from (practically) *any unrepentant* sinners, in the hope that they may repent *some day*. According to the Talmud, the reason for their doing so is rather clear: the rabbis envisioned a temple that was open to (practically) all Jews. I think we can extrapolate from this tradition, and explain the similarly lenient rabbinic approach to ill-gotten sacrifices: because the rabbis desired to include all those who would participate, the principle of including all trumped the concern that this or that offering may have been acquired unethically. Their vision was indeed quite different from the exclusive view espoused in the Qumran literature.

The Temple's Funds

There is one further way the rabbis envisioned all Jews participating in the temple worship, and it involved money: by paying the annual half-sheqel temple tax. According to tannaitic sources, the annual tax was to be used to defray the costs of the daily sacrificial offerings (*m. Sheqalim* 4:1–4).[69] Yet rabbinic sources also recall a dispute on this matter: according to traditions generally believed to be tannaitic, the Sadducees—or possibly the Boethusians— maintained that the daily offerings would be funded by voluntary donations from wealthy individuals, but the sages opposed this view (*b. Menahot* 65a, scholion to *Megillat Ta'anit* 1).[70]

If the Sadducees (or Boethusians) did oppose the public funding of daily worship through the annual temple tax, they may not have been alone. We know from Qumranic sources that at least some Jews opposed the idea of an annual temple tax, believing instead that the tax was to be paid only once, when a man reached his twentieth year (4Q159 *Ordinances*[a] frag. 1, II: 6–7; cf. 11QT XXXIX:7–11).[71] An opposition to the tax in theory (whether one-time or annual) is also expressed in Matthew 17:24–27, though in this case, Jesus is said to have grudgingly approved paying the tax, so as not to offend the authorities (this passage will be discussed further in chapter 7). Possibly, but not necessarily, those who opposed the annual tax would agree with the position the rabbis attribute to the Sadducees (or Boethusians), that the daily offerings were to be funded by wealthy benefactors.

In agreement with the later rabbis, Josephus states on more than one occasion that the daily offerings were funded from public money (*Ant.* 3:237, 255). Yet he does not explicitly say that these funds came from the money raised by the temple tax.[72] Philo is even less clear on the matter. The philosopher regularly speaks of the gifts sent to the temple locally and from abroad, and he notes that the daily offering is presented "on behalf of the world" (*Spec.* 1:97). Yet Philo does not explicitly say that the daily offering is to come exclusively from public money. While some scholars try to equate Philo's position with the rabbinic approach to these matters, it is better to recognize that he leaves the specific question of sacrificial funding unanswered.[73]

Indeed, it is not at all uncommon to find scholars suggesting that Josephus—and even Philo—agree not just with rabbinic law but also with the *Pharisaic* law on this matter.[74] The problem is that we don't have an explicit testimony on the matter of the Pharisaic position. The rabbinic sources noted above speak of a dispute between the Sadducees and the *sages*—the rabbinic sources don't mention the Pharisees at all. Scholars have simply assumed, since the rabbinic sources speak of a dispute with the Sadducees (or Boethusians), that the other view must have been articulated by the Pharisees of pre-70 C.E., even though they are not mentioned.[75] Since we don't have a single source—of any date—testifying explicitly to the Pharisaic answer to this question, we can hardly treat the supposed Pharisaic articulation of the later rabbinic position as a fact. But even if it is not a Pharisaic tradition, we still have a dispute between those who said that the sacrifices were funded by public money (Josephus, the rabbinic sages) and those who said they could be funded privately (Sadducees or Boethusians, according to rabbinic sources).

And how does this relate to the issue at hand? Whether the dispute between the sages and the Sadducees (or Boethusians) was historical or not—and regardless of what was actually done in the temple—the differences among these sources testify further to the significance of the matters we have been reviewing in this chapter. The rabbinic position on the temple tax—that it was paid annually, by *all* Jews, and used to defray the costs of the daily offering—virtually ensures that the sacrificial service would depend for its day-to-day operation on funds that others would question. Practically by definition—and certainly by any definition acceptable to, for instance, the *Damascus Document*—the revenues from an annual and widely collected temple tax would include at least some money tainted by theft or some other transgression. For the rabbis, presumably, the concern to include all over-rides the concern to maintain a taint-free temple purse. It's not difficult to imagine that various groups of predestruction Jews might have opposed such a policy, had it been suggested or implemented.

We have seen that the rabbis were rather open and honest about the fact that the Second Temple was funded by aristocrats, of whom some could surely have been accused of being greedy, and others, like Herod, were surely immoral people. The rabbis were similarly open and practical when it came to considering the impact of theft and robbery on the daily practice of the temple. While they were interested in the issue of stolen sacrifices, they were not sympathetic to the approach that could lead either to a rejection of the temple or to the implementation of an exclusivist policy. The rabbis chose a course that condemned the act of sacrificing ill-gotten goods but at the same time refrained from considering such acts to be a threat to the purity of temple worship. The rabbis, therefore, waver in their treatment of the robbed sacrifice itself, refraining from explicitly disqualifying such offerings. And even those rabbis who would ban the robbed or stolen sacrifice don't go much farther than that. Thieves and tainted money seem to be beyond their general concern when discussing the status of sacrificial offerings. They would have welcomed practically all sinful Jews into the temple, just as they imagined collecting money for the temple from the sinful as well as from the righteous. In short, the rabbis recall with equanimity that the temple was funded by transgressors and open to sinners, some of whose offerings, naturally, were prone to being tainted by theft.

In the previous section, we observed that postmishnaic rabbinic sources were fully willing to recall that the temple and its priests were from time to time—and especially toward the end of its history—tainted by various crimes and corruptions. As we also noted, the tannaitic sources recall with approval that the temple was repeatedly ritually defiled by pilgrims. And despite all this, the rabbis were unwilling to indict the priests or even the general late Second Temple period populace with the charge of sanctuary defilement, even when they wished to explain why the temple was destroyed. By contrast, Josephus, as we have seen, explicitly connected the temple's destruction to the sins that were committed there, and in this the historian followed the precedent of the prophet Ezekiel. The Qumran sectarians, as we have also seen, repeatedly spoke of the temple's defilement by sin, and presumably their rejection of the Jerusalem temple was closely connected to this idea. Despite these precedents and parallels, the rabbis do not embrace the notion of sanctuary defilement as an explanation for the temple's destruction. Indeed, their nostalgia for the temple appears to prevent them from accepting the idea that the temple itself was particularly responsible for its own destruction.

At first, it may be simpler to appreciate the ethical high ground assumed in the Qumran literature: moral transgressions are flatly rejected, and the temple is held to a high ethical standard. No sinners allowed, no tainted offerings tolerated. In CD, the temple's worship was considered compromised because sacrificial system operated in a manner that fell well short of the sectarian economic ideal. The pious are therefore to be "closers of the door." The sectarians envisioned an ideal institution, operating on the highest ritual and ethical plain, and open only to those they deemed worthy to participate. The temple remembered by the rabbis—funded by aristocrats, and open to the participation of thieves—was surely well below sectarian standards. The challenge is to appreciate equally the ethics of the looser, rabbinic approach to these matters. After all, the desire to keep the central institutions open to the participation of as many as possible can also be understood as a moral position. The rabbis envisioned an open institution, one perhaps not free of all taint, but one that could then serve its purpose: welcoming all Jews who wish to worship. The doors of the temple remembered by the rabbis—which were endowed by an aristocrat named Nicanor—were wide open.

Judaism without a Temple

In this section we will see that the rabbis' nostalgia for the Second Temple can be seen in two more phenomena: (1) their continued hope for the temple's eventual reconstruction, and (2) their varied efforts at emulating the temple's sanctity by "templizing" certain rituals, particularly those relating to food and prayer. In line with the foregoing analysis, neither of these phenomena constitutes a rejection of the past; to the contrary, both are further examples of the rabbis' rather consistently nostalgic view of the Second Temple. The analysis of these two themes will lead to the fourth and final section of this chapter, in which we reconsider a number of the scholarly reconstructions of the rabbinic response to the destruction. As we will see, the scholarly analysis has been unduly influenced by the biases we have seen all along in the second part of this book.

The Rabbinic Hope for Restoration

A significant amount of evidence can be marshaled to the effect that the rabbis hoped for the temple's eventual rebuilding, and held no expectation for a future devoid of a temple. If the continued interest in the temple's procedures—as detailed especially in Mishnah *Seder Qodashim*—isn't evidence enough, we could point to explicit expressions hoping for the temple's rebuilding, interspersed throughout even the Mishnah—though at least some of these passages are later glosses (e.g., *m. Ma'aser Sheni* 5:2; *m. Ta'anit* 4:8; *m. Tamid* 7:3).[76] Perhaps a more certain line of evidence is to be found in the traditional liturgies, which contain repeated, explicit appeals for the temple to be rebuilt. We can hardly present a full listing, but the following examples should suffice. The daily eighteen benedictions include two such prayers: One blessing (now beginning "And to Jerusalem Your City"; no. 14 in Elbogen's enumeration) is concerned in its various versions with the future rebuilding of Jerusalem and the temple.[77] Another blessing (now beginning with the words "Accept, oh Lord"; no. 17 in Elbogen's enumeration) is concerned more explicitly with the rebuilding of the temple and the return of sacrifices.[78] In many versions—including the custom in use among traditional Jews today—the blessing concludes with a plea for the return of God's presence to Zion.[79]

Dating these prayers poses great difficulties,[80] but surely they date at least to the amoraic period, for partial versions of the prayers, and discussions of their themes, appear in various rabbinic documents (blessing 14: e.g., *b. Berakhot* 29a; blessing 17: e.g., *Lev. Rabbah* 7:2).[81] Interestingly, we find that similar prayers—including the hope for the rebuilding of the temple—were offered at least by some individuals long before the temple's destruction (Ben Sira 36:17–19; 51:12, lines 7 and 8 of material preserved only in Hebrew MS). While we cannot use these parallels to date the rabbinic versions of the eighteen benedictions to the predestruction era, the parallels demonstrate that we cannot assume that prayers for the building of the temple must postdate 70 c.e. Scholars generally believe, reasonably enough, that the basic hopes contained in the rabbinic prayers—if not the particular expressions known to us—reflect not only wishes of the amoraic age but those of the tannaitic era as well.

Added to this liturgical evidence is the fact that a number of aggadic traditions explicitly affirm that the temple, the priesthood, and the sacrificial service will not only return but are meant to be eternal. We find one such tradition preserved (anonymously) in *Sifre Numbers*, sec. 92 (on Num. 11:16; ed. Horovitz 92):

> "Gather for me" (Num. 11:16): That there should be a Sanhedrin for
> my name. For in every instance where "for me" [לי, which can
> also mean "mine"] is said, what is spoken of is to last forever and
> ever. With regard to the priests, it is said: "And they shall minister for

me" (Exod. 28:41). With regard to the Levites, it is said: "And the Levites shall be mine" (Num. 8:14). With regard to Israel, it is said: "For the children of Israel are servants for me" (Lev. 25:55). With regard to the land, it is said: "For the land is mine" (Lev. 25:23). With regard to the first-born, it is said: "For every first-born of Israel is mine" (Num. 8:17). With regard to the temple, it is said: "And they shall make for me a sanctuary" (Exod. 25:8). With regard to the altar, it is said: "Make for me an earthen altar" (Exod. 20:24). With regard to the anointing oil, it is said: "Sacred anointing oil there shall be for me" (Exod. 30:31). With regard to the kingship, it is said: "For I have seen among his sons a king for me" (1 Sam. 16:1). With regard to the sacrifices it is said, "To offer for me at its time" (Num. 28:2). And so in every instance where "for me" is said, behold this will last forever and ever.

Substantially similar traditions appear in other aggadic works, including *Leviticus Rabbah* 2:2 (ed. Margulies, 1:37–38).[82] While we find here and there an item added to or missing from the list, the eternity of the temple, the sacrifices, and the priesthood is asserted in all these traditions.[83]

We also find a tradition, attributed to a group of Palestinian amoraim, that asserts that all types of sacrifice other than the thanksgiving offering will be annulled in the future age (*Lev. Rabbah* 9:7; ed. Margulies, 1:185; 27:12 [2:747]; *Pesikta de-Rab Kahana* 9:12; ed. Mandelbaum, 1:159). This tradition is not infrequently noted, particularly in New Testament scholarship, as will be seen in chapter 7. Less frequently noted—but crucial for appreciating the thrust of the passage—is that these sages also assert that forms of prayer other than those relating to thanksgiving will also be annulled in the future age. Indeed, this source testifies to the eternity of both prayer and sacrifice, claiming only that in the future, when there will be no transgression, there will be no need for atonement or supplication, whether in sacrificial or in prayer form.[84] These traditions are no more critical of the temple and its worship than they are of synagogues and prayer. Although these traditions assert that some kinds of sacrifice—those relating to repentance—will become obsolete, the traditions also assert that sacrifice will continue in the future age. Indeed, one would be hard pressed to find rabbinic sources that speak of a future without a temple.[85] It is therefore all the more surprising that various scholars of rabbinic literature have endeavored to demonstrate that the rabbis harbored misgivings about the temple or its sacrificial service.

One further point requires emphasis here. Had the rabbis been dissatisfied with the Second Temple in any significant way—rejecting its priests, practices, or physical structure—we might expect to find expressions of such judgments in their eschatological hopes. Along the lines of Ezekiel, the *New Jerusalem Texts*—or even the New Testament book of Revelation—the rabbis could have put forth visions of the future that in some fashion imply an overturning of the past by imagining a temple of vastly greater size, operating by different rules, run by different personnel. But this, too, they don't do. The mishnaic discussions of temple practice are, as we have seen, practical and realistic. Moreover, the measurements for the temple supplied in Mishnah Tractate *Middoth*—while not entirely in agreement with Josephus—are by no means extraordinary or beyond what Jerusalem's physical landscape would easily allow. While some rabbinic and medieval rabbinic traditions speak of a jewel-encrusted future temple,[86] the dominant trend is to imagine a future without even implying any deficiency or critique of what was lost. And this too further confirms one of the central themes of this chapter: the rabbis—in contrast with other ancient Jewish voices—were rather reluctant to voice dissatisfaction with the temple that was destroyed by Titus in 70 C.E.

Emulations of the Temple in Rabbinic Thought and Practice

The rabbis' nostalgia for the temple can also be seen in the various ways in which they supported the "templization" of synagogues and the "sacrificial-ization" of both prayer and food practices. As we have seen, literary and archaeological evidence suggests that various groups of ancient Jews sought purity and sanctity even when they were away from Jerusalem. Evidence that the bounds of purity extended beyond the temple is also to be found in rabbinic literature, as Alon famously argued decades ago.[87] For example, we note the early rabbinic interest in the defilement of hands, and the consequent requirement to wash hands before eating (e.g., *m. Berakhot* 8:1–2).[88] Eventually, the rabbis applied this requirement to prayer as well (*b. Berakhot* 14b).[89] Another characteristic example of this phenomenon can be found in *m. Berakhot* 3:4–6, which requires those rendered ritually impure by contact with semen to immerse before reciting the *shema* or the daily benedictions. This ruling is based in part on Deut. 23:10–15, which concerns the defilement of semen and the purity of the Israelite war camp (cf. *Sifre Deut.*, sec. 258).[90] According to the Mishnah, the prohibition applies to prayer as well, and other tannaitc sources extend the prohibition to Torah study (*t. Berakhot* 2:11–12). Yet despite the rabbis' application of the Deuteronomic prohibition to new contexts, the rabbinic interpretation does not fully generalize the biblical ruling. The restrictions still apply only to those affected by the specific form of defilement mentioned in Deuteronomy 23; those suffering from other impurities do not fall under the prohibition (*m. Berakhot* 3:6, cf. *t. Berakhot* 2:12).

What is the motivation for these rules? Were the rabbis acting like priests or following purity for its own sake? In my view, it is difficult to believe that the meaning of these rites could be divorced, in part or in whole, from their obvious, scriptural, ritual context: purity is first and foremost the prerequisite for entry to the temple. As such, the maintenance of ritual purity beyond the temple is evidence of the effort to "templize" other aspects of religious life. Moreover, what is "templized" or "sacrificialized" here are those aspects of daily life—particularly prayer and eating—that were already conceptually related to temple worship. According to all, sacrifice involved food, and according to rabbinic sources (as we will see), the temple service involved prayer too. Thus these rabbinic rulings hardly constitute a criticism of the temple.

Indeed, the Mishnah asserts that the holy of holies is the holiest place on earth, and no source will question that assertion (*m. Kelim* 1:6–9). Some rabbinic rulings even explicitly ascribe continuing sanctity to the site of the destroyed temple (e.g., *m. Berakhot* 9:5). The sacralization of synagogues and prayer in no way implies a desacralization of the temple or the worship that took place there.

As we also noted in the previous chapter, various structural and decorative motifs of ancient synagogues hearken back to the Jerusalem temple. Extant synagogue floors frequently depict seven-branched candelabra and the ark of the covenant (frequently, as noted in chapter 4, juxtaposed with images of the zodiac).[91] Structurally, some synagogues partially resembled the temple (as well as contemporary churches) in that the more sacred areas were marked off—or blocked off—by chancel screens.[92] And yet this process appears to be a restrained one: for instance, no synagogue was built to fully resemble the temple of old.[93] Without supposing that the rabbis controlled the synagogues or designed their decoration,[94] it can be demonstrated that the rabbis supported or at least agreed with the templization of synagogues and the service performed there. Various rabbinic rulings—such as those noted above—reinforce the sanctity of synagogues and the purity of the study and worship that takes place within them.

Some have argued that the rabbinic approach to extratemple holiness constitutes a distinct and even revolutionary response to the temple's destruction. With an appeal to Jonathan Z. Smith's work, the rabbis are seen as replacing the old, place-centered, "locative" temple ritual with newer "utopian" patterns of religion, ones that were less tied to the old sacred center.[95] But this approach is problematic. Smith's analysis itself postulates that the transition from locative to utopian was a common development among religions in the Greco-Roman period. The process was not necessarily occasioned by a crisis, or inevitably spearheaded by a religious elite.[96] Smith's theoretical work describes a bottom-up process, whereby people of various religious traditions sought purity and sanctity even when away from the older sacred centers.

Indeed, we now know that the rabbis cannot be credited with setting this process in motion among ancient Jews. The literary and archaeological evidence testifying to the building of ritual baths, the use of stone vessels, and the custom of washing hands all suggests that the process of seeking holiness while away from Jerusalem was well underway long *before* the destruction of the temple, without the sponsorship of the rabbinic (or Pharisaic) elites. Even though the rabbinic rulings themselves can only be dated to the tannaitic (postdestruction) period,[97] the general process of which these rulings are only a part is not an effort we can credit the tannaim with inventing; nor is it something that can be seen as a novel or revolutionary response to the temple's loss. Rather, the rabbis' unquestionable support for the sacrificialization of prayer and the templization of synagogues can be understood as further evidence of their nostalgic approach to the temple that was destroyed.

Sacrifice, Prayer, and Jewish Supersessionism

In the opening pages of his history of Jewish prayer, Ismar Elbogen claimed that "Jewish liturgy has unparalleled importance in the history of religions, for it was the first to free itself completely from the sacrificial cult, thus deserving to be called 'The Service of the Heart.' "[98] In this brief formulation, we have the hallmarks of the supersessionist attitudes articulated by many modernist Jewish scholars when writing about ancient Jewish sacrifice and the various practices—typically prayer, acts of loving-kindness, or Torah study—that are understood to succeed or replace the temple's service. First, we have the *presumption* that what replaces sacrifice (in this case, prayer) is in fact better than it—whether spiritually or morally. Second, we have the attempt to root this judgment in the rabbinic texts themselves, as if to claim that the rabbis too were already aware that sacrifice was meant only for a time, just as the medieval Maimonideans and modern reformers would later claim. Needless to say, Elbogen's work is not unique in this regard. The same phenomena are at work in Jacob Milgrom's approach to sacrifice (and his interpretation of *Lev. Rabbah* 22:8). Elias Bickerman's rather offensive reference to Titus as a religious reformer also bears recalling. Other denigrations of sacrifice by modernist Jewish scholars can easily be identified.[99]

In recent years, some scholarship on these matters has added a new twist to the classic understanding of the rabbis' replacing sacrifice with prayer. According to this view, early rabbinic Judaism was too shocked by the events of 70 C.E. to mount an effective response.[100] Drawing an analogy to survivors of modern catastrophes such as the Holocaust or the bombing of Hiroshima, Baruch Bokser suggests that the rabbinic response was delayed and protracted.[101] Only after some time had passed could the rabbis fully acknowledge the loss, and accept that sacrifice has been replaced—and in truth bettered—by prayer and acts of loving-kindness.

Others have rightly questioned whether the rabbis were hopelessly stunned by the events of 70 C.E. One could just as well claim, on the basis of the same lack of evidence, that the tannaim determinedly asserted a sense of normalcy, consciously avoiding addressing the temple's loss head-on.[102] Similarly, we have to ask whether the shock is more in the minds of the interpreters than in the evidence of early rabbinic sources.[103] In fact, the Holocaust analogy is hopelessly flawed. First of all, there is an extreme imbalance between the two ostensibly delayed reactions. It is one thing to suppose that fully thought-out responses to the Holocaust took decades to appear. It is something else entirely to suggest, by comparison, that it took ancient Jews *hundreds* of years to come to terms with the temple's destruction. As it happens, moreover, there are good reasons to question whether the theory of delayed response applies even in the case of the Holocaust. Many literary works responding to the atrocities were composed even before 1945 (among numerous examples, one could note the diaries and archival work by

Emmanuel Ringelblum in the Warsaw Ghetto).[104] Moreover, even if after a few decades the rate of publication increased and the attention such works received multiplied, supposing a delayed *Jewish* response to the tragedy is only one possible historical explanation.[105]

We may do better if we try to understand the rabbinic response to 70 C.E. without drawing analogies to contemporary catastrophes. In what follows, we will review a number of the rabbinic sources that are commonly cited when scholars seek to demonstrate that the rabbis consciously replaced sacrifice with something of their own invention. Indeed, a number of rabbinic traditions—almost all of which can be dated to the amoraic period—do suggest that sacrifice is either equaled or in some cases even bettered by something else, whether it is the study of Torah (e.g., *b. Menahot* 110a), acts of loving-kindness (e.g., *Avot de-Rabbi Natan* 4), or prayer (e.g., *b. Berakhot* 32b).[106] What these sources lack, however, is any assertion that prayer, acts of loving-kindness, or Torah study constitute *later* and distinctly *rabbinic* substitutes for the *original* and now lost practice of sacrifice. These particular assertions stem not from the rabbinic sources themselves but from modernist Judaism, and its supersessionist approach to sacrifice and the temple.

We begin by looking at the tradition Elbogen alluded to in the passage quoted above. The tannaitic tradition in question appears anonymously in *Sifre Deuteronomy*, sec. 41 (ed. Finkelstein 87–88) as well as in the talmudim (*b. Ta'anit* 2a; *y. Berakhot* 4:1, 7a/31). Commenting on Deuteronomy 11:13, "and you shall serve him with all your heart," the passage asks whether or not the verse speaks of sacrifice or some other sort of service. The first possibility entertained is that the command concerns Torah study, which is then identified as a type of "service," through a creative exegesis of Genesis 2:15 ("to till it and guard it," with the first verb sharing the same root as "serve"). Then an alternate understanding is presented:

> "And serve him (with all your heart and will all your soul)...." (Deut.
> 11:13): This refers to prayer. You say this is prayer, but perhaps it
> refers to sacrificial service? Yet scripture states "with all your heart
> and with all your soul" (11:13, cf. 6:5). But is there a service that
> pertains to the heart? Behold scripture states "and serve him." This
> is prayer....[107] So just as worship at the altar is called service, so too
> prayer is called service.

By virtue of its being alluded to on the first pages of Elbogen's work, one might expect that the sentiment expressed here—or even the phrase "service of the heart"—were commonplace in rabbinic literature. Yet the catch phrase appears only in the single exegetical tradition, which itself appears all of three times in classic rabbinic sources. The degree to which the tradition has become well known in modern times is surely related to the fact that the phrase "service of the heart" has become in modern times a slogan for Jewish prayer.

Not only is the catch phrase less common than it might be thought, the tradition in question is also much less radical than one might expect. Some scholars assert that the exegesis here clearly identifies prayer and Torah study as equivalents to or better than sacrifice.[108] But the question at hand is an exegetical one: what kind of "service" is meant in Deut. 11:13? At most, what the tradition does is create an overarching category of "service" and identifies all three—sacrifice, study, and prayer—as included therein. No relative judgments are made, nor are the three equalized. Nor, in fact, is the possibility even considered that one form of service may cease. The tradition is hardly a response to the destruction. The subsequent valorization of the "service of the heart" has compelled scholars to read that sentiment into this passage, but it's not there.

As for the other option entertained by this tradition—that the "service" spoken of here is Torah study—here, too, we do not find the suggestion that sacrifice had been replaced. The valorization of Torah study is commonplace in rabbinic literature. The locus classicus—m. Peah 1:1—already asserts that Torah study holds its own against giving to the poor, honoring one's parents, acts of loving-kindness, and reconciling one person to another. A few traditions in particular juxtapose Torah study with sacrifice, and it is even suggested that the public teaching of Torah compares to priestly ministering at the sanctuary (Avot de-Rabbi Natan A 4; ed. Schechter 9b; cf. B 8, ed. Schechter 11b): "the Sage who sits and expounds to the congregation, scripture accounts to him as if he had offered fat and blood upon the altar."

Perhaps the most famous text suggesting that the goals of sacrifice may be achieved by another means can also be found in Avot de-Rabbi Natan (A 4; ed. Schechter 11a–b; cf. B 8, ed. Schechter 11b). According to this tradition, Rabban Yohanan ben Zakkai and Rabbi Joshua were walking by the temple's ruins. When Joshua bewailed the loss—and the inability to atone for Israel's sins— ben Zakkai said: "my son, do not be grieved, for we have another atonement that is just like it. And which is it? Acts of loving-kindness, as it is said: 'For I desire loving-kindness, and not sacrifice' (Hos. 6:6)."[109] In the Babylonian Talmud (b. Berakhot 32b) we find a similar statement, attributed to Rabbi Eleazar, to the effect that prayer is the surrogate for sacrifice: "prayer is greater than all the sacrifices, as it is said: 'What need have I with all your offerings?' (Isa. 1:11), and it is written, 'And when you lift your hands' (Isa. 1:15)."[110]

Those who believe that sacrifice has been "transcended" or even "superseded" in rabbinic thought find support for these claims in these traditions.[111] That these sources do not unquestionably claim that sacrifice has been superseded can be seen first and foremost by context. The passage from Avot de-Rabbi Natan is preceded by various traditions affirming the religious and even cosmic significance of the temple service; it is followed shortly thereafter by a version of the legend concerning ben Zakkai and Vespasian, which concludes with the sages mourning the temple's loss (ed. Schechter 10a–13a). The passage from b. Berakhot 32b quoted above is juxtaposed with other statements attributed to the same Rabbi Eleazar, one of which asserts that since the destruction of the temple, the gates of prayer have been closed, and an iron wall has separated Israel from God. Clearly, according to Rabbi Eleazar—at least as the Talmud preserves his opinions—the destruction of the temple has brought about changes that not only prevent the performance of sacrifice but interfere with the power of prayer as well.[112] Even as prayer becomes the means by which certain obligations can be fulfilled in the absence of the temple, the relative efficacy of prayer has been dramatically decreased by the lack of a temple service. Taken as a whole, the message here can hardly be that animal offerings are relatively unimportant or second rate.[113] Prayer may have its distinct values when compared to sacrifice, but even the efficacy of prayer is negatively impacted by the lack of sacrifice.

A closer look at the exegesis of Isaiah attributed to Rabbi Eleazar demonstrates that this understanding is the correct one. The choice of proof-texts is curious: while the first statement—"what need have I of all your offerings" (1:11)—can surely be utilized to demote sacrifice, it is difficult to understand how the next phrase quoted—"and when you lift your hands" (1:15)—can be used to assert the priority of prayer. Indeed, as the verse continues, the prophet emphasizes that neither sacrifice nor prayer will be acceptable before God: "even though you make many prayers, I will not listen." How can this be construed as a pronouncement of prayer's greater importance? The traditional reading of the talmudic passage—following Rashi—proceeds like this: because Isaiah first states that God rejects sacrifice (1:11) and only second (1:15) that God rejects prayer too, we can therefore infer that prayer is in fact greater than sacrifice, and not subsumed by it. If sacrifice were greater than prayer, Isaiah would not have had to say that prayers would be rejected too, for that point would be obvious by the rejection of sacrifice.[114] In other words, the very fact that prayer is rejected here on its own terms proves that prayer is better than sacrifice. One can safely wonder whether this is the only way of understanding the exegesis involved here.

Significantly, another verse from the first chapter of Isaiah is quoted in the talmudic passage as well: a statement attributed to Rabbi Yohanan maintains that the priestly benediction (which involves the raising of hands, as mentioned also in Isa. 1:15a) should not be offered by priests who have killed a man, for "their hands are full of blood" (Isa. 1:15b; b. Berakhot 32b). Clearly, the talmudic understanding of the Isaiah passage presupposes a situation in which prayer and sacrifice are both being offered at the temple. Thus the exegesis at work here perfectly matches the sentiments expressed in the other traditions attributed in this passage to Rabbi Eleazar: the relative evaluation of prayer is a qualified one, for the situation being considered is one in which sacrifice and prayer are both being offered, and both being rejected.

One of the challenges in understanding these traditions is to avoid superimposing scholarly knowledge of history onto the rabbis. It is generally assumed by scholars that statutory prayer—the idea that somewhat fixed liturgies would be recited regularly—is a quintessentially rabbinic institution. Indeed, clear prerabbinic evidence of fixed regimens of daily prayer is generally lacking—except at Qumran.[115] It has been asserted, therefore, that statutory prayer was at origin a *substitute* for sacrifice, one that was first practiced at Qumran, by those who rejected the temple. Only later—in the absence of the temple—was the practice endorsed by the rabbis and, eventually, adopted by all Israel.[116]

We cannot fully evaluate this construction of the history of Jewish liturgy here.[117] But it should be noted here that much of the liturgical material from Qumran exhibits very little or no distinctively sectarian jargon. Thus the possibility remains quite strong that at least some of the liturgical documents preserved at Qumran—like the vast majority of the literature discovered there—are nonsectarian in origin.[118] Moreover, the present state of evidence simply does not allow us to determine the role played by prayer in the Jerusalem temple, and I have already questioned the assumption that the sacrificial service was silent.[119] Thus the possibility remains, historically speaking, that prayer did not replace sacrifice at all but that prayer and sacrifice at first coexisted, and then one ceased while the other continued.[120]

What is truly important for our concerns, however, is not what actually happened but what the rabbis in the amoraic period—when these traditions emerged—perceived as having happened. In order to maintain that the rabbis replaced sacrifice with prayer—that what was "original" was "replaced" or otherwise bettered by a "rabbinic" substitute[121] and that sacrifice was deemed by them to be "inferior"[122]—we would have to also claim that the rabbis acknowledged the novelty of prayer. But the rabbis hardly do so; to the contrary, they frequently assert its antiquity.[123] Perhaps the rabbis knew that Abraham didn't keep the entire oral law (*b. Yoma* 28b), and they probably didn't all really believe that the patriarchs invented the three daily prayer services (*b. Berakhot* 26b; *y. Berakhot* 7a/32). But we have no reason to doubt that the amoraic sages themselves believed fully that regular prayer was a part of the temple service (as asserted in, e.g., *m. Tamid* 5:1, 7:2) or that it had long been a fixture of predestruction extratemple piety as well. Again, the facts of the matter—as far as we scholars can adduce them—are irrelevant to the point at hand. What is significant is that the amoraic sages juxtaposed prayer with acts of loving-kindness or Torah study as ways to worship in the absence of sacrifice. The rabbis could hardly claim that acts of loving-kindness are a novelty, and they would hardly claim that Torah study is something new either. Surely they make no such claim for prayer. To the contrary, by appealing to the prophetic passages and other biblical precedents, it is clear that for the rabbis, both prayer and acts of loving-kindness *always* coincided with, and were *always* more important than, sacrifice. And either can continue without it. Because of their insistence that prayer was an ancient part of the temple practice, the rabbis cannot be accused of replacing sacrifice with an extratemple act: in their view (whether true or not) one act that was performed in the temple—prayer—can continue, while another—sacrifice—cannot.

As Baruch Bokser observed, the rabbinic assertions that prayer or other behavior is better than sacrifice appear only in later rabbinic texts.[124] But we ought not to see this as evidence for a gradual or delayed response to the destruction. In my view, an alternate explanation presents itself: perhaps the rabbis assert that prayer is greater than sacrifice only when it has become firmly established that institutionalized statutory prayer was around a good long time before 70 C.E. That is to say, only when statutory prayer has become fully and unquestionably established—so that its novelty is forgotten and its temple-based antiquity accepted by all—does it become safe to assert that prayer is better than sacrifice. At any rate, there is no "replacement" in the rabbinic assertions (qualified as they are) that prayer or acts of loving-kindness can be better than sacrifice. The rabbinic sources themselves do not seek to assert that the original rite of sacrifice has been replaced by something *rabbinic* that came *later*. The amoraim demonstrate an affinity for prayer without denigrating the temple or its ritual. In *their* view, prayer was no novelty; nor was it disconnected from the temple. Because some of these sources concern prayer—and because we scholars "know" that Jewish prayer became fixed and ritualized only after the destruction of the temple—the discussion has become muddled. What has happened here is this: the narrative of prayer being the later replacement for inadequate and outmoded sacrificial practice—a predominant ideal of modernist Judaism—has intruded itself too much on the scholarly discussion of the history of rabbinic Judaism.

Of course, it is impossible to disprove the claim that the amoraic rabbis consciously asserted the superiority of an institution they knew they invented over the one ordained in Leviticus. What can be done is demonstrate the unlikelihood of this construction of events. We can be rather certain that by the amoraic period, the basic liturgical expressions of hope for the temple's restoration were in place, along with the repeated liturgical and aggadic assertions that sacrifice is eternal, and prayer functions for now as a temporary substitute for temple worship. It is also in the amoraic age that the "templization" of the synagogue and the "sacrificialization" of its service proceeds apace. These phenomena cannot be understood as assertions of the synagogue's ascendancy over the temple. Quite the contrary, these phenomena acknowledge that the opposite is the case, and try nonetheless to channel what they can from the temple's sanctity and significance to the synagogue.

Further, once we are in the amoraic period, we can point to various traditions—cited and discussed in chapter 4—that assert the temple's cosmic significance, and speak also of a temple in heaven that corresponds to what will exist again below. There was no synagogue in heaven; and the synagogue represents the cosmos only in the sense that it sees itself as emulating the temple. The earth's foundation stone is located by the temple, and not by any synagogue. And even though the temple was destroyed, the foundation stone is still there.[125] Thus the theory that asserts a gradual acceptance of the idea that prayer replaces sacrifice—as a delayed response to the temple's destruction—does not really fit what we know about rabbinic Judaism's attitude toward the temple and sacrifice in the amoraic period.

The rabbinic approach to temple and synagogue, sacrifice and prayer is extremely complicated. Some traditions assert that the functions of sacrifice can be achieved by other means, or that the obligations to bring sacrifice can, at least for now, be fulfilled by performing other actions. But the thrust of rabbinic material on the matter is better understood if we approach matters from the other direction. It's not that the rabbis sought to replace sacrifice with something entirely different, of their own invention. Rather, the rabbis clung to the temple ritual that they could still perform—prayer—and emphasized its overall importance even when compared to the sacrificial ritual that they could no longer perform, but still wished to.

Conclusion

We began this chapter by looking at a number of rabbinic sources that constitute parallels (and perhaps responses) to the criticisms of the temple surveyed in the previous chapter. On the one hand, we found that the rabbis were willing—in texts other than the Mishnah—to recall that the temple service was from time to time marred by corrupt priests and other improper practices. On the other hand—and in contrast with the Dead Sea sectarians—the rabbis were not willing to indict the Second Temple as a whole. Nor did they seem very interested in the idea that the Second Temple had been defiled morally by transgressions that took place there.

In the second section of this chapter, we examined the rabbinic approach to a set of related issues: how was the temple and its service affected by the fact that the sanctuary's funds and offerings could come from tainted sources? The rabbis' response to these questions was rather practical: they recognized that without aristocratic gifts, the temple could not have been built, let alone glorified. The rabbis also recognized—and here we can speak accurately of tannaim specifically—that there simply was no way to be certain that all contributions to the temple came from proper sources. While the Dead Sea sectarians appeared to have held the temple to a high (and perhaps unobtainable) ideal, the rabbis were rather practical in their recognition that the temple's funding and contributions may have been tainted in various ways. Moreover, according to the Talmud, the rabbis' approach was not only a practical one but a moral one as well: in their view, the desire to welcome all Jews to the temple trumped the concern to ensure that the temple remained untainted by unrighteousness.

In the third and fourth sections, we reviewed a number of rabbinic sources relating especially to prayer and sacrifice. I have been arguing all along in this book that the scholarly treatment of sacrifice has been unduly influenced by various contemporary biases—religious and cultural—that typically work to the detriment of a sympathetic understanding of the temple and its sacrificial service. I showed this to be true here as well, especially when with regard to some of the current scholarly understandings of the rabbis' attitude toward sacrifice and prayer. According to a number of scholars, the rabbis eventually came to replace the older outmoded sacrificial ritual with something newer and more palatable: prayer. This historical reconstruction suspiciously matches a perspective—traceable to Maimonides—that came into its own with the rise of movements calling for synagogue reform. In truth, it is a form of Jewish supersessionism—and the term itself is sometimes used in the scholarship.

The temple has been replaced by something better that came later, synagogue prayer.

In addition to being unabashedly evolutionist, the narrative is problematic in that it attributes to the rabbis attitudes they most likely never held. In the rabbinic mindset, sacrifice cannot be superseded by prayer, because prayer isn't new, and sacrifice is to return. In some versions, the scholarly narrative also suffers from a well-intentioned but ill-applied analogy to contemporary crises: the idea that ancient Jews in general and the rabbis in particular were too shocked by the destruction to respond to it.

It is altogether odd that documents composed three, four, or even five centuries after the destruction are labeled as delayed responses to the destruction, especially when we may be able to discern certain responses to the catastrophe in the earliest layers of rabbinic material. Moreover, the suggestion that it took the rabbis centuries to respond to the destruction, because it ostensibly took that long to assert that the temple could be bested by something else, is insulting both to the rabbis themselves and the institution whose loss they mourned. In my view, the extant tannaitic sources allow us to describe certain aspects of the early rabbinic response to the destruction, aspects that have been overlooked because of the scholarly focus on the supersessionist narrative. The early rabbis were fully equal to the task at hand; they were not shocked into silence. And the rabbis' love for the temple that was lost was not a failure to respond: it was part of their response.

The comparison with Josephus and Qumran yields one important facet of the rabbinic response. The Qumran sectarians were wont to consider the Second Temple ritually and morally defiled. Josephus too argues that the temple was destroyed largely because of the unrighteousness committed within it. The rabbis, by contrast, do not go in this direction: to the contrary, the rabbinic treatments of the temple seem largely nostalgic in nature. In the rabbinic view, the Second Temple was as ritually and morally pure as can be expected, and the institution was not particularly blamed for falling short. The Qumran sectarians also considered the Second Temple to be both ritually and structurally inadequate. The rabbis may not remember the temple's structure with reliable accuracy, but they hardly distinguish between the temple that was and the one they wish to have again. For them, there was nothing particularly wrong about the temple that was destroyed. Theirs is not a reformist vision of the future; they simply want back what they lost.

In my view, all this constitutes a distinctly rabbinic response to the catastrophe: in disagreement with Josephus and, presumably, other Jews after 70 C.E. who followed the same biblical or even Qumranic precedents, the rabbis refused to blame the calamity of 70 C.E. on the temple, its practices, or its personnel. So if there was little or nothing wrong with the Second Temple, why, then, in the rabbinic tradition, was the temple destroyed? In the rabbinic view, no single institution or group was responsible: there was plenty of blame to spread around, and the guilt was communal: as the traditional Jewish liturgy simply puts it: "we were exiled on account of our sins."

In short, the tannaitic response to the destruction consists of the attitudes toward the temple we have seen in this chapter: (1) a generally sympathetic discussion of the practices of the Second Temple, combined with (2) a desire to absolve the Second Temple of practically any guilt connected to its own destruction, along with (3) a sincere hope for the temple's restoration. The authentic early rabbinic response to the destruction, therefore, was simply wanting the temple back, *just the way it was.* This is a full-blown response to the destruction, and attempts to suggest otherwise underestimate the religious integrity of the temple-centered tannaim on the one hand and the institution they mourned the loss of on the other. But as we have seen throughout this book, such underestimations are the rule, not the exception.

7

The Last Supper,
the Temple Incident,
and the "Spiritualization"
of Sacrifice in the
New Testament

In this chapter, we consider some of the attitudes expressed toward the temple in the New Testament. In particular, we will focus on two gospel narratives, both central to many contemporary understandings of the historical Jesus: the Last Supper, and the overturning of the tables in the temple. In recent years, a number of scholars have articulated interpretations of these New Testament traditions that set both *against* the Jewish temple.[1] The scholars whose work we will consider (and counter) here represent a broad spectrum of approaches and views. Some take these events as historical, while others either reject their historicity or are less interested in such matters.[2] A few scholars articulate harsh and offensive criticisms of the Jewish religion, while most carefully nuance their analyses to direct their criticisms against the inadequacy of sacrifice or improper priestly practices.[3] But there are a sufficient number of common features that justify grouping these approaches together. In a nutshell, these theories seek to understand the narrative of the temple incident as evidence of Jesus' rejection of the Jerusalem temple, and the narrative of the Last Supper as Jesus' establishment of a more suitable replacement. In this perspective, the temple incident articulates an absolute rejection of an institution that was "utterly corrupt,"[4] whether because it was overly exclusive,[5] "economically exploitative,"[6] or the "talisman of nationalist violence."[7] The eucharistic narrative then explains the origin of the newer and more effective "surrogate for sacrifice"[8] that serves to "replace provisionally the temple cult which had become obsolete."[9]

That these judgments are in line with later Christian views is quite apparent. Of course, the fact that these views complement traditional supersessionist claims does not by itself demonstrate that these analyses are invalid; it just raises suspicions. As we proceed, however, we will see that the suspicions in this case are well founded. Each facet of these constructions is flawed. The highly condensed and complicated traditions concerning the temple incident are hardly unambiguous rejections of the temple. The Last Supper narratives are even more complicated, and even less rejectionist. Indeed, the understanding of these narratives as rejections of the temple is contradicted by a good deal of other evidence from the earliest strata of the New Testament.

In what follows, we will take each narrative on its own, but we will begin with the eucharist and then turn back to the temple incident. By doing so, we will avoid the temptation of interpreting the eucharist in light of the temple incident. Instead, we will interpret the temple incident in light of our understanding of the eucharist. In raising some challenges to those who interpret the eucharist in light of the temple incident—and both as rejections of the temple—the goals of this chapter are: (1) to contribute to the ongoing scholarly discussion of these traditions, and (2) to raise some questions regarding the ways in which these issues have been and continue to be approached in New Testament scholarship. These questions, as we will see, are directly related to the issues we have been paying attention to throughout this book: the selective determination of what is and isn't symbolic, and the troubling tendencies to assume the worst of the temple, presuming that all that is good (and symbolic) in ancient Judaism is to be found elsewhere.

The Last Supper: Spiritualization, Sacrifice, and Imitation

We turn now to the eucharistic traditions of the New Testament (Matt. 26: 26–29; Mark 14:22–25; Luke 22:15–20; 1 Cor. 11:23–26; cf. John 6:51–59).[10] According to the Synoptic Gospels and Paul, Jesus is said to have gathered with his disciples, shortly before he was killed. At the meal, bread and wine were consumed, and Jesus in some fashion declared the bread to be his body, the wine his blood. In addition to the sources cited above, we have other early church accounts that may impact on the understanding of the eucharist (e.g., Acts 2:46–47 and *Didache* 9–10). In addition to the standard source-critical problems of determining which of these sources are to be preferred over others, there are some thorny textual problems, including particularly the Gospel of Luke.[11]

We cannot construct a history of the textual tradition here. The goal here, rather, will be to situate the Last Supper narrative—in its various versions—in the context of ancient Jewish and early Christian attitudes toward the temple cult in Jerusalem. It is, of course, rather common for New Testament scholars to set the Last Supper in one Jewish context or another. While few scholars today would endorse without qualification Joachim Jeremias's identification of the Last Supper as a Passover Seder, practically all scholars currently working on these materials consider the Seder ritual to be one of a small number of Jewish rites that are viewed as possible backgrounds for the Last Supper.[12] Other candidates typically considered include Jewish meal practices more generally, Qumranic meal practices in particular, and then variations on these themes such as prayers before meals or prayers after meals. For the most part, however, ancient Jewish sacrificial rituals tend to play a different role in the current discussion. Sacrifice is not one of those contexts within which Last Supper traditions are typically placed. Ancient Jewish sacrifice, rather, tends to be the context which Last Supper traditions are typically set *against*.[13]

History, Symbol, and Metaphor

Although we have put aside the question of historicity,[14] we can appropriately begin our analysis by considering one kind of argument that is frequently raised against the historicity of these traditions. This is the claim that the Last Supper traditions are too scandalous to be credible. This understanding has been championed in particular by the Jesus Seminar, which interprets the eucharistic traditions as if they were violations of Jewish purity codes: how could Jews drink blood?[15] The Jesus Seminar rejects the historicity of these traditions, precisely because such a perspective is deemed too radical to be historical. In this approach, the essence of the "bread from heaven" discourse in John 6:35–59 is taken at face value and turned on its head. Where Jesus is said to have said "I am the bread come down from heaven" (6:41), Jesus' Jewish opponents are depicted as objecting, "How can this man give us his flesh to eat?" (6:52). If the Jews contemporary to Jesus could not believe or understand that a Jewish person would say—or even think of—something to the effect of "Eat my flesh" or "Drink my blood," then it must in fact be impossible for Jesus to have equated his body with bread and his blood with wine.

In a similar vein, but among less skeptical scholars, it is not uncommon to find discussions of the *relative* dating of Last Supper traditions that give priority to whichever version of the saying can be inferred to be less offensive to Jewish ears. For example, some prefer the Pauline formulation "This is the new covenant in my blood" (1 Cor. 11:25; cf. Luke 22:20) over the Markan "This is my blood of the (new) covenant" (Mark 14:24; cf. Matt. 26:28) because the latter ostensibly draws greater attention to the scandal of drinking blood.[16] The closer we come to an image of people drinking blood—so this argument goes—the further we must be from any authentic first-century Jewish context.

It is essential, however, to note two important facts regarding the sixth chapter of the Fourth Gospel. First, the passage with its depiction of the Jews as murmurers (John 6:41; cf. LXX to Exod. 16:2) is quite obviously polemical. Second, the text provides no reason to assume that concerns with purity per se are at work here. The thrust of the entire passage—in a fashion typical of the Fourth Gospel—is to present the Jews of Jesus' time as unduly incredulous.[17]

In addition to questioning how Jesus can give them his body to eat, they are also said to have wondered how Jesus—whose parents were known to all—could possibly have been sent from heaven (6:42). The Jews here are depicted as theologically challenged: they reject the practical possibilities both of Jesus' coming down from heaven and of his feeding people with his own flesh. The "scandal" (6:61) of the passage need not have anything to do with the blood taboo in particular.

One important starting point for any analysis of the Last Supper traditions must be the recognition that the eucharistic words ascribed to Jesus in Mark 14:22–25, 1 Corinthians 11:23–26—even John 6:35–59—are not nearly as unambiguous as Jesus' stock Jewish opponents in John 6 make them out to be. It is indeed nearly impossible to conceive of a plausible Jewish teacher of the first century c.e. who advocates the eating of human flesh, or the drinking of blood of any species. Yet, as has been often pointed out,[18] neither human flesh nor blood of any species was consumed by Jesus, his followers, members of the early church, or even, for that matter, by Catholics after the fourth Lateran Council in 1215. Even when performed by Christians with a firm belief in the doctrine of transubstantiation, no violation of *Jewish* purity codes is taking place in any enactment of eucharistic traditions.

How then are we to understand the actions and words attributed to Jesus in the Last Supper traditions? Jesus' words can be best understood when we keep in mind much of what was said earlier (especially, in chapter 2) with regard to metaphor. I have argued that metaphor is often primary and fundamental, and it is at the very least expressive. Since biblical and ancient Jewish literature is chock full of metaphor, we cannot by any means accept the depiction of Jews in the sixth chapter of John's Gospel as accurate: ancient Jews were certainly capable of understanding metaphors (both old and new), and they were even adept at creating new ones themselves. We can certainly accept as reasonable the picture we get from all our sources that Jesus from time to time spoke in parables (i.e., metaphorically).[19] Indeed, it is difficult to conceive of any understanding of Jesus' words at the Last Supper that does not grant on some level (stated or not) that Jesus' equation of wine with blood and bread with flesh is a metaphor of some sort.[20]

With regard to Jesus' actions, the interpretive framework to keep in mind is that of the symbolic act. It is indeed rather common for scholars to contextualize the Last Supper within the tradition of the symbolic actions of Israel's prophets.[21] Of course, such symbolic acts are, practically by definition, provocative ones (as seen in chapter 3). When we keep in mind the long tradition of provocative prophetic symbolic actions, Jesus' behavior at the Last Supper—even when coupled with his surprising metaphors—comes off as rather tame. Certainly these two well-documented phenomena—metaphor and symbolic action—provide sufficient cultural context to allow for one to situate the words and actions attributed to Jesus in Last Supper traditions within a plausible first-century Jewish context.

But these considerations are still insufficient for full understanding of the Last Supper traditions. In fact, the danger here lies precisely in the fact that symbolic acts were often provocative ones. This has encouraged scholars to take Jesus' metaphorical words and symbolic actions as an expression of his alleged rejection of the temple cult. Nonetheless, there is a troubling double standard in many of these treatments, for they operate on the assumption that the balance of symbol and metaphor in ancient Judaism is tipped in Jesus' favor. When compared to the Last Supper, sacrifice always comes up short, whether it is deemed to be corrupt, flawed, outmoded, or spiritually inadequate.

In order to evaluate more carefully the language attributed to Jesus in the eucharistic traditions, we have to keep in mind not only the symbolic acts of Israel's prophets but also the symbolic actions of Israel's priests: animal sacrifice. In recognizing the symbolic dimensions of ancient Jewish sacrifice, a good deal of progress has been made of late, in part by some of the scholars who interpret the eucharist as a rejection of the cult.[22] But there are two inherent problems with any interpretation of the eucharistic traditions that attempts to ascribe to them an articulation of a cultic critique; each of these will be explored in what follows. The first problem is a historical one: Jesus' followers did not separate themselves from the temple and its sacrificial worship. The second problem is a methodological one: there is good reason to question some of the assumptions with which early Christian sacrificial metaphors are typically interpreted.

The Last Supper and the Temple in the Early Church

One good place to begin an evaluation of early Christian approaches to the temple and the eucharist is with Acts' account of the apostles' activity in Jerusalem (Acts 2:46–47; cf. 3:1, 5:42): "(46) Day by day, as they spent much time together in the temple, they broke bread at home and ate their food with glad and generous hearts, (47) praising God and having the goodwill of all the people. And day by day the Lord added to their number those who were being saved." This description of the disciples' daily gathering to break bread and praise God is often understood as evidence of early Christian eucharistic practice,[23] but it must be admitted that we are not told explicitly that these communal meals were eucharistic in nature. The passage clearly has idyllic aspects to it as well. We must surely doubt that the coterie of Jesus' early followers had the goodwill "of all the people" (2:47). What is striking here is the fact that the early disciples are remembered as having visited the temple repeatedly, not so long after Jesus' death. And it's certainly not as if Luke-Acts is thoroughly enamored of the temple: Stephen's antitemple polemic (7:1–53) is one of the sharpest in the entire New Testament, with its assertion that God resides *only* in heaven, and not in any earthly sanctuary constructed by people (7:48–50). Setting aside the question of historicity, the passage quoted above tells us quite clearly that Luke did not interpret the Last Supper event as an unambiguously antitemple action: if he had, then he would have depicted the disciples as abandoning the temple immediately thereafter.[24] But the question is, can we trust what Acts says of the early apostles—did they also refrain from interpreting the Last Supper event as an antitemple action?

The testimony of Acts 2:46–47 can be confirmed in a number of ways. First, it cannot be questioned that the early Christian community chose to be headquartered in Jerusalem. This is claimed explicitly by Acts and confirmed by Paul in Galatians (1:18, 2:1), and virtually every Church historian follows suit. As Paula Fredriksen has emphasized, depicting the apostles as remaining in Jerusalem is a curious choice indeed if a radically antitemple program was part of the picture from the earliest stage.[25] Another argument against an antisacrificial reading of the early eucharistic traditions is the fact that in the explicitly antitemple passages of the New Testament, reference to the eucharist is notable by its absence. This is true of Stephen's speech in Acts, and it is equally true of Hebrews. If the Last Supper really had been an unambiguously antitemple act, why not bring it up in such contexts?

A third realm of evidence contradicting the antitemple reading of the eucharist can be found in the assorted (and often overlooked) sayings attributed to Jesus that assume his followers worship in the temple, and will continue to do so.[26] Such sayings come from various strands of the gospel traditions. For instance, Matthew 8:4, Mark 1:44, and Luke 5:14 depict Jesus commanding the cured leper to show himself to the priest, and offer the sacrifice commanded in the law. In Matthew 5:23–24, Jesus instructs his followers to reconcile themselves, and then bring their offerings to the altar. Perhaps most important, in Matthew 23:21 (cf. Matt. 5:34–35) Jesus is said to have said: "whoever swears by the sanctuary swears by it and the one who dwells within it." The italicized phrase confirms that for Matthew at least the temple remains (at least for now) the location of God's earthly presence.[27] Finally, returning to the complex of passages at the center of our concern, surely it is significant that Jesus' disciples are said to have visited the temple to prepare for and participate in the Passover following the temple incident and immediately before the Last Supper (Matt. 26:17–20; Mark 14:12–17; Luke 22:7–14). If these traditions were unambiguously antitemple, why would the disciples have visited the sanctuary, presumably with their master's blessing?

A fourth confirmation of the impression conveyed by Acts 2 is to be found in Didache 9–10.[28] Assuming these two chapters to be relatively early,[29] what we find discussed here could be the sort of ritual practiced by the early apostles, even after a visit to the temple. The ritual context is that of a meal: bread is broken, and prayers of thanksgiving are recited—prayers that strikingly resemble Jewish after-meal prayers.[30] The liturgies of Didache 9–10 recall the figure of Jesus and express eschatological hopes. Importantly, nothing explicitly antitemple is articulated. Didache 9–10 fits perfectly with the picture related in Acts 2: the earliest Christians did not view the eucharist as an inherently antitemple ritual.

A fifth confirmation of the general tenor of Acts 2 can be found in Paul's letters, undeniably the oldest Christian documents we have. A number of scholars—including Robert J. Daly, W. D. Davies, Bertil Gärtner, Michael Newton, and, more recently, Paula Fredriksen—have surveyed the key passages, and the consensus is that Paul did not articulate an outright rejection of the temple.[31] To the contrary, the temple remained an important institution

in Paul's thought and life. Indeed, even Paul's discussion of the eucharist
speaks positively of the temple (1 Cor. 10:14–21):

> (14) Therefore, my dear friends, flee from the worship of idols. (15) I
> speak as to sensible people; judge for yourselves what I say. (16) The
> cup of blessing that we bless, is it not a sharing (κοινωνία) in the
> blood of Christ? The bread that we break, is it not a sharing in
> the body of Christ? (17) Because there is one bread, we who are many
> are one body, for we all partake of the one bread. (18) Consider
> the people of Israel[32] (βλέπετε τὸν Ἰσραὴλ κατὰ σάρκα); are not
> those who eat the sacrifices partners in the altar (κοινωνοὶ τοῦ
> θυσιαστηρίου)? (19) What do I imply then? That food sacrificed to
> idols is anything, or that an idol is anything? (20) No, I imply that
> what pagans sacrifice, they sacrifice to demons and not to God. I do
> not want you to be partners with demons. (21) You cannot drink the
> cup of the Lord and the cup of demons. You cannot partake of the
> table of the Lord and the table of demons.

One of the striking aspects of this passage is the fact that Paul draws an
analogy between eucharist and sacrifice. But the analogy is not drawn to make
the eucharist out to be a better alternative or even a replacement for Israel's
service in the sanctuary. To the contrary, the point of the passage is to underscore the seriousness, legitimacy, and efficacy of Israel's sacrificial service,
and to present the eucharist as similarly serious, legitimate and efficacious. It
is true that Paul refers in verse 10:18 to Israel *according to the flesh*. But
regardless of how we are to understand (or translate) this phrase, it ought to
be rather clear that Paul is *not* drawing a black-and-white contrast between
Israel's service of the flesh and Christians' service of the spirit. To the contrary, the thrust of Paul's treatment of the eucharist in 1 Corinthians is to
claim that Christian worship—like its analogue in Jerusalem—is not dis-
embodied or abstract but physical, tangible, and even threatened by defilement and profanation (see 1 Cor. 11:27–31; cf. 2 Cor. 7:1).[33]

This passage is not unique in the Pauline corpus, at least not in terms of its
evaluation of Jewish sacrificial worship. Throughout his letters, Paul draws a
number of comparisons between Jewish sacrificial worship and the practices of
the early Gentile Christians in his milieu. Famously, Paul compares the
community of believers to the temple in Jerusalem (1 Cor. 3:16–17, 6:19; 2 Cor.
6:16).[34] He also makes a habit of using sacrificial terminology when speaking
of the work of early Christian apostles, including himself (Rom. 1:9; Phil.
2:17).[35] Paul also compares converts to the first fruits (ἀπαρχή) offered to the
temple (Rom. 16:5; 1 Cor. 16:15) and the monetary contributions of Christian
communities to the sacred contributions that Jews devoted to the temple (Rom.
15:25–32; 2 Cor. 9:13–14; Phil. 4:18). And as we have seen, Paul compares
Christian worship to sacrificial service (Rom. 12:1; 1 Cor. 10–11).[36] In each of
these passages, Paul employs cultic language—speaking of the temple, of
sacrifices, of sacred fragrances and libations—in the service of describing the

significance of his own experience and work as an apostle. In each of these passages, the comparison drawn between one kind of service and another is both positive and constructive. Even Romans 12:1, with its reference to "your rational service" (τὴν λογικὴν λατρείαν ὑμῶν; too frequently translated as "your *spiritual* worship"), needs to be read in this light.

Indeed, when we look a little deeper into Paul's descriptions of sacrificial worship, we find that Paul affirms many of the fundamental theological tenets upon which ancient Jewish sacrificial worship is based. Paul speaks of God's presence in the sanctuary (1 Cor. 3:16; 2 Cor. 6:16; cf. Rom. 9:4). He asserts that sacrifice is a mode of achieving close interaction between the worshiper and God (1 Cor. 9:13, 10:18). Paul also speaks of the pleasing aroma sacrifice sent up to God (2 Cor. 2:15; Phil. 4:18). All of these are widely attested biblical and ancient Jewish understandings of what sacrifice achieved. In his letters, Paul affirms and even praises these notions, all without articulating any explicit critique of the cult, or even alluding to any such critique ostensibly offered by Jesus.

Yet all too often, Paul's discussions of Jewish sacrificial worship are understood as examples of the so-called spiritualization of sacrifice.[37] Granted, the term is often presented in quotation marks, and frequently accompanied by an apology (usually an affirmation that "spiritualization" can be found within Judaism as well as without).[38] So while it is precarious to generalize the disparate ways the term is used by New Testament scholars, virtually every use of the referent articulates a critique of sacrifice, practically by definition.[39] It is indeed a useful exercise to catalogue Paul's sacrificial metaphors alongside Philo's allegories, and other metaphorical applications of sacrificial terminology—including those attributed to Jesus. Yet it is another exercise altogether—and indeed, a flawed exercise—to group sacrificial metaphors along with cultic critiques, leaving temple ritual alone as the only thing that is *not* a "spiritual" sacrifice.[40] As I have been arguing all along, it is high time to abandon the term "spiritual sacrifice" altogether, at least as a scholarly category. Instead, perhaps, we should speak more neutrally of metaphorical use of sacrificial language—a phenomenon that we can see in Paul, Philo, the rabbis, and even the Last Supper traditions. Then we also need to acknowledge that sacrifice itself is meaningful and symbolic, which is precisely the reason why sacrificial terms are used metaphorically. Finally, we need to treat metaphorical use of sacrificial terminology sympathetically, recognizing that these metaphors frequently help us understand and appreciate the various ways in which sacrifice was understood.

To turn sacrificial metaphors into "spiritualizations" *of* sacrifice is to misread them. These metaphors are, rather, *borrowings from* sacrifice. Sacrificial metaphors operate on the assumption of the efficacy and meaning of sacrificial rituals, and hope to appropriate some of that meaning and apply it to something else. Thus, Paul's metaphors can be compared to the efforts exerted by various groups of ancient Jews to infuse aspects of daily life with some of the holiness that pertained more directly to the temple. As we discussed in chapters 5 and 6, the application of temple purity rules to practices concerning food and prayer can be understood as an active effort to draw on and to channel some of the temple's sanctity toward these other practices. These efforts, I argued, can accurately be understood as "sacrificializations" of modes of worship that do not explicitly involve the performance sacrifice, all in order to make a rather straightforward statement: "this too is divine service." Paul's sacrificial metaphors can and should be understood accordingly.

Returning to 1 Corinthians 10:14–22, one striking aspect of the passage remains to be noted: the contrast that is drawn between proper worship on the one hand and idolatry on the other. This contrast—which is drawn elsewhere (1 Cor. 8:4–6, 13; 2 Cor. 6:16)—is instructive, and it allows us to juxtapose the picture of early Christian worship in a Pauline, Diaspora community with Acts' picture of the apostles' worship in Jerusalem. In Acts 2, we are presented with a picture of early Christians performing both eucharistic and Jewish sacrificial rituals. In 1 Corinthians 10, we are presented with a different picture: that of Gentile Christians in Corinth who do not have the option of performing sacrificial rites and eucharistic rites. Jewish sacrificial devotion outside of Jerusalem is out of the question. Other local forms of sacrificial devotion are equally out of the question, because they are idolatrous. And what is Paul's message? That early Christians must choose one or the other: it's either idolatry or the worship of God, either sacrifice or eucharist.

When we try to picture the social reality motivating Paul's statements here, I think we can begin to understand better the origin of the antisacrificial perspectives offered in the New Testament. Paul himself did not articulate a broadly antisacrificial perspective. In his view, the Jewish cult is proper and effective, though it pertains primarily to the people of Israel (cf. Rom. 9:4). The sacrificing he does reject as ineffective—and worse—is idolatry. But to a Gentile in the Diaspora, rejecting all sacrifice but the Jerusalem cult is little different from rejecting all sacrifice whatsoever. The origin of the idea that the eucharist is a replacement for sacrifice is likely to be found in this kind of social reality, among those who—unlike the disciples in Jerusalem—actually had to choose between two distinct options: eucharist *or* sacrifice.[41]

The Last Supper as Sacrificial Metaphor

We can now offer a brief analysis of the Last Supper traditions (Matt. 26:26–29; Mark 14:22–25; Luke 22:17–20; and 1 Cor. 11:23–26). The goal in this short survey is simply to present some reflections that, it is to be hoped, avoid the historical and interpretive errors that I have traced above. I will not assume that sacrificial language in these traditions must be—by virtue of some alleged violation of Jewish purity codes—inauthentic. Nor will I assume that sacrificial language in these traditions ought to be read as spiritualizations of or critiques of the temple cult. We cannot, of course, survey the texts in great detail, nor can we attempt here to determine which elements can reliably be attributed to the historical Jesus.[42] We will first simply catalogue the aspects of these traditions that are frequently understood in relation to Israel's sacrificial ritual. Second, I will suggest some ways of reaching a balanced understanding of these traditions.

The following aspects of the Last Supper traditions are frequently understood as sacrificial on some level. First, references to flesh and blood (which appear in all of the eucharistic traditions) have certain sacrificial connotations, though the implications may not be exclusively sacrificial.[43] Second, the symbolic value of Jesus' act of giving (bread or wine; present in all the narrative traditions) may well draw meaning from the presence of the notion of giving in sacrificial traditions.[44] Third, the expressions "for you" (Luke 22:19, 20; 1 Cor. 11:24) and "for many" (Matt. 26:28, Mark 14:24) may well have expiatory implications.[45] Fourth, the immediate juxtaposition of blood with covenant alludes rather clearly to the sacrificial covenant ceremony of Exodus 24 (Matt. 26:28; Mark 14:24; Luke 22:20; and 1 Cor. 11:25).[46] Fifth, the Paschal context of the gospel traditions has clear sacrificial implications.[47] Finally, the command to do the act as a remembrance has possible sacrificial overtones as well (Luke 22:19, 1 Cor. 11:24; cf. Lev. 2:2 [MT and LXX]).[48]

It is nearly impossible for all of these aspects of the tradition to be authentic. Indeed, there are competing sacrificial ideologies at work in these traditions. For example, expiation and Passover are two distinct concerns, although they are from time to time jumbled together in the literature.[49] Importantly, all of these ideas can be found in the tradition recorded in 1 Corinthians 11, with the exception of a clear allusion to Passover (though Paul does speak of Jesus as a Paschal lamb in 1 Cor. 5:7). Without attempting to argue that the Pauline text is the most authentic record of this tradition, I think we ought to take seriously 1 Corinthians 11:23–26 as a likely source of information regarding the earliest understandings of Last Supper. Moreover, 1 Corinthians 11:23–26 provides the proper control for a more balanced evaluation of the significance of the sacrificial language attributed to Jesus in the Last Supper traditions. If we take 1 Corinthians 11 as evidence that Jesus spoke in sacrificial metaphors, then we ought not to push the sacrificial language attributed by Paul to Jesus in this passage any further than Paul himself has pushed it in the context of 1 Corinthians 10–11. If Paul understood this sacrificial language to mean that Jesus came to the point where he rejected the temple outright, then why can Paul still speak of the temple so positively? Surely there had been no major reform of temple practices since Jesus' death. The same sort of priesthood was in charge; the power of the Pharisees was probably pretty much the same. If we are to accept from Paul that Jesus' eucharistic words had sacrificial overtones, we must equally accept from Paul that those overtones need not be understood as an outright rejection of the Jerusalem temple. To the contrary, we are to understand Jesus' sacrificial metaphors as we understand Paul's: not as a spiritualization of, or a critique of, the cult but as an appropriation of, a borrowing from, the cult. "This too is divine service" is what, and all, Jesus may have meant.

The Temple Incident: Rejection, Prophecy, Reform

In this section, we will turn to the gospel traditions concerning Jesus' demonstration in the temple. As we will see, it is assumed in the scholarship on these passages, with some frequency, that the Jerusalem temple was in fact a corrupt institution, serviced by greedy priests or thieving money changers—and that Jesus therefore had much to be angry about when he visited. Of course, not all accept this view, by any means. A number of scholars insist that whatever commerce Jesus did see in the temple must have been a practical necessity, and therefore right and proper. To be sure, a variety of other approaches have also been considered. After surveying a number of understandings of the temple incident, I will suggest a new way of understanding Jesus' attitude toward the temple.

I will not claim to solve the question of what Jesus did or what he meant by it. But I do hope to shed new light on the subject by presenting an explanation that has not yet been considered. Moreover, I hope to illustrate some problems inherent in much of the scholarship on the temple incident. On the one hand, we will find that there is often much less evidence that Jesus articulated strong antitemple polemics than is supposed. On the other hand, we will also see that there *is* some reason to suppose that Jesus criticized an aspect of temple practice. But it is better to see Jesus as furthering and nuancing certain prophetic arguments of old rather than endorsing the kind of approach taken by the Qumran sectarians, even perhaps in his own day. The challenge here is to identify the social and moral issues involved without falling into the trap of accepting ancient criticisms of the temple as a modern scholarly understanding of it. As I argued with regard to the prophetic traditions (chapter 3), I will try to demonstrate here too that conflicts between disparate parties—priests and prophets in any age—can only be fully understood when the different positions' motivations are evaluated and appreciated. By doing so, we can avoid the problematic but still frequent tendency to place Jesus *against* ancient Judaism instead of *within* ancient Jewish disputes on matters cultic and moral.

The Gospel Accounts of Jesus in the Temple

The gospel accounts of the temple incident differ more widely than the accounts concerning the Last Supper (Matt. 21:12–13; Mark 11:15–17; Luke 19:45–46; John 2:14–17). The description in Luke is the briefest: Jesus comes to the temple, he expels the traders, and he recites a statement incorporating two distinct prophetic verses: "it is written, 'My house shall be a house of prayer' (Isa. 56:7) but you have made it a 'den of robbers' (Jer. 7:11)." In Matthew we are told that Jesus also overturned the tables of the money changers and those who sold pigeons. The Markan version is even longer: in addition to expelling the traders and overturning the tables of the money changers and the pigeon sellers, we are told that Jesus "would not allow anyone to carry anything through the temple" (11:16). It is also suggested that Jesus quoted more of Isaiah 56:7, referring to the temple as a place of prayer "for all the nations" (11:17). The account in John includes most of what we find in Matthew, though it also refers to "sellers of oxen" (2:14) and describes the whip of cords used by Jesus against the merchants (2:15). Jesus' statement in John is also less based on the earlier prophetic passages: "take these things away; you shall not make my Father's house a house of trade" (2:16). Upon hearing this, the disciples were said to have remembered the verse "Zeal for your house will consume me" (Ps. 69:9).

These traditions present an irony to those who maintain the theory of Markan priority: if true, the earliest tradition is also the longest. But as we will see, the curious statement in Mark 11:16 has early rabbinic analogues (e.g., *m. Berakhot* 9:5), so it is possible that it was intelligible only to an original Jewish-Christian audience. Indeed, one scholar has recently attempted to reconstruct the Aramaic original on which Mark 11:15–17 was based.[50] Some scholars of Luke then present its shorter account as dependent upon Mark.[51] On the other hand, there are those who maintain that the shortest formulation—in Luke—is the earliest.[52] There are also those who defend John as an early report independent of the Synoptics.[53] Without denying the entire authenticity of John's report, it must be noted that his reference to *oxen* being sold in the temple is rather unlikely.[54]

Obviously, these brief passages have received much attention, and while many debates remain unresolved, we can speak of a general consensus concerning two matters. The first is the traditions' importance:[55] as we have already discussed, for some scholars the temple incident is to be linked to the ever-important Last Supper narrative, the first demonstrating Jesus' rejection of the Jewish sacrificial cult, and the second his establishment of a better replacement. For a number of scholars, the temple incident also provides the key to unlocking the mystery of Jesus' death at the hands of the authorities who crucified him.[56] Those who focus on Jesus' political or social message also are sure to find much significance in Jesus' overturning of the money changers' tables, the expulsion of the traders, and his apparent reference to the temple as a place for *all* people.[57] Whether the traditions relate to Jesus' social message, his violent death, the Last Supper, or more than one of these, we can at least speak of a broad agreement on the significance of the event. And all this despite the little space devoted to the temple incident, even in all four Gospels taken together. The second point of consensus concerns the historicity of the event: even the rather skeptical Jesus Seminar overwhelmingly accepts that *something* happened in the Jerusalem temple shortly before Jesus' death.[58] Needless to say, more conservative scholars accept the historicity of the temple incident as well.

There are, however, some important debates concerning the nature and meaning of this event. We can begin with terminology: while the event is often referred to as the "cleansing of the temple," it is increasingly recognized that this referent is inappropriate and inaccurate.[59] It has no basis in the New Testament texts themselves, for no explicit concerns with purity (ritual or moral) are expressed in *any* of the gospel traditions on the temple incident. The term is also inappropriate, for it implies that something practical was achieved by Jesus' act, that some filth was cleansed or some sin purged. This conclusion too is something that the all-too-brief gospel accounts simply cannot support. I will therefore speak more accurately and more neutrally of Jesus' action in the temple—a phrase that is becoming increasingly common.[60]

For many scholars, the temple incident is not just any "action" but a *symbolic* action. According to E. P. Sanders, Jesus' action was not directed toward any particular priestly abuse or ritual inadequacy. The act, rather, was a symbolic destruction of the current temple, constituting an inauguration of Jesus' messianic era.[61] Perhaps in reaction to Sanders's influential analysis, some of those scholars who understand Jesus' action as one intended to counter specific social ills also reject the understanding of the incident as a symbolic action.[62] Yet others rightly note that prophetic "symbolic actions" were often pointed at real problems.[63] Indeed, even Hamerton-Kelly describes the temple incident as a symbolic action—one that foretells the end of sacrifice and repudiates "sacrificial exclusiveness" and all the violence entailed therein.[64]

The similarities between the accounts of Jesus' demonstration in the temple and other prophetic symbolic actions described in the Hebrew Bible are striking and undeniable.[65] Moreover, the placing of the eucharist within the context of symbolic action would suggest that the temple incident should similarly be understood. But even as I accept an understanding of the temple incident as a symbolic action, I once again emphasize the disparity between the scholarly recognition of prophetic actions as symbolic ones, against the typically dryer scholarly discussions of priestly rituals. To speak of prophetic symbolic actions criticizing priestly rituals is to stack the deck unnecessarily in favor of the meaningfulness of the former against the meaninglessness of the latter. If we are to employ the term "symbolic action" with regard to prophetic reformers, we should do so only in a context where sacrificial ritual too is recognized as symbolic action.

As we proceed to review various interpretations of the temple incident, we will consider the possibility that Jesus' symbolic action had a practical dimension to it. We will begin by reviewing those understandings of the temple incident that are predicated upon priestly abuse, and we will proceed from there to consider other possible sources of Jesus' social criticism of the temple. Some of these approaches illustrate the problems we have been facing all along: the presumption of priestly guilt, and the biased acceptance of prophetic symbolism. Yet pursuing this line of inquiry is hardly hopeless. In fact, I will suggest that a more nuanced and evenhanded consideration of the ethical questions inherent in ancient Israel's sacrificial system could lead to an understanding of the temple incident that allows both Jesus and those he argued against to articulate morally legitimate positions.

Jesus versus Greedy Priests

There was a time when it was practically taken for granted that the Jerusalem temple was a corrupt institution, supervised by priests whose primary concern was their own economic gain.[66] There were some lonely voices of

dissent—including, not surprisingly, Jewish scholars—who pleaded otherwise. In a still frequently cited classic work, Israel Abrahams argued that
commerce in the temple was a practical necessity, and that whatever abuses
occurred were the exception, not the rule.[67] In more recent days, Abrahams's
position has been defended consistently and eloquently by Sanders.[68] But the
older, more conservative approach has by no means disappeared: it is still
frequently asserted that the Jerusalem temple was indeed a flawed institution,
serviced by greedy or even crooked priests.[69] The power of this argument
stems in part from the fact that ancient Jewish literature provides various
reasons for us to think that the temple was in fact corrupt or flawed.

We need, however, to be careful not to accept as modern understandings
of the temple ancient texts that articulate—or seem to articulate—indictments
of the temple. In chapter 3, we reviewed the prophetic traditions, and I argued
that they constitute much less of an unambiguous cultic critique than is often
assumed. Those who seek to build the case against the temple in Jesus' day
often begin with the prophets, despite the anachronism and despite all that
can be said about the prophets' fidelity to both the temple and sacrifice.[70] One
can also find plenty of criticism leveled at the temple and its priests in the
literature of the Second Temple period, as we have seen. But much of this
evidence too is problematic. We find, for instance, that scholars cite the criticisms leveled against corrupt priests in *Assumption of Moses* and *T. Levi*.[71] We
have already noted the possibly Christian nature of the latter, and the former
is also of uncertain date. Some scholars look also to the criticisms leveled
against the temple, its cult, and its personnel in the literature from Qumran.[72]
But the bulk of this evidence articulates critiques of the temple that are far
from the concerns that can be credibly attributed to Jesus, for, as we have
already observed, there is little evidence that Jesus rejected or boycotted the
temple, and he certainly did not advocate the kind of positions we find articulated in literature such as 4QMMT.

In a number of ways, the rabbinic evidence may provide the best chance
of confirming that the Jerusalem temple was prone to corruption. If the
rabbis, who clearly respected the temple in principle and hoped for its future rebuilding, believed that the priests of the late Second Temple period
were morally obtuse, why should the case be doubted? Indeed, those who
want to claim that the priests were in fact crooked often call on rabbinic
evidence to corroborate this claim. As we saw in the previous chapter, a good
number of rabbinic sources recall stories of priestly corruption and immorality, and these stories are frequently catalogued by those scholars who wish
to argue that the temple in Jesus' day was in fact a flawed institution.[73] For
instance, scholars frequently point to the story preserved in *m. Keritot* 1:7,
pressing the interpretation (mistaken, in my view) that the narrative concerns
an instance of priestly extortion.[74] Also frequently noted are the traditions
preserved in the Babylonian Talmud (*b. Pesahim* 57a; see chapter 6), which
depict the temple itself crying out over a series of sinful, gluttonous high
priests.[75] In addition to these stories—and many others—we can also find
brief statements here and there in rabbinic literature that speak generally of

priestly greed or worse (e.g., *Lev. Rabbah* 21:9) or that note that many of the later high priests achieved their position only through bribery (e.g., *b. Yoma* 8b). At times, rabbinic sources even blame the destruction of the temple on these factors (e.g., *t. Yoma* 1:12, *t. Menahot* 13:22).

There are a number of scholars who deny altogether the possibility of utilizing rabbinic sources for the history of the Second Temple period.[76] Obviously such historians would not use these sources in any reconstruction of the historical Jesus (assuming such skeptical historians would condone that exercise at all). Surely we cannot treat the rabbis as historians, or their literary products as historical books.[77] Moreover, these stories are *narratives*, and need to be studied as such as well.[78] Literary analysis could lead one to conclude that the effort to extract historical kernels from such stories is hopeless. We might then consider an alternative approach: instead of attempting to prove the historicity of specific events, would it be possible to assert that only the general impression is accurate—that the rabbinic sources testify in general that the priests were a sinful lot? The problem with this kind of an approach is that much of rabbinic ideology is shaped by a polemic against— and possibly competition with—the priesthood itself, as well as, perhaps, the priestly claims of the Qumran sectarians.[79]

Over against all this skepticism, however, it is important to recognize that on occasion (albeit rare), isolated rabbinic memories can be verified by external evidence. For example, we noted above the traditions concerning a Nicanor and the doors he endowed for the temple (*m. Yoma* 3:10). While we would have to dismiss the miracle stories as legends, we know from Josephus and from epigraphic finds that there was in fact a Nicanor, from Alexandria, who was able to purchase a family burial plot on Mt. Scopus, and whose epitaph suggests he wanted to be remembered for doors he made.[80] With regard to the sinful priests mentioned in rabbinic literature, we can find similar accounts of a greedy, gluttonous priesthood in book 20 of Josephus' *Antiquities*. In a number of cases, both Josephus and the rabbis are equally judgmental of late Second Temple high priests bearing the same names.[81]

What is really surprising—and what truly demonstrates the inherent plasticity of the rabbinic evidence—is the fact that there is a wide array of approaches to these sources, even among those who are willing to accept their general historicity. Of course, some accept the Gospels' and the rabbinic sources' general historicity and argue that the temple was in fact corrupt in Jesus' day. But many are able to accept the historicity of the rabbinic sources without granting that the temple was necessarily flawed in Jesus' day. Adolph Büchler suggested long ago that the rabbinic memory of the Second Temple largely pertains to the last decade or so of that institution's existence.[82] Indeed, many of the above-noted correspondences between Josephus and rabbinic sources pertain to the 60s c.e. Some writers therefore feel justified in claiming that the rabbinic accounts testify primarily—or possibly *only*—to abuses in the decades after Jesus' death.[83] This in turn can be taken as an argument against reading the New Testament to the effect that Jesus had some substantial dispute with the priests of his day concerning ethical matters.[84]

Yet other historians who are also convinced of the historicity of both the New Testament and the rabbinic accounts come to a very different conclusion. Shmuel Safrai, for instance, was willing to grant that there were priests who exploited the sacrificial system to add to their own wealth.[85] Safrai also accepts the gospel accounts to the effect that there were traders *in* the temple precincts. Indeed, Safrai goes on to suggest that the rabbis would agree with Jesus that the trade should have taken place elsewhere.[86] Thus the rabbis and Jesus are presented by Safrai—and by David Flusser[87] too—as comrades-in-arms against the dishonorable practices of the priesthood in the early first century C.E. This approach—which accepts the historicity of both the rabbinic sources and the Gospels—comes close to the more conservative approaches taken by New Testament scholars to the temple incident: the difference is not so much in the evaluation of Jesus, the priests, or the temple but in the evaluation of the rabbis. Some New Testament scholars seem to group the rabbis and the priests together, pitting Jesus against them all; Flusser and Safrai present Jesus and the rabbis as allied against the priests.

I am not at all certain that this dispute can ever be resolved. The New Testament sources are all too brief, and the rabbinic evidence is so vast and diverse that practically any conclusion could be reached. The problem, however, is the fact that so many of these theories stretch far beyond the realm of proof. To suppose that priestly abuse never happened is to be naïve.[88] To assert that abuse may have happened at a later date but not in Jesus' day rests on narrow readings of the evidence.[89] Indeed, this view rests on having already interpreted what we seek to explain: to deny that there is *any* evidence for priestly corruption in Jesus' day is to assert that the New Testament accounts of Jesus' action in the temple cannot be read to that effect. On the other hand, to claim that systematic abuse was endemic to the temple system is to deny any integrity to ancient Jewish temple-goers.[90] To maintain that a few priests in Jesus' day abused the system for their own gain is to go beyond what our evidence can responsibly demonstrate. Indeed, this explanation rests on a coincidence: Jesus just *happened* to come to the temple on a bad day. While this is possible, this is hardly a satisfying historical reconstruction of events. Moreover, it must be emphasized that the gospel narratives and the prophetic verses cited therein are hardly unambiguous evidence for economic *abuse* on behalf of the priests or their cohorts. And—to add a touch of reality—it should also be noted that these evaluations of the Second Temple rarely consider whether it is reasonable to assume that whatever priestly corruption there was (if any) would have been any worse than economic oppression in general in the ancient world or any abuse carried out by tax collectors, other Roman authorities, or even members of Jerusalem's aristocracy who were not priests or not directly associated with the temple.[91]

In the end, the possibility that Jesus opposed priestly abuse in his day cannot be excluded, but it can't be proven either. The question that needs to be asked is whether or not priestly abuse is the *only* way of making sense of Jesus' action in the temple. It is my belief that priestly abuse is not a necessary background for understanding this event, even if we still wish to understand

Jesus' act as articulating a practical social message. In order to work toward this conclusion, we now turn to consider some interpretations of the temple incident that focus on matters concerning the temple's economics, without asserting that priests were criminals.

Jesus versus the Annual Half-Sheqel Tax

For a number of scholars, the explanation of the temple incident is to be found in disputes concerning the payment of the annual half-sheqel temple tax. Only one tradition in the New Testament explicitly addresses the temple tax, and this passage appears only in Matthew 17:24–27.[92] In this passage, tax collectors ask Peter whether Jesus pays the tax. He replies that Jesus does. Later, Jesus himself brings up the issue, telling a parable, comparing God to an earthly king: just as an earthly king would collect taxes not from his family but from others, so too the people of Israel—God's children—should be exempt from payment. But Jesus then says the tax should be paid, so as not to cause offense. The story concludes with Peter being told to find a coin in the mouth of a fish, and to pay the tax for both of them with the coin.

As with all gospel traditions, there are disputes here too concerning historicity and meaning. A number of scholars assert that the tradition is too late to attribute to the historical Jesus.[93] Indeed, the Jesus Seminar prints the words attributed to Jesus in Matthew 17:24–27 in black ink, which constitutes the Seminar's lowest rating for authenticity.[94] Yet a number of other scholars defend the passage as an authentic saying of Jesus. Flusser published a brief study in Hebrew some time ago, in which he argued (1) that Jesus' parable can be compared to similar rabbinic tales comparing God to a "king of flesh and blood" (e.g., b. Berakhot 33b); (2) that the parable's identification of the king's children with the Jews, to the detriment of Gentiles, is more likely to be an earlier tradition than a later one; and (3) that Jesus' opposition to the tax finds a greater Jewish context in the Qumranic texts also opposed to the temple tax.[95] Other scholars have more recently defended the authenticity of the passage, for these as well as other reasons.[96]

Besides the debate over authenticity, scholars also ponder whether or not this tradition has anything to do with the temple incident. The arguments in favor of connecting the two are thematic and textual.[97] The textual argument rests primarily on the reference to the tables of money changers (τῶν κολλυβιστῶν) in three of the four Gospels (Matt. 21:12; Mark 11:15; John 2:15). For those familiar with rabbinic literature, this reference seems like a striking correspondence with the rules outlined in Mishnah Tractate *Sheqalim*, which speak of money changers employed by the temple authorities, who set up tables at or near the temple, shortly before Passover, in order to collect the temple tax (1:3).[98] As emphasized long ago by Abrahams, and more recently by Sanders,[99] the money changers were a practical necessity because the only accepted currency was the relatively well-regulated silver coinage of Tyre (on this currency, see below). What is more, these rules speak of a surcharge, a "kalbon" (קלבון), consisting of a small fraction of a sheqel (1:6); is this what the money changer would collect in Jesus' day?[100] For those willing to interpret the Gospels in light of rabbinic evidence, it can be quite tempting to understand Jesus' overturning of the tables as an opposition to the tax, the surcharge, or the money changers who helped collect these funds.

The thematic arguments connecting the temple incident and the temple tax proceed from this textual base, and depend on the particular theory being developed. Those who view the priests as inherently corrupt can find further justification in this tax or the surcharge.[101] Those who suppose that Jesus opposed occasional abuses can find opportunities for such in these transactions.[102] It is also possible to imagine that Jesus was opposed to the idea of the surcharge, even if all the transactions involved were otherwise honest.[103] Against these approaches are those who defend the general integrity of the priests, and who describe the surcharge as necessary and practical, and therefore inherently unoffensive.[104] But here we face the same issue noted earlier with regard to corruption in general: we simply cannot prove that it did or didn't happen during Jesus' visit to the temple. On the other hand, to assert that the tax with its surcharge was a practical necessity is to miss an important point: the fact that that the collection was practical doesn't mean that it remained unopposed. Prophetic reformers are not always bound by practicality.

But there are other reasons to be cautious. First, the textual arguments are less convincing than they may at first appear. Money changers would have had work to do—exchanging currencies—even without the assessment of a surcharge. The fact that later rabbinic texts use the term *kalbon* to refer to the surcharge does not definitively prove that the money changers in Jesus' day were collecting such a charge. What is more problematic for this thesis is the fact that the *only* New Testament text that speaks explicitly of the temple tax (Matt. 17:24–27) knows nothing of a surcharge, and certainly does not oppose the tax on those grounds. Finally, it is important to note, with regard to the temple incident, that the surcharge theory fails to explain other aspects of the gospel traditions, such as Jesus' expulsion of the pigeon sellers. Even if true, the surcharge theory does not constitute on its own a full theory for explaining either the temple incident or Matthew 17:24–27.

Another approach to Matthew 17:24–27 is to suggest that Jesus did not oppose the tax categorically but asserted priestly prerogatives by claiming for himself and his followers an exemption from the tax.[105] According to *some* rabbinic sources, priests were in theory exempt from paying the half-sheqel tax, though they could pay it if they so chose (*m. Sheqalim* 1:4). On the other hand, other rabbinic sources exempt priests only from the surcharge, suggesting that they were in fact required to pay the half-sheqel (*m. Sheqalim* 1:3, 6). Besides the ambiguous rabbinic evidence, this argument is problematic and unconvincing. The argument is unconvincing since nothing in the gospel passage itself suggests that priestly prerogatives are being asserted. The argument is problematic because in the end it still amounts to an opposition to the tax per se: if Jesus and his disciples can claim the exemption, couldn't anyone?

We are left with one further possibility: that Jesus opposed the tax entirely. Again, we could not consider this a complete explanation of the temple incident, for opposition to the tax does not explain Jesus' action against the pigeon sellers. But it remains possible that Jesus did oppose the tax and overturned the tables for that reason. We do know that the temple tax was the subject of disputes in ancient Judaism. According to rabbinic sources, the sages and the Sadducees (or Boethusians) disputed over whether or not the tax revenues should defray the costs of the daily offering (e.g., b. Menahot 65a). A few scholars have tried to understand Jesus' temple action or his approach to the temple tax in light of this dispute. For instance, Hugh Montefiore believed that Jesus rejected the idea that even the poor should have to pay this tax, and that the sacrifices should be paid for in some other manner.[106] Jacob Neusner, on the other hand, asserted that Jesus assumed (like the later rabbis) that the sacrifices would be paid for by everyone, through the temple tax; Jesus' rejection of the tax is therefore tantamount to his rejection of the temple.[107] While it is possible that Jesus took a side on these matters, it must be emphasized that the rabbinic sources speak of a dispute over how the tax money should be spent, without any reference to one group or another opposing the tax per se. In addition, there is little reason to believe that Jesus' overturning the money changers' tables could effectively communicate any opposition to the more specific matter of how the money was spent.

There is, however, other evidence of ancient Jews who opposed this tax: some of the Dead Sea texts oppose the *annual* collection of the tax, maintaining that the tax should be paid only once, when a man reached his twentieth year (e.g., 4Q159 frag. 1, II:6–7).[108] For the sake of accuracy, we must distinguish carefully between a complete opposition to the tax (as suggested in theory in Matt. 17:24–27) and an opposition to its annualization (as articulated in 4Q159). But in practice, an opposition to the annualization of the tax amounts to pretty much the same thing as a complete opposition to the tax. The only time the two approaches would dictate a different practice would be in a person's twentieth year; the rest of the time, according to either position, the tax would not be paid. If we are to suppose that Jesus opposed the tax—on whatever grounds—we cannot necessarily describe such an opposition as "radical."[109] There were indeed Jews who opposed the idea of an annual half-sheqel tax, and Jesus could well have been one of them. Indeed, that Jesus opposed in principle collecting money *every year* from *all* Israel—including the poor—is rather possible, and matches much of what we read about Jesus elsewhere in the gospel traditions. We will return to this aspect of the temple tax below.

Jesus versus the Idolatrous Sheqels of Tyre

According to rabbinic sources—and rabbinic testimony in this respect is widely accepted—the temple tax was to be paid in the form of sheqels of Tyre (m. Sheqalim 2:4, m. Bekhorot 8:7). In his analysis of this coinage, Ya'akov

Meshorer identifies changes in the coins' style and quality that apparently occurred during the time when King Herod ruled Judea. The dean of ancient Jewish numismatics then ventures further, suggesting that these differences result from the fact that these coins were, from the time of Herod on, minted at Jerusalem by the temple authorities.[110] Among other evidence, Meshorer points to a curious rabbinic source that refers to the Tyrian sheqel as Jerusalemite (t. Ketubot 13:20). Some New Testament scholars have picked up on this, believing that Meshorer's theory allows the identification of yet another problem Jesus would have had with the priesthood. The Tyrian sheqels—by definition—bear an eagle on one side and the head of Melqart/Hercules on the other. Jesus, it is argued, would have found such symbols patently offensive. Jesus' opposition to the temple authorities (and to the temple tax) would have only been strengthened if he knew that the coins were minted by the Jerusalem authorities.[111]

There are two problems with this line of argument. First, it needs to be emphasized that Meshorer's theory is just that—a *theory*. While there are many reasons to believe that later series of sheqels were not minted at Tyre, there is no evidence proving they were minted in Jerusalem, and a number of numismatists remain unconvinced by Meshorer's argument.[112] Second, that Jesus opposed the use of the Tyrian sheqels because of their idolatrous symbols is difficult to maintain, and is based upon false assumptions concerning broad ancient Jewish opposition to all idolatrous images—an assumption that simply is not supported by the evidence. Certainly there is no evidence in the Gospels to suggest that Jesus was concerned with idolatrous imagery.[113] Indeed, the sheqel of Tyre is a prime example of what Steven Fine calls "tolerated imagery."[114] Hoards of such coins have been discovered all over Israel, including Qumran.[115] If Meshorer is just partially correct, that only *some* Tyrian sheqels were minted in Jerusalem, then the case that the sheqels were considered idolatrous is all the more weakened, not strengthened. In the end, the extant literary and numismatic evidence simply cannot support the argument that Jesus opposed the temple authorities' issuing of coins bearing idolatrous images.

Jesus versus Trade in the Temple

A further approach to the temple incident—one that also relates to the temple tax collectors—is based on the idea that what's at stake isn't systemic or occasional abuse of commercial transactions by priestly authorities but the physical location of the commerce. According to this theory, Jesus challenged the traders and money changers because he opposed their having been *in* the temple in the first place. Jesus is thus defending the sanctity of the sanctuary against an encroachment of commerce into the temple's outer courts.[116] The textual support for these arguments includes (1) the fact that Jesus is said in all four Gospels to have *expelled* traders from the temple (Matt. 21:12; Mark 11:15; Luke 19:45; John 2:15), and (2) the curious reference in Mark to Jesus' having prevented anyone from carrying anything within the temple (11:16). The latter is sometimes understood in light of similar rabbinic efforts to maintain the sanctity of the temple by forbidding one to enter there carrying one's money purse or simply in order to take a shortcut (e.g., *m. Berakhot* 9:5).[117]

The Herodian expansion of the Temple Mount certainly brought about a "monumentalization" of the sacred precincts.[118] This in turn encouraged a number of changes—including increased pilgrimage—that had economic and practical consequences for the day-to-day operation of the temple.[119] Thus there could have been any number of recent innovations that Jesus might have opposed, including the specific placement of the pigeon sellers or the money changers.[120] Again, protestations that the commerce was practical and necessary does not preclude the possibility that Jesus opposed their placement within the temple precincts.

But the question is not whether it was possible that Jesus opposed the placement of the traders; the question is whether it is likely that he opposed it: does such an opposition fit in well with his overall message and preaching? Some see Jesus' opposition to the location of the traders as part of his broader message opposing the commercialism of sacrifice in general.[121] But to the degree to which Jesus is seen as interested in a broader reform of sacrifice— seeking, perhaps, to put the emphasis on the "purity of the heart"[122]—the less clear it becomes that Jesus would have been satisfied had the traders merely moved outside of the temple. Moreover, once the argument is generalized to the point of being concerned with commercialism in general and "purity of the heart," the argument has lost its connection to any changes brought about by Herod. As Sanders has correctly emphasized, there was no "original" time when the sacrificial service was free of commercialism.[123] Sacrifice presupposes ownership, and ownership often requires commerce.

Another possibility is to align Jesus' concern with the placement of the traders with the ideal-temple perspectives as laid out in the final chapters of Ezekiel and in the *Temple Scroll*.[124] But there are problems with viewing Jesus' action as expressing hope for the building of an ideal temple of expanded dimensions. First, while it is possible that Jesus hoped for such a temple, there is no explicit testimony to that effect in the Gospels (or, for that matter, in other early Christian literature). Second, while it is possible that Jesus was influenced by Ezekiel or the *Temple Scroll* in this respect, it is difficult to point out very many other ways in which these texts or their general approaches to matters ritual or moral have impacted the Jesus tradition. Third, had Jesus expected to find Jerusalem and its temple structured along the lines laid out in either Ezekiel or the *Temple Scroll*, he would have been sorely disappointed long before he entered the temple precinct. The temples imagined by these texts are so vast that one could tell even from a rather significant distance that the Herodian temple in all its glory was not up to measure. Jesus would not have needed to enter the temple to learn that it fails by these standards, and had he believed in those standards he probably would have known not to enter. For these reasons, it is in my view unlikely that Jesus' expressed a vision for an ideal temple in his expulsion of the traders and money changers.

Jesus and the Ownership of Sacrifices

Bruce Chilton has recently advanced a new interpretation of what he refers to as Jesus' "occupation" of the temple.[125] Chilton's theory is complicated and it depends on his own interpretation of a rather obscure passage from the Babylonian Talmud. His theory is of particular interest here because it focuses on an issue pertaining to the ownership of sacrificial offerings. Indeed, Chilton deserves credit for paying attention to issue of ownership, which has been too often overlooked. Chilton's work is also notable in that his is among the few works written of late on the temple in ancient Judaism that also directly and productively engages the theoretical literature on sacrifice.

According to Chilton, Jesus' opposition to the temple was based on a rather subtle point. While common sacrificial practice allowed for visitors to purchase their offerings at (or near) the temple itself, Jesus rejected this view. Of course the common practice was rather sensible, as we have noted, for one could come to the temple and then purchase an offering guaranteed to be acceptable by the priests. Even so, according to Chilton, Jesus rejected two aspects of this practice. First, Jesus opposed making a necessity out of commerce in the sanctuary. But more to the point is Jesus' belief that one must sacrifice what one truly owned. For Jesus, this meant that one could not sacrifice one minute something that one purchased the moment before.[126] Thus by expelling the traders, Jesus was striking a blow in favor of a "'peasants' view of purity."[127] Jesus opposed the exclusivist practices of the temple, advocating instead a program that was "radically inclusive."[128] Where the temple authorities—and particularly the Pharisees—focus on the purity of the temple and who must be excluded, Jesus redefines things in a more liberal way, hoping to open the doors to those otherwise left out.[129]

Chilton finds support for his theory in a debate between the houses of Hillel and Shammai first recorded in the Mishnah (*m. Betzah* 2:4) and then amplified in the Talmud (*b. Betzah* 20a–b).[130] This debate—about the permissibility of "laying hands" (Lev. 1:4) on certain sacrifices brought by individuals—is taken by Chilton as evidence that the Hillelites advocated the generally accepted view that sacrifices could be purchased on site, and that ownership was effected when the individual laid hands on the animal just before offering it. The Shammaites—and Jesus—are understood by Chilton as rejecting this view. Chilton's theory goes into greater detail, and reviews other sources as well. But the aspects of it that I have just paraphrased are extremely problematic, and the rabbinic sources that constitute the cornerstone of his theory have been fundamentally misunderstood.[131]

The Mishnaic debate between the Houses of Hillel and Shammai (*m. Betzah* 2:4) on which Chilton's thesis rests does not in fact concern sacrifice in general.[132] To the contrary, the debate is about a rather fine point: the permissibility of "laying of hands" on sacrifices brought by individuals *on holidays during which "work" is prohibited*. The house of Shammai prohibits the rite, while the Hillelites permit it. But the issue at stake here—and throughout much of *m. Betzah*—is the degree to which sabbatical restrictions apply on holidays, with Hillelites taking a consistently lenient approach, and the Shammaiites a stricter one (see *m. Betzah* 2:1–5).

In defense of his claim that the dispute about laying hands concerns ownership, Chilton cites the work of David P. Wright (which we discussed in chapter 3). But here too is an error on Chilton's part. Wright's work suggests that in the ancient Near East (over a thousand years before the Mishnah) there was a distinction between laying *two* hands, as required in certain atonement rituals (see, e.g., Lev. 16:21), and the laying of only *one* hand, as in standard sacrificial rituals (see, e.g., Lev. 1:4). Wright suggests that while the former ritual conveys the notion of designation or selection, the latter—the laying of a single hand—conveys the notion of ownership. Wright's work has important ramifications for the understanding of Leviticus, which may indeed envision the worshiper laying a single hand on the offering, in order to connote ownership. But the ramifications for rabbinic literature are less clear, because the rabbis, curiously, do away with the distinction between the two types of hand-laying rites altogether. According to tannaitic literature, the laying of hands is *always* done with *two* hands, even if scripture speaks in the singular.[133] Thus Wright's work would suggest, if anything, that the rabbinic sources understand the laying of hands not as connoting ownership but rather as designation. To take Wright's article as justification for the argument that the rabbis believed the laying of hands connoted ownership involves misunderstanding both Wright's thesis and rabbinic praxis.

Chilton's interpretation of *m. Betzah* 2:4 is also problematic, in that he leaves the Shammaiite position largely unexplained.[134] According to Chilton, the Shammaites believe that purchasing sacrifices immediately before offering them is unacceptable. So at what point is the purchase acceptable? What if someone is an artisan and does not regularly keep animals—how then can one sacrifice at all? Moreover, in Chilton's reading, we would have to ask whether the Shammaites believe that purchasing something in general does not constitute true ownership. But there can be little doubt that in tannaitic law in general (even, surely, according to the House of Shammai) monetary purchases do indeed constitute ownership, provided the buyer takes possession of the object—this is a fundamental assumption of rabbinic law concerning such transactions (*m. Bava Qamma* 4:1–2). If the Shammaites had rejected the fundamental rabbinic definition of what constitutes a proper purchase, we would certainly have heard a lot about it.

One further point needs to be noted. Even had there been some dispute about the ownership of sacrifice as related to the permissibility of the rite of laying of hands, it is highly doubtful that such a dispute would provide the "background" for understanding Jesus' overturning of the tables in the temple. One common thread running through many of the accounts is Jesus' attack on the "sellers of pigeons" (Matt. 21:12; Mark 11:15; John 2:16). With regard to Chilton's theory, it ought to be noted that according to both the Hebrew Bible and rabbinic literature, the rite of "laying hands" was not performed on birds![135]

Chilton's theory therefore does not stand up to scrutiny. Still, he should indeed be commended for calling attention to the issue of ownership. The issue has been largely overlooked in the scholarship, and I have tried to rectify this oversight at various points in this analysis. Chilton is not only correct to call attention to the issue; he may also be right, if only in the most general sense, that the temple incident can be explained by keeping in mind issues concerning sacrificial ownership.

Jesus, the Gifts of the Poor, and Alms to the Poor

I have reviewed a number of approaches to the temple incident, and have found reason to question these approaches. Some analyses rest on the assumption that the ancient Jewish temple was inherently flawed, and in need of replacement. This kind of approach is contradicted by the rather significant evidence that can be marshaled to the effect that early Christians remained loyal to the Jerusalem temple, long after Jesus' death. Such an approach is also problematic in that it cannot be objectively demonstrated that the temple was an inherently flawed institution. Whatever evidence can be marshaled (from Qumran, from rabbinic literature, or from the apocalypses) is both ahistorical and biased. Moreover, this approach contains within it at least an implicit and sometimes an explicit criticism of ancient Judaism altogether. Obviously, many Jews (and a good number of early Christians too) remained loyal to the Jerusalem temple until 70 C.E. and even well beyond that. Were they just blindly, foolishly, or slavishly loyal to an obviously corrupt institution?

Some approaches rest on the assumption that the system was prone to abuse. In an extreme form, this is no different from that noted above: a temple with widespread systemic abuse is little different from a temple that is inherently flawed. Of course, it is quite possible that the system was abused from time to time—indeed, we could hardly suppose, to say nothing of prove, otherwise. But the problem with this approach is that it rests on coincidence: Jesus happened to come to the temple on an "off day," when he could encounter a wicked priest or a crooked money changer. Once the coincidence becomes a likely one, we are back to the idea of the temple as *inherently* corrupt. While this kind of unlikely coincidence is surely possible, we would do better as historians to look for an explanation that rests on a firmer basis.

The theories that avoid the pitfalls just noted typically suffer from one further weakness or another. Some seem entirely removed from Jesus' overall social and religious teaching (e.g., that Jesus was concerned with an ideal temple along the lines of 11QT). Others seem entirely removed from a plausible first-century ancient Jewish context (e.g., Jesus' supposed opposition to the images on sheqels of Tyre). How then can we proceed? We need an approach that allows Jesus to articulate a message that can be reasonably attributed to a temple-going Jewish person of the first century C.E. Yet we would hope to understand Jesus' incident in the temple in such a way that we are not at the same time denying any integrity to those who might reject

Jesus' message. I think we can find such a theory if we look further into one of the issues we have touched on now and again throughout this book: the moral issues at the nexus between sacrifice and property.

I would suggest—and for now it must remain just a suggestion—that we take our cue from two shared features of three of the four versions of the temple incident: in Matthew, Mark, and John, Jesus is said to have expelled both the money changers and the pigeon sellers. And the common denominator here is that both of these types of traders would have a marked impact on poor pilgrims in particular. The money changers have their impact on the impoverished because only the poor would feel pinched by the small surcharge assessed at the temple (again, following rabbinic sources). The pigeon sellers have their impact on the destitute because the birds are the cheapest of the animal sacrifices, and presumably it's the poor who are buying pigeons, as opposed to more expensive animals such as lambs or goats. As emphasized above, both the selling of pigeons and the money changers' surcharge are practical and reasonable. But that doesn't mean they are entirely unobjectionable, especially to a group or movement that has different ideas about how one should relate to the poor. It could be argued that *any* given tax or fee is practical and reasonable; but surely practically every tax or charge has had its opponents. In my view, Jesus opposed those aspects of the temple system—the temple tax and the pigeon sellers—that required exacting money or goods from the poor.

The poor seem to have held a special place in Jesus' teaching (Luke 6:20, cf. Matt. 5:3).[136] Jesus' praises for the poor are matched by a consistent renunciation of wealth—even, in many cases, a condemnation of it. A number of sayings and parables attributed to Jesus revolve around this general theme. It will be particularly difficult for the rich to get into heaven; indeed, as the famous saying goes, it will be easier for a camel to pass through the eye of a needle (Matt. 19:23–24; Mark 10:23–25; Luke 18:24–25).[137] Jesus' concerns don't remain solely on the level of rhetoric or ideology. They seem to have motivated certain aspects of his social program:[138] his followers are to choose between serving God or Mammon (Matt. 6:24; Luke 16:13).[139] Presumably, they were expected to renounce their homes and property (Matt. 19:27; Mark 10:28),[140] even their cloaks, if necessary (Matt. 5:40, Luke 6:29; cf. *Did.* 1:4–5).[141] The wealthy were advised to give all of what they have to those in need (Matt. 19:16–22; Mark 10:17–22; Luke 18:18–23).[142] But the poor are not only to receive. Giving alms was expected of everyone (Matt. 5:42; Luke 6:30; cf. Matt. 6:1–4).[143] The gospel tradition even has praises for the poor who give what they can to the temple, as the famous "widow's mite" passage relates (Mark 12:41–44; Luke 21:1–4).[144]

If wealth is to be renounced, and if even the poor are supposed to give, whence then comes the community's material support? They are to rely in part on divine providence. According to a number of gospel narratives, Jesus himself miraculously provides for his followers. At a wedding in Cana, Jesus is said to have turned water into wine (John 2:1–11). On the Sea of Galilee, Jesus' disciples gather a wondrously large catch of fish, at the time and place

that Jesus tells them to cast their nets (Luke 5:1–11; John 21:1–11). Most famously, Jesus multiplies loaves and fishes at various times and places, feeding
four thousand in one instance (Matt. 15:32–39; Mark 8:1–10), and five thousand in another (Matt. 14:13–21, Mark 6:32–44, Luke 9:10b–17, John 6:1–15).[145]
Jesus' own provision for the poor and needy was very likely meant as an
illustration of God's capacity to do the same (Matt. 6:25–34; Luke 12:23–32).[146]

But the community's well-being was not entirely dependent upon miracles. It *appears* that they enacted a communitarian ethic, sharing among all
whatever anyone happened to have. Although the evidence for this practice is
less prevalent than might be expected, the sharing of goods is strongly implied
in all the various sayings and narratives concerning alms listed above. But we
do have a few explicit statements with regard to the community of goods
shared by the early Christian community. According to Acts 2:44–45, "all who
believed were together and had all things in common; they would sell their
possessions and goods and distribute the proceeds to all, as any needed."[147]
And the point is driven home again in 4:32–35:

> (32) Now the whole group of those who believed were of one heart
> and soul, and no one claimed private ownership of any possessions,
> but everything they owned was held in common.... (34) There was
> not a needy person among them, for as many as owned lands or
> houses sold them and brought the proceeds of what was sold.
> (35) They laid it at the apostles' feet, and it was distributed to each as
> they needed. (36) There was a Levite, a native of Cyprus, Joseph, to
> whom the apostles gave the name Barnabas (which means "son
> of encouragement"). (37) He sold a field that belonged to him, then
> brought the money, and laid it at the apostles' feet.

The report in Acts continues, relating the miraculous punishments that fell
upon a married couple when the husband foolishly and greedily withheld
from the community some of what he owned (5:1–11). These reports are, of
course, "idealized."[148] But I am not concerned so much with whether the
early church really lived up to its stated ideals. What is of interest here is
whether these ideals can help us understand the gospel narratives.

And what has any of this to do with the temple incident? It could be
telling—and it certainly is intriguing—that the clearest evidence of the early
church's community of goods is juxtaposed *immediately* with the clearest report of their continued adherence to the temple. Acts 2:44–45 (quoted above)
is followed by the assertion quoted at the beginning of this chapter, to the
effect that the community worshiped in the temple on a daily basis (2:46—
also admittedly an "idealized" report). How might the movement's community of goods be related to their continued adherence to the temple? I would
suggest that the early church's communitarianism allowed the group to cir-
cumvent whatever it was that Jesus opposed when he visited the temple. By
reading the temple incident in light of Acts 2, we find that Jesus drove out the
money changers and the pigeon sellers because he in principle opposed the

idea that the poor should be required to pay for their own offerings, or—by paying the temple tax—the offerings of the community. Jesus did indeed seek exemptions from payments to the temple, but the principle behind the exemptions he sought was not the assertion of priestly prerogatives on behalf of himself or his followers. Jesus believed that the poor should not have to pay what they could not easily afford. Another clue in support of this reading comes from the very end of the story in Matthew about the temple tax. Surely we have reason to be skeptical when we are told that Peter should expect to find a coin in the fish's mouth, and then miraculously does so. But there is an important issue in this report, one that is often overlooked but directly related to the issue of ownership: Yes, Jesus and his disciple Peter will pay the tax, *but it won't cost them anything.*[149]

I suggest—with all the caveats mentioned at the beginning of this section still in mind—that the temple incident is a further reflection of Jesus' consistent concern with giving to the poor, which was balanced by a firm renunciation of wealth.[150] In Jesus' view, wealth was not something to collect but something to give away. Coming to the temple, Jesus encountered a sight that he should have expected: the rather well-off temple authorities and their authorized traders were assessing a surcharge for money changing, and charging the poor for their sacrificial pigeons.[151] But whether he was prepared for it or not, the phenomenon seems to have bothered him, possibly getting the better of him.

I must emphasize once again that protestations that the fees or collections were practical and necessary are beside the point: the passages quoted above concerning Jesus' and the Gospels' attitudes toward the poor strongly suggest that practicality was not the guiding force here. Of course, any claims that the collections were inherently unjust or that the collectors were dishonest have now been rendered irrelevant. I am not speaking now about whether the burden is unjustified, whether a surcharge is excessive, or even whether the charges are exacted with undue abuse. I am suggesting that Jesus felt the temple should pose *no financial burden to the poor at all.* Those with money should give, those without should be exempt.[152] If anything, the system should provide for the poor. But this did not amount to a rejection of the temple, for his followers could easily continue to worship in the temple by circumventing the ill effects from the traders. By sharing wealth among themselves, they could provide the sacrificial needs for the poor among them (and perhaps for other poor folk as well). Hence, I suggest, the juxtaposition in the book of Acts of the community of goods with the continued Christian worship in the temple. The good of the sharing of goods trumps the bad from the exaction of fees from the poor.

I have already eliminated many varied attempts at illuminating the temple incident—and I have also admitted that the reports, in their brevity and complexity, may be beyond what can be firmly be explained by any scholarly theory. A new explanation should therefore be offered only with hesitation. While the theory proposed here takes its cues from various temple-related New Testament passages, the textual support for it is not in all cases that much stronger than some of the arguments I have rejected. But this proposal is worth considering as a possibility, if only because it attempts to do what so many theories have failed to do: make good sense of *both* sides of the argument between Jesus and his opponents. We can understand Jesus' temple incident as substantial, without making a mockery of those who disagreed with him.

And what principle could possibly support Jesus' opponents? For the sake of the argument, we take our cue from rabbinic sources—which admittedly may or may not be of help in understanding first-century Judaism. I have already emphasized that the rabbis, in their memory or imagination of the Second Temple, place a great priority on inclusion. The rabbis' principle of inclusion leads to certain leniencies. For instance, it trumps the concern to rid the temple of tainted wealth (which we saw expressed at Qumran), as well as the concern to keep the temple free from sinners (which we saw expressed in Philo). On the other hand, the rabbis' principle of inclusion leads to a few stringencies, particularly when it comes to the temple's funds. The temple tax was to be paid by all, on an annual basis—*and there's no exemption for the poor.* Moreover, because sacrifices are to be duly owned, the poor must in fact pay for their sacrifices either before the fact or on site. Of course, rabbinic sources praise giving to the poor, and obviously they would have looked kindly upon any efforts at helping the poor out. But that doesn't change the fact that there *are* financial burdens placed on the poor. There's simply no way around that, because that's the way the temple and its service technically become everyone's. As noted in the previous chapter, the rabbis consider the gifts of the poor to be particularly praiseworthy (e.g., *Lev. Rabbah* 3:5). But the rabbis don't exempt the poor from their financial obligations.

A rabbinic tradition may help us illustrate further the issues at stake here. According to *b. Sukkah 30a*—a passage discussed in chapter 6 with regard to the ownership of sacrifices—the following parable is supposed to illustrate the prohibition of offering stolen sacrifices.

> The matter is likened to an earthly king who passed a toll-booth, and told his servants to pay the collectors. They said to him: "But [what is collected from the] the toll is entirely yours!" He said to them: "Let all who pass by learn from my example, and not evade paying the toll." Similarly, the Holy One, blessed be He, said: " 'I the Lord hate robbery with a burnt offering' (Isa. 61:8): Let all learn from my example, and keep themselves clear of robbery."

The passage bears surprising structural similarities to Matthew 17:25–26.[153] But it has the opposite message: where Jesus' parable leads to the statement "the sons are free," the rabbinic source emphasizes that all must pay the tax in question. If God were making pilgrimage (so the parable would imply), then even *He* would pay the tax. No one is exempt. The message here is the ideal that the temple belongs to everyone and performs sacrifices for everyone. That ideal (and it too is a moral perspective) requires that the minimum payment be brought by each individual. There's a place for alms—but that place is not the temple. In the temple, the focus is on each person's obligation to give to the sanctuary, and the point is to emphasize that all are included by participating in this fashion.

To be clear, I am not suggesting that *b. Sukkah* 30a is an authentic first-century document, nor am I suggesting that Jesus knew of this particular parable. I do think it is possible that the rabbinic parable is a response to the gospel text, but there is no specific evidence for this claim (other than the fact that the parables share some striking structural and thematic aspects). Still, what's important is that a comparison of the rabbinic and Matthean texts allows us to see two very different sides of a real moral conundrum, one that is certainly worthy of debate and one that from an objective standpoint has no obvious winner or loser. On the one side, we have the position articulated by Jesus: he believed (so I suggest) that the system should not force the poor to pay. Their personal contribution should not be coerced, and ideally their offerings should be provided for them. This provision can occur miraculously through Jesus' presence, or it can occur more practically through the community's sharing of goods. The latter, presumably, explains how the early Christians could continue to worship at the temple: through the sharing of wealth, the community's poor were provided for. Against this view stands the approach taken by the rabbis: every person (who is male, and of age) must pay his minimum to the temple. The question of alms is a good one, but it's a separate issue. The financial burden for the temple's upkeep applies to all. What we have here, indeed, is the conflict of two principles.

I look forward to hearing responses to this suggestion by New Testament scholars. But even if the suggestion itself is not accepted, I hope my purpose in making the suggestion is. That purpose is to emphasize that where scholars all too often see just black and white, there are in fact many shades of gray. Scholars too often portray the disputes concerning the temple in ancient Judaism as a story of good versus evil, the haves versus the have-nots, the priests versus the prophets, or what have you. But as emphasized now and again throughout this book, a number of the moral issues regarding sacrifice are rather complicated. Indeed, we all know of this complexity in our own world. Not everyone who is truly concerned for the poor would agree that it is morally appropriate to give cash to a beggar on an urban street, or pledge money to every charity that manages to reach one by phone at home. We all know that contemporary issues of relating to the poor and to society are complicated, and there's more than one right approach (and more than one wrong one too, to be sure). We would do well to understand that ancient Jewish society—though very different from our own—was also complicated, and that there was possibly more than one principled answer to a number of moral questions of the day.

Antitemple Polemics in the New Testament

While I have tried here to demonstrate that the two gospel narratives being considered are not inherently critical of the temple, the same thing cannot be said of the New Testament in its entirety. There are, to be sure, less ambiguously antitemple polemics in the New Testament, and for the sake of clarity and completeness we identify and comment briefly on some of the key texts.

Because of the importance the book of Acts played in this analysis, it is fitting to turn first to Stephen's speech, particularly its conclusion as recorded in Acts 7:48–50.[154] Stephen's harangue against the people of Jerusalem retells biblical history in a negative light, leading toward the assertion that "the Most High does not dwell in a house made with human hands; as the prophet says (Isa. 66:1–2), 'Heaven is my throne, and the earth is my footstool. What kind of house will you build for me, says the Lord, or what is the place of my rest? Did not my hand make all these things?'" We have discussed previously—at some length—the biblical and ancient Jewish idea that God's true dwelling place is in heaven. It was argued earlier that discussions of God dwelling in heaven are not necessarily antitemple polemics, for very often it can be assumed that the understanding of God living in heaven is balanced with the understanding that God's glory, presence, or name dwells in the earthly sanctuary below, endowing the lower place too with its own sanctity (as for example, 1 Kgs. 8:27 is balanced by 6:13 and 8:10–13). Indeed, many visions of the heavenly sanctuary serve to reinforce the sanctity of its earthly counterpart. But we can be rather certain that Stephen is to be understood as polemicizing against the temple. First of all, we are told as much in Acts 6:13–14: the crowd accuses Stephen of speaking against the temple.[155] More important, the passage quoted above is followed by a sentence beginning "You stiffnecked people." Clearly, Stephen is criticizing the people's faith in their sanctuary. Finally, nowhere in Stephen's speech is the sanctuary defended against these charges. Thus what we find in Acts 7 is qualitatively different from the various references to heavenly sanctuaries we reviewed in chapter 4. Discussions of heavenly sanctuaries per se are not necessarily antitemple. But when we find the assertion that God dwells *only* in the heavenly temple, and not in any earthly one, then clearly we have entered the realm of antitemple polemic. Indeed, this kind of polemic is remarkable precisely because it undercuts an essential and common facet of ancient Jewish theology: that God's presence, glory, or name dwells in the Jerusalem temple. We must, therefore, recognize Acts 7 for the polemic that it is, with its exceptional rejection of traditional Jewish theology. At the same time, we must avoid assuming— based in part on Acts 7—that other references to heavenly sanctuaries are necessarily antitemple. And we also must avoid assuming that Jesus himself said what Luke-Acts tells us that Stephen said. Indeed it is striking and important that in Luke-Acts, the antitemple polemic comes not during the life of Jesus but shortly thereafter, as relations between the early church and other Jews begin to sour.

In the book of Revelation, we find a different antitemple polemic, one that is also connected to imagining God's extra-worldly dwelling place. In the final chapters of this complicated document (21:1–22:5), we find a vision of the New Jerusalem, one that exhibits certain continuities with other visions we have seen earlier (e.g., the Qumran *New Jerusalem* texts).[156] This sort of vision, as I pointed out earlier, imagines structures ready and waiting in heaven to descend onto earth in the final days. In Revelation, a seer is shown the New Jerusalem, and it is a city of divine construction (21:10) built from wondrous materials (21:11, 18–21), with twelve gates, one for each of the tribes (21:12). But as is not the case of other visions with the New Jerusalem, we are explicitly told in this case that the seer "saw no temple in the city, for its temple is the Lord God the Almighty and the Lamb" (21:22). Clearly, in this vision of the future, the temple holds no place, and the Jerusalem of the future will not suffer from its absence: "and the city has no need of sun or moon to shine on it, for the glory of God is its light, and its lamp is the Lamb" (21:23). For the final chapters of Revelation, there is no place for a future temple, and this repudiates an assumption that was common and very likely predominant among ancient Jews—the idea that there would be some sort of temple in any future age. So here, too, what is truly polemical is also what is strikingly exceptional.

We turn, finally, to the letter to the Hebrews.[157] I have alluded to Hebrews now and again throughout this book, for the epistle lays out a clear, supersessionist approach in its contrast between the old order and the new. In the old scheme, a number of earthly, mortal priests (7:21, 23) administered in a temple that was a mere copy of the true sanctuary above (8:1–5).[158] They offered an ineffective atonement (9:9–10, 10:4, 11). But in the new scheme, the earthly models become irrelevant. In Jesus, people now have access to a single, immortal, ideal high priest (7:22, 24–26), one who dispenses true atonement (9:11–14), in a sanctuary not made by human hands (9:11, 14). The antitemple, antisacrificial, and antipriestly polemics here are simply unmistakable: and what we encounter here is certainly of a different order than what we find in the Gospels, Qumran, or in the other ancient Jewish literature we have surveyed. Here the temple is seen to be inherently inferior. It always was so, and humanity simply had to wait until Jesus' day for an effective means of atonement to be provided. Everything that came before was simply inadequate. This text is the basis of Christian supersessionist approaches to the temple, and, by extension, it is the ancestor of many modern scholarly approaches to the temple and its ritual.

Conclusion

In current discussions of the historical Jesus, a number of scholars interpret both the temple incident and the Last Supper as antitemple acts. In this chapter, however, alternative interpretations have been presented. The Last Supper traditions have been understood here within the context of ancient Jewish understandings of sacrificial worship. It was argued, first of all, that the sacrificial overtones in Jesus' words and actions—and especially the statement over the cup—ought not to lead scholars to dismiss the Last Supper tradition as inauthentic because of some ostensible violation of Jewish purity laws. Those who argue in this manner forget two things: (1) that during the

Last Supper, the disciples drank wine, not blood, and (2) that ancient Jews could recognize a metaphor when they encountered one. It was then argued that a good deal of evidence—especially in Acts and Paul—strongly suggests that the temple remained an important institution in early Christian practice and thought. According to Acts, the Jerusalem Church was not radically anti-temple; according to his epistles, Paul also regarded Jersualem's sacrificial worship positively. Finally, it was also argued that both Paul's metaphors and Jesus' eucharistic words and deeds find a likely context in the multifarious and well-attested ancient Jewish efforts to channel the temple's sanctity into various other ritual activities, such as prayer and eating. Reaching this conclusion, however, requires some rethinking of the ways these issues are typically approached. If we grant, as we must, that sacrificial rituals had broad symbolic significance for ancient Jews, then we can come one step closer to breaking down the analytic categories that dominate the discussion: the empty performance of sacrificial rituals on the one hand and the "spiritualization" of sacrifice on the other. In their place, we could put rituals pregnant with symbolism on the one hand and metaphoric expansions of such symbolisms on the other. The Last Supper traditions, in their various forms, fit well within the context of ancient Jewish applications of temple significance to nontemple rituals. And thus the historical Last Supper was most likely not an antitemple symbolic action. "This too is divine service" is probably what and all Jesus originally intended to say.

It was also argued above that the temple incident ought not be understood as a rejection of the temple. Here too, an important piece of evidence is the fact that early Christians continued to speak highly of and visit the temple, long after Jesus' death. Indeed, Jesus' own apostles continued to visit the temple—presumably with Jesus' permission and blessing—after the temple incident. We surveyed here many approaches to the temple incident, and found them all lacking in some respect. Those that operate on the assumption that the temple was completely corrupt are to be rejected out of hand. Such approaches blindly trust all the critical sources, and refuse to consider the possibility that the temple authorities may have had a different—and at least equally legitimate—response. Those who suggest that the temple was simply prone to abuse now and then must in the end suppose that the temple incident resulted from a coincidence: Jesus came to the temple on a bad day, and just happened to catch a corrupt money changer or a crooked trader. While this approach remains possible, it is less than satisfying to resort to coincidence.

I have suggested a new explanation, one that may not be convincing but exhibits two particular strengths, in addition to avoiding the problems mentioned above: (1) it takes its cues from other temple-related New Testament passages (especially Acts 2:44–46 and Matt. 17:24–27), and (2) it seeks to explain both sides of the dispute in a sympathetic manner. Jesus, in my view, articulates an idealized approach to dealing with the poor, one that prioritizes giving alms over a number of other temple-related concerns. Taking our cues from rabbinic sources, I suggest that a different view perhaps motivated the temple authorities of that time. They may have believed that the temple funds must come from all worshipers—the poor included—as a way to establish that the temple is for everyone.

Needless to say, the approaches suggested here for understanding the Last Supper and the temple incident are ones rarely taken or even considered. It's simpler—and more attractive, it would seem—to take both traditions as antitemple polemics. But, as I have argued throughout this book, simpler and attractive assumptions have for too long negatively impacted the understanding of the ancient Jewish temple and the rituals practiced there. There is no escaping the fact that some New Testament texts—especially Hebrews—are clearly rejectionist in their approach to the temple. Yet it is surely interesting that the three documents that most clearly express antitemple messages in the New Testament (Acts 7, Revelation 21–22, Hebrews) themselves do not connect that message to Jesus, his Last Supper, or his temple incident. Christian theology followed in the direction set out by Acts 7, Revelation 21–22, and Hebrews; eventually the Last Supper and the temple incident were understood accordingly. And in some quarters, they continue to be understood accordingly.

Conclusion

Throughout this book, I have argued that contemporary scholarship on ancient Jewish cultic matters has been unduly influenced by three ideological stances that are negatively predisposed toward the ancient Jewish temple. One such stance is Christian superesessionism. Because Jesus' death is understood as doing what the Jerusalem temple could not do, the latter is often presented as flawed in one way or another. Another such stance is a medieval and modernist Jewish form of supersessionism, whereby the synagogue is understood as the better and foreseen successor to the temple, an institution that had long ago outlasted its usefulness in weaning Israel from idolatry. The third ideology is the distinctly contemporary association of animal sacrifice with human violence. This approach disparages all sacrifice in the search for the origins of the human proclivity to murder our own kind. All three of these views approach the ancient Jewish temple through the lens of presumption: it was a flawed institution, with an unspiritual, unjust, and even immoral ritual at its core.

These three biases have resulted in two problematic tendencies. The first is to place sacrifice as an early element in a broad evolutionary scheme. Sacrifice meant something only long ago, when the practice was taken literally—and foolishly—as an attempt to feed the gods or give to the gods. Sacrifice continued in later stages—as it did among ancient Israelites—only as a fossilized vestige. Finally—whether by Jesus' death, by the synagogue, or by the triumph of modern wisdom—sacrifice has been eliminated altogether, and for the better. The second tendency is related to the first: the assumption that the only true meaning of sacrifice is a literal one. Symbolic understandings of sacrifice—if any are identified at all—are typically attributed not to those who practiced sacrifice but to those who ostensibly began to move beyond it, be they philosophers and mystics who "spiritualized" sacrifice, or prophets and visionaries who rejected it.

In order to avoid these biases and tendencies, this analysis has proceeded with a few simple guidelines. First, the effort has been made here to understand the temple, its practices, and its priests with a reasonable degree of sympathy—in line with the consideration scholars more typically reserve for better liked rituals (such as purity) or better liked figures (such as prophets). Second, in order to provide something of a check and balance to previous biases, this book seeks to expand the focus of the scholarly discussion: we have looked at the sacrificial process broadly conceived, including ritual purity; we considered the approaches of priests and prophets; we examined the literature of the Hebrew Bible and ancient Judaism; and we considered sources as diverse as the Gospels and *Midrash Tadshe*. The third rule of thumb followed here is to resist the tendency to plug the data into any linear, evolutionary schemes. As a result of these guidelines, this book is somewhat apologetic, certainly lengthy, and structured topically, not chronologically.

In the first chapter of this book, we observed how rarely scholars entertain the possibility that sacrificial practice had symbolic meanings for the Israelites who practiced it. The fact that this reluctance is rooted in bias can be demonstrated by the fact that the reluctance is selective. Other ancient Israelite rituals—such as purity rites—are frequently understood as symbolic, while sacrifice is derided as a fossilized vestige. In the second chapter, I tried to model a different way of looking at ancient Israel's cult. Sacrifice should be understood as a broad process, one that includes rites of purification. Therefore, it is necessary to apply to the sacrificial process the scholarly sympathy that is typically reserved for ritual purity. The resulting hypothesis suggests that sacrifice, broadly conceived, was understood by ancient Israelites as an act of *imitatio Dei*, performed in the hope of attracting and maintaining God's presence in the sanctuary, among the community.

In chapter 3, we turned to the prophetic literature, with an eye toward reevaluating those well-known passages that are often taken as criticisms of ritual in general or the temple cult in particular. We found that here too, the biases against sacrifice have impacted negatively on the discussion. Of course, (mis)understandings of these prophetic passages in part drive the biases with which this book is concerned. But we also found that a number of the standard counterarguments—offered by scholars to temper the prophetic critique—are themselves at times too reflective of contemporary religious rhetoric. I attempted to steer a middle course between those on the one hand who suggest that prophets and priests shared little if anything when it came to religiosity and those on the other who would gloss over the differences between them. I also flatly rejected those constructions that see prophecy as a chronological stage in ancient Israel's religious development. Following Wellhausen, some see the prophetic stage as a golden age of Israelite thought, followed by a period of priestly ossification; following Kaufmann, others view the prophets as having introduced ethics to older, dryer, priestly texts. In my view, evolutionist constructions of either type are methodologically flawed, and motivated by invalid presuppositions concerning the nature of ritual and the development of religious traditions.

When we reviewed the key texts that pertain to this discussion—including Jeremiah's temple sermon and the final chapters of Ezekiel—we were able to see how much the priests and prophets shared, especially with regard to what is often considered "priestly" theology: the concern to maintain God's presence in the sanctuary, and the fear that grave sin could threaten that presence, through the process of moral defilement. It was also suggested in the course of this chapter that the hard-and-fast distinction between ritual and ethics has prevented scholars from appreciating the degree to which ritual and ethics are inherently connected—and virtually inseparable—when it comes to sacrifice. Sacrifice became anathema for the prophets not because God preferred a loftier form of worship, nor because the temple service was performed by people who had other things on their minds. The prophetic critique of contemporary cultic practice stemmed from the fact that many sacrifices were being offered by those whose property was unduly earned, being proceeds from the exploitation of the poor. Because proper sacrifice presupposes due ownership, a thieving society cannot render due offerings, at least not in the prophetic understanding of these matters.

When we turned to the final chapters of Ezekiel, we found something rather surprising: a prophet whose vision of a future temple is actually more exclusive than the rules we find in the priestly codes. This contrast may point the way toward understanding the priestly side of the disagreements between priestly and prophetic traditions. Where the prophets found sin everywhere, and therefore spoke negatively of the present cultic system, the priests just might have disagreed, believing that Israel's worship was not so easily threatened by the sins of the people. I cannot *prove* that this description of the state of affairs in ancient Israel is accurate. However, I would argue that many of the interpretations put forward here are at least as plausible as the more common ones, which too frequently operate on flawed assumptions regarding the inherent inadequacy of sacrifice or the limited religious vision of ancient Israel's priests.

In chapter 4, we traced the two most important symbolic understandings of cultic practice in ancient Judaism. According to one perspective, the temple in Jerusalem represents the cosmos; according to the other, the temple on earth parallels a heavenly sanctuary. Both of these ideas are commonly understood as "spritualizations" of the cult or as "desacralizations" of the temple. But such approaches were articulated by those—like Philo, Josephus, and the rabbis—who fully believed in the centrality and efficacy of the Jerusalem temple. These ideas, therefore, are not "spiritualizations" of sacrifice but, simply, symbolic understandings of it. Indeed, with either approach, both purity and sacrifice can be understood as aspects of a ritual process that imitates divine prerogatives and summons some sort of divine presence into the earthly temple. According to the first perspective—that the temple represents the cosmos—people can, by building the temple, emulate and imitate the divine act of creation. By maintaining and supporting the symbol of the cosmos, people play roles that are god-like or angelic in nature. According to the second perspective—that the earthly temple corresponds to a heavenly one—we again find that both purity and sacrifice can be understood in light of modified notions of *imitatio Dei*, for what is done in the earthly temple below emulates what the angels do in the heavenly temple above. To the degree to which angelology becomes more pronounced in these texts, we should perhaps speak more accurately of *imitatio angeli*. Nonetheless, once again, the processes of purification and sacrifice take on the meaning of being god-like or angel-like. And although God resides in heaven, a divine presence still dwells in the earthly analogue to the heavenly shrine.

In chapter 5, we turned to those ancient Jewish texts that articulate criticisms of the temple and its service, especially as found in the literature from Qumran. In a number of ways, the analysis of chapter 5 develops that of chapter 3. On the one hand, it was argued that even the Qumran sectarians— like the most radical of the prophets who preceded them—continued to believe in the eventual restoration of sacrifice, and never questioned its theoretical religious value. But—again like the prophets of old—the Qumran sectarians did pay close attention to the threat posed to the temple system by economic sin. Indeed, taking the prophetic critique one step further, the Qumran sectarians not only spoke against the contemporary temple but also *did* actively reject it (at least at certain points in their history). As a result, they removed themselves from ancient Jewish society, and came to see their own worship as a temporary stand-in for the temple that they now shunned.

We identified a number of specific charges raised against the temple in this literature. Various texts from Qumran articulate the concern that (1) the temple was morally defiled, by virtue of grave sins (especially ones performed in close proximity to the temple) as well as by the economic transgressions of the people at large; (2) the temple was ritually defiled, by virtue of the fact that the priests were not following the right rules of purification; (3) the temple practice was ritually inadequate, by virtue of the fact that the priests were failing to adhere to other important religious requirements, such as those concerning the calendar; and, finally, (4) the temple was structurally inadequate, by failing to meet the design requirements laid out in, especially, the *Temple Scroll* (which itself builds in part on traditions going back to Ezekiel 40–48). The various arguments are distinct and separable, and frequently appear independently of one another. And each argument has its own ramifications for the question of whether or not the temple was rejected in full by the Qumran sectarians. Yet when taken together, what we find in the Qumran sectarian texts differs from what we find either earlier in the prophets or elsewhere in the Second Temple period: a deep and sustained criticism of the temple, one that seems to be backed up by a social program involving rejection of the temple.

But here, too, we find that scholars are too quick to assert that the sectarians in some way "spiritualized" the temple, as if the temple lacked spirit to begin with, or as if the sectarians' religious life was in some fashion more valid religiously than even a properly maintained temple would be. Scholars have also been too quick to overestimate the degree to which the sectarians were satisfied with their rejection of the temple. While some scholars suggest that the sectarians viewed their community as if it could provide atonement as effective as the temple that they left behind, other scholars suggest that the sectarians understood their forms of atonement as better than the sacrifices of the temple. I argued that both views overstate the case. When we take into consideration the sect's own penal code—which ought to demonstrate more than anything else the degree to which the sect thought their rituals could effect atonement—we find that the sectarians did not claim to possess powers of atonement that surpassed that of the temple they left behind. To the contrary, sectarian sinners were often believed to be in a rather difficult position, with the required penance involving exclusion from the community for long periods of time, even for transgressions that other Jews would have believed could be effectively and speedily atoned for (at least in part) by sacrifice at the temple.

We also find at Qumran evidence for an important phenomenon seen in other realms of ancient Jewish literature as well: the belief that aspects of the temple service can be emulated by performing cultic practices beyond the bounds of the temple site. Extra-temple purity practices were surely a regular facet of life at Qumran. The desire to emulate the temple beyond its confines—and before its destruction in 70 C.E.—was characteristic of other strata of ancient Jews too, as can be seen in literary and archaeological evidence concerning stone vessels and water rites. A similar effort—aptly referred to by some as *imitatio templi*—can also be seen after 70 C.E. in the decoration of ancient synagogues. With regard to this phenomenon, the Qumran sectarians differ from other ancient Jews only by degree. They cultivated a particularly strict form of purity. But the cultivation of purity beyond the temple cannot be understood, in and of itself, as a rejection of the temple. To the contrary, the emulation of the temple was based on a belief in the intrinsic value of the institution. Imitation is the heart of flattery—so goes the cliché. But this is no mere catch phrase. Scholars have been too reluctant to recognize these efforts for what they are: affirmations that the temple was a meaningful (even if controversial) institution in ancient Jewish religious life.

In chapter 6, we examined a number of rabbinic sources relating to the temple, its worship, purity, and prayer. Here too we find that evolutionist perspectives have clouded the historical record. Some scholars unabashedly attempt to suggest that the rabbis replaced sacrifice with prayer, even believing that the latter "superseded" the former. Others have been too quick to assume that the rabbis' approach to the temple was inchoate, uninteresting, or unprincipled. We reviewed a number of sources, with an eye toward reaching different conclusions.

We began by looking at sources that may constitute parallels to, and possibly responses to, the approaches to the temple taken at Qumran. Over and against the Qumran sectarians, the rabbis fundamentally rejected the idea that the Second Temple was inherently defiled, whether ritually or morally. Indeed, while postmishnaic sources are willing to recall (or imagine) that the

Second Temple was prone, at least from time to time, to moral corruption, the rabbis were not generally willing to go the next step to suggest that the Second Temple had been ritually or morally defiled by this corruption. Where the rabbis do exhibit an interest in moral defilement, in almost all cases that interest is directed not toward the temple itself but toward the land in general.

Taking cues from suggestions and analyses presented in chapters 3 and 5, we then considered the rabbinic approach to a number of issues relating to the nexus between sacrifice and money. The Qumran sectarians—and the biblical prophets who preceded them—articulated criticisms of the temple and its ritual based at least in part on the idea that rampant economic transgression had rendered it difficult or impossible to offer a proper, duly owned sacrifice. The rabbinic approach to such matters is surprisingly different. Rabbinic lore remembers well that the Second Temple was funded by aristocrats—and substantially rebuilt by the evil, despotic Herod. Yet while the sectarians condemned the temple as having been defiled by a wicked priest, the rabbis come to terms with Herod's temple, on largely practical grounds. Moreover, rabbinic *halakhah* reflects the same, relaxed attitude: even sacrifices consisting of stolen animals were not inherently or in all cases disqualified or seen as a threat to the purity of the temple. Indeed, rabbinic law also insisted that the temple tax had to be collected from *all* Israel: this ruling (whether historical or not) surely would lead to the funding of the temple from money that others would question. And we find in rabbinic literature what may have been implied in earlier priestly literature. Where ethical idealism can lead to exclusivist policies (as in the prophets and at Qumran), the rabbinic position articulates an ideology of openness. According to rabbinic sources, the temple belongs to all Israel, and therefore practically all are welcome, even unrepentant sinners (excluding, of course, apostates and a few others).

Rabbinic literature allows us to see much more than what the rabbis would have said to the Qumran sectarians, had they been in conversation. It is at times supposed that the rabbis were shocked into silence by the destruction of the temple, mounting an effective response only centuries later. I have argued here that the earliest rabbinic sources can be understood as articulating a full-fledged response to the temple's destruction. This consisted of one point just mentioned—(1) that the temple, its practices, and its personnel were *not* largely responsible for the temple's defilement or destruction— wedded with two related points: (2) the unquestioned hope for the temple's return, and (3) a vision of the future temple that would be in all essentials like the one that was lost. In the second of these, we find a point of agreement between the rabbis and the Qumran sectarians; in the first and third points, we find significant disagreements between the two realms of literature. While some visionaries looked for a future cult entirely different and better than what preceded it, the rabbinic approach was notably conservative. What was lost was what they wanted back. This is hardly the supersessionist approach sometimes imputed to them.

One further point of agreement between Qumran and rabbinic literature was identified in this chapter. In rabbinic literature, too, we find evidence of the concern to emulate the temple beyond its bounds by practicing purity or other temple-related practices even when not in or near the temple. The comparison between Qumran, the rabbis, and other literary and archaeological evidence drives home the point that these efforts cannot accurately be identified as part of the rabbinic response to the destruction. These efforts were long part of Jewish religiosity, well before the destruction of the temple.

In chapter 7, we turned to the New Testament, taking a close look at two narratives both related on some level to the temple or sacrifice: the Last Supper and the temple incident. As we noted, a number of scholars link the two stories together, understanding one as Jesus' rejection of the temple and the other as Jesus' establishment of a better alternative. The greatest impediment to this perspective, historically speaking, is the fact that much evidence can be mustered to the effect that a number of early Christians maintained fidelity to the temple: had Jesus unambiguously rejected the institution, or clearly established a full replacement for it, we would not expect to find continued Christian fidelity to the temple.

The eucharistic statements uttered at the Last Supper can be understood as yet another example of a phenomenon we have seen throughout this book: the efforts exerted by various ancient Jews to conceive of their own daily practices in cultic terms, as an effort not to replace the temple but to emulate it. Far from being an effort to do without the temple, the eucharist can be easily understood as yet further evidence that the temple in Jerusalem was a powerful source of religious meaning for many ancient Jews. They believed in it so much that they wanted to make the temple a part of their daily lives.

The temple incident, in its brevity and ambiguity, poses a greater challenge to interpreters. But most of the suggestions offered thus far either ascribe too much criticism of the temple to Jesus or seem too interested in downplaying the possibility that Jesus had anything constructive or critical to say. Indeed, in my view, the problems inherent in explaining the temple incident are not entirely unlike those faced in chapter 3 with regard to the prophetic critique. Sometimes it seems that all sides of the debate have been unduly influenced by other religious disputes. Some unreasonably depict the ancient Jewish temple as a flawed institution, without regard to the fact that many Jews clearly did worship there regularly. Perhaps such Jews were blind after all. On the other hand, other scholars assert that Jesus would never have disagreed with anything ancient Jewish priests might have done. As in chapter 3, here, too, the challenge is to try to understand two sides to a debate on principle. And I proposed—tentatively—just such a solution, one that takes its cue from observations concerning sacrifice and ownership put forth first in chapter 3.

Finally, we briefly examined those New Testament texts that do explicitly and completely reject sacrifice, for all time. Such texts set forth the presumption that sacrifice really was by the Second Temple period a fossilized vestige, something doomed to disappear, an activity we should be proud we no longer do. The Christian tradition followed this line of thought practically from the time these texts were composed. In the Middle Ages, certain Jewish thinkers adopted similar perspectives, and the idea firmly took root among Jews with the rise of synagogue reform in the nineteenth century. Ironically, it is these exceptional texts that set us on the road that much scholarship—be it Christian or Jewish—continues to follow.

We have surveyed a good deal of literature in this book: texts from various time periods, and sources relating to what have often been considered to be different topics, possibly even different fields. The resulting analysis differs in many ways from other studies of ancient Judaism. By examining both purity and sacrifice, especially in Part I, we were able to note and evaluate the unsound disparity between the ways the two topics are approached in the theoretical and exegetical literature. By looking at more than one period of history and eschewing the tendency to plug every text into a single, linear, chronological scheme, we were able to make note of, avoid, and even counter various evolutionist and supersessionist approaches to our themes. By consistently attempting when possible to understand *both* sides of disputes—whether between prophets and priests, between Qumran and the rabbis, or among Jesus and his contemporaries—we were able to avoid the mistake of putting forth an interpretation of one perspective that makes a mockery of the other. By consistently giving cultic rituals and personnel the benefit of the doubt, we have been able to find what so many have overlooked: various texts that allow us to understand better what the temple cult meant to those ancient Jews who believed in its meaning, willingly participated in its rituals, and sincerely hoped for its eventual restoration.

As scholars of ancient Judaism, this is our job: to attempt to understand what ancient Jews believed. While we may be interested in—as we should be—the rabbinic response to the destruction, Jesus' distinctive message, the curious community at Qumran, and even contemporary moral or political issues, we cannot abdicate our responsibility to come to terms with the living religion of biblical Israel and Second Temple period Jews. There are any number of reasons why Jewish, Christian, or even secularist moderns may wish to believe that cult sites and animal sacrifice ought to remain things of the past. But scholarship that attempts to prove that point, or that simply rests on it, becomes a tool of theology or politics.

It can hardly be expected that all the interpretations suggested in this book—some of them admittedly speculative—will be accepted in full. Even fewer will withstand the test of time without modification or correction, for rare indeed is the exegesis that cannot be improved upon by close rereading. And rarer still is a broadly conceived book that does not stumble along its way. But there is a larger goal here, one greater than the specific understandings offered here of either the rabbis or Qumran, of either Amos 2 or Acts 2. That goal is to call attention to the ways the scholarship on the ancient Jewish cult in general—and on sacrifice in particular—has been dominated by various religious and cultural biases for far too long. It's time for a change. And if this work hasn't brought us there, it is my hope that it at least points in the right direction.

Notes

INTRODUCTION

   1. Turner, "Sacrifice as Quintessential Process."

   2. Hubert and Mauss, *Sacrifice*, 19–28.

   3. E.g., Miller, *Religion of Ancient Israel*, 106–130 (on sacrifice) and 131–161 (on purity and holiness).

   4. Virtually every subsequent treatment of purity in the Hebrew Bible has at least reckoned with the possibilities raised by Douglas's insights. One noteworthy treatment, with ample bibliography, can be found in Eilberg-Schwartz, *Savage*.

   5. For purity rules as expressing notions concerning body and cosmos, see Douglas, *Purity and Danger*, and Eilberg-Schwartz, *Savage*. With regard to purity and its symbolic relation to justice, see Douglas, "Forbidden Animals" and "Holy Joy."

   6. There are exceptions, of course: one recent work that treats sacrifice (but not impurity) symbolically is Anderson, *Sacrifices and Offerings*; see also Hendel, "Sacrifice as a Cultural System."

   7. E.g., Milgrom, *Leviticus 1–16*, 1003.

   8. For a general definition and review, see Waller and Edwardsen, "Evolutionism," and Evans-Pritchard, *Theories of Primitive Religion*, 20–47.

   9. On Tylor and Frazer, see Pals, *Seven Theories of Religion*, 16–53, in addition to the works cited in the previous note. See also McCalla, "Evolutionism," which discusses a number of pre-Darwinian histories of religion that are decidedly evolutionist.

   10. See Arnold and Weisberg, "Centennial Review."

   11. For a classic articulation of this view, see de Vaux, *Studies in Old Testament Sacrifice*, 38–42. For a more recent articulation of this view, see Milgrom, *Leviticus 1–16*, 440. See discussion of Milgrom's work in chapter 1, and see further discussion of the matter of divine food in chapter 2.

12. See, for instance, the views of Milgrom, discussed in chapter 1.

13. See chapter 3.

14. On Hebrews, see Attridge, *Epistle*, and further discussion in chapter 7.

15. E.g., Jostein Ådna, "Jesus' Symbolic Act in the Temple (Mark 11:15–17): The Replacement of the Sacrificial Cult by his Atoning Death," in Ego et al., *Gemeinde ohne Tempel*, 461–475; see further Ådna's German monographs referred to in this article. See also Chilton, *Temple of Jesus*, 91–154, and see discussion of Chilton's work in chapters 1 and 7.

16. See, e.g., Chilton, *Temple of Jesus*, 150–154; Feeley-Harnik, *Lord's Table*, 139, 168; Hamerton-Kelly, *Gospel and the Sacred*, 19–20, 43–44.

17. So, e.g., Feeley-Harnik, *Lord's Table*, 139–140, 168.

18. So, e.g., Chilton, *Temple of Jesus*, 121–136.

19. Hamerton-Kelly, *Gospel and the Sacred*, 18–19.

20. See, e.g., Philip P. Jenson, "Levitical Sacrificial System," in Beckwith and Selman, *Sacrifice in the Bible*, esp. 37–38. Compare Hartley, *Leviticus*, 25, and Wenham, *Leviticus*, 28–29.

21. Maimonides, *Guide of the Perplexed*, III:32, 69b–73b (trans. Pines, 2:525–32). For a discussion, see Harvey, "Sacrifices," and Kellner, "Maimonides," xx–xxix (I thank Menachem Kellner for sending me a copy of this article).

22. For a brief survey of the Maimonidean controversy addressed to nonmedievalists and nonphilosophers, see Jospe, "Faith and Reason."

23. For a brief survey, see Elbogen, *Jewish Liturgy*, 308–332. For a more comprehensive history of this phenomenon, see Petuchowski, *Prayerbook Reform*.

24. For Geiger's views on sacrifice and liturgical reform, see Petuchowski, *Prayerbook Reform*, 33–35, 165–171.

25. Quoted in (and translated by) Petuchowski, *Prayerbook Reform*, 166–167.

26. Bickerman, *Jews in the Greek Age*, 139. This book was published "in cooperation with The Jewish Theological Seminary of America," an institution with which Bickerman had been associated since 1942.

27. See for instance the treatment in the following commentaries, meant for use in modern English-speaking synagogues: Hertz, *Pentateuch*, 486 (on Lev. 17:7) and 560–562; Plaut, *Torah*, 750–755 (comments on sacrifice by Bernard J. Bamberger) and 1217–1218 (comments by W. Gunther Plaut); and now also: Lieber, *Etz Hayim*, 585–586 (comments by Harold Kushner), 1446–1450 (essay by Gordon Tucker). A more sympathetic modernist treatment of temples (but not sacrifice) can be found in certain strains of Zionist thought, where thinkers imagined various modern institutions taking the place of the ancient temple: see Roitman, *Envisioning the Temple*, 127–148, esp. the quotations from Theodore Herzl and Moses Hess on 129–130.

28. For a translation of Sallustius, *On the Gods*, see Murray, *Five Stages of Greek Religion*, 191–212 (quotation from 207). For a discussion of this figure and his day, see Belayche, "Sacrifice and Theory of Sacrifice."

29. See Evans-Pritchard, *Theories of Primitive Religion*, 14–17.

CHAPTER 1

1. Generally, on Douglas's life and work, see Fardon, *Mary Douglas*, esp. 75–105, on *Purity and Danger*.

2. Durkheim, *Elementary Forms*, 337–433; see further discussion of Durkheim later in this chapter.

3. Freud, *Totem and Taboo*, 24–93 (ch. 2).

4. Robertson Smith, *Lectures*, 446–454. There are some significant differences between the first edition of this work (Edinburgh: A. and C. Black, 1889) and the second edition of 1894. As most reprints follow the pagination of the second edition, all citations here do likewise.

5. Robertson Smith, *Lectures*, 447.

6. Robertson Smith, *Lectures*, 447.

7. Robertson Smith, *Lectures*, 447, 449.

8. Douglas, *Purity and Danger*, 7–40 (chs. 1–2).

9. Douglas, *Purity and Danger*, 29–57 (chs. 2–3).

10. Douglas, *Purity and Danger*, 41–57, 114–128 (chs. 3 and 7).

11. Douglas, *Purity and Danger*, 41–57 (ch. 3).

12. Douglas, *Purity and Danger*, 114–179 (chs. 7–10).

13. Douglas, *Purity and Danger*, 18–19, 62–63.

14. Douglas, *Purity and Danger*, 58–72 (ch. 4).

15. Douglas, *Purity and Danger*, 62.

16. See, e.g., Davies, "Interpretation," and Leach, *Culture and Communication.*

17. Lévi-Strauss, *Myth and Meaning*, 16, here summarizing the thrust of *Totemism*, and *Savage Mind*. See also *Savage Mind*, 13–16, 73–74, and *Structural Anthropology*, 230.

18. Lévi-Strauss, *Totemism*, esp. 16, 28; cf. *Structural Anthropology*, 210.

19. For the simplest statement to this effect, see Lévi-Strauss, *Myth and Meaning*, 8; cf. *Structural Anthropology*, 21; *Totemism*, 90. See Douglas's critique, "The Meaning of Myth," reprinted in *Implicit Meanings*, 153–172, as well as Strenski, *Religion in Relation*, 57–74.

20. We must, in the words of Wendy Doniger, "jump off Lévi-Strauss's bus one stop before he does." See Doniger's forward to *Myth and Meaning*, xiv.

21. Lévi-Strauss, *Naked Man*, 667–675; see discussion by J. Z. Smith, "The Domestication of Sacrifice," in Hamerton-Kelly, *Violent Origins*, esp. 193–196, and Smith, *To Take Place*, 111–112. Compare also the sadly comical comments in Eribon, *Conversations*, 6. When commenting on the traditional Jewish observances maintained by his relatives, Lévi-Strauss moves effortlessly from recalling these relatives' ritual proclivities to discussing their bouts with mental illness. Should we not expect the anthropologist to recognize that the correlation between ritual observance and insanity is not a direct one?

22. Lévi-Strauss, *Savage Mind*, 224; cf. *Totemism*, 72–91.

23. Lévi-Strauss, *Totemism*, 101–102; cf. *Structural Anthropology*, 186–205.

24. For Douglas's appreciative comments on Lévi-Strauss, see *Leviticus as Literature*, 22–24.

25. de Heusch, *Sacrifice in Africa*, 1–2, 23–26.

26. Lévi-Strauss, *Savage Mind*, 224; quoting Evans-Pritchard, *Nuer Religion*, 128.

27. Lévi-Strauss, *Savage Mind*, 227. On the distinction between metaphor and metonymy, see Lakoff and Johnson, *Metaphors We Live By*, 35–40. Lévi-Strauss's approach to sacrifice will be revisited further in chapter 2; we will find there that Lévi-Strauss had things backward: if the distinction applies here at all, sacrifice is to be seen as metaphorical, and purity as metonymic.

28. Lévi-Strauss, *Savage Mind*, 228.

29. Lévi-Strauss, *Totemism*, 89.

30. There are indeed very few structuralist interpretations of biblical sacrifice. Edmund Leach's work will be considered further in this chapter. One other treatment deserves mention as a curiosity: Rigby, "Structural Analysis." This work—which is

infrequently cited in the scholarly literature—constitutes one of the few attempts at applying Lévi-Strauss's own methods to Israelite sacrifice. Rigby's essay disappoints, however. Despite his desire to present a synchronic approach, he consistently dates the priestly traditions late, and focuses on material he deems to be earlier (322, 342, 347).

31. Girard, *Violence and the Sacred*, 274.

32. Works that develop the Girardian approach include Hamerton-Kelly, *Gospel and the Sacred* and *Sacred Violence;* Williams, *Bible, Violence, and the Sacred*, and some of the articles collected in *Semeia* 33 (1985): 43–108. The many other scholars who endorse the Girardian approach, at least in part, include Gorman, *Ideology*, 181–189; Gruenwald, *Rituals and Ritual Theory*, 216–217, 259–260, and Rogerson, "What Was the Meaning of Animal Sacrifice."

33. For Girard's own brief summary (on which the following relies), see "Generative Scapegoating," in Hamerton-Kelly, *Violent Origins*, 73–105. On Girard and his work in general, see Burton Mack, introduction to Hamerton-Kelly, *Violent Origins*, 6–22.

34. Girard, *Violence and the Sacred*, 143–168; cf. *Things Hidden*, 3–47, 283–298 as well as Girard's comments in the discussion following his "Generative Scapegoating," in Hamerton-Kelly, *Violent Origins*, 121–129.

35. Girard, *Violence and the Sacred*, 27, 55.

36. Girard, *Violence and the Sacred*, 85, 93; "Generative Scapegoating," in Hamerton-Kelly, *Violent Origins*, 100.

37. Girard, *Violence and the Sacred*, 19, 93.

38. Girard, *Violence and the Sacred*, 93.

39. See, e.g., Girard, "Generative Scapegoating," in Hamerton-Kelly, *Violent Origins*, 107; *Things Hidden*, 443–434; and *Scapegoat*, 140.

40. Girard, *Violence and the Sacred*, 8

41. Girard, *Violence and the Sacred*, 23.

42. Girard, *Violence and the Sacred*, 5; cf. "Generative Scapegoating," in Hamerton-Kelly, *Violent Origins*, 82, 94.

43. For criticisms of Girard, see, e.g., Hecht, "Studies on Sacrifice," 257–258; de Heusch, *Sacrifice in Africa*, 15–17; Smart, review of *Violence and the Sacred*, and Strenski, *Religion in Relation*, 202–216. For a critique focused more directly on biblical studies, see Chilton, *Temple of Jesus*, 15–25, 163–172; see also Chilton, "Hungry Knife."

44. Dunnill, "Methodological Rivalries," 112; compare (without reference to Gnosticism), Strenski, *Religion in Relation*, esp. 204–205, 214–215.

45. Girard, *Violence and the Sacred*, 20–21.

46. See e.g., Girard, *Scapegoat*, 101, 147, 165.

47. See e.g., Girard, *Things Hidden*, 158; *Scapegoat*, 103, 147, 165, 205; cf. the critique in Boyarin, *Radical Jew*, 327–328 n. 30. Boyarin's comments could also apply to supersessionistic comments by another one of Girard's followers; see Williams, *Bible, Violence, and the Sacred*, 175–176.

48. See e.g., Girard, *Things Hidden*, 167; *Scapegoat*, 100–111, 210–211; cf. the critique in Chilton, *Temple of Jesus*, 25.

49. See Hamerton-Kelly, *Gospel and the Sacred* and *Sacred Violence*. See again Boyarin's pointed critique in *Radical Jew*, 214–219, 327–328 nn. 24–31.

50. Girard, "Generative Scapegoating," in Hamerton-Kelly, *Violent Origins*, 121; *Things Hidden*, 231; *Scapegoat*, 147, 179, 212. See also the critique of Chilton, *Temple of Jesus*, 24–25.

51. Compare Douglas, "Go-Away Goat," 121–141, esp. 124.

52. Chilton, *Temple of Jesus*, 25.

53. See Girard, *Violence and the Sacred*, esp. 28–38; cf. Hamerton-Kelly, *Gospel and the Sacred*, 145 (here summarizing Girard's approach): "the essential ingredient in all ritual pollution is violence."

54. Girard, *Violence and the Sacred*, 91.

55. Burkert, "The Problem of Ritual Killing," in Hamerton-Kelly, *Violent Origins* (italics added). See Burkert's rather dismissive comments toward sacrifice, 163; and *Homo Necans*, 7–8. See Douglas's brief comments with regard to Girard and Burkert in "Go-Away Goat," 124.

56. As in, primarily, Hamerton-Kelly, *Violent Origins*; see especially J. Z. Smith's contribution to that volume, "Domestication of Sacrifice," 211–212; but cf., e.g., Milgrom, *Leviticus 1–16*, 442.

57. Burkert, "Problem of Ritual Killing," in Hamerton-Kelly, *Violent Origins*, 171–172; cf. Girard's comments in the discussion following his "Generative Scapegoating," 107–108.

58. See, e.g., Burkert, *Homo Necans*, 82 and 296–297.

59. Burkert, "Problem of Ritual Killing," in Hamerton-Kelly, *Violent Origins*, 172; cf. Burkert, *Structure and History*, 59–77.

60. Burkert, *Homo Necans*, xii, 22–34; "Problem of Ritual Killing," in Hamerton-Kelly, *Violent Origins*, 155–159; *Structure and History*, 1–58.

61. Burkert, "Problem of Ritual Killing," in Hamerton-Kelly, *Violent Origins*, 176.

62. Burkert, *Homo Necans*, 5, 21, 38; cf. Kirk, "Some Methodological Pitfalls," 66–67, and Vernant, "General Theory," 294–295.

63. See Smith, "Domestication of Sacrifice," in Hamerton-Kelly, *Violent Origins*, and see further discussion of these matters in chapter 2.

64. Among recent commentaries and guidebooks, the following exhibit disparities between their generally sympathetic, symbolic (and nonhistoricist) treatment of purity and a notably less sympathetic treatment of sacrifice (usually concerned with the origins of sacrifice): Bernard J. Bamberger, "Leviticus," in Plaut, *Torah*; Budd, *Leviticus*; Gerstenberger, *Leviticus*; Grabbe, *Leviticus*; Hartley, *Leviticus*; Lieber, *Etz Hayim: Torah and Commentary*; Levine, *Leviticus*; and Wenham, *Leviticus*. An important exception to this trend is Gorman, whose works exhibit a broad and sustained interest in the symbolism of ritual, including sacrifice and purity (see esp. *Ideology*, 7–38). Moreover, Gorman helpfully tracks and convincingly counters many of the antiritual biases that have plagued scholarship on priestly matters ("Ritual Studies and Biblical Studies"). Curiously, however, Gorman casts a vote in favor of the Girardian approach (*Ideology*, 181–189). And although his approach is largely sympathetic, he too does not integrate his analyses of purity and sacrifice.

65. I leave aside here Milgrom's treatment of *moral* impurity, which, while interesting, is less germane to the analysis here. For a fuller assessment of Milgrom's approach to ritual and moral purity, see Klawans, "Ritual Purity, Moral Purity, and Sacrifice."

66. Milgrom, *Leviticus 1–16*, 45–46.

67. See Milgrom, *Leviticus 1–16*, 934–935; see also 667, 746, and the general statement on 983.

68. See especially *Leviticus 1–16*, 825–826, 953–968, and 976–1000 (parts of which were prepared with the help of David Wright). For similar approaches to these rules, see Harrington, *Impurity Systems*, and Wright, *Disposal*, both of which originated as dissertations under Milgrom's tutelage.

69. For fuller discussion, see Milgrom, *Leviticus 1–16*, 763–68, 816–820, 948–953, 1000–1004.

70. Milgrom, *Leviticus 1–16*, 46, 766–768, and 1000–1004; quotation from 1002. For further discussion and analysis, see chapter 2.

71. Milgrom, *Leviticus 1–16*, 718–736; see also *Leviticus 23–27*, 2437.

72. Milgrom, *Leviticus 1–16*, 49.

73. Milgrom has also been influenced in this respect (as in many others) by Yehezkel Kaufmann. For a similarly evolutionist approach to sacrifice, see Kaufmann, *Toledot ha-Emunah*, 2:396–403, 560–574; cf. Kaufmann, *Religion of Israel*, 53–55, 110–115.

74. Milgrom, *Leviticus 1–16*, 440.

75. The interpretation is attributed to the fourth-generation amoraic sage, Rabbi Pinhas, who is said to have cited the tradition in the name of the third-generation amoraic sage, Rabbi Levi. If we can accept these attributions, the tradition is to be dated to some time in the early to mid–fourth century C.E., which is approximately a century earlier than the generally accepted date of *Lev. Rabbah* as a whole. At any rate, this is a relatively late rabbinic tradition.

76. On the long dispute over the correct text and proper understanding of *Lev. Rabbah* 22:8, see: Hertz, *Pentateuch*, 562; Heschel, *Theology*, 1:33–53, esp. 42–43; Hirsch, "Sacrifice," 627–628; and Hoffmann, *Leviticus*, 1:79–92. Note that, for instance, Hirsch as a Reform rabbi favored liturgical reforms eliminating sacrificial references from the liturgy and rather disliked sacrifice; he also favored the Maimonidean approach ("Sacrifice," 627–628). Hoffmann, as a traditionalist, explicitly opposed such reforms (*Leviticus*, 1:86), rejected Maimonides' view (1:83), and defended sacrifice as meaningful, expressive, and even symbolic (see esp. 1:86–87).

77. As we will see in Chapter 6, hopes for the restoration of sacrifice appear throughout rabbinic literature and liturgy, even in *Lev. Rabbah*. Maimonides' historicism was truly revolutionary, and the search for ostensible rabbinic precedents is misguided.

78. See also, e.g., Exod. 27:22, 28:43, and Lev. 3:17 and 16:34.

79. See, e.g., Philip P. Jenson, "The Levitical Sacrificial System," in Beckwith and Selman, *Sacrifice in the Bible*, 37–38. Compare Hartley, *Leviticus*, 25, and Wenham, *Leviticus*, 28–29.

80. Milgrom, *Leviticus 1–16*, 440 (italics added); see also 1003 and *Leviticus 23–27*, 2091–2093. Compare the comments of de Vaux, *Studies in Old Testament Sacrifice*, 38–42 and Haran, *Temples and Temple-Service*, 17, 221–225. For the contrary view, see Anderson, *Sacrifices and Offerings*, 14–19, and "Sacrifice and Sacrificial Offerings (OT)," *ABD* 5:872.

81. Milgrom, *Leviticus 1–16*, 442–443; Milgrom here quotes from Bourdillon, introduction to Bourdillon and Fortes, *Sacrifice*, 23.

82. See Milgrom, *Leviticus 1–16*, esp. 440 and 1003; compare Robertson Smith, *Lectures*, 446–456, quoted in part earlier.

83. Milgrom, *Leviticus 1–16*, 307–318, 999; see (on sacrifices) 1002–1003.

84. Milgrom, *Leviticus 1–16*, 35–38; *Leviticus 17–22*, 1325–1330, 1353, 1579, 1702; but see 1578, where he asserts that H's purity is not metaphoric.

85. *Leviticus 17–22*, 1345–1347 (on inner growth of H) and 1579 (from D to H).

86. Blenkinsopp, "Assessment," and Douglas, *Leviticus as Literature*, 33–40 and 128–130.

87. On Robertson Smith's life and work see Beidelman, *W. Robertson Smith*; on sacrifice in particular, see 53–61. For a fuller analysis of his works in their contemporary Christian context, see Bediako, *Primal Religion*.

88. Robertson Smith, *Lectures*, 226–227; cf. 345.

89. Robertson Smith, *Lectures*, 244–245, 385–386.

90. Robertson Smith, *Lectures*, 336–337, 397–398.

91. Robertson Smith, *Lectures*, 395.

92. Robertson Smith, *Lectures*, 240, 252–253.

93. Robertson Smith, *Lectures*, 237–239; but compare Hubert and Mauss, *Sacrifice*, 5–6, and more recently, Milgrom, *Leviticus 1–16*, 172–177. The question remains unsettled.

94. Robertson Smith, *Lectures*, 137–138, 269–311, and 338–339. On Robertson Smith's totemic assumptions, see Beidelman, *W. Robertson Smith*, 35–38, and Bediako, *Primal Religion*, 334–339.

95. Evans-Pritchard, *Theories of Primitive Religion*, 51–53.

96. See, e.g., Robertson Smith, *Lectures*, 15, 24, 439–440. On Robertson Smith's evolutionism, see Beidelman, *W. Robertson Smith*, 29–30, 38–42, 50–51.

97. Robertson Smith, *Lectures*, 85–89.

98. See Bediako, *Primal Religion*, 178–218 and 305–348. On his heresy trial, see Beidelman, *W. Robertson Smith*, 13–22.

99. Robertson Smith, *Lectures*, 269; italics added.

100. Robertson Smith, *Lectures*, 312.

101. Robertson Smith, *Lectures*, 396.

102. Beidleman, *W. Robertson Smith*, 53.

103. Bediako, *Primal Religion*, 371. Robertson Smith may never have resolved fully in his own mind the relationship between the original sacrificial communion and the final Christian one. On these tensions in Robertson Smith's views—and on the curious deletions of certain paragraphs from the first edition of *Lectures*—see Bediako, *Primal Religion*, 366–372.

104. Generally, see Beidelman, *W. Robertson Smith*, 29, 42–49, 58–61, 66–68; Evans-Pritchard, *Theories of Primitive Religion*, 51–53, and Douglas, *Purity and Danger*, 7–28 (ch. 1).

105. See, for instance, Durkheim, *Elementary Forms*, 377–381.

106. See, for instance, Freud, *Totem and Taboo*, 164–173, and note Frazer's dedication of *The Golden Bough* to Robertson Smith.

107. For a full account of this remarkable publication in its social context, see especially Strenski, *Theology and the First Theory of Sacrifice*. See also the same author's *Contesting Sacrifice*, and "Social and Intellectual Origins of Hubert and Mauss's Theory." While overlapping, all three treatments are essential for a fuller understanding of Hubert and Mauss's *Sacrifice*.

108. See, for example, Anderson, "Sacrifice and Sacrificial Offerings (OT)," *ABD* 5:871–872; de Heusch, *Sacrifice in Africa*, 1; Vernant, "General Theory," 290.

109. Strenski, "Social and Intellectual Origins," 511; cf. *Contesting Sacrifice*, 163–164, and *Theology and the First Theory*, 19–20.

110. Mauss and Hubert do not deny all forms of historical development, and they even trace certain ways in which the "Christian imagination has built upon ancient models" (94). But unlike Robertson Smith and Frazer, Mauss and Hubert are just as likely to emphasize continuities with the remote past; the thrust of their work, even if it does not deny all forms of development (or evolution) is to counter the crude and presumptuous evolutionist schemes of Robertson Smith and Frazer. See Strenski, *Religion in Relation*, 77, 83–85, and "Social and Intellectual Origins," 524–526.

111. See Hubert and Mauss, *Sacrifice*, 2–7.

112. Hubert and Mauss, *Sacrifice*, 106–7 n. 9.

113. Hubert and Mauss, *Sacrifice*, 6–7, 17–18, 58–60, 95–97.

114. Hubert and Mauss, *Sacrifice*, 7.

115. Hubert and Mauss, *Sacrifice*, 19–28.

116. Hubert and Mauss, *Sacrifice*, 22–26.

117. Hubert and Mauss, *Sacrifice*, 22.

118. Hubert and Mauss, *Sacrifice*, 20.

119. Burkert, *Structure and History*, 36 and 160 n. 16.

120. De Heusch, *Sacrifice in Africa*, 3–4.

121. See de Heusch, *Sacrifice in Africa*, 3–4, and Detienne and Vernant, *Cuisine of Sacrifice*, 13–16.

122. See, e.g., Hubert and Mauss, *Sacrifice*, 77–94, 100–101; cf. Neusner, *History of the Mishnaic Law of Holy Things*, 6:279 n. 2, with gloss by Richard Sarasson.

123. Strenski, *Contesting Sacrifice*, esp. 156–179; *Theology and the First Theory*, esp. 173–191, and "Social and Intellectual Origins."

124. Strenski, *Contesting Sacrifice*.

125. Hubert and Mauss, *Sacrifice*, 100; see Strenski, *Contesting Sacrifice*, 156–179; *Theology and the First Theory*, 173–191, and "Social and Intellectual Origins."

126. On Lévi and his influence on Hubert, Mauss, and Durkheim, see esp. Strenski, *Durkheim and the Jews of France*, 82–148; cf. "Social and Intellectual Origins," 526–533.

127. Strenski, *Religion in Relation*, 180–201; *Durkheim and the Jews of France*, esp. 124–130.

128. Strenski, *Contesting Sacrifice*; more briefly, see "Social and Intellectual Origins," 512; cf. "Between Theory and Speciality," esp. 12.

129. Girard, *Violence and the Sacred*, 89–90.

130. Strenski, *Religion in Relation*, 76–77; "Social and Intellectual Origins," 516–518; and "Durkheim's Bourgeois Theory of Sacrifice." Strenski focuses on the Durkheimians' approach to sacrifice; he does not note (as it is not part of his project) the degree to which Hubert and Mauss on the one hand and Durkheim on the other approach purity differently.

131. Durkheim, *Elementary Forms*, 378–379, 384–385.

132. Durkheim, *Elementary Forms*, 384–385.

133. On Durkheim's evolutionism—which is certainly more restrained than that of Robertson Smith or Frazer—see Belier, "Durkheim, Mauss, Classical Evolutionism." Compare Strenski, *Religion in Relation*, 77, 83–85, and "Social and Intellectual Origins," 524–526 (calling the Durkheimians "evolutionists"), with Pals, *Seven Theories*, 112–113, who asserts that even Durkheim was an evolutionist in "only a limited way." The differences among these scholars seem to concern more the definition of the term *evolutionism* than the evaluation of Durkheim's work. No one could credibly claim that Durkheim's work was as evolutionist as Frazer's.

134. Durkheim, *Elementary Forms*, 348–349, 365.

135. Durkheim, *Elementary Forms*, 366.

136. Durkheim, *Elementary Forms*, 388–389.

137. See, for instance, Evans-Pritchard, *Theories of Primitive Religion*, 53–69. Compare 70–71, ostensibly criticizing Hubert and Mauss but apparently applying more to Durkheim's chapter on sacrifice in *Elementary Forms*.

138. On Steiner's life and works, see Adler and Fardon, *Franz Baermann Steiner*; a biography of Steiner introduces vol. 1; an essay on his anthropological works introduces vol. 2.

139. See Mary Douglas, "Franz Steiner: A Memoir," in Adler and Fardon, *Franz Baermann Steiner*, 1:3–15; see also Douglas, *Purity and Danger*, vii and 4.

140. Steiner, *Taboo*, 51; reprinted in Adler and Fardon, *Franz Baermann Steiner*, 1:133.

141. See the comments of Marcel Detienne (3) and Jean-Louis Durand (88) in Detienne and Vernant, *Cuisine of Sacrifice*. See also Douglas, *Leviticus as Literature*, 66–67.

142. On these and other charges raised against the food industry, see Schlosser, *Fast Food Nation*. I thank David Seed for bringing this book to my attention.

143. On the moral issues involved with animal research, see Orlans, *In the Name of Science*, and Orlans et al., *Human Use of Animals*.

144. Orlans, *In the Name of Science*, 11, 14; Orlans et al., *Human Use of Animals*, 35, 196.

145. See Leach, *Culture and Communication*, 1–7; see also "Structure of Symbolism."

146. Leach, *Culture and Communication*, 96; Fardon, *Mary Douglas*, 204 n. 2; but see the excerpt from Leach's review of *Natural Symbols* quoted on 103, and Douglas's statement on Leach in her "Franz Steiner: A Memoir," in Adler and Fardon, *Franz Baermann Steiner*, 1:11.

147. See "Logic of Sacrifice," in *Culture and Communication*, 81–94.

148. Leach, *Culture and Communication*, 12–16, 37–45, 83–84.

149. Leach, *Culture and Communication*, 83.

150. Leach, *Culture and Communication*, 92.

151. Working in a similar vein—and at precisely the same time—Douglas Davies authored an essay that explicitly attempted to apply the lessons of Mary Douglas's *Purity and Danger* to the sacrificial rules of Leviticus; see Davies, "Interpretation of Sacrifice," 151–162. Like Leach in his essay, Davies focused on sacrifice in isolation from ritual purity and on atonement above all other motivations for sacrifice. But here too we find one of the rare instances in which Douglas's methods were applied to the study of sacrifice. See 162 n. 28 for Davies's statement regarding the similarity of his essay with Leach's.

152. Eilberg-Schwartz, *Savage*, 125.

153. Eilberg-Schwartz, *Savage*, 141–176.

154. Eilberg-Schwartz, *Savage*, 122–126.

155. Eilberg-Schwartz, *Savage*, 133–138.

156. Chilton, *Temple of Jesus*, 3–42, 163–180.

157. Chilton, *Temple of Jesus*, 41, citing Detienne and Vernant, *Cuisine of Sacrifice*.

158. Detienne and Vernant, *Cuisine of Sacrifice*, 4–5.

159. Chilton does spend a little time discussing the notion that the temple represents the cosmos, as noted by Josephus (*Temple of Jesus*, 80). But he barely mentions Philo's symbolic discussions of sacrifice, and he says little if anything about other ancient Jewish symbolic understandings of the temple or sacrifice, such as will be discussed in chapter 4. Rather, Chilton's discussions of symbolism are largely contained in his general discussions of sacrificial theory.

160. For the author's fuller assessment of this work, see Klawans, "Rethinking Leviticus." I reproduce here only what pertains directly to the themes at hand.

161. Douglas, *Leviticus as Literature*, 1.

162. Douglas, *Leviticus as Literature*, 59.

163. Douglas, *Leviticus as Literature*, 221–222, with chart on 223.

164. Douglas, *Leviticus as Literature*, 68.

165. Douglas, *Leviticus as Literature*, 20–25, which largely reformulates the methodological insights of *Purity and Danger*. For the term "piecemeal" see *Purity and Danger*, 41.

166. Douglas, *Leviticus as Literature*, 62, 79.

167. Douglas, *Leviticus as Literature*, 71–72, 81–86.

168. Douglas, *Leviticus as Literature*, 163–166.

169. Douglas, *Leviticus as Literature*, 77–78.

170. Kirk, "Some Methodological Pitfalls," 54.

171. Milgrom, *Leviticus 1–16*, 440–444; cf. Anderson, "Sacrifice and Sacrificial Offerings (OT)," *ABD* 5:871.

172. Baruch A. Levine spoke of an "organizing principle" as an alternative to theory in his "Prolegomenon" to Gray, *Sacrifice in the Old Testament*, vii–xliv, esp. xxxi.

CHAPTER 2

1. For a brief treatment of the nature and contours of the Priestly strand (P), see Jacob Milgrom, "Priestly ('P') Source," *ABD* 5:454–461; for a brief treatment of the Holiness Code, see Henry T. C. Sun, "Holiness Code," *ABD* 3:254–257. See also the discussions in Knohl, *Sanctuary of Silence*, and Milgrom, *Leviticus 1–16*, 1–63, and *Leviticus 17–22*, 1319–1364. Leviticus 27 is generally recognized to be an appendix to the book and thus not originally integral to either source; most view Leviticus 27 as closer to H than P. Generally, see Milgrom, *Leviticus 23–27*, 2407–2409.

2. For the history of distinction between P and H, see Sun, "Holiness Code," *ABD* 3:254–257, and Kugler, "Holiness, Purity," 3–8. See also Rolf Rendtorff, "Is It Possible to Read Leviticus as a Separate Book?" in Sawyer, *Reading Leviticus*, 27–29.

3. Wellhausen, *Prolegomena*, 86 n. 1, 376–384.

4. See Knohl, *Sanctuary of Silence*; see also Milgrom, *Leviticus 23–27*, 2440–2446.

5. See, e.g., Kaufmann, *Toledot ha-Emunah*, 2:532–588 (cf. Kaufmann, *Religion of Israel*, 101–121); Haran, *Temples and Temple-Service*, 1–12 and 132–148; Weinfeld, *Deuteronomy and the Deuteronomic School*, 179–190; cf. Blenkinsopp, "Assessment," 496–499.

6. Briefly, see Blenkinsopp, *Pentateuch*, 11–12, and Silberman, "Wellhausen and Judaism."

7. On Kaufmann's evolutionism, see Blenkinsopp, "Assessment," 496–499. Milgrom's response ("Antiquity of the Priestly Source") does not respond to the charge of evolutionism.

8. Knohl, *Sanctuary of Silence*, 138–139; see also 175–180, 214–216, and 222–224.

9. Knohl, *Sanctuary of Silence*, 223. Theoretically, one could describe P as being less interested in ethics without being critical of P—one could posit, for instance, that the purposes and audiences of the traditions are so different that P's (alleged) failure to address ethics is not necessarily indicative of a total disinterest in ethics. Nonetheless, it is clear from Knohl's rhetoric here and in the passages cited in the previous note that he views H in a more positive light than P.

10. Milgrom, *Leviticus 1–16*, 21–26; *Leviticus 17–22*, 1400–1404; and *Leviticus 23–27*, 2440–2446.

11. Douglas, *Leviticus as Literature*, 33–34, 128–131; term used on 129.

12. Knohl, *Sanctuary of Silence*, 1–7 and 199–224; see also Milgrom, *Leviticus 17–22*, 1319–1364.

13. Milgrom, *Leviticus 23–27*, 2444.

14. Blenkinsopp, "Assessment"; Douglas, *Leviticus as Literature*, 1; Rendtorff, "How to Approach Leviticus," 13–20; Rendtorff, "Is It Possible to Read Leviticus as a Separate Book?" in Sawyer, *Reading Leviticus*; Rendtorff, "Two Kinds of P." See also Rendtorff's commentary-in progress, *Leviticus*. An earlier articulation of this approach

can be found in Brichto, "On Slaughter and Sacrifice," 43, 47, and 50–55. See also the comments of Eilberg-Schwartz, *Savage*, 124 and Geller, *Sacred Enigmas*, 62–64.

15. Blenkinsopp, "Assessment," 497. For further reflections on the (limited) value of dating documents, see Rendtorff, "Paradigm," 49–50.

16. J. Z. Smith's comments were uttered in a conversation transcribed in Hamerton-Kelly, *Violent Origins*, 210. Compare the more recent comments to the same general effect in J. Z. Smith, "Religion Up and Down, Out and In," in Gittlen, *Sacred Time, Sacred Place*, 3–10.

17. Knierim, *Text and Concept*, 17–22, 98–101. Knierim explicitly discusses the structuralist reading of Rigby ("Structural Analysis"), which is a rather "orthodox" application of Levi-Strauss's own structuralism. Knierim's critique does not explicitly address the approaches by Davies, Leach, or Douglas. See Wright, review of Knierim's *Text and Concept*.

18. See, esp., Gorman, *Ideology*.

19. Gorman senses this: see *Ideology*, 7.

20. See Geertz, *Interpretation of Cultures*, 3–32, esp. 9–10 and 29.

21. For a fuller summary of ancient Israelite sacrificial worship see Anderson, "Sacrifice and Sacrificial Offerings (OT)," *ABD* 5:870–886.

22. Anderson, "Sacrifice and Sacrificial Offerings (OT)," *ABD* 5:871.

23. Ancient Israel's sacrificial worship included (among other things) offerings of grain (Lev. 2:1–16), bread (Lev. 24:5–9), and incense (Exod. 30:34–38). On the significance of the incense altar, for example, see Carol Meyers, "Realms of Sanctity: The Case of the 'Misplaced' Incense Altar in the Tabernacle Texts of Exodus," in Fox et al., *Texts, Temples, and Traditions*, 33–46.

24. The nature and significance of this distinction is the subject of Klawans, *Impurity and Sin*. The reader is referred to the introduction and first chapter of that work for fuller description of the distinction, and the history of the discussion. Other important discussions include Büchler, *Studies in Sin and Atonement*; Frymer-Kensky, "Pollution"; Hoffmann, *Leviticus*; and Wright, "Unclean and Clean (OT)," *ABD* 6:729–741.

25. The intricacies of the ritual purity laws are covered well, as we have observed, in Milgrom's works, especially *Leviticus 1–16*.

26. An important exception in this regard is King Uzziah's leprosy, which continued until his death (2 Chron. 26:21).

27. E.g., Wright, "Spectrum," and "Unclean and Clean (OT)," *ABD* 6:729–741; see also Miller, *Religion of Ancient Israel*, 149–155.

28. See 1 Kgs. 14:24 (sexual sins); Jer. 2:7, 23 (idolatry); Jer. 3:1 (sexual sins); Ezek. 20:30–31 (idolatry); 33:25–26 (sexual sins and bloodshed); Hos. 5:3, 6:10 (general unfaithfulness); and also Ps. 106:35–40 (idolatry and bloodshed); cf. Amos 2:7 (sexual immorality as a profanation of God's name).

29. On sacrifice, atonement, and purification, see Milgrom, *Leviticus 1–16*, 254–278, 373–378.

30. Milgrom, *Leviticus 1–16*, 766–768 and 1000–1004, quotation from 1002. For a critical discussion of the impurity-as-death theory, see Eilberg-Schwartz, *Savage*, 182–186 and 248 n. 16.

31. On the dietary laws in general as understood in this light, see Milgrom, *Leviticus 1–16*, 704–742, 732–733, and 741–742. On the pig's role in chthonic worship, see Milgrom, *Leviticus 1–16*, 649–653; on the blood prohibition, see Gorman, *Ideology*, 181–189; and Milgrom, *Leviticus 1–16*, 704–713; on the role of blood in sacrificial rituals, see discussion later in this chapter. For a critique of Milgrom's approach to the

food laws, and for more on the dietary prohibitions, see Houston, *Purity and Monotheism*.

32. Milgrom, *Leviticus 1–16*, 732–733.

33. We discussed earlier in chapter 1 Leach's observation regarding the fluidity of the terms "theory" and "metaphor." We have seen that scholars take some metaphors of sacrifice (i.e., sacrifice as gift) and elevate them to the level of theory. The observation could apply here as well, though what we have in this case is, strictly speaking, not metaphor but metonymy. Briefly put, the difference is this: in metaphor, there is generally no direct relationship between the tenor and the vehicle; the relation is indirect, through some analogy. A metonym, however, exhibits a more direct, indexical, relationship with the item it stands for. According to Milgrom and those who preceded him, each of the substances that defiles ritually is one step or more removed—but still connected directly, not by analogy—to the phenomenon of death. This relationship, is therefore, strictly speaking, *metonymic*, and not metaphorical. On the distinction between metaphor and metonym, see Lakoff and Johnson, *Metaphors We Live By*, 35–40.

34. Milgrom, *Leviticus 1–16*, 766 and 1001–1002. See for instance, Feldman, *Biblical and Post-Biblical Defilement*, 13–30.

35. Edersheim, *Temple*, 348–350.

36. See Meigs, "Papuan Perspective," which Milgrom cites in his discussion (*Leviticus 1–16*, 1001). On the centrality of death to the Zoroastrian impurity system, see Choksy, *Purity and Pollution*, 16–19. Death also figures prominently in ancient Greek conceptions of impurity; see Parker, *Miasma*, 32–73.

37. In ancient Egyptian religion, for instance, corpses were purified in order to secure their safe passage into the next world, but corpses were not considered a source of ritual defilement for the living. Indeed, corpses were brought into sanctuaries; see Blackman, "Purification (Egyptian)."

38. This same question is also posed by Eilberg-Schwartz, *Savage*, 186.

39. Frymer-Kensky, "Pollution," 401; Frymer-Kensky, *In the Wake*, 189; Wright, "Unclean and Clean (OT)," *ABD* 6:739. See also Maccoby, *Ritual and Morality*, 30–31, 49–50. On the more general question of the role of gender in the ritual purity system, see Eilberg-Schwartz, *Savage*, 178–182, and Klawans, *Impurity and Sin*, 38–41. For an analysis of ancient Israelite sacrifice under the lens of gender studies, see Jay, *Throughout Your Generations*. But note the pointed critique in Strenski, "Between Theory and Speciality," 13–17. Jay is followed in part (but with regard to Greek sacrifice, not Israelite) by Stowers, "Greeks Who Sacrifice."

40. Wright, "Unclean and Clean (OT)," *ABD* 6:739; cf. Wright, "Holiness, Sex, and Death."

41. Frymer-Kensky, *In the Wake*, 189.

42. Hubert and Mauss, *Sacrifice*, 20; see also 84–85.

43. On the issue of control and its relationship to ancient Israelite ritual purity and sacrifice, see Eilberg-Schwartz, *Savage*, 186–194; cf. Klawans, "Pure Violence," 144–145.

44. On Walter Burkert's theory of sacrificial origins, see chapter 1. Whether or not sacrifice finds its origins in some form of the domestication of the hunt, it must be kept in mind that sacrifice is generally—and certainly in ancient Israel— performed on domesticated animals by agrarians and pastoralists. See discussion of this issue in the next section.

45. Jonathan Z. Smith, "The Domestication of Sacrifice," in Hamerton-Kelly, *Violent Origins*, 191–205, quotation from 199.

46. Smith, "Domestication of Sacrifice," in Hamerton-Kelly, *Violent Origins*, 197.

47. Smith, "Domestication of Sacrifice," in Hamerton-Kelly, *Violent Origins*, 204; this is the thesis of Isaac, "On the Domestication of Cattle"; see also Girard, *Things Hidden*, 68–73.

48. Smith, "Domestication of Sacrifice," in Hamerton-Kelly, *Violent Origins*, 206.

49. Smith, in conversation transcribed in Hamerton-Kelly, *Violent Origins*, 213.

50. Smith, "Domestication of Sacrifice," in Hamerton-Kelly, *Violent Origins*, 191–196; see also Smith's comments in the discussion that follows, 206–214, 224–225.

51. Smith, "Domestication of Sacrifice," in Hamerton-Kelly, *Violent Origins*, 199.

52. B. D. Smith, *Emergence of Agriculture*, 18. With special attention to the animals of the biblical world, see also Edwin Firmage, "Zoology (Fauna)," *ABD* 6:1111–1167.

53. B. D. Smith, *Emergence of Agriculture*, 18.

54. See B. D. Smith, *Emergence of Agriculture*, 28–33.

55. On Israel's dietary rules, see Milgrom, *Leviticus 1–16*, 641–742; Eilberg-Schwartz, *Savage*, 125–126, 218–221, and Houston, *Purity and Monotheism*. Douglas, *Purity and Danger*, 41–57, remains important, but Douglas herself has revisited the topic and changed her views a number of times: see "Deciphering a Meal" and "Self-Evidence" (both reprinted in *Implicit Meanings*, 249–318). Douglas's more recent treatments include: "A Bird, a Mouse;" "The Forbidden Animals," and *Leviticus as Literature*, 134–175.

56. Milgrom, *Leviticus 1–16*, 721–726.

57. On animal metaphors in ancient Israel, see Eilberg-Schwartz, *Savage*, 115–140. With regard to domestication and Greek sacrifice, see Stowers, "Greeks Who Sacrifice," esp. 329; Stowers's analysis also builds on Eilberg-Schwartz and J. Z. Smith.

58. Eilberg-Schwartz, *Savage*, 120–121, and 247 n. 5.

59. For the image of God protecting his flock, see, e.g., Gen. 49:24, Isa. 40:11, and Jer. 31:10. For the image of God guiding his flock see, e.g., Isa. 40:11, 49:10–11, 63:13–14; Jer. 23:3–4, 31:10, 50:19; Ezek. 34:13; Mic. 2:12, 7:14; Ps. 23:1–3, 78:52, and 80:2. For the image of feeding see Jer. 50:19; Ezek. 34:13–15; Hos. 4:16; Mic. 7:14; and Ps. 23:1–3. For the image of slaughter, see Isa. 53:7; Jer. 12:3, 51:40; Ezek. 34:16; and Ps. 44:12, 23. Other general references to God as shepherd include Jer. 13:17; Ps. 74:1, 79:13, 95:7, and 100:3. For extended passages incorporating many of the foregoing images (and others as well) see Ezekiel 34 and Zechariah 10–13. At times, God is depicted as ruling over Israel's shepherds—dismissing Israel's failed leaders, and appointing new ones (e.g., Jer. 23:1–4, and Ezek. 34:1). But even in these passages, it is also asserted that God too is to play the role of shepherd (Jer. 23:3–4; Ezek. 34:10). Some have creatively argued that passages such as Psalm 23:1–3 do not mean that Israel understood God as a shepherd: see Matthews and Benjamin, *Social World of Ancient Israel*, 63–64. The prevalence of these images, however, compels us to take them seriously.

60. For this approach, see Rogerson, "What Was the Meaning of Animal Sacrifice," 8–17.

61. On the vagaries of the term "vegetarian," see, e.g., Osborne, "Ancient Vegetarianism."

62. See, e.g., Gruenwald, *Rituals and Ritual Theory*, 40–93.

63. For literary and archaeological evidence on farming and herding in ancient Israel, see Matthews and Benjamin, *Social World of Ancient Israel*, 37–66.

64. On the tabernacle and the temple, see Frank Moore Cross, *From Epic to Canon*, 84–95. See also Haran, *Temples and Temple Service*.

65. Generally, on temples and the cosmos, see Clements, *God and Temple*; compare the broad theoretical discussion in Eliade, *Myth of the Eternal Return*, 3–48. On cosmic symbolism as manifested in the tabernacle and Solomonic temple, see Bloch-Smith, " 'Who Is the King of Glory,' " Levenson, *Sinai and Zion*, 111–137; Stager, "Jerusalem and the Garden of Eden," and Wenham, "Sanctuary Symbolism." For reviews of the ancient Near Eastern evidence, see Lundquist, "Common Temple Ideology," and "What Is a Temple." For an even broader survey, see Fox, *Temple in Society*.

66. Levenson, *Creation and the Persistence of Evil*, 78–99 and 100–120; *Sinai and Zion*, 142–145; see also Fishbane, *Text and Texture*, 3–16. For some observations on *imitatio Dei* relating more directly to sacrifice, see also Levenson, *Death and Resurrection*, 25–32.

67. Hubert and Mauss, *Sacrifice*, 19–49.

68. Anderson, "Sacrifice and Sacrificial Offerings (OT)," *ABD* 5:875.

69. Gerstenberger, *Leviticus*, 26–27. Of course, other commentators provide their own lists, more or less similar to Anderson's or Gerstenberger's. See, for instance, Hartley, *Leviticus*, 15, and Wenham, *Leviticus*, 52–55.

70. Gerstenberger, *Leviticus*, 26, 29; cf. Wenham, *Leviticus*, 55.

71. E.g., Lev. 1:10, 3:1, 6; 4:3, and so on; see also Deut. 17:1. See Milgrom, *Leviticus 17–22*, 1873–1874.

72. On these regulations, see Milgrom, *Leviticus 17–22*, 1870–1892.

73. On this regulation in particular, see Douglas, "Forbidden Animals," 18–23; "Holy Joy," 10–14; and "Sacred Contagion," in Sawyer, *Reading Leviticus*, 101–106.

74. Douglas, *Purity and Danger*, 53–54; Milgrom, *Leviticus 17–22*, 1873.

75. See Gerstenberger, *Leviticus*, 26, 29; and Wenham, *Leviticus*, 55.

76. See Buckley, "Matter of Urgency," especially 68: "as if prepared for war—loins girded, feet sandaled, staff in hand (v. 11)—they are to eat on the run, which is what God is doing."

77. See Jer. 11:20, 12:3, 17:10, 20:12; Ps. 7:10; Prov. 17:3; 1 Chron. 29:17; cf. Ezek. 21:26.

78. The NJPS reads "test the thoughts and the mind"; the NRSV reads: "who try the heart and mind"; the RSV reads "who triest the heart and the mind." For a more literal reading one must go back to the KJV, which reads: "that triest the reins and heart." See also Brown, Driver, and Briggs, *Lexicon*, s.v. "כליות."

79. We cannot consider here all the complex issues involved in blood symbolism in sacrificial rites. On blood in the Hebrew Bible in general, see S. David Sperling, "Blood," *ABD* 1:761–763. On blood and sacrifice, see Brichto, "On Slaughter and Sacrifice"; on blood symbolism, see the contributions of Hendel, "Sacrifice as a Cultural System," and Geller, *Sacred Enigmas*, 62–86. Gorman's treatment of blood symbolism, by contrast, is nearly Girardian; see *Ideology*, 181–189.

80. Generally, on God as divine warrior, see Cross, *Canaanite Myth*, 91–215; and Miller, *Divine Warrior*.

81. Generally, on the notion of holy war, see Von Rad, *Holy War*, and Niditch, *War in the Hebrew Bible*. On sacrificial aspects of holy war ideology see Niditch, *War in the Hebrew Bible*, 28–55. In the (priestly) wilderness traditions, God's residence finds its place in the midst of a war camp. Moreover, ritual purity is a prerequisite for holy war, just as it is for sacrifice (Deut. 23:10–15; Josh. 3:5, 7:13; 1 Sam. 21:6; 2 Sam. 11:11); see Von Rad, *Holy War*, 42.

82. I thank Jon D. Levenson for bringing this aspect of Isa. 63 to my attention.

83. We discuss this aspect of the sacrificial process in greater detail in chapter 3.

84. See also Jer. 46:10 and Ezek. 39:17–20; see Isa. 30:27, in which God's "sifting" of the nations is described with the same term as the priestly "waving" of sacrificial offerings (e.g., Lev. 9:21).

85. Haran, *Temples and Temple Service*, 17; see also 221–225. Haran here follows Kaufmann, *Toledot ha-Emunah*, 2:396–403 and 560–574; cf. *Religion of Israel*, 53–55 and 110–105. Essentially the same approach was taken by de Vaux, *Studies in Old Testament Sacrifice*, 38–42. For a more recent articulation of this view, see Milgrom, *Leviticus 1–16*, 440. For a critique of this kind of approach, see Anderson, *Sacrifices and Offerings*, 14–19, and "Sacrifice and Sacrificial Offerings (OT)," *ABD* 5:872.

86. See, e.g., Deut. 4:24, 9:3, 32:22, Isa. 30:27, and Lam. 2:3; see also 2 Kgs. 1:10–11, Ps. 18:9, and 2 Sam. 22:9. This phenomenon represents yet another interrelationship between sacrifice and holy war.

87. See, e.g., Exod. 24:17; Lev. 9:24; 10:2; Num. 9:15, 16:35; Judg. 6:21, 13:20; 1 Kgs. 18:38; see also Gen. 15:17 and 1 Chron. 21:26.

88. For a useful and readable survey of the complex philosophical debates on metaphor and their impact on contemporary understandings of religious language, see Stiver, *Philosophy of Religious Language*, 112–133. Further on philosophy and metaphor, see the helpful collection of essays in Sacks, *On Metaphor*, which contains seminal essays by, among others, Donald Davidson and Paul Ricoeur. Perhaps the most challenging (and most readable) contemporary philosophical work on metaphor is Lakoff and Johnson, *Metaphors We Live By*. On the linguistic side of the question, see Kittay, *Metaphor*. For an anthropological perspective on metaphor, see. e.g., Fernandez, *Persuasions and Performances*, 3–70, and Lévi-Strauss, *Totemism*. For a brief survey of some of the relevant anthropological literature, with specific attention to biblical metaphors, see Eilberg-Schwartz, *Savage*, 115–140. Another useful and readable work that is more directly related to the Hebrew Bible is Caird, *Language and Imagery*. Despite the fact that this work is often confessional (e.g., 271) and at times offensive (e.g., 143, where Jewish dietary laws are described as "tyranny"), it contains helpful discussions of meaning in general (35–84) and metaphor in particular (see 131–159).

89. On the antimetaphorical bias in Western philosophy, see Ted Cohen, "Metaphor and the Cultivation of Intimacy," in Sacks, *On Metahpor*, 1–3; Lakoff and Johnson, *Metaphors We Live By*, 189–192, and Stiver, *Philosophy of Religious Language*, 8–13, 112–114.

90. See especially Lakoff and Johnson, *Metaphors We Live By*. See also Fernandez, *Persuasions and Performances*, 32–36, 58; Lévi-Strauss, *Totemism*, 102, and Stiver, *Philosophy of Religious Language*, 112–133. On biblical metaphors in particular, see Eilberg-Schwartz, *Savage*, 117–121.

91. Eilberg-Schwartz is a notable exception.

92. Actually, this statement deserves qualification. Some sacrificial metaphors, like those we catalogued here, are systematically ignored. Other sacrificial metaphors—like the analogy between sacrifices and gifts (e.g., Num. 18:12) or between sacrifice and food (e.g., Ezek. 44:16)—receive attention. But these metaphors have been elevated arbitrarily to the level of "theory." See Leach, *Culture and Communication*, 83, and my comments on Leach's essay in chapter 1.

93. Caird, *Language and Imagery*, 185–197.

94. Caird, *Language and Imagery*, 246.

95. Generally, see Fernandez, *Persuasions and Performances*, 23–24; Lakoff and Johnson, *Metaphors We Live By*, 147–155. On biblical metaphors in particular, see Eilberg-Schwartz, *Savage*, 122–126.

96. On metaphor and ritual generally, see Fernandez, *Persuasions and Performances*, 21–23, 41–50; Geertz, *Interpretation of Cultures*, 412–453; Lakoff and Johnson, *Metaphors We Live By*, 233–235, and Turner, *Dramas, Fields, and Metaphors*, 23–59. With regard to the Hebrew Bible specifically, see Eilberg-Schwartz, *Savage*, 119, 122–129. Some prefer to understand rituals as metonymic. On the distinction between metaphor and metonymy, see Lakoff and Johnson, *Metaphors We Live By*, 35–40. For a theory of sacrifice as metonymic, see Lévi-Strauss, *Savage Mind*, 222–228.

97. I follow Leach in this respect against Lévi-Strauss. Where Lévi-Strauss dismissed sacrifice as metonymic and largely nonsensical (*Savage Mind*, 222–228), Leach defended sacrifice in general (and ancient Israelite sacrifice in particular) as logical, symbolic, and metaphorical (*Culture and Communication*, 81–93). Going one step further than Leach, it is worth observing that this analysis constitutes a near reversal of Lévi-Strauss's approach, which dismissed sacrifice as metonymic and praised totemism as metaphorical. In my view, ritual purity—which constitutes the shunning of substances one or two steps removed from death—is the more metonymic of the two structures, while sacrifice is the metaphorical one.

98. On ritual, analogy, and metaphor—and for further arguments in defense of the kind of approach pursued here—see Wright, "Analogy in Biblical and Hittite Ritual," "Blown Away Like a Bramble," and "Ritual Analogy in Psalm 109."

99. Compare the situation with other ritual structures that can be understood in light of *imitatio Dei:* e.g., Israelites resting on the recurring seventh day of the week while God rested on the eternal seventh day of creation; Israelites constructing a temple on earth while God constructed the earth itself. On the limits of and problems relating to *imitatio Dei*, see Eilberg-Schwartz, *Savage*, 192–194.

100. See J. David Sapir, "Anatomy of Metaphor," in Sapir and Crocker, *Social Use of Metaphor*, 3–32, esp. 5–12; see also Geertz, *Interpretation of Cultures*, 210–211.

101. J. Z. Smith, *To Take Place*, 109.

102. Bell, *Ritual Theory*, 19–46, is rather critical of many symbolic approaches to ritual, and J. Z. Smith, *To Take Place*, 83–86, 96–117, speaks of certain biblical practices in particular as examples of arbitrary ritual. Of those currently working on biblical ritual, perhaps the most emphatic proponent of the nonsymbolic nature of ritual in general and biblical sacrifice in particular is Gruenwald, *Ritual and Ritual Theory*. See Klawans, review of Gruenwald's *Ritual and Ritual Theory*.

103. See Turner, *Forest of Symbols*, 20–47, 50–52, 292–296.

104. Turner, *Forest of Symbols*, 50–51; cf. Anderson, "Sacrifice and Sacrificial Offerings (OT)," *ABD* 5:871.

105. On this issue, see Douglas, *Leviticus as Literature*, 66–86.

106. For discussions concerning the divine presence in ancient Israel, see Kaufmann, *Toledot ha-Emunah*, 5:473–476; Levine, "On the Presence of God," and Wenham, *Leviticus*, 16–18. See also Gorman, *Divine Presence*, 10–17, 20. For some recent rethinking of the biblical conceptions of the divine presence, see Sommer, "Conflicting Constructions," and "Expulsion as Initiation."

107. Elizabeth Bloch-Smith, "Solomon's Temple: The Politics of Ritual Space," in Gittlen, *Sacred Time, Sacred Place*, 83–94, and Haran, *Temples and Temple Service*, 225–226, 246–259.

108. On the term "tabernacle," see Cross, *Canaanite Myth*, 298–300.

109. On this term, see Fox, *Five Books of Moses*, 497; Levine, "On the Presence of God," 80; and Milgrom, *Leviticus 1–16*, 145.

110. See Levine, *In the Presence*, 22–27; and "On the Presence of God," 79–80; cf. Anderson, "Sacrifice and Sacrificial Offerings (OT)," *ABD* 5:878.

111. See also Abraham's covenant of pieces (Gen. 15:17), which may or may not technically be a sacrifice.

112. Anderson, *Sacrifices and Offerings*, 91–126.

113. Translation quoted earlier by Anderson, from his discussion in *Sacrifices and Offerings*, 14–19. Anderson builds on Tigay, *Evolution*, 227–229 and 296. See also Pritchard, *Ancient Near Eastern Texts*, 95.

114. For a different view on sacrifice as a means of maintenance, see Gorman, *Divine Presence*, 7–8, and *Ideology*, 54–55, 220–221. Gorman categorizes the daily burnt offering as a "ritual of maintenance" (his two other categories are rituals of "founding" and "restoration"). Though somewhat commensurate with the analysis suggested here, Gorman's work focuses more on the functions of sacrifice and less on its possible symbolic values. Gorman also does not seek to link his understanding of sacrifice with an understanding of purity (whether ritual or moral).

115. See also Exod. 19:12, 22, 28:43, 30:20; Lev. 10:9; but cf. Lev. 21:23.

116. Wenham, *Leviticus*, 25–29.

117. See, e.g., Eilberg-Schwartz, *Savage*, 134–136; Milgrom, *Leviticus 1–16*, 153–154 and 172–177; and Wenham, *Leviticus*, 25–29 and 59–63.

118. See Anderson, *Sacrifices and Offerings*, 91–126; Gray, *Sacrifice in the Old Testament*, 1–54; Kaufmann, *Toledot ha-Emunah*, 2:560–574; Levine, *In the Presence*, 22–27, and "On the Presence of God," 79–80, and Marx, "Theology of the Sacrifice."

119. There is another form of ritual killing that, at least in a way, does serve more directly to undo the effects of moral impurity: capital punishment. On capital punishment as an antidote to moral defilement, see, e.g., Gen. 9:4–7 and Num. 35:30–4; for a later tradition, see *Jubilees* 7:33. That sacrifice and capital punishment conceptually can be seen in shared terminology (e.g., compare "laying hands" in Lev. 1:4 and Lev. 24:14) and in parallel rules (e.g., compare Deut. 21:22 and Lev. 22:19; see Eilberg-Schwartz, *Savage*, 123). Compare too the earlier-noted conceptual overlap between sacrifice and holy war. But capital punishment cannot properly be understood as a sacrifice per se, for there is no selection, no altar, no dissection, no daubing of blood, and no consumption (except in the case of burning).

CHAPTER 3

1. See, for example, Burkert, *Homo Necans*, 7; Girard, *Violence and the Sacred*, 43, and Williams, *Bible, Violence, and the Sacred*, 129–162. For ancient and medieval precedents, see, e.g., Hebrews 10:4–9 and Maimonides, *Guide of the Perplexed*, III:32, 72a–73a (trans. Pines, 2:529–531).

2. See, for example, Wellhausen, *Prolegomena*, 392–401, 422–425, and (reprinted from his encyclopedia article "Israel") 473–474. For a survey of the history of scholarship on prophecy, see Blenkinsopp, *History of Prophecy*, 16–26, and Wilson, *Prophecy and Society*, 1–20. For a general treatment of prophecy, see John J. Schmitt, "Prophecy (Preexilic Hebrew)," *ABD* 5:482–489. For a brief book-by-book assessment of current trends in scholarship on Isaiah, Jeremiah, and Ezekiel, see Sweeney, "Latter Prophets."

3. On the circumstances of Weber's *Wirtschaft und Gesellschaft* in general and on the portions pertinent to our interests in particular, see Ephraim Fischoff's preface to Weber, *Sociology of Religion*, xix–xxvii.

4. Weber, *Sociology of Religion*, 30; compare Wellhausen, *Prolegomena*, 397–398.

5. Weber, *Sociology of Religion*, 46; again, compare Wellhausen, *Prolegomena*, 397–398.

6. For further references to works from the days of Weber and Wellhausen, see discussions in Blenkinsopp, *History of Prophecy*, 16–26, and Wilson, *Prophecy and Society*, 1–8. For a recent articulation of such an approach—much more nuanced, to be sure, than Wellhausen's—see Albertz, *History of Israelite Religion*, 1:171–175.

7. Berger, "Charisma and Religious Innovation," 942. See also Anderson, "Sacrifice and Sacrificial Offerings (OT)," *ABD* 5:881.

8. See, e.g., Kaufmann, *Toledot ha-Emunah*, 2:538; cf. *Religion of Israel*, 103.

9. Kaufmann (in the passage noted earlier) speaks of "development" and not a stark Wellhausen-like contrast. Kaufmann also notes that the prophetic rejection of the cult—even Amos's—is not categorical: *Toledot ha-Emunah*, 7:71–76, 194–195, 282–283; 8:443–446; cf. *Religion of Israel*, 364–365, 385, 396–397, 418–419. We will discuss the approach taken by Milgrom later in this chapter. Note, however, the rather sharp contrast drawn in Knohl, *Sanctuary of Silence*, as discussed in chapter 2.

10. See, for instance, the discussions of priests and prophets in Blenkinsopp, *Sage, Priest, Prophet*, 66–114 (on priests), and 115–165 (on prophets).

11. Ronald S. Hendel, "Prophets, Priests, and the Efficacy of Ritual," in Wright et al., *Pomegranates*, 191 (italics in the original).

12. Hendel, "Prophets, Priests," in Wright et al., *Pomegranates*, 190–191; see also Williams, "Social Location."

13. McKane, "Prophet and Institution," 266.

14. McKane, "Prophet and Institution," 253.

15. Buber's work is discussed in McKane, "Prophet and Institution," 260–261, and "Prophecy and the Prophetic Literature," 177. More generally, see Ulrich E. Simon, "Martin Buber and the Interpretation of the Prophets," in Coggins et al., *Israel's Prophetic Tradition*, 250–261.

16. Source-critical problems run throughout the prophetic books: questions are raised, for example, concerning the authenticity of oracles in Amos 2 and even Isaiah 1. For a source-critical evaluation of the status of Amos 2:4–5 (e.g.), see Andersen and Freedman, *Amos*, 294–306. A number of scholars now maintain that the first two chapters of Isaiah (or at least parts of them) serve as an introduction to the *entire* book of Isaiah; as such, the chapter was redacted (and perhaps partially composed) as late as the fifth century B.C.E. See, e.g., Sweeney, *Isaiah 1–39*, 67–69. For the contrary view, see Tomasino, "Isaiah 1.1–2.4 and 63–66."

17. Following scholarly convention, based primarily on the works of Martin Noth (1902–1968), we recognize the strong influence of Deuteronomy's phraseology and ideology on the telling of Israel's history in Joshua through 2 Kings. Also following scholarly convention we refer to this ideology as Deuteronomism; hence the term used earlier, "Deuteronomistic," to refer to those historical books. The term "Deuteronomic" refers to the book of Deuteronomy itself. See Noth, *Deuteronomistic History*; Weinfeld, *Deuteronomy and the Deuteronomic School*, and Cross, *Canaanite Myth*, 274–289.

18. For a sustained treatment of Israelite prophecy sensitive to this distinction, see Wilson, *Prophecy and Society*, 37–41, and the literature cited there.

19. Among the brief studies dedicated exclusively to prophets and the cult, see, e.g., Carroll, "Prophecy and Society," esp. 211–215, and Murray, "Prophecy and the Cult," in Coggins et al., *Israel's Prophetic Tradition*. Longer treatments of prophecy address our themes as a matter of course: see, e.g., Blenkinsopp, *History of Prophecy*,

30–38; Lindblom, *Prophecy in Ancient Israel*, 351–360, and Rofé, *Introduction to the Prophetic Literature*, 94–97. Some studies attempt to make use of social science to account for and understand better the differences between the experiences and messages of ancient Israel's prophetic figures: see, e.g., Long, "Prophetic Authority," and "Social Dimensions." For a critical evaluation of some contemporary social-scientific approaches to prophecy (especially Wilson, *Prophecy and Society*), see Carroll, "Prophecy and Society." On the problem of cross-cultural comparison, see Overholt, "Prophecy."

20. So NRSV; the difference between Amos and Hosea here is obscured, unfortunately, in NJPS. See Heschel, *Prophets*, 60 and 195.

21. So Williams, "Social Location," and Hendel, "Prophets, Priests," in Wright et al., *Pomegranates*, 190–191. Generally, on the question of literary dependence among prophetic writings, see Blenkinsopp, *Sage, Priest, and Prophet*, 143–144.

22. Murray, "Prophecy and the Cult," in Coggins et al., *Israel's Prophetic Tradition*, 200–202.

23. Wilson, *Prophecy and Society*, 270–271.

24. Blenkinsopp, *History of Prophecy*, 194–212; Wilson, *Prophecy and Society*, 287–294.

25. See Mowinckel, *Psalms*, 2:53–58, and *Psalmenstudien* 3:4–29 (reprinted as "Cult and Prophecy"). Generally, on the designation "cultic prophet" in works by Mowinckel and beyond, see Rowley, "Ritual and the Hebrew Prophets," in *From Moses to Qumran*, 111–138, and Wilson, *Prophecy and Society*, 8–10, 259–260. On the designation as applied to Amos, see Wilson, *Prophecy and Society*, 268; for Isaiah, see 271; for Nahum, Habakkuk, and Zephaniah, see 276–280; for Joel and Malachi, see 290. For a critical evaluation of the designation "cultic prophet" as applied to Nahum, Habakkuk, and Joel in particular, see Richard Coggins, "An Alternative Prophetic Tradition," in Coggins et al., *Israel's Prophetic Tradition*, 77–94, and the literature discussed there. For a less guarded critique of Mowinckel, see Williams, "Social Location." There are still those who use the designation; Blenkinsopp, for instance, discusses Nahum and Habakkuk as cult prophets in *History of Prophecy*, 121–129.

26. See Douglas, "Holy Joy," 8–10; quotation from 10; cf. Douglas, "Forbidden Animals," 23, and "Sacred Contagion," in Sawyer, *Reading Leviticus*, 104; and Anderson, "Sacrifice and Sacrificial Offerings (OT)," *ABD* 5:881–882.

27. Heschel, *Prophets*, 196; Kaufmann, *Toledot ha-Emunah*, 7:72, 194; 8:444; cf. *Religion of Israel*, 365, 385, 418; de Vaux, *Ancient Israel*, 454.

28. Milgrom, *Leviticus 1–16*, 482; Kaufmann, *Toledot ha-Emunah*, 7:72, 194; 8:445; cf. *Religion of Israel*, 365, 385, 418; Rofé, *Introduction to the Prophetic Literature*, 96.

29. Anderson, "Sacrifice and Sacrificial Offering (OT)," *ABD* 5:882.

30. See Long, "Social Dimension"; Rowley, *From Moses to Qumran*, 124–130, and Schmitt, "Prophecy (Preexilic Hebrew)," *ABD* 5:486.

31. Anderson, "Sacrifice and Sacrificial Offering (OT)," *ABD* 5:882; Heschel, *Prophets*, 6–10.

32. Rofé, *Introduction to the Prophetic Literature*, 96–97. A similar problem has dogged New Testament research, in the interpretation of sayings such as Mark 7:15. See Klawans, *Impurity and Sin*, 147, and the literature cited on 213 n. 87.

33. Milgrom, *Leviticus 1–16*, 482–484; quotation from 483.

34. See Milgrom, *Leviticus 1–16*, 236–238.

35. Anderson, "Sacrifice and Sacrificial Offerings (OT)," *ABD* 5:881–882; Hendel, "Prophets, Priests," in Wright et al., *Pomegranates*, 190 n. 20; Meir Weiss,

"Concerning Amos' Repudiation of the Cult," in Wright et al., *Pomegranates*, 206–207. Significantly, both Hendel's and Weiss's analyses are printed in a Milgrom *festschrift*. Even Kaufmann, apparently, would reject Milgrom's argument here: see Kaufmann, *Toledot ha-Emunah*, 7:72, 103; cf. *Religion of Israel*, 365, 385.

36. De Vaux, *Ancient Israel*, 454–456; see also, e.g., Orlinsky, *Ancient Israel*, 128–130, and Rowley, *From Moses to Qumran*, 83–87.

37. Heschel, *Prophets*, 195.

38. See, e.g., Bernard J. Bamberger, "Leviticus," in Plaut, *Torah*, 752–753; Blenkinsopp, *Sage, Priest, Prophet*, 152; Ernest C. Lucas, "Sacrifice in the Prophets," in Beckwith and Selman, *Sacrifice in the Bible*, 59–74; Milgrom, *Leviticus 1–16*, 482; Miller, *Religion of Ancient Israel*, 188–189; Shalom Paul, "Prophecy and Prophets," in Lieber, *Etz Hayim*, 1407–1412, esp. 1411–1412; Ringgren, *Israelite Religion*, 264–265, 270; Rowley, *From Moses to Qumran*, 116–118, and Gordon Tucker, "Sacrifices," in Lieber, *Etz Hayim*, 1449–1450.

39. Hendel, "Prophets, Priests," in Wright et al., *Pomegranates*, 190–191; McKane, "Prophet and Institution," 253; see also Weiss, "Concerning Amos' Repudiation," in Wright et al., *Pomegranates*, esp. 213.

40. Cf. McKane, "Prophet and Institution," 257.

41. See, e.g., Carroll, *From Chaos to Covenant*, 96–106.

42. So Weiss, "Concerning Amos' Repudiation," in Wright et al., *Pomegranates*, 214.

43. E.g., Blenkinsopp, *History of Prophecy*, 146, 157, 167; Lindblom, *Prophecy in Ancient Israel*, 165–173; Matthews and Benjamin, *Social World of Ancient Israel*, 215–217; Miller, *Ancient Israelite Religion*, 186; Paul, "Prophecy and Prophets," in Lieber, *Etz Hayim*, 1408–1409; Ringgren, *Israelite Religion*, 214–215, 256–257, and 284; Rofé, *Introduction to the Prophetic Literature*, 71–73; Sweeney, *Isaiah 1–39*, 19–20.

44. See Hendel, "Prophets, Priests," in Wright et al., *Pomegranates*, 188–189, who contrasts symbolic actions with ritual.

45. Rowley, *From Moses to Qumran*, 137–138.

46. Mauss, *Gift*.

47. Barr and Kennedy, "Sacrifice and Offering," 871. Barr's comments are noted and approvingly reiterated by Milgrom, *Leviticus 1–16*, 441, and *Leviticus 17–22*, 1875–1876. See also de Vaux, *Studies in Old Testament Sacrifice*, 28–29.

48. One recent work that pays due attention to the issue of ownership is Chilton, *Temple of Jesus;* we consider this aspect of Chilton's work in chapter 7.

49. See, e.g., Gruenwald, *Rituals and Ritual Theory*, 40–93.

50. See the comments of Barr and Milgrom, cited earlier. See especially Milgrom, *Leviticus 1–16*, 441, for a brief discussion of the biblical sacrificial terms that connote the idea of giving. For a fuller discussion of ancient Israelite sacrifice as an act of giving, see Gray, *Sacrifice in the Old Testament*.

51. The following commentaries (e.g.) understand the rite as one of transfer: Gerstenberger, *Leviticus*, 26–28; Noth, *Leviticus*, 22, and Wenham, *Leviticus*, 61–62.

52. See, e.g., Hartley, *Leviticus*, 19–21; see Wenham, *Leviticus*, 61–62.

53. Knierim, *Text and Concept*, 34–40, quotation from 38.

54. Wright, "Gesture."

55. Wright, "Gesture," 436.

56. Wright, "Gesture," 437–438; see also Rendtorff, "How to Approach," 19.

57. One further ruling related to our theme can be found in the Pentateuch: Deut. 23:18 (MT 23:19), we find a prohibition against bringing to the sanctuary for the

fulfillment of a vow the "fee of a prostitute." The verse continues, speaking also literally of the "pay of a dog," which is frequently understood as a reference to male cult prostitution. So, e.g., NIV, NRSV. However, NJPS, NASB, NKJV, KJV, and many others translate MT literally. While the greater context lends support to the figurative understanding (see Deut. 23:17 [MT 23:18]), the case can still be made that the verse intends to speak literally of a dog: See Elaine Adler Goodfriend, "Could *Keleb* in Deuteronomy 23:19 Actually Refer to a Canine?" in Wright et al., *Pomegranates*, 381–397. Compare Tigay, *Deuteronomy*, 216. Regardless of how the verse is understood, what we find here is an explicit prohibition placed on bringing tainted funds into the holy precincts. What is more, the prohibition finds justification in the fact that the practices mentioned (whatever they may be) are "abominations" to the Lord. While there are no echoes of this ruling in other Hebrew Bible laws or narratives, we will see that subsequent interpreters do take up again the issue of tainted money.

58. McCarter, *I Samuel*, 267.

59. Many translations (including RSV, JB, NEB, NAB, NIV, NJB, and NRSV) follow LXX, Targum, and other authorities in rendering the verse "I hate robbery with violence." MT (translated earlier) is followed by KJV, NASB, and NJPS, and is also attested by Rashi and Ibn Ezra; RSV, NJB, and NRSV present MT as an alternate. Among modern scholars, the MT reading is preferred, e.g., by Childs, *Isaiah*, 500–506.

60. So KJV, RSV, JB, NEB, NAB, NASB, NIV, NJPS, NJB, and NRSV. See the discussion of the term in Hill, *Malachi*, 184–185.

61. Heschel, *Prophets*, 14–16.

62. Wellhausen, *Prolegomena*, 72–75, 108–112.

63. See, e.g., de Vaux, *Ancient Israel*, 418–421, and *Studies in Old Testament Sacrifice*, 91–112; Douglas, "Atonement in Leviticus," esp. 126–128; see also Hubert and Mauss, *Sacrifice*, 16–17. See also Gray, *Sacrifice in the Old Testament*," esp. 55–95, which helpfully introduces an important and overlooked distinction between sacrificial expiation (in response to known sin) and propitiation (the desire to appease the deity independent of knowledge of specific transgression). Helpful as this distinction is, Gray's evolutionism (54) remains partisan and problematic.

64. For general matters on Jeremiah, see Blenkinsopp, *History of Prophecy*, 129–147; Carroll, *Jeremiah*, and (briefly) Sweeney, "Latter Prophets," 81–88. Since the days of Mowinckel, scholars have commonly spoken of four distinct sources in the book (usually referred to by the letters A through D). See Carroll, *Jeremiah*, 38–50.

65. On the text of Jeremiah in the Greek and Hebrew versions, see Carroll, *Jeremiah*, 50–55.

66. Carroll, *From Chaos to Covenant*, esp. 9–11.

67. E.g., Carroll, *From Chaos to Covenant*, esp. 1–30 (in general) and 84–106 (on the temple sermon); we will return to this matter later in this chapter.

68. On Baruch and his ostensible role in shaping the Jeremiah traditions, see Jack R. Lundbom, "Baruch," *ABD* 1:617.

69. E.g., Blenkinsopp, *History of Prophecy*, 138–141; Bright, *Jeremiah*, lxxii–lxxiii, 58–59, 171–172, and Sa-Moon Kang, "The Authentic Sermon of Jeremiah in Jeremiah 7:1–20," in Fox et al., *Texts, Temples, and Traditions*, 147–162.

70. On this doctrine, and Zion traditions generally, see Levenson, *Sinai and Zion*, 89–184.

71. So NRSV (cf. BHS), following the Hebrew consonantal text, ancient translations, and predominant scriptural usage (e.g., Exod. 25:8); NJPS, following the vocalization of MT, understands the final words of verse 7 (also v. 3) to say that the Lord will allow the Israelites to dwell by the sanctuary.

72. Interestingly, by a strict reading of Deuteronomic standards (Deut. 18:22), Micah's prophecy has been proven to be false! See Carroll, *From Chaos to Covenant*, 94–95.

73. See Levenson, *Sinai and Zion*, esp. 165–169, as well as our discussion in chapter 2 here.

74. Levenson, *Sinai and Zion*, 168–169.

75. See Sweeney, *Isaiah 1–39*, 80–81, who suggests that Isaiah's critique of the cult is similarly related to the notion of the temple as a symbol.

76. On Deuteronomism in Jeremiah, see Blenkinsopp, *History of Prophecy*, 130–138; Carroll, *From Chaos to Covenant*, 13–18, and Weinfeld, *Deuteronomy and the Deuteronomic School*, 27–32 (on Jeremiah specifically) and 320–365 (for a catalogue of Deuteronomistic phraseology).

77. For further illustrations of Deuteronomic and Deuteronomistic influences on these passages, see Carroll, *From Chaos to Covenant*, 84–95.

78. See especially Milgrom, *Leviticus 1–16*, 253–261.

79. Milgrom, *Leviticus 1–16*, 260–261.

80. See Eilberg-Schwartz, *Savage*, 136–137. Eilberg-Schwartz is close to the mark here, but his comments are too centered on sacrificial atonement. As we have observed, expiation is but one motivation for sacrifice in ancient Israel.

81. See Long, "Social Dimensions of Prophetic Conflict," on the social locations of Jeremiah's priestly and prophetic interlocutors.

82. *Contra*, e.g., Williams, "Social Location," 15–169.

83. On the book of Ezekiel generally, see Blenkinsopp, *History of Prophecy*, 165–180; Greenberg, *Ezekiel 1–20*, and Zimmerli, *Ezekiel 1*. For a comparison of Greenberg's and Zimmerli's works, see Levenson, "Ezekiel." For the history of scholarship on Ezekiel in general, see Sweeney, "Latter Prophets," 88–94, and Zimmerli, *Ezekiel 1*, 3–8; on recent trends see Darr, "Ezekiel among the Critics."

84. For an approach to the book of Ezekiel that is consistently skeptical about the state of the text and the attribution of certain portions to the prophet, see esp. Zimmerli, *Ezekiel 1* and *Ezekiel 2*. For doubts on the authenticity of Ezekiel 40–48, see *Ezekiel 1*, 35; *Ezekiel 2*, 327–328.

85. So especially Greenberg, *Ezekiel 1–20*, 12–17, on the historical setting, and 18–27, on the book's literary unity.

86. Greenberg, "Design and Themes."

87. Such an approach was taken earlier in this century by Gustav Hölscher; see discussion with brief quotes in Sweeney, "Latter Prophets," 90, and Zimmerli, *Ezekiel 1*, 4–5.

88. Sweeney, "Latter Prophets," 90–91.

89. On priestly aspects of the book of Ezekiel, see Blenkinsopp, *History of Prophecy*, 169–171, 178–180, and Sweeney, "Latter Prophets," 91–94.

90. Milgrom, *Leviticus 17–22*, 1362; Zimmerli, *Ezekiel 1*, 46–52.

91. Greenberg, "Design and Themes," 183–189.

92. Wellhausen, *Prolegomena*, 59–60, 404–409; cf. Zimmerli, *Ezekiel 1*, 52.

93. Kaufmann, *Toledot ha-Emunah*, 7:475–583; cf. *Religion of Israel*, 426–446; Greenberg, "Design and Themes," 183–189; Greenberg, *Ezekiel 1–20*, ix; Haran, "Law Code of Ezekiel"; Milgrom, *Leviticus 1–16*, 3–8, *Leviticus 17–22*, 1362, and *Leviticus 23–27*, 2348–2363. The case, however, is not closed: see Blenkinsopp, "Assessment," 511.

94. Levenson, *Theology of the Program*, 1–2.

95. Greenberg, "Design and Themes"; Levenson, *Theology of the Program*; Smith, *To Take Place*, esp. 47–73, and Stevenson, *Vision of Transformation*.

96. Stevenson, *Vision of Transformation*, 149.

97. Greenberg, "Design and Themes," 194–199; Stevenson, *Vision of Transformation*, 21–23, 49–78.

98. The development is discussed in Smith, *To Take Place*, 62–63.

99. Stevenson, *Vision of Transformation*, 24–30, 76; Greenberg, "Design and Themes," 193–194, 206.

100. Greenberg, "Design and Themes," 193–194, 206.

101. Stevenson, *Vision of Transformation*, 89–95.

102. On the status of the Levites before and within Ezekiel's vision, see Stevenson, *Vision of Transformation*, 63–78. On the Zadokite priesthood in Ezekiel, see Greenberg, "Design and Themes," 195–196.

103. Levenson, *Theology of the Program*, 55–107; Smith, *To Take Place*, 61–62; Stevenson, *Vision of Transformation*, 109–123, 151–154.

104. Stevenson, *Vision of Transformation*, 153.

105. On the land allotments, see Levenson, *Theology of the Program*, 111–128; Smith, *To Take Place*, 65–71; Stevenson, *Vision of Transformation*, 81–84, and Greenberg, "Idealism and Practicality." On the aliens' portion, see Stevenson, *Vision of Transformation*, 83–5.

106. Stevenson, *Vision of Transformation*, 149; cf. Greenberg, "Design and Themes," 203–208, and Levenson, *Theology of the Program*, 124.

107. See George W. Ramsey, "Zadok," *ABD* 6:1034–1036.

108. This line of argument owes its inspiration to the recent studies of Mary Douglas concerning the dispute between Ezra and the priests. See Douglas, "Stranger in the Bible," and, more recently, "Responding to Ezra."

109. Greenberg, "Idealism and Practicality," and "Biblical Attitudes toward Power."

110. Greenberg, "Biblical Attitudes toward Power," 52 and 58.

111. Greenberg, "Biblical Attitudes toward Power," 60.

INTRODUCTION TO PART II

1. Busink, *Tempel*, 2:1062–1233 (on the temple in Herod's day in general), and 1529–1574 (on the temple as recalled in *m. Middot*); Ralph Marcus's notes in the LCL edition of Josephus (on *Jewish War* 5:201–226) discuss briefly the parallels between Josephus and *m. Middot* (LCL 3:260–269). For more recent reviews of the archaeological evidence see Mazar, *Complete Guide*.

2. Sanders, *Judaism*, 103–118; Schmidt, *How the Temple Thinks*, 76–97. Schürer, Vermes et al., *History*, 2:292–308.

3. Chilton, *Rabbi Jesus*, 26–32, 214–216; Fredriksen, *Jesus of Nazareth*, 42–50; Sanders, *Judaism*, 112–116 and Schmidt, *How the Temple Thinks*, 77–85.

4. In addition to the works just cited, for general surveys of the Second Temple and its religious significance, see Roitman, *Envisioning the Temple*, esp. 57–94, and Safrai, "Temple and the Divine Service."

5. See, e.g., Grabbe, *Judaic Religion*, 129–149; Sanders, *Judaism*, 47–169; Schürer, Vermes et al., *History*, 2:237–313, and Schwartz, *Imperialism and Jewish Society*, 49–66.

6. On pilgrimage to the Second Temple, see Safrai, *Pilgrimage*. For a briefer English treatment, see Safrai, "Temple and the Divine Service," 324–332. We will discuss issues pertaining to the temple tax in chapters 5, 6, and 7.

7. On these offerings, see Sanders, *Judaism*, 146–169, and Safrai, "Temple and the Divine Service," 321–324.

8. Safrai, "Temple and the Divine Service," 332–337.

9. See Schüssler Fiorenza, "Cultic Language," and Kampen, "Significance of the Temple."

10. On this phrase and its use in scholarship, see chapter 6.

11. This criticism applies, for instance, to Hayward, *Jewish Temple*.

12. A prime example of this phenomenon can be found throughout Elior, *Three Temples*.

13. See, e.g., Schmidt, *How the Temple Thinks*, discussed later in this section; cf. Chilton, *Temple of Jesus*, discussed (among many other works) in chapter 7.

14. Hayward, *Jewish Temple*, i.

15. Hayward, *Jewish Temple*, 6–13.

16. See Hayward, *Jewish Temple*, 1–2. Although rabbinic literature is not treated systematically in this work, Hayward liberally peppers his analysis of other material with parallels in rabbinic sources. See, e.g., *Jewish Temple*, 1.

17. E.g., Himmelfarb, *Ascent to Heaven*, and now also Elior, *Three Temples*.

18. Hayward, *Jewish Temple*, 3–4, citing 1QS VIII:4–12.

19. Surprisingly, Hayward suggests that the *Temple Scroll* (11QT) "has little to say about what the meaning and significance of the service to be offered in the ideal sanctuary might be" (*Jewish Temple*, 4).

20. Hayward, *Jewish Temple*, 4.

21. See Pomykala, review of Hayward, *Jewish Temple*.

22. See, e.g., Schmidt, *How the Temple Thinks*, esp. 22, 96 n. 54.

23. Schmidt, *How the Temple Thinks*, 34–38, 259–263.

24. Schmidt, *How the Temple Thinks*, 138–142.

25. Schmidt, *How the Temple Thinks*, 39–40, 141.

26. Schmidt, *How the Temple Thinks*, 40–44.

27. Schmidt, *How the Temple Thinks*, 89.

28. Schmidt, *How the Temple Thinks*, 85–97; Douglas and others influenced by her early work on purity are cited throughout this chapter.

29. Schmidt, *How the Temple Thinks*, 98–131; cf. Klawans, "Notions of Gentile Impurity," and Hayes, *Gentile Impurities*.

30. Schmidt, *How the Temple Thinks*, 98–101.

31. Safrai, *Pilgrimage*, 135–141, and Israel Knohl, "Post-Biblical Sectarianism and the Priestly Schools of the Pentateuch: The Issue of Popular Participation in the Temple Cult on Festivals," in Trebolle Barrera and Vegas Montaner, *Madrid Qumran Congress*, 2:601–609. See also Baumgarten, *Studies in Qumran Law*, 64–65.

32. See Klawans, "Notions of Gentile Impurity," 297–299, and the literature cited there. For a fuller discussion on Gentiles and the temple, see Hayes, *Gentile Impurities*, 34–37, 59–63.

33. See discussion of 11QT in chapter 5.

34. See Klawans, *Impurity and Sin*, 200–201 n. 85, and the literature cited there.

35. See, e.g., Douglas, *Leviticus as Literature*; see discussion in Klawans, *Impurity and Sin*, 7–10, 18–19, and Klawans, "Rethinking Leviticus."

CHAPTER 4

1. For a classic brief survey of this notion in the ancient Near East, Hebrew Bible, and postbiblical Jewish literature, see Patai, *Man and Temple*, 105–117.

2. For a classic survey of this notion in ancient Jewish sources, see Aptowitzer, "Heavenly Sanctuary."

3. While studies of one or another of these notions can be found, analyses that distinguish clearly between the two notions are much more difficult to come by. The most sophisticated treatment of these two approaches—one that clearly recognizes the difference between them—is Gray, *Sacrifice in the Old Testament*, 148–178. Gray, however, gives equal treatment to a third and entirely less significant theme: the idea that the temple was constructed according to plans shown to Moses in heaven (153–156). This theme—which develops the explicit testimony of Exod. 25:9—is entirely compatible with either of the two notions we are dealing with here, and as such is best viewed as an ancillary idea, one with fewer distinct implications for the understanding of temples and sacrifice in ancient Judaism. Nonetheless, Gray is correct to isolate the idea, for too many other scholars, as we will see below, refer to texts that recall the models shown to Moses as evidence for the idea of a temple in heaven, in which God is worshiped. See further discussion later in this chapter. For a more recent, brief survey that distinguishes between the various notions, see C. C. Rowland, "The Second Temple: Focus of Ideological Struggle?" in Horbury, *Templum Amicitiae*, 175–198.

4. So, for example, Clements, *God and Temple*, 65; see esp. n. 3.

5. See, for example, Himmelfarb, *Ascent to Heaven*, 15, and Davila, "Macrocosmic Temple," 1–5, 17. See also Elior, *Three Temples*, 70–71.

6. See, for instance, Barker, *Gate of Heaven*, 104–132 (on the cosmic symbolism of the sanctuary's veil) and 133–177 (on visions of God's heavenly throne). Note also Barker's juxtaposition of Philo's cosmic symbolism with the depiction of heavenly worship in *Songs of the Sabbath Sacrifice* in "Temple Imagery in Philo: An Indication of the Origin of the Logos?" in Horbury, *Templum Amicitiae*, 70–102, esp. 90–91.

7. See, for instance, Hayward, *Jewish Temple*, 8–13, who sees the two approaches as largely related.

8. On the significance of this notion to Jews of the Second Temple period, see G. I. Davies, "The Presence of God in the Second Temple and Rabbinic Doctrine," in Horbury, *Templum Amicitiae*, 32–36.

9. E.g., Himmelfarb, *Ascent to Heaven*, 13.

10. See Hayward, *Jewish Temple*, 6–8.

11. On Josephus generally, see Harold W. Attridge, "Josephus and His Works," in Stone, *Jewish Writings*, 185–232; on Josephus' attitude toward the temple, see Hayward, *Jewish Temple*, 142–153. On Josephus' *Antiquities*, see Feldman, *Judean Antiquities 1–4*, xii–xxxvi.

12. On Josephus' relationship to Scripture, see Feldman, "Use, Authority, and Exegesis of Mikra in the Writings of Josephus," in Mulder, *Mikra*, 455–518.

13. It is possible that Josephus reserved his symbolic interpretations for a planned treatise on rituals, referred to in *Ant.* 1:25 and again in 3:205. But it is also possible that at least some of the material originally intended to be published elsewhere was eventually worked into *Antiquities*: see Ralph Marcus's note a to *Ant.* 3:205 in the LCL edition, 2:414–415; see Feldman, *Judean Antiquities 1–4*, 10 n. 34 (on *Ant.* 1:25) and 283 n. 541 (on 3:205).

14. For more detail on all these passages, see Feldman, *Judean Antiquities 1–4*, 256–283.

15. For a comparison of Josephus' and Philo's cosmological interpretations of the tabernacle, see Koester, *Dwelling of God*, 59–63. Feldman, *Judean Antiquities 1–4*, provides many references to parallel passages in both Philo and rabbinic literature; see esp. 263 n. 286 (on *Ant.* 3:123), 280 nn. 474–475 (on 3:180), 270 n. 361 on 3:146. A number of the passages cited by Feldman are discussed in sections that follow.

16. See Swartz, "Semiotics," 57–80.

17. On these depictions, see Hayward, *Jewish Temple*, 49–55 (on 50:5–11, as translated from the Hebrew) and 67–68 (on 45:8–12, as translated from the Hebrew); and see 78, 83–84 on the Greek texts.

18. On the text and translation of this phrase—and on the entire passage—see Hayward, *Jewish Temple*, 30, 34–36.

19. See Winston, *Wisdom of Solomon*, 321–322, who identifies various Hellenistic (especially Stoic and Cynic) parallels for the motif in question. We will note further antecedents in Ben Sira and *Aristeas* later in this chapter.

20. So, too, Hayward, *Jewish Temple*, 146.

21. For the ancient Near Eastern evidence of this analogy, see Lundquist, "Common Temple Ideology," and "What Is a Temple."

22. See Bloch-Smith, "'Who Is the King of Glory'"; Levenson, *Sinai and Zion*, 111–137; Stager, "Jerusalem and the Garden of Eden"; and Wenham, "Sanctuary Symbolism."

23. See chapter 2; see Fishbane, *Text and Texture*, 3–16, and Levenson, *Creation and the Persistence of Evil*, 78–99 and 100–120.

24. On this passage, see also Feldman, *Judean Antiquities 1–4*, 9–10 nn. 28–33.

25. Further on Josephus and the priesthood, see Thoma, "High Priesthood."

26. Compare also *JW* 5:459, where Josephus indicates that the rebels continue to believe that God's protective presence dwells in the sanctuary.

27. See also *JW* 2:30, 4:183, 201; 5:16–19, 100–105 (on violence in or near the sancta) and 4:200–201, 242; 5:402; 6: 95, 99; 6:110, 122, 126 (on the desecration of the sancta by Jewish bloodshed).

28. On Josephus' self-understanding as a prophet, see Cohen, "Josephus, Jeremiah."

29. See also *JW* 4:323, 388; 5:566; 6:110, 250, 288–315. Briefly, on Josephus' theology in general, see Harold W. Attridge, "Josephus and His Works," in Stone, *Jewish Writings*, 203–206, and Feldman, "Use, Authority and Exegesis," in Mulder, *Mikra*, 503–507. Curiously, the divine departure from Jerusalem's temple is also noted in Tacitus' account of the revolt: see *Histories* 5:13; cf. Stern, *Greek and Latin Authors*, 2:60–61.

30. Generally on Philo, see Peder Borgen, "Philo," in Stone, *Jewish Writings*, 233–282, and, more extensively, *Philo of Alexandria*. On ritual and moral purity in Philo's thought, see Klawans, *Impurity and Sin*, 64–65. On sacrifices in Philo's thought, see Hayward, *Jewish Temple*, 108–141, and Nikiprowetzky, "Spiritualisation des sacrifices." But for its unfortunate use of the problematic term "spiritualization," this study presents some well-balanced analyses of Philo's thought on sacrifice. Nikiprowetzky does not argue that Philo rejects the sacrifices on a literal level (see esp. 109–116), only that he—as in all things—seeks truth beyond the material. On sacrifices as related especially to prayer, see Wolfson, *Philo* 2:241–248. Also helpful for its treatment of both purity and sacrifice is Laporte, "Sacrifice and Forgiveness." For a treatment of temple ritual practiced as described by Philo in comparison to the rules described by the tannaitic sages, see Belkin, *Philo and the Oral Law*, 49–88. Belkin is not at all interested in analyzing Philo's symbolic understandings of the rituals.

31. We follow Colson's LCL edition for titles and enumeration of Philo's works. On the various subtopics treated in *Spec. Laws* 1—and the subheadings provided by various manuscripts and some modern editors and translators—see Colson's notes in that edition, 7:xvii–xviii and 137, note d. Translations of Philo are also based closely on

Colson and Whitaker, with modifications for clarity, partially in comparison with Philo, *Works*, as translated by Yonge.

32. On Philo and his relation to the Hebrew Bible, see Yehoshua Amir, "Authority and Interpretation of Scripture in the Writings of Philo," in Mulder, *Mikra*, 421–453.

33. Nikiprowetzky, "Spiritualisation," 109–116.

34. According to Josephus, *Against Apion*, 1:199, the Greek philosopher Hecateus of Abdera made a similar observation, perhaps around 300 B.C.E. On (Pseudo-?) Hecateus' description of the temple, see Hayward, *Jewish Temple*, 18–25. Generally, see Holladay, *Historians*, 1:277–336, and Stern, *Greek and Latin Authors*, 1:20–44. Holladay questions the authenticity of the fragments, while Stern generally accepts their authenticity.

35. Goodenough, *By Light, Light*, and *Jewish Symbols*, 1:3–32.

36. So, respectively, argue Wolfson, *Philo*, and Belkin, *Philo and the Oral Law*. On our topic specifically, note the judgment of Ginzberg, *Legends*, 6:67 n. 346: "the symbolic explanation of the tabernacle as given by Philo . . . has many points of contact with that of the Rabbis."

37. See Baer, "Sacrificial Service," which focuses especially on Philo, *Who Is the Heir*.

38. So argues Margaret Barker, "Temple Imagery," in Horbury, *Templum Amicitiae*.

39. Therefore, with respect to our themes, the helpful models are to be found in the more evenhanded approaches taken by both Hayward, *Jewish Temple*, and Laporte, "Sacrifice and Forgiveness."

40. For earlier discussions of this symbolism, see Goodenough, *By Light, Light*, 95–120; Hayward, *Jewish Temple*, 109–112, and Nikiprowetzky, "Spiritualisation," 102–109.

41. See also *On Dreams* 1:215.

42. Hayward, *Jewish Temple*, 112–116; Swartz, "Semiotics," 68–69.

43. The *Questions and Answers* are extant primarily in Armenian manuscripts, with some Greek and Latin fragments also preserved. Briefly, on this work, see Borgen, "Philo," in Stone, *Jewish Writings*, 241–242. On the passages concerning the cult in particular, see Goodenough, *By Light, Light*, 112–114. For translations from the Armenian, along with the Greek and Latin fragments in their original and in translation, see Ralph Marcus's supplementary volumes to the LCL edition of Philo. For Marcus's thoughts on the scope of the original work, see the first of the supplementary volumes, ix–xv.

44. The significance of this material is disputed. Goodenough considered this section of the *Questions and Answers* to be "the most detailed source of all for the explanation of the Mystery of the temple and priesthood" (*By Light, Light*, 12). Curiously, and by contrast, Hayward devotes little attention to this material in his survey of Philo's works in *Jewish Temple* (see e.g., 124–125). The truth is somewhere in between: much of what we find in *QA on Exod.* confirms the thrust of what we have already seen in *Spec. Laws* and *Moses*. On the other hand, there are some differences on the level of detail: for instance, in *QA on Exod.*, the symbolism of the candelabrum is decoded through allusions to the zodiac (2:73–81) in addition to the planets, as in *Moses* 2:101–103). But as the *Questions and Answers* are extant largely in translation, and because the interpretations of many key cultic passages from Exodus (e.g., Exodus 29 and 40) are no longer extant, evaluating the significance of what we do have will remain a challenge.

45. See Laporte, "High Priest"; see Barker, "Temple Imagery in Philo," in Horbury, *Templum Amicitiae*, 90–95.

46. On the "cosmic significance" of Judaism in Philo, see Borgen, "Philo" in Stone, *Jewish Writings*, 269–272.

47. See Nikiprowetzky, "Spiritualisation," 100–102.

48. Klawans, *Impurity and Sin*, 64–65.

49. Philo does not state, however, that sinners are ritually impure; the sinners are excluded because of their morally impure souls, not because of their ritually impure bodies. See Klawans, *Impurity and Sin*, 65.

50. Philo, however, like the later tannaim, understands the rite as requiring the laying of *both* hands upon the animal's head. Compare *Spec. Laws* 1:202 with *m. Menahot* 9:8, and see our discussion of this rite in chapter 7, with regard to the works of Bruce Chilton.

51. See Wolfson, *Philo*, 2:241–242. Wolfson characteristically (and not all that helpfully) describes Philo's insistence that sacrifice be combined with morality as "essentially Jewish." See also Nikiprowetzky, "Spiritualisation," who recognizes prophetic and Greek philosophical backgrounds to Philo's approach (97–99).

52. See Klawans, *Impurity and Sin*, 64–65.

53. For the rabbinic approach, see Klawans, *Impurity and Sin*, 115.

54. Philo here builds on the accounts of God's fiery presence, e.g., Exod. 24:17 and Lev. 9:24. For legends concerning the divine nature of the Second Temple's fire, see 2 Macc. 1:19–2:18.

55. Barker, "Temple Imagery in Philo," in Horbury, *Templum Amicitiae*, 90–95; Hayward, *Jewish Temple*, 111; Goodenough, *By Light, Light*, 115–117; and Laporte, "High Priest," 74–77.

56. For a brief review of Philo's Logos, see Borgen, "Philo," in Stone, *Jewish Writings*, 273–274; with regard to our theme in particular, see Barker, "Temple Imagery in Philo," in Horbury, *Templum Amicitiae*, 70–71; Barker dialogues, in part, with Segal, *Two Powers in Heaven*, esp. 159–181. For extended treatments, see Wolfson, *Philo*, 1:200–332, and Winston, *Logos and Mystical Theology*.

57. E.g., Himmelfarb, *Ascent to Heaven*, 12; Himmelfarb follows Clements, *God and Temple*, 87–99; Kaufmann, *Religion of Israel*, 289–290, and Weinfeld, *Deuteronomy and the Deuteronomic School*, 191–209. Predictably, the Kaufmann school views the development from literal to metaphor, as taking place from P to D. Clements (*God and Temple*, 90–92, 113–118) argues, however, that the development is from D to P, with the understanding that P believes in the indwelling of God's *glory*, while God remains in heaven. The same approach is articulated in McKelvey, *New Temple*, 26–27.

58. Tigay, *Deuteronomy*, 120, on Deut. 12:4. Italics reproduced as in original.

59. See Clements, *God and Temple*, 90–92.

60. Barker, "Temple Imagery in Philo," in Horbury, *Templum Amicitiae*, 83–85.

61. This is especially true of Chronicles—see Clements, *God and Temple*, 128–129.

62. On the divine presence in P as compared to D (a comparison allowing for similar complexity) see Clements, *God and Temple*, 113–118.

63. See Barker, "Temple Imagery in Philo," in Horbury, *Templum Amicitiae*, 70–102. Barker's particular claim regarding the origin of Philo's Logos in distinctly *royal* cultic ideologies is beyond our concern. For Barker's theory of the origin of Jewish mythology in the Israelite royal cult, see her *Older Testament*.

64. Laporte, "Sacrifice and Forgiveness," 34, 38.

65. For general methodological reflections on the study of aggadic sources, see Bloch, "Methodological Note." Of course, an important exception in this regard is the mystical literature of the rabbinic period, now well studied (see further in this chapter).

66. See, e.g., Bialik and Ravnitzky, *Book of Legends*, 160–161. Also helpful is the more eclectic collection by Vilnay, *Legends of Jerusalem*, 3–16.

67. E.g., esp. Aptowitzer, "Heavenly Sanctuary."

68. See Levenson, *Creation and the Persistence of Evil*, 95–99, who builds on Patai, *Man and Temple*, 54–139. Note also the brief treatment of these themes in Tishby, *Wisdom of the Zohar* 3:867–869. Tishby, incidentally, clearly recognizes the difference between conceiving of the temple as representing the cosmos and imagining the existence of a temple in the cosmos (3:867).

69. The phrase in Ezekiel is consistently understood in this fashion in rabbinic literature, and this interpretation goes back at least to the Septuagint. A similar understanding of Jerusalem is reflected in both *1 Enoch* 26:1 (discussed briefly earlier) and *Jub.* 8:19, and some modern translations of Ezekiel follow suit (e.g., NJPS, NRSV). It has also been argued that the concept first arose among Jews in the Hellenistic period, and that the biblical phrase itself is simply geographic in meaning, referring to a hill (see Judg. 9:37). See Talmon, "The 'Navel of the Earth' and the Comparative Method," in *Literary Studies*, 50–75, and, in the same volume, "The Comparative Method in Biblical Interpretation: Principles and Problems," 11–49, esp. 40–44. Compare Levenson, *Sinai and Zion*, 115–117, who defends the meaning "navel" even for understanding Ezek. 38:12.

70. E.g., *Tanhuma va-Ayra* 18 (ed. Buber 17a–b); *Tanhuma Qedoshim* 10 (ed. Buber 39b); *Midrash Psalms* 91:7; *Midrash be-Khokhmah Yesod ha-Aretz* (Jellinek, *Beth ha-Midrasch* 5:63). For discussions, see Philip S. Alexander, "Jerusalem as *Omphalos* of the World: On the History of a Geographical Concept," in Levine, *Jerusalem: Its Sanctity*, 104–119, esp. 114–115; Levenson, *Sinai and Zion*, 117–121, and Patai, *Man and Temple*, 85–86 and 101 n. 100.

71. E.g., *m. Yoma* 5:2; *t. Yoma* 2 (3):14; *b. Yoma* 53b; *y. Yoma* 5:2, 42c/584; *b. Sanhedrin* 26b; *Num. Rabbah* 12:4; *Tanhuma Aharei Mot* 4 (ed. Buber 30a); *Tanhuma Qedoshim* 10 (ed. Buber 39b); *Midrash Psalms* 11:2, 91:7; *Pirkei de-Rabbi Eliezer* 9; *Song Rabbah* 3:23 (to 3:9). On these traditions—and on the term "foundation stone" (translated variously), see Alexander, "Jerusalem as *Omphalos*," in Levine, *Jerusalem: Its Sanctity*, 114–115; Busink, *Tempel*, 2:1174–1178; Ginzberg, *Legends*, 5:14–16 n. 39, and Patai, *Man and Temple*, 57–58, 85–86. Presumably, this is the same stone that is now located within the Dome of the Rock. According to the Bordeaux Pilgrim, Jews in the early fourth century c.e., would come once a year to lament over and anoint a "pierced stone" at the site of the temple. For a discussion of this text— with a quotation of the relevant passage—see Glenn Bowman, "'Mapping History's Redemption' Eschatology and Topography in the *Itinerarium Burdigalense*," in Levine, *Jerusalem: Its Sanctity*, 163–187 (key passage quoted on 180). For a photograph of the pierced stone in the Dome of the Rock, see Vilnay, *Legends of Jerusalem*, 12. Compare also the traditions that speak of the temple as the access point to (and therefore the seal of) the watery abyss below the earth: *b. Sukkah* 53a–b, discussed in Patai, *Man and Temple*, 54–59 and Levenson, *Creation and the Persistence of Evil*, 99.

72. I translate Ezek. 38:12 here according to the rabbinic understanding.

73. The tradition is quoted and discussed briefly in Levenson, *Creation and the Persistence of Evil*, 96–97.

74. See, e.g., *b. Berakhot* 55a; *Mekilta Shirah* 10 (ed. Horovitz and Rabin 150); *Pesikta Rabbati* 6; *Pesikta de-Rab Kahana* 1:5 (ed. Mandelbaum 10–11); *Tanhuma*

Va-Yakhel (ed. Buber 61b–62a); and *Num. Rabbah* 12:12. Compare *Gen. Rabbati* 32 (ed. Albeck), which juxtaposes the building of the tabernacle with God's creation of the human body.

75. See also Ginzberg, *Legends*, 3:165–167, and 6:67–68, nn. 346–350; Ginzberg here surveys various traditions concerning the symbolism of the tabernacle, not all of which are cosmic in nature. The priestly garb—mentioned above in our earlier discussions of Josephus and Philo—is generally interpreted in rabbinic sources as a symbol not of the cosmos but of the people of Israel. See Swartz, "Semiotics," 69–72.

76. *Midrash Tadshe* was first published the middle of the nineteenth century by A. Jellinek in *Bet ha-Midrasch*, 3:164–193; see Jellinek's introduction, xxxiii–xxxvi. A fuller edition with introduction and annotation was published later in 1887 by Epstein in his *Me-Qadmoniot*. For *Midrash Tadshe*, see 130–171, with additional notes on 173–174. Much of the tradition in question is also preserved in the *Yalqut Shim'oni* to Kings, sec. 185; see Epstein, *Me-Qadmoniot*, 145 n. 5.

77. Certainly a number of later Kabbalistic texts develop many fascinating symbolic interpretations of the tabernacle, temple, and sacrificial practice—but these take us well beyond the confines of this study. A number of fascinating traditions are discussed in Tishby, *Wisdom of the Zohar*, 3:867–940.

78. Epstein, *Me-Qadmoniot*, 139–140, followed by Theodor, "Midrashim," 578. Not all accept this attribution: see Strack and Stemberger, *Introduction to the Talmud and Midrash*, 345, and the literature cited there.

79. On these and other parallels, see Epstein, "Livre des Jubilés."

80. Epstein, *Me-Qadmoniot*, 133–139.

81. Epstein, *Me-Qadmoniot*, 135; the fuller treatment of this thesis can be found in Epstein's "Livre des Jubilés."

82. Belkin, "Midrash Tadshe."

83. For a summary statement, see Belkin, "Midrash Tadshe," 5. At times, Belkin appears to state that *Midrash Tadshe* drew from Philo (e.g., 17, 26). Elsewhere, however, he clarifies that Philo and the Midrash drew on common Hellenistic sources (e.g., 10, 30).

84. Ladermann, "Parallel Texts."

85. See Mintz-Manor, "Creation, the *Mishkan* and Mosheh HaDarshan." The *piyyut* is quoted on 266. Note also the general discussion of such liturgical poems with regard to the synagogues (and their decoration) in Schwartz, *Imperialism and Jewish Society*, 263–274.

86. Scholars of the origins of the Kabbalah face precisely the same methodological problem—see Idel, *Kabbalah*, 17–34.

87. For one example of a scholar who prefers to leaves this mystery unsolved, see Fine, *This Holy Place*, 124. For more detailed analyses, see Foerster, "Zodiac," and Hachlili, "Zodiac in Ancient Jewish Synagogal Art," which updates her earlier treatment, "Zodiac in Ancient Jewish Art." A classic, but dated, treatment can be found in Goodenough, *Jewish Symbols*, 8:167–218 and 12:152–157. For a recent critical assessment of the scholarly interpretations of Jewish synagogue art (without sustained focus on the zodiac in particular) see Schwartz, *Imperialism and Jewish Society*, 240–274.

88. Briefly, on the dates of each of these mosaics, see the related entries in Stern, *New Encyclopedia*, "Beth Alpha" (by Nahman Avigad; 1:190–192); "Hammath-Tiberias" (by Moshe Dothan; 2:573–577); "Husifa" (by Michael Avi-Yonah; 2:637–638); "Na'aran" (by Michael Avi-Yonah; 3:1075–1076); "Susiya, Khirbet" (by Zeev Yeivin; 4:1417–1421). For convenience of reference, we follow here the

transliterations adopted by Stern. For the Sepphoris mosaic—discovered in 1993, and therefore not discussed in the *New Encyclopedia*—see Weiss and Netzer, *Promise and Redemption*, but compare the critical comments by Schwartz, *Imperialism and Jewish Society*, 248–252. For Hammath, see also Dothan, *Hammath Tiberias*, which presents a detailed discussion of the most striking of these mosaics.

89. So Hachlili, "Zodiac in Ancient Jewish Synagogal Art," 232–237; Dothan, *Hammath Tiberias*, 45–49; cf. Fine, *This Holy Place*, 121–124. Hachlili credits Michael Avi-Yonah with this insight, and her original study is dedicated to him.

90. See, e.g., Schwartz, *Imperialism and Jewish Society*, pp, 255, 257 n. 44.

91. See Chiat, "Synagogues and Churches," 13–14; cf. Gideon Foerster, "Beth-Shean," in Stern, *New Encyclopedia*, 1:230–234.

92. Wilkinson, "Beit Alpha Synagogue Mosaic," esp. 26–27.

93. On the broader concept of ascent to heaven in ancient Judaism, see Himmelfarb, *Ascent to Heaven*, and Segal, "Heavenly Ascent." For a review of the theme in the Qumran material, see James R. Davila, "Heavenly Ascents in the Dead Sea Scrolls," in Flint et al., *The Dead Sea Scrolls after Fifty Years*, 2:461–485.

94. For a survey and discussion of these traditions, see Lee, *New Jerusalem*. The Qumran texts will be discussed in greater detail in the next chapter. The idea also appears in rabbinic traditions, as will be noted later in this chapter.

95. Gray, *Sacrifice in the Old Testament*, 153–157. Gray counters Charles, *Pseudepigrapha*, 306. Note, as Gray does (156 n. 2), that Charles later withdrew the statement. It should also be noted that even later in *Pseudepigrapha*, Charles says more clearly that what is expressed in *T. Levi* has no precedent in the book of Exodus, for *T. Levi* represents "the earliest reference to the heavenly temple" (*Pseudepigrapha*, 307, on *T. Levi* 5:1).

96. See, e.g., Davila, "Macrocosmic Temple"; Elior, *Three Temples*, 70–71; and McKelvey, *New Temple*, 41. It does not help that Eliade, too, jumped from one idea to the other (e.g., *Myth of the Eternal Return*, 7–9). Lee, *New Jerusalem*, also confuses the matter by speaking of the "New/Heavenly Temple/Jerusalem" (52) and interpreting the *Songs of a Sabbath Sacrifice* (discussed later) as if it speaks also of a future temple to be constructed on earth (105–111).

97. In the index to Charlesworth's *Pseudepigrapha*, the entry for "temple in heaven" refers to the reader to various passages, some of which (like *T. Levi* 3:5) speak of angelic worship in a heavenly temple, while others (like 2 Baruch 4:5) speak of seers who see in heavenly temples that are waiting to be constructed on or descend to earth (2:999; cf. 1:622 n. 4b [on 2 Baruch] and 789 n. 3d [on *T. Levi*]). In the index to Spark's edition, the entry "Heavenly Temple" (984) presents no references, and simply directs the reader to the heading "Archetypal Temple" (981).

98. For an example of a more guarded approach in scholarship, see García Martínez, *Qumran and Apocalyptic*, 207–208.

99. There is one brief passage in Philo's corpus that is taken by at least one interpreter as evidence that Philo believed in (or at least acknowledged) the notion of a temple *in* heaven (*QA on Exod.* 2:28, in which Philo comments on Moses' ascent as recorded in Exod. 24:1–2). Borgen suggests that Philo's reference here to the "forecourt of the palace of the father" alludes to and builds upon the ancient Jewish notion of a temple *in* heaven, as developed in apocalyptic literature (*Philo of Alexandria*, 202). It is more likely, however, that Philo is speaking here of the parts of heaven that correspond to the forecourt of the earthly temple, in line with his general view that the temple represents the cosmos. Philo on more than one occasion remarks on the ascent to heaven undertaken by Moses (*Moses* 1:149–162), philosophers

(*Spec. Laws* 1:37–50), and the Jewish people (2:164–166). But, decidedly unlike the heavenly tours in the apocalypses, ascent in Philo does not involve encountering a heavenly temple, as it would if Philo believed there to be a temple in heaven. For Philo, rather, ascent to heaven involves encountering and being taken into the cosmos that the earthly temple represents. Generally, on ascent in Philo, see Borgen, *Philo of Alexandria*, 194–205, 235–242.

100. As does, e.g., Gray, *Sacrifice in the Old Testament*, 156–157.

101. Himmelfarb, for instance, claims that the vision of a temple in heaven connotes a "desacralization" of the earthly temple, or results from the notion that the earthly temple is in some fashion "defiled" (*Ascent to Heaven*, 13 and 22, respectively). Compare 66, where Himmelfarb asserts that the vision of heaven as a temple (in the Apocalypse of Abraham) "confirms the importance of the earthly temple."

102. On Enoch's ascent in the *Book of Watchers*, see Himmelfarb, *Ascent to Heaven*, 9–28; for a brief history of scholarship on *1 Enoch*, see Nickelsburg, *1 Enoch 1*, 109–124.

103. Nickelsburg, *1 Enoch 1*, 7, and Stone, "Enoch, Aramaic Levi." The Qumran manuscripts are conveniently accessible in García Martínez and Tigchelaar, *Study Edition* 1:399–445 (4Q 201–212); 2:1162–1163 (7Q 4, 8, 11–14). The earliest complete manuscripts of *1 Enoch* are in Ethiopic, and date from the early modern era; fortunately for our purposes, however, much of the *Book of Watchers* is extant in early Greek manuscripts as well. On the various versions and manuscripts of *1 Enoch*, see Nickelsburg, *1 Enoch 1*, 9–20. For the Greek text, see Black, *Apocalypsis*, 2–44.

104. See Klawans, *Impurity and Sin*, 56–57.

105. Nickelsburg, *1 Enoch 1*, 261–262.

106. As Himmelfarb correctly notes (*Ascent to Heaven*, 14), Enoch passes through three barriers, suggesting a parallel with the three zones of the earthly temple (14:9, 10, 15).

107. On the text-critical problem associated with the (probable) mention of cherubim in 14:18, see Himmelfarb, *Ascent to Heaven*, 116–117 n. 4, and the literature cited there.

108. See also *Jub.* 8:19 and Ezek. 38:12. On this concept, see Philip Alexander, "Jerusalem as the *Omphalos*," in Levine, *Jerusalem: Its Sanctity*, 104–119. Rabbinic parallels have been noted earlier in this chapter.

109. Nickelsburg, *1 Enoch 1*, 54–55. Elior too assumes that *1 Enoch* was composed by what she calls "secessionist priests" who departed from the Second Temple (*Three Temples*, 88–134). Although Himmelfarb rejects those views that pit apocalyptic seers against the cult (*Ascent to Heaven*, 27–28), Himmelfarb still concludes that *1 Enoch* does in fact constitute a muted or "milder" critique of the temple (20–23, quotation from 22). Barker finds antipriestly elements within the work but doubts that cultic disputes of the second or third century B.C.E. provide the *original* context for *1 Enoch*. She traces elements of *1 Enoch* back to the mythology of ancient Israel's royal cult. See Barker, *Older Testament*, 8–80 (on *1 Enoch* as a whole) and esp. 20–32, 64–66 (on the *Book of Watchers* in particular).

110. E.g., Elior, *Three Temples*, 29–44 (generally), 93–94,112–113 (on Enoch particularly); Himmelfarb, *Ascent to Heaven*, 22; Nickelsburg, *1 Enoch 1*, 54–55.

111. E.g., Himmelfarb, *Ascent to Heaven*, 22; Nickelsburg, *1 Enoch 1*, 54; Suter, "Fallen Angel, Fallen Priest." See also Elior, *Three Temples*, 111–134; for Elior, however, a key feature of the priestly transgression is their reluctance to follow the 364-day calendar spoken of especially in *1 Enoch* 72–82; see Klawans, review of Elior, *Three Temples*, and further discussion of the calendar in chapter 5, under the heading "The Temple as Ritually Inadequate."

112. Nickelsburg, *1 Enoch 1*, 119; for a fuller statement see Nickelsburg, "Enoch, Levi, and Peter."

113. This argument is considered (but not favored) in Barker, *Older Testament*, 26.

114. Nickelsburg, "Enoch, Levi, and Peter," 581.

115. See the photographs in Nickelsburg, *1 Enoch 1*, 238–247.

116. Nickelsburg, *1 Enoch 1*, 54–55.

117. For a detailed assessment and commentary, see Hollander and de Jonge, *Testaments*. For the Greek text of *T. Levi*, see de Jonge et al., *Testaments*, 24–50.

118. So Howard Clark Kee, in Charlesworth, *Pseudepigrapha*, 1: 777.

119. The main proponent of this view is de Jonge; see, in particular, "Christian Influence" and "Transmission of the Testaments." Himmelfarb concurs (*Ascent to Heaven*, 30 and 126 n. 1), as does Stone, "Ideal Figures," 578.

120. The Geniza and Dead Sea manuscripts of the *Aramaic Levi Document* are conveniently available in García Martínez and Tigchelaar, *Study Edition*, 1:48–59 (Geniza and 1Q23); 446–455 (4Q213a–214b), 2:1078–1081 (4Q540–541). The *editio princeps* of the Dead Sea material, prepared by Michael E. Stone and Jonas C. Greenfield, can now be found in Brooke et al., *DJD XXII*, 1–72. For a recent thorough survey of the *Aramaic Levi Document* see Kugler, *From Patriarch to Priest*, esp. 23–138. While most posit a direct dependence of *T. Levi* on the earlier Aramaic document, Kugler attemps to reconstruct the contours of a Jewish *Testament of Levi*, a document ostensibly composed in the Hasmonean era, which later served as the basis for the Christian *T. Levi* that we now have (*From Patriarch to Priest*, 171–220). For de Jonge's more guarded response, see "Levi in Aramaic Levi." For an alternative review of the tradition-history, see Kugel, "Levi's Elevation to the Priesthood."

121. We proceed here in line with de Jonge's caution, that we should assume the documents are Christian except where it can be reasonably demonstrated otherwise; see "Transmission of the Testaments," 19–22.

122. On the relationship between the Enochic and Levi traditions, see Nickelsburg, "Enoch, Levi, and Peter," and Stone, "Enoch, Aramaic Levi, and Sectarian Origins." For discussions of Levi's ascent to a heavenly temple, see Gray, *Sacrifice in the Old Testament*, 157–158, and Himmelfarb, *Ascent to Heaven*, 29–37.

123. See Himmelfarb, *Ascent to Heaven*, 32–33. Some scholars claim that an earlier tradition (possibly reflected in 2:7–9) may have known of only three heavens, but the sevenfold heaven appears intrinsic to the complete Testament as we have it. See Himmelfarb, *Ascent to Heaven*, 126–127 n. 7, and the literature cited there; cf. Kugler, *From Patriarch to Priest*, 181, esp. n. 36.

124. On this passage see Himmelfarb, *Ascent to Heaven*, 36–37, and Kugler, *From Patriarch to Priest*, 184–185.

125. Translation from Hollander and de Jonge, *Testaments*, 136.

126. So Hollander and de Jonge, *Testaments*, 138. There have been some voices dissenting from this view. Assuming *T. Levi* to be a Jewish document composed in Hebrew, Aptowitzer hypothesized that the original text spoke not of an offering that was "rational" (נבון) but of an offering that was secure, enduring, or properly established (נכון). Thus the current reading results from a scribal error. See Aptowitzer, "Heavenly Sanctuary," 259 n. 4, and compare Gen. 43:25, Zeph. 1:7 and Ps. 141:2. The suggestion is fascinating but hardly convincing, especially in light of so much evidence for Christian interpolation in, if not composition of, the *Testaments*.

127. Himmelfarb, *Ascent to Heaven*, 36.

128. On the exegetical motivations for much of *T. Levi*, see Kugel, "Levi's Elevation to the Priesthood," esp. 30–42.

129. See Hollander and de Jonge, *Testaments*, 129, 154; de Jonge, "Christian Influence," 214–219, 230–235, and Kugler, *From Patriarch to Priest*, 187–189.

130. See Kugler, *From Patriarch to Priest*, 216–220, and the literature cited there. For an alternative reconstruction, see Kugel, "Levi's Elevation to the Priesthood," 42–46, 60–63.

131. Compare Kugel, "Levi's Elevation to the Priesthood," 42–46.

132. Various editions of the work now exist: the first complete publication was Newsom, *Songs of the Sabbath Sacrifice*, which itself was a revision of the author's Harvard doctoral dissertation, with a similar title, completed in 1982. Newsom is largely responsible for the official publication of the Qumran Cave 4 manuscripts in Eshel et al., *DJD XI*, 173–401, and she also produced an alternative edition, which includes the Masada MS and a reconstructed composite text, in Charlesworth and Newsom, *Angelic Liturgy*. The official publication of 11Q17 appears in García-Martínez et al., *DJD XXIII*, 259–304. For an alternative introduction and reconstructed composite text (in translation only), see Davila, *Liturgical Works*, 83–167.

133. On the paleography of the manuscripts and the date of the work, see Newsom, introduction to Charlesworth and Newsom, *Angelic Liturgy*, 1–2 and 4–5. For fuller discussion, see the treatment of each Cave 4 fragment in Eshel et al., *DJD XI*, and of 11Q17 in García Martínez et al., *DJD XXIII*. Like many scholars, I too am skeptical of the confidence with which paleographers working on the Dead Sea Scrolls assign dates with rather narrow ranges to the various scripts. See further comments in chapter 5.

134. Newsom and others associate the songs with the *first* thirteen Sabbaths of the year (Newsom, introduction to Charlesworth and Newsom, *Angelic Liturgy*, 3–4; *Songs of the Sabbath Sacrifice*, 13–21). Some, however, suggest that the cycle of thirteen songs would be repeated four times in the course of a fifty-two-week year; see Johann Maier, "Shîrê 'Ôlat hash-Shabbat: Some Observations on their Calendric Implications and on their Style," in Trebolle Barrera and Vegas Montaner, *Madrid Qumran Congress*, 2:543–560, and Elior, *Three Temples*, 51.

135. On the 364-day calendar in the *Songs*, see Maier, "Shîrê 'Ôlat hash-Shabbat," in Trebolle Barrera and Vegas Montaner, *The Madrid Qumran Congress* 2:544–552. See further discussion of the calendar in chapter 5, under the heading "The Temple as Ritually Inadequate."

136. Newsom presents her arguments in her introduction to Charlesworth and Newsom, *Angelic Liturgy*, 4–5, and in Newsom, "'Sectually Explicit' Literature from Qumran," 179–185. Compare Davila, *Liturgical Works*, 88–89, who reviews the basic arguments, leaving the question open.

137. See Fletcher-Louis, "Heavenly Ascent," 377–381, who points out, for example, that 4Q 400 frag. 1 I:16 seems to echo 1QS IX:3–6. Newsom too originally believed the *Songs* to be sectarian, a position she later retracted; see *Songs of the Sabbath Sacrifice*, 1–5, 59–72, and discussion in Murray-Jones, "Temple Within," 409–411. Devorah Dimant has also argued that the *Songs* are closely tied (conceptually) to the *Rule of the Community*, with the *Songs* describing the angels as doing various activities (such as maintaining purity and offering expiation) that are performed by the community in the *Rule*. See Dimant, "Men as Angels." Dimant's survey is provocative, but the parallels she describes are too general, and the differences between the *Songs* and the *Rule* remain great—including the all-important fact that while the *Rule* does speak of the community in cultic terms (see chapter 5), the *Songs* don't speak of the community at all.

138. Himmelfarb, *Ascent to Heaven*, 22, 36; cf. Elior, *Three Temples*, 70–74, 167–170, 183–191, which consistently discusses the *Songs* as an example of "secessionist" priestly literature.

139. According to Davila (*Liturgical Works*, 89–90), the "liturgical use of these songs may have served as a validation of their self-identification as a spiritual temple. By identifying themselves with the cult of the heavenly temple they could exalt their own rank above the priesthood of the mere earthly temple in Jerusalem." Similarly, Newsom understands the work as a sort of "communal mysticism," practiced by those who thought they were the true priests, even though they were no longer functioning in any earthly temple. See Newsom, introduction to Charlesworth and Newsom, *Angelic Liturgy*, 4; cf. *Songs of the Sabbath Sacrifice*, 59–72. Lee, *New Jerusalem*, 105–111, largely follows Newsom, though he also assumes that the *Songs* are to be interpreted in light of *4QFlorilegium* (discussed in chapter 5), with both documents assuming that the true temple is the community itself.

140. Chazon, "Liturgical Communion."

141. For surveys of the heavenly temple in the Songs, see Charlesworth and Newsom, *Angelic Liturgy*, 7–8, and Newsom, *Songs of the Sabbath Sacrifice*, 39–58. The following summary draws heavily on Newsom's discussions. Because the references are so cumbersome, only a single textual reference is provided for each item cited; for fuller annotation see Newsom, *Songs of the Sabbath Sacrifice*.

142. One term that appears throughout the work is תבנית (e.g., 4Q403 frag.1, II:3), the term used in Exod. 25:9 and elsewhere with reference to the "pattern" shown to Moses on Sinai. As Newsom correctly observes, the biblical idea of the heavenly pattern "may have been an impetus to speculation about a heavenly temple in later tradition (cf. Heb. 8:5), but it does not in itself necessarily reflect a belief in a heavenly temple corresponding to an earthly one" (*Songs of the Sabbath Sacrifice*, 60 and 314–315).

143. Fletcher-Louis makes some fascinating suggestions regarding the significance of these vestments—particularly the breastplate—for the Qumran sectarians: see "Heavenly Ascent," 398–399.

144. See Davila, *Liturgical Works*, 103.

145. On the heavenly sacrifice in the *Songs*, see Newsom, *Songs of the Sabbath Sacrifice*, 47, 371–373; Davila, *Liturgical Works*, 157–161; and Himmelfarb, *Ascent to Heaven*, 33–36.

146. For a thorough review of this question, see Allison, "Silence of the Angels."

147. In defense of the claim that the *priests* (but not Levites or others) maintained silence in the temple, see Knohl, "Between Voice and Silence," esp. 24–26. Many scholars, however, reject the idea of a silent earthly temple service as impractical or even nonsensical: see Hayward, *Jewish Temple*, 32–37. On various traditions (especially biblical and rabbinic) concerning instrumental and choral music in the temple, see Werner, "Liturgical Music in Hellenistic Palestine," in *Sacred Bridge, Volume II*, 1–24.

148. So Chazon, "Liturgical Communion," 98–102, 104–105. Allison, "Silence of the Angels," 190–191, considers this argument as well but favors the notion discussed earlier, that the angelic service is a silent one.

149. On the influence of Ezekiel, see Charlesworth and Newsom, *Angelic Liturgy*, 8–9, and Newsom, *Songs of the Sabbath Sacrifice*, 51–58.

150. On seven heavens or seven temples in the *Songs*, see Newsom, *Songs of the Sabbath Sacrifice*, 48–51; see also 120–121, 177–178.

151. See discussion in Davila, *Liturgical Works*, 137–138, 141–145.

152. Davila, *Liturgical Works*, 145–146; Fletcher-Louis, "Heavenly Ascent," 384–388; Newsom, *Songs of the Sabbath Sacrifice*, 54–57.

153. Davila, *Liturgical Works*, 109; cf. Newsom, *Songs of the Sabbath Sacrifice*, 65, 115–116, and Chazon, "Liturgical Communion," 98–102.

154. See Fletcher-Louis, "Heavenly Ascent," and on other such transformations see Himmelfarb, *Ascent to Heaven*, 29–46.

155. See Schuller, "Petitionary Prayer."

156. So Chazon, "Liturgical Communion," 98–102, 104–105, who is followed by Abusch, "Sevenfold Hymns," 236–237.

157. See Himmelfarb, *Ascent to Heaven*, 15–16.

158. See Maier, "*Shîrê 'Ôlat hash-Shabbat*," in Trebolle Barrera and Vegas Montaner, *Madrid Qumran Congress*, 2:552–553.

159. There are three distinct forms of the *qedushah*, each of which in turn is extant in various versions; generally, see Elbogen, *Jewish Liturgy*, 54–66, as well as the literature cited the discussion later in this chapter.

160. Modern translations (e.g., NRSV) typically emend Ezek. 3:12 so that it speaks of noise made during the ascent of the Lord's glory. The traditional Jewish liturgy, of course, follows the Masoretic text, as do all Jewish translations of Ezekiel (e.g., NJPS) and most premodern translations (e.g., KJV). Thus Ezek. 3:12 (like Isa. 6:3) is understood as a direct quotation of angelic praise.

161. For discussions of the origins of (various forms of) this prayer, see (in addition to Elbogen), Heinemann, *Prayer*, 145–147; and Werner, "The Doxology in Synagogue and Church," in *Sacred Bridge*, esp. 282–291.

162. See Fiensy, *Prayers Alleged to Be Jewish*, 66–73, and 225–227, where the author argues that seven of these prayers—including 7:35.1–10—preserve a version of the Sabbath *amidah* along with its *qedushah*. For a recent review of the issues involved with the study of this text (without reference to the *qedushah* in particular) see Pieter W. van der Horst, "The Greek synagogue Prayers in the Apostolic Constitutions, book VII," in Tabory, *From Qumran*, 19–45.

163. Flusser, "Jewish Roots," 42–43. Flusser's thesis (intimated in the article's full title) is rejected by Werner, "The Genesis of the *Sanctus* in Jewish and Christian Liturgies," in *Sacred Bridge, Volume II*, 108–126. Werner's thesis too is intimated in his title: not all that is shared in Jewish and Christian liturgies stems from the former: the traditions remained interdependent, and thus influence continued to exert itself in both directions throughout the early history of the church and synagogue.

164. Elior, "From Earthly Temple to Heavenly Shrines," 230–235.

165. See Chazon, "The *Qedushah* Liturgy and Its History in Light of the Dead Sea Scrolls," in Tabory, *From Qumran*, 7–17; and Chazon, "Liturgical Communion." In addition to the *Songs*, Chazon focuses in these studies on 4Q503 *Daily Prayers*, which similarly juxtaposes heavenly and earthly praise.

166. See Elior, "From Earthly Temple to Heavenly Shrines," 230–235, 262.

167. See Chazon, "Liturgical Communion," 103, and "*Qedushah* Liturgy," in Tabory, *From Qumran*, 15–16.

168. Aptowitzer, "Heavenly Temple." Virtually every subsequent survey of the theme (including what follows) builds largely on Aptowitzer's well-organized and rather thorough survey of the sources. Note, however, that Aptowitzer does not include the mystical traditions (e.g., *Hekhalot Rabbati*) in his survey.

169. For a brief statement on Scholem's contribution and impact on the field, see Idel, *Kabbalah*, 10–13.

170. For a work on later Jewish mysticism that proves helpful in tracing the earlier rabbinic traditions, see Tishby, *Wisdom of the Zohar*, 3:867–869. For the early Jewish mystical texts known as *Hekhalot* or *Merkabah* traditions, see esp. Schäfer, *Synopse*.

171. See, for example, Flusser, "Jerusalem" (first published in 1974); Safrai, "Heavenly Jerusalem" (1969); Urbach, "Heavenly and Earthly Jerusalem" (1968); and Vilnay, *Legends of Jerusalem*, 128–132 (first published in 1973).

172. Among the texts cited and discussed in Aptowitzer, "Heavenly Temple," are *Midrash Aseret ha-Dibrot* (text: Jellinek, *Beth ha-Midrasch* 1:62–90; mention of heavenly temple: 1:64), *Midrash Elleh Ezkereh* (text: Jellinek, *Beth ha-Midrasch* 2:64–72; mention of heavenly temple: 2:66), and *Midrash be-Khokhmah Yesod ha-Aretz*, version B (text: Jellinek, *Beth ha-Midrasch* 5:63–69; mention of heavenly temple: 5:63). For brief discussion and bibliography concerning the first two of these texts, see Strack and Stemberger, *Introduction to the Talmud and Midrash*, 333, 338–339). See also *Gen. Rabbati* 136–137 (ed. Albeck), extensively quoted (in English translation) in Safrai, "Heavenly Jerusalem," 12. Like *Midrash Tadshe*, *Gen. Rabbati* is attributed by some scholars to R. Moshe ha-Darshan of Narbonne; see Strack and Stemberger, *Introduction to the Talmud and Midrash*, 355–356.

173. Aptowitzer, "Heavenly Temple," 140–145 (followed by Urbach, "Heavenly and Earthly Jerusalem," 158) argued that the origin of the notion is to be found in Isaiah's vision of the angels in the sanctuary (Isa. 6:1–7). Flusser, "Jerusalem," 59, and Safrai, "Heavenly Jerusalem," 11, 16, more reasonably trace the idea back to the Second Temple period.

174. See Aptowitzer, "Heavenly Sanctuary," 264, who also quotes from the *Alphabet of Rabbi Akiva* (Jellinek, *Beth ha-Midrasch* 3:20) to the effect that the sanctuary is located in the third heaven. See also Safrai, "Heavenly Jerusalem," 15, for an English discussion (and translation) of these sources.

175. See also *Pesikta de-Rab Kahana* 1:3 (ed. Mandelbaum 7–8); *Num. Rabbah* 12:8; *Song Rabbah* 3:25 (to 3:11); see discussion in Aptowitzer, "Heavenly Temple," 13–17. Some traditions imagine Moses seeing these models in heaven (*Pesikta de-Rab Kahana* 1:3); others imagine that the models were sent down from heaven to Sinai (b. *Menahot* 29a).

176. See also *Gen. Rabbah* 2:5 (ed. Theodor and Albeck 18); *Gen. Rabbah* 56:10 (608), 65:23 (744); 69:7 (797) and *Peskita de-Rab Kahana* 21:5 (ed. Mandelbaum 322). On these traditions, see Flusser, "Temple of the End of Days."

177. See also *Pesikta Rabbati* 5:18 (22b); *Tanhuma Naso* 18 (traditional eds. only).

178. So MT. NRSV, NJPS: "and I will not come in wrath," both noting that the meaning of Hebrew is uncertain.

179. Text and translation follows Malter, *Treatise Ta'anit*, 53–54; see 54 n. 64. The text continues with an editorial comment: "but is there a heavenly Jerusalem? Yes: for it is written (Ps. 122:3): 'Jerusalem is built as a city that is bound firmly together.'" On the meaning of this see Rashi, to b. *Ta'anit* 5a, and Malter, *Treatise Ta'anit*, 54 n. 65. See also Urbach, "Heavenly and Earthly Jerusalem," 156–157, esp. n. 1.

180. Safrai, "Heavenly Jerusalem," 16. For further traditions on the divine presence in exile, see *Impurity and Sin*, 118–134.

181. This idea also appears in a number of the more "exotic" midrashim—the ones whose history are difficult, if not impossible, to track—such as those reproduced in Jellinek's *Beth ha-Midrasch*. See Aptowitzer, "Heavenly Sanctuary," 257–259, which quotes the key passages from the midrashic sources, and 264–265 for his analysis of their approaches to heavenly sacrifice.

182. See Jellinek, *Beth ha-Midrasch*, 3:137, discussed in Aptowitzer, "Heavenly Sanctuary," as cited in the previous note.

183. Urbach, "Heavenly and Earthly Jerusalem," 157; see also Safrai, "Heavenly Jerusalem," 14.

184. Generally on these texts, see Schäfer, *Hidden and Manifest God*; with regard to our themes see also Elior, "From Earthly Temple to Heavenly Shrines."

185. See Abusch, "Sevenfold Hymns," for the relationship between the *Hekhalot* texts and the Qumran *Songs*.

186. Elior, "From Earthly Temple to Heavenly Shrines," 226–232; Lieber, "Where Is Sacrifice."

187. Elior, "From Earthly Temple to Heavenly Shrines," 231. In *Three Temples*, 165–200, Elior places the *Hekhalot* traditions firmly within the trajectory of the literature composed by the "secessionist priesthood." Compare Himmelfarb, *Ascent to Heaven*, 36 (speaking of the apocalyptic traditions).

188. Lieber, "Where Is Sacrifice." For examples of the violence imagined in the *Hekhalot* literature, see, e.g., *Hekhalot Rabbati* 19:6, 26:1–2 (Schäfer, *Synopse*, sec. 224, 258–259) and *Hekhalot Zutarti* (Schäfer, *Synopse*, sec. 410; cf. *b. Hagigah* 14b). On these traditions, see Schäfer, *Hidden and Manifest God*, 33, 37–39, and Scholem, *Jewish Gnosticism*, 14–19.

189. See Schäfer, *Hidden and Manifest God*, 2–3 n. 4, and the literature cited there, including esp. Scholem, *Jewish Gnosticism*, 20 n. 1.

190. Elior, "From Earthly Temple to Heavenly Shrine," 224, 226–230.

191. Schäfer, *Synopse*, sec. 151; Elior, "From Earthly Temple to Heavenly Shrine," 228 n. 28.

192. See Elior, "From Earthly Temple to Heavenly Shrine," 244 n. 55; Lesses, *Ritual Practices to Gain Power*, 117–160, and Swartz, "'Like the Ministering Angels.'"

193. Schäfer, *Synopse*, secs. 225–228. Had the sages truly defiled Nehunia's body, he would have been killed; had they left his body untouched, he would have remained in heaven. By bringing Nehunia in contact with a substance of questionable purity, they are able to secure his safe dismissal from heaven. The narrative is discussed in Scholem, *Jewish Gnosticism*, 9–13. See also Swartz, "'Like the Ministering Angels,'" 162–164, and the literature cited there.

194. Swartz, "'Like the Ministering Angels,'" 157–162.

195. Schäfer, *Synopse*, sec. 181, quoted and discussed in Swartz, "'Like the Ministering Angels,'" 161–162.

196. Scholem, *Major Trends*, 40–79; see also Scholem, *Jewish Gnosticism*.

197. Halperin, *Merkabah*, 65–105, 179–181. Compare Elior, *Three Temples*, 201–265.

198. Aptowitzer, "Heavenly Sanctuary," 272; Elior, *Three Temples*, 6, 264–265; Urbach, "Heavenly and Earthly Jerusalem," 167–171.

199. Flusser, "Jerusalem," 59; Safrai, "Heavenly Jerusalem," 11, 16.

CHAPTER 5

1. One very good survey of the basic issues—with ample bibliography—is Lawrence H. Schiffman, "Community without Temple: The Qumran Community's Withdrawal from the Jerusalem Temple," in Ego et al., *Gemeinde ohne Tempel*, 267–284. See also Johann Maier, "Temple," in Schiffman and VanderKam, *Encyclopedia*, 2:921–927. One of the earlier studies that continues to be frequently cited is J. Baumgarten, "Sacrifice and Worship" (also reprinted in Baumgarten, *Studies*, 39–56). Baumgarten published a subsequent essay, "The Essenes and the Temple: A Reappraisal," in which he revisits some of the conclusions of his earlier study—see *Studies*, 57–74, and see also *Studies*, ix–x, where he explicitly reevaluates (without entirely rejecting) his earlier analysis.

2. See, e.g., García Martínez and Trebolle Barrera, *People of the Dead Sea Scrolls*, 77–96, on the history of the community, and "The Problem of Purity: The Qumran Solution," 139–157 (both by García Martínez).

3. This possibility has been suggested by, e.g., Baumgarten, "Essenes and the Temple," in *Studies*, 68.

4. The classic and often-cited study is Cross, "Development." See also his more recent discussion of typological method in *From Epic to Canon*, 233–245. It is fair to say that Cross's work provides the basis on which virtually every Qumran document published in the DJD series is dated.

5. For these and other concerns with paleography as carried out by Qumran scholars, see Eisenman, *Maccabees, Zadokites*, 80–97. Perhaps Eisenman's embrace of some rather bizarre ideas in this book explains why the important methodological questions he raises with regard to paleography have not received due attention.

6. For comments on medieval Hebrew paleography, see Golb, *Who Wrote*, 249–254. I rely on the testimony of colleagues in classics who assure me that virtually no one working with Greek papyri would presume to be able to date documents on paleographic grounds to a twenty-five-year period.

7. Consider Cross's appeal to the historical validity of Hegelian dialectic, in *From Epic to Canon*, 239.

8. Wilson, *Magic and the Millennium*, 18–26. For applications of Wilson's typology of sects—which actually consists of seven types of groups—to ancient Judaism, see A. Baumgarten, *Flourishing*, 13–14 and Saldarini, *Pharisees, Scribes and Sadducees*, 70–73, 285–287.

9. For fuller analysis of these passages, see Klawans, *Impurity and Sin*, 48–56 (11QT and CD) and 69–72 (1QpHab); these passages—and some of those noted in the following paragraphs—are also discussed in Regev, "Abominated Temple." I thank Eyal Regev for sharing this manuscript with me in advance of its publication.

10. Dimant, *DJD XXX*, refers to the document as *4QJeremiah Apocryphon*; see general discussion, 1–3, and see also 244–249 for the fragment quoted here. García Martínez and Tigchelaar print the relevant parabliblical texts under an earlier name, *4QPseudo-Moses* (*Study Edition* 2:770–785).

11. For the readings, reconstructions, and discussion see Dimant, *DJD XXX*, 136–138 (4Q385a), 175–179 (4Q387), 204–205 (4Q388a).

12. It is possible that this passage assumes that the sanctuary has been defiled by failure to properly practice certain ritual purity rules (as understood, for instance, by Knibb, *Qumran Community*, 43–44, 75). If I am correct, however, in understanding CD IV:20, V:6–9, as speaking of moral defilement, then presumably the same would hold here. But it is also possible that this passage—like many others in sectarian literature—reflects a perspective where no distinction is drawn between ritual and moral defilement. In this case, however, the passage would be unique in CD.

13. On this ruling, see Yadin, *Temple Scroll*, 1:312–314; cf. 4QMMT B 36–38, on which see Qimron, *DJD X*, 157–158, and Kugler, "Rewriting Rubrics," 104–106.

14. Nothing in the extant portions of 4QMMT B 36–38 suggests that such an offering is ritually or morally impure. The question regarding the interpretation of 11QT LII:5 is a difficult one, and perhaps not fully resolvable. The key characteristic of a moral defilement is that it would defile the temple even at a distance, but since, according to 11QT, sacrifice is only performed at the temple, this litmus test cannot be applied.

15. One further passage can be mentioned—4Q183—which speaks of the defilement of the sanctuary (line 1) and later speaks of evil wealth as well. The fragment

is too poorly preserved to allow any definite understanding of the defilement in question. It is quite possible that in this case, the temple is defiled not by sin but by the enemies mentioned immediately before the reference to sanctuary defilement.

16. Trans. O. S. Wintermute, in Charlesworth, *Pseudepigrapha*, 2:101. Unfortunately, no Qumran copy of the passage survives.

17. Trans. Hollander and de Jonge, *Testaments*, 168. Greek text in de Jonge et al., *Testaments*, 42–43. We noted in the previous chapter the difficulties concerning this text's date and provenance.

18. For translation and introduction, see R. B. Wright in Charlesworth, *Pseudepigrapha*, 2:639–670, and S. Brock in Sparks, *Apocryphal Old Testament*, 649–682. The Greek text is in Rahlfs, *Septuaginta*, 471–489, whose versification is followed here.

19. See discussion of these passages in Klawans, *Impurity and Sin*, 50–51, 122–123; cf. Hayes, *Gentile Impurities*, 87, for further examples of this sort of exegesis.

20. For a thorough treatment of issues pertaining to property in the Dead Sea corpus, see Murphy, *Wealth in the Dead Sea Scrolls.*

21. In addition to 1QpHab VIII:11–12 and XII:10 (both cited previously), note especially 1QS VI:19–22, and CD passages to be discussed later in this chapter. On wealth in CD, see Murphy, *Wealth in the Dead Sea Scrolls*, 25–102, and "Disposition of Wealth." On the phrase "evil wealth," see Murphy, *Wealth in the Dead Sea Scrolls*, 36–40.

22. This is true as well of the passages cited previously from *T. Levi, Assumption of Moses, Jubilees,* and *Psalms of Solomon.*

23. On this passage, see Murphy, *Wealth in the Dead Sea Scrolls*, 61–66, 476–477. Murphy supposes that this ruling breaks new ground by extending "the biblical law to prohibit the cultic use of wealth tainted by violence" (64). Murphy is correct that no biblical *law* explicitly prohibits such an offering. But we can hardly be certain that CD inveighs here against what were "probably dominant cultic practices" (62). Indeed, as Murphy also notes, there are a host of prophetic and wisdom traditions (such as those discussed in chapter 3) on which CD could rely for its ruling (62 n. 85).

24. This is among the passages pointed to by those who wish to assert that the sectarian rejection of the temple in Jerusalem was not complete: see, e.g., Davies, "Ideology of the Temple," 293–294. We obviously cannot deal with that larger question here, but this law in particular is not necessarily evidence of active participation in the temple cult, any more than the tannaitic laws of *m. Nedarim* (concerning vows) and *m. Shevu'ot* (concerning oaths) are evidence that the temple still stood in the late second century c.e. By analogy to rabbinic literature, if the system of temple dedication can persist in the absence of the temple (as it does in the Mishnah), laws concerning vows to the temple can persist along with the rejection of the temple as well (as, perhaps, at Qumran).

25. Translation based on Daniel R. Schwartz, in Charlesworth, *Damascus Document*, 23–25, and on Baumgarten's translation (and reconstruction) of 4Q266, as presented in *DJD XVIII*, 41–43. On this passage, see also (among many other studies): Davies, "Ideology"; Grossman, "Priesthood as Authority," 128–131; Murphy, *Wealth in the Dead Sea Scrolls*, 75–78, 460–461; and Murphy-O'Connor, "Translation of Damascus Document VI," and "Literary Analysis of Damascus Document VI."

26. Schwartz translates the Hebrew חנם as "in vain," as do all other translations of CD known to me. On the meaning of the verse from Malachi, see discussion in chapter 3. As reconstructed by Baumgarten, 4Q266 does not include the word חנם at this point in the document, and it is also phrased in the singular. According to this

reading, he who enters the covenant is not to enter the sanctuary (at all), for if he were—as Malachi states—he would light the altar at no cost.

27. Schwartz translates רג as "proselyte," following usage in rabbinic literature, and CD XIV:5–6. "Stranger" fits the immediate context better, in my view; compare Wise's assessment in *Critical Study*, 169–170 n. 29.

28. On wealth in 1QS in general, see Murphy, *Wealth in the Dead Sea Scrolls*, 103–162, on 1QS V:20 see 133–134, 498–499.

29. There has been a long debate on whether this passage articulates a rejection of the temple. In his earliest treatment of these themes, J. Baumgarten believed that the passage did indeed articulate a rejection of the temple ("Sacrifice and Worship," 143–144). In his later assessment ("Essenes and the Temple," in *Studies*, 70–71), he stepped back from that judgment. Davies, "Ideology," 295–298, develops this approach further, claiming (1) that not lighting the altar is not the main concern of the passage but just the first of a number of injunctions, and (2) that the phrase "in vain" is meant restrictively: as long as they don't light the altar in vain, they can still light the altar. In *DJD XVIII*, 43, Baumgarten dismisses Davies's first point as syntactically difficult. As for Davies's second point, once we drop the translation of חנם as "in vain" and adopt something more suitable to the context of Mal. 1:10 and CD VI:11, it becomes clear that the point of the passage is that there is no way to light the altar properly at all in the current situation. Among the recent interpreters who view the passage as a rejection of the temple are Regev, "Abominated Temple," 258, and Schmidt, *How the Temple Thinks*, 150–151.

30. On Ben Sira's attitude toward sacrifice and the temple in general, see Hayward, *Jewish Temple*, 38–84. On this passage in particular, see Skehan and Di Lella, *Wisdom of Ben Sira*, 411–423. But we have to disregard their understanding of the passage to the effect that "external cultic practices are efficacious only when joined to interior conversion and repentance" (417–418); see our discussion under the heading "Priests, Prophets, Sacrifice and Theft" in chapter 3. See also Büchler's brief comments in *Studies in Sin and Atonement*, 404–407.

31. On the laws in 4QMMT, see Kister, "Studies in 4Miqsat Ma'aseh ha-Torah"; Qimron, *DJD X*, 123–177, and Sussmann, "History of *Halakha*," which is the fully annotated version of what is presented in Qimron, *DJD X*, 179–200. In a recent survey, Regev claims that *all* the rulings listed in 4QMMT can be understood in relation to ritual impurity ("Abominated Temple," 245–249). In my view, this conclusion goes beyond what the extant evidence permits. On the purity laws in 11QT, see Yadin, *Temple Scroll*, 1:277–343.

32. Presumably the three-day extension comes by exegetical analogy to Exod. 19:15; see Yadin, *Temple Scroll*, 1:285–288.

33. See Yadin, *Temple Scroll*, 1: 340, and Qimron, *DJD X*, 153–154, 169–170.

34. Schiffman, "Pharisaic and Sadducean Halakhah," and see also Grabbe, "4QMMT and Second Temple Jewish Society," 91–93, and Kister, "Studies in 4QMMT," 327.

35. On these passages, see Yadin, *Temple Scroll*, 1:289–291, and Qimron, *DJD X*, 160–161.

36. Klawans, *Impurity and Sin*, 67–91.

37. See Qimron, *DJD X*, 152–154, 169–170; on the other 4Q texts concerning this rite, see J. Baumgarten et al., *DJD XXXV*, 79–122. See also articles cited earlier with regard to the "Tevul Yom."

38. Schiffman, "Exclusion from the Sanctuary," and Yadin, *Temple Scroll*, 1:277–343.

39. See, e.g., Yadin's comments to this effect, *Temple Scroll*, 2:127–128.

40. Unfortunately, this aspect of the *Temple Scroll*'s theology has not been suitably studied to date. Typically, analyses of presence theology in 11QT build on the alleged distinction between Deuteronomy's "abstract" theology and the Priestly strand's "concrete" one. See, for example, Shemesh, "Holiness." In my view, the theology of most of these documents is largely consistent: God will cause some divine aspect to dwell in a temple, provided it is pure. Whether that temple is large or small, and whether its sanctity extends into the surrounding city or not, the theology is essentially the same.

41. Schiffman, "Theology of the Temple Scroll," and *Reclaiming the Dead Sea Scrolls*, 262–266. Schiffman subsequently has suggested that there is indeed a difference between biblical theology and that of 11QT. Noting that 11QT's temple consists of concentric square courts, while the Solomonic and Herodian temples consisted of off-center, rectangular courts, Schiffman identifies different theologies in the two models—one focused on penetration into the sacred (Solomonic and Herodian), and the other focused on the radiation of the sacred outward (the *Temple Scroll*). See "Architecture and Law," 282–284; "Community without Temple," in Ego et al., *Gemeinde ohne Tempel*, 277–278, and "Sacred Space," 402–404. In my view, the suggestion that a different theology is implied by the architectural contrasts is outweighed by the more well-documented fact that the basic presence-theology explicitly stated in 11QT is essentially what we find in the biblical sources, as Schiffman, "Theology," demonstrates.

42. On the *Temple Scroll*'s sources, see Wise, *Critical Study*, 21–23, 197–198 (in general), and 133–136 (on purity laws in particular); see also the literature cited there. On the possible priestly origins of the *Temple Scroll* see 155–194.

43. Klawans, *Impurity and Sin*, 67–91.

44. See Qimron, *DJD X*, 150–152 and Yadin, *Temple Scroll*, 2:89–90; cf. Kugler, "Rewriting Rubrics," 99–100.

45. See Qimron, *DJD X*, 164–166, and Kugler, "Rewriting Rubrics," 109–110.

46. See discussion of these regulations in Yadin, *Temple Scroll*, 1:143–168.

47. See, for example, Cross, *Ancient Library of Qumran*, 100–120; De Vaux, *Archaeology and the Dead Sea Scrolls*, 3–5, and Vermes, *Complete Dead Sea Scrolls*, 49–66. See discussion in Kugler, "Priesthood at Qumran," 97–103, and the literature cited there.

48. Metso, *Textual Development* 27–28, 41–42, 78, 80; see also Baumgarten, "Zadokite Priests."

49. Magness, *Archaeology of Qumran*, 47–72.

50. So Schechter, *Fragments of a Zadokite Work*, 34–35, followed more recently by Grossman, "Priesthood as Authority," 126–128. For fuller discussions of this passage—and the variants between CD's quotation of Ezekiel and MT—see Klinzing, *Umdeutung des Kultus*, 130–142; for references to recent debates about this passage, see A. Baumgarten, "Zadokite Priests," 151 n. 38.

51. On this calendar, see VanderKam, "Origin, Character, and Early History," which revisits the theories presented in Jaubert, *Date of the Last Supper*. On this calendar at Qumran, see Uwe Glessmer, "Calendars in the Qumran Scrolls," in Flint et al., *The Dead Sea Scrolls after Fifty Years*, 2:213–278, and VanderKam, "Calendrical Texts." Many of the Qumran calendar texts are now available in Talmon et al., *DJD XXI* (and see also Talmon's introduction, 1–6).

52. For a comprehensive history of the traditional Jewish calendar and its system of intercalation (with reference to the early solar calendar as well), see Stern, *Calendar and Community*.

53. On the Egyptian and Roman calendars, see Finegan, *Handbook*, 18–25 (Egypt) and 64–68 (Rome), and Richards, *Mapping Time*, 150–160 (Egypt) and 206–219 (Rome).

54. Glessmer, "Calendars in the Qumran Scrolls," in Flint et al., *The Dead Sea Scrolls After Fifty Years*, 2:223–230, 240–252.

55. It is, however, commonly asserted that the calendar *must* have been intercalated: so, e.g., Elior, *Three Temples*, 43, 92–93 n. 17; Jaubert, *Date*, 52, 97, and 148 n. 9; and Talmon's introduction to *DJD XXI*, 6. Glessmer, "Calendars," in Flint et al., *The Dead Sea Scrolls After Fifty Years*, 2:265–268 suggests that 4Q319 (4QOtot) can be understood in part as reflecting the effort to correlate the 364-day Qumran calendar with the actual solar year. But see Ben-Dov's comments on 4Q319 in Talmon et al., *DJD XXI*, 210–211: because no extant Qumran text explicitly speaks of the true solar year, 4Q319 should not be understood in this way.

56. *Contra* Elior, *Three Temples*, 44–45, 82–87.

57. *Contra* Elior, *Three Temples*, 57, 86.

58. Compare the similar assessment in Stegemann, *Library of Qumran*, 176.

59. This passage speaks of Jerusalem as a whole, but presumably the temple too is included; cf. Tob. 14:5–7, and Isa. 54:11–12. For discussion, see Lee, *New Jerusalem*, 82–86.

60. On these documents, see García Martínez, "The Temple Scroll and the New Jerusalem," in Flint et al., *The Dead Sea Scrolls after Fifty Years*, 2:431–460, esp. 445–460; García Martínez, *Qumran and Apocalyptic*, 202–213, and Lee, *New Jerusalem*, 123–127.

61. This is the standard view, taken by (among others): García Martínez, *Qumran and Apocalyptic*, 204–205, and "Temple Scroll and the New Jerusalem," in Flint et al., *The Dead Sea Scrolls After Fifty Years*, 2:438–440; Lee, *The New Jerusalem*, 91–96; Schiffman, "Theology of the Temple Scroll," 115–118, and especially Yadin, *Temple Scroll*, 1:182–188. For the perspective that links 11QT with the *New Jerusalem* texts, see Wise, *Critical Study*, 64–84; see also his interpretation of 11QT XXIX, 157–161. Wise's arguments regarding the *New Jerusalem* texts are effectively countered by García Martínez; Wise's reading of 11QT XXIX is effectively countered by Schiffman and Yadin.

62. On this passage, see Yadin, *Temple Scroll*, 2:125–129. For a slightly different reading of this important passage see Qimron, *Temple Scroll*, 44 (on the damage to this particular column of the manuscript, see Qimron, *Temple Scroll*, 2). See also Schiffman, "Theology of the Temple Scroll," 115–118.

63. Generally, see Yadin, *Temple Scroll*, 1:177–276; see also Schmidt, *How the Temple Thinks*, 167–173, and the articles by Schiffman cited later.

64. For this comparison (with a superimposed map), see Roitman, *Envisioning the Temple*, 43–46. On the outer court, see Yadin, *Temple Scroll*, 1:249–275.

65. Yadin, *Temple Scroll*, 1:188–200.

66. Schiffman, "Structures of the Inner Court," 176; see also Schmidt, *How the Temple Thinks*, 183 n. 32, and Yadin, *Temple Scroll*, 1:211–271, 412–413. For other details concerning the temple in 11QT, see Yadin, *Temple Scroll*, 1:177–276; Schiffman, "Architecture and Law" and "Construction of the Temple."

67. For a comparison of these various structures, see Yadin, *Temple Scroll*, 1:188–197, and Schiffman, "Architecture and Law," "Construction of the Temple," and "Descriptions of the Jerusalem Temple."

68. See, e.g., Regev, "Abominated Temple," 242; Roitman, *Envisioning the Temple*, 43; Sussmann, "The History of the Halakha," in Qimron, *DJD X*, 187.

69. See e.g., Schiffman, "Exclusion from the Sanctuary."

70. See Elman, "Some Remarks," 99–105.

71. On the gates, see Yadin, *Temple Scroll*, 1:246–247, 253–256.

72. See Yadin, *Temple Scroll*, 1:151, and the sources cited there; Schiffman, "*Shelamim* Sacrifices."

73. See Yadin, *Temple Scroll*, 1:154–159, and Jacob Milgrom, "The Shoulder for the Levites," in Yadin, *Temple Scroll*, 1:169–176.

74. So, e.g., Baumgarten, "Essenes and the Temple," in *Studies*, 69, 74, and Davies, "Ideology," 300–301.

75. Davies, "Ideology," 290; see Regev, "On Blood," 12.

76. E.g., Cross, *Ancient Library of Qumran*, 85–86, and Humbert, "L'espace Sacré à Qumrân," 184–191, 199–201. For a critical evaluation with fuller bibliography, see Magness, *Archaeology of Qumran*, 105–133. In a sense, this dispute began even before the Dead Sea Scrolls were discovered. In *Fragments of a Zadokite Work* (xv), Schechter maintained that the sect performed sacrifices on its own (presumably in Damascus). Ginzberg objected, believing instead that the sect offered prayers in lieu of sacrifice (*Unknown Jewish Sect*, 70–71).

77. On the bone burials in particular, see de Vaux, *Archaeolgy and the Dead Sea Scrolls*, 12–16; on archaeological evidence pertaining to cultic practices in general (including the bone burials) see Magness, *Archaeology of Qumran*, 105–133. Humbert, "L'espace Sacré à Qumrân," tries to interpret the layout of the Qumran site as if it were a temple; Magness's account—which denies this possibility—is more convincing.

78. For a full discussion of *Ant.* 18:19, see A. Baumgarten, "Josephus on Essene Sacrifice," and J. Baumgarten, *Studies in Qumran Law*, 57–74, as well as Louis Feldman's notes to *Ant.* 18:19 in the LCL edition.

79. So, e.g., J. Baumgarten, "Sacrifice and Worship," 155; cf. "Essenes and the Temple," in *Studies*, 67. But see Feldman's notes to *Ant.* 18:19; A. Baumgarten, "Josephus on Essene Sacrifice," 170 n. 4.

80. E.g., Baumgarten, "Essenes and the Temple," in *Studies*, 61–62; Klinzing, *Umdeutung des Kultus*, 48–49; Schiffman, "Community without Temple," in Ego et al., *Gemeinde ohne Tempel*, 272.

81. Generally, see Jena Jörg Frey, "Temple and Rival Temple—The Cases of Elephantine, Mt. Gerizim, and Leontopolis," in Ego et al., *Gemeinde ohne Tempel*, 171–203; the case of Araq el-Emir is also discussed, 194–195.

82. See Elgvin and Pfann, "Incense Altar."

83. Schiffman, "Community without Temple," in Ego et al., *Gemeinde ohne Tempel*, 272, and *Eschatological Community*, 64–67; cf. Baumgarten, "Essenes and the Temple," in *Studies*, 59–60.

84. Magness, *Archaeology of Qumran*, 116–128, 132–133.

85. On the red heifer rite at Qumran, see Bowman, "Did the Qumran Sect Burn." As Bowman points out (78), the potential conceptual separation of this rite from temple-centered sacrifices can be seen by analogy to the Samaritans, who apparently performed the red heifer ritual well into the fourteenth century c.e., long after their temple at Mount Gerizim was destroyed. Bowman is followed more recently by A. Baumgarten, "Josephus on Essene Sacrifice," 177–183 (who suggests that when Josephus speaks of Essene sacrifice beyond the temple, he has the red heifer rite in mind), and García Martínez, "Priestly Functions in a Community without Temple," in Ego et al., *Gemeinde ohne Tempel*, 315–316, who bases his argument in part on the documents pertaining to this rite uncovered at Qumran

(e.g., 4Q277). For the key Qumran texts see Baumgarten, *DJD XXXV*, 79–122, 81–92. It is also possible—but beyond verification—that the sectarians performed the Passover offering of Exodus 12 at Qumran; see, briefly, Stegemann, *Library of Qumran*, 176.

86. See *m. Parah* 3:5, and the Samaritan evidence summarized by Bowman, "Did the Qumran Sect Burn," 78.

87. A number of studies have been devoted to this theme, particularly as it appears in both Qumran and the New Testament. See especially Gärtner, *Temple and the Community*, and Klinzing, *Umdeutung des Kultus*. For a critical review of these comparative analyses, see Schüssler Fiorenza, "Cultic Language." On Qumran in particular, see Schmidt, *How the Temple Thinks*, 138–197.

88. In addition to often-cited classic works (such as Baumgarten, "Sacrifice and Worship," and Gärtner, *Temple and the Community*), the following recent studies describe the community as a "spiritual" temple or their worship as "spiritual" sacrifices: Brooke, "Miqdash Adam," in Ego et al., *Gemeinde ohne Tempel*, 297; García Martínez, *Qumran and Apocalyptic*, 206; Knibb, *Qumran Community*, 130–131 (see also Knibb, "Rule of the Community," in Schiffman and VanderKam, *Encyclopedia*, 2:793–797); Regev, "Abominated Temple," 271; and Roitman, *Envisioning the Temple*, 88–93. See, in addition, Wise, Abegg, and Cook, *Dead Sea Scrolls*, 126; although the term "spiritualization" is not used here, the argument presumes that the sectarians replaced sacrificial worship with a better alternative.

89. For discussions of these options, see Kugler, "Rewriting Rubrics," 90–92; on the less common idea that their exegetical activity served in this capacity, see 92–94, 112. Surely the sect studied sacrificial laws; but the idea that they "satisfied themselves" by such study (94) has hardly been proven. For a more restrained survey of this evidence, see Schiffman, "Community without Temple," in Ego et al., *Gemeinde ohne Tempel*, 272–276.

90. E.g., Dimant, "Men as Angels," 97, and Lee, *New Jerusalem*, 96–104; see discussion further in this chapter.

91. The *editio princeps* of 4Q174 was prepared by Allegro and published in *DJD V*, 53–57. This edition has been considered woefully inadequate virtually since its publication: see Strugnell, "Notes en marge," 220–225. A revised version of *DJD V* is still awaited.

92. Strugnell, "Notes en Marge," 177, 220.

93. On these exclusions, see J. Baumgarten, "Exclusion of 'Netinim.'" Against the idea that the text concerns proselytes per se, see Wise, *Critical Study*, 168–172.

94. See, e.g., Gärtner, *Temple and the Community*, 18–19, 30–42, who finds in the phrase *miqdash adam* further confirmation of the idea that the Qumran community understood itself as a "spiritualized" temple; see J. Baumgarten, "Exclusion of 'Netinim,'" 94–96 (esp. n. 29, which cites Gärtner approvingly with regard to the "spiritual" temple). García Martínez, *Qumran and Apocalyptic*, 206, also uses the term "spritualization," even though he interprets *miqdash adam* in a different way; Lee, *New Jerusalem*, 118–122, does not speak of "spiritualization," but, like Gärtner, he believes that the eschatological temple will be a temple consisting of the community.

95. Yadin, "Midrash on 2 Sam vii" (see also *Temple Scroll*, 1:182–188), and Flusser, "Two Notes on the Midrash on 2 Sam. vii," in *Judaism and the Origins of Christianity*, 88–98. Yadin and Flusser have been followed in essence (but not in all particulars) by, among others, Klinzing, *Umdeutung des Kultus*, 80–87, and McKelvey, *New Temple*, 50–51; see also García Martínez, *Qumran and Apocalyptic*, 208–211.

96. Yadin, *Temple Scroll*, 1:187–188 n. 13; cf. McKelvey, *New Temple*, 50–51.

97. For the reading "acts of Torah," see Allegro, *DJD V*, 53, who is followed by Baumgarten, "Exclusion of 'Netinim,'" 94–95; Gärtner, *Temple and the Community*, 34; Schmidt, *How the Temple Thinks*, 164; and Dimant, "*4QFlorilegium*," 169, who asserts that the early photograph supports Allegro's reading. Klinzing, *Umdeutung des Kultus*, 81, notes the question concerning the reading but translates following Allegro. For the reading "acts of thanksgiving" (*todah*), see Strugnell, "Notes en marge," 121, now followed by Brooke, "Miqdash Adam," in Ego et al., *Gemeinde ohne Tempel*, 288 n. 13: "all those who have recently studied the actual manuscript together with the photographs are agreed that *daleth* should be read as Strugnell originally tentatively suggested." García Martínez and Tigchelaar, *Study Edition*, 1:352, print the text with the *daleth*.

98. Schwartz, "Three Temples," 88.

99. García Martínez, *Qumran and Apocalyptic*, 208–209.

100. Dimant, "*4QFlorilegium*," 177–178.

101. Brooke, "Miqdash Adam," in Ego et al., *Gemeinde ohne Tempel*, 288–291, building on (and in some ways refuting) Wise, "*4QFlorilegium*."

102. Schmidt, *How the Temple Thinks*, 163–164, for instance, understands the document to be speaking of a "temple of men"—consisting of the community—that exists only provisionally, until the final physical temple will be rebuilt.

103. So, e.g., Maier, "Temple," in Schiffman and VanderKam, *Encyclopedia*, 2:925.

104. See Yadin, *Scroll of the War*, 198–201, 264–265, 272–273; see also García Martínez, *Qumran and Apocalyptic*, 209–213, and Klinzing, *Umdeutung des Kultus*, 34–35.

105. Yadin, *Temple Scroll*, 1:186–188, esp. nn. 12 and 13; cf. Lee, *New Temple*, 91–96.

106. Hannah K. Harrington, "Atonement," in Schiffman and VanderKam, *Encyclopedia*, 1:69.

107. For discussions of these passages in light of this theme, see Gärtner, *Temple and the Community*, 22–30; Knibb, *Qumran Community*, 120–140; Klinzing, *Umdeutung des Kultus*, 37–41, 50–74, 93–105; Licht, *Rule Scroll*, 168–173; McKelvey, *New Temple*, 46–50, and Schiffman, "Community without Temple," in Ego et al., *Gemeinde ohne Tempel*, 272–273. Note also the more significant 4Q parallels: 4QSb (4Q256) frag. 5, 5–6 and 4QSd (4Q258) frag. 1, 1:4–5//1QS V:5–6; 4QSe (4Q259) II:11–16//1QS VIII:5–10; 4QSd (4Q258) frag. 3, 1:4–6//1QS IX:3–5. These texts are published in Alexander and Vermes, *DJD XXVI*, and Charlesworth, *Rule of the Community*.

108. So, e.g., Charlesworth, *Rule of the Community*, 39; García Martínez and Tigchelaar, *Study Edition*, 1:91; Knibb, *Qumran Community*, 138–139; Kilinzing, *Umdeutung des Kultus*, 37–41, 64–66; Vermes, *Complete Dead Sea Scrolls*, 110. For a discussion that concludes in favor of this possibility, see Lichtenberger, "Atonement and Sacrifice," 161–162.

109. E.g., J. Baumgarten, "Exclusion of 'Netinim,'" 94–95; cf. "Sacrifice and Worship," 149, and "Essenes and the Temple," in *Studies*, 67–68; Gaster, *Dead Sea Scriptures*, 63; Leaney, *Rule of Qumran*, 210.

110. So, e.g., Wise, Abegg, and Cook, *Dead Sea Scrolls*, 139, and Wernberg-Møller, *Manual of Discipline*, 35, 133. See discussion in Schmidt, *How the Temple Thinks*, 140–141.

111. Gärtner, *Temple and the Community*, 29 (n. 2), 30; compare McKelvey, *New Temple*, 47, 50, who understands the key phrase to be speaking of atonement "without

the flesh of burnt offerings" but still claims that the new temple spoken of here "displaces" and "supersedes" the old. With reference to 1QS IX:4, Wise introduces his discussion of 1QS with the rather offensive assertion that "many thinking people in the period of the New Testament had difficulties with the notion of animal sacrifice" (Wise, Abegg, and Cook, *Dead Sea Scrolls*, 126).

112. E.g., Charlesworth, *Rule of the Community*, 39 n. 222. See also Lichtenberger, "Atonement and Sacrifice," 161–162.

113. So, e.g., Baumgarten, "Essenes and the Temple," in *Studies*, 57; García Martínez, *Qumran and Apocalyptic*, 206; Schiffman, "Community without Temple," in Ego et al., *Gemeinde ohne Tempel*, 274, and Schmidt, *How the Temple Thinks*, 141.

114. E.g., Knibb, *Qumran Community*, 134; Leaney, *Rule of Qumran*, 221; Schiffman, "Architecture and Law," 270; Schmidt, *How the Temple Thinks*, 145–150; cf. Yadin, *Temple Scroll*, 1:189.

115. Schwartz, "Temple and Desert: On Religion and State in Second Temple Period Judaea," in *Studies in the Jewish Background*, 29–43.

116. Talmon, "The Desert Motif in the Bible and in Qumran Literature," in *Literary Studies*, 216–254.

117. Schmidt, *How the Temple Thinks*, 143–144.

118. Talmon, *Literary Studies*, 246–254.

119. Koester, *Dwelling of God*, 26–33. Contrast, e.g., Schiffman, "Architecture and Law," but see also Schiffman, "Construction of the Temple," 570, which comes closer to Koester's position.

120. So, for example, Schmidt, *How the Temple Thinks*, 162.

121. Licht, *Rule Scroll*, 179; see also 171–172.

122. Gärtner, *Temple and the Community*, 25; Licht, *Rule Scroll*, 171–172. Of course, scripture itself (2 Sam. 7:1–29) plays with the various meanings of this term—including "temple," "palace," and "dynasty." Christine Hayes (personal communication, June 15, 2004) suggests the possibility that the Qumranic references to a "sure house" are to be understood, at least in part, in the genealogical sense.

123. On this passage, see Klinzing, *Umdeutung des Kultus*, 75–80. Compare CD XI:21–XII:1 (cf. 4Q271 frag. 5, I:15), which speaks of the community's "house of prostration," again stopping short of using the term for sanctuary. See Ginzberg, *Unknown Jewish Sect*, 71, and Steudel, "Houses of Prostration." But see Baumgarten, "Essenes and the Temple," 70 (cf. *DJD XVIII*, 182), and Solomon, "Prohibition against Tevul Yom," 10–12, where the phrase is understood as applying to the temple (or at least some part of it).

124. See also 4Q266 frag. 6, II:9, as reconstructed by Baumgarten in *DJD XVIII*, 55–57.

125. Licht, *Rule Scroll*, 23, 171–172, 174. See also Lee, *New Jerusalem*, 113–116, which discusses the appearance of this metaphor in 1QH XIV:15. Here, too, Lee interprets the entire column of 1QH in light of the community-as-temple hypothesis.

126. On this metaphor in Qumran literature (especially its function in 4QFlorilegium), see Brooke, "Miqdash Adam," in Ego et al., *Gemeinde ohne Tempel*, 291–293.

127. Schiffman, "Community without Temple," in Ego et al., *Gemeinde ohne Tempel*, 274; see Lee, *New Jerusalem*, 100.

128. See VanderKam's edition of 4Q216 in Harold Attridge et al., *DJD XIII*, 1–22. *Jubilees* also knows of various mediating angels, but in the first chapter we are told of God's presence and glory. On *Jubilees'* angelology, see VanderKam, "Angel of Presence."

129. Schiffman, *Eschatological Community*, 49–51.

130. Gärtner, *Temple and the Community*, 94–96, McKelvey, *New Temple*, 37–38.

131. Jacobus A. Naudé, "Holiness in the Dead Sea Scrolls," in Flint et al., *Dead Sea Scrolls after Fifty Years*, 2:171–199, esp. 186–189.

132. So, e.g., Gärtner, *Temple and the Community*, 32–34; Hayward, "Jewish Temple at Leontopolis," 443; Sanders, *Paul and Palestinian Judaism*, 314–316; Schmidt, *How the Temple Thinks*, 152, 162–164, 193–197; and Wise, Abegg, and Cook, *Dead Sea Scrolls*, 126. The opposite assertion—that the sectarians believed God still dwelled in the Jerusalem temple—is expressed more rarely; but see, e.g., Stegemann, *Library of Qumran*, 176.

133. E.g., Knibb, *Qumran Community*, 138–139; Klinzing, *Umdeutung des Kultus*, 104–105; Lichtenberger, "Atonement and Sacrifice at Qumran," 164; Maier, "Temple," in Schiffman and VanderKam, *Encyclopedia*, 2:924; Regev, "Abominated Temple," 269, 278; Schiffman, "Community without Temple," in Ego et al., *Gemeinde ohne Tempel*, 273.

134. J. Baumgarten, "Exclusion of 'Netinim,'" 94–95; Gaster, *Dead Sea Scriptures*, 63; Leaney, *Rule of Qumran*, 210. Not all scholars overestimate the sectarian beliefs in their community's power of atonement. Contrast the foregoing with, e.g., Garnet, *Salvation and Atonement*, 57–81. Still, I am left with the impression that scholars are more likely to overestimate than underestimate the sectarians' faith in their community's power to effect atonement.

135. On the penal code of 1QS, see Licht, *Rule Scroll*, 153–166, 183–186; Schiffman, *Sectarian Law*, 155–190.

136. On this punishment in the Hebrew Bible, see Milgrom, *Leviticus 1–16*, 457–460.

137. For a detailed comparison of the biblical, Qumranic, and rabbinic approaches to these matters, see Shemesh, *Punishments and Sins*. For a study comparing the three approaches to sacrificial atonement, see Anderson, "Interpretation of the Purification Offering."

138. Shemesh, *Punishments and Sins*, 57–82; cf. J. Baumgarten, *DJD XVIII*, 74–78, 162–166, and Baumgarten, "Cave 4 Versions."

139. On this passage, and on the distinction between willful and unintentional sin at Qumran, see Gary Anderson, "Intentional and Unintentional Sin in the Dead Sea Scrolls," in Wright et al., *Pomegranates and Golden Bells*, 49–64.

140. Schuller, "Petitionary Prayer."

141. For these and other examples from the sectarian literature, see Schuller, "Petitionary Prayer," esp. 39–43.

142. E.g., Dimant, "Men as Angels," 97; Gärtner, *Temple and the Community*, 4–15; Klinzing, *Umdeutung des Kultus*, 106–114; Lee, *New Jerusalem*, 96–104; Regev, "Abominated Temple," 275–277; Roitman, *Envisioning the Temple*, 92–93; Schiffman, "Community without Temple," in Ego et al., *Gemeinde ohne Tempel*, 273–274; Schmidt, *How the Temple Thinks*, 132–197. One of the more interesting recent reviews of these issues can be found in Murphy, *Wealth in the Dead Sea Scrolls*, 137–155.

143. See discussion in Murphy, *Wealth in the Dead Sea Scrolls*, 137–141.

144. Murphy, *Wealth in the Dead Sea Scrolls*, 141–143.

145. See García Martínez, "Priestly Functions in a Community without Temple," in Ego et al., *Gemeinde ohne Tempel*, 303–319, and Kugler, "Priesthood at Qumran," in Flint et al., *The Dead Sea Scrolls After Fifty Years* 2:93–116; and with regard to Levites in particular, Kugler, "Priesthood at Qumran."

146. Generally, see Himmelfarb, "'Kingdom of Priests,'" Regev, "Non-Priestly Purity," and Regev, "Pure Individualism." The evidence is also surveyed briefly—but

with additional bibliography—in Poirier, "Purity beyond the Temple," 259. See Harrington, *Holiness*, for a broader analysis of holiness in ancient Judaism.

147. See Regev, "Non-Priestly Purity," 225–228, and "Pure Individualism," 177–178, and the literature cited in these articles concerning Tobit, Judith, *Aristeas*, and the *Sibylline Oracles*. Regev's discussion of these sources is based on Alon, "The Bounds of the Laws of Levitical Cleanness," in *Jews, Judaism, and the Classical World*, 190–234, esp. 201–203. On handwashing before eating in Mark, see Booth, *Jesus and the Laws of Purity*. Booth argues correctly that certain groups of ancient Jews required a *supererogatory* washing of the hands—even beyond what the laws of ritual purity may have required (189–203). (See also Booth, 160, on the textual problems surrounding *Sib. Or.* 3:591.) Generally, on the sacralization of food practices among ancient Jews, see also Schmidt, *How the Temple Thinks*, 198–244. Schmidt correctly emphasizes the ritual and conceptual overlap between food practices of ancient Jews and the sacrificial practices of the temple. He also correctly understands these phenomena as popular attempts at seeking holiness, ones that are not directed *against* the temple but along with it.

148. The fullest treatment of ritual baths discovered in the land of Israel and dated to the Second Temple period is Reich, "Miqwa'ot." Some of Reich's research is distilled in Sanders, *Jewish Law*, 214–227. For the latest on the ritual baths from Qumran, see Magness, *Archaeology of Qumran*, 134–162. With regard to ritual baths and extratemple purity specifically, see Regev, "Non-Priestly Purity," 234–236, and "Pure Individualism," 184–185.

149. See Reich, "Synagogue and Ritual Bath." Note also Acts 16:13, and the location of certain Diaspora synagogues near rivers or bodies of water (e.g., Delos, Ostia). A number of Diaspora synagogues also had their own cisterns (e.g., Delos, Dura, Sardis). See Poirier, "Purity beyond the Temple," 249–250.

150. For the latest on stone vessels in the Second Temple period, see Magen, *Stone Vessel Industry*, esp. 138–147, on the literary sources, and 148–162, 168–173, on the geographic distribution of the finds. For a brief account of the finds, see also Regev, "Non-Priestly Purity," 229–234, and "Pure Individualism," 181–184.

151. Regev, "Non-Priestly Purity," and "Pure Individualism." See also Himmelfarb, "Kingdom of Priests."

152. Notably, Sanders, *Jewish Law*, 131–254.

153. Himmelfarb, "Impurity and Sin," esp. 37.

154. See Magness, *Archaeology of Qumran*, 134–162.

155. See Baumgarten, *DJD XXXV*, 79–80 (note errata to 80); Harrington, *Impurity Systems*, 267–281, and Schmidt, *How the Temple Thinks*, 235–236 n. 119.

156. Alon, "Bounds," in *Jews, Judaism, and the Classical World*, 190–234. For a sustained discussion of Alon's position, see Poirier, "Purity beyond the Temple."

157. Alon, "Bounds," in *Jews, Judaism, and the Classical World*, 233.

158. So Büchler, *Galiläische 'Am-ha' Ares*. In this debate, we take the side of Alon against Büchler.

159. In dating (the nonsectarian) movements in this direction to later than 70 c.e., Büchler has been followed more recently by Baruch Bokser, whose works will be discussed in the next chapter.

160. Himmelfarb, "Kingdom of Priests"; see Hayes, *Gentile Impurities*, 73–75.

161. See Schwartz, " 'Kingdom of Priests'—a Pharisaic Slogan?" in *Studies in the Jewish Background*, 57–80. The same is true of another phrase used often in scholarship: "service of the heart" (see discussion in chapter 6).

162. See Himmelfarb, "Kingdom of Priests," 98 n. 21.

163. Sanders suggested that the Pharisees maintained purity "for its own sake," rejecting the idea that nonpriests wished to be priests; see *Jewish Law*, 184, 192, 245, 248; cf. Regev, "Non-Priestly Purity," 237–244, and "Pure Individualism," 186–190. Both of these scholars overlook the nuances of Alon's original position (see "Bounds," in *Jews, Judaism, and the Classical World*, 231), which did not assume that the maximalists thought they were becoming priests in all respects.

164. Poirier ("Purity beyond the Temple," 253) states with regard to any evidence concerning the temple orientation of the purity laws, that "apart from one dubious quotation from Josephus, *none* exists for the second temple period."

165. Poirier, "Purity beyond the Temple," 259, dismisses the evidence from *Against Apion* out of hand. The other texts noted earlier are not considered.

166. This connection, too, is dismissed out of hand by Poirier; see "Purity beyond the Temple," 253 n. 18.

167. See Fine, *This Holy Place*; see also the brief survey of temple imagery in ancient synagogue decoration in Roitman, *Envisioning the Temple*, 102–111 (this section authored by Shulamit Laderman).

168. Fine, *This Holy Place*, 32, 55 ("templization"), 41–55, 79–94, 132–134 (*imitatio templi*). Fine credits Ziony Zevit with coining the second neologism (184 n. 44). Some similar observations regarding synagogue holiness are also made by Branham, "Vicarious Sacrality." While offering some helpful observations on synagogue sanctity, this study is problematic in its use of Girard's model of mimetic rivalry (see esp. 320–323, 339–345). Girard's theory is an unfortunate choice when evaluating the relationship between the synagogue and the temple, for Girardian theory stacks the deck against the temple and sacrifice.

CHAPTER 6

1. Generally, on the temple as remembered by the rabbis, see Safrai, *Pilgrimage*, and "Temple and the Divine Service." For a recent comparative survey, see Harrington, *Holiness*, 45–90. It is my impression that there is significantly less scholarship on what the rabbis thought about the Second Temple compared to all that we find concerning those who (ostensibly) reject the temple. Useful, detailed analyses of the tannaitic sources can be found in Neusner, *History of the Mishnaic Law of Holy Things*, 6:273–290, also published as "Mapping Sacrifice and Sanctuary," in *HR* 19 (1979): 103–127. Important earlier analyses of the temple, its practice, and personnel in rabbinic literature include Büchler, *Priester*, and Lieberman, *Hellenism in Jewish Palestine*, 128–179.

2. On the possibility that rabbinic literature preserves responses to Qumranic texts or perspectives, see Magen Broshi, "Anti-Qumranic Polemics in the Talmud," in Trebolle Barrera and Vegas Montaner, *Madrid Qumran Congress*, 2:589–600. On the chronological issues involved (which are, again, of less interest to us here) see also Goodman, "Sadducees and Essenes after 70 C.E."

3. Klawans, *Impurity and Sin*, 118–135.

4. See discussion in Klawans, *Impurity and Sin*, 50–51, 122–123.

5. See Klawans, *Impurity and Sin*, 51. See also 88–90, where I suggested that the idea that sin defiles the land might have played some role in the sectarian withdrawal to the desert on the boundary of Israel. Explicit evidence to support that claim cannot be offered in part because so little Qumran evidence speaks at all of the defilement of the land.

6. For a fuller account, see Klawans, *Impurity and Sin*, 127–128, and 206, nn. 40 and 41, for fuller lists of traditions expressing the longer and shorter forms, respectively.

7. Perhaps the simplest way to find such sources is to survey the scholarship on Jesus' turning the tables in the temple. On this—and for the literature discussing this event—see chapter 7.

8. See, e.g., Fraenkel, *Iyyunim*, 119–121.

9. See discussion in Neusner, *History of the Mishnaic Law of Holy Things*, 6:202.

10. Epstein, *Introductions to Tannaitic Literature*, 25–58, defends the antiquity of such passages. Even in a later stage of his work, Neusner, *Judaism*, 71, 248–250, speaks of a priestly legacy in evidence in the Mishnah; but see 100–101 for more skeptical comments. For the classic expression of the theory that *m. Tamid* contains early, priestly material, see Ginzberg, "Mishnah Tamid" (often more readily available in its Hebrew translation, which appeared in Ginzberg, *'al Halakha ve-'Aggadah* [Tel Aviv: Dvir, 1960], 41–65, 269–284). For a critical discussion of Ginzberg's theory, see Neusner, *History of the Mishnaic Law of Holy Things*, 6:196–207.

11. See, e.g., Herr, "Continuum."

12. See also *Lev. Rabbah* 21:9; *y. Yoma* 1:1, 38c/562; *b. Yoma* 9a. On these traditions—and the issue of high priests bidding for office—see Alon, "Par'irtin," in *Jews, Judaism, and the Classical World*, esp. 48–49 and 65–69.

13. This understanding becomes clear by comparing the tradition quoted here with others in which the saying (or something similar to it) appears (*b. Shabbat* 116a–b; *Pesikta de Rab Kahana* 15:9, ed. Mandelbaum 260–261). In all three cases, the point of the saying is that the highest bidder will win. See Margulies's comments to *Lev. Rabbah* 21:9, on 2:489 of his edition. For what it's worth—considering the small sample—the tradition quoted is unique in utilizing the saying with regard to priestly corruption; the other tales tell of (nonpriestly) judges who took bribes.

14. The historicity of rabbinic attributions is not assumed (or denied). Whether or not rabbinic sources are historically accurate with regard to such attributions, it remains potentially significant for the evaluation of rabbinic perspectives to pay attention to who says what, and thus attributions will be noted here whenever relevant.

15. Again, we find that the details provided in the Mishnah are much less condemnatory than what we find in the subsequent rabbinic literature.

16. See Alon, "Par'irtin," in *Jews, Judaism, and the Classical World*, 57 and Herr, "Continuum."

17. For a brief survey of the methodological issues relating to the study of rabbinic stories, see Rubenstein, *Talmudic Stories*, 3–15.

18. Who received the money is less clear; again, see Alon, "Par'irtin," in *Jews, Judaism, and the Classical World*, 65–69.

19. In *Jewish War* 4:151–154, Josephus claims that until the eve of the war the priesthood carried on in an unbroken succession of inheritance. This is contradicted by Josephus' own account in *Antiquities*, where he speaks explicitly of priests from various families being appointed and fired by kings and governors.

20. Alon, "Par'irtin," in *Jews, Judaism, and the Classical World*, 62–63, cites and quotes from "In inscriptionem Altaris" (J.-P. Migne, *Patrologia graeca*, 162 vols. [Paris: 1844–1864], 51:73).

21. On *b. Pesahim* 57a and the various traditions preserved there, see Schwartz, "KATA TOYTON TON KAIPON," esp. 262–263. The translation here follows Schwartz, as compared to MS Vatican 125; see Rabbinovicz, *Diqduqe Soferim*, to *b. Pesahim* 57a.

22. So reads the version in *b. Pesahim*. While substantially similar, in *t. Menahot*, the fourth woe (and what follows) reads: "woe is me because of the House of Elisha, woe is me for their fist! Woe is me because of the House of Ishmael ben Phiabi, for they are high priests."

23. On this baraitha, see Schwartz, "KATA TOYTON TON KAIPON," 263–266, and Fraenkel, *Iyyunim*, 121–123. For the version in *b. Pesahim*, as compared to the parallel in *b. Keritot* 28a–b, see Schwartz, "KATA TOYTON TON KAIPON," 267 n. 74, who reasonably concludes that the version in *b. Keritot* is dependent upon the version in *b. Pesahim*. Again, the translation here follows Schwartz, as compared to MS Vatican 125; see Rabbinovicz, *Diqduqe Soferim*, to *b. Pesahim* 57a.

24. The italicized words are an Aramaic gloss, added to the otherwise Hebrew, tannaitic source.

25. And many modern interpreters have followed suit, as catalogued in Schwartz, "KATA TOYTON TON KAIPON," 264 n. 61. See, for example, Büchler, *Studies in Jewish History*, 37–39. Büchler points out that Ishmael ben Ph(i)abi is remembered for good—and called a rabbi!—in *m. Sotah* 9:15. The generally negative tone of this passage should not be ignored, however, by appeal to other possibly contradictory sources, especially mishnaic sources, which, as we have noted, are consistently less critical of the priesthood than later rabbinic material.

26. So Schwartz, "KATA TOYTON TON KAIPON," 262–264.

27. For the house of Boethus, see, e.g., *Ant.* 15:320–323, 17:339; the house of Ananus: *Ant.* 18:26–27, 20:197–207; the house of Kantheros: *Ant.* 19:297, 342, 20:15; Ishmael ben Ph(i)abi: 18:34, 20:179–196 (probably two distinct priests; see Feldman's note f. to *Ant.* 18:34 (LCL, 9:29).

28. See also *Ant.* 20:205–207, on the greed of an Ananus. On the variable spelling of Ph(i)abi in the manuscripts of Josephus, see, e.g., LCL, 9:484 n. 3. For more on this figure and the sources concerning him, see Schwartz, "Ishmael ben Phiabi and the Chronology of Provincia Judaea," in *Studies in the Jewish Background*, 218–242.

29. See Schwartz, "KATA TOYTON TON KAIPON," 264–265.

30. Schwartz, "KATA TOYTON TON KAIPON," 262–268.

31. Virtually the same answer is given in *y. Yoma* 1:1, 38c/562; in *b. Yoma* 9a, we are told only that senseless hatred caused the destruction (greed is not mentioned). We find here and elsewhere in rabbinic literature different reasons given for the destruction of the Second Temple, and therefore different evaluations of that generation's behavior are offered. As we will see, not all rabbinic sources acquit the people of the Second Temple period of the charge of murder.

32. On the *t. Yoma* text and its parallels, see Lieberman, *Tosefta Ki-Fshutah*, 4:735–736. Compare *m. Yoma* 2:2, where we find once again that the Mishnah's parallel is much less condemnatory of the priests. For a literary analysis of this story, see Fraenkel, "Hermeneutic Problems," 157–163, cf. Fraenkel, *Iyyunim*, 133–135. I thank Alon Goshen-Gottstein for bringing Fraenkel's analysis of this story to my attention. See also Klawans, *Impurity and Sin*, 121–122.

33. Curiously, there are some rabbinic sources to the effect that corpses themselves could not defile the temple at all; see *t. Kelim BQ* 1:8, which recalls Joseph's bones being carried out of Egypt, and cf. *Sifre Zutta* to Num. 19:11 (ed. Horovitz 305).

34. These and other leniencies are noted and discussed briefly by J. Baumgarten, in "Essenes and the Temple," 63–64. For a fuller treatment, see Safrai, *Pilgrimage*, 134–141.

35. See also *y. Yoma* 1:1, 38c/562, *b. Yoma* 9a. On differences between the two temples in general, see, e.g., *b. Yoma* 18a, 21b, and *b. Menahot* 27b.

36. *Lam. Rabbah*, proem 5 (ed. Buber 3b; see n. 8), proem 23 (ed. Buber 11a); *Lam. Rabbah* 2:2 (ed. Buber 54b), 4:13 (ed. Buber 74b–75a); *Pesikta de Rab Kahana* 15:7 (ed. Mandelbaum 257–258).

37. See, with minor variations (not always amounting to seven sins), *Lam. Rabbah* proem 23, *Lam. Rabbah* 4:13, and *Pesikta de Rab Kahana* 15:7.

38. See especially Rubenstein, *Talmudic Stories*, 139–175, whose translation is utilized here; see 290–292 for the text of the story following MS Arras 969, and 173–185 for a listing of variants among other manuscripts.

39. On this sage's curious—and, no doubt, legendary—name, see Rubenstein, *Talmudic Stories*, 348 n. 27.

40. See *Lam. Rabbah* 4:2 (ed. Buber 71b–72a), where Zechariah's meekness is connected directly to the event concerning Qamza and Bar Qamza: he was one of the sages who acquiesced to the latter's embarrassment. See discussion in Rubenstein, *Talmudic Stories*, 149–150, 172–173.

41. *B. Gittin* 55b, 57a; the former may well be a later gloss. See Rubenstein, *Talmudic Stories*, 140.

42. See discussion in Rubenstein, *Talmudic Stories*, 149–151.

43. See also *Mekilta de-Rabbi Ishmael* Bahodesh 1, on Exod. 19:1 (ed. Horovitz and Rabin, 203–204); *b. Bava Metzia* 30b; *b. Hagigah* 14a, and *Lam. Rabbah* 1:3 (ed. Buber 31b). For a discussion of the *Lam. Rabbah* traditions in particular, see Cohen, "Destruction," 25–28.

44. See Klawans, *Impurity and Sin*, 127–129.

45. See Klawans, *Impurity and Sin*, 118–133; cf. Anderson, "Interpretation of the Purification Offering," esp. 34–35.

46. I think Christine Hayes for helping me develop this line of argument.

47. Compare the traditions collected in *Lev. Rabbah* 3:5 (ed. Margulies, 1:65–68), discussed also in Fraenkel, *Iyyunim*, 1329–132.

48. Translation follows printed editions, as compared to MS Kaufmann.

49. On this device, see Lieberman, *Hellenism in Jewish Palestine*, 177–179.

50. Josephus, *Ant.* 20:17–53.

51. See *m. Middot* 1:4; 2:3; *t. Yoma* 2:4; *b. Yoma* 38a; Josephus, *JW* 5:201. On these traditions, see Wiesenberg, "Nicanor Gate." Again, we make no assumption here concerning the historicity of these rabbinic sources—our primary concern is with the ideology that emerges from the rabbis' recollection of such donations. With regard to Nicanor, however, it is important to note the Greek and Aramaic burial inscription from the Second Temple period discovered on Mt. Scopus, mentioning an Alexandrian named Nicanor "who made the doors." See Avigad, "Jewish Rock-Cut Tombs," 119–125. The ossuary is now in the British Museum, and a photograph of the ossuary and its inscription can be found on the museum's web site, by typing "Nicanor" into the search engine for the online collections database.

52. On one level, the building of the temple can be seen as an act of repentance on Herod's part: the restoration is seen as countering the killing of the sages. On the other hand, there are many other sins recounted here, and Herod's wish that he didn't kill the sages has less to do with his repentance than his recognition that his action against the sages was unwise. Compare the brief but compelling analysis of *b. Bava Batra* 3b-4a in Rubenstein, *Rabbinic Stories*, 33–37.

53. For a survey of the rabbinic approach to the guilt offering—with special attention to theft—see Büchler, *Studies in Sin and Atonement*, 376–461.

54. *Sifra Dibura de-Nedaba* parashah 5:2, on Lev. 1:10, ed. Finkelstein 2:49, see 4:49, and ed. Weiss 7c. The fourth-generation Babylonian amora Abbaye (c. 300 C.E.) is said to have quoted the same tradition in *b. Bava Qamma* 66b and 67b.

55. Two additional anonymous and otherwise unparalleled tannaitic traditions appear in *Sifra Tzav Mekilta de-Miluim* 15, on Lev. 8:15 (ed. Weiss 41d), and *Sifre Zutta Shelach* 15:3, on Num. 15:3 (ed. Horovitz 281). An amoraic tradition that excludes robbed animals appears in *Lev. Rabbah* 2:7, attributed to the fifth-generation Palestinian amora R. Berakhiah of the late fourth century C.E. (ed. Margulies 1:45).

56. Rabbinic sources consistently interpret Deut. 23:19 literally as referring to a dog; on Deut. 23:19, see further in this chapter.

57. See *m. Zevahim* 8:1, *m. Bekhorot* 6:12, 7:7, 9:4; *m. Temurah* 6:1–5; *t. Zevahim* 8:1–2, 9:1–3, *t. Temurah* 1:9, 12, 4:1–10; cf. *t. Nazir* 4:9; *t. Makkot* 5 (4):4; *t. Menahot* 8:18; *b. Temurah* 28a–31b; *Sifra Dibura de Nedaba* parashah 2:7, on Lev. 1:2 (ed. Finkelstein 2:22–25, see also 4:24–25; ed. Weiss 4d–5a); *Sifre Deut.*, sec. 147, on 17:1 (ed. Finkelstein 201–202); *Sifre Deut.*, sec. 261, on 23:19 (ed. Finkelstein 283–284).

58. *Sifra Dibura de-Nedaba* parashah 2:7 (ed. Finkelstein 2:22–23), *b. Temurah* 28b, cf. *b. Sota* 46b. *Sifra Dibura de-Nedaba* parashah 5:2 (ed. Finkelstein 2:49–50), which preserves a tradition attributed to R. Yudah, also explicitly permits animals that have been used in violation of Sabbaths, holidays, or other commandments.

59. The reading and meaning of this phrase are obscure. The reading here follows *m. Gittin* 5:5 and *m. Eduyyot* 7:9 in MS Kaufmann and MS Parma, as well as in the printed editions of the Mishnah, and both Talmuds. Rashi on *b. Gittin* 55a–b reads "following the decree concerning the altar," and so reads Maimonides, *Laws of Altar Prohibitions* 5:7. See Epstein, *Introduction to the Text*, 657–658. In the first reading, the phrase is rather obscure; in the second reading, the phrase refers to an otherwise unknown rabbinic decree. Either way, the thrust of the passage remains the same: the offering in question is deemed effective.

60. Translation follows printed edition, as compared to MS Munich and MS Vatican Ebr. 134; see Rabbinovicz, *Diqduqe Soferim*, to *b. Sukkah* 29b–30a. Compare the alternative amoraic tradition in *y. Gittin* 5:5, 47b/1076, which interprets Mal. 1:13 as support for *m. Gittin* 5:5: just as the lame and sick are "revealed," so too all other exclusions apply when they are "revealed" (known).

61. A related ideal is articulated in a number of amoraic, aggadic traditions that note that the domesticated animals offered on the altar are chosen by virtue of the fact that these animals, unlike wild carnivores, do not steal. See, e.g., *Lev. Rabbah* 3:4 (ed. Margulies, 1:64) and *Lev. Rabbah* 27:5 (ed. Margulies, 2:631–632).

62. Cf. *b. Bava Qamma* 114a. Maimonides grants this point too, and states (*Altar Prohibitions* 5:7) that stolen offerings (when the robbery is unknown to the community) offered after the original owner despairs are perfectly acceptable. It is also worth noting that for some sages, among the differences between robbery and theft is whether or not the issue of despair applies (e.g., *m. Kelim* 26:8): one can hope to recover what was stolen by the petty thief, but one cannot hope to recover what was robbed by violence.

63. Translation follows printed edition, as compared to MS Munich and MS Vatican Ebr. 134. For the variants (which are numerous, but rather minor with regard to the overall sense of the tradition), see Rabbinovicz, *Diqduqe Soferim*, to *b. Sukkah* 30a, who at times prefers the printed edition over the MSS.

64. The translation of Deut. 23:19 here follows the rabbinic interpretation, which consistently understands the prohibition as referring to a dog.

65. *Sifra Qedoshim* perek 4:1, on Lev. 19:15 (ed. Weiss 88d–89a), and *Mekilta de-Rabbi Ishmael, Yitro*, sec.9 (ed. Horovitz and Rabin 238), both discussed in *Impurity and Sin*, 122–123.

66. Klawans, *Impurity and Sin*, 92–117.

67. See Klawans, *Impurity and Sin*, 109–116.

68. Translation follows printed edition, as compared to MS Munich (and see Rabbinovicz, *Diqduqe Soferim* to *b. Eruvin* 69b). A parallel version is preserved in *b. Hullin* 5a; cf. *b. Hullin* 13b and *Sifra Dibura de-Nedaba* parashah 2:3, on Lev. 1:2 (ed. Finkelstein 2:20–21, see also 4:22; ed. Weiss 4c).

69. On the history of this tax, see Liver, "Half-Shekel Offering," and Mandell, "Who Paid the Temple Tax?" In general, there is less conclusive evidence for the regular practice of an annual half-sheqel tax in the Second Temple period than many assume. Certainly—as Liver argues—the tax was not an age-old institution but an innovation of the late Second Temple period.

70. On the passage from the scholion to *Megillat Ta'anit*—and its relation to other rabbinic sources such as *b. Menahot* 65a—see Noam, *Megillat Ta'anit*, 57–59 (text of scholion), 133–135 (text of *b. Menahot* 65a), and 165–173 (Noam's analysis, including a history of scholarship on the passage). Note that the Oxford MS speaks of Boethusians, while the Parma MS speaks of Sadducees. Compare Lichtenstein, "Fastenrolle," 290–292 (comment) and 323 (text). On the historicity of this dispute, see also Baumgarten, "Rabbinic Literature as a Source," 20–21, and the literature cited there.

71. On 4Q159, see Schiffman's edition and commentary in Charlesworth, *Rule of the Community*, 145–157; on the 11QT passage, consult Yadin, *Temple Scroll*, 1:248, 2:166–167; and, with reference also to the book of *Jubilees*, see Schiffman, "Sacrificial System," 219–220. There may also be a disagreement between the sages and the sectarians on the matter of at what age the tax should be paid. Some rabbinic sources suggest that the tax would be paid beginning when one reaches puberty (y. *Sheqalim* 1:3, 46a/605). The sectarian ruling is based presumably on Exod. 30:14. See further Broshi, "Anti-Qumranic Polemics in the Talmud," in Trebolle Barrera and Vegas Montaner, *The Madrid Qumran Congress*, 2:593, and Schiffman, *Eschatological Community*, 16–20, and *Sectarian Law*, 58–60.

72. Feldman, *Judean Antiquities 1–4*, 297 n. 656; see also 384–384 nn. 508–509, on *Ant.* 3:104–196, for Josephus' treatment of the half-sheqel tax, which makes no explicit connection to the funding of the daily offerings.

73. I agree with Belkin, *Philo and the Oral Law*, 54, on this point.

74. For the opinion that Josephus agrees with the Pharisees on this matter, see Feldman, *Judean Antiquities 1–4*, 297 n. 656; and Regev and Nakman, "Josephus and the Halakhah," 407. Hayward, *Jewish Temple*, 119 states that Philo agrees with the Pharisees on this matter; on Philo's approach to Jewish law in general, see Regev and Nakman, "Josephus and the Halakhah," 423–428, and the literature cited there.

75. This assumption is quite commonplace: e.g., Lichtenstein, "Fastenrolle," 290; Liver, "Half-Shekel Offering," 189; Noam, *Megillat Ta'anit*, 165; Regev and Nakman, "Josephus and the Halakhah," 407; Safrai, "Temple and the Divine Service," 318. See also Albeck's introduction to *m. Sheqalim* (*Shishah Sidre Mishnah*, ed. Albeck, 2:184).

76. On *m. Ta'anit* 4:8, see Malter, *Treatise Ta'anit*, 406–407 n. 390, and Epstein, *Introduction to the Text*, 686–687.

77. On the eighteen benedictions in general, see Elbogen, *Jewish Liturgy*, 24–54. On the fourteenth blessing in particular, see 47–48, and the Geniza fragment printed on 396 n. 4.

78. See Elbogen, *Jewish Liturgy*, 50–51, and the Geniza fragment printed on 396 n. 4.

79. In a series of recent studies, Uri Ehrlich has attempted to rewrite the history of the development of this blessing, and he has done so by arguing that the earliest versions are those that do not contain requests for the divine presence to return to the temple, as do the traditional editions of the Jewish prayer book; see Ehrlich, "The Earliest Version of the *Amidah*: The Blessing about the Temple Worship" [Hebrew], in Tabory, *From Qumran*, 17–38; "Location of the *Shekhina*," and "Place of the *Shekhina*." In these studies, Ehrlich constructs his history of the prayers on the basis of the idea that only later sages—in the amoraic period—would have prayed for God's presence to return to the temple. Ehrlich's assertion that tannaitic sources are not aware of the idea that the divine presence has departed from the temple is mistaken. Virtually every tannaitic text other than the Mishnah expresses the notion (as I have argued already and in *Impurity and Sin*), and the idea can also be found in Josephus, though as I have noted, the former connects the departure of the divine presence with the defilement of the land, while the latter connects it to the defilement of the sanctuary. Similarly problematic—for missing much of the tannaitic material as well as the Josephan precedent—is N. Cohen, "Shekhinta ba-Galuta."

80. On the history of the *amidah*, see Elbogen, *Jewish Liturgy*, 25–27, and note Heinemann's comments quoted on 37; cf. Heinemann, *Prayer in the Period of the Tanna'im*, 29–51.

81. For fuller discussion of the early versions as cited in rabbinic texts, see Ehrlich, "The Location of the *Shekhina*," 9–18; cf. Heinemann, *Prayer in the Period of the Tanna'im*, 39–40, 48–49.

82. See also *Num. Rabbah* 15:17 and *Tanhuma Terumah* 3 (ed. Buber 45a). For fuller listing of the parallels, partial and complete, with a discussion of their main differences, see Margulies's comments on *Lev. Rabbah*, 2:2, on 1:37 of his edition.

83. As noted already, the appearance of such traditions in *Lev. Rabbah* underscores that Milgrom's reading of *Lev. Rabbah* 22:8—discussed in chapter 1—is problematic.

84. See Mirkin's comments on *Lev. Rabbah* 9:7 (in *Midrash Rabbah*, ed. Mirkin 7:96) and Mandelbaum's comments to *Pesikta de-Rab Kahana* 9:12, 1:159.

85. Only one such source is known to me: *Deut. Rabbah* 5:3, to Deut. 16:18 (ed. Lieberman 96; ed. Mirkin 11:86). The text is difficult to date, and the midrashic collection of which it is part had a "turbulent textual history," according to Strack and Stemberger, *Introduction to the Talmud and Midrash*, 308.

86. E.g., *Pesikta de-Rab Kahana* 18:6 (ed. Mandelbaum 299–300), discussed in Urbach, "Heavenly and Earthly Jerusalem," 170–171, and *Gen. Rabbati* (attributed to Moshe ha-Darshan, ed. Albeck 136–137), discussed in Safrai, "Heavenly Jerusalem," 12.

87. Alon, "Bounds," in *Jews, Judaism, and the Classical World*.

88. On handwashing in rabbinic sources, see Booth, *Jesus and the Laws of Purity*, 161–187, and Sanders, *Jewish Law*, 228–231.

89. Alon, "Bounds," in *Jews, Judaism, and the Classical World*, 201–203.

90. For a discussion of the various understandings of this prohibition in ancient Judaism, see Bokser, "Approaching Sacred Space," and "Rabbinic Continuity."

91. On temple motifs in synagogue decorations, see Fine, *This Holy Place*, 95–126 (synagogues in Israel) and 137–157 (Greco-Roman Diaspora). See also Branham, "Vicarious Sacrality," esp. 330–336.

92. On the screens (in both the synagogue and the temple), see Branham, "Vicarious Sacrality," 325–333, and Fine, *This Holy Place*, 110–111.

93. Fine, *This Holy Place*, 93.

94. On the relationship between the rabbis and the synagogue, see Lee I. Levine, "The Sages and the Synagogue in Late Antiquity: The Evidence of the Galilee," in Levine, *Galilee*, 201–222, and cf. S. Schwartz, *Imperialism and Jewish Society*, 103–128, 215–239.

95. Bokser, "Approaching Sacred Space," 287–288, 298–299; see also Neusner, *History of the Mishnaic Law of Holy Things*, 6:273–290. In a subtler fashion, see Neusner, *Judaism*, 25–44; see also the comments by Cohen, "Jacob Neusner, Mishnah, and Counter-Rabbinics," 57–58.

96. See Smith, *Map Is Not Territory*, xiii–xiv, 130–142, 160–166, and esp. 185–189; note also his comments on the Jewish temple on 128.

97. In this we agree with Bokser and Neusner, against Alon, who tries to prove the antiquity of the rabbinic rulings by pointing to the practices described in, e.g., Jdt. 12:7 ("Bounds," in *Jews, Judaism, and the Classical World*, 201–203).

98. Elbogen, *Jewish Liturgy*, 3. The phrase "Service of the Heart" appears in *Sifre Deut.*, sec. 41, ed. Finkelstein 87–88, and a few other rabbinic sources; see further in this chapter.

99. For Glatzer, rabbinic Judaism went in quest of substitutes for sacrifices in the wake of the destruction, with the result that "sacrifice in the old sense was taken out of the circumscribed realm of cult and ritual and was given a broader implication. Now, study, prayer, charity, and loving kindness, etc., are accounted as sacrifice or better, they are new forms of sacrifice" ("Concept of Sacrifice," 52). In a justifiably classic essay on rabbinic Judaism ("The Rabbinic Heritage," in *Studies*), G. Cohen asserts that "prayer became the surrogate of sacrifice not only in the sense that it was now the vehicle for supplication to God, but in the sense that it made of each Jew a sacerdotal officer, who must ever stand on duty. In one sense, however, Rabbinic prayer was the very opposite of sacrifice; or, to put it in another way, Talmudic prayer followed in the tradition of Hosea rather than Leviticus. Prayer was supplicatory and emotional, varying from day to day and from one person to another" (*Studies*, 80; see also 71). Needless to say, I cannot accept as valid the dismissal of sacrifice as a dry, fixed, unemotional, and unchanging ritual. It is certainly by no means clear that the rabbis themselves viewed things this way.

100. Bokser, "Rabbinic Responses," 61. Bokser is not alone in this supposition: compare, Kirschner, "Apocalyptic and Rabbinic Responses," 28–29, 44–45. A more recent variant of the thesis has been presented by Seth Schwartz, who posits that Judaism was entirely "shattered" by the events of 70 C.E. (and 135 C.E.) and basically disappeared into near oblivion, only to emerge centuries later, coinciding with the Christianization of Rome. See *Imperialism and Jewish Society*, esp. 15–16, 108–110, 175. In disagreement with Schwartz, I don't presume that Judaism was shattered by the calamities of 70 C.E. (though surely many Jewish lives were shattered).

101. See Bokser, "Rabbinic Responses," 59–61, and the literature cited there. See also Bokser, "*Ma'al* and Blessings over Food," 570–571, and Cohen, "Temple and the Synagogue," 316 (Bokser's work—and his psychological analogy—are cited approvingly in n. 66, despite the judgment offered on 314 and n. 60). For a similar approach to the book of Lamentations, see Moore, "Human Suffering," 537.

102. Cohen, "Temple and the Synagogue," 316, and Neusner, *History of the Mishnaic Law of Holy Things*, 6:280–284.

103. Cohen, "Temple and the Synagogue," 314, and n. 60.

104. For a fuller accounting of the literature produced during and immediately after the Holocaust, see Roskies, *Literature of Destruction*, 3–12 (Roskies's introduction) and 381–564 (anthology of literary works written *during* the Holocaust).

105. At the risk of venturing far beyond my expertise, I would suggest that the increased public discourse on the Holocaust in the 1960s is directly tied to societal changes during that time. American society in the 1940s and 1950s was beset by various taboos, such that words like "cancer" would be uttered in a whisper. Yet even today, the Holocaust can hardly be discussed or illustrated accurately without raising in some quarters issues of obscenity. I think it reasonable to consider the possibility that the Holocaust could be discussed more openly in the 1960s precisely because some of the societal barriers preventing its public discussion had broken down.

106. See also *b. Megillah* 3b (Torah study greater than the daily offering), *b. Sukkah* 49b (charity over sacrifice; acts of loving-kindness over charity) and *b. Ta'anit* 27b (reciting the Torah portions relating to sacrifice as equivalent to performing them). For a catalogue of such traditions, see Glatzer, "Concept of Sacrifice." The important analytic surveys of these traditions include Bokser, "Rabbinic Responses"; Cohen, "Temple and the Synagogue"; Goldenberg, "Broken Axis," and Reif, *Judaism and Hebrew Prayer*, 95–102.

107. In *b. Ta'anit* 2a and *y. Berakhot* 4:1, 7a/31 the tradition is clearly understood as referring not to prayer in the abstract but to "the prayer"—the *amidah*.

108. Cohen, "Temple and the Synagogue," 315; Goldenberg, "Broken Axis," 874; cf. Reif, *Judaism and Hebrew Prayer*, 98–99. Contrast the treatment of the tradition in Heinemann, *Prayer in the Period of the Tanna'im*, 17–18.

109. Translation based on Bokser, "Rabbinic Responses," 38.

110. Translation based on Bokser, "Rabbinic Responses," 49. Also with Bokser (p. 49 n. 24), we follow various manuscripts over the printed editions, in reading "greater than *all the* sacrifices." See Rabbinovicz, *Diqduqe Soferim* to *b. Berakhot* 32a. For a fuller analysis, see Bokser, "Wall Separating," discussed and critiqued further in this chapter.

111. According to Bokser, "Rabbinic Responses," the amoraic traditions "agree in directly confronting and transcending the Temple cult, setting nonsacrificial rites over against the Temple ones" (52); "the more they accepted the Temple's loss, the greater on a practical level did they openly speak of superseding it" (58); "at a certain point they fully admitted a discontinuity, asserting that the past institutions are superseded by the present ones and the latter are superior to the former" (61).

112. Bokser's rereading of the traditions—to the effect that R. Eleazar views all these developments as positive—is entirely unconvincing (see Bokser, "Wall Separating," 352–365). He glosses the iron wall tradition so that it says the very opposite (that the wall has been lifted), and then he creatively limits the force of the tradition concerning the closed gates. Bokser thus reinterprets the entire passage in light of his maximalist understanding of the claim attributed to R. Eleazar that prayer is better than sacrifice. We proceed here in the opposite fashion, seeking to understand R. Eleazar's assertions about prayer in light of the sage's clearer statements regarding the temple and its loss.

113. *Contra* Bokser, "Rabbinic Responses," 49–50, and "Wall Separating."

114. For those unable to follow Rashi's comments, Bokser paraphrases Rashi's reading in his translation of the passage, "Rabbinic Responses," 49.

115. Talmon, "The Emergence of Institutionalized Prayer in Israel in Light of Qumran Literature," in *World of Qumran from Within*, 200–243.

116. Fleischer, "On the Beginnings of Obligatory Jewish Prayer;" cf. Talmon, "Emergence," in *The World of Qumran*.

117. For a fuller evaluation, see the studies collected in Tabory, *From Qumran*, and Tabory's introduction, 5–6.

118. See Falk, "Qumran Prayer Texts."

119. Note that Philo speaks of prayer in the temple (e.g., *Special Laws* 1:97), and prayer is juxtaposed with sacrifice in Ben Sira 35:1–26. On rabbinic sources concerning prayer in the temple, see Elbogen, *Jewish Liturgy*, 189–191, and Heinemann, *Prayer in the Period of the Tanna'im*, 78–98. For a contrary interpretation of the evidence, see Fleischer, "On the Beginnings of Obligatory Jewish Prayer," 419–425.

120. So, Falk, "Qumran Prayer Texts." Compare the comments of Elbogen, *Jewish Liturgy*, 199: "the destruction of the Temple and the cessation of sacrifices did not result in any tremendous upheaval in the manner of worship; the status of the synagogue in religious life was already so firmly established that no noteworthy shift occurred."

121. Cohen uses these terms twice each in "Temple and the Synagogue," 318; see also Bokser, "Rabbinic Responses," 52, 58, 61.

122. Bokser uses this term in "Rabbinic Responses," 50.

123. See, e.g., *b. Berakhot* 33a, *b. Megillah* 18a; see Heinemann, *Prayer in the Period of the Tanna'im*, 17–18 and the sources cited there.

124. Bokser, "Rabbinic Responses," 52, 58, 61.

125. Goldberg, "Broken Axis," 871. According to a few rabbinic traditions, the foundation stone was split or cut off at the time of the temple's destruction (*y. Pesahim* 4:1, 30d/517, *y. Ta'anit* 1:6, 64c/709). This led, according to these traditions, to the custom whereby women refrained from weaving during the nine days leading to the ninth of Av, the day commemorating the temple's loss. (Presumably, the custom emerged because the Aramaic term for weaving shares the same root as the Hebrew term usually translated as "foundation" in the expression "foundation stone.")

CHAPTER 7

1. Jostein Ådna, "Jesus' Symbolic Act," in Ego et al., *Gemeinde ohne Tempel*, 461–475; Chilton, *Feast of Meanings*, 46–74 (cf. *Temple of Jesus*, 150–154, and *Rabbi Jesus*, 250–254); Feeley-Harnik, *Lord's Table*, 107–164; Hamerton-Kelly, *Gospel and the Sacred*, 15–34, 43–45; Neusner, "Money-Changers in the Temple," 287–290. Theissen and Merz, *Historical Jesus*, 405–439; and Wright, *Jesus and the Victory*, 405–428, 554–564.

2. Those cited earlier who are interested in the historical Jesus include: Ådna, Chilton, Theissen and Merz, and Wright. Those less interested in the historical Jesus per se include Feeley-Harnik, Hamerton-Kelly, and Neusner.

3. As we have already noted, Hamerton-Kelly's work—which is inspired by Girard's—is thoroughly critical of ancient Jewish religion. None of the other works cited above (with the possible exception of Feeley-Harnik) comes even close to Hamerton-Kelly's attack on ancient Judaism. By contrast, for instance, Chilton and Wright both carefully balance their interpretations with relatively sympathetic treatments of ancient Jewish sacrifice (Chilton, *Temple of Jesus* 45–67, and Wright, *Jesus and the Victory*, 406–412).

4. Wright, *Jesus and the Victory*, 419.

5. Borg, *Conflict, Holiness, and Politics*, 174–212.

6. Borg, more recently, in the new preface to *Conflict, Holiness, and Politics*, 14–15; cf. Horsely, *Jesus and the Spiral*, 29–30, 285–317.

7. Wright, *Jesus and the Victory*, 420; cf. Hamerton-Kelly, *Gospel and the Sacred*, 17–20.

8. Chilton, *Feast of Meanings*, 46–74; *Temple of Jesus*, 113–154.

9. Theissen and Merz, *Historical Jesus*, 434.

10. On the Last Supper texts generally and for summaries of scholarly views, see (in addition to standard Gospel commentaries): Léon-Dufour, *Sharing the Eucharistic Bread*, 77–179; R. F. O'Toole, "Last Supper," *ABD* 4:234–241, and Theissen and Merz, *Historical Jesus*, 405–439. The classic treatment is still Jeremias, *Eucharistic Words*. For a more recent review of the eucharist (going beyond the New Testament), see Mazza, *Celebration*.

11. On debate regarding the shorter and longer forms of Luke, see, e.g., Fitzmyer, *Luke X–XXIV*, 1387–1389 (prefers longer version), and Ehrman, *Orthodox Corruption*, 197–209 (prefers the shorter text). Though Jeremias originally preferred the shorter version, subsequent editions of his work joined what was then the consensus favoring the longer text; see Jeremias, *Eucharistic Words*, 139–159.

12. See, for instance, Jeremias, *Eucharistic Words*, 26–36; Mazza, *Celebration*, 19–28; O'Toole, "Last Supper," *ABD* 4:236; and Theissen and Merz, *Historical Jesus*, 412–413.

13. Some scholars consider the *todah* ("thanksgiving") sacrifice to be a possible background for the Last Supper, sometimes building on the idea (see *Lev. Rabbah* 9:7 discussed in chapter 6) that only this sacrifice will continue in the end of days. But typically, if the *todah* is considered, it is only in its alleged "nonsacrificial" form: see O'Toole, "Last Supper," *ABD* 4:236–237, and Léon-Dufour, *Sharing the Eucharistic Bread*, 40–44, both building on Gese, "Origin of the Lord's Supper." One modern interpreter who places the eucharist squarely within the context of Jewish sacrificial rites is Douglas—see her essay "Eucharist."

14. Some arguments in defense of the traditions' historicity are presented in Klawans, *Interpreting the Last Supper*, 1–6.

15. See Funk et al., *The Acts of Jesus*, 139; cf. Chilton, *Temple of Jesus*, 139, and *Rabbi Jesus*, 252–253. Further examples cited in Klawans, *Interpreting the Last Supper*, 5 n. 14.

16. See, for example, O'Toole, "Last Supper," *ABD* 4:238, and Theissen and Merz, *Historical Jesus*, 421–422, who use this kind of logic to give priority to the Pauline formulation over the Markan. Beck, "Last Supper," puts forth an even bolder argument, claiming that the saying over the cup in any formulation is inherently offensive to Jews, and that therefore only the saying over the bread has a strong claim for authenticity. Jeremias, on the other hand, evaluates the traditions in a similar fashion, but then argues—by *lectio difficilior*—that the Markan formulation (ostensibly the most offensive) must be more authentic (*Eucharistic Words*, 170–171, 212).

17. See, e.g., Sandmel, *Anti-Semitism*, 101–119; esp. 103: "the Jews in John are depicted as lacking all religious insight."

18. Davies, *Paul and Rabbinic Judaism*, 245–256.

19. Theissen and Merz, *Historical Jesus*, 316–346.

20. Caird's brief treatment is to the point; see *Language and Imagery*, 101–102. This view holds true only with the provision that we view metaphor as creative and expressive, not merely ornamental. For an anthropological take on symbolism and metaphor—dealing directly with the eucharist—see Fernandez, *Persuasions and Performances*, 28–70.

21. E.g., Beck, "Last Supper," 192–198; Fredriksen, *Jesus of Nazareth*, 242; O'Toole, "Last Supper," *ABD* 4:238; Theissen and Merz, *Historical Jesus*, 431–436; Wright, *Jesus and the Victory*, 558–561. For a more thorough treatment, see McKnight, "Jesus and Prophetic Actions."

22. As noted toward the beginning of this chapter, sympathetic treatments of ancient Jewish sacrifice can be found in both Chilton, *Temple of Jesus*, 45–67, and Wright, *Jesus and the Victory*, 406–412.

23. Jeremias, *Eucharistic Words*, 115–122.

24. Compare the assessment of C. K. Barrett, "Attitudes to the Temple in the Acts of the Apostles," in Horbury, *Templum Amicitiae*, 345–397, esp. 361–362. In contrast, Horsley attempts to downplay the significance of Acts 2:46–47 in *Jesus and the Spiral*, 291–292.

25. Fredriksen, *Jesus of Nazareth*, 94–96, 106, 147.

26. What follows builds on Fredriksen, *Jesus of Nazareth*, 204, and Sanders, "Jerusalem and Its Temple in Early Christian Thought and Practice," in Levine, *Jerusalem: Its Sanctity*, 90–103, esp. 91.

27. On this passage, see G. I. Davies, "The Presence of God in the Second Temple and Rabbinic Doctrine," in Horbury, *Templum Amicitiae*, 35.

28. Generally on the *Didache* and the eucharist, see Johannes Betz, "Eucharist in the Didache," and Enrico Mazza, "Didache 9–10: Elements of a Eucharistic Interpretation," both in Draper, *Didache in Modern Research*, 244–275 and 276–299, respectively. See also Draper's introduction, esp. 26–31.

29. See Jeremias, *Eucharistic Words*, 117–118, and the literature cited in the previous note.

30. The classic treatment of this parallel is still Finkelstein, "Birkat Ha-Mazon." Briefly, see Mazza, *Celebration*, 15–17, 307–308.

31. Daly, *Christian Sacrifice*, 230–250; Davies, *Gospel and the Land*, 185–194; Fredriksen, *Jesus of Nazareth*, 34–41, and "Ultimate Reality," 66–67; Gärtner, *Temple and the Community*, 47–70; Newton, *Concept of Purity*, 52–78.

32. So NRSV. On this phrase (traditionally translated as "Behold Israel according to the flesh"), see further in this chapter.

33. Compare Schüssler Fiorenza, "Cultic Language," 172–173 (with regard to 1 Cor. 6:19). On Paul's understanding of moral defilement as a threat to the sacred, see Klawans, *Impurity and Sin*, 150–155.

34. Davies, *Gospel and the Land*, 190–194; Gärtner, *Temple and the Community*, 47–60; Newton, *Concept of Purity*, 53–60; cf. Daly, *Christian Sacrifice*, 232–236, and 256–260.

35. Newton, *Concept of Purity*, 60–70; Daly, *Christian Sacrifice*, 240–256.

36. Newton, *Concept of Purity*, 70–75.

37. See, e.g., Daly, *Christian Sacrifice*, 1–5, 256; Ferguson, "Spiritual Sacrifice," 1162–1165; Gärtner, *Temple and Community*, 47–71; McKelvey, *New Temple*, 92–124.

38. E.g., Daly, *Christian Sacrifice*, 4–5; Gärtner, *Temple and Community*, 18–19, Léon-Dufour, *Sharing the Eucharistic Bread*, 43. H. J. Klauck, "Sacrifice and Sacrificial Offerings (NT)," in *ABD* 5:886–891, rejects the term, but for all the wrong reasons: Klauck argues (891) that the term "spiritualization" shortchanges the novelty and the originality of the *Christian* approach to sacrifice!

39. See Schüssler Fiorenza, "Cultic Language," esp. 159–164.

40. E.g., Daly, "Power of Sacrifice"; Ferguson, "Spiritual Sacrifices," 1156–1162; Gärtner, *Temple and Community*, esp. 84–85; McKelvey, *New Temple*, 42–57; Ringgren, *Sacrifice in the Bible*, 54–72.

41. See the assessment of Barrett (with regard to Stephan's speech in Acts 7), "Attitudes to the Temple," in Horbury, *Templum Amicitiae*, 365–366.

42. For fuller treatments, see Jeremias, *Eucharistic Words*, and Léon-Dufour, *Sharing the Eucharistic Bread*. For briefer treatments, see Theissen and Merz, *Historical Jesus*, and O'Toole, "The Last Supper" *ABD* 4:234–241.

43. Chilton, *Feast of Meanings*, 66–74; Jeremias, *Eucharistic Words*, 220–225; Léon-Dufour, *Sharing the Eucharistic Bread*, 117–156.

44. Jeremias, *Eucharistic Words*, 231–237; see also Chilton, *Feast of Meanings*, 73, who speaks of the *sharing* of the eucharistic elements in light of sacrificial sharing.

45. Chilton, *Feast of Meanings*, 71–72; Jeremias, *Eucharistic Words*, 225–231.

46. Léon-Dufour, *Sharing the Eucharistic Bread*, 144–154.

47. Jeremias, *Eucharistic Words*, 220–225.

48. Jeremias, *Eucharistic Words*, 237–255; Léon-Dufour, *Sharing the Eucharistic Bread*, 102–116.

49. E.g., Jeremias, *Eucharistic Words*, 225–226; Wright, *Jesus and the Victory*, 557.

50. Casey, "Culture and Historicity."

51. E.g., Fitzmyer, *Luke X–XXIV*, 1260–1268.

52. E.g., Flusser, *Jesus*, 138 (on the temple incident); see 21–22 (on Lukan priority in general).

53. Matson, "Contribution to the Temple Cleansing."

54. Safrai, *Pilgrimage*, 147.

55. See Wright, *Jesus and the Victory*, 405: "one of the chief gains of the last twenty years of Jesus-research is that the question of Jesus and the Temple is back where it belongs, at the centre of the agenda."

56. Sanders in particular has focused on the temple incident as the explanation of why authorities executed Jesus (*Jesus and Judaism*, 296–308). Sanders has been followed in this respect by, among others, Fredriksen, *Jesus of Nazareth*, 207–218; see also Crossan, *Historical Jesus*, 360; Flusser, *Jesus*, 141, and Wright, *Jesus and the Victory*, 405.

57. See, e.g., Horsley, *Jesus and the Spiral*, 29–30, 285–317, and Borg, *Conflict, Holiness, and Politics*, 174–212.

58. Funk et al., *Acts of Jesus*, 121–122, 231–232, 338–339, 373–374.

59. Sanders, *Jesus and Judaism*, 67–68; so too Bauckham, "Jesus' Demonstration," 72–73, and Betz, "Jesus and the Purity," 459.

60. So, e.g., Betz, "Jesus and the Purity," esp. 459, and Collins, "Jesus' Action in Herod's Temple." For a defense of the referent "cleansing" (and much that it implies), see Evans, "Jesus' Action."

61. Sanders, *Jesus and Judaism*, 69–90; compare Crossan, *Historical Jesus*, 357, and Wright, *Jesus and the Victory of God*, 413–428.

62. So, e.g., Chilton, *Temple of Jesus*, 91–100, and cf. Evans, "Jesus' Action," 395–402.

63. Betz, "Jesus and the Purity," 459–460.

64. Hamerton-Kelly, *Gospel and the Sacred*, 17–19.

65. See e.g., McKnight, "Jesus and Prophetic Actions."

66. See Sanders, *Jesus and Judaism*, 61–63 and the literature cited there.

67. Abrahams, *Studies in Pharisaism*, 82–89.

68. Sanders, *Jesus and Judaism*, 61–76.

69. See, for example, Evans, "Jesus' Action," 395–439, and Horsley, *Jesus and the Spiral*, 285–317. For the temple as a flawed institution—without necessarily the corrupt priests—see, e.g., Borg, *Conflict, Holiness, and Politics*, esp. 174–212, and Wright, *Jesus and the Victory*, 413–428.

70. E.g., Evans, "Jesus' Action," 410–413.

71. E.g., Evans, "Jesus' Action," 414, 417–418.

72. E.g., Evans, "Jesus' Action," 424–426.

73. See, e.g., Evans, "Jesus' Action," esp. 421–424, and Casey, "Culture and Historicity," 313–316.

74. This story is cited by, among others, Bauckham, "Jesus' Demonstration," 77; Casey, "Culture and Historicity," 314; Chilton, Temple of Jesus, 102–103, and Evans, "Jesus' Action," 423.

75. Cited or referred to by Bauckham, "Jesus' Demonstration," 79; Casey, "Culture and Historicity," 315; Chilton, Temple of Jesus, 185; Evans, "Jesus' Action," 422; Horsley, Jesus and the Spiral, 47, and Wright, Jesus and the Victory, 413 n. 163. See also Collins, "Jesus' Action in Herod's Temple," 51–53, who puts the passage to a different use. I have sometimes wondered if this might be the most frequently cited page of Talmud in all New Testament scholarship.

76. For a brief discussion of the issues at stake, see Rubenstein, Talmudic Stories, 3–8. The most consistent advocate of the skeptical approach to rabbinic sources with regard to history has been Jacob Neusner. See, for instance, Neusner, Judaism, 307–328. Rubenstein cites further bibliography in his discussion.

77. See Herr, "Conception of History," and Yerushalmi, Zakhor, 14–26.

78. See Rubenstein, Talmudic Stories, esp. 3–15.

79. See Broshi, "Anti-Qumranic Polemics in the Talmud," in Trebolle Barrera and Vegas Montaner, Madrid Qumran Congress, 2:589–600, and Herr, "Continuum."

80. Avigad, "Jewish Rock-Cut Tombs."

81. See Schwartz, "KATA TOYTON TON KAIPON," 262–268, and our discussion of b. Pesahim 57a in chapter 6.

82. Büchler, Priester, 7–47, and Studies in Jewish History, 24–63.

83. E.g., Büchler, Priester, 67–90; Büchler describes a series of conflicts between sinful aristocratic priests and more pious priests of lower social class.

84. So, e.g., Collins, "Jesus' Action," 53, following Abrahams, Studies in Pharisaism, 86.

85. Safrai, "Temple and the Divine Service," 286.

86. Safrai, Pilgrimage, 146–149.

87. Flusser, Jesus, 138, cites and follows Safrai.

88. On this point I agree with Evans, "Jesus' Action," 420.

89. On this point I agree with Bauckham, "Jesus' Demonstration," 79–80.

90. On this point I agree with the broad thrust of Sanders's Jesus and Judaism.

91. On tax/toll collectors in the Gospels, a good place to begin is Wills, "Methodological Reflections." On Jerusalem's aristocracy, see Goodman, Ruling Class.

92. On this passage, see Bauckham, "Coin in the Fish's Mouth," Chilton, "Coin of Three Realms," and William Horbury, "The Temple Tax," in Bammel and Moule, Jesus and the Politics, 265–286.

93. Collins, "Jesus' Action in the Temple," 50–51; compare Chilton, "Coin of Three Realms."

94. Funk et al., Five Gospels, 212–213.

95. Flusser, "Matthew XVII, 24–27." Curiously, unlike many of his other articles on Jesus, this study was not incorporated into Flusser's final word on the matter, his book Jesus.

96. Bauckham, "Coin in the Fish's Mouth;" cf. "Jesus' Demonstration," 73–74.

97. The thematic connections are stressed by, e.g., Bauckham, "Jesus' Demonstration," 73–74, and Richardson, "Why Turn the Tables." The textual connections were noted long ago by Abrahams, Studies in Pharisaism, 84.

98. For further details on these correspondences, with translated selections of the key rabbinic texts, see Richardson, "Why Turn the Tables," 512–513, and Neusner, "Money-Changers in the Temple."

99. Abrahams, *Studies in Pharisaism*, 83–85; Sanders, *Jesus and Judaism*, 63–64.

100. See Lachs, *Rabbinic Commentary*, 347.

101. E.g., Casey, "Culture and Historicity," 313–316.

102. E.g., Abrahams, *Studies in Pharisaism*, 87–88, and Safrai, "Temple and the Divine Service," 286.

103. Lachs, *Rabbinic Commentary*, 347.

104. So Sanders, *Jesus and Judaism*, esp. 63–64.

105. So, e.g., Chilton, "Coin of Three Realms," 350. For a fuller analysis along these lines, see Daube, "Temple Tax."

106. Montefiore, "Jesus and the Temple Tax," 70–71.

107. Neunser, "Money-Changers in the Temple," 289–290. Neusner is followed by, e.g., Ådna, "Jesus' Symbolic Act," in Ego et al., *Gemeinde ohne Tempel*, 467–469, and Wright, *Jesus and the Victory*, 423.

108. See discussion in chapter 6.

109. Chilton, "Coin of Three Realms," 342.

110. Meshorer, "One Hundred Ninety Years."

111. Richardson, "Why Turn the Tables," is followed by Collins, "Jesus' Action," 58–60. For a refutation of this view in light of the gospel evidence, see Chilton, *Feast of Meanings*, 172–176.

112. See discussion in Hendin, *Guide*, 288–293. For a full refutation of Meshorer's theory, see Levy, "Tyrian Shekels." I thank Brooks Levy for providing me a copy of this article; and I thank both Brooks Levy and David Hendin for their helpful personal communications on this matter.

113. Cf. Chilton, *Feast of Meanings*, 174.

114. Fine, "Art and Identity," 22; see also 30–31.

115. Three jugs were discovered at Qumran containing over five hundred sheqels of Tyre. For a description of these finds, and a discussion of their relation to Qumran literature, see Magness, *Archaeology of Qumran*, 188–193, 206–207, and the literature cited there. Magness interprets the find in light of 4Q159—that the collection consists of the one-time payments to the community by its membership. Magness grants, however, that other interpretations cannot be ruled out (193). See Yaakov Meshorer, "Numismatics," in Schiffman and VanderKam, *Encyclopedia*, 2:619–620.

116. One form of this theory was suggested years ago by Eppstein in "Historicity." The theory has been endorsed by both Flusser, *Jesus*, 138, and Safrai, *Pilgrimage*, 148. The theory has been refined and augmented by both Betz, "Jesus and the Purity," 461–462, 467–469, and Collins, "Jesus' Action," 53–58. Aspects of the theory (in Betz's formulation) are endorsed by Evans ("Jesus' Action," 436–437), but note Evans's critical discussion of Eppstein (429–432).

117. Ådna, "Jesus' Symbolic Act," in Ego et al., *Gemeinde ohne Tempel*, 465–466; Casey, "Culture and Historicity," 310–311; Evans, "Jesus' Action," 407–408.

118. Betz, "Jesus and the Purity," esp. 432–437.

119. Martin Goodman, "The Pilgrimage Economy of Jerusalem in the Second Temple Period," in Levine, *Jerusalem: Its Sanctity*, 69–76.

120. See Collins, "Jesus' Action," esp. 57–58, and the literature cited there.

121. So Betz, "Jesus and the Purity," esp. 461, 465, 467; compare Evans, "Jesus' Action," 436–437.

122. So Betz, "Jesus and the Purity," 469–472.

123. Sanders, *Jesus and Judaism*, 63.

124. Collins, "Jesus' Action," 55–58.

125. Chilton has presented his thesis in a number of venues: much of it appears in *Temple of Jesus*, 91–136. Chilton reiterates and to some degree refines his theory in *Feast of Meanings*, 57–63, "Eucharist," 36–43, *Pure Kingdom*, 115–123, and, most recently, *Rabbi Jesus*, 213–230. Generally, on the latter, see Klawans, review of *Rabbi Jesus*.

126. So runs the theory following *Temple of Jesus*, 108–111; see also 128.

127. Chilton, "Eucharist," 39.

128. Chilton, *Temple of Jesus*, 134.

129. Chilton, *Temple of Jesus*, 121–136; in this respect, Chilton's understanding of the Second Temple is not so far from Francis Schmidt's—see discussion of Schmidt's work in the introduction to part II of this book.

130. Chilton, *Temple of Jesus*, 101–103; *Feast of Meanings*, 57–59, and *Rabbi Jesus*, 226.

131. An additional problem with Chilton's theory is his use of the term "purity" to apply to issues—such as the acceptability of certain sacrifices—that have nothing to do with purity per se. See, e.g., *Temple of Jesus*, 109, 123. As we argued in chapter 6, improperly procured sacrifices would not be considered ritually impure by most Jews, except perhaps those at Qumran.

132. We leave aside for the present all concerns with standard methodology: Chilton assumes the sixth-century Babylonian Talmud (in *b. Betzah* 20a–b) accurately preserves a story concerning Hillel, who lived before Jesus.

133. See *m. Menahot* 9:8; *b. Menahot* 93a; *Sifra Aharei Mot* parashah 4:4, to Lev. 16:21 (ed. Weiss 82a). Compare also Philo, *Special Laws* 1:202–204 (mentioned in chapter 4), which speaks of a two-handed rite as well.

134. Chilton, *Temple of Jesus*, 101; the amplification in *Feast of Meanings*, 58—"sacrifice as a self-contained action"—is not at all clear.

135. Compare Lev. 1:14–15 with 1:4; cf. *Sifra Dibura de Nedaba* perek 4:4, 7. According to rabbinic sources, the hand-laying rite was also not performed on grain offerings or any public offerings: see *m. Menahot* 9:7, 9.

136. On these passages—and the difference between their concerns—see Betz, *Sermon on the Mount*, 571–576.

137. This saying is often taken as authentic. See Funk et al., *Five Gospels*, 91–92, 222–223, 370–371, where the saying is printed in pink type, the Jesus Seminar's second highest rating. See also Luke 16:19–31.

138. Treatments of Jesus' economic/social message are legion. For brief reviews, see, e.g., Horsley, *Jesus and the Spiral*, 246–255, and Flusser, *Jesus*, 93–96. Flusser's fuller treatments of the theme include "Blessed are the Poor in Spirit," "Jesus' Opinion about the Essenes," and (with S. Safrai), "The Slave of Two Masters," all reprinted in *Judaism and the Origins*, 102–114, 150–168, and 169–172, respectively.

139. Betz, *Sermon on the Mount*, 453–459.

140. On such advice, see Wright, *Jesus and the Victory*, 403–405.

141. Betz, *Sermon on the Mount*, 290–291.

142. On these sayings, see Funk et al., *Five Gospels*, 90–91, 222, 370–371, where the sayings are printed in gray type: possibly authentic, and in agreement with Jesus' message. See also Luke 12:33, and 3:11, this saying attributed to the Baptist.

143. Betz, *Sermon on the Mount*, 292–293, 351–361, 597–599.

144. On these sayings, see Funk et al., *Five Gospels*, 106–107, 381 (printed in gray type: possibly authentic, and in agreement with Jesus' message). Importantly, this aspect

of Jesus' teaching (if authentic) is rather unexceptional: rabbinic literature, as I have noted, preserves similar traditions considering the contributions from the poor to be particularly praiseworthy (e.g., *Lev. Rabbah* 3:5). Betz, "Jesus and the Purity," 466–467, points out Greek parallels to this concern, without identifying the rabbinic sources.

145. On these traditions, see Bammel, "The Feeding of the Multitude," in Bammel and Moule, *Jesus and the Politics*, 211–240.

146. Compare Bauckham, "Jesus' Demonstration," 74.

147. On this passage—and on the sharing of goods in Acts—see Conzelmann, *Acts*, 23–24. On the sharing of goods in the early church, see Dupont, *Salvation*, 85–102, and (compared to the Qumran community) Johnson, "Dead Sea Manual," esp. 131–133.

148. Conzelmann, *Acts*, 24.

149. Cf. Horsley, *Jesus and the Spiral*, 282.

150. See Wright, *Jesus and the Victory*, 403–405; see also 294–295.

151. As noted earlier, Jesus does not appear to have prohibited the poor from giving at the temple, and Jesus—like the rabbis—praises the poor for the contributions they make. But still, there appears to be a difference here: I think we are to understand that Jesus would praise the individual poor who contribute *voluntarily*, while condemning the system that would exact anything from them as *obligatory*. For the rabbis, the *voluntary* contributions remain praiseworthy, and the obligations remain obligations.

152. Our suggestion is not entirely unlike Montefiore's understanding of Jesus' approach to the temple tax; see "Jesus and the Temple Tax," 70. We differ from Montefiore in (1) applying this approach to the temple incident; (2) drawing support from the evidence from Acts; and (3) attempting also to understand sympathetically Jesus' opposition (which may have been Pharisaic, but not exclusively so).

153. So Lachs, *Rabbinic Commentary*, 264–265. On rabbinic parables in general, see Stern, *Parables in Midrash*; on the King/God parables, see 19–21; on the comparison between rabbinic and New Testament parables in particular, see 188–206, and the literature cited there. (Stern does not discuss *b. Sukkah* 30a.)

154. See Conzelmann, *Acts*, 49–59, and Koester, *Dwelling of God*, 79–87. See also Barrett, "Attitudes to the Temple," in Horbury, *Templum Amicitiae*, 350–351, 362, and compare J. P. M. Sweet, "A House Not Made with Hands," also in Horbury, *Templum Amicitiae*, 368–390, esp. 384–388.

155. Barrett, "Attitudes to the Temple," in Horbury, *Templum Amicitiae*, 352, 361. Presumably, the falsehood of the testimony lies not in the content of 6:13 but in the next verse, where words are attributed to Jesus that Luke never has Jesus say. Compare Acts 6:14 with Matt. 26:61 and Mark 14:58, and see the treatments of Barrett and Sweet mentioned in the previous note.

156. On the New Jerusalem vision in Revelation, see, e.g., Lee, *New Jerusalem*, 239–304 (keeping in mind the criticisms raised against this work in chapter 4). See also Flusser, "No Temple in the City," in *Judaism and the Origins*, 454–465.

157. On Hebrews, see Attridge, *Epistle*; see esp. 222–224 on the heavenly temple in Hebrews and earlier Jewish literature.

158. As we noted in chapter 4, we find in Hebrews the juxtaposition of two distinct heavenly temple ideas: (1) the notion of a temple in heaven in which God is worshiped, and (2) the idea that Moses was shown in heaven copies or images that he was to reproduce on earth. The combination of the two ideas—which may be original with the author of Hebrews—furthers the antitemple polemic, by driving home the point that the earthly temple is a *mere* copy of the temple above.

Abbreviations of Journals and Series

AB	Anchor Bible
ABD	*Anchor Bible Dictionary*, edited by David Noel Freedman
AJS	*Association for Jewish Studies*
BibInt	*Biblical Interpretation*
CBQ	*Catholic Bible Quarterly*
CRINT	Compendia rerum iudaicarum ad Novum Testamentum
DJD	Discoveries in the Judaean Desert
DSD	*Dead Sea Discoveries*
EI	*Eretz-Israel*
HR	*History of Religions*
HTR	*Harvard Theological Review*
HUCA	*Hebrew Union College Annual*
JAAR	*Journal of the American Academy of Religion*
JBL	*Journal of Biblical Literature*
JJS	*Journal of Jewish Studies*
JQR	*Jewish Quarterly Review*
JSJ	*Journal for the Study of Judaism in the Persian, Hellenistic and Roman Periods*
JSNT	*Journal for the Study of the New Testament*
JSOT	*Journal for the Study of the Old Testament*
JSQ	*Jewish Studies Quarterly*
LCL	Loeb Classical Library
NTS	*New Testament Studies*
OTL	Old Testament Library
PTSDSSP	Princeton Theological Seminary Dead Sea Scroll Project
RB	*Revue Biblique*
REJ	*Revue des études juives*
RevQ	*Revue de Qumran*

RelSRev	*Religious Studies Review*
SBLSP	*Society of Biblical Literature Seminar Papers*
ZAW	*Zeitschrift für die alttestamentliche Wissenschaft*
ZNW	*Zeitschrift für die neutestamentliche Wissenschaft*

Bibliography

Abrahams, Israel. *Studies in Pharisaism and the Gospels*. 2 vols. 1917, 1924; reprint, New York: Ktav, 1967.

Abusch, Ra'anan. "Sevenfold Hymns in the *Songs of the Sabbath Sacrifice* and the Hekhalot Literature: Formalism, Hierarchy, and the Limits of Human Participation." In *The Dead Sea Scrolls as Background to Postbiblical Judaism and Early Christianity: Papers from an International Conference at St. Andrews in 2001*, edited by James R. Davila, 220–247. Leiden: Brill, 2003.

Academy of the Hebrew Language. *The Historical Dictionary of the Hebrew Language: Talmud Yerushalmi: According to Ms. Or. 4720 (Scal. 3) of the Leiden University Library with Restorations and Corrections*. Jerusalem: Academy of the Hebrew Language, 2001.

Adler, Jeremy, and Richard Fardon, eds. *Franz Baermann Steiner: Selected Writings*. 2 vols. New York: Berghahn Books, 1999.

Albeck, Chanoch, ed. *Midrash Bereshit Rabbati ex libro R. Mosis Haddarshan collectus e codice Pargensi cum adnotationibus et introductione*. Jerusalem: Mekize Nirdamim, 1940.

———, ed. *Shishah Sidre Mishnah*. 6 vols. Jerusalem: Bialik Institute, 1952–58.

Albertz, Rainer. *A History of Israelite Religion in the Old Testament Period*. Translated by John Bowden. 2 vols. Louisville, Ky.: Westminster John Knox Press, 1994.

Alexander, Philip, and Geza Vermes. *Qumran Cave 4, XIX: Serekh Ha-Yahad and Related Texts. DJD XXVI*. Oxford: Clarendon Press, 1998.

Allegro, John M. *Qumran Cave 4, I (4Q158–4Q186). DJD V*. Oxford: Clarendon Press, 1968.

Allison, Dale C., Jr. "The Silence of the Angels: Reflections on the Songs of the Sabbath Sacrifice." *RevQ* 49–52/13.1–4 (1988): 189–197.

Alon, Gedalyahu. *Jews, Judaism, and the Classical World*. Translated by Israel Abrahams. Jerusalem: Magnes Press, 1977.

Andersen, Francis I., and David Noel Freedman. *Amos: A New Translation with Introduction and Commentary.* AB 24a. New York: Doubleday, 1989.

Anderson, Gary A. "The Interpretation of the Purification Offering in the *Temple Scroll* (11QTemple) and Rabbinic Literature." *JBL* 111.1 (1992): 17–35.

———. *Sacrifices and Offerings in Ancient Israel: Studies in Their Social and Political Importance.* Atlanta: Scholars Press, 1987.

Aptowitzer, Avigdor. "The Heavenly Sanctuary According to the Aggadah" [Hebrew]. *Tarbiz* 2 (1931): 137–153; 257–287.

Arnold, Bill T., and David B. Weisberg. "A Centennial Review of Friedrich Delitzsch's 'Babel und Bibel' Lectures." *JBL* 121.3 (2002): 441–457.

Attridge, Harold W. *The Epistle to the Hebrews: A Commentary on the Epistle to the Hebrews.* Hermeneia. Philadelphia: Fortress Press, 1989.

Attridge, Harold W., Torleif Elgvin, Józef T. Milik, Saul Olyan, John Strugnell, Emanuel Tov, James VanderKam, and Sidnie White. *Qumran Cave 4, VIII: Parabiblical Texts.* Part 1. *DJD XIII.* Oxford: Clarendon Press, 1994.

Avigad, Nahman. "Jewish Rock-Cut Tombs in Jerusalem and in the Judean Hill-Country" [Hebrew]. *EI* 8 (1967): 119–142.

Baer, Isaac. "The Sacrificial Service in the Second Temple Period" [Hebrew]. *Zion* 40.3–4 (1975): 95–153 (English summary, xxxix–xli).

Bammel, Ernst, and C. F. D. Moule, eds. *Jesus and the Politics of His Day.* Cambridge: Cambridge University Press, 1984.

Barker, Margaret. *The Gate of Heaven: The History and Symbolism of the Temple in Jerusalem.* London: SPCK, 1991.

———. *The Older Testament: The Survival of Themes from the Ancient Royal Cult in Sectarian Judaism and Early Christianity.* London: SPCK, 1987.

Barr, James, and A. R. S. Kennedy. "Sacrifice and Offering." In *Dictionary of the Bible,* edited by James Hastings, 868–876. New York: Scribner's, 1963.

Bauckham, Richard. "The Coin in the Fish's Mouth." In *Gospel Perspectives 6: The Miracles of Jesus,* edited by David Wenham and Craig Blomberg, 219–252. Sheffield, England: JSOT Press, 1986.

———. "Jesus' Demonstration in the Temple." In *Law and Religion: Essays on the Place of the Law in Israel and Early Christianity by Members of the Ehrhardt Seminar of Manchester University,* edited by Barnabas Lindars, 72–89, 171–176. Cambridge: James Clark, 1988.

Baumgarten, Albert I. *The Flourishing of Jewish Sects in the Maccabean Era: An Interpretation.* Leiden: Brill, 1997.

———. "Josephus on Essene Sacrifice." *JJS* 45.2 (1994): 169–183.

———. "Rabbinic Literature as a Source for the History of Jewish Sectarianism in the Second Temple Period." *DSD* 2.1 (1995): 14–57.

———. "The Zadokite Priests at Qumran: A Reconsideration." *DSD* 4.2 (1997): 137–156.

Baumgarten, Joseph M. "The Cave 4 Versions of the Qumran Penal Code." *JJS* 43.2 (1992): 268–276.

———. "The Exclusion of 'Netinim' and Proselytes in 4Q Florilegium." *RevQ* 29/8.1 (1972): 87–96.

———. *Qumran Cave 4, XIII: The Damascus Document (4Q266–73). DJD XVIII.* Oxford: Clarendon Press, 1996.

———. "Sacrifice and Worship among the Jewish Sectarians of the Dead Sea (Qumran) Scrolls." *HTR* 46.3 (1953): 141–159.

———. *Studies in Qumran Law.* Leiden: Brill, 1977.

Baumgarten, Joseph M., Torleif Elgvin, Esther Eshel, Erik Larson, Manfred R. Lehmann, Stephen Pfann, and Lawrence H. Schiffman. *Qumran Cave 4, XXV: Halakhic Texts. DJD XXXV.* Oxford: Clarendon Press, 1999.

Beck, Norman. "The Last Supper as an Efficacious Symbolic Act." *JBL* 89.2 (1970): 192–198.

Beckwith, Roger T., and Martin J. Selman, eds. *Sacrifice in the Bible.* Grand Rapids, Mich.: Baker Book House, 1995.

Bediako, Gillian M. *Primal Religion and the Bible: William Robertson Smith and His Heritage.* Sheffield, England: Sheffield Academic Press, 1997.

Beidelman, T. O. *W. Robertson Smith and the Sociological Study of Religion.* Chicago: University of Chicago Press, 1974.

Belayche, Nicole. "Sacrifice and Theory of Sacrifice during the 'Pagan Reaction': Julian the Emperor." In *Sacrifice in Religious Experience,* edited by Albert I. Baumgarten, 101–126. Leiden: Brill, 2002.

Belier, Wouter W. "Durkheim, Mauss, Classical Evolutionism and the Origin of Religion." *Method and Theory in the Study of Religion* 11.1 (1999): 24–46.

Belkin, Samuel. "Midrash Tadshe or the Midrash of Rabbi Phineas: An Early Hellenistic Midrash" [Hebrew]. *Horeb* 11.21–22 (1951): 1–52.

———. *Philo and the Oral Law: The Philonic Interpretation of Biblical Law in Relation to the Palestinian Halakah.* Cambridge, Mass.: Harvard University Press, 1940.

Bell, Catherine. *Ritual Theory, Ritual Practice.* New York: Oxford University Press, 1992.

Berger, Peter L. "Charisma and Religious Innovation: The Social Location of Israelite Prophecy." *American Sociological Review* 28.6 (1963): 940–950.

Berlin, Adele. *Lamentations.* OTL. Louisville, Ky.: Westminster John Knox Press, 2002.

Betz, Hans Dieter. "Jesus and the Purity of the Temple (Mark 11:15–18): A Comparative Religion Approach." *JBL* 116.3 (1997): 455–472.

———. *The Sermon on the Mount: A Commentary on the Sermon on the Mount, including the Sermon on the Plain (Matthew 5:3–7:27 and Luke 6:20–49).* Hermeneia. Minneapolis: Fortress Press, 1995.

Bialik, Hayim Nahman, and Yehoshua Hana Ravnitzky. *The Book of Legends, Sefer Ha-Aggadah: Legends from the Talmud and Midrash.* Translated by William G. Braude. New York: Schocken Books, 1992.

Bickerman, Elias J. *The Jews in the Greek Age.* Cambridge, Mass.: Harvard University Press, 1988.

Black, Matthew, ed. *Apocalypsis Henochi Graece.* Leiden: Brill, 1970.

Blackman, Aylward M. "Purification (Egyptian)." In *The Encyclopedia of Religion and Ethics,* edited by James Hastings, 10:476–482. 13 vols. New York: Scribner's, 1908–26.

Blenkinsopp, Joseph. "An Assessment of the Alleged Pre-Exilic Date of the Priestly Material of the Pentateuch." *ZAW* 108.4 (1996): 495–518.

———. *A History of Prophecy in Israel: Revised and Enlarged.* Louisville, Ky.: Westminster John Knox Press, 1996.

———. *The Pentateuch: An Introduction to the First Five Books of the Bible.* New York: Doubleday, 1992.

———. *Sage, Priest, Prophet: Religious and Intellectual Leadership in Ancient Israel.* Louisville, Ky.: Westminster John Knox Press, 1995.

Bloch, Renée. "Methodological Note for the Study of Rabbinic Literature." In *Approaches to Ancient Judaism: Theory and Practice,* edited by William Scott Green, 51–75. Missoula, Mont.: Scholars Press, 1978.

Bloch-Smith, Elizabeth. "'Who Is the King of Glory?' Solomon's Temple and Its Symbolism." In *Scripture and Other Artifacts: Essays on the Bible and Archaeology in Honor of Philip J. King*, edited by Michael D. Coogan, J. Cheryl Exum, and Lawrence E. Stager, 18–31. Louisville, Ky.: Westminster John Knox Press, 1994.

Bokser, Baruch M. "Approaching Sacred Space." *HTR* 78.3 (1985): 279–299.

———. "*Ma'al* and Blessings over Food: Rabbinic Transformation of Cultic Terminology and Alternative Modes of Piety." *JBL* 100.4 (1981): 557–574.

———. "Rabbinic Continuity and Revisions in the Notion of Sacred Space—Applying Deuteronomy 23:10–15." In *Proceedings of the Ninth World Congress of Jewish Studies, Jerusalem, August 4–12, 1985, Division C: Jewish Thought and Literature*, 7–14. Jerusalem: World Union of Jewish Studies, 1988.

———. "Rabbinic Responses to Catastrophe: From Continuity to Discontinuity." *Proceedings of the American Academy for Jewish Research* 50 (1983): 37–61.

———. "The Wall Separating God and Israel." *JQR* 73.4 (1983): 349–374.

Booth, Roger P. *Jesus and the Laws of Purity: Tradition History and Legal History in Mark 7.* Sheffield, England: JSOT Press, 1986.

Borg, Marcus J. *Conflict, Holiness, and Politics in the Teachings of Jesus.* New ed. Harrisburg, Pa.: Trinity Press International, 1998.

———. *Jesus, a New Vision: Spirit, Culture, and the Life of Discipleship.* San Francisco: Harper and Row, 1987.

Borgen, Peder. *Philo of Alexandria: An Exegete for His Time.* Leiden: Brill, 1997.

Bourdillon, M. F. C., and Meyer Fortes, eds. *Sacrifice.* London: Academic Press, 1980.

Bowman, John. "Did the Qumran Sect Burn the Red Heifer?" *RevQ* 1/1.1 (1958): 73–84.

Boyarin, Daniel. *A Radical Jew: Paul and the Politics of Identity.* Berkeley: University of California Press, 1994.

Branham, Joan R. "Vicarious Sacrality: Temple Space in Ancient Synagogues." In *Ancient Synagogues: Historical Analysis and Archaeological Discovery*, edited by Dan Urman and Paul V. M. Flesher, 2:319–345. 2 vols. Leiden: Brill, 1995.

Brichto, Herbert Chanan. "On Slaughter and Sacrifice, Blood and Atonement." *HUCA* 48 (1976): 19–55.

Bright, John. *Jeremiah: Introduction, Translation, and Notes.* AB 21. Garden City, N.Y.: Doubleday, 1965.

Brooke, George J., John Collins, Torleif Elgvin, Peter Flint, Jonas Greenfield, Erik Larson, Carol Newsom, Émile Puech, Lawrence Schiffman, Michael Stone, and Julio Trebolle Barrera. *Qumran Cave 4, XVII: Parabiblical Texts, Part 3. DJD XXII.* Oxford: Clarendon Press, 1996.

Brown, F., S. R. Driver, and C. A. Briggs. *A Hebrew and English Lexicon of the Old Testament.* Oxford: Clarendon Press, 1907.

Brownlee, William H. *The Midrash Pesher of Habakkuk.* Missoula, Mont.: Scholars Press, 1979.

Buber, Martin. *The Prophetic Faith.* New York: MacMillan, 1949.

Buber, Salomon, ed. *Midrash Echah Rabbah.*1899. Reprint, Jerusalem: Wagshal, n.d.

———, ed. *Midrash Tanhuma.* 2 vols. 1885. Reprint, Israel: Book Export Enterprises, n.d.

Büchler, Adolph. *Der galiläische 'Am-ha' Ares des zweiten Jahrhunderts: Beiträge zur innern Geschichte des palästinischen Judentums in den ersten zwei Jahrhunderten.* Vienna: Alfred Hölder, 1906.

———. *Die Priester und der Cultus im letzten Jahrzehnt des jerusalemischen Tempels.* Vienna: Alfred Hölder, 1895.

———. *Studies in Jewish History: The Adolph Büchler Memorial Volume.* Edited by I. Brodie and J. Rabbinowitz. London: Oxford University Press, 1956.

————. *Studies in Sin and Atonement in the Rabbinic Literature of the First Century*. London: Oxford University Press, 1928.

Buckley, Jorunn Jacobsen. "A Matter of Urgency: A Response to 'The Passover Supper in Exodus 12:1–20.'" *Semeia* 67 (1984): 63–71.

Budd, Philip J. *Leviticus*. New Century Bible. Grand Rapids, Mich.: Eerdmans, 1996.

Burkert, Walter. *Homo Necans: The Anthropology of Ancient Greek Sacrificial Ritual and Myth*. Translated by Peter Bing. Berkeley: University of California Press, 1983.

————. *Structure and History in Greek Mythology and Ritual*. Berkeley: University of California Press, 1979.

Busink, Th. A. *Der Tempel von Jerusalem, von Salomo bis Herodes: Eine archäologisch-historische Studie unter Berücksichtigung des westsemitischen Tempelbaus*. 2 vols. Leiden: Brill, 1970, 1980.

Caird, G. B. *The Language and Imagery of the Bible*. London: Duckworth, 1980.

Carroll, Robert P. *From Chaos to Covenant: Prophecy in the Book of Jeremiah*. New York: Crossroad, 1981.

————. *Jeremiah*. OTL. London: SPCK, 1986.

————. "Prophecy and Society." In *The World of Ancient Israel: Sociological, Anthropological and Political Perspectives*, edited by R. E. Clements, 203–225. Cambridge: Cambridge University Press, 1989.

Casey, P. M. "Culture and Historicity: The Cleansing of the Temple." *CBQ* 59.2 (1997): 306–332.

Charles, R. H. *Pseudepigrapha*. Vol. 2 of *The Apocrypha and Pseudepigrapha of the Old Testament in English*. 2 vols. Oxford: Oxford University Press, 1913.

Charlesworth, James H., ed. *Damascus Document, War Scroll, and Related Documents*. PTSDSSP 2. Tübingen: Mohr Siebeck, 1995.

————, ed. *The Old Testament Pseudepigrapha*. 2 vols. Garden City, N.Y.: Doubleday, 1983.

————, ed. *Rule of the Community and Related Documents*. PTSDSSP 1. Tübingen: Mohr Siebeck, 1995.

Charlesworth, James H., and Carol A. Newsom, eds. *Angelic Liturgy: Songs of a Sabbath Sacrifice*. PTSDSSP 4B. Tübingen: Mohr Siebeck, 1999.

Chazon, Esther G. "Liturgical Communion with the Angels at Qumran." In *Sapiential, Liturgical and Poetical Texts from Qumran: Proceedings of the International Organization for Qumran Studies, Oslo 1998 (Published in Memory of Maurice Baillet)*, edited by Daniel K. Falk, Florentino García Martínez, and Eileen M. Schuller, 95–105. Leiden: Brill, 2000.

Chiat, Marilyn J. "Synagogues and Churches in Byzantine Beit She'an." *Journal of Jewish Art* 7 (1980): 6–24.

Childs, Brevard S. *Isaiah*. OTL. Louisville, Ky.: Westminster John Knox Press, 2001.

Chilton, Bruce. "A Coin of Three Realms (Matthew 17:24–27)." In *Jesus in Context: Temple, Purity, and Restoration*, edited by Bruce Chilton and Craig A. Evans, 340–351. Leiden: Brill, 1997.

————. "The Eucharist: Exploring Its Origins." *Bible Review* 10.6 (1994): 36–43.

————. *A Feast of Meanings: Eucharistic Theologies from Jesus through Johannine Circles*. Leiden: Brill, 1994.

————. "The Hungry Knife: Towards a Sense of Sacrifice." In *Jesus in Context: Temple, Purity, and Restoration*, edited by Bruce Chilton and Craig A. Evans, 91–108. Leiden: Brill, 1997.

————. *Pure Kingdon: Jesus' Vision of God, Studying the Historical Jesus*. Grand Rapids, Mich.: Eerdmans, 1996.

————. *Rabbi Jesus: An Intimate Biography*. New York: Doubleday, 2000.

————. *The Temple of Jesus: His Sacrificial Program within a Cultural History of Sacrifice*. University Park: Pennsylvania State University Press, 1992.

Choksy, Jamsheed K. *Purity and Pollution in Zoroastrianism*. Austin: University of Texas Press, 1989.

Clements, R. E. *God and Temple*. Philadelphia: Fortress Press, 1965.

Coggins, Richard, Anthony Phillips, and Michael Knibb, eds. *Israel's Prophetic Tradition: Essays in Honour of Peter R. Ackroyd*. Cambridge: Cambridge University Press, 1982.

Cohen, Gerson D. *Studies in the Variety of Rabbinic Cultures*. Philadelphia: Jewish Publication Society, 1991.

Cohen, Norman J. "Shekhinta ba-Galuta: A Midrashic Response to Destruction and Persecution." *JSJ* 13.1–2 (1982): 147–159.

Cohen, Shaye J. D. "The Destruction: From Scripture to Midrash." *Prooftexts* 2.1 (1982): 18–39.

————. "Jacob Neusner, Mishnah, and Counter-Rabbinics: A Review Essay." *Conservative Judaism* 37.1 (1983): 48–63.

————. "Josephus, Jeremiah and Polybius." *History and Theory* 21.3 (1982): 366–381.

————. "The Temple and the Synagogue." In *The Cambridge History of Judaism*, vol. 3, *The Early Roman Period*, edited by William Horbury, W. D. Davies, and John Sturdy, 298–325. Cambridge: Cambridge University Press, 1999.

Collins, Adela Yarbro. "Jesus' Action in Herod's Temple." In *Antiquity and Humanity: Essays on Ancient Religion and Philosophy, Presented to Hans Dieter Betz on His Seventieth Birthday*, edited by Adela Yarbro Collins and Margaret M. Mitchell, 45–61. Tübingen: Mohr Siebeck, 2001.

Conzelmann, Hans. *Acts of the Apostles: A Commentary on the Acts of the Apostles*. Hermeneia. Philadelphia: Fortress Press, 1987.

Cross, Frank Moore. *The Ancient Library of Qumran*. 3rd ed. Minneapolis: Fortress Press, 1995.

————. *Canaanite Myth and Hebrew Epic: Essays in the History of the Religion of Israel*. Cambridge, Mass.: Harvard University Press, 1973.

————. "The Development of the Jewish Scripts." In *The Bible and the Ancient Near East: Essays in Honor of William Foxwell Albright*, edited by G. E. Wright, 133–202. Garden City, N.Y.: Doubleday, 1961.

————. *From Epic to Canon*. Baltimore: Johns Hopkins University Press, 1998.

Crossan, John Dominic. *The Historical Jesus: The Life of a Mediterranean Jewish Peasant*. San Francisco: HarperCollins, 1991.

Daly, Robert J. *Christian Sacrifice: The Judaeo-Christian Background before Origen*. Washington, D.C.: Catholic University of America Press, 1978.

————. "The Power of Sacrifice in Ancient Judaism and Christianity." *Journal of Ritual Studies* 4.2 (1990): 181–198.

Danby, Herbert. *The Mishnah: Translated from the Hebrew with Introduction and Brief Explanatory Notes*. Oxford: Oxford University Press, 1933.

Darr, Katheryn Pfisterer. "Ezekiel among the Critics." *Currents in Research: Biblical Studies* 2 (1994): 9–24.

Daube, David. "Temple Tax." In *Jesus, The Gospels, and the Church: Essays in Honor of William R. Farmer*, edited by E. P. Sanders, 121–134. Macon, Ga.: Mercer University Press, 1987.

Davies, Douglas. "An Interpretation of Sacrifice in Leviticus." In *Anthropological Approaches to the Old Testament*, edited by Bernhard Lang, 151–162. Philadelphia: Fortress Press, 1985.

Davies, Philip R. "The Ideology of the Temple in the Damascus Document." *JJS* 33 (1982): 287–301.

Davies, W. D. *The Gospel and the Land: Early Christianity and Jewish Territorial Doctrine.* Berkeley: University of California Press, 1974.

———. *Paul and Rabbinic Judaism: Some Rabbinic Elements in Pauline Theology.* London: SPCK, 1968.

Davila, James R. *Liturgical Works.* Grand Rapids, Mich.: Eerdmans, 2000.

———. "The Macrocosmic Temple, Scriptural Exegesis, and the Songs of the Sabbath Sacrifice." *DSD* 9.1 (2002): 1–19.

de Heusch, Luc. *Sacrifice in Africa: A Structuralist Approach.* Translated by Linda O'Brian and Alice Morton. Bloomington: Indiana University Press, 1985.

de Jonge, Marinus. "Christian Influence in the Testaments of the Twelve Patriarchs." *Novum Testamentum* 4.3 (1960): 182–235.

———. "Levi in Aramaic Levi and in the Testament of Levi." In *Pseudepigraphical Perspectives: The Apocrypha and Pseudepigrapha in Light of the Dead Sea Scrolls*, edited by Esther G. Chazon and Michael Stone, with the collaboration of Avital Pinnick, 73–89. Leiden: Brill, 1999.

———. "The Transmission of the Testaments of the Twelve Patriarchs by Christians." *Vigiliae Christianae* 47 (1993): 1–28.

de Jonge, Marinus, in cooperation with H. W. Hollander, H. J. de Jonge, and Th. Korteweg. *The Testaments of the Twelve Patriarchs: A Critical Edition of the Greek Text.* Leiden: Brill, 1978.

Detienne, Marcel, and Jean-Pierre Vernant, eds. *The Cuisine of Sacrifice among the Greeks.* Translated by Paula Wissing. Chicago: University of Chicago Press, 1989.

de Vaux, Roland. *Ancient Israel.* New York: McGraw-Hill, 1961.

———. *Archaeology and the Dead Sea Scrolls: The Schweich Lectures of the British Academy 1959.* London: Oxford University Press, 1973.

———. *Studies in Old Testament Sacrifice.* Cardiff: University of Wales Press, 1964.

Dimant, Devorah. "4QFlorilegium and the Idea of the Community as Temple." In *Hellenica et Judaica: Hommage á Valentin Nikiprowetzky*, edited by A. Caquot, M. Hadas-Level, and J. Riaud, 165–189. Paris: Peeters, 1986.

———. "Men as Angels: The Self-Image of the Qumran Community." In *Religion and Politics in the Ancient Near East*, edited by Adele Berlin, 95–103. College Park: University Press of Maryland, 1996.

Dimant, Devorah, partially based on earlier texts by John Strugnell. *Qumran Cave 4, XXI: Parabiblical Texts, Part 4: Pseudo-Prophetic Texts. DJD XXX.* Oxford: Clarendon Press, 2001.

Dothan, Moshe. *Hammath Tiberias: Early Synagogues and the Hellenistic and Roman Remains.* Jerusalem: Israel Exploration Society, 1983.

Douglas, Mary. "Atonement in Leviticus." *JSQ* 1.2 (1993–1994): 109–130.

———. "A Bird, a Mouse, a Frog, and Some Fish: A New Reading of Leviticus 11." In *Literary Imagination, Ancient and Modern: Essays in Honor of David Grene*, edited by Todd Breyfogle, 110–126. Chicago: University of Chicago Press, 1999.

———. "The Eucharist: Its Continuity with the Bread Sacrifice of Leviticus." In *Catholicism and Catholicity: Eucharistic Communities in Historical and Contemporary Perspectives*, edited by Sarah Beckwith, 97–112. Oxford: Blackwell, 1999.

————. "The Forbidden Animals in Leviticus." *JSOT* 59 (1993): 3–23.

————. "The Go-Away Goat." In *The Book of Leviticus: Composition and Reception*, edited by Rolf Rendtorff and Robert A. Kugler, with the assistance of Sarah Smith Bartel, 121–141. Leiden: Brill, 2003.

————. "Holy Joy: Rereading Leviticus: The Anthropologist and the Believer." *Conservative Judaism* 46.3 (1994): 3–14.

————. *Implicit Meanings: Essays in Anthropology*. London: Routledge and Kegan Paul, 1975.

————. *Leviticus as Literature*. Oxford: Oxford University Press, 1999.

————. *Purity and Danger: An Analysis of the Concepts of Pollution and Taboo*. London: Routledge and Kegan Paul, 1966.

————. "Responding to Ezra: The Priests and the Foreign Wives." *BibInt* 10.1 (2002): 1–23.

————. "The Stranger in the Bible." *Archives Européennes de Sociologie* 35.1 (1994): 283–298.

Draper, Jonathan A., ed. *The Didache in Modern Research*. Leiden: Brill, 1996.

Dunnill, John. "Methodological Rivalries: Theology and Social Science in Girardian Interpretations of the New Testament." *JSNT* 62 (1996): 105–119.

Dupont, Jacques. *The Salvation of the Gentiles: Essays on the Acts of the Apostles*. New York: Paulist Press, 1979.

Durkheim, Emile. *The Elementary Forms of the Religious Life*. Translated by Joseph Ward Swain. New York: Free Press, 1965.

Edersheim, Alfred. *The Temple: Its Ministry and Services as They Were at the Time of Jesus Christ*. London: Religious Tract Society, 1874.

Ego, Beate, Armin Lange, and Peter Pilhofer, in cooperation with Kathrin Ehlers, eds. *Gemeinde ohne Tempel: Zur Substituierung und Transformation des Jerusalemer Tempels und seines Kults im Alten Testament, antiken Judentum und frühen Christentum*. Tübingen: Mohr Siebeck, 1999.

Ehrlich, Uri. "The Location of the *Shekhina* in the early Versions of the *Shemone Esre*" [Hebrew]. *Sidra* 13 (1997): 5–23.

————. "The Place of the *Shekhina* in the Consciousness of the Worshipper" [Hebrew]. *Tarbiz* 45.2 (1996): 315–329 (English summary, x–xi).

Ehrman, Bart D. *The Orthodox Corruption of Scripture: The Effect of Early Christological Controversies on the Text of the New Testament*. New York: Oxford University Press, 1993.

Eilberg-Schwartz, Howard. *The Savage in Judaism: An Anthropology of Israelite Religion and Ancient Judaism*. Bloomington: Indiana University Press, 1990.

Eisenman, Robert M. *Maccabees, Zadokites, Christians and Qumran: A New Hypothesis of Qumran Origins*. Leiden: Brill, 1983.

Elbogen, Ismar. *Jewish Liturgy: A Comprehensive History*. Translated by Raymond P. Scheindlin. Philadelphia: Jewish Publication Society, 1993.

Elgvin, Torleif, in collaboration with Stephen J. Pfann. "An Incense Altar from Qumran?" *DSD* 9.1 (2002): 20–33.

Eliade, Mircea. *The Myth of the Eternal Return: Or, Cosmos and History*. Translated by Willard R. Trask. Second printing, with corrections, 1965. Reprint, Princeton: Princeton University Press, 1991.

Elior, Rachel. "From Earthly Temple to Heavenly Shrines: Prayer and Sacred Song in the Hekhalot Literature and Its Relation to Temple Traditions." *JSQ* 4.3 (1997): 217–267.

————. *The Three Temples: On the Emergence of Jewish Mysticism*. Translated by David Louvish. London: Littman Library of Jewish Civilization, 2004.

Elman, Yaakov. "Some Remarks on 4QMMT and the Rabbinic Traditions: or, When Is a Parallel Not a Parallel?" In *Reading 4QMMT: New Perspectives on Qumran Law and History*, edited by John Kampen and Moshe J. Bernstein, 99–128. Altanta, Ga.: Scholars Press, 1996.

Eppstein, Victor. "The Historicity of the Gospel Account of the Cleansing of the Temple." *ZNW* 55.1–2 (1964): 42–58.

Epstein, Abraham. "Le Livre des Jubilés, Philon, et le Midrasch Tadshé." *REJ* 21 (1890): 80–97; 22 (1891): 1–25.

———. *Me-Qadmoniot ha-Yehudim*. In *The Writings of Rabbi A. Epstein* [Hebrew], edited by A. M. Haberman, 2:130–171, 173–174. 2 vols. Jerusalem: Mossad ha-Rav Kook, 1950, 1957.

Epstein, Isidore, ed. *The Babylonian Talmud Translated into English with Notes, Glossary, and Indices*. 18 vols. London: Soncino Press, 1961.

Epstein, Jacob N. *Introduction to the Text of the Mishnah* [Hebrew]. 2nd ed. 2 vols. Jerusalem: Magnes Press, 1964.

———. *Introductions to Tannaitic Literature: Mishna, Tosephta, and Halakhic Midrashim* [Hebrew]. Edited by E. Z. Melamed. Jerusalem: Magnes Press, 1957.

Eribon, Didier. *Conversations with Claude Lévi-Strauss*. Translated by Paula Wissing. Chicago: University of Chicago Press, 1991.

Eshel, Esther, Hannan Eshel, Carol Newsom, Bilhah Nitzan, Eileen Schuller, and Ada Yardeni. *Qumran Cave 4, VI: Poetical and Liturgical Texts, Part 1. DJD XI*. Oxford: Clarendon Press, 1997.

Evans, Craig A. "Jesus' Action in the Temple: Cleansing or Portent of Destruction?" In *Jesus in Context: Temple, Purity, and Restoration*, edited by Craig A. Evans and Bruce Chilton, 395–439. Leiden: Brill, 1997.

Evans-Pritchard, E. E. *Nuer Religion*. New York: Oxford University Press, 1956.

———. *Theories of Primitive Religion*. Oxford: Clarendon Press, 1965.

Falk, Daniel K. "Qumran Prayer Texts and the Temple." In *Sapiential, Liturgical and Poetical Texts from Qumran: Proceedings of the International Organization for Qumran Studies, Oslo 1998 (Published in Memory of Maurice Baillet)*, edited by Daniel K. Falk, Florentino García Martínez, and Eileen M. Schuller, 106–126. Leiden: Brill, 2000.

Fardon, Richard. *Mary Douglas: An Intellectual Biography*. London: Routledge, 1999.

Feeley-Harnik, Gillian. *The Lord's Table: The Meaning of Food in Early Judaism and Christianity*. Washington, D.C.: Smithsonian Institution Press, 1994.

Feldman, Emanuel. *Biblical and Post-Biblical Defilement and Mourning: Law as Theology*. New York: Yeshiva University Press, 1977.

Feldman, Louis H. *Judean Antiquities 1–4: Translation and Commentary*. Vol. 3 of *Flavius Josephus: Translation and Commentary*, edited by Steve Mason. Leiden: Brill, 2000.

Ferguson, Everett. "Spiritual Sacrifice in Early Christianity and Its Environment." In *Aufstieg and Niedergang der römischen Welt: Geschicht and Kultur Roms im Spiegel der neurern Forschung*. Part 2, *Principat*, edited by Hildegard Temporini and Wolfgang Haase, 23.2:1152–1189. New York, de Gruyter, 1980.

Fernandez, James W. *Persuasions and Performances: The Play of Tropes in Culture*. Bloomington: Indiana University Press, 1986.

Fiensy, D. A. *Prayers Alleged to Be Jewish: an Examination of the Constitutiones Apostolorum*. Chico, Calif.: Scholars Press, 1985.

Fine, Steven. "Art and Identity in Later Second Temple Period Judaea: The Hasmonean Royal Tombs at Modi'in." Rabbi Louis Feinberg Memorial Lecture in Jewish Studies. Cincinnati: University of Cincinnati, 2001.

———. *This Holy Place: On the Sanctity of the Synagogue during the Greco-Roman Period.* Notre Dame: University of Notre Dame Press, 1997.

Finegan, Jack. *Handbook of Biblical Chronology.* Revised ed. Peabody, Mass.: Hendrickson, 1998.

Finkelstein, Louis. "The Birkat Ha-Mazon." *JQR* (n.s.) 19 (1928–1929): 211–262.

———, ed. *Sifra on Leviticus: According to Vatican Manuscript Assemani 66 with Variants from the Other Manuscripts, Genizah Fragments, Early Editions and Quotations by Medieval Authorities and with References to Parallel Passages and Commentaries.* 5 vols. New York: Jewish Theological Seminary, 1983–91.

———. *Sifre on Deuteronomy.* 1939. Reprint, New York: Jewish Theological Seminary, 1993.

Fishbane, Michael. *Text and Texture: Close Readings of Selected Biblical Texts.* New York: Schocken Books, 1979.

Fitzmyer, Joseph A. *The Gospel According to Luke X–XXIV: A New Translation with Introduction and Commentary.* AB 28a. New York: Doubleday, 1985.

Fleischer, Ezra. "On the Beginnings of Obligatory Jewish Prayer" [Hebrew]. *Tarbiz* 59 (1989–90): 397–441.

Fletcher-Louis, Crispin H. T. "Heavenly Ascent or Incarnational Presence? A Revisionist Reading of the *Songs of the Sabbath Sacrifice.*" *SBLSP* 37.1 (1998): 367–399.

Flint, Peter W., and James C. VanderKam, with the assistance of Andrea E. Alvarez, eds. *The Dead Sea Scrolls after Fifty Years: A Comprehensive Assessment.* 2 vols. Leiden: Brill, 1999.

Flusser, David. "Jerusalem in the Literature of the Second Temple" [Hebrew]. In David Flusser, *Judaism of the Second Temple Period: Sages and Literature*, edited by Serge Ruzer, 36–67. Jerusalem: Magnes Press, 2002.

———. "Jewish Roots of the Liturgical Trishagion." *Immanuel* 3 (1973): 37–43.

———. *Judaism and the Origins of Christianity.* Jerusalem: Magnes Press, 1988.

———. "Matthew XVII, 24–27 and the Dead Sea Sect" [Hebrew]. *Tarbiz* 31.2 (1961): 150–156 (English summary, iii).

———. "The Temple of the End of Days." [Hebrew]. In David Flusser, *Judaism of the Second Temple Period: Qumran and Apocalypticism*, edited by Serge Ruzer, 179–183. Jerusalem: Magnes Press, 2002.

Flusser, David, in collaboration with R. Steven Notley. *Jesus.* 2nd ed., corrected and augmented. Jerusalem: Magnes Press, 1998.

Foerster, Gideon. "The Zodiac in Ancient Synagogues and Its Place in Jewish Thought and Literature" [Hebrew]. *EI* 19 (1987): 225–234.

Fox, Everett. *The Five Books of Moses.* Vol. 1 of *The Schocken Bible.* New York: Schocken Books, 1995.

Fox, Michael V., ed. *Temple in Society.* Winona Lake, Ind.: Eisenbrauns, 1988.

Fox, Michael V., Victor Avigdor Hurowitz, Avi Hurvitz, Michael L. Klein, Baruch J. Schwartz, and Nili Shupak, eds. *Texts, Temples, and Traditions: A Tribute to Menahem Haran.* Winona Lake, Ind.: Eisenbrauns, 1996.

Fraenkel, Jonah. "Hermeneutic Problems in the Study of the Aggadic Narrative" [Hebrew]. *Tarbiz* 47.3–4 (1978): 139–172 (English summary, ii–iii).

———. *Iyyunim be-Olamo ha-Ruchani shel Sippur ha-Aggadah.* Tel Aviv: Hakibbutz Hameuchad, 1981.

Fredriksen, Paula. *Jesus of Nazareth, King of the Jews: A Jewish Life and the Emergence of Christianity.* New York: Knopf, 1999.

———. "Ultimate Reality in Ancient Christianity: Christ and Redemption." In *Ultimate Realities*, edited by Robert Cummings Neville, 61–73. Albany: State Univesity of New York Press, 2000.

Freedman, David Noel, ed. *The Anchor Bible Dictionary*. 6 vols. New York: Doubleday, 1992.

Freud, Sigmund. *Totem and Taboo: Some Points of Agreement between the Mental Lives of Savages and Neurotics*. Translated by James Strachey. 1950. Reprint, New York: Norton, 1989.

Frymer-Kensky, Tikva. *In the Wake of the Goddesses: Women, Culture and the Biblical Transformation of Pagan Myth*. New York: Fawcett Columbine, 1992.

———. "Pollution, Purification, and Purgation in Biblical Israel." In *The Word of the Lord Shall Go Forth: Essays in Honor of David Noel Freedman in Celebration of His Sixtieth Birthday*, edited by Carol L. Meyers and M. O'Connor, 399–410. Winona Lake, Ind.: Eisenbrauns, 1983.

Funk, Robert W., Roy W. Hoover, and the Jesus Seminar. *The Five Gospels: The Search for the Authentic Words of Jesus*. New York: Macmillan, 1993.

Funk, Robert W., and the Jesus Seminar, eds. *The Acts of Jesus: The Search for the Authentic Deeds of Jesus*. New York: HarperCollins, 1998.

García Martínez, Florentino. *Qumran and Apocalyptic: Studies on the Aramaic Texts from Qumran*. Leiden: Brill, 1992.

García Martínez, Florentino, and Julio Trebolle Barrera. *The People of the Dead Sea Scrolls: Their Writings, Beliefs and Practices*. Leiden: Brill, 1995.

García Martínez, Florentino, and Eibert J. C. Tigchelaar, eds. *The Dead Sea Scrolls Study Edition*. 2nd ed. 2 vols. Leiden: Brill, 2000.

García Martínez, Florentino, Eibert J. C. Tigchelaar, and A. S. van der Woude. *Qumran Cave 11, II: 11Q2–18, 11Q20–31. DJD XXIII*. Oxford: Clarendon Press, 1998.

Garnet, Paul. *Salvation and Atonement in the Qumran Scrolls*. Tübingen: Mohr Siebeck, 1977.

Gärtner, Bertil. *The Temple and the Community in Qumran and the New Testament: A Comparative Study in the Temple Symbolism of the Qumran Texts and the New Testament*. Cambridge: Cambridge University Press, 1965.

Gaster, Theodor H. *The Dead Sea Scriptures: With Introduction and Notes*. 3rd ed., rev. and enl. New York: Doubleday, 1976.

Geertz, Clifford. *The Interpretation of Cultures*. New York: Basic Books, 1973.

Geller, Stephen A. *Sacred Enigmas: Literary Religion in the Hebrew Bible*. London: Routledge, 1996.

Gerstenberger, Erhard S. *Leviticus: A Commentary*. OTL. Louisville, Ky.: Westminster John Knox Press, 1996.

Gese, Hartmut. "The Origin of the Lord's Supper." In *Essays on Biblical Theology*, 117–140. Translated by Keith Crim. Minneapolis: Augsburg, 1981.

Ginzberg, Louis. *Legends of the Jews*. Translated by Henrietta Szold and Paul Radin. 7 vols. Philadelphia: Jewish Publication Society, 1909–1938.

———. "The Mishnah Tamid: The Oldest Treatise of the Mishnah." *Journal of Jewish Lore and Philosophy* 1 (1919): 33–44, 197–209, 265–295

———. *An Unknown Jewish Sect*. New York: Jewish Theological Seminary, 1976.

Girard, René. *The Scapegoat*. Translated by Yvonne Freccero. Baltimore: Johns Hopkins University Press, 1986.

———. *Things Hidden since the Foundation of the World*. Translated by Stephen Bann and Michael Metteer. Stanford: Stanford University Press, 1987.

———. *Violence and the Sacred.* Translated by Patrick Gregory. Baltimore: Johns Hopkins University Press, 1977.

Gittlen, Barry M., ed. *Sacred Time, Sacred Place: Archaeology and the Religion of Israel.* Winona Lake, Ind.: Eisenbrauns, 2002.

Glatzer, Nahum N. "The Concept of Sacrifice in Post-Biblical Judaism: Quest for Substitutes for Sacrifices after the Destruction of the Second Temple." In *Essays in Jewish Thought*, 48–57. Tuscaloosa: University of Alabama Press, 1978.

Golb, Norman. *Who Wrote the Dead Sea Scrolls? The Search for the Secret of Qumran.* New York: Scribner's, 1995.

Goldenberg, Robert. "The Broken Axis: Rabbinic Judaism and the Fall of the Temple." *JAAR supp.* 45.3 (1977): F 869–882.

Goodenough, Erwin R. *By Light, Light: The Mystic Gospel of Hellenistic Judaism.* New Haven: Yale University Press, 1935.

———. *Jewish Symbols in the Greco-Roman Period.* Vols. 1–12. New York: Pantheon Books, 1953–65. Vol. 13. Princeton: Princeton University Press, 1968.

Goodman, Martin. *The Ruling Class of Judaea: The Origins of the Jewish Revolt against Rome* A.D. *66–70.* Cambridge: Cambridge University Press, 1987.

———. "Sadducees and Essenes after 70 CE." In *Crossing the Boundaries: Essays in Biblical Interpretation in Honour of Michael D. Goulder*, edited by Stanley E. Porter, Paul Joyce, and David E. Orton, 347–356. Leiden: Brill, 1994.

Gorman, Frank H., Jr. *Divine Presence and Community: A Commentary on the Book of Leviticus.* International Theological Commentary. Grand Rapids, Mich.: Eerdmans, 1997.

———. *The Ideology of Ritual: Space, Time and Status in the Priestly Theology.* Sheffield, England: JSOT Press, 1990.

———. "Ritual Studies and Biblical Studies: Assessment of the Past; Prospects for the Future." *Semeia* 67 (1984): 13–36.

Grabbe, Lester L. *Judaic Religion in the Second Temple Period: Belief and Practice from the Exile to Yavneh.* London: Routledge, 2000.

———. *Leviticus.* OTG. Sheffield England: JSOT Press, 1993.

———. "4QMMT and Second Temple Jewish Society." In *Legal Texts and Legal Issues: Proceedings of the Second Meeting of the International Organization for Qumran Studies, Cambridge 1995, Published in Honour of Joseph M. Baumgarten*, edited by Moshe Bernstein, Florentino García Martínez, and John Kampen, 89–108. Leiden: Brill, 1997.

Gray, George Buchanan. *Sacrifice in the Old Testament: Its Theory and Practice.* 1925. Reprint, New York: Ktav, 1971.

Greenberg, Moshe. "Biblical Attitudes toward Power: Ideal and Reality in Law and Prophets." In *Religion and Law: Biblical-Judaic and Islamic Perspectives*, edited by Edwin B. Firmage, Bernard G. Weiss, and John W. Welch, 101–112. Winona Lake, Ind.: Eisenbrauns, 1990.

———. "The Design and Themes of Ezekiel's Program of Restoration." *Interpretation* 38.2 (1984): 181–208.

———. *Ezekiel 1–20: A New Translation with Introduction and Commentary.* AB 22. Garden City, N.Y.: Doubleday, 1983.

———. *Ezekiel 21–37: A New Translation with Introduction and Commentary.* AB 22a. New York: Doubleday, 1997.

———. "Idealism and Practicality in Numbers 35:4–5 and Ezekiel 48." *JAOS* 88.1 (1968): 59–65.

Grossman, Maxine. "Priesthood as Authority: Interpretive Competition in First-Century Judaism and Christianity." In *The Dead Sea Scrolls as Background to Postbiblical Judaism and Early Christianity: Papers from an International Conference at St. Andrews in 2001*, edited by James R. Davila, 117–131. Leiden: Brill, 2003.

Gruenwald, Ithamar. *Rituals and Ritual Theory in Ancient Israel*. Leiden: Brill, 2003.

Hachlili, Rachel. "The Zodiac in Ancient Jewish Art: Representation and Significance." *Bulletin of the American Schools of Oriental Research* 228 (1977): 61–77.

———. "The Zodiac in Ancient Jewish Synagogal Art." *JSQ* 9.3 (2002): 219–258.

Halperin, David J. *The Merkabah in Rabbinic Literature*. New Haven: American Oriental Society, 1980.

Hamerton-Kelly, Robert G. *The Gospel and the Sacred: Poetics of Violence in Mark*. Minneapolis: Fortress Press, 1994.

———. *Sacred Violence: Paul's Hermeneutic of the Cross*. Minneapolis: Fortress Press, 1992.

———, ed. *Violent Origins: Walter Burkert, René Girard, and Jonathan Z. Smith on Ritual Killing and Cultural Formation*. Stanford: Stanford University Press, 1987.

Haran, Menahem. "The Law Code of Ezekiel XL–XLVIII and its Relations to the Priestly School." *HUCA* 50 (1979): 45–72.

———. *Temples and Temple-Service in Ancient Israel: An Inquiry into Biblical Cult Phenomena and the Historical Setting of the Priestly School*. Winona Lake, Ind.: Eisenbrauns, 1985.

Harrington, Hannah K. *Holiness: Rabbinic Judaism and the Graeco-Roman World*. London: Routledge, 2001.

———. *The Impurity Systems of Qumran and the Rabbis*. Atlanta, Ga.: Scholars Press, 1993.

Hartley, John E. *Leviticus*. Word Biblical Commentary. Dallas: Word Books, 1992.

Harvey, W. Zéev. "Les Sacrifices, La Prière, et l'Étude chez Maïmonide." *REJ* 154.1–2 (1995): 97–103.

Hayes, Christine E. *Gentile Impurities and Jewish Identities: Intermarriage and Conversion from the Bible to the Talmud*. New York: Oxford University Press, 2002.

Hayward, C. T. R. *The Jewish Temple: A Non-Biblical Sourcebook*. London: Routledge, 1996.

Hayward, Robert. "The Jewish Temple at Leontopolis: A Reconsideration." *JJS* 33 (1982): 429–443.

Hecht, Richard D. "Studies on Sacrifice, 1970–1980." *RelSRev* 8.3 (1982): 253–259.

Heinemann, Joseph. *Prayer in the Period of the Tannai'm and Amorai'm: Its Nature and Its Patterns* [Hebrew]. 4th ed. Jerusalem: Magnes Press, 1984.

Hendel, Ronald S. "Sacrifice as a Cultural System: The Ritual Symbolism of Exodus 34,3–8." *ZAW* 101.3 (1989): 366–390.

Hendin, David. *Guide to Biblical Coins*. 3rd ed. New York: Amphora, 1996.

Herr, Moshe David. "The Conception of History among the Sages" [Hebrew]. In *Proceedings of the Sixth World Congress of Jewish Studies, Jerusalem, August 13–19, 1973: Volume 3, Division C*, 129–142. Jerusalem: World Union of Jewish Studies, 1977.

———. "Continuum in the Chain of Torah Transmission" [Hebrew]. *Zion* 44.1 (1979): 43–56 (English summary, x–xi).

Hertz, Joseph H., ed. *The Pentateuch and Haftorahs: Hebrew Text, English Translation and Commentary*. London: Soncino Press, 1961.

Heschel, Abraham Joshua. *The Prophets*. Philadelphia: Jewish Publication Society, 1962.

————. *Theology of Ancient Judaism.* Vol. 1. [Hebrew]. London: Soncino Press, 1962.

Hill, Andrew E. *Malachi: A New Translation with Introduction and Commentary.* AB 25d. New York: Doubleday, 1998.

Himmelfarb, Martha. *Ascent to Heaven in Jewish and Christian Apocalypses.* New York: Oxford University Press, 1993.

————. "Impurity and Sin in 4QD, 1QS, and 4Q512." *DSD* 8.1 (2001): 9–37.

————. " 'A Kingdom of Priests': The Democratization of the Priesthood in the Literature of Second Temple Judaism." *Journal of Jewish Thought and Philosophy* 6.1 (1997): 89–104.

Hirsch, Emile. "Sacrifice." In *The Jewish Encyclopedia,* edited by Isidore Singer. 10:615–628. 12 vols. New York: Funk and Wagnall's, 1905.

Hoffmann, David Z. *Das Buch Leviticus.* 2 vols. Berlin: M. Poppelauer, 1905–6.

Holladay, Carl R. *Historians.* Vol. I. of *Fragments from Jewish Hellenistic Authors.* Chico, Calif.: Scholars Press, 1983.

Hollander, H. W., and Marinus de Jonge. *The Testaments of the Twelve Patriarchs: A Commentary.* Leiden: Brill, 1985.

Horbury, William, ed. *Templum Amicitiae: Essays on the Second Temple Presented to Ernst Bammel.* Sheffield, England: Sheffield Academic Press, 1991.

Horovitz, H. S., ed. *Siphre D'Be Rab, Fasciculus primus: Siphre ad Numeros adjecto Siphre zutta.* 1917. Reprint, Jerusalem: Shalem, 1992.

Horovitz, H. S., and I. A. Rabin, eds. *Mechilta D'Rabbi Ismael.* 1930. Reprint, Jerusalem: Wahrmann Books, 1970.

Horsley, Richard A. *Jesus and the Spiral of Violence: Popular Jewish Resistance in Roman Palestine.* San Francisco: Harper and Row, 1987.

Houston, Walter. *Purity and Monotheism: Clean and Unclean Animals in Biblical Law.* Sheffield, England: JSOT Press, 1993.

Hubert, Henri, and Marcel Mauss. *Sacrifice: Its Nature and Functions.* Translated by W. D. Halls. Chicago: University of Chicago Press, 1964.

Humbert, Jean-Baptiste. "L'espace Sacré à Qumrân: Propositions pour l'archéologie." *RB* 101.2 (1994): 161–214.

Idel, Moshe. *Kabbalah: New Perspectives.* New Haven: Yale University Press, 1988.

Isaac, Erich. "On the Domestication of Cattle." *Science* 137 (1962): 195–204.

Isenberg, Sheldon R., and Dennis E. Owen. "Bodies, Natural and Contrived: The Work of Mary Douglas." *RelSRev* 3.1 (1977): 1–17.

Jaubert, Annie. *The Date of the Last Supper.* New York: Alba, 1965.

Jay, Nancy. *Throughout Your Generations Forever: Sacrifice, Religion, and Paternity.* Chicago: University of Chicago Press, 1992.

Jellinek, Adolph, ed. *Bet ha-Midrasch.* 6 vols. 1853–77. Reprint, Jerusalem: Wahrmann Books, 1967.

Jeremias, Joachim. *The Eucharistic Words of Jesus.* Translated by Norman Perrin. 3rd ed. London: SCM Press, 1966.

Johnson, Sherman E. "The Dead Sea Manual of Discipline and the Jerusalem Church of Acts." In *The Scrolls and the New Testament,* edited by Krister Stendahl, 129–142. New York: Harper, 1957.

Josephus, Flavius. *Works.* Translated and edited by H. St. J. Thackeray, Ralph Marcus, Allen Wikgren, and Louis H. Feldman, 9 vols. LCL. Cambridge, Mass.: Harvard University Press, 1926–1965.

Jospe, Raphael. "Faith and Reason: The Controversy over Philosophy." In *Great Schisms in Jewish History,* edited by R. Jospe and Stanley M. Wagner, 73–117. New York: Ktav, 1981.

Kampen, John. "The Significance of the Temple in the Manuscripts of the Damascus Document." In *The Dead Sea Scrolls at Fifty: Proceedings of the 1997 Society of Biblical Literature Qumran Section Meetings*, edited by Robert A. Kugler and Eileen M. Schuller, 185–197. Atlanta, Ga.: Scholars Press, 1999.

Kaufmann, Yehezkel. *The Religion of Israel: From Its Beginnings to the Babylonian Exile.* Translated by Moshe Greenberg. Chicago: University of Chicago Press, 1960.

———. *Toledot ha-Emunah ha-Yisraelit.* 8 vols. Tel Aviv: Dvir, 1937–58.

Kellner, Menachem. "Maimonides on the Nature of Ritual Purity and Impurity." *Daat* 50–52 (2002–3): I–XXX.

Kirk, G. S. "Some Methodological Pitfalls in the Study of Ancient Greek Sacrifice (in Particular)." In *Le Sacrifice dans L'antiquité: Huit exposés suivis de discussions,* edited by Olivier Reverdin, Bernard Grange, and Jean-Pierre Vernant, 41–80. Geneva: Fondation Hardt, 1980.

Kirschner, Robert. "Apocalyptic and Rabbinic Responses to the Destruction of 70." *HTR* 78.1–2 (1985): 27–46.

Kister, Menahem. "Studies in 4QMiqsat Ma'aseh ha-Torah and Related Texts: Law, Theology, Language and Calendar" [Hebrew]. *Tarbiz* 68.3 (1998–99): 317–372.

Kittay, Eva Feder. *Metaphor: Its Cognitive Force and Linguistic Structure.* Oxford: Clarendon Press, 1987.

Klawans, Jonathan. *Impurity and Sin in Ancient Judaism.* New York: Oxford University Press, 2000.

———. "Interpreting the Last Supper: Sacrifice, Spiritualization, and Anti-Sacrifice." *NTS* 48.1 (2002): 1–17.

———. "Notions of Gentile Impurity in Ancient Judaism." *AJS Review* 20.2 (1995): 285–312.

———. "Pure Violence: Sacrifice and Defilement in Ancient Israel." *HTR* 94.2 (2001): 133–155.

———. "Rethinking Leviticus and Rereading *Purity and Danger*: A Review Essay." *AJS Review* 27.1 (2003): 89–101.

———. Review of *Rabbi Jesus*, by Bruce Chilton. *Bible Review* 18:1 (2002): 42–44.

———. Review of *Rituals and Ritual Theory in Ancient Israel*, by Ithamar Gruenwald. *AJS Review*, forthcoming.

———. Review of *The Three Temples*, by Rachel Elior. *AJS Review*, forthcoming.

———. "Ritual Purity, Moral Purity, and Sacrifice in Jacob Milgrom's *Leviticus*." *RelSRev* 29.1 (2003): 19–28.

Klinzing, Georg. *Die Umdeutung des Kultus in der Qumrangemeinde und im Neuen Testament.* Göttingen: Vandenhoeck and Ruprecht, 1971.

Knibb, Michael A. *The Qumran Community.* Cambridge: Cambridge University Press, 1987.

Knierim, Rolf P. *Text and Concept in Leviticus 1:1–9.* Tübingen: Mohr Siebeck, 1992.

Knohl, Israel. "Between Voice and Silence: The Relationship between Prayer and Temple Cult." *JBL* 115.1 (1996): 17–30.

———. *The Sanctuary of Silence: The Priestly Torah and the Holiness School.* Minneapolis: Fortress Press, 1995.

Koester, Craig R. *The Dwelling of God: The Tabernacle in the Old Testament, Intertestamental Jewish Literature, and the New Testament.* Washington, D.C.: Catholic Biblical Association of America, 1989.

Kugel, James. "Levi's Elevation to the Priesthood in Second Temple Writings." *HTR* 86.1 (1993): 1–64.

Kugler, Robert A. *From Patriarch to Priest: The Levi-Priestly Tradition from Aramaic Levi to Testament of Levi.* Atlanta, Ga.: Scholars Press, 1996.

———. "Holiness, Purity, the Body, and Society: The Evidence for Theological Conflict in Leviticus." *JSOT* 76 (1997): 3–27.

———. "The Priesthood at Qumran: The Evidence of the References to Levi and the Levites." In *The Provo International Conference on the Dead Sea Scrolls: Technological Innovations, New Texts, and Reformulated Issues*, edited by Donald W. Parry and Eugene Ulrich, 465–479. Leiden: Brill, 1999.

———. "Rewriting Rubrics: Sacrifice and Religion of Qumran." In *Religion in Qumran*, edited by John J. Collins and Robert A. Kugler, 90–112. Grand Rapids, Mich.: Eerdmans, 2000.

Lachs, Samuel Tobias. *A Rabbinic Commentary on the New Testament: Matthew, Mark, and Luke*. Hoboken, N.J.: Ktav, 1987.

Ladermann, Shulamith. "Parallel Texts in a Byzantine Christian Treatise and Sections of Midrash Attributed to Rabbi Moshe Hadarshan" [Hebrew]. *Tarbiz* 70.2 (2001): 213–226 (English summary, vii–viii).

Lakoff, George, and Mark Johnson. *Metaphors We Live By*. Chicago: University of Chicago Press, 1980.

Laporte, Jean. "The High Priest in Philo of Alexandria." *Studia Philonica Annual* 3 (1991): 71–82.

———. "Sacrifice and Forgiveness in Philo of Alexandria." *Studia Philonica Annual* 1 (1989): 34–42.

Leach, Edmund. *Culture and Communication: The Logic by Which Symbols Are Connected*. Cambridge: Cambridge University Press, 1976.

———. "The Structure of Symbolism." In *The Interpretation of Ritual: Essays in Honour of A. I. Richards*, edited by J. S. La Fontaine, 239–275. London: Tavistock, 1972.

Leaney, A. R. C. *The Rule of Qumran and Its Meaning: Introduction, Translation and Commentary*. Philadelphia: Westminster Press, 1966.

Lee, Pilchan. *The New Jerusalem in the Book of Revelation*. Tübingen: Mohr Siebeck, 2001.

Léon-Dufour, Xavier. *Sharing the Eucharistic Bread: The Witness of the New Testament*. New York: Paulist Press, 1987.

Lesses, Rebecca Macy. *Ritual Practices to Gain Power: Angels, Incantations, and Revelation in Early Jewish Mysticism*. Harrisburg, Pa.: Trinity Press International, 1998.

Levenson, Jon D. *Creation and the Persistence of Evil: The Jewish Drama of Divine Omnipotence*. Princeton: Princeton University Press, 1988.

———. *The Death and Resurrection of the Beloved Son: The Transformation of Child Sacrifice in Judaism and Christianity*. New Haven: Yale University Press, 1993.

———. "Ezekiel in the Perspectives of Two Commentaries." *Interpretation* 38.2 (1984): 210–217.

———. *Sinai and Zion: An Entry into the Jewish Bible*. San Francisco: Harper and Row, 1985.

———. *Theology in the Program Restoration of Ezekiel 40–48*. Missoula, Mont.: Scholars Press, 1976.

Lévi-Strauss, Claude. *Myth and Meaning*. New York: Schocken, 1979.

———. *The Naked Man*. Translated by John and Doreen Weightman. New York: Harper and Row, 1981.

———. *The Savage Mind*. Chicago: University of Chicago Press, 1966.

———. *Structural Anthropology*. Translated by Claire Jacobson and Brooke Grundfest Schoepf. New York: Basic Books, 1963.

————. *Totemism*. Translated by Rodney Needham. Boston: Beacon Press, 1962.

Levine, Baruch A. *In the Presence of the Lord: A Study of Cult and Some Cultic Terms in Ancient Israel*. Leiden: Brill, 1974.

————. *The JPS Torah Commentary: Leviticus*. Philadelphia: Jewish Publication Society, 1989.

————. "On the Presence of God in Biblical Religion." In *Religions in Antiquity: Essays in Memory of Erwin Ramsdell Goodenough*, edited by Jacob Neusner, 71–87. Leiden: Brill, 1968.

————. Prolegomenon to *Sacrifice in the Old Testament*, by George Buchanan Gray, vii–xliv. Ktav: 1971, 1971.

Levine, Lee I., ed. *The Galilee in Late Antiquity*. New York: Jewish Theological Seminary, 1992.

————. *Jerusalem: Its Sanctity and Centrality to Judaism, Christianity, and Islam*. New York: Continuum, 1999.

Levy, Brooks. "Tyrian Shekels and the First Jewish War." In *Proceedings of the Eleventh International Numismatic Congress, September 8–13, 1991*, 267–274. Louvain-la-Neuve, Belgium: International Numismatic Commission, 1993.

Licht, Jacob. *The Rule Scroll: A Scroll from the Wilderness of Judaea* [Hebrew]. Jerusalem: Bialik Institute, 1965.

Lichtenberger, Hermann. "Atonement and Sacrifice in the Qumran Community." In *Approaches to Ancient Judaism*, vol. 2, edited by William Scott Green, 159–171. Chico, Calif.: Scholars Press, 1980.

Lichtenstein, Hans. "Die Fastenrolle: Eine Untersuchung zur Jüdische-Hellenistischen Geschichte." *HUCA* 8–9 (1931–32): 257–351.

Lieber, Andrea Beth. "Where Is Sacrifice in the Heavenly Temple? Reflections on the Role of Violence in Hekhalot Traditions." *SBLSP* 37.1 (1998): 432–446.

Lieber, David L., ed. *Etz Hayim: Torah and Commentary*. New York: The Rabbinical Assembly, 2001.

Lieberman, Saul. *Hellenism in Jewish Palestine: Studies in the Literary Transmission, Beliefs and Manners of Palestine in the First Century* B.C.E. *to Fourth Century* C.E. New York: Jewish Theological Seminary, 1950.

————. *Tosefta Ki-Fshutah: a Comprehensive Commentary on the Tosefta*. 10 vols. New York: Jewish Theological Seminary, 1955–88.

————, ed. *Midrash Debarim Rabbah: Edited for the First Time from the Oxford MS, no. 147*. With an introduction and notes. 2nd ed. Jerusalem: Shalem, 1992.

Lindblom, J. *Prophecy in Ancient Israel*. Oxford: Blackwell, 1962.

Liver, Jacob. "The Half-Shekel Offering in Biblical and Post-Biblical Literature." *HTR* 56.3 (1963): 173–198.

Long, Burke O. "Prophetic Authority and Social Reality." In *Canon and Authority: Essays in Old Testament Religion and Theology*, edited by George W. Coats and Burke O. Long, 3–20. Philadelphia: Fortress Press, 1977.

————. "Social Dimensions of Prophetic Conflict." *Semeia* 21 (1981): 30–53.

Lundquist, John M. "The Common Temple Ideology of the Ancient Near East." In *The Temple in Antiquity: Ancient Records and Modern Perspectives*, edited by Truman G. Madsen, 53–76. Provo, Utah: Religious Studies Center, Brigham Young University, 1984.

————. "What Is a Temple? A Preliminary Typology." In *The Quest for the Kingdom of God: Studies in Honor of George E. Mendenhall*, edited by H. B. Huffmon, F. A. Spina, and A. R. W. Green, 205–219. Winona Lake, Ind.: Eisenbrauns, 1983.

Maccoby, Hyam. *Ritual and Morality: The Ritual Purity System and Its Place in Judaism.* Cambridge: Cambridge University Press, 1999.

Magen, Yitzhak. *The Stone Vessel Industry in the Second Temple Period: Excavations at Hizma and the Jerusalem Temple Mount.* Edited by Levana Tsafania. Jerusalem: Israel Exploration Society, 2002.

Magness, Jodi. *The Archaeology of Qumran and the Dead Sea Scrolls.* Grand Rapids, Mich.: Eerdmans, 2002.

Maimonides, Moses. *Guide of the Perplexed.* Translated with an introduction and notes by Shlomo Pines. 2 vols. Chicago: University of Chicago Press, 1963.

Malter, Henry, ed. *The Treatise Ta'anit of the Babylonian Talmud: Critically Edited and provided with a Translation, Introduction, and Notes.* Philadelphia: Jewish Publication Society, 1928.

Mandelbaum, Bernard. *Pesikta de Rav Kahana: According to an Oxford Manuscript, with Variants from All Known Manuscripts and Genizoth Fragments and Parallel Passages.* With commentary and introduction. 2 vols. New York: Jewish Theological Seminary, 1987.

Mandell, Sara. "Who Paid the Temple Tax When the Jews Were under Roman Rule?" *HTR* 77.2 (1984): 223–232.

Margulies, Mordecai, ed. *Midrash Wayyikra Rabbah: A Critical Edition Based on Manuscripts and Genizah Fragments with Variants and Notes.* 3rd ed. 2 vols. New York: Jewish Theological Seminary, 1993.

Marx, Alfred. "The Theology of the Sacrifice According to Leviticus 1–7." In *The Book of Leviticus: Composition and Reception,* edited by Rolf Rendtorff and Robert A. Kugler, with the assistance of Sarah Smith Bartel, 103–120. Leiden: Brill, 2003.

Matson, Mark A. "The Contribution to the Temple Cleansing by the Fourth Gospel." *SBLSP* 31 (1992): 489–506.

Matthews, Victor H., and Don C. Benjamin. *Social World of Ancient Israel, 1250–587 BCE.* Peabody, Mass.: Hendrickson, 1993.

Mauss, Marcel. *The Gift: The Form and Reason for Exchange in Archaic Societies.* Translated by W. D. Halls. New York: Norton, 1990.

Mazar, Eilat. *The Complete Guide to the Temple Mount Excavations.* Translated by Don Glick and Nava Panitz-Cohen. Jerusalem: Shoham Academic Research and Publication, 2002.

Mazza, Enrico. *The Celebration of the Eucharist: The Origin of the Rite and the Development of Its Interpretation.* Translated by Matthew J. O'Connell. Collegeville, Minn.: Liturgical Press, 1999.

McCalla, Arthur. "Evolutionism and Early Nineteenth-Century Histories of Religions." *Religion* 28.1 (1998): 29–40.

McCarter, P. Kyle, Jr. *I Samuel: A New Translation with Introduction and Commentary.* AB 8. New York: Doubleday, 1980.

McKane, William. "Prophecy and the Prophetic Literature." In *Tradition and Interpretation: Essays by Members of the Society for Old Testament Study,* edited by G. W. Anderson, 163–188. Oxford: Clarendon Press, 1979.

———. "Prophet and Institution." *ZAW* 94.2 (1982): 251–266.

McKelvey, R. J. *The New Temple: The Church in the New Testament.* London: Oxford University Press, 1969.

McKnight, Scot. "Jesus and Prophetic Actions." *Bulletin for Biblical Research* 10.2 (2000): 197–232.

Meigs, Anna S. "A Papuan Perspective on Pollution." *Man* 13.2 (1978): 304–318.

Mendelssohn, Moses. *Jerusalem: Or on Religious Power and Judaism.* Translated by Allan Arkush. Hanover, N.H.: University Press of New England, 1983.

Meshorer, Ya'akov. "One Hundred Ninety Years of Tyrian Shekels." In *Festschrift für/ Studies in Honor of Leo Mildenberg: Numismatics, Art History, Archaeology,* edited by Arthur Houghton, Silvia Hurter, Patricia Erhart Mottahedeh, and Jane Ayer Scott, 171–179, pl. 26. Wetteren, Belgium: NR, 1984.

Metso, Sarianna. *The Textual Development of the Community Rule.* Leiden: Brill, 1997.

Milgrom, Jacob. "The Antiquity of the Priestly Source: A Reply to Joseph Blenkinsopp." *ZAW* 111.1 (1999): 10–22.

———. *Leviticus 1–16: A New Translation with Introduction and Commentary.* AB 3. New York: Doubleday, 1992.

———. *Leviticus 17–22: A New Translation with Introduction and Commentary.* AB 3a. New York: Doubleday, 2000.

———. *Leviticus 23–27: A New Translation with Introduction and Commentary.* AB 3b. New York: Doubleday, 2001.

Miller, Patrick D. *The Divine Warrior in Early Israel.* Cambridge, Mass.: Harvard University Press, 1973.

———. *The Religion of Ancient Israel.* Louisville, Ky.: Westminster John Knox Press, 2000.

Mintz-Manor, Ophir. "Creation, the *Mishkan* and Moseh HaDarshan: A Response to Sh. Ladermann" [Hebrew]. *Tarbiz* 71.1–2 (2001–2): 265–267 (English summary, x).

Mirkin, Moshe Aryeh, ed. *Midrash Rabbah: Meforash Perush Mada'i Hadash.* 11 vols. Tel Aviv: Yavneh, 1987.

Montefiore, Hugh. "Jesus and the Temple Tax." *NTS* 11.1 (1964): 60–71.

Moore, Michael S. "Human Suffering in Lamentations." *RB* 90.4 (1983): 534–555.

Mowinckel, Sigmund. "Cult and Prophecy." Translated by James L. Schaaf. In *Prophecy in Israel: Search for an Identity,* edited by David L. Petersen, 74–98. Philadelphia: Fortress Press, 1987.

———. *Psalmenstudien III: Kultprophetie und prophetische Psalmen.* Oslo: Jacob Dybwad, 1922.

———. *The Psalms in Israel's Worship.* Translated by D. R. Ap-Thomas. 2 vols. New York: Abingdon Press, 1967.

Mulder, Martin Jan, ed. *Mikra: Text, Translation, Reading and Interpretation of the Hebrew Bible in Ancient Judaism and Early Christianity.* CRINT 2.1. Assen, the Netherlands: Van Gorcum, 1990.

Murphy, Catherine M. "The Disposition of Wealth in the *Damascus Document* Tradition." *RevQ* 73/19.1 (1999): 83–129.

———. *Wealth in the Dead Sea Scrolls and in the Qumran Community.* Leiden: Brill, 2002.

Murphy-O'Connor, Jerome. "A Literary Analysis of Damascus Document VI, 2–VIII, 3." *RB* 78.2 (1971): 210–232.

———. "The Translation of Damascus Document VI, 11–14." *RevQ* 28/7.4 (1971): 553–556.

Murray, Gilbert. *Five Stages of Greek Religion.* Garden City, N.Y.: Doubleday, 1955.

Murray-Jones, C. R. A. "The Temple Within: The Embodied Divine Image and Its Worship in the Dead Sea Scrolls and Other Early Jewish and Christian Sources." *SBLSP* 37.1 (1998): 400–431.

Neusner, Jacob. *A History of the Mishnaic Law of Holy Things.* 6 vols. Leiden: Brill, 1978–1980.

———. *Judaism: The Evidence of the Mishnah.* Chicago: University of Chicago Press, 1981.

———. "Money-Changers in the Temple: The Mishnah's Explanation." *NTS* 35.2 (1989): 287–290.

Newsom, Carol A. "'Sectually Explicit' Literature from Qumran." In *The Hebrew Bible and Its Interpreters*, edited by William Henry Propp, Baruch Halpern, and David Noel Freedman, 167–187. Winona Lake, Ind.: Eisenbrauns, 1990.

———. *Songs of the Sabbath Sacrifice: A Critical Edition*. Atlanta: Scholars Press, 1985.

Newton, Michael. *The Concept of Purity at Qumran and in the Letters of Paul.* Cambridge: Cambridge University Press, 1985.

Nickelsburg, George W. E. "Enoch, Levi, and Peter: Recipients of Revelation in Upper Galilee." *JBL* 100.4 (1981): 575–600.

———. *1 Enoch 1: A Commentary on the Book of 1 Enoch, Chapters 1–36, 81–108.* Hermeneia. Philadelphia: Fortress Press, 2001.

Niditch, Susan. *War in the Hebrew Bible: A Study in the Ethics of Violence.* New York: Oxford University Press, 1993.

Nikiprowetzky, Valentin. "La spiritualisation des sacrifices et le culte sacrificiel au Temple de Jérusalem chez Philon d'Alexandrie." *Semitica* 17 (1967): 97–116.

Noam, Vered. *Megillat Ta'anit: Versions, Interpretation, History, with a Critical Edition.* Jerusalem: Yad Ben-Zvi Press, 2003.

Noth, Martin. *The Deuteronomistic History.* Translated by Jane Doull and John Barton. Sheffield, England: JSOT Press, 1981.

———. *Leviticus.* OTL. Philadelphia: Westminster Press, 1977.

Orlans, F. Barbara. *In the Name of Science: Issues in Responsible Animal Experimentation.* New York: Oxford University Press, 1993.

Orlans, F. Barbara, Tom L. Beauchamp, Rebecca Dresser, David B. Morton, and John P. Gluck. *The Human Use of Animals: Case Studies in Ethical Choice.* New York: Oxford University Press, 1998.

Orlinsky, Harry M. *Ancient Israel.* Ithaca, N.Y.: Cornell University Press, 1960.

Osborne, Catherine. "Ancient Vegetarianism." In *Food in Antiquity*, edited by John Wilkins, David Harvey, and Mike Dobson, 214–224. Exeter, England: University of Exeter Press, 1995.

Overholt, Thomas W. "Prophecy: The Problem of Cross-Cultural Comparison." *Semeia* 21 (1981): 55–78.

Pals, Daniel L. *Seven Theories of Religion.* New York: Oxford University Press, 1996.

Parker, Robert. *Miasma: Pollution and Purification in Early Greek Religion.* Oxford: Clarendon Press, 1983.

Patai, Raphael. *Man and Temple in Ancient Jewish Myth and Ritual.* London: Thomas Nelson, 1947.

Petuchowski, Jakob J. *Prayerbook Reform in Europe.* New York: World Union for Progressive Judaism, 1968.

Philo of Alexandria. *Works.* Translated and edited by F. H. Colson and G. H. Whitaker. 10 vols. LCL, with 2 supplemental volumes by Ralph Marcus. Cambridge, Mass.: Harvard University Press, 1929–62.

———. *The Works of Philo Judaeus: The Contemporary of Josephus,* Translated by Charles Duke Yonge. London: H. G. Bohn, 1854–90.

Plaut, W. Gunther, ed. *The Torah: A Modern Commentary.* New York: Union of American Hebrew Congregations, 1981.

Poirier, John C. "Purity beyond the Temple in the Second Temple Era." *JBL* 122.2 (2003): 247–264.

Pomykala, Kenneth E. Review of *The Jewish Temple*, by C. T. R. Hayward. *JBL* 118.4 (1999): 547–549.

Pritchard, James B., ed. *Ancient Near Eastern Texts Relating to the Old Testament.* 3rd ed. Princeton: Princeton University Press, 1969.

Qimron, Elisha. *The Temple Scroll: A Critical Edition with Extensive Reconstructions.* Beer Sheva, Israel: Ben Gurion University of the Negev Press, 1996.

Qimron, Elisha, and John Strugnell. *Qumran Cave 4, V (Miqsat Ma'aseh ha-Torah).* DJD X. Oxford: Clarendon Press, 1994.

Rabbinovicz, Raphaelo. *Sefer Diqduqe Soferim: Variae Lectiones in Mischnam et in Talmud Babylonicum.* 1866–97. Reprint, 2 vols., New York: M. P. Press, 1976.

Regev, Eyal. "Abominated Temple and a Holy Community: The Formation of the Notions of Purity and Impurity in Qumran." *DSD* 10.2 (2003): 243–278.

———. "Non-Priestly Purity and Its Religious Aspects According to Historical Sources and Archaeological Findings." In *Purity and Holiness: The Heritage of Leviticus,* edited by M. J. H. M. Poorthuis and J. Schwartz, 223–244. Leiden: Brill, 2000.

———. "On Blood, Defilement, and the Attitude toward the Body among the Halakhic Schools in the Times of the Second Temple, the Mishnah, and the Talmud" [Hebrew]. *AJS Review* 27.1 (2003): 1*-23*.

———. "Pure Individualism: The Idea of Non-Priestly Purity in Ancient Judaism." *JSJ* 31.2 (2000): 176–202.

Regev, Eyal, and David Nakman. "Josephus and the Halakhah of the Pharisees, the Sadducees, and Qumran" [Hebrew]. *Zion* 77.4 (2002): 401–433 (English summary, xxxii).

Reich, Ronny. "Miqwa'ot (Jewish Ritual Immersion Baths) in Eretz-Israel in the Second Temple and the Mishnah and Talmud Periods" [Hebrew]. Ph.D. diss., Hebrew University, 1990.

Reich, Ronny. "Synagogue and Ritual Bath during the Second Temple and the Period of the Mishna and Talmud" [Hebrew]. In *Synagogues in Antiquity,* edited by A. Kasher, A. Oppenheimer, and U. Rappaport, 205–212 (English summary xiii–xiv). Jerusalem: Yad Ben-Zvi, 1987.

Reif, Stefan C. *Judaism and Hebrew Prayer: New Perspectives on Jewish Liturgical History.* Cambridge: Cambridge University Press, 1993.

Rendtorff, Rolf. "How to Approach Leviticus." In *Proceedings of the Tenth World Congress of Jewish Studies, Jerusalem, August 16–23, 1989, Division A: The Bible and Its World,* 13–20. Jerusalem: World Union of Jewish Studies, 1990.

———. *Leviticus.* Vol. 3.1. *Biblischer Kommentar: Altes Testament.* Neukirchen-Vluyn, Germany: Neukirchener Verlag, 1985.

———. "The Paradigm Is Changing: Hopes and Fears." *BibInt* 1.1 (1993): 34–53.

———. "Two Kinds of P? Some Reflections on the Occasion of the Publishing of Jacob Milgrom's Commentary on Leviticus 1–16." *JSOT* 60 (1993): 75–81.

Richards, E. G. *Mapping Time: The Calendar and Its History.* Oxford: Oxford University Press, 1998.

Richardson, Peter. "Why Turn the Tables? Jesus' Protest in the Temple Precincts." *SBLSP* 31 (1992): 507–523.

Rigby, Paul. "A Structural Analysis of Israelite Sacrifice and Its Other Institutions." *Église et Théologie* 11 (1980): 299–351.

Ringgren, Helmer. *The Faith of Qumran: Theology of the Dead Sea Scrolls.* Philadelphia: Fortress Press, 1963.

———. *Israelite Religion.* Philadelphia: Fortress Press, 1966.

———. *Sacrifice in the Bible.* London: United Society for Christian Literature, 1962.

Robertson Smith, William. *Lectures on the Religion of the Semites: The Fundamental Institutions.* 3rd ed., with an introduction and notes by Stanley A. Cook. New York: Macmillan, 1927.

Rofé, Alexander. *Introduction to the Prophetic Literature.* Translated by Judith H. Seeligmann. Sheffield, England: Sheffield Academic Press, 1997.

Rogerson, J. W. "What Was the Meaning of Animal Sacrifice?" In *Animals on the Agenda: Questions about Animals for Theology and Ethics,* edited by Andrew Linzey and Dorothy Yamamoto, 8–17. Urbana: University of Illinois Press, 1998.

Roitman, Adolfo, with a contribution by Shulamit Laderman. *Envisioning the Temple: Scrolls, Stones, and Symbols.* Translated by David Louvish. Jerusalem: Israel Museum, 2003.

Roskies, David G. *The Literature of Destruction: Jewish Responses to Catastrophe.* Philadelphia: Jewish Publication Society, 1988.

Rowley, H. H. *From Moses to Qumran.* New York: Association Press, 1963.

Rubenstein, Jeffrey L. *Rabbinic Stories.* New York: Paulist Press, 2002.

———. *Talmudic Stories: Narrative Art, Composition, and Culture.* Baltimore: Johns Hopkins University Press, 1999.

Sacks, Sheldon, ed. *On Metaphor.* Chicago: University of Chicago Press, 1978.

Safrai, Shmuel. "The Heavenly Jerusalem." *Ariel* 23 (1969): 11–16.

———. *Pilgrimage at the Time of the Second Temple* [Hebrew]. 2nd ed., corrected and updated. Jerusalem: Akademon, 1985.

———. "The Temple and the Divine Service." In *The World History of the Jewish People,* vol. 7, *The Herodian Period,* edited by Michael Avi-Yonah and Zvi Baras, 284–337. New Brunswick, N.J.: Rutgers University Press, 1975.

Saldarini, Anthony J. *Pharisees, Scribes and Sadducees in Palestinian Society: A Sociological Approach.* Wilmington, Del.: Michael Glazier, 1988.

Sanders, E. P. *Jesus and Judaism.* Philadelphia: Fortress Press, 1985.

———. *Jewish Law from Jesus to the Mishnah.* London: SCM Press, 1990.

———. *Judaism: Practice and Belief 63 BCE to 66 CE.* London: SCM Press, 1992.

———. *Paul and Palestinian Judaism: A Comparison of Patterns of Religion.* Minneapolis: Fortress Press, 1977.

Sandmel, Samuel. *Anti-Semitism in the New Testament?* Philadelphia: Fortress Press, 1978.

Sapir, J. David, and J. Christopher Crocker, eds. *The Social Use of Metaphor: Essays on the Anthropology of Rhetoric.* Philadelphia: University of Pennsylvania Press, 1977.

Sawyer, John F. A., ed. *Reading Leviticus: A Conversation with Mary Douglas.* Sheffield, England: Sheffield Academic Press, 1996.

Schäfer, Peter. *The Hidden and Manifest God: Some Major Themes in Early Jewish Mysticism.* Translated by Aubrey Pomerance. Albany: State University of New York Press, 1992.

Schäfer, Peter, in cooperation with Margarete Schlüter, and Hans Georg von Mutius, eds. *Synopse zur Hekhalot-Literatur.* Tübingen: Mohr Siebeck, 1981.

Schechter, Solomon, ed. *Aboth de Rabbi Nathan.* 1887. Reprint, New York: Jewish Theological Seminary, 1997.

———. *Fragments of a Zadokite Work.* Vol. 1 of *Documents of Jewish Sectaries.* 2 vols. Cambridge: Cambridge University Press, 1910.

Schiffman, Lawrence H. "Architecture and Law: The Temple and Its Courtyards in the Temple Scroll." In *From Ancient Israel to Modern Judaism: Intellect in Quest of Understanding: Essays in Honor of Marvin Fox,* edited by Jacob Neusner, Ernest S. Frerichs, and Nahum M. Sarna, 1:267–284. 4 vols. Atlanta, Ga.: Scholars Press, 1989.

———. "The Construction of the Temple According to the *Temple Scroll.*" *RevQ* 65–68/17.1–4 (1996): 555–571.

———. "Descriptions of the Jerusalem Temple in Josephus and the *Temple Scroll.*" In *Historical Perspectives: From the Hasmoneans to Bar Kokhba in Light of the Dead Sea Scrolls; Proceedings of the Fourth International Symposium of the Orion Center for the Study of the Dead Sea Scrolls and Associated Literature, 27–31 January, 1999*, edited by David Goodblatt, Avital Pinnick, and Daniel R. Schwartz, 69–82. Leiden: Brill, 2001.

———. *The Eschatological Community of the Dead Sea Scrolls.* Atlanta, Ga.: Scholars Press, 1989.

———. "Exclusion from the Sanctuary and the City of the Sanctuary in the Temple Scroll." *Hebrew Annual Review* 9 (1985): 301–320.

———. "Pharisaic and Sadducean Halakhah in Light of the Dead Sea Scrolls: The Case of Tevul Yom." *DSD* 1.3 (1994): 285–299.

———. *Reclaiming the Dead Sea Scrolls: The History of Judaism, the Background of Christianity, the Lost Library of Qumran.* Philadelphia: Jewish Publication Society, 1994.

———. "Sacred Space: The Land of Israel in the *Temple Scroll.*" In *Biblical Archaeology Today, 1990: Proceedings of the Second international Congress on Biblical Archaeology, Jerusalem, June–July 1990*, edited by Avraham Biran and Joseph Aviram, 398–410. Jerusalem: Israel Exploration Society, 1990.

———. "The Sacrificial System of the *Temple Scroll* and the Book of Jubilees." *SBLSP* 24 (1985): 217–233.

———. *Sectarian Law in the Dead Sea Scrolls: Courts, Testimony and the Penal Code.* Atlanta, Ga.: Scholars Press, 1983.

———. "*Shelamim* Sacrifices in the *Temple Scroll.*" *EI* 20 (1989): 176*–183*.

———. "The Structures of the Inner Court of the Temple according to the Temple Scroll" [Hebrew]. In *Fifty Years of Dead Sea Scrolls Research: Studies in Memory of Jacob Licht*, edited by Gershon Brin and Bilhah Nitzan, 171–180. Jerusalem: Yad Ben-Zvi Press, 2001.

———. "The Theology of the Temple Scroll." *JQR* 85.1–2 (1994): 109–123.

Schiffman, Lawrence H., and James C. VanderKam, eds. *The Encyclopedia of the Dead Sea Scrolls.* 2 vols. New York: Oxford, 2000.

Schlosser, Eric. *Fast Food Nation: The Dark Side of the All-American Meal.* Boston: Houghton-Mifflin, 2001.

Schmidt, Francis. *How the Temple Thinks: Identity and Social Cohesion in Ancient Judaism.* Translated by J. Edward Crowley. Sheffield, England: Sheffield Academic Press, 2001.

Scholem, Gershom G. *Jewish Gnosticism, Merkabah Mysticism, and Talmudic Tradition.* New York: Jewish Theological Seminary, 1965.

———. *Major Trends in Jewish Mysticism.* New York: Schocken, 1961.

Schuller, Eileen. "Petitionary Prayer and the Religion of Qumran." In *Religion in the Dead Sea Scrolls*, edited by John J. Collins and Robert A. Kugler, 29–45. Grand Rapids, Mich.: Eerdmans, 2000.

Schürer, Emil, revised and edited by Geza Vermes and Fergus Millar, with Matthew Black, Martin Goodman, and Pamela Vermes. *The History of the Jewish People in the Age of Jesus Christ.* 4 vols. Edinburgh: T. and T. Clark, 1973–87.

Schüssler Fiorenza, Elizabeth. "Cultic Language in Qumran and in the NT." *CBQ* 38.2 (1976): 159–177.

Schwartz, Daniel R. "KATA TOYTON TON KAIPON: Josephus' Source on Agrippa II." *JQR* 72.4 (1982): 241–268.

————. *Studies in the Jewish Background of Christianity*. Tübingen: Mohr Siebeck, 1992.

————. "The Three Temples of 4Q Florilegium." *RevQ* 37/10.1 (1979): 83–91.

Schwartz, Seth. *Imperialism and Jewish Society, 200 B.C.E. to 640 C.E.* Princeton: Princeton University Press, 2001.

Segal, Alan F. "Heavenly Ascent in Hellenistic Judaism, Early Christianity and Their Environment." In *Aufstieg und Niedergang der römischen Welt: Geschicht und Kultur Roms im Spiegel der neurern Forschung. Part 2, Principat*, edited by Hildegard Temporini and Wolfgang Haase, 23.2: 1333–1394. New York, de Gruyter, 1980.

————. *Two Powers in Heaven: Early Rabbinic Reports about Christianity and Gnosticism*. Leiden: Brill, 1977.

Shemesh, Aharon. "The Holiness According to the *Temple Scroll*." *RevQ* 75/19.3 (2000): 369–382.

————. *Punishments and Sins: From Scripture to the Rabbis* [Hebrew]. Jerusalem: Magnes Press, 2003.

Silberman, Lou H. "Wellhausen and Judaism." *Semeia* 25 (1982): 75–82.

Skehan, Patrick W., and Alexander A. Di Lella. *The Wisdom of Ben Sira: A New Translation with Notes, Introduction and Commentary*. AB 39. New York: Doubleday, 1987.

Smart, Ninian. Review of *Violence and the Sacred*, by René Girard. *RelSRev* 6.3 (1980): 173–177.

Smith, Bruce D. *The Emergence of Agriculture*. New York: Scientific American Library, 1995.

Smith, Jonathan Z. *Map Is Not Territory: Studies in the History of Religions*. Leiden: Brill, 1978.

————. *To Take Place: Toward Theory in Ritual*. Chicago: University of Chicago Press, 1987.

Solomon, Avi. "The Prohibition against Tevul Yom and Defilement of the Daily Whole Offering in the Jerusalem Temple in CD 11:21–12:1: A New Understanding." *DSD* 4.1 (1997): 1–20.

Sommer, Benjamin D. "Conflicting Constructions of Divine Presence in the Priestly Tabernacle." *BibInt* 9.1 (2001): 41–63.

————. "Expulsion as Initiation: Displacement, Divine Presence, and Divine Exile in the Torah." In *Beginning/Again: Toward a Hermeneutics of Jewish Texts*, edited by Aryeh Cohen and Shaul Magid, 23–48. New York: Seven Bridges Press, 2002.

Sparks, H. F. D., ed. *The Apocryphal Old Testament*. Oxford: Clarendon Press, 1984.

Staal, Frits. "The Meaninglessness of Ritual." *Numen* 26.1 (1979): 2–22.

Stager, Lawrence E. "Jerusalem and the Garden of Eden." *EI* 26 (1999): 183*–194*.

Stegemann, Hartmut. *The Library of Qumran: On the Essenes, Qumran, John the Baptist, and Jesus*. Grand Rapids, Mich.: Eerdmans, 1998.

Steiner, Franz. *Taboo*. London: Cohen and West, 1956.

Stern, David. *Parables in Midrash: Narrative and Exegesis in Rabbinic Literature*. Cambridge, Mass.: Harvard University Press, 1991.

Stern, Ephraim, ed. *The New Encyclopedia of Archaeological Excavations in the Holy Land*. 4 vols. Jerusalem: Israel Exploration Society, 1993.

Stern, Menahem. *Greek and Latin Authors on Jews and Judaism: Edited with Introductions, Translations, and Commentary*. 3 vols. Jerusalem: Israel Academy of Sciences and Humanities, 1976–84.

Stern, Sacha. *Calendar and Community: A History of the Jewish Calendar, Second Century BCE to Tenth Century CE*. Oxford: Oxford University Press, 2001.

Steudel, Annette. "The Houses of Prostration *CD* XI, 21–XII, 1: Duplicates of the Temple." *RevQ* 61/16.1 (1993): 49–68.

Stevenson, Kalinda Rose. *The Vision of Transformation: The Territorial Rhetoric of Ezekiel 40–48*. Atlanta, Ga.: Scholars Press, 1996.

Stiver, Dan R. *The Philosophy of Religious Language: Sign, Symbol, and Story*. Malden, Mass.: Blackwell, 1996.

Stone, Michael E. "Enoch, Aramaic Levi and Sectarian Origins." *JSJ* 19.2 (1988): 159–170.

————. "Ideal Figures and Social Context: Priest and Sage in the Early Second Temple Age." In *Ancient Israelite Religion: Essays in Honor of Frank Moore Cross*, edited by Patrick D. Miller, Jr., Paul D. Hanson, and S. Dean McBride, 575–586. Philadelphia: Fortress Press, 1987.

————, ed. *Jewish Writings of the Second Temple Period: Apocrypha, Pseudepigrapha, Qumran Sectarian Writings, Philo, Josephus*. CRINT 2.2. Assen, the Netherlands: Van Gorcum, 1984.

Stowers, Stanley K. "Greeks Who Sacrifice and Those Who Do Not: Toward an Anthropology of Greek Religion." In *The Social World of the First Christians: Essays in Honor of Wayne A. Meeks*, edited by L. Michael White and O. Larry Yarbrough, 293–333. Minneapolis: Fortress Press, 1995.

Strack, H. L., and Günter Stemberger. *Introduction to the Talmud and Midrash*. Translated by Marcus Bockmuehl. Second Printing. Minneapolis: Fortress Press, 1996.

Strenski, Ivan. "Between Theory and Speciality: Sacrifice in the 90's." *RelSRev* 22.1 (1996): 10–20.

————. *Contesting Sacrifice: Religion, Nationalism, and Social Thought in France*. Chicago: University of Chicago Press, 2002.

————. *Durkheim and the Jews of France*. Chicago: University of Chicago Press, 1997.

————. "Durkheim's Bourgeois Theory of Sacrifice." In *On Durkheim's Elementary Forms of Religious Life*, edited by N. J. Allen, W. S. F. Pickering, and W. Watts Miller, 116–126. London: Routledge, 1998.

————. *Religion in Relation: Method, Application, and Moral Location*. Columbia: University of South Carolina Press, 1993.

————. "The Social and Intellectual Origins of Hubert and Mauss's Theory of Ritual Sacrifice." In *India and Beyond: Aspects of Literature, Meaning, Ritual and Thought*, edited by Dick van der Meij, 511–537. London: Kegan Paul International, 1997.

————. *Theology and the First Theory of Sacrifice*. Leiden: Brill, 2003.

Strugnell, John. "Notes en marge du Volume V des 'Discoveries in the Judaean Desert of Jordan.'" *RevQ* 26/7.2 (1969–71): 163–276.

Sussmann, Yaakov. "The History of *Halakha* and the Dead Sea Scrolls: A Preliminary to the Publication of 4QMMT" [Hebrew]. *Tarbiz* 59.1 (1989–90): 11–76.

Suter, David. "Fallen Angel, Fallen Priest: The Problem of Family Purity in 1 Enoch 6–16." *HUCA* 50 (1979): 115–135.

Swartz, Michael D. "'Like the Ministering Angels': Ritual and Purity in Early Jewish Mysticism and Magic." *AJS Review* 19.2 (1994): 135–167.

————. "Ritual about Myth about Ritual: Towards an Understanding of the *Avodah* in the Rabbinic Period." *Journal of Jewish Thought and Philosophy* 6.1 (1997): 135–155.

————. "The Semiotics of the Priestly Vestments in Ancient Judaism." In *Sacrifice in Religious Experience*, edited by Albert I. Baumgarten, 57–80. Leiden: Brill, 2002.

Sweeney, Marvin A. *Isaiah 1–39: With an Introduction to Prophetic Literature*. Grand Rapids, Mich.: Eerdmans, 1996.

————. "The Latter Prophets (Isaiah, Jeremiah, Ezekiel)." In *The Hebrew Bible Today: An Introduction to Critical Issues*, edited by Steven L. McKenzie and M. Patrick Graham, 69–94. Louisville, Ky.: Westminster John Knox Press, 1998.

Tabory, Joseph, ed. *From Qumran to Cairo: Studies in the History of Prayer: Proceedings of the Research Group Convened under the Auspices of the Institute for Advanced Studies of the Hebrew University of Jerusalem 1997*. Jerusalem: Orhot Press, 1999.

Talmon, Shemaryahu. *Literary Studies in the Hebrew Bible: Form and Content*. Jerusalem: Magnes Press, 1993.

————. *The World of Qumran from Within: Collected Studies*. Jerusalem: Magnes Press, 1989.

Talmon, Shemaryahu, Jonathan Ben-Dov, and Uwe Glessmer. *Qumran Cave 4, XVI: Calendrical Texts. DJD XXI*. Oxford: Oxford University Press, 2001.

Theodor, Julius. "Midrashim: Midrash Tadshe." In *The Jewish Encyclopedia*, edited by Isidore Singer, 12 vols. 8:578. New York: Funk and Wagnall's, 1904.

————, ed. *Midrash Bereshit Rabba: Critical Edition with Notes and Commentary*. 2nd ed., with additional corrections by Chanoch Albeck. 3 vols. Jerusalem: Wahrmann, 1965.

Theissen, Gerd, and Annette Merz. *The Historical Jesus: A Comprehensive Guide*. Minneapolis: Fortress Press, 1996.

Thoma, Clemens. "The High Priesthood in the Judgment of Josephus." In *Josephus, the Bible, and History*, edited by Louis H. Feldman and Gohei Hata, 196–215. Detroit: Wayne State University Press, 1989.

Tigay, Jeffrey H. *The Evolution of the Gilgamesh Epic*. Philadelphia: University of Pennsylvania Press, 1982.

————. *The JPS Torah Commentary: Deuteronomy*. Philadelphia: Jewish Publication Society, 1996.

Tishby, Isaiah. *The Wisdom of the Zohar: An Anthology of Texts*. Translated by David Goldstein. 3 vols. Oxford: Littman Library of Jewish Civilization, 1989.

Tomasino, Anthony J. "Isaiah 1.1–2.4 and 63–66, and the Composition of the Isaianic Corpus." *JSOT* 57 (1993): 81–98.

Trebolle Barrera, Julio, and Luis Vegas Montaner, eds. *The Madrid Qumran Congress: Proceedings of the International Congress on the Dead Sea Scrolls, Madrid 18–21 March, 1991*. 2 vols. Leiden: Brill, 1992.

Turner, Victor. *Dramas, Fields, and Metaphors: Symbolic Action in Human Society*. Ithaca, N.Y.: Cornell University Press, 1974.

————. *The Forest of Symbols: Aspects of Ndembu Ritual*. Ithaca, N.Y.: Cornell University Press, 1967.

————. "Sacrifice as Quintessential Process: Prophylaxis or Abandonment?" *HR* 16.3 (1977): 189–215.

Urbach, Ephraim E. "Heavenly and Earthly Jerusalem" [Hebrew]. In *Jerusalem through the Ages: The Twenty-Fifth Archaeological Convention, October 1967*, edited by Joseph Aviram, 156–171. Jerusalem: Israel Exploration Society, 1968.

VanderKam, James C. "The Angel of Presence in the Book of Jubilees." *DSD* 7.3 (2000): 378–393.

————. "Calendrical Texts and the Origins of the Dead Sea Scroll Community." In *Methods of Investigation of the Dead Sea Scrolls and the Khirbet Qumran Site: Present Realities and Future Prospects*, edited by Michael O. Wise, Norman Golb, John J.Collins and Dennis G. Pardee, 371–388. New York: New York Academy of Sciences, 1994.

———. "The Origin, Character, and Early History of the 364-Day Calendar: A Reassessment of Jaubert's Hypotheses." *CBQ* 41.3 (1979): 390–411.

Vermes, Geza. *The Complete Dead Sea Scrolls in English*. New York: Allen Lane, 1997.

Vernant, Jean-Pierre. "A General Theory of Sacrifice." In *Mortals and Immortals: Collected Essays*, edited by Froma I. Zeitlin, 290–302. Princeton: Princeton University Press, 1991.

Vilnay, Zev. *Legends of Jerusalem*. Vol. 1 of *The Sacred Land*. 3 vols. Philadelphia: Jewish Publication Society, 1973.

Von Rad, Gerhard. *Holy War in Ancient Israel*. Translated by Marva J. Dawn. Grand Rapids, Mich.: Eerdmans, 1991.

Waller, James, and Mary Edwardsen. "Evolutionism." In *The Encyclopedia of Religion*, edited by Mircea Eliade, 4:214–218. 16 vols. New York: Macmillan, 1987.

Weber, Max. *The Sociology of Religion*. Translated by Ephraim Fischoff. Boston: Beacon Press, 1963.

Weinfeld, Moshe. *Deuteronomy and the Deuteronomic School*. Oxford: Clarendon Press, 1972.

Weiss, Isaac H., ed. *Sifra D'Be Rab (Torat Kohanim)*. Vienna: Jacob Schlossberg, 1862.

Weiss, Ze'ev, and Ehud Netzer. *Promise and Redemption: A Synagogue Mosaic from Sepphoris*. Jerusalem: Israel Museum, 1996.

Wellhausen, Julius. *Prolegomena to the History of Israel: With a Reprint of the Article "Israel" from the Encyclopaedia Britannica*. Translated by J. Sutherland Black and Allan Menzies. 1885. Reprint, New York: Meridian Books, 1957.

Wenham, Gordon J. *The Book of Leviticus*. New International Commentary on the Old Testament. Grand Rapids, Mich.: Eerdmans, 1979.

———. "Sanctuary Symbolism in the Garden of Eden Story." In *"I Studied Inscriptions from before the Flood": Ancient Near Eastern, Literary, and Linguistic Approaches to Genesis 1–11*, edited by Richard S. Hess and David Toshio Tsumura, 399–404. Winona Lake, Ind.: Eisenbrauns, 1994.

Wernberg-Møller, P. *The Manual of Discipline: Translated and Annotated*. Leiden: Brill, 1957.

Werner, Eric. *The Sacred Bridge: The Interdependence of Liturgy and Music in Synagogue and Church in the First Millennium*. New York: Columbia University, 1959.

———. *The Sacred Bridge: The Interdependence of Liturgy and Music in Synagogue and Church in the First Millennium*. Vol. 2. New York: Ktav, 1984.

Wiesenberg, E. "The Nicanor Gate." *JJS* 3.1 (1952): 14–29.

Wilkinson, John. "The Beit Alpha Synagogue Mosaic: Towards an Interpretation." *Journal of Jewish Art* 5 (1978): 16–28.

Williams, James G. *The Bible, Violence, and the Sacred: Liberation from the Myth of Sanctioned Violence*. San Francisco: HarperSanFrancisco, 1991.

———. "The Social Location of Israelite Prophecy." *JAAR* 37.2 (1969): 153–165.

Wills, Lawrence M. "Methodological Reflections on the Tax Collectors in the Gospels." In *When Judaism and Christianity Began: Essays in Memory of Anthony J. Saldarini*, edited by Alan J. Avery-Peck, Daniel Harrington, and Jacob Neusner, 1:251–266. 2 vols. Leiden: Brill, 2003.

Wilson, Bryan R. *Magic and the Millennium: A Sociological Study of Religious Movements of Protest among Tribal and Third-World Peoples*. London: Heinemann, 1973.

Wilson, Robert R. *Prophecy and Society in Ancient Israel*. Philadelphia: Fortress Press, 1980.

Winston, David. *Logos and Mystical Theology in Philo of Alexandria*. Cincinnati: Hebrew Union College Press, 1985.

――――. *The Wisdom of Solomon: A New Translation with Introduction and Commentary.* AB 43. New York: Doubleday, 1979.

Wise, Michael Owen. *A Critical Study of the Temple Scroll from Qumran Cave 11.* Chicago: Oriental Institute, 1990.

――――. "4QFlorilegium and the Temple of Adam." *RevQ* 57–58/15.1–2 (1991–92): 103–132.

Wise, Michael Owen, Martin Abegg, Jr., and Edward Cook. *The Dead Sea Scrolls: A New Translation.* San Francisco: Harper San Francisco, 1999.

Wolfson, Harry Austryn. *Philo: Foundations of Religious Philosophy in Judaism, Christianity, and Islam.* Cambridge, Mass.: Harvard University Press, 1947.

Wright, David P. "Analogy in Biblical and Hittite Ritual." In *Religionsgeschtliche Beziehungen zwischen Kleinasien, Nordsyrien, und dem Alten Testament: Internationales Symposion Hamburg 17.–21. März 1990,* edited by Bernd Janowski, Klaus Koch, and Gernot Wilhelm, 473–506. Freiburg: Universitätsverlag Freiburg Schweiz, 1993.

――――. "Blown Away Like a Bramble: The Dynamics of Analogy in Psalm 58." *RB* 103.2 (1996): 213–236.

――――. *The Disposal of Impurity: Elimination Rites in the Bible and in Hittite and Mesopotamian Literature.* Atlanta, Ga.: Scholars Press, 1987.

――――. "The Gesture of Hand Placement in the Hebrew Bible and in Hittite Literature." *Journal of the American Oriental Society* 106 (1986): 433–446.

――――. "Holiness, Sex, and Death in the Garden of Eden." *Biblica* 77.3 (1996): 305–329.

――――. Review of *Text and Concept,* by Rolf P. Knierim. *JBL* 113.1 (1994): 123–124.

――――. "Ritual Analogy in Psalm 109." *JBL* 113.3 (1994): 385–404.

――――. "The Spectrum of Priestly Impurity." In *Priesthood and Cult in Ancient Israel,* edited by Gary A. Anderson and Saul M. Olyan, 150–181. Sheffield, England: JSOT Press, 1991.

Wright, David P., David Noel Freedman, and Avi Hurvitz, eds. *Pomegranates and Golden Bells: Studies in Biblical, Jewish, and Near Eastern Ritual, Law, and Literature in Honor of Jacob Milgrom.* Winona Lake, Ind.: Eisenbrauns, 1995.

Wright, N. T. *Jesus and the Victory of God.* Vol. 2 of *Christian Origins and the Question of God.* Minneapolis: Fortress Press, 1996.

Yadin, Yigael. "A Midrash on 2 Sam vii and Ps i–ii (4QFlorilegium)." *Israel Exploration Journal* 9.2 (1959): 95–98.

――――. *The Scroll of the War of the Sons of Light against the Sons of Darkness.* Translated by Chaim Rabin. Oxford: Clarendon Press, 1962.

――――. *The Temple Scroll.* 3 vols. Jerusalem: Israel Exploration Society, 1983.

Yerushalmi, Yosef Hayim. *Zakhor: Jewish History and Jewish Memory.* With a new preface and postcript. New York: Schocken, 1989.

Zimmerli, Walther. *Ezekiel 1: A Commentary on the Book of the Prophet Ezekiel, Chapters 1–24.* Translated by Ronald E. Clements. Hermeneia. Philadelphia: Fortress Press, 1979.

――――. *Ezekiel 2: A Commentary on the Book of the Prophet Ezekiel, Chapters 25–48.* Translated by James D. Martin. Hermeneia. Philadelphia: Fortress Press, 1983.

Index of Scripture
and Ancient Texts

General Index

70231941R00217

Made in the USA
San Bernardino, CA
26 February 2018